Frommer's®

Budapest & the Best of Hungary

7th Edition

by Ryan James

Here's what the critics say about Frommer's:

"Amazingly easy to use. Very portable, very complete."

—*Booklist*

"Detailed, accurate, and easy-to-read information for all price ranges."
—*Glamour Magazine*

"Hotel information is close to encyclopedic."

—*Des Moines Sunday Register*

"Frommer's Guides have a way of giving you a real feel for a place."
—*Knight Ridder Newspapers*

WILEY

Wiley Publishing, Inc.

Wiley Publishing, Inc.

111 River St.
Hoboken, NJ 07030-5774

ISBN: 978-0-470-22701-5
Editor: Stephen Bassman
Production Editor: Jonathan Scott
Cartographer: Elizabeth Puhl
Photo Editor: Richard Fox
Production by Wiley Indianapolis Composition Services

Front cover photo: Szechenyi Lanchid (Chain Bridge) at dusk; Parliament in background
Back cover photo: Young musicians on Margaret Island, Budapest

For information on our other products and services or to obtain technical support, please contact our Customer Care Department within the U.S. at 800/762-2974, outside the U.S. at 317/572-3993 or fax 317/572-4002.

Wiley also publishes its books in a variety of electronic formats. Some content that appears in print may not be available in electronic formats.

Manufactured in the United States of America

5 4 3 2 1

Contents

6   Where to Dine in Budapest   94

7   Exploring Budapest   132

8   Strolling Around Budapest   168

9   Budapest Shopping   195

List of Maps

An Invitation to the Reader

In researching this book, we discovered many wonderful places—hotels, restaurants, shops, and more. We're sure you'll find others. Please tell us about them, so we can share the information with your fellow travelers in upcoming editions. If you were disappointed with a recommendation, we'd love to know that, too. Please write to:

Frommer's Budapest & the Best of Hungary, 7th Edition
Wiley Publishing, Inc. • 111 River St. • Hoboken, NJ 07030-5774

An Additional Note

Please be advised that travel information is subject to change at any time—and this is especially true of prices. We therefore suggest that you write or call ahead for confirmation when making your travel plans. The authors, editors, and publisher cannot be held responsible for the experiences of readers while traveling. Your safety is important to us, however, so we encourage you to stay alert and be aware of your surroundings. Keep a close eye on cameras, purses, and wallets, all favorite targets of thieves and pickpockets.

Author's Acknowledgments

I wish to thank my student helpers who came to my rescue when my Hungarian was not enough: Anikó Bálint, Balázs Kántor, Gergely Hubai, Anna Rázsi, and Balázs Varga. I am indebted to Ron Schmitz (a.k.a. Mr. Map) for his map assistance, dining with me, his support, and suggestions. I want to also thank my editor, Stephen Bassman, for helping me with the learning curves needed along the way. Last, but not least, special thanks to those who paved the way by creating a foundation for this book in previous editions.

About the Author

Dr. Ryan James was born and raised in Long Branch, New Jersey. He earned his doctorate in education from the University of San Francisco, and has taught English at ELTE University in Budapest since 2002. He and his partner own BudaBaB, a bed and breakfast on the Pest side. He welcomes questions and comments about this guide, and his email address is drryanjames@gmail.com.

Other Great Guides for Your Trip:

Frommer's Star Ratings, Icons & Abbreviations

Every hotel, restaurant, and attraction listing in this guide has been ranked for quality, value, service, amenities, and special features using a **star-rating system.** In country, state, and regional guides, we also rate towns and regions to help you narrow down your choices and budget your time accordingly. Hotels and restaurants are rated on a scale of zero (recommended) to three stars (exceptional). Attractions, shopping, nightlife, towns, and regions are rated according to the following scale: zero stars (recommended), one star (highly recommended), two stars (very highly recommended), and three stars (must-see).

In addition to the star-rating system, we also use **seven feature icons** that point you to the great deals, in-the-know advice, and unique experiences that separate travelers from tourists. Throughout the book, look for:

Finds	Special finds—those places only insiders know about
Fun Fact	Fun facts—details that make travelers more informed and their trips more fun
Kids	Best bets for kids and advice for the whole family
Moments	Special moments—those experiences that memories are made of
Overrated	Places or experiences not worth your time or money
Tips	Insider tips—great ways to save time and money
Value	Great values—where to get the best deals

The following **abbreviations** are used for credit cards:

AE	American Express	DISC	Discover	V	Visa
DC	Diners Club	MC	MasterCard		

Frommers.com

Now that you have the guidebook to a great trip, visit our website at **www.frommers.com** for travel information on more than 3,600 destinations. With features updated regularly, we give you instant access to the most current trip-planning information available. At Frommers.com, you'll also find the best prices on airfares, accommodations, and car rentals—and you can even book travel online through our travel booking partners. At Frommers.com, you'll also find the following:

- Online updates to our most popular guidebooks
- Vacation sweepstakes and contest giveaways
- Newsletter highlighting the hottest travel trends
- Online travel message boards with featured travel discussions

What's New in Budapest & Hungary

"**W**hat's new" makes the assumption that you know what was here before. This chapter will give you some information about both, so you don't feel like you have missed out on a thing.

GETTING TO KNOW BUDAPEST
If you have been here before and have attended a performance at the Erkel Theater, you will be saddened to know that it permanently closed in May 2007. Though not a pretty structure either inside or out being a lackluster communist block design, it was enormous. It could hold up to 4,000 people and was the largest entertainment venue in the city. Due to the cost of repairs, it is instead slated for destruction at some time in the future.

TRANSPORTATION In 2006, the old trams were replaced with new more efficient trams, but to accommodate them, all tram stops had to be remodeled to raise the platform to meet the floor of the tram. This is the only wheelchair- and stroller-compliant transportation in the city. In addition, work has started on the construction of a fourth metro line. Due to the construction, there has been some disruption of services for other forms of transportation. Some tram routes have been diverted, while others have been completely changed. In some areas, buses are running in place of the tram for part of the route and then the tram picks up carrying passengers for the balance of the ride. Most of the changes are on the Buda side at traditional transport hubs. When

in doubt, the **Budapest Sun** has traffic alerts, which include public transportation concerns in each issue. The BKV (www.bkv.hu), the company that runs the transportation systems, has a good English section on their website.

In 2007, MÁV, the Hungarian railroad, announced its intent to cut 14 branch lines with another 60 lines being considered. Although we do not believe this will affect any trips discussed in this book, it is best to double check the MÁV website (www.elvira.hu; click on the British flag for English) for the most current information. MÁV has also announced that it will start offering online ticketing by early 2008, so this is something worth checking on.

WHERE TO STAY There are many new hotels for every price range in the city with new ones in the final construction phases and others breaking ground for construction. Some of the most beautiful current hotels include the historic Gresham Palace, which is now the **Four Seasons Hotel Gresham Palace** (p. 75), the crown jewel among hotels in Hungary, probably in the entire central European region. The developers have beautifully restored the grand Art Nouveau structure at the head of the Chain Bridge in Pest. The hotel also includes the Páva Restaurant with its six-course meals served in a refined style and crowning elegance. The **Gresham Kávéház** (p. 99) is a full service restaurant. Check out chapter 1 "The Best of Budapest" or chapter 5,

"Where to Stay in Budapest" for more on Budapest's accommodations.

WHERE TO DINE   Although the law requires that all restaurants offer a non-smoking section, it is not always a separate room or even a ventilated one. However, more and more of the newer places are considering nonsmoking customers by being completely nonsmoking or completely segregating the two areas. Bars on the other hand continue to be smoking paradises.

Budapest has seen an explosion in the variety of culinary choices with samples from many countries. Typical and traditional Hungarian cuisine consists of large portions and many foods are fried. Traditional recipes call for goose fat, which really adds a distinctive and delicious flavor to the meal. Of course, you will want to try some of the many excellent traditional Hungarian dishes since that is such an important part of any cultural experience.

Restaurants that earn their reputation by word of mouth are where you will find the most delicious meals. Some are tucked away and sometimes difficult to find, but worth the effort. In the center of town, we suggest **Kőleves Vendéglő** (p. 118) with their modern versions of Hungarian dishes and a lively atmosphere, or one with the simple name, **M** (p. 111). Both are affordable, have a fun atmosphere, and are comfy. **Tabáni Terasz** (p. 125) and the **Szép Ilona** (p. 127) are the best if you're looking for traditional Hungarian fare.

EXPLORING BUDAPEST   The **Ludwig Múzeum (Ludwig Museum of Contemporary Art),** now located in the Palace of Arts overlooking the Danube, houses a permanent exhibition of contemporary Hungarian and international art. The collection consists primarily of American pop art and central European contemporary works. It includes several late Picassos, Andy Warhol's *Single Elvis,*

and a Jean Tinguely. The museum's temporary exhibits often outshine its permanent collection. The design of the space is a feat in and of itself, since it is the first important Hungarian museum created for the display of contemporary art. See p. 144.

The private art gallery scene has also gained renewed interest with exciting art galleries such as the **Kogart Gallery** (p. 120) and the newer **Art Factory Gallery** (p. 201), while increasing interest in the older established galleries at the same time, including the **Ernst Gallery** (p. 201). The Ernst Gallery has a long history in the city and presents a number of different exhibitions of Hungarian art as well as special and unusual temporary exhibitions, such as an exhibit of the famous coffeehouses of the city. For more art galleries, see chapter 9, "Budapest Shopping."

BUDAPEST SHOPPING   The city has been flooded with huge Western-style malls and the largest of them all should be open sometime in 2008. Before this, the largest mall in Central Europe was the **West End Center,** right behind Nyugati Railway Station. This is the first and allegedly, the last mall built right in central Pest, most likely for lack of space. In addition to the malls, international designers have also discovered the city. Shops like Louis Vuitton and Chanel are now open on Andrássy. If you have children with you, you may find the **Tropicarium** of interest; it is located in a mall in Southern Buda called **Campona,** at Nagytétényi út 35–47.

For more on Budapest's best shopping, see chapter 9, "Budapest Shopping."

BUDAPEST AFTER DARK   Prices for concerts, opera, and the theater continue to rise, but most are still a bargain compared to other major cities. There are few if any events in Budapest beyond the means of the average Western budget traveler. It is still possible to get a balcony seat, albeit high up, in the Opera House for less than 1,150 Ft ($6.20/£3.25), but for a splurge, some performances sell tickets in the orchestra section for as little as 8,050 Ft ($43/£22). All theater productions are in Hungarian and rarely are they supertitled, but they can be superb nevertheless.

Trafó (located in a funky old converted electric power station; p. 226) has been the rising star as the venue for modern dance. Trafó brings in Hungarian and international dance troupes with a diverse range of styles for performances. Over the years, word has spread and the theater is usually jampacked in not too comfortable, but inexpensive seating. See p. 226.

A complete rundown of Budapest's nightlife can be found in chapter 10, "Budapest After Dark."

THE DANUBE BEND The annual **Visegrád International Palace Tournament** has grown in scale in recent years and is now a must-see for medieval enthusiasts or those who love Renaissance fairs. The tournament recreates an authentic medieval festival replete with dueling knights on horseback and early music and dance. See p. 250.

In Esztergom, you'll find a new sign of better days ahead for peaceful coexistence in central Europe. Though deeply rooted tension between the Hungarians and the Slovaks never seems to abate, Esztergom is once again connected by **bridge** across the Danube to the Slovak town of Sturovo. The Germans blew up the old bridge connecting these towns in World War II. All that remained was a curious stump on the river's edge, along with four unconnected pylons in the river, stark testimonials to the German rampage in Europe as well as to the continuing regional hostilities.

For more suggestions on what to do in the Danube region, see chapter 11, "The Danube Bend."

SOUTHERN HUNGARY: THE MECSEK HILLS & THE GREAT PLAIN
Szeged, the proud paprika capital of the world, located in the Great Plains is a lovely little city to spend a day or two after immersing yourself in the capital. Szeged and Pécs jointly share the European Capital of Culture for 2010 designation, being of the same regions.

For other great things to do in the South of Hungary, see chapter 14, "Southern Hungary: The Mecsek Hills & the Great Plain."

1

The Best of Budapest

It never occurred to me when living in Modesto, California that someday, I would live in Budapest, Hungary and have the opportunity to write this book.

After graduating with a doctorate in International and Multicultural Education in 2000 (with over 20 years of teaching experience at that point), it was time to make a major move. A year abroad seemed to be in order for me and my partner to revitalize our spirits before transferring to the east coast of the U.S. Our European travels eventually took us to Budapest during a cold spell, and we decided to hunker down and stay until spring. Back then, all an American had to do was leave the country for a day and return to refresh your Visa for another ninety days—we did this several times. Then we started teaching English at private schools; when we were told we could avoid work and residency permits if we had our own business, we started a private language school. It turns out we did need those permits after all, which cost us a trip to NYC and a wait in line at the Hungarian Consulate. We submitted our applications and were back in Hungary the next day.

After more than 6 years and several Visas renewals later, we're still here.

We've found teaching jobs at universities and several years ago opened up a bed and breakfast (BudaBaB; see p. 91). We've also seen Budapest and Hungary grow and evolve before our eyes.

In those days, Budapest was not on the travel radar, still considered too exotic, while many still did not realize it was no longer a Communist country. (People still ask us this question.) During our first year, Hungary had its third democratic election for Prime Minister. Each of the three elections put a different political party into control causing continual upheaval in the laws from one party's whims to the next.

Tourism has been greatly aided by the budget airlines, which have started to spring up in the last few years. Budapest now boasts fourteen budget airlines flying from destinations throughout Europe, with new ones in the works. With this, the hotel industry has blossomed. Boutique hotels and new 4- and 5-star hotels have been built or have taken over historic buildings, creating a wide offering of accommodations for all budgets.

Up until a couple of years ago, a new restaurant would open after extensive remodeling only to close within 6 months. This has changed with the influx of tourism, which has stabilized the business scene. Menus in English were once uncommon, and ordering an entrée was a grab bag surprise; tourism has changed all this and is changing customer services across the board. Shop clerks have had to be re-trained to deal with English-speaking tourists and to offer friendlier customer service. (For the most part, it is working.) Culturally, the country (and especially Budapest) continues to thrive, with nightlife, arts, and fashion scenes that are infused with more youthful exuberance than ever before, and an underground party scene that is well worth seeking out.

Since Hungary joined the European Union in 2004, those extended visits we enjoyed in 2001 are somewhat trickier for today's American traveler; the official EU law still allows 90 day visits, but then requires Americans to leave the EU for 6 months before returning. I hope that regardless of how long you are visiting, you enjoy yourself enough to extend your stay, just as we did.

1 The Best Little Adventures in Budapest

- **The Best Photographic Viewpoints in the City:** If you want to start at the highest point, you will have to go to János-Hegy or John Hill where the tower is 529m (1,736 ft.) high. On a clear day, you might just see the Tatra Mountains. The best way to get there is the chairlift (p. 156). The next highest vista is the Citadel on Gellért Hill. The bus only gets you so far, and then you hike up the rest, but it is worth the effort. This is where you will find the Lady of Liberty statue viewable from the Pest side. Castle Hill is of course an excellent viewpoint for photographs from both the front of the castle and Fisherman's Bastion. Margit Bridge, the side across from the island, has a breathtaking view of the river from where the bridge elbows.

- **Shopping the Courtyards of Budapest:** What travelers find confusing are the windows displaying interesting merchandise, but with no store in the vicinity to buy the merchandise. With a little investigative work, you will realize that the stores are often in the commercialized courtyards. Like little hidden shopping districts, the courtyards offer bargains and unusual items in locations seemingly known only by those in the know. The best courtyards to explore are those off the well-known Váci utca. Many designer stores are hidden away in nooks and crannies. See chapter 9, "Budapest Shopping" for some ideas of where to start, but don't limit yourself to this district. These courtyards are all over the city.

- **Architecture Not to Be Missed:** Many people do not bother to look up at the top of buildings, missing much. Aside from the historic listings, Posta Takarékpénzter on Hold utca across from where Perczel Mór utca comes into it is one of my favorite buildings in the city (p. 183). It is now part of the National Bank. Move around so the trees don't obstruct your view. Párizsi udvar in the Art Nouveau style where Kigyo utca meets Ferenciek tere is sumptuous both outside and inside. Walk in the courtyard and look at the ceiling. On the korut, near Blaha Lujza is the New York Palace built in eclectic style with an emphasis on Italian renaissance and baroque. For something more modern, don't pass up the Lehel Tér market at the blue metro stop by the same name. It looks like a beached boat.

- **Riding the Trams:** With your transit pass in hand, tour the city and orient yourself from the windows of the city's many trams. Hop on a tram and ride it to the end of the line, get out, and take it back again. This is also an inexpensive hop-on, hop-off way to sightsee, checking out things that catch your eye along the way. Tram 4 or 6 will take you along the large ring road. Tram 2 at night provides a lovely view of Parliament, and of Castle Hill all lit up. Bus no. 15 gives a good overview of the city. See

"Getting Around" in chapter 4, "Getting to Know Budapest," for details on public transportation.

- **Packing a Picnic for an Outing:** Any day when pleasant weather is in the forecast, people flock to one of the parks or Margaret Island to enjoy the fresh air and one another's company. Families stroll along with their young children while young lovers enjoy each other's company, and the older folks reminisce about the old and better times. A quick and easy way to pack a picnic is to pick up an already roasted chicken. See the tip on p. 152.
- **Taking a Walk in the Buda Hills:** It's hard to believe that such a large expanse of hilly forest is right here within the capital city. There are hiking trails aplenty; every Budapest native has a favorite. Ask around. See chapter 7, "Exploring Budapest," for more about the Buda Hills.
- **Strolling through the Jewish District:** Budapest still has a large Jewish population. Pest's historic Jewish neighborhood is disappearing at a sorrowfully rapid rate due to modernization, commercialization, and new construction. Run-down historic areas that once resonated with the magic and tragedy of the past have been bulldozed into oblivion. See "Walking Tour 4: The Jewish District" in chapter 8, "Strolling Around Budapest."

2 The Best Places to Enjoy a Sunset in Budapest

- **From the Riverside:** As the sun sets, you will find many locals and visitors flocking to the riverside to enjoy people-watching, watching the sunset, and just plain relaxing. Depending on how busy your day was, you may either want to find a bench to sit on and unwind or take a stroll onto one of the bridges that span the mighty Danube, the second longest river in Europe. See chapter 7, "Exploring Budapest," for more about Budapest's bridges and riverside walks.
- **Széchenyi Thermals:** This thermal is open until 10pm. Relax in the hot spring waters while watching the end of the day's suns rays as they fade into the horizon. For more on the thermals see p. 166.
- **Margaret Island (Margit Sziget):** This island, once called Rabbit Island, was home to the cloistered nuns' convent founded by Princess Margaret, daughter of Béla IV, who promised his daughter to the nunnery. Enjoy the flower gardens or the singing fountain as the sun sinks into the western sky.
- **Fisherman's Bastion:** Sip a glass of wine in this romantic sunset spot. On Castle Hill, it overlooks the city on one side and St. Matthias Church on the other.
- **Academy of Sciences Park:** For a casual place to relax, sit in the park across the street from the academy and take in the engaging architecture, the river view, and a beautiful sunset on Roosevelt tér.
- **The Sculptural Grounds at Buda Castle:** There is a powerful statue called the Matthias Fountain. It is based on a legend of King Matthias, who, while on a hunting trip through the forest, came across a woman stranger, Ilona; she fell in love with him instantly, not realizing he was the king. He reciprocated the love.

Hungary

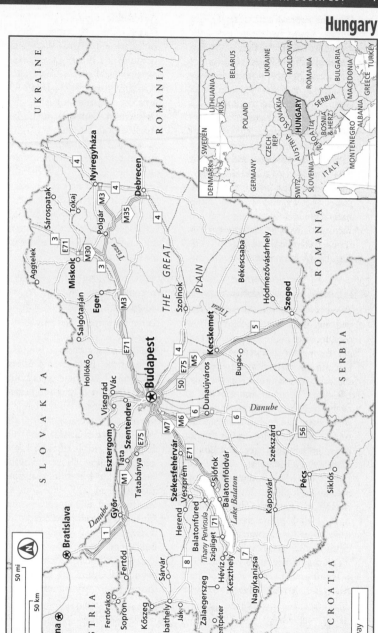

3 The Best Off-the-Beaten-Track Museums

- **Bélyegmúzeum (Postal Stamp Museum):** Philatelists the world over have recognized the artistic creativity of the Magyar Posta creations. Here you'll find incredibly beautiful and well-organized collections of Hungary's finest stamps and those of many other countries. See p. 136.

- **Miksa Róth Memorial House:** This is the last home of the famed stained glass and mosaic artist whose work graces the Parliament and other places throughout the city and the world. It is truly an exceptional collection not to be missed. See p. 137.

- **Ráth Gőrgy Museum:** A personal collection of Asian art from different countries, each displayed in separate rooms, makes this Budapest museum a treasure trove of exotic collections, at Varosligeti fasor 12 (© 1/342-3916; www.hoppmuzeum.hu).

- **Holokauszt Emlékközpont (Budapest Holocaust Memorial Center):** Surrounded by modern architecture is the Páva Synagogue. The center has special exhibits and documents the Jewish history of Hungary during the Holocaust. See p. 132.

- **Underground Railway Museum:** Located at Deák metro underground, this small exhibit shows the history of the tram lines in the city.

4 The Best Places to Kill an Hour in Budapest

- **Central Market Hall:** Not only a good place to pick up souvenirs, but also a fun place for people-watching. The second floor balcony overlooking the whole market is an experience you should not miss. See p. 215.

- **Castle Hill:** Ignore the tourist sights for an hour and just stroll along the side streets, winding around and allowing yourself to get lost in admiring the buildings.

- **The Baths:** The Király or Rudas baths are steeped in history and are the perfect way to relax while soaking in the history of the culture at the same time. See "Budapest's Most Popular Thermal Baths" in chapter 7, "Exploring Budapest."

- **A Traditional Coffeehouse:** Coffeehouses are a cultural icon in the city, dating back over a 100 years. Enjoy a cup of coffee or tea and linger with a book or newspaper for as long as you like without feeling any pressure to leave. See "Coffeehouses: Historic & Traditional" in chapter 6, "Where to Dine in Budapest."

- **Browse the Shelves in a Bookstore:** With three used English bookstores, there are many opportunities to find something that will catch your eye. Perhaps you will find that special book as a remembrance of your visit. See chapter 9, "Budapest Shopping."

- **Art Factory Gallery and Studio:** Open to the public and located in the ABB Building at Váci út 152–156, it is small enough to enjoy for an hour or longer if you have the time. See "Shopping" in chapter 9, for more information.

5 The Best Day Trips Outside Budapest

- **Cruising the Danube:** There's nothing like a boat ride on a fine sunny day. From Budapest, head up the river to the charming towns of Szentendre and Visegrád along the Danube Bend. See "Railing through the Danube Bend" in chapter 11, "The Danube Bend."

- **Visiting Szentendre:** Only 45 minutes outside the city by HÉV, this small Serbian village boasts a number of tiny museums, shopping opportunities, and wonderful views of the Danube. See chapter 11, "The Danube Bend.

- **Vác:** A delightful little town that took me 6 years to discover and I wish I had earlier. The center square is a mix of historic buildings with a modern square completed in 2006. The river walk is fantastically beautiful. See p. 247.

- **Swimming in the Thermal Lake at Hévíz:** Even in the bitterest spells of winter, the temperature in Europe's largest thermal lake seldom dips below 85° to 90°F (29°–32°C). Hungarians swim here year-round and you can too! If you're here in winter, it'll be a particularly memorable experience. See p. 262.

- **Visit Esztergom:** Hungary's seat of Catholicism, Esztergom is located 46km (29 miles) northwest of Budapest. St. István, the first Christian king of Hungary was crowned here on Christmas Day A.D. 1000.

The cathedral has impressive views of the Danube and the rest of the city. See chapter 11, "The Danube Bend."

- **Explore the Monastery at Pannonhalma:** Prince Géza founded the monastery in 969. This is where the gothic cloisters are housed as well as a magnificently ornate 19th-century library, with the most important collection of Hungarian historical documents. It sits on a hill between the forested slopes of the Bakony region and the low-lying *Kisalföld* (Little Plain), with a fantastic view.

- **Sleepy Historical Visegrád:** Located 40km (25 miles) north of Budapest to Nagymaros, then a ferry to Visegrád, you can find the ruins of King Béla IV's reign. The Citadel and the reconstructed Royal Palace are among the places worth seeing. See p. 249.

- **Medve Otthon:** Visit the bears at the bear sanctuary, which holds 42 bears that were once stars in Hungarian movies then rescued due to mistreatment. You can feed them honey, and kids can have their face painted. It is just 1 hour from the city. See p. 40.

6 The Best Hotels in Budapest

- **Best Splurge Hotel:** The magnificent **Four Seasons Hotel Gresham Palace,** V. Roosevelt tér 5–6 (☎ 1/268-6000), has gained the reputation as Hungary's foremost hotel. The workmanship of the recreated Art Nouveau architecture is breathtaking. Guests get the royal treatment, with customer care that will enamor you for a long time. See p. 75.

- **Best for a Romantic Getaway:** After entering the **Corinthia Grand Hotel Royal,** VII. Erzsébet krt. 43–49 (☎ 1/479-4000), you will not want to leave the gorgeous building and with the pool, spa, and restaurants, there is no need to do so. See p. 75.

- **Best for Families:** The accommodations at **Charles Apartment House,** I. Hegyalja út 23 (☎ 1/212-9169), are comfortable and clean flats with fully equipped kitchens in a Buda-side apartment building. See p. 87.

- **Best Moderately Priced Hotel:** The jazzy **Cotton House Hotel,** VI. Jókai u. 26 (☎ 1/354-2600), conveniently located near the Opera House and Liszt Ferenc tér, will soothe the blues away. See p. 80.

- **Best Budget Hotel:** The accommodations at **Medosz,** VI. Jókai tér 9 (☎ 1/374-3001) are comfortable and clean and close to Octogon and Liszt Ferenc tér. See p. 82.

- **Best Pension:** The charming **Leo Panzió,** XII. Kossuth Lajos u. 2/A. (© **1/266-9041**), is in a quiet apartment building with the perfect location to start your shopping expedition and transportation is right outside the door. See p. 81.
- **Best Location and Views:** This one is a tie between two hotels, one on each side of the river. On the Pest side, it is the **Four Seasons Hotel Gresham Palace,** V. Roosevelt tér 5–6 (© **1/268-6000**), with the Chain Bridge outside its door. On the Buda the **Hilton Budapest,** I. Hess András tér 1–3 (© **1/899-6600;** p. 87), is a luxurious lodging right next door to the Matthias Church and the Fisherman's Bastion square.

7 The Best Dining Bets in Budapest

- **Best for a Romantic Dinner:** At **Gerlóczy Kávéház,** V. Gerlóczy u. 1 (© **1/235-0953**), you can dine under the canopy of the leafy trees shading you, with excellent service, all the while being serenaded by live music at night. See p. 107.
- **Best Decor:** The legends of the benevolent King Mátyás are painted as murals on the walls with stained glass decorating the windows at **Mátyás Pince,** V. Március 15 tér 7–8 (© **1/266-8008**). See p. 102.
- **Best Wine List: Gundel,** XIV. Állatkerti út 2 (© **1/468-4040**), the city's fanciest, most expensive, and (we think) most overrated restaurant, nonetheless has an impressive wine list. See p. 120.
- **Best Beer List:** You will have difficulty choosing from the 10 draft beers or 50 bottled beers at **Mosselen Belgian Beer Café** at XIII. Pannónia u. 14 (© **1/452-0535**). The food is also excellent making it a double treat. See p. 112.
- **Best Wild Game:** At **Paprika Vendéglő,** VII. Dozsa Gyorgy 72., 4½ blocks from Heroes Square (© **06/70-574-6508**), you can relish the savory dishes of wild boar or venison. There are many other choices for the less adventurous. See p. 121.
- **Best Traditional Coffeehouse: Centrál Kávéház,** V. Károly Mihály u. 9 (© **1/266-2110**), is the closest to the classic coffeehouse of the city's past traditions. Even today, it is the meeting place for intellectuals, tourists, families, and more. This is a Budapest must see. See p. 127.
- **Best Nontraditional Coffeehouse:** For coffee or hot chocolate, **Aztek Choxolat Café** at V. Karoly korut 22 or Semmelweiss u. 19. (© **1/266-7113**), has a tremendous selection of both. See p. 129.
- **Best Pastries:** Our favorite pastry shop is the **Művész Kávéház,** VI. Andrássy út 29 (© **1/352-1337**). It has many traditional desserts such as somlói galuska, considered a national dessert, plus pastries, and an ice cream bar. See p. 128.
- **Best Rétes:** Melt-in-your-mouth strudel is available at the **Rétesbár,** I. Balta köz 4, the alley on Castle Hill. Directly across from Tourinform, look for the red banner hanging outside, in the brick alleyway.

2

Planning Your Trip to Budapest

Now that you've decided to travel to Budapest or the rest of the country, you may have dozens of questions: Do I need a visa? What currency is used in Hungary, and can I get my hands on the currency before leaving home? Will any festivals take place during my trip? What's the best route to get there? This chapter is devoted to providing answers to these and other questions.

1 Visitor Information

The tourism infrastructure has been developing at a furious pace in Hungary with great support from the Ministry of Tourism. There are many high-quality hotels and restaurants already and it seems new ones are appearing every few months. Major improvements in the service sector have been noticeable over the past few years. In most cities you will find tourism-related information offices called **Tourinform** (© 1/438-8080 or 06/80-630-800; www.tourinform.hu), a branch of the Hungarian National Tourist Office, at V. Sütő u. 2, Budapest; open daily from 8am to 8pm. You'll also find a branch office in the heart of Budapest's Broadway, at Liszt Ferenc tér 11 (© 1/322-4098; fax 1/342-2541), open daily from 9am to 7pm. These offices distribute pamphlets on events and attractions that can be found in the area where you are visiting, and help you with finding appropriate accommodations and restaurants. The tourism authority, **Magyar Turizmus Rt** (© 1/488-8701; www.hungarytourism.hu), also has offices throughout the world, and it is their mandate to promote Hungary as a destination for tourism.

For general country information and a variety of pamphlets and maps before you leave home, contact the government-sponsored **Hungarian National Tourist Office,** 350 Fifth Ave., New York, NY 10118 (© 212/695-1212; www.gotohungary.com). In London, the **Hungarian National Tourist Office** is at 46 Eaton Place, London SW1X 8AL (© 020/7823-1032). The Hungarian National Tourist Office's main website, a great source of information, is **www.gotohungary.co.uk**.

Other sites with lots of helpful bits of information containing news, shopping, entertainment, and current venues for music, dance, and theatrical events for visitors and English-speaking locals are the Internet sites of the printed periodicals *Funzine* at www.funzine.hu and the *Budapest Sun* www.budapestsun.com, and the *Budapest Times* at www.budapesttimes.hu. City and sightseeing information is available at www.budapestinfo.hu, but it is sometimes out of date. To get news about Hungary, check out the Hungarian News Agency at **www.english.mti.hu**. It's updated daily.

2 Entry Requirements & Customs

ENTRY REQUIREMENTS

For information on how to get a passport, go to "Passports" in the "Fast Facts: Budapest" section in chapter 4. The websites listed provide downloadable passport applications as well as the current fees for processing passport applications. For an up-to-date, country-by-country listing of passport requirements around the world, go to the "Foreign Entry Requirement" Web page of the U.S. State Department at **http://travel.state.gov**.

CUSTOMS

WHAT YOU CAN BRING INTO HUNGARY

You're allowed to bring duty-free into Hungary 250 cigarettes, 2 liters of wine, and 1 liter of spirits. There is no limit to the amount of money you may bring into the country. However, you may not take out of the country more than 1,000,000 forints in Hungarian currency.

WHAT YOU CAN TAKE HOME FROM HUNGARY

Returning **U.S. citizens** who have been away for at least 48 hours are allowed to bring back, once every 30 days, $800 worth of merchandise duty-free. You'll pay a flat rate of duty on the next $1,000 worth of purchases. Any dollar amount beyond that is subject to duties at whatever rates apply. On mailed gifts, the duty-free limit is $200. Be sure to keep your receipts or purchases accessible to expedite the declaration process. *Note:* If you owe duty, you are required to pay on your arrival in the United States using cash, personal check, government or traveler's check, money order, or, in some locations, a Visa or MasterCard.

To avoid paying duty on foreign-made personal items you owned before your trip, bring along a bill of sale, insurance policy, jeweler's appraisal, or receipts of purchase. You can also register items that can be readily identified by a permanently affixed serial number or marking, for instance laptop computers, cameras, and CD players, with Customs before you leave. Take the items to the nearest Customs office or register them with Customs at the airport from which you're departing. You'll receive, at no cost, a Certificate of Registration, which allows duty-free entry for the life of the item.

With some exceptions, you cannot bring fresh fruits or vegetables into the United States; however, if your trip continues from here to other European countries, you will need to know their restrictions also. Some countries in Europe are now restricting the transport of Hungarian salami, for which Pick is a famous brand. For specifics on what you can bring back, download the invaluable free pamphlet *Know Before You Go.* Many rules change frequently, so it is best to have the most current information on hand. Go to www.cbp.gov/xp/cgov/travel and click on "Know Before You Go! Online Brochure." Or contact the **U.S. Customs & Border Protection (CBP),** 1300 Pennsylvania Ave., NW, Washington, DC 20229 (© **877/287-8667**) and request the pamphlet.

For a clear summary of **Canadian** rules, write for the booklet *I Declare,* issued by the **Canada Border Services Agency** (© **800/461-9999** in Canada, or 204/983-3500; www.cbsa-asfc.gc.ca). Canada allows its citizens a C$750 exemption, and you're allowed to bring back duty-free one carton of cigarettes, one can of tobacco, 40 imperial ounces of liquor, and 50 cigars. In addition, you're allowed to mail gifts to Canada valued at less than C$60 a day, provided they're unsolicited and don't contain alcohol or tobacco (write on the package "Unsolicited gift, under C$60 value"). All valuables should be declared on the Y-38 form

Tips Passport Savvy

New laws requiring passports to countries where passports were never needed in the past has increased passport processing time considerably. Allow plenty of time before your trip to apply for a passport; processing can take up to 6 weeks but can take longer during busy periods (especially spring). And keep in mind that expediting a passport when in a rush will cost you a higher processing fee. When traveling, safeguard your passport in an inconspicuous, inaccessible place like a money belt and keep a copy of the critical pages with your passport number in a separate place. If you lose your passport, visit the nearest consulate or embassy of your native country as soon as possible for a replacement, but bear in mind that temporary passport replacements come with a hefty fee. Once you get to Hungary, by law you are required to have your passport with you at all times. Unless you think you may have some legal problem, you probably won't need it. No police officer is going to ask you to produce it. The only other times you will need it is if you are going to a bank for a transaction, are making a large credit card purchase, or are driving a vehicle. Best bet: Carry a photocopy of your passport's identification pages and leave the real deal in a safe or locked suitcase at your hotel. However, someone you trust should be able to access it in case of a legal need. If you do have a legal issue, then the police can hold you until your passport is presented by someone.

---

before departure from Canada, including serial numbers of valuables you already own, such as expensive foreign cameras. *Note:* The C$750 exemption can be used only once a year and only after an absence of 7 days.

Citizens of the U.K. who are **returning from a European Union (EU) country** will go through a separate Customs exit especially for EU travelers. In essence, there is no limit on what you can bring back from an EU country, provided the items are for personal use (this includes gifts), and you have already paid the necessary duty and tax. Customs laws, however, set out guidance levels. If you bring in more than these levels, you may be asked to prove that the goods are for your own use. Guidance levels on goods bought in the EU for personal use are 3,200 cigarettes, 200 cigars, 400 cigarillos, 3 kilograms of smoking tobacco, 10 liters of spirits, 90 liters of wine, 20 liters of fortified wine (such as port or sherry), and 110 liters of beer.

The duty-free allowance in **Australia** is A$400 or for those under 18, A$200. Citizens can bring in 250 cigarettes or 250 grams of loose tobacco, and 1,125 milliliters of alcohol. If you're returning with valuables you already own, such as foreign-made cameras, you should file form B263. A helpful brochure is available from Australian consulates or Customs offices called *Know Before You Go.* For more information, call the **Australian Customs Service** at © **1300/363-263,** or log onto www.customs.gov.au.

The duty-free allowance for **New Zealand** is NZ$700. Citizens over 17 can bring in 200 cigarettes, 50 cigars, or 250 grams of tobacco (or a mixture of all three if their combined weight doesn't exceed 250g), plus 4.5 liters of wine and beer, or 1.125 liters of liquor. New Zealand currency does not carry import or export restrictions. Fill out a certificate of export, listing the valuables you are taking out of the country; that way, you can bring them back without paying duty. Most questions are answered in a free pamphlet available at New Zealand consulates and Customs offices: *New Zealand Customs Guide for Travellers,* *Notice no. 4.* For more information, contact **New Zealand Customs,** The Customhouse, 17–21 Whitmore St., Box 2218, Wellington (© **04/473-6099** or 0800/428-786; www.customs.govt.nz).

3 Money

The basic unit of currency in Hungary is the **forint (Ft)**. Coins come in denominations of 1, 2, 5, 10, 20, 50, and 100 Ft. Banknotes come in denominations of 200; 500; 1,000; 5,000; 10,000; and 20,000 Ft.

The U.S. dollar has weakened considerably over the past several years and inflation has hit Hungary. These factors combined have made Hungry only slightly less expensive for travelers than most Western countries. Labor-intensive services, such as picture framing, tailoring, shoe and watch repair, and the like, are still inexpensive.

As of this writing, the rate of exchange is **$1 = 185 Ft (or 100 Ft = 54¢)**, and this is the rate used to calculate all the U.S. dollar prices in this book. Of course, exchange rates fluctuate over time. Go to www.oanda.com/convert/cheatsheet, to print out a cheat sheet for currency exchange rates to save using a calculator all of the time.

Note: Most hotels and pensions in Budapest list their prices in euros, while others still list them in forints. They have done this predominantly as a hedge against forint inflation; Hungary became a member of the European Union in May 2004, but is not planning to introduce the euro until, optimistically, 2012. All hotels in Budapest accept payment in Hungarian forints as well as in many foreign currencies.

CURRENCY

The best official exchange rates for cash are usually at the exchange booths all over the city. Many of them are associated with an Arany Pók clothing store, but others are independent. Their rates are always better than what you will get at a bank. The exchanges do not charge an additional commission, but build it into their conversions, which change daily. Traveler's checks can only be cashed at one Western Union outlet and very few banks. With the conversion factor and the commission, you will lose handsomely on the exchange. Neither restaurants nor shops will accept traveler's checks and we strongly urge travelers against using them here. Bank machines are common and the city center has a tremendous number of them, while exchange booths are also located throughout the city center, in train stations, and in most luxury hotels. Other than the Arany Pók exchange booths, those in the airport or hotels will almost uniformly offer less favorable rates than if you used your bankcard at an ATM. You may withdraw forints at the daily exchange rate from your home account through the Cirrus and PLUS networks (see "ATMs," below).

If you are approached by someone on the street to exchange money, ignore them or tell them to leave you alone. This is a not only illegal if they really have the cash, but many times, it is a scam. If caught exchanging money from anyone other than an authorized change booth or bank, you could be arrested.

The Hungarian forint is convertible back to any other currency; however, when you look at the rate board, the buy rate is never as good as the sell rate. It does not matter if it is an exchange booth or a bank. This is standard procedure throughout the world. Coins are never

The Hungarian Forint

For American Readers   At this writing $1 = approximately 185 Ft (or 100 Ft = 54¢), and this was the rate of exchange used to calculate the dollar values given in this chapter.

For British Readers   At this writing £1 = approximately $1.90 and this was the rate of exchange used to calculate the pound values in the table below.

Note: The rates given here fluctuate and may not be the same when you travel to Hungary. Therefore, this table should be used only as a guide.

Ft	US$	UK£	Ft	US$	UK£
5	0.03	0.01	3,000	16.21	8.52
10	0.05	0.03	4,000	20.62	11.36
25	0.14	0.07	5,000	27.02	14.20
50	0.27	0.14	6,000	32.43	17.04
75	0.41	0.21	7,000	37.83	19.88
100	0.54	0.28	8,000	43.24	22.72
200	1.08	0.57	9,000	48.64	25.56
300	1.62	0.85	10,000	54.05	28.40
400	2.15	1.13	15,000	81.08	42.60
500	2.70	1.42	20,000	108.10	56.80
750	4.05	2.13	25,000	135.14	71.10
1,000	5.40	2.84	30,000	162.16	85.20
1,500	8.10	4.26	40,000	216.20	113.60
2,000	10.80	5.68	50,000	270.27	142.24

accepted for exchange regardless of the currency, so if you have accumulated many of them, you may want to try to use them first before breaking more bills. You no longer have to retain your currency exchange receipts as proof of exchange.

Most people never think to use the airport ATMs (automated teller machines) only to pay higher rates by exchanging some money at home first, to cover airport incidentals. If you want to bypass any line, pay for your shuttle ride by credit card and then go to an ATM once you settle into your hotel. If you feel you need to have some cash, you can exchange money at your local American Express or Thomas Cook office or at your bank. American Express also dispenses traveler's checks and foreign currency via www.americanexpress.com or ℂ **800/ 807-6233,** but they'll charge a $15 order fee and additional shipping costs. American Express cardholders should dial ℂ **800/221-7282;** this number offers service in several foreign languages, and exempts Amex gold and platinum cardholders from the 1% fee. Take note that the American Express office has closed in Hungry.

ATMs

The easiest and best way to get cash away from home is from an ATM (automated teller machine). The **Cirrus** (ℂ **800/ 424-7787;** www.mastercard.com) and

PLUS (✆ 800/843-7587; www.visa.com) networks span the globe; look at the back of your bank card to see which network you're on, then call before you leave home as these numbers will not work in Europe or check online for ATM locations. Note that 800 numbers **do not** work from Europe, regardless if your company tells you they do, so be sure to call before leaving home or take the international collect number with you. Be sure you know your personal identification number (PIN) and daily withdrawal limit before you depart. *Note:* Remember that many banks impose a fee every time you use a card at another bank's ATM, and that fee can be higher for international transactions (up to $5 or more) than for domestic ones (where it is rarely more than $2). In addition, the bank from which you withdraw cash may charge its own fee. To compare banks' ATM fees within the U.S., use **www.bankrate.com**. For international withdrawal fees, ask your bank. Some banks have been known to waive fees temporarily for good customers or they may have a cooperative agreement with a foreign bank to waive fees. It pays to ask.

You can use your credit card to receive cash advances at ATMs, but you will need to know your PIN number. Keep in mind that credit card companies protect themselves from theft by limiting maximum withdrawals outside their home country, so call your credit card company before you leave home. Keep a record of your credit card phone numbers that are *not* toll free, but can be called collect in case of need. And keep in mind that you'll pay interest from the moment of your withdrawal, even if you pay your monthly bills on time.

TRAVELER'S CHECKS

Traveler's checks are the dinosaurs of travel. ATMs make cash accessible at any time. Given the fees you'll pay for ATM use at banks other than your own,

however, you might be better off with traveler's checks if you're withdrawing money often, but then you are dependent on finding a bank that will cash them. Not all banks provide this service and those that do are not open on weekends. Travelers checks are not as good as cash here in Hungary, so rethink using them. I have only seen one bank that advertises that they accept traveler's checks, but not even at all of their branches. Many banks will flatly refuse.

However, you can buy traveler's checks at most banks at home. **American Express** offers denominations of $20, $50, $100, $500, and (for cardholders only) $1,000. You'll pay a service charge ranging from 1% to 4%. By phone, you can buy traveler's checks by calling ✆ 800/807-6233. American Express cardholders should dial ✆ 1/800-528-4800 or 1/336-393-1111 collect international; this number accepts collect calls, offers service in several foreign languages, and exempts Amex gold and platinum cardholders from the 1% fee.

Foreign currency traveler's checks are useful if you're traveling to one country, or to the euro zone; **American Express and Thomas Cook** offer foreign currency traveler's checks. You'll pay the rate of exchange at the time of your purchase (so it's a good idea to monitor the rate before you buy), and both companies charge a transaction fee per order (and a shipping fee if you order online). I have had problems with traveler's checks in other countries within Europe and quit using them years ago.

If you do choose to carry traveler's checks, keep a record of their serial numbers separate from your checks in the event that they are stolen or lost. You'll need the numbers to get a refund faster.

CREDIT CARDS

Credit cards are another safe way to carry money. They also provide a convenient record of all your expenses, plus they generally offer relatively good exchange rates. You can also withdraw cash advances from your credit cards at banks or ATMs, provided you know your PIN specifically for that card. If you don't know yours, call the number on the back of your credit card and ask the company to send it to you. It usually takes 5 to 7 business days, though some banks will provide the number over the phone if you tell them your mother's maiden name or some other personal information. This practice is becoming more rare with heightened security. Keep in mind that many banks now assess a 1%-to-3% "transaction fee" that they call a currency conversion charge on **all** charges you incur abroad (whether you're using the local currency or U.S. dollars). But credit cards still may be the smart way to go when you factor in things like exorbitant ATM fees and the higher exchange rates and service fees you'll pay with traveler's checks.

4 When to Go

Budapest has a relatively mild climate—the annual mean temperature in Hungary is 50°F (10°C). Nevertheless, summer temperatures often exceed 80° to 85°F (27°–29°C), and sweltering hot, humid days are typical in July and August. In July 2007, all heat records were broken when the temperature soared to 100° to 104°F (38°–40°C) for days on end and stayed just under that for weeks, causing power interruptions. Most hotels with air-conditioning were on restrictions due to the overload of electric usage. January and February are the coldest months, averaging 30°F (−1°C), though temperatures can dip well below that on any given day. Be prepared for damp and chilly weather in winter. It may snow often, but rarely does it last more than 1 day and with no accumulation. Spring is usually mild and, especially in May, wet. Autumn is usually quite pleasant, with mild, cooler weather through October.

HOLIDAYS

Hungarian holidays are: January 1 (New Year's Day), March 15 (National Holiday), Easter Sunday and Easter Monday, May 1 (May Day), Whit Monday, August 20 (St. Stephen's Day), October 23 (Republic Day), November 1 (All Saints' Day), and December 25 and 26 (Christmas). Shops and banks are closed on all holidays, some museums stay open on some holidays.

HUNGARY CALENDAR OF EVENTS

With a little planning you can come to Budapest at a time that will coincide with one or more of the city's cultural events; however, if you miss these, there is always something worthy happening; it is a city of festivals. All inquiries about ticket availability and locations of events can first be checked online where you can also buy tickets for many venues at www.jegymester.hu. For other information, contact Budapest's main tourist information office, **Tourinform** (see "Visitor Information," earlier in this chapter).

March

Budapest Spring Festival. For 2 weeks, performances of everything from opera to ballet, from classical music to drama, are held at all the major halls and theaters of Budapest. Simultaneously, temporary exhibitions

Budapest's Average Daily Temperatures & Rainfall

	Jan	Feb	Mar	Apr	May	June	July	Aug	Sept	Oct	Nov	Dec
Temp. (°F)	30	34	38	53	62	68	72	71	63	52	42	35
Temp. (°C)	−1	1	3	12	17	20	22	22	17	11	6	2
Rainfall (in.)	1.3	1.2	1.1	1.5	2.2	2.5	2	2	1.6	1.3	2	1.6

open in many of Budapest's museums. Tickets are available at the **Festival Ticket Service,** V. 1053 Egyetem tér 5 (© **1/486-3300;** www.fesztivalvaros.hu; Blue line: Ferenciek tere), and at the individual venues. Hotels book quickly for this time of year, so plan ahead. Mid- to late March.

Hollókő's Easter Festival. During Easter in this charming small town in northeastern Hungary, villagers wear traditional costumes and participate in a folk festival. It features traditional song, dance, and foods. For information, contact the **Hungarian Arts Festivals Federation** (© **1/202-1095;** www.artsfestivals.hu). Held on Easter Day, it is just as popular with Hungarians as with travelers, so expect a crowd.

June, July & August

Open-Air Theater Programs, Budapest. A rich variety of open-air performances are given throughout Budapest during the summer. Highlights include opera and ballet at the Margaret Island Open-Air Theater, folklore and dance at the Buda Park Theater, musicals in Városmajor Theater, and classical music recitals in the Dominican Courtyard at the Hilton Hotel. For information, contact the Hungarian Arts Festivals Federation (© **1/202-1095;** www.artsfestivals.hu). June through August.

Sziget Summer Festival, Szeged. Szeged, the proud capital of the Great Plain, is home to a summer-long series of cultural events (ballet, opera, rock opera, open-air theater). For information, call © **62/471-411;** www.szeged iszabadteri.hu. June through August.

Organ Concerts, Budapest. Concerts are given in the Matthias Church, in the lovely Castle District of Buda. See p. 223 for details. June through August. In addition, Budapest's largest church, St. Stephen's Basilica (p. 141), also hosts concerts outside the front doors. If you don't care about sitting, you can listen for free. July through August.

International Palace Tournament, Visegrád. Each summer, this ancient town on the Danube hosts an authentic medieval festival replete with dueling knights on horseback, and early music and dance. Contact **Visegrád Tours,** RÉV u. 15 in Visegrád (© **26/398-090;** www.palotajatekok.hu). Second weekend in July.

"Budafest" Summer Opera and Ballet Festival, Budapest. This summer festival (usually held during most of July and August) is the only time to see a summer performance at the wonderful Hungarian State Opera House in Budapest. Tickets are available at the **opera house** box office at VI. Andrássy út 20 (© **1/331-2550;** www.opera.hu).

International Guitar Festival, Esztergom. This stately little town on the Danube hosts a guitar festival that features performers from around the world. The Basilica hosts the classical concert performances. For information, contact **Gran Tours,** Esztergom at Széchenyi tér 25 (© **33/502-001;** www.guitarfestival.hu). First week of August every other year; the next festival is scheduled for 2009.

Formula One Grand Prix, Budapest. One of the European racing circuit's most important annual events is held at Budapest's HungaroRing in Mogyoród. Hotels book quickly for this event, so plan ahead. They also increase their rates considerably. Call © **28/444-444** or check out **www. hungaroring.hu.** First week or second weekend in August.

Island Festival (Sziget Fesztivál), Óbuda Island in the Danube. Established in 1994 as Hungary's very own Woodstock, the Sziget Festival (© **1/372-0650;** www.sziget.hu) is a weeklong music festival that draws young people from all over Europe. It is now one of the largest music festivals in Europe. The event features foreign and local rock, folk, jazz, world music, and other groups on dozens of stages playing each day from early afternoon to the wee hours of the morning. Camping is available. You can get details and pick up a program schedule at **Tourinform** (p. 11) or check out their website. Usually begins the second week of August.

Traditional Handicraft Fair, Budapest. The Castle District is the site of a 3-day annual handicraft fair, which draws vendors from across Hungary and from Hungarian enclaves in neighboring countries, especially Romania. The wares are generally handmade and of high quality. This is a part of the St. Stephen's Day celebrations. August 20.

St. Stephen's Day, Budapest. This is Hungary's national day. The country's patron saint is celebrated with cultural events and a dramatic display of fireworks over the Danube at 9pm. Hungarians also celebrate their constitution on this day and ceremoniously welcome the first new bread from the recent crop of July wheat. August 20.

National Jewish Festival, Budapest. In 1999 this annual festival arrived on the Hungarian cultural scene. The festival features a variety of Jewish culture–related events. Features range from klezmer music to a book fair, from ballet to cabaret held at various locations for the different venues offered. For information, contact the Tourism and Cultural Center of the Budapest Jewish Community, Síp u. 12 (© **1/343-0420;** www.jewish festival.hu). Late August into early September; call for exact dates.

September

Budapest International Wine Festival. This festival, in Budapest's Castle District, features wine tastings, displays, and auctions, as well as folk and classical music performances. Each year, there is a guest country that shares its wines. In 2007, it was South Africa. The sponsor is the **Hungarian Viniculture Foundation,** XI. Bartók Béla út 152 (© **1/203-8507;** www.winefestival.hu). Early September.

Budapest International Fair. For 10 days, Budapest's HungExpo grounds fill up with displays of Europe's latest consumer goods. Call © **1/263-6000** or go to www.hungexpo.hu. Mid-September.

Budapest Art Weeks. In celebration of the opening of the fall season, special classical music and dance performances spring up for 3 weeks in all the city's major halls. For information, contact the Hungarian Arts Festivals Federation (© **1/318-8165**). The festivals' traditional start is September 25, the day of Béla Bartók's death.

Contemporary Music Weeks, Budapest. Held in conjunction with the Budapest Art Weeks, this 3-week festival features contemporary music performances in all the capital's major halls. For information, contact the Hungarian Arts Festivals Federation (© 1/318-8165). Starts September 25.

5 Travel Insurance

Check your existing insurance policies and credit card coverage before you buy travel insurance. You may already be covered for lost luggage, canceled tickets, or medical expenses.

The cost of travel insurance varies widely, depending on the cost and length of your trip, your age and health, and the type of trip you're taking, but expect to pay between 5% and 8% of the vacation itself. If you buy your tickets through a travel agent, be sure to ask about insurance, but also ask if you can purchase it at a later date if you need to. Then you have the flexibility to get estimates from various providers through websites such as **InsureMyTrip.com**. Enter your trip cost and dates, your age, and other information for prices from more than a dozen companies. If you're over 65, obtaining insurance is a bit trickier. Medicare does not cover you outside of the U.S. In this case, your travel agent may be able to get the only deal for you, but at a higher premium.

TRIP-CANCELLATION INSURANCE

Trip-cancellation insurance will help retrieve your money if you have to back out of a trip or depart early, or if your travel supplier goes bankrupt. Permissible reasons for trip cancellation can range from sickness to natural disasters to the State Department declaring a destination unsafe for travel. (Insurers usually won't cover vague fears, though, as many travelers discovered when they tried to cancel their trips in Oct 2001.) In this unstable world, trip-cancellation insurance is a good buy if you're purchasing tickets well in advance. One never knows what the state of the world, or of your airline, will be 9 months in the future. Insurance policy details vary, so read the fine print to make sure that your airline or cruise line is on the list of carriers covered in case of bankruptcy. A good resource is **"Travel Guard Alerts,"** a list of companies considered high-risk by Travel Guard International (see website below). Protect yourself further by paying for the insurance with a credit card. The law provides for consumers to get their money back on goods and services not received if they report the loss within 60 days after the charge is listed on their credit card statement.

Note: Many tour operators, particularly those offering trips to remote or high-risk areas, include insurance in the total trip cost or can arrange insurance policies through a partnering provider, which is a convenient and often cost-effective way for the traveler to obtain insurance. Make sure the tour company is a reputable one, however, and be aware that some experts suggest you avoid buying insurance from the tour or cruise company you're traveling with. They contend it's more secure to buy from a third party than to put all your money in one place.

For more information, contact one of the following recommended insurers: **Access America** (© **800/284-8300;** www.accessamerica.com); **Travel Guard International** (© **800/826-4919;** www.travelguard.com); **Travel Insured International** (© **800/826-4919;** www.travelinsured.com); and **Travelex Insurance Services** (© **800/228-9792;** www.travelexinsurance.com).

MEDICAL INSURANCE For travel overseas, most health plans (including Medicare and Medicaid) do not provide coverage, and those that do often require you to pay for services upfront and only reimburse you after you return home. Even if your plan does cover overseas treatment, most out-of-country hospitals make you pay your bills upfront, and send you a refund only after you've returned home and filed the necessary paperwork with your insurance company. As a safety net, you may want to buy travel medical insurance, particularly if you're traveling to a remote or high-risk area where emergency evacuation is a possible scenario. If you require additional medical insurance, try **MEDEX Assistance** (© **800/732-5309;** www.medexassist.com) or **Travel Assistance International** (© **800/821-2828;** www.travelassistance.com) for general information on services.

LOST-LUGGAGE INSURANCE On domestic flights, checked baggage is covered for up to $2,500 per ticketed passenger. On international flights (including

U.S. portions of international trips), baggage coverage is limited to approximately $9.07 per pound, up to approximately $635 per checked bag. If you plan to check items more valuable than what's covered by the standard liability, see if your homeowner's policy covers your valuables, get baggage insurance as part of your comprehensive travel-insurance package, or buy Travel Guard's "BagTrak" product. Don't buy insurance at the airport, where it's usually overpriced. Be sure to take any valuables or irreplaceable items with you in your carry-on luggage, because many valuables (including books, money, and electronics) aren't covered by airline policies.

If your luggage is lost, immediately file a lost-luggage claim at the airport, detailing the luggage contents. Photographing the contents with a digital camera will expedite claims. Most airlines require that you report delayed, damaged, or lost baggage within 4 hours of arrival. The airlines are required to deliver luggage, once found, directly to your house or destination free of charge.

6 Health & Safety

STAYING HEALTHY

No shots or inoculations are required for entry to Hungary. To be on the safe side, bring enough of any prescription or other medication you may need. It is also good practice to bring along a copy of all prescriptions in their generic form in case you run out of any medications, but you will need a Hungarian doctor to write a prescription for the pharmacy to dispense it. Sunscreen and other toiletries are readily available.

GENERAL AVAILABILITY OF HEALTH CARE

Emergency medical treatment is available in Hungary, but with new laws, you will have to pay a fee for service, but not anywhere as much as a visit in the U.S. You'll have to pay for prescription medications and for nonemergency care. In some cases, your existing health plan will provide the coverage you need, but double-check; you may want to buy **travel medical insurance** instead. Your insurance at home may not accept forms in Hungarian and the forms will not be provided in English here unless you go to a private clinic. (See "Medical Insurance," above.) Bring your insurance ID card with you when you travel.

Contact the **International Association for Medical Assistance to Travelers (IAMAT;** ℭ **716/754-4883** or, in Canada, **519/836-0102;** www.iamat.org) for tips on travel and health concerns in the countries you're visiting, and for lists of local, English-speaking doctors. The United States **Centers for Disease Control and Prevention** (ℭ **800/311-3435;** www.cdc.gov) provides up-to-date information on health hazards by region or country and offers tips on food safety. The website **www.tripprep.com**, sponsored by a consortium of travel medicine practitioners, may also offer helpful advice on traveling abroad. You can find listings of reliable clinics overseas on the **International Society of Travel Medicine** website (www.istm.org).

WHAT TO DO IF YOU GET SICK AWAY FROM HOME

Any foreign consulate can provide a list of doctors in the area who speak English. If you get sick, consider asking your hotel concierge to recommend a local doctor or clinic. In Budapest, there are a couple of clinics where English is the primary language. You can also try the emergency room at a local hospital. We list hospitals and emergency numbers under "Fast Facts: Budapest," p. 65.

If you suffer from a chronic illness, consult your doctor before your departure. For conditions like epilepsy, diabetes, or heart problems, wear a **MedicAlert identification tag** (© 888/633-4298; www.medic alert.org), which will immediately alert doctors to your condition and give them access to your records through MedicAlert's 24-hour hot line.

Pack **prescription medications** in your carry-on luggage in their original containers, with pharmacy labels—otherwise they won't make it through airport security. Also carry copies of your prescriptions in case you lose your pills or run out. Don't forget an extra pair of contact lenses or prescription glasses. Carry the generic name of prescription medicines, in case a local doctor is unfamiliar with the brand name; they are different from country to country.

For domestic trips, most reliable healthcare plans provide coverage if you get sick away from home. For travel abroad, you may have to pay all medical costs upfront and be reimbursed later. See "Medical Insurance," above.

STAYING SAFE

Budapest is a safe city, and violent street crime is almost nonexistent. There were political upheavals in 2006 and 2007, but staying away from the action will keep you safe. However, you should always be on the lookout for pickpockets, especially on crowded buses, trains, and trams. Pickpockets generally work in teams, with one or more creating a distraction (bumping into people, falling down, staging a fake argument, and so on), while a partner takes advantage of the distracted victim. Protect yourself by always carrying valuables in an inside pocket or a money belt. There is no shortage of rowdy drunks at night in Budapest, but they don't pose danger to others. Many of them are other travelers who are here to party thanks to cheap flights and they get rowdy. Budapest is a city filled with underpasses. Be careful at night; you can sometimes cross a street above ground if an underpass appears deserted and traffic allows it.

7 Specialized Travel Resources

TRAVELERS WITH DISABILITIES

Disabilities shouldn't stop anyone from traveling. There are more options and resources out there than ever before. With that said, Hungary is not a friendly country to the disabled traveler. Access is limited and it is difficult for wheelchairs to get into most hotels, restaurants, and public transportation. There are only a few exceptions to the rule, the 4 and 6 tram lines have platforms level with the tram door; however, other trams do not have accessibility. The metros have stairs and escalators, not elevators. For the few metro stops that have wheelchair elevators, a key is needed, but there is no attendant available to acquire it. Sidewalks do not have ramps or slopes for a wheelchair and the majority of the stores have barriers that would make wheelchair

access improbable to impossible. The disabled in Hungary have been fighting for better access since the change in government, but change is very slow.

With that said, many travel agencies offer customized tours and itineraries for travelers with disabilities. **Flying Wheels Travel** (© 507/451-5005; www.flying-wheelstravel.com) offers escorted tours and cruises that emphasize sports and private tours in minivans with lifts. **Access-Able Travel Source** (© 303/232-2979; www.access-able.com) offers extensive access information and advice for traveling around the world with disabilities. **Accessible Journeys** (© 800/846-4537 or 610/521-0339; www.disabilitytravel.com) caters specifically to slow walkers and wheelchair travelers, their families, and friends.

Avis Rent a Car has an "Avis Access" program that offers such services as a dedicated 24-hour toll-free number (© 888/879-4273) for customers with special travel needs; special car features such as swivel seats, spinner knobs, and hand controls; and accessible bus service. Not all of these services may be available at locations in Hungary.

Organizations that offer assistance to travelers with disabilities include **Moss Rehab** (www.mossresourcenet.org),which provides a library of accessible-travel resources online; the **American Foundation for the Blind (AFB;** © 800/232-5463; www.afb.org), a referral resource for the blind or visually impaired that includes information on traveling with Seeing Eye dogs; and **SATH** (Society for Accessible Travel & Hospitality; © 212/447-7284; www.sath.org; annual membership fees: $45 adults, $30 seniors and students), which offers a wealth of travel resources for all types of disabilities and informed recommendations on destinations, access guides, travel agents, tour operators, vehicle rentals, and companion services. **AirAmbulanceCard.com** is now partnered with SATH and allows you to preselect top-notch hospitals in case of an emergency for $195 a year ($295 per family), among other benefits.

Also check out the quarterly magazine *Emerging Horizons* (www.emerging horizons.com; $16.95 per year, $21.95 outside the U.S.); and *Open World* magazine, published by SATH (© 212/447-7284).

GAY & LESBIAN TRAVELERS

Being part of the EU, Hungary has had to modify its laws regarding gay and lesbian rights, though some older gay people say they had it better under Socialism. Either way, sexual orientation is not an issue in Hungary for the most part. Gays and lesbians do have a tendency to try to stay invisible as much as possible though. In Hungary, there are far fewer lesbian

events and no bars specifically for women. **The International Gay and Lesbian Travel Association (IGLTA;** © 800/448-8550 or 954/776-2626; www.iglta.org) is the trade association for the gay and lesbian travel industry, and offers an online directory of gay- and lesbian-friendly travel businesses; go to their website and click on "Members."

Many agencies offer tours and travel itineraries specifically for gay and lesbian travelers. **Above and Beyond Tours** (© 800/397-2681; www.abovebeyond tours.com) is the exclusive gay and lesbian tour operator for United Airlines. **Now, Voyager** (© 800/255-6951; www.nowvoyager.com) is a well-known San Francisco–based, gay-owned and -operated travel service. **Olivia Cruises & Resorts** (© 800/631-6277; www. olivia.com) charters entire resorts and ships for exclusive lesbian vacations and offers smaller group experiences for both gay and lesbian travelers. (In 2005, tennis great Martina Navratilova was named Olivia's official spokesperson.)

Gay.com Travel (© 415/834-6500; www.gay.com/travel or www.outand about.com) is an excellent online successor to the popular *Out & About* print magazine. It provides regularly updated information about gay-owned, gay-oriented, and gay-friendly lodging, dining, sightseeing, nightlife, and shopping establishments in every important destination worldwide. It also offers trip planning information for gay and lesbian travelers for more than 50 destinations, along various themes, ranging from sex and travel to vacations for couples.

The following travel guides are available at many bookstores, or you can order them from any online bookseller: *Frommer's Gay & Lesbian Europe* (www. frommers.com), an excellent travel resource to the top European cities and resorts; *Spartacus International Gay Guide* (Bruno Gmünder Verlag;

www.spartacusworld.com/gayguide) and *Odysseus: The International Gay Travel Planner* (Odysseus Enterprises Ltd.), both good, annual, English-language guidebooks focused on gay men; and the *Damron* guides (www.damron.com), with separate, annual books for gay men and lesbians.

SENIOR TRAVEL

If you are a senior, check with different groups such as **AARP**, 601 E St. NW, Washington, DC 20049 (© **888/687-2277**; www.aarp.org), to see if you can get any discounts on hotels, airfares, and car rentals. AARP offers members a wide range of benefits, including *AARP: The Magazine* and a monthly newsletter, but the travel industry has changed many of the perks it once offered, so you may not find as many savings as in the past, but it is worth checking. They may be domestic offers only. Anyone over 50 can join for $12 a year.

Many reliable agencies and organizations target the 50-plus market. **Elderhostel** has become less of a bargain over the years, but they still maintain a good reputation (© **800/454-5768**; www.elderhostel.org). It arranges study programs for those age 55 and over (and a spouse or companion of any age) in the U.S. and in more than 80 countries around the world. Most courses last 5 to 7 days in the U.S. (2–4 weeks abroad), and many include airfare, accommodations in university dormitories or modest inns, meals, and tuition. **ElderTreks** (© **800/741-7956** or © **0808-234-1714** from the United Kingdom; www.eldertreks.com) offers small-group tours to off-the-beaten-path or adventure-travel locations, restricted to travelers 50 and older. **INTRAV** (© **800/456-8100**; www.intrav.com) is a high-end tour operator that caters to the mature, discerning traveler (not specifically seniors), with trips around the world that include trips down the Nile, polar expeditions, private-jet adventures, and excursion tours to South Africa, relieving you of having to make too many decisions, but if you are free-spirited, they may not be for you as they also curb your free time.

There are some recommended publications specifically targeting the needs of the older traveler. One such magazine with five issues a year for $14 is *Travel 50 & Beyond* (www.travel50andbeyond.com). Books about the travel industry need to be as current as possible to be of value, since change happens fast. Look at *Travel Unlimited: Uncommon Adventures for the Mature Traveler* (Avalon, 2000) for any possible tips, but since it is from 2000, it may be out of date; and *Unbelievably Good Deals and Great Adventures That You Absolutely Can't Get Unless You're Over 50, 2007–2008.* (McGraw-Hill), by Joann Rattner Heilman. There are older editions, so make sure you get this one in particular.

Seniors in Hungary do not usually qualify for a discount. When you see it on signs, it is usually reserved for Hungarians or if extended further to EU citizens. However, I always recommend asking. Some workers will not bother asking your country of origin and let you have the discount.

AFRICAN-AMERICAN TRAVELERS

The African-American traveler should not have any concerns about a trip to Budapest. In the countryside, people may be more curious, but there is no reason for any concern. In Budapest, there have been a number of immigrants from some of the poorer African countries and the population has been accepting.

The Internet offers a number of helpful travel sites for African-American travelers. **Black Travel Online** (www.blacktravelonline.com) posts news on upcoming events and includes links to articles and travel-booking sites. **Soul of America** (www.soulofamerica.com) is a comprehensive website, with travel tips, event and family reunion postings, and sections on historically black beach resorts, active vacations, and even black innkeepers.

Agencies and organizations that provide resources for black travelers include: **Rodgers Travel** (© **800/825-1775;** www.rodgerstravel.com), a Philadelphia-based travel agency with an extensive menu of tours in destinations worldwide, including heritage and private-group tours; the **African American Association of Innkeepers International** (© **877/ 422-5777;** www.africanamericaninns. com), which provides information on member B&Bs in the U.S., Canada, the Caribbean and Ghana; and **Henderson Travel & Tours** (© **800/327-2309** or 301/650-5700; www.hendersontravel. com), which has specialized in trips to Africa since 1957. For more information, check out the following collections and guides: *African American Travel Guide to Hot, Exotic & Fun Filled Places* by Jon Haggins (Amber Communications, 2002); *Go Girl: The Black Woman's Guide to Travel & Adventure* (English Mountain Press, 1997), a compilation of travel essays by writers including Jill Nelson and Audre Lorde, with some practical information and trip-planning advice; *The African American Travel Guide* by Wayne Robinson (Hunter Publishing; www.hunterpublishing.com), with details on 19 North American cities; *Steppin' Out: An African-American Guide to Our 20 Favorite Cities* by Carla Labat (Avalon), with details on 20 cities; *Travel and Enjoy Magazine* (© **866/266-6211;** subscription: $15 for 4 issues per year), which focuses on discounts and destination reviews; and the more narrative *Pathfind-ers Magazine* (© **877/977-PATH;** www.pathfinderstravel.com; subscription: $18 per year), which includes articles on everything from Rio de Janeiro to Ghana as well as information on upcoming ski, diving, golf, and tennis trips.

STUDENT TRAVEL

Students should look into the **International Student Identity Card (ISIC),** which offers discounts on entrance fees and some hostels. There may or may not be a discount on railroad tickets, but rarely plane tickets. Remember, you have to have the card with you to get the discount if it is available. If you purchase your airline tickets through STA, you do receive basic health and life insurance and a 24-hour help line. The card is available for $22 from **STA Travel** (© **800/ 781-4040** in North America; www.sta. com or www.statravel.com), the biggest student travel agency in the world. If you're no longer a student but are still under 26, you can get an **International Youth Travel Card (IYTC)** for the same price from the same people, which entitles you to fewer discounts. Travel CUTS (© 866/246-9762; www.travelcuts.com) offers similar services for both Canadians and U.S. residents. Irish students may prefer to turn to USIT (© 01/602-1904; www.usitnow.ie), an Ireland-based specialist in student, youth, and independent travel. Note that in Hungary, student discounts are only given at some hostels, not all of them. Museums and other attractions may reserve the student discounts for Hungarian students only, but others will offer a discount with a valid card. Some discounts are listed in this guide.

SURFING FOR AIRFARES

The "big three" online travel agencies, **Expedia.com, Travelocity.com,** and **Orbitz.com,** sell most of the air tickets bought on the Internet. (Canadian travelers should try Expedia.ca and Travelocity.ca; U.K. residents can go for Expedia.co.uk and opodo.co.uk.) **Kayak.com** is also gaining popularity and uses a sophisticated search engine (developed at MIT). Each has different business deals with the airlines and may offer different fares on the same flights, so it's wise to shop around. Expedia, Kayak, and Travelocity will also send you an **e-mail notification** when a cheap fare becomes available to your favorite destination. Of the smaller travel-agency websites, **SideStep** (www.sidestep.com) has gotten the best reviews from Frommer's authors. The website (with optional browser add-on) purports to "search 140 sites at once," but in reality only beats competitors' fares as often as other sites do. One megasite that allows you to enter your information once, but choose different search engines is Smarter Travel (www.smartertravel.com). If you want to check flights and schedules within Europe, go to **SkyScanner** at www.skyscanner.com or www.flylc.com for the best fares.

When you think you have found the best deal available on the Internet, go directly to the **airline's website,** to see if you can get a better deal by booking directly with them. Often times, low-fare carriers such as Southwest, JetBlue, Air-Tran, WestJet, Ryanair, or many of the European budget airlines are either missing from travel websites or their inventory of seats is not updated efficiently. Major airlines are now trying to cut out the intermediary as often as possible by offering specials on their websites, which are not available anywhere else. Some of the low-cost airlines are charging extra for calling their phone agents, making Web fares even more attractive. For the websites of airlines that fly to and from your destination, go to "Getting There," p. 28.

If you are flexible in your travel times, it is a good idea to sign up for e-mail alerts from different airlines or travel sites. You will get first-hand information on great **last-minute deals** as they are offered. Most announcements come on Tuesday or Wednesday and must be purchased online. Most are only valid for travel within specific periods, but some (such as Southwest's) can be booked weeks or months in advance.

For last-minute trips, **site59.com** and **lastminutetravel.com** in the U.S. and **lastminute.com** in Europe often have better air-and-hotel package deals than the major-label sites.

If you're willing to give up some control over your flight details, use what is called an **"opaque" fare service** like **Priceline** (www.priceline.com; www.priceline.co.uk for Europeans) or its smaller competitor, **Hotwire** (www.hotwire.com). Both offer rock-bottom prices in exchange for travel on a "mystery airline" at a mysterious time of day, often with a mysterious change of planes en route. The mystery airlines are all major, well-known carriers and the possibility of being sent from Philadelphia to Chicago via Tampa is remote; the airlines' routing computers are a lot better than they used to be. Your chances of getting a 6am or 11pm flight, however, are still high. Hotwire tells you flight prices before you buy; Priceline usually has better deals than Hotwire, but you have to play their "name our price" game. If you're new at this, the helpful folks at **Bidding-ForTravel** (www.biddingfortravel.com) do a good job of demystifying Priceline's prices and strategies. Priceline and Hotwire are great for flights within North America and between the U.S. and Europe. But for flights to other parts of the world, consolidators will almost always beat their fares. *Note:* Priceline also has non-opaque services available. You now have the option to pick exact flights, times, and airlines from a list of offers, or opt to bid on opaque fares as before. Note that with the Priceline and Hotwire, you usually do not accrue frequent flyer miles for your flights.

SURFING FOR HOTELS

Shopping online for a hotel can be done in a few different ways: You may use a hotel booking agency, or a service such as

Priceline or Hotwire, but you may also try to book through the hotel's own website, where like the airlines, they will offer specials not found elsewhere. Internet hotel agencies have multiplied exponentially and new start-ups appear weekly all competing for the business of millions of consumers surfing for accommodations around the world. Competition can be a traveler's best friend if you have the know-how, the patience, and time to shop around and compare what each site is offering. The same property can vary considerably from site to site. And keep in mind that hotels at the top of a site's listing may be there for no other reason than that they paid money to get the placement.

Of the "big three" sites, **Expedia** offers a long list of special deals and virtual tours or photos of available rooms so you can see what you're paying for (a feature that helps counter the claims that the best rooms are often held back from bargain-booking websites). **Travelocity** posts unvarnished customer reviews and ranks its properties according to the AAA rating system. **Trip Advisor** (www.tripadvisor.com) is another excellent source of unbiased user reviews of hotels around the world. While even the finest hotels can inspire a misleadingly poor review from a picky or crabby traveler, the body of user opinions, when taken as a whole, is usually a reliable indicator.

Other reliable online booking agencies include **Hotels.com** and **Quikbook.com.** An excellent free program, **TravelAxe** (www.travelaxe.net), can help you search multiple hotel sites at once, even ones you may never have heard of. **Orbitz** is a popular site, conveniently listing the total price of the room, including the taxes and service charges. Another booking site, **Travelweb** (www.travelweb.com), is partnered with Priceline. The Italian-based **Venere** (www.venere.com) is a great site for European accommodations from bed-and-breakfasts to five-star hotels. Another site that offers pension and bed-and-

breakfast options are **Great Bed and Breakfasts** found at www.betterbedandbreakfasts.com. It allows you to be in direct contact with the supplier, allowing you to make your own decisions without having to pay a commission.

For the gay and lesbian traveler, we recommend **Purple Roofs** at www.purpleroofs.com for listings of gay-owned or gay-friendly accommodations or **Enjoy Bed and Breakfast** at www.ebab.com.

More than once, travelers have arrived at their hotel, only to be told that they have no reservation. We always recommend sending an e-mail or phoning the hotel to reconfirm the reservation has been made and keep a record of the person corresponded with or the name of the person you spoke with. It's a good idea to **get a confirmation number** and **make a printout** of any online booking transaction.

In the opaque website category, **Priceline** and **Hotwire** are even better for hotels than for airfares; through both, you're allowed to pick the neighborhood and quality level of your hotel before paying. Priceline's hotel product even covers Europe and Asia, though it's much better at getting five-star lodging for three-star prices than at finding anything at the bottom of the scale. On the downside, many hotels stick Priceline guests in their least desirable rooms. Be sure to go to the BiddingForTravel website (see above) before bidding on a hotel room on Priceline; it features a somewhat up-to-date list of hotels that Priceline uses in major cities. For both Priceline and Hotwire, you pay upfront, and the fee is nonrefundable. *Note:* Some hotels do not provide loyalty program credits, points, or other frequent-stay amenities when you book a room through opaque online services.

SURFING FOR RENTAL CARS

For booking rental cars online, the best deals are usually found at rental-car company websites, although all the major online travel agencies also offer rental-car reservations services. Priceline and Hotwire work well for rental cars, too, but the only "mystery" is which major rental company you get, and for most travelers the difference between Hertz, Avis, and Budget is negligible. For Hungary, we found that dealing direct with the rental-car agency websites produced much better deals.

9 Getting There

BY PLANE

Northwest Airlines (© 800/447-4747) and **Malév** (© 800/877-5429, 800/262-5380, or 800/223-6884), the former Hungarian state airline, offer non-stop service between North America and Budapest. Other leading carriers include **Lufthansa** (© 800/645-3880), **British Airways** (© 800/247-9297), **Delta Airlines** (© 800/241-4141), and **Austrian Air** (© 800/843-0002).

Budapest is served by two adjacent airports, **Ferihegy 1** and **Ferihegy 2,** both located in the XVII district in southeastern Pest. Ferihegy 1 is the airport that all budget airlines use, while Ferihegy 2 (which has a **Terminal A** and a **Terminal B**) serves the flagship carriers and other traditional airlines. The distance between the terminals is about 1 block, so there is no need to be concerned if you arrive at the airport for your flight and are at the wrong terminal, but there is some concern if you arrive at the wrong airport. There are several main information numbers: For airport information call © 1/296-5959; and for general information, call © 1/296-7000. For ease of language, use the airport's English version website at www.bud.hu/english/transport for flight arrival information.

All arriving flights are international since there is no domestic air service in Hungary. Arriving passengers need to pass through the Passport Control and Customs before they emerge into the bustling arrivals halls of the respective airports. **Ferihegy 1** was remodeled and enlarged just a few years ago, but due to the number of budget airlines, the demand has exceeded this retrofit. **Ferihegy 2** is larger, but still not overwhelmingly large. You will not have any fears of getting lost in it like some other airports in major cities. In each airport, you will find accommodations offices, rental-car agencies, shops, and exchange booths, plus a Tourinform desk. Note that exchange rates are much less favorable here than in the city, so rather than change money, take it out of the ATM. Even with bank fees, you will come out ahead in the end.

Twenty-four-hour left-luggage service is available at **Ferihegy 2** Terminal B (© 1/296-8802).

GETTING THROUGH THE AIRPORT

With the ever-changing federalization of airport security screening procedures at U.S. airports, we strongly urge you to ask your airline carrier what their requirements are regarding check-in times. We have heard different rules being applied at different U.S. airports, so it is best to check ahead of time. The general rule of thumb is to arrive at the airport **1 hour** before a domestic flight and **2 hours** before an international flight. Airline personal are not as sympathetic to people who are late to arrive at the airport as in the past, so plan for long lines at security.

Bring a **current, government-issued photo ID** such as a driver's license or passport (passport only for international travel). Many times now, you will have to present your passport when checking in for an international flight, show it again at the security checkpoint, and yet again as you are handing over your boarding pass as you enter the plane. (Children under 18 do not need government-issued photo IDs for domestic flights, but they do for international flights to most countries.)

In order to get through security, you have to show a boarding pass. E-tickets have almost made paper tickets obsolete and airlines who are trying to save on labor costs are using airport **electronic kiosks** and some even offer **online check-in** from your home computer. Online check-in involves logging on to your airline's website, accessing your reservation, and printing out your boarding pass. The airline may even offer you bonus miles to do so! If you're using a kiosk at the airport, bring the credit card you used to book the ticket or your frequent-flier card. Print out your boarding pass from the kiosk and simply proceed to the security checkpoint with your pass and a photo ID. If you're checking bags or looking to snag an exit-row seat, you will be able to do so using most airline kiosks. For checking baggage, there is usually a separate line for dropping it off. Even the smaller airlines are employing the kiosk system, but charging passengers extra when they use the usual check-in counter. Call your airline to see if these alternatives are available and while you have them on the phone, check to see if they allow **curbside check-in.** This is not something you will find in Europe, but may be available when leaving the U.S.

Security checkpoint lines can be cumbersome and the rules and regulations sometimes differ at different airports. One may require you to take off your shoes, while others do not. Since 2006, there is a restriction on liquids that can be brought through security. To avoid holding up the line, drink your liquids before you go through security, take off your belt if it has a buckle, remove all jewelry and coins from your pockets. If you've got metallic body parts, a note from your doctor can prevent a debate with the security screeners, especially in a foreign country where language is an issue. If you have trouble standing for long periods of time, tell an airline employee; the airline will provide a wheelchair Keep in mind that only **ticketed passengers** are allowed past security, except for people escorting either passengers with disabilities or children.

Federalization and international laws have established **what you can carry on** and **what you can't.** The general rule is that sharp things are out, nail clippers are okay, and food must pass through the X-ray machine. Security screeners will make you drink or toss all liquids. Bring food in your carry-on rather than checking it, as explosive-detection machines used on checked luggage have been known to mistake food (especially chocolate, for some reason) for bombs. Travelers in the U.S. are allowed one carry-on bag, plus a "personal item" such as a purse, briefcase, or laptop bag. Carry-on hoarders can stuff all sorts of things into a laptop bag; as long as it has a laptop in it, it's still considered a personal item. The Transportation Security Administration (TSA) has issued a list of restricted items; check its website(www.tsa.gov/travelers/airtravel/prohibited/permitted-prohibited-items.shtm) for details. Some international airlines with flights within Europe have imposed strict rules on carry-on pieces going so far as not allowing a carry-on other than one personal item. Check before you get to the airport to save time and aggravation later.

Airport screeners may decide that your checked luggage warrants a hand search. You can now purchase luggage locks that allow screeners to open and relock a checked bag if hand searching is necessary. Look for Travel Sentry certified locks (www.travelsentry.org) at luggage or travel shops or check the website for a store near you. The locks are more than readily available. Luggage inspectors can open these TSA-approved locks with a special code or key rather than having to cut them off the suitcase, as they normally do to conduct a hand search.

BY TRAIN

Countless trains arrive in Budapest from most corners of Europe. Many connect through Vienna, where 18 daily trains depart for Budapest from either the Westbahnhof or Sudbahnhof station. Ten daily trains connect Prague and Budapest, while four connect Berlin with Budapest and one connects Warsaw with Budapest.

The train trip between Vienna and Budapest takes about 3 hours on an IC train. For more information on Vienna trains, contact the **Austrian National Tourist Board,** 500 Fifth Ave., Suite 800, New York, NY 10110 (*©* **212/944-6885**); 11601 Wilshire Blvd., Suite 2480, Los Angeles, CA 90025 (*©* **310/477-3332**); 30 St. George St., London W1R 0AL (*©* **020/7629-0461**); 2 Bloor St. E., Suite 3330, Toronto, ON M4W 1A8 (*©* **416/ 967-3381**); or 1010 Sherbrooke St. W., Suite 1410, Montreal, PQ H3A 2R7 (*©* **514/849-3708**).

Train travel within Hungary is generally very efficient; trains almost always depart right on time and usually arrive on time. You can access a full, user-friendly timetable on the Web, at **www.elvira.hu**. Hungarian ticket agents generally speak little English, so you will need to know some basic terminology in Hungarian. *Indul* means "departure" and *érkezik* means "arrival." The timetables for arrivals are displayed in big white posters *(érkező vonatok),* while departures *(induló vonatok)* are on yellow posters. The relevant terms in the timetables are *honnan* (from where), *hova* (to where), *vágány* (platform), *munkanap* (weekdays), *hétvége* (weekend), *munkaszüneti nap* (Sat), *ünnepnap* (holiday), *gyors* (fast train, these stop only at major cities, as posted), and *IC* (intercity, stops only once or twice en route; you must reserve a seat

for IC trains). Ticket terminology is as follows: *jegy* (ticket), *oda* (one-way), *odavissza* (round-trip), *helyjegy* (reservation), *első osztály* (first class), *másodosztály* (second class), *nem dohányzó* (nonsmoking), *ma* (today), and *holnap* (tomorrow).

A train posted as *személy* is a local train, which stops at every single village and town on its route. Always opt for a *gyors* (fast) or intercity train to get to your destination in a timely manner. All intercity trains (but no other domestic trains) require a *helyjegy* (seat reservation); ask for the reservation when purchasing your ticket; the agent may not offer the information that it is mandatory. On intercity trains, you must sit in your assigned seat. You may find a local sitting there, trying to avoid the extra charge, but if you show your reservation, he or she will move. All intercity trains now comply strictly with a new law imposing constraints on smoking in public spaces; if there is a smoking car at all, it is in first class and only a single car, while the rest of the train is nonsmoking. If you want a seat in the smoking car, you need to ask for *dohányzó* when buying your ticket. The *gyors* train is typically an old, gritty, wellworn train with the classic eight-seat compartments. The intercity, a state-ofthe-art, clean, modern train without compartments, is said to travel faster, but our experience has shown us that there's seldom more than 30 minutes difference if that between the two in terms of speed.

During the day, MÁV operates a call center called **MÁVDIREKT** (*©* **1/371- 9449**). Purchase tickets at train station ticket windows. You need at least an hour before departure time to make a reservation. MÁV announced in the fall of 2007 that it would be making ticket purchase online possible sometime in 2008. Check the website at www.elvira.hu (click on the British flag for English). It could be a timesaver if you have access to a printer.

TRAIN PASSES

Regional passes, which include Hungary are available. One pass covers Austria and Hungary; one includes Hungary, Slovenia, and Croatia; and one is for Romania and Hungary. Each pass is good for 5 to 10 days of travel within a 2-month period (4 to 10 days for Austria-Hungary). You must purchase the pass from a travel agent or Rail Europe (see contact information below) before you leave for Europe. You can also purchase a **Hungarian Flexipass** (www.eurorailways.com), which covers 5 days of travel within a 15-day period in Hungary or 10 days within 1 month. If you plan to visit only one European country or region, bear in mind that a country or regional pass will cost less than a Eurailpass, but may be more expensive than point-to-point tickets.

EURAILPASS   The **Eurail Globalpass** entitles travelers to unlimited first-class travel over the 160,900km (99,979-mile) national railroad network in 18 western European countries, except Britain, but including Hungary and Romania. It's also valid on some lake steamers and private railroads. A Eurailpass may be purchased for as short a period as 15 days or as long as 3 months. The passes are not available to residents of the countries where the pass is valid or to residents of the United Kingdom.

The Eurailpass, which is ideal for extensive trips, eliminates the hassles of buying tickets—just show your pass to the ticket collector. You should note, however, that some trains require seat reservations. Also, many of the trains have couchettes, or sleeping cars, for which an additional fee is charged.

The pass cannot be purchased in Europe, so you must secure one before leaving on your trip (see www.raileurope.com). Children under 4 travel free if they don't occupy a seat (otherwise the fee is half the fare); the fee is half the fare for children under 12.

If you're 25 or under on your first day of travel, you can obtain unlimited second-class travel, wherever Eurailpass is honored, on a **Eurail Youthpass.**

Groups of two or more people can save on train fairs with the **Eurailpass Saver Flexi,** and the company offers a **Eurail Flexipass** and a **Youth Eurail Flexipass,** which allows more flexibility in travel times.

These passes are available from travel agents in North America, or you can contact **Rail Europe** by calling 🕿 **800/ 848-7245** or surf over to **www.rail europe.com**.

For British travelers, many different rail passes are available in the U.K. for travel in Europe. Stop in at the **International Rail Centre,** Victoria Station, London SW1V 1JY (🕿 **171/834-2345**); or Wasteels, 121 Wilton Rd., London SW1V 1JZ (🕿 **171/834-7066**).

BY BUS

Buses to and from western and eastern Europe and points in Hungary west of the Danube come into **Népliget** bus station. You reach this station by getting off at the Népliget metro stop on the Red line. Buses to and from the Danube Bend and other points north of Budapest depart and arrive at the **Árpád híd bus station** (🕿 **1/320-9229** or 1/317-9886). Take the Blue line metro to Árpád híd. For domestic and international bus information, call 🕿 **1/219-8080,** though you should be aware that it can be rather difficult to get through to the bus stations over the telephone and then getting an English speaker will be a miracle. Your best bet is perhaps to gather your information in person or ask for assistance at the Tourinform office (p. 11).

BY CAR

Several major highways link Hungary to nearby European capitals. The recently modernized **E60** (or M1) connects Budapest with Vienna and points west; it is a toll road from the Austrian border to the city of Györ. The **E65** connects Budapest with Prague and points north.

The **border crossings** from Austria and Slovakia (from which countries most Westerners enter Hungary) are hassle-free for the most part, but there is still border control. In addition to your passport, you may be requested to present your driver's license, vehicle registration, and proof of insurance (the number plate and symbol indicating country of origin are acceptable proof). A green card is required of vehicles bearing license plates of Bulgaria, France, the former USSR, Greece, Poland, Italy, Romania, and Israel. Hungary no longer requires the international driver's license. Cars entering Hungary are required to have a decal indicating country of registration, a first-aid kit, and an emergency triangle. For traffic regulations, see "Getting Around," in chapter 4.

Driving distances are: from Vienna, 248km (154 miles); from Prague, 560km (348 miles); from Frankfurt, 952km (592 miles); and from Rome, 1,294km (804 miles).

BY HYDROFOIL

The Hungarian state shipping company **MAHART** operates hydrofoils on the Danube between Vienna and Budapest in the spring and summer months. It's an extremely popular route, so you should book your tickets well in advance. In North

America or Britain, contact the Austrian National Tourist Board (see "By Train," above). In Vienna you can contact MAHART, Handelskai 265 (© **43/729-2161;** fax 43/729-2163) or visit www.besthotelz.com/hungary/hydrofoil/hydrofoil.htm.

From April 7 through July 2 the MAHART hydrofoil departs Vienna at 9am daily, arriving in Budapest at 3:20pm, with a stop in Bratislava when necessary (passengers getting on or off). From July 3 to August 29, two hydrofoils make the daily passage, departing Vienna at 8am and 1pm, arriving in Budapest at 1:30 and 6:30pm, respectively. From August 30 to November 1, the schedule returns to one hydrofoil daily, departing Vienna at 9am and arriving in Budapest at 2:30pm. The dates and times may change depending on water levels, so check with MAHART for the current information. Customs and passport control begin 1 hour prior to departure. Eurailpass holders also receive a discount, as long as they buy the ticket before boarding. ISIC holders also receive a discount. The Budapest office of MAHART is at V. Belgrád rakpart (© 1/318-1880). Boats and hydrofoils from Vienna arrive at the international boat station next door to the MAHART office on the Belgrád rakpart, which is on the Pest side of the Danube, between the Szabadság and Erzsébet bridges.

10 Packages for the Independent Traveler

Before you start your search for the lowest airfare, you may want to consider booking your flight as part of a travel package. Package tours are not the same thing as escorted tours. Package tours are simply a way to buy the airfare, accommodations, and other elements of your trip (such as car rental, airport transfers, and sometimes even activities) at the same time and often at discounted prices making it kind of like one-stop shopping.

Packages are sold in bulk to tour operators who in turn resell them to the public at a cost that usually undercuts standard rates.

One good source of package deals is the airlines themselves. Most major airlines offer air/land packages, including **American Airlines Vacations** (© **800/321-2121;** www.aavacations.com), **Delta Vacations** (© 800/221-6666; www.deltavacations.com), **Continental Airlines**

Vacations (© 800/301-3800; www. covacations.com), and **United Vacations** (© 888/854-3899; www.united vacations.com). Several big **online travel agencies**—Expedia, Travelocity, Orbitz, site59, and Lastminute.com also do a brisk business in packages. If you're unsure about the pedigree of a smaller packager, check with the Better Business Bureau in the city where the company is based, or go online at www.bbb.org. If a packager won't tell you where they're based, don't fly with them.

Travel packages are also listed in the travel section of your local Sunday newspaper. You can also check ads in the national travel magazines such as *Arthur Frommer's Budget Travel Magazine*, *Travel & Leisure*, *National Geographic Traveler*, and *Condé Nast Traveler*.

Package tours can run the gambit of services and prices. Some offer a better class of hotels than others, while some offer the same hotels for lower prices. Some offer flights on scheduled airlines, while others book charters. Some limit your choice of accommodations and travel days. You are often required to make a large payment upfront. On the plus side, packages can save you money, offering group prices but allowing for independent travel. Some even let you add on a few guided excursions or escorted day trips (also at prices lower than if you booked them yourself) without booking an entirely escorted tour.

Before you invest in a package tour, get some answers. Ask about the **accommodations choices** and prices for each. Then look up the hotels' review in a Frommer's guide and check their rates online for your specific dates of travel. You'll also want to find out what **type of room** you get. If you need a certain type of room, ask for it; don't take whatever is thrown your way. Request a nonsmoking room, a quiet room, a room with a view, or whatever you need to enjoy your trip. If the provider of the package is not willing to accommodate your needs, perhaps you need to look elsewhere.

Finally, look for **hidden expenses.** Ask whether airport departure fees and taxes, for example, are included in the total cost.

11 Recommended Books & Movies

Many books published by Corvina, a Budapest-based English-language press, are recommended below. They can be purchased at English-language bookstores in Budapest, or you can write for a free catalog: **Corvina kiadó,** P.O. Box 108, Budapest H-1364, Hungary.

HISTORY & POLITICS For an overview of Hungarian history, try László Kontler's *A History of Hungary* (Palgrave/Macmillan, 2002). Try Amazon.com or ABE.com, but if you can't obtain it before your journey, you can pick one up at the Central European University's bookshop (V. Nádor u. 9–11) in Budapest, where the author happens to be head of the History Department. *A History of Hungary* (Indiana University Press, 1990), edited by Peter Sugar, is an anthology with a number of good essays. *The Habsburg Monarchy, 1809–1918* (London: Hamish Hamilton, 1948), by A. J. P. Taylor, is a lively and readable analysis of the final century of the Austro-Hungarian Empire.

The Holocaust in Hungary: An Anthology of Jewish Response (University of Alabama Press, 1982), edited and translated by Andrew Handler, is notable for the editor's excellent introduction. Elenore Lister's *Wallenberg: The Man in the Iron Web* (Prentice Hall, 1982) recounts the heroic life of Raoul Wallenberg in Nazi-occupied Budapest.

When Angels Fooled the World (University of Wisconsin Press, 2008), by Charles Fenyvesi is an excellent recounting of those who saved Jews during the war.

MEMOIRS Two memoirs of early-20th-century Budapest deserve mention: *Apprentice in Budapest: Memories of a World That Is No More* (University of Utah Press, 1988) by anthropologist Raphael Patai; and *Budapest 1900* (Weidenfeld & Nicolson, 1989), by John Lukacs, which captures the feeling of a lively but doomed imperial city at the turn of the 20th century. Post-communist Budapest is described in Marion Merrick's *Now You See It, Now You Don't; Seven Years in Hungary 1982–89* (Mágus, 1998). Another book of note is *In Search of the Mother Book* (University of Nebraska Press, 1999), a memoir by the American feminist literary figure Susan Rubin Suleiman, who fled Hungary after World War II and returned to the land of her birth in the late 1980s.

CULTURE, CUISINE & WINE Tekla Domotor's *Hungarian Folk Beliefs* (Corvina and Indiana University Press, 1981) covers witches, werewolves, giants, and gnomes. Zsuzsanna Ardó's *How to Be a European: Go Hungarian* (Biográf, 1994) is a witty little guidebook to Hungarian culture, etiquette, and social life.

Julia Szabó's *Painting in Nineteenth Century Hungary* (Corvina, 1985) contains a fine introductory essay and over 300 plates. In our opinion, the best traveler-oriented coffee-table book available in Budapest is *Budapest Art and History* (Flow East, 1992), by Delia Meth-Cohn.

Hungary in the *Culinaria* series (Konemann, 2001) by Aniko Gergely provides an excellent and thorough cultural introduction to Hungarian cooking, in addition to a bunch of authentic recipes. The *Cuisine of Hungary* (Bonanza Books, 1971), by the famous Hungarian-born restaurateur George Lang, also contains a great deal of material on the subject.

Hungary: Its Fine Wines and Winemakers (Print X Budavar RT, 2007) by David Copp has been given rave reviews by all of the Budapest press.

FICTION Not all the best examples of Hungarian literature are available in translation, but *Fateless* by 2002 Nobel Prize–winner Imre Kertész is a must. You should also look for any translations of highly esteemed contemporary authors Péter Nádas and Péter Esterházy. Of particular interest is Esterházy's *Helping Verbs of the Heart* (Weidenfeld & Nicolson, 1991), a gripping story of grief following a parent's death, and Nádas's *A Book of Memories* (Penguin, 1998), which was assessed by Susan Sontag as the best European novel of the 20th century. You may also want to find and read the following: Gyula Illyés' *The People of the Puszta* (Corvina, 1979), an unabashedly honest look at peasant life in the early 20th century; *The Tragedy of Man* (1862) is a Magyar classic, by Imre Madách; István Örkény's *The Toth Family and The Flower Show* (New Directions, 1966), a book with two stories: the first an allegorical story about fear and authority, and the second a fable about different types of reality in modern life; Zsolt Csalog's *Lajos M., Aged 45* (Budapest: Maecenas, 1989), an extraordinary memoir of life in a Soviet labor camp; Kálmán Mikszáth's *St. Peter's Umbrella* (Corvina, 1962); and Zsigmond Móricz's *Seven Pennies* (Corvina, 1988), a collection of short stories by one of Hungary's most celebrated authors.

MOVIES In the movie *Sunshine* (1999), Hungarian director István Szabó tells the life of three generations of Jews before, during, and after the war. A wonderfully dark, but metaphorically powerful movie is *Kontroll* (2003), in Hungarian with English subtitles. The movie *Munich* (2005) was partially filmed by the opera house.

3

Suggested Budapest & Hungary Itineraries

Most people who only arrange a day or two in Budapest find that they have shortchanged themselves and pledge to return for a longer visit in the future. However, if your time in the city is limited, you will find ways in this chapter to maximize your trip. Historic Budapest is basically a small area and many sights listed in this book are relatively easy to walk to, and you'll have the added pleasure of perusing the architecture along the way. However, if you are severely limited by time, I suggest you invest in a transport pass, covering the number of days you will be here, so you can get around

more quickly. Conversely, if you scheduled more than a week in the city, you may want to balance it out with one or two side trips with Budapest as your base. (Be warned that Budapest is my favorite city in Hungary and I will do my best to keep you here.) In an easy day of travel and touring, you can visit the small, quaint villages of Szentendre, Vác, Gödöllő, or Esztergom, each within an hour of the capital.

You many want to consider the information here as a supplement for the itineraries of the walking tours listed in chapter 8, "Strolling Around Budapest."

1 The Best of Budapest in 1 Day

If you only have 1 day in Budapest, you'll want to see a bit of both Buda and Pest, and this tour lets you do both. You'll start off with a cultural and historic tour of Pest, then you'll cross Chain Bridge (an attraction in itself) for a brief tour of the Castle District in Buda, where you can enjoy a meal and a stop in a pub. **Start:** Inner Pest.

❶ Inner City & Central Pest ✪
Budapest is a city where wide boulevards intersect with some really narrow streets. It is a reminder that it was once part of the Austrian-Hungarian Empire. Wide boulevards were especially well suited for accommodating carriages for royals and others of wealth. This is definitely a city to be walked, so start in the center, wander the grand boulevards, and admire the architecture. Make sure you look up. So many interesting features on buildings are not at eye level.

Depending on your travel tastes, you may want to visit a few museums and highlights of the area. You may find the Greek-looking **Hungarian National Museum** ✪✪ (p. 133), the **Budapest Holocaust Memorial Center** ✪✪ (p. 132), or the **Inner City Parish Church** ✪ (p. 141) to your liking. As you wander through the area, remind yourself of two facts: Unlike Prague, much of Budapest was bombed during World War II and that the communist regime only ended in 1989. In a relatively short time, the city has made tremendous strides, although it still has far to go. Many historic buildings have been torn down to be replaced with modern conveniences such as boutiques, apartment complexes, or restaurants. Others have been renovated to their former glory, but in my opinion, certainly not enough. History is being replaced by sterility of the new and modern.

Váci utca is the perennially favorite shopping and walking street of Budapest. Developed after the regime changes in 1989, it has blossomed with many international stores and some Hungarian ones as well. For examples of Hungarian crafts, visit the **Vali Folklór** folk craft shop (p. 212), the **VAM Design Gallery,** at Váci utca 64, and various clothing stores (avoid the touristy cafes here).

Walk from Váci utca to the Danube Promenade and stroll along the river. Following the 2 tram line, you will be making your way to Kossuth tér for:

❷ Parliament ✸✸✸

Budapest's exquisite Parliament building is the second largest in Europe after England's Westminster. I've taken the tour six times and could still do it again. The main facade faces the Danube. Designed by Imre Steindl and completed in 1902, the building mixes neo-Gothic style with a neo-Renaissance dome reaching 96m (315 ft.), significant as the country's millennium was 1896 and the conquest of the kingdom of Hungary was 896. St. Stephens is also 96m (315 ft.) high for the same reasons. It is by far one of our favorite buildings in Budapest. At the top of a grandly ornamented staircase, there is a hexadecagonal (16-sided) central hall that leads to an impressive chamber. The fabled Hungarian crown jewels of St. Stephen are on display. Unfortunately, you can enter only on guided tours (the ¾–hour tour is worth the chance to go inside). See p. 140 for tour times and information.

---

③ SZABADSAG TÉR (FREEDOM SQUARE) ✸

This beautifully maintained park is the home of a large obelisk statue that commemorates when the Soviet Union liberated Hungary at the end of World War II. It is the last remaining memorial to the Soviet Union in the city. You may want to rest in the park or have a coffee at Farger's Café at Zoltán u. 18, right on the square. You will be directly across from the U.S. Embassy.

Walk back to Parliament and then south about .4km (¼ mile) toward the historic Chain Bridge, which you will see in the distance:

❹ Chain Bridge ✸

Known as the Széchenyi Bridge or the Chain Bridge, this bridge holds the distinction of being the first permanent crossing to link Buda and Pest. The idea for the bridge was instigated and funded by 19th-century Hungarian reformer Count István Széchenyi. Legend has it that due to storms, he was not able to cross the river to be with this dying father. While Széchenyi waited 8 days for the storms to subside so he could cross the river, his father died and he missed the funeral. Designed by William Tierney Clark, an Englishman, the bridge was also one of the largest suspension bridges of its time when it opened in 1849. According to legend, the omission of sculpted tongues on the lions, which guard the bridge at either end, caused the sculptor to drown himself in the river out of shame; however, the lions do have tongues, just not visible from the ground. See p. 147. (**Note:** You might duck into the **Four Seasons Hotel Gresham Palace** ✸✸✸ while you're here to view its breathtaking interiors; p. 75).

Walk across the Chain Bridge, and take the funicular up to the:

❺ Castle District ✸✸

Castle Hill, a UNESCO World Cultural Heritage site, consists of two parts: the

Royal Palace itself and the so-called Castle District. Most of this area is a reconstructed medieval city, but the original castle was destroyed in World War II and replaced with the current Royal Palace. For a detailed 3-hour itinerary of this area, see "Walking Tour 2: The Castle District," in chapter 8, "Strolling Around Budapest."

This is an interesting area for walking and wandering. There are many cobblestone streets, so choose your shoes carefully. You might also wish to stop and visit the **Hungarian National Gallery** (p. 145) and the **Budapest History Museum** (p. 144).

---

⑥ RIVALDA CAFÉ & RESTAURANT

After a long day of walking and sightseeing, one option for a meal while still on the hill is the Rivalda Café & Restaurant. This restaurant is housed in a building that was once a monastery of Carmelite monks who disbanded in 1786. The building was then given to the people of Buda by Joseph II to become a theater. Opened as a restaurant in 2000, it has saxophone or piano music nightly. I. Szinház u. 5–9; © **1/489-0236.** See p. 126.

After dinner, you might head back to your hotel to relax for a bit so you'll be ready to:

⑦ Socialize at a Bar, Club, or Bistro

Budapest has a variety of lively nightlife possibilities to suit every taste. You'll find all levels of partying available, whether you're looking for hardcore clubbing or just a pub for drinks with the locals. Clubs such as **The Old Man's Music Pub** (p. 230) and **Paris, Texas** (p. 233) have nightly music. Both are quite popular places for nighttime drinks and socializing, where you'll find locals of all ages mingling here. See chapter 10, "Budapest After Dark."

2 The Best of Budapest in 2 Days

Once you have discovered the charms of Inner Pest and the Castle District on Day 1, it is time to broaden the scope with a walk around the **Outer Ring Boulevard (körút).** Note that as you walk the *körút*, the name changes from district to district. *Start:* New York Palace Hotel.

---

① New York Palace Hotel

The New York Life Insurance Company originally commissioned the building, which opened on October 23, 1894. During the 1900s, its cafe was a center of intellectual life in the city, with writers and journalists as frequent patrons. After many years of remodeling and revitalizing the original eclectic style with a strong Italian renaissance influence, the Boscolo hotel chain reopened the hotel and its legendary cafe in 2006. The detailed reconstruction is worth admiring and returning to see in the evening when lit up. Walk toward Oktogon, noting the grand turn-of-the-20th-century architecture of Pest.

At Oktogon turn right and walk up to Andrássy u. 60:

② Terror Háza (House of Terror)

First the headquarters of the secret police of the Nazi Arrow Cross regime, when the Soviets liberated Hungary, it immediately turned into the headquarters for the communist secret police. This building is the setting of some of the most horrific days of 20th-century Hungary, which lasted for over 50 years. Hundreds were tortured and murdered in the basement by both regimes. The Nazis' primary victims were Jews, but the communists targeted anyone who spoke out against the government. The building is a museum functioning as a memorial to the victims of both fascism and communism and is an everlasting reminder of the effect of oppressive regimes in Hungary. However; it has caused continual controversy since it opened in 2002, especially because the building's overhang has the word "TERROR" stenciled on it, which is quite striking when the sun shines through it.

❸ Andrássy Boulevard 🐾

Strolling up the majestic Andrássy Boulevard toward Heroes' Square and City Park, you are taking the UNESCO World Heritage Site tour. The boulevard is lined with trees and a wealth of beautiful apartment buildings, many of which are now used as embassies. In addition, there are restaurants and museums scattered along the way leading to Heroes' Square. This is Pest's greatest boulevard.

If you are ready for a break,

🍵 KOGART GALLERY AND RESTAURANT 🐾🐾🐾
Designed by Ignác Alpar, who also designed the Vajdahunyad Castle in City Park, this historic building is now home to a beautiful cafe and restaurant. Take your coffee and read a paper while sitting on a leather sofa in a quiet corner of the room. If you are so inclined, the art gallery upstairs has rotating exhibits of superior quality. Andrássy út 112. ✆ 1/354-3830. See p. 120.

Once you reach the end of Andrássy Boulevard, adjacent to the Museum of Fine Arts, the Múcsarnok, and City Park, you'll find:

❺ Heroes' Square 🐾🐾

Heroes' Square was created for the millennium in 1896 (remember the reoccurring 96), which celebrates the arrival of the Magyar tribes in the Carpathian Basin in 896. The statues represent the chronology of some 1,000 years of Hungarian history. The seven statues on the

left side are all Hungarian kings. On the right side, they are all famous Hungarians, but only one was a king. In 1896 during the famous world exhibition, this space was the apex of some 200 pavilions that made up the festivities. Many festivals are still held here.

To your left you will find the **Museum of Fine Arts** 🐾 (p. 133). The museum is the main repository of foreign art in Hungary. It has one of central Europe's major collections and it is considered one of the most important art collections in Europe. Free 1-hour tours are offered by highly trained docents Tuesday through Friday at 11am and 2pm and Saturday at 11am.

Walk through the park and you will arrive at the Széchenyi Thermal Bath:

❻ The Széchenyi Baths 🐾🐾

After a long day, you deserve to rest and relax. Nothing could be better after a day of touring than a soak in a thermal. This is one of the largest spa complexes in Europe and the first thermal bath on the Pest side. Chances are if you have seen photos of men playing chess on floating chessboards, the men were in this thermal. It is mixed men and women and bathing suits are mandatory.

See p. 166 and the box, "Thermal Bathing 101," on p. 164.

After your afternoon of thermal bathing, you may want to head back to your hotel to rest, but if you have done so at the thermals, then head out for dinner. You can take the Yellow metro from Széchenyi and go one stop to Mexikói or choose a dining spot from chapter 6, "Where to Dine in Budapest," but either way make a reservation.

❼ Trófea Grill Étterem 🐾🐾🐾

You have had a full day of exercise, so treat yourself to the best Hungarian all-you-can-eat restaurant in the city. With over 100 choices from soups to desserts and everything in between, everyone is sure to leave satisfied. See p. 121.

❽ Attend Some Nighttime Culture 🏅🏅

Spend an evening attending a concert at the **Ferenc Liszt Music Academy** (p. 224), or an opera at the **Opera House** 🏅🏅🏅. Both are premier venues. The first is a more classical hall, while the Opera House is magnificently beautiful inside. The fine arts are alive and well in Budapest, and a nighttime cultural event is the way to round out your short stint in the city. Note that performances usually start at 7pm not the customary 8pm.

3 The Best of Hungary's Side-Trip Options

Now that you have had a taste of Budapest, perhaps now you want to experience other parts of the country and see how life differs outside of the capital. Since the average visitor to Hungary usually spends a few days in the country, we've opted to give you a few side-trip options from Budapest, rather than a 1-week or longer tour of the entire country. All rail tracks lead to Budapest, so regardless of which direction you go chances are you will have to return to Budapest when changing from one geographical area to another, making a full Hungarian tour both difficult and time-consuming. You'd need several weeks to see it all. Traveling by bus is even more time-consuming and not as comfortable as the train. Driving a car can be downright dangerous if you're not used to European driving, not to mention the cost. Trains, though not quite luxurious, are easy and safe, and they usually cost less than 5,000 Ft ($27/£14) round-trip, depending on the destination.

For more information on the following regions, see the regional chapters later in the book.

Option 1: A Day in Szentendre 🏅🏅

After some time in Budapest, you might visit Szentendre (pronounced *Sen*-ten-dreh), just north of Budapest on the Danube and one of the most-visited spots in all of Hungary. Take the HÉV (regional train) from Budapest's Batthyány tér metro for a 45-minute ride.

Visit the **Margit Kovács Museum** 🏅🏅🏅 and see the interesting collection of the late Margit Kovács. She was primarily a ceramicist, and her depictions of peasant life in Hungary are charming. Have a late lunch at the **Aranysárkány Vendéglő** 🏅, and take a walk along the river. Then spend your afternoon exploring the many shops, museums, churches, and galleries in town. Fő tér, the main drag, is enticing, but explore all the side streets of this small, manageable town. Try **Chez Nicolas Restaurant** 🏅🏅 Kígyó utca 10.

For more information on Szentendre, see section 2 in chapter 11.

Option 2: A Day in Vác 🏅🏅🏅

Just past Szentendre along the Danube, but actually faster to reach, Vác can be reached by direct train from Budapest in as little as 25 minutes. This is a very historic little town, and it also has one of the most beautiful Danube parks I have seen. All along the river is a wide promenade with winding walking and biking paths with play areas for children interspersed along the way. To the side of these are wide sidewalks providing a lovely walk under the chestnut-tree-lined street.

Vác is a town for strolling, since most of the historic sights are to be seen from the outside, with the exception of peeking through the glass of the doorways of churches and one must-see museum. Starting at the main square, **Március 15 tér** 🏅🏅🏅, there is the historic **White Friar's Church** 🏅🏅 and the impressive statute and fountain of **St. Hedwig** on the side of the church. Directly across from the church is the **Memento Mori** ✶✶✶ with the preserved crypts that were uncovered accidentally when renovations took place on White Friar's Church. Also on the square are many historic and interesting baroque buildings. The **Cathedral of the Assumption** on Konstantin tér is the only building in Hungary influenced by Parisian revolutionary architecture. At Géza Király tér is the **Franciscan or "Brown" Church,** which sits next to the castle, the oldest building in Vác. An Italian architect designed the synagogue on Eötvös utca in romantic style. The river walk is a glorious relaxing escape.

For more information on Vác, see section 3 in chapter 11.

Option 3: A Few Hours in Gödöllő ✶

Gödöllő is the home to the largest Baroque palace in Hungary, which was originally built for the aristocratic Grassalkovich family. Later Franz Josef, emperor of Austria, king of Hungary, and his wife Elisabeth, or "Sisi" as she was affectionately known, used this as their summer residence. Gödöllő is less than an hour away from Budapest by HÉV, making this an ideal getaway for a short day trip. At Christmastime, the decoration of the palace is well worth seeing. While in Gödöllő, you may want to have dinner at **Kastélykert Étterem** (Palace Park Restaurant) at Szabadság út 4; ✆ **28/527-020.** They are open daily from noon to 11pm. For transportation to Gödöllő, see chapter 4, "Getting to Know Budapest."

Option 4: Visit the Bears ✶✶ *(Kids*

Medve Otthon or Bear Sanctuary is the place to go when the kids or the adults for that matter are tired of the city and need some nature-loving activity. Here you can visit the 42 brown bears at the bear sanctuary, just 50 minutes from Nyugati Station. Some of the bears were stars in Hungarian films, but were rescued due to mistreatment. Don't ask for their autographs, but you can feed them honey bought from the gift shop using a long spoon. If you find this unbearable, there are two packs of 26 wolves living here also. On weekends, there are pony rides, a bouncy castle, and face painting. The sanctuary is located at Patak u. 39, Veresegyház and it is open daily from 8am to 7pm. Take the train from Nyugati Station to Ivacs, the nearest station. Depending on the train, the tickets will cost either 450 Ft ($2.40/£1.30) or 900 Ft ($4.85/£2.55) with the lesser expensive trains actually being faster: 46 minutes as opposed to 1 hour and 5 minutes. From the train station, follow the clearly marked route 2km (1.2 miles) to the sanctuary. Admission is 200 Ft ($1.10/55p) per person.

Option 5: Győr ✶✶

Győr is located halfway between Budapest and Vienna (131km/81 miles) in the northwestern corner, making it a perfect stop if you are coming from or going to Vienna. Considered one of the more important cities in Hungary, it is known as the town of rivers; it sits at the meeting point of three rivers, the Danube, Rába, and Rábca. There are six fast trains leaving Budapest, which will get you into Győr in 1½ hours for 2,560 Ft ($14/£7.30), but you will need a reservation for these trains.

First inhabited by the Celts, then the Romans in the first century B.C., Győr has been populated ever since. During the Ottoman invasion, the commander of the town didn't think it was worth defending, so he ordered the entire town to be burned to the ground. When the Ottomans arrived, they only found piles of ashes. When they left, the town was rebuilt and the top Italian builders completed the work, filling the city with baroque buildings. World War II brought destruction, but a massive campaign in the '70s renewed the buildings to their former status, thus earning them the

European Award for monument protection. Buildings surrounding each square give them a unique feel from the others.

Things to see include the **Győ Basilica** on Káptalandomb, where King Stephan established the Episcopate in his first decade as king. The baroque church with its Blessed Virgin picture is one of the most significant pilgrimage sites in Hungary. It is open 8am to noon and 2 to 6pm. The **Esterházy Palace** at Király u. 17 (© **96/322-695**), consists of three monumental buildings from the 18th century. Originally the palace of Count Gábor Esterházy, it is now the City Art Museum, open Tuesday through Sunday 10am to 6pm. At the **Zichy-Palota** on Liszt Ferenc utca 20 (© **96/311-316**), you will find the permanent puppet collection of 72 puppets, accessories, and furniture. It is open Tuesday through Thursday 8am to 3:30pm and Friday 8am to 1pm. If you miss the bath experience in Budapest, you can visit the **Rába-Quelle Medicinal, Thermal and Pleasure Bath** at Fürdő tér 1 (© **96/514-900**). It is open 9am to 10pm. If your visit brings you here between April and August, the city has a number of fairs and celebrations. One dining option among the many is Komédiás Étterem at Czuczor G. utca 30 (© **96/527-217**). It is open 11am to midnight and accepts all credit cards.

For hotel recommendations or further information, contact Tourinform in Győr at Árpád utca 32 (© **96/311-771;** www.gyortourism.hu). From June through August it's open weekdays from 8am to 8pm and weekends 9am to 6pm, and during the rest of the year, it's open weekdays 9am to 5pm and weekends 9am to 1pm.

Option 6: Two Days in Keszthely 𝕲 & Héviz 𝕲𝕲

Keszthely and Héviz are located on the western corner of Hungary's very own little "sea," Lake Balaton, almost 200km (124 miles) from Budapest. The towns sit right in a microclimate area, with warm summers, clear skies, and beautiful vistas and hills.

From Budapest, take a 3-hour express (*gyors*) train from Déli or Keleti stations to Keszthely. Then explore the **Festetics Mansion** 𝕲, **Carriage Museum,** or try the **Dolls Museum,** which has Europe's largest collection of dolls, with the **Parliament of Snails.**

After roaming around Keszthely, have a traditional Hungarian meal, with a traditional Unicum, at the **Margaréta Étterem.** At night, you may want to consider an event at the **Balaton Congress Center and Theater,** and stay either in a "private room" or at the **Barbara Wellness Pension.**

The next day take a bus to Héviz, 8km (5 miles) northeast of Keszthely. Here you'll find a wide range of hotel choices from pensions to five-star luxury hotels to fit any budget. One choice is **Hotel Erzsébet** in the town center. Take a dip in **Europe's largest thermal lake,** or spend your whole day unwinding at the hotel. Spa treatments include a selection of health cures, sports, wellness, or even medical treatment programs.

You might shorten this side trip by heading straight to Héviz, then tour Keszthely a bit and relax in the spa hotel at night.

For more information about Keszthely, see section 3 in chapter 12.

Option 7: Two Days in Pécs 𝕲𝕲𝕲

The popular Pécs is the most culturally vibrant Hungarian city outside of the capital—warm and arid, with lots of museums, galleries, and a large student population from the university.

Take an early morning intercity train from Budapest's Déli Station to Pécs, a 3-hour ride. Walk down Káptalan utca, the street of museums which are all housed in medieval houses. Visit the **Tivadar Csontváry Museum** 𝕲 and the **Victor Vasarely Museum** 𝕲, institutions that celebrate two of Hungary's most notable artists. In the **Zsolnay Museum** ✦✦✦, housed in a Gothic residence, you will find displays of the finest pieces of award-winning porcelain, even paintings. Then check out the hustle and bustle of the **Pécsi Vásár** ✦✦ flea market, where you can find traditional Hungarian wares. Head up hill for dinner at the Vadasz-tanya (Hunters' Lodge) ✦✦, where you can enjoy a fine Hungarian wine before checking in at the fun, centrally located **Hotel Főnix** ✦✦.

For a midmorning snack, stop for coffee and pastry at the **Mecsek Cukrászda** before checking out Pécs' houses of worship, the **Pécs Cathedral,** the **Pécs Synagogue** ✦, and the largest-standing Turkish structure, the **Mosque of Pasha Gazi Kassim.**

For more information about Pécs, see section 1 in chapter 14.

Option 8: Two Days in Szeged ✦

The southeastern Hungarian town of Szeged is the cultural center of the region. With a thriving university, it is overflowing with students. If you're in Hungary in the summer, come here for the **Szeged Summer Open Air Festival** ✦✦ in Dóm tér, which offers rock operas, classical music, ballet, and contemporary dance,

in July and August, making it the largest festival of its kind in Hungary.

From Budapest, take the train from Nyugati Station for a 2½-hour ride. Start off with a coffee and pastry at the famous **Virág Cukrászda.** Enjoy some of the impressive architecture; visit the Votive **Church of Our Lady of Hungary** ✦✦✦, the cathedral built in Hungarian Ecclesiastic architecture.

Take a walk on the river's edge, then head back to **Kárász utca** ✦✦, the main walking street which is usually bustling with students. Have a casual dinner on the terrace at the **Gödör Restaurant** or for a more upscale meal try **Göry Restaurant & Terrace** ✦. Try to get a room at the reasonably priced and clean **Family Pension,** not far from the train station and Dóm tér.

On your second day here, check out the **Polish Market (Lengyel Piac)** ✦ on the southern edge of town and visit the beautiful and historic **synagogue** ✦. Then head for some hearty fish stew at **Kiskörössy Halaszcsarda** ✦ for which Szeged is famous. The Szeged fish soup uses fish from the Tiza River, not the Danube.

For more information about Szeged, see section 3 in chapter 14.

4

Getting to Know Budapest

In this chapter, you'll find the nuts and bolts of practical information for you to use as a reference again and again during your stay in Budapest. There are neighborhood orientation listings, transportation options, and advisories on how to avoid taxi hustlers; and that is just for starters. Read through this chapter before your arrival and mark it for ready reference once you are here. I like to use little self-stick flags in different colors to mark the sections I know I will be referring to often.

1 Orientation

ARRIVING

BY PLANE   Budapest has two airports: **Ferihegy 1 and 2,** both are in district XVII. All budget airlines fly into **Ferihegy 1.** This was the old airport, but was remodeled specifically to accommodate the ever-growing number of budget airlines. It is now more modern looking than the newer airport Ferihegy 2. **Ferihegy 2** has two terminals, though it is still a small airport considering it is the primary airport for a capital city. The positive side is that you cannot get lost nor do you have to worry about running a great distance to catch a flight. Terminal A is used almost exclusively by **Malév,** the Hungarian airlines. Terminal B is for all other airlines, other than budget airlines mentioned above. If you happen to be meeting someone here, he or she can check the status of your flight on the airport website by entering the airline and flight number (www.bud.hu/english).

If you are planning travels in other parts of Europe before or after coming to Budapest, you may want to check out the numerous budget airlines flying in and out of the city. The oldest of the economy airlines are **Air Berlin** (www.airberlin.com), **Wizz Air** (www.wizzair.com), and **German Wings** (www.germanwings.com). However, there are currently 13 nontraditional airlines flying into Budapest from 62 different destinations within Europe. Although, some of these routes are summertime only, you can check the current routes on **www.skyscanner.com** or **www.flylc.com**.

There are three ways into the city. I will start with the most expensive and then describe the others in descending order.

Although in the past, taxis were notorious for scamming tourists at the airport, the airport authority with a nudge from the Ministry of Tourism, took steps to correct this situation. The airport now exclusively contracts with **Zóna Taxi** services (© **1/365-5555**), making this the official taxi service of both airports. The fares are fixed rates per cab, not per person and adhere to predestined zones within the city. Fares run from zones 1–4 and cost from 3,000 Ft to 4,300 Ft ($16–$23/£8.55–£12). These taxis are also metered, so if the metered fare is less than the zone rate, you pay the reduced fare. By law, all taxis must give you a paper receipt for your fare. If you know of another taxi company and prefer them, you will need to call them. The unauthorized taxi stand pick-up area is away from the general taxi area, but there are signs in English.

Airport Shuttle (© 1/296-8555; www.bud.hu/english), is a public service owned and operated by the Budapest Airport Authority. There is a clearly visible kiosk in each of the terminals for the shuttle. If you know you will use this service to return to the airport, it will be less expensive to buy a round-trip ticket than two one-way tickets. A round-trip fare is 3,900 Ft ($21/£11) per person and one way is 2,300 Ft ($12/£6.55) per person. The fares are the same for both airports. Depending on the number of people, you may find the taxi service to be less expensive. When you purchase your tickets for the shuttle, you will be asked which district that you are going to since many districts have streets with the same name. Once a minibus is sufficiently full, the driver will call out your destination and direct you to the right vehicle and load your luggage. This can take anywhere from 10 minutes to as much as an hour, depending on how busy it is at any given time of day. The shuttle takes you directly to the door of any address in the city. The trip takes from 30 minutes to an hour, depending on traffic and how many stops are made. To arrange your return to the airport from where you are staying, call the number above 24 hours *in advance,* but not longer than 24 hours in advance and absolutely not less than 12 hours in advance. The shuttle office is open from 6am to 10pm, but be warned that you may have to wait on hold for some time and may possibly get disconnected in the process. The shuttle will pick up passengers virtually anywhere in the Budapest area from their front door. You will be given a 10-minute time frame for when the shuttle will arrive to pick you up based on your flight departure. You will be asked to wait outside the door during this 10-minute period to facilitate the pick up process.

There are also two public transportation options with the trip taking about 1 hour total on either. Two buses leave the airport for the metro. From **Ferihegy 2,** you will take **bus no. 93** to the last stop, Kőbánya-Kispest. From there, the Blue metro line runs to the Inner City of Pest. The cost is two transit tickets, which is 460 Ft ($2.50/£1.30) for both; tickets can be bought from the automated vending machine at the bus stop (coins only and not recommended) or from any newsstand in the airport. From **Ferihegy 1,** there are two bus options: **bus no. 93** and **bus no. 200.** We recommend bus no. 200 as it is a new route that is shorter with less stops, but with the same end point.

The newest option as of August 2007 is the airport train, which runs from **Ferihegy 1** to **Nyugati** train station. The cost is 300 Ft ($1.60/85p) for one way. There are over 30 trains daily. If you arrive at **Ferihegy 2,** take either bus above to **Ferihegy 1** in order to catch the train. Plans are to extend the train tracks to the newer airport, but this most likely will not happen any time soon.

BY TRAIN   Budapest has three major train stations: **Keleti** pályaudvar (Eastern Station), **Nyugati** pályaudvar (Western Station), and **Déli** pályaudvar (Southern Station). The stations' names, curiously, have no correspondence to anything, so don't try to use any logic here. Each has a metro station beneath it and an array of accommodations offices and currency-exchange booths, which we recommend avoiding (see below), plus other services including food. Under no circumstances should a traveler take a taxi from any of the train stations unless you have called the company yourself. This is the most often used scam separating tourists and their cash. The taxis charge inflated prices and take 20 minutes to get to a 5-minute destination.

Most international trains pull into bustling **Keleti Station** (© **1/314-5010**), an impressively elegant European train station on the outside. It is located in Pest's old and tired Baross tér, beyond the Outer Ring on the border of the VII and VIII districts. Various people from old ladies to young men will be offering rooms and taxis to travel-weary tourists, but a polite smile, while you continue walking is all that is needed to tell them you are not interested. The Red line of the metro is below the station; numerous bus, tram, and trolleybus lines serve Baross tér as well.

Some international trains arrive at **Nyugati Station** (© **1/349-0115**), another classic designed by the Eiffel Company and completed in 1877. This is the site of the first Hungarian train station dating back to 1846. The current station is located on the Outer Ring, at the border of the V, VI, and XIII districts. The Blue line metro is beneath Nyugati alongside numerous snack shops, small independent stores, and bakeries. Numerous tram and bus lines serve busy Nyugati tér.

Few international trains, but some from Vienna, arrive at **Déli Station** (© **1/375-6293**), an ugly modern building that lacks any architectural accoutrements. It borders on the depressing. It is the only station on the Buda side; the terminus of the Red metro line is beneath this train station.

MÁV operates a minibus that will take you from any of the three stations to the airport. However, the pricing system is complicated and depends on how many passengers are traveling, which station you are leaving from, and enough other variables to recommend calling a legitimate taxi service instead. If you are not dissuaded by this, then call the minibus at © **1/353-2722** (see "Getting Around," later in this chapter). Personally, I have never used it and don't know anyone who has.

BY BUS The Népliget Bus Station is the city's recently opened modern main bus terminal on the Red metro line at the **Stadionok** stop. The Blue line goes to the much smaller **Árpád híd bus station** that caters only to the domestic bus service.

VISITOR INFORMATION

Since Budapest continues to undergo rapid changes, much of the tourist information on the Internet is often out-of-date, with the exception of the Frommer's website, where we update the information. The city's best source of visitor information is **Tourinform,** the official Budapest Tourism offices. They have a booth at each of the airports, plus three offices in the city. The office at V. Liszt Ferenc tér 11, in Pest (© **1/322-4098;** www.tourinform.hu; metro: Opera, Yellow line; tram: Oktogon, no. 4–6) is open daily from 10am to 6pm. The office at V. Süt_ street 2 (Deák Square; metro: Deák tér) is open from 8am to 8pm daily. The office at Buda Palace on Castle Hill (bus no. 10) offers summer and winter hours: From May 5 through October 31, it is open Monday through Sunday 9am to 8pm, and from November 2 through April 30 it is open Monday through Sunday 9am to 6pm. The staff in all offices speak English.

You can also attempt to access city information through the **"Touch Info"** user-friendly computer terminals located at the airport, Déli railway station, several of the larger metro stations, and in the market hall at Fővám tér; however, many times, the terminal software is corrupted, so *attempt* is the key word.

Of the various free informational magazines in English that you will find at tourist offices, pubs, restaurants, and elsewhere in the city and the most useful for English speakers are ***Funzine*** (www.funzine.com) and ***Where.*** Both have a current story of a festival or area to be explored in each issue. In addition they each have extensive listings of events, restaurants, and shopping in and around Budapest. Published every

2 weeks, *Funzine* is an independent magazine that is fresh, hip, and a fun read with lots of pictures useful to travelers. Each issue has basic Hungarian words and phrases with phonetic pronunciations. *Where* is a monthly published by the Ministry of Tourism and has excellent information. The listings in *Pesti Est* and *Exit,* free weeklies, are in Hungarian only, but are widely available at clubs, bookstores, and many other places. Other useful and free publications are *Budapest Passport,* a pocket-size guide published monthly, with a map, and the *Budapest Guide,* both of which are available at tourist offices and some hotels. These contain information on scheduled cultural events. The tourist office also has excellent free maps of the city.

The *Budapest Sun* (www.budapestsun.com), published every 2 weeks, and the *Budapest Times* (www.budapesttimes.hu), published weekly, are both English language, which have listings for concerts, theater, dance, film, and other events, along with restaurant reviews and current event happenings. They are available at most hotels and many newsstands. You can get a free copy of both at the Tourinform office at V. Liszt Ferenc tér 11. One website that attempts to map out Budapest's cultural and social scene is **www.pestiside.hu**, which provides an impertinent and saucy look at the city. Its sister site, **www.chew.hu**, provides some great restaurant news on new places to eat as they open.

CITY LAYOUT

To really appreciate the city and the layout, you will need a short history lesson. The city of Budapest came into being in 1873, making it relatively young in its present form. It is the result of a union of three separate cities: **Buda, Pest,** and **Óbuda** (literally meaning Old Buda) consisting of 23 self-governing municipal districts. Budapest is divided by the **River Danube (Duna)** with Pest, almost completely flat, on the eastern shore, making up almost two-thirds of the city. On the western bank is Buda and farther yet, Óbuda, which has the hilly areas; these areas being much older settlements. The entire Danube River flows eastward for a distance of some 2,850km (1,771 miles) making some strange twists and turns as it goes flowing through or forming part of a border of ten European countries, making it the longest river in the European Union.

The stretch of the Danube flowing through the capital is fairly wide (the average width is 400m/1,312 ft.), and most of the city's historic sites are on or near the river. Nine bridges connect the two banks, but two are for rail travel only, with five in the city center. The Széchenyi Chain Bridge (Lánchíd) built in 1873, was the first permanent bridge across the Danube uniting Óbuda, Buda, and Pest. Although it was blown up by the Nazis in 1945, it was rebuilt after the war, reopening in November 1949. If you look at a map of the city, you will see that the districts are numbered in a spiral pattern for the most part with districts I, II, and III on the Buda side and then IV starts the Pest side until XI, which again is the Buda side.

MAIN STREETS & SQUARES

PEST   Pest is as flat as a *palacsinta* (pancake), spread over a number of districts, taking in two-thirds of the city. Pest is the heartbeat with the commercial and administrative center of the capital and of all of Hungary. *Central Pest,* the term used in this guide, is that part of the city between the Danube and the semicircular **Outer Ring Boulevard (Nagykörút),** where stretches of it are named after former Austro-Hungarian monarchs: Ferenc körút, József körút, Erzsébet körút, Teréz körút, and Szent

Hungarian Address Terms

Navigating in Budapest will be easier if you are familiar with the following words (none of which are capitalized in Hungarian):

utca (abbreviated as *u.*)	street
út	road
útja	road of
körút (abbreviated as *krt.*)	boulevard
tér	square
tere	square of
köz	alley or lane
körönd	circle
rakpart	quay
liget	park
sziget	island
híd	bridge
sor	row
part	riverbank
pályaudvar (abbreviated as *pu.*)	railway station
állomás	station

István körút, changing names as the district changes. The Outer Ring begins at the Pest side of the Petőfi Bridge in the south and wraps itself around the center, ending at the Margit Bridge in the north. Several of Pest's busiest squares are found along the Outer Ring, and Pest's major east-west avenues bisect the ring at these squares.

Central Pest is further defined by the **Inner Ring (Kiskörút),** which lies within the Outer Ring. It starts at Szabadság híd (Freedom Bridge) in the south and is alternately named Vámház körút, Múzeum körút, Károly körút, Bajcsy-Zsilinszky út, and József Attila utca, depending on the district, before ending at the Chain Bridge. Inside this ring is the **Belváros,** the actual city center and the historic Inner City of Pest. For the traveler, the Pest side is our recommended side for accommodations since this is where the lion's share of the action is and it is easy to walk to where you want to go.

Váci utca (distinct from Váci út) is a popular pedestrian-only, touristy, shopping street between the Inner Ring and the Danube. It spills into **Vörösmarty tér,** one of the area's best-known squares. The **Dunakorzó (Danube Promenade),** a popular evening strolling spot, runs along the river in Pest between the Chain Bridge and the Erzsébet Bridge. The historic Jewish district of Pest is in the **Erzsébetváros (Elizabeth Town),** between the two ring boulevards.

Margaret Island (Margit-sziget) is in the middle of the Danube. Accessible via the Margaret Bridge or the Árpád Bridge, it's an enormously popular recreation park with restricted vehicular traffic. It is extremely popular in the summer for sunbathing, sports, jogging, and bike riding. It has a small petting zoo for children and the remnants of an old monastery.

BUDA & ÓBUDA   On the left bank of the Danube is Buda; to its north, beyond the city center, lies Óbuda. Buda is as hilly as Pest is flat and a good place for hiking.

The two most advantageous vista points in the city are in central Buda on Castle Hill and the even higher Gellért Hill. Streets in Buda, particularly in the hills, are not as logically arranged as those in Pest.

Castle Hill is one of the most beautiful parts of Budapest with its magnificent view of Pest. Castle Hill is accessed by steep steps, walking paths, and small roads that are not open to general traffic. There are three less aerobic ways to access Castle Hill for those who want to conserve their energy for other adventures. From Clark Ádám tér (at the head of the Chain Bridge) you can take the funicular; from Várfok utca (near Moszkva tér) you can take the no. 10 bus; or from Deák, take the no. 16 bus, all of which will take you to the top. Castle Hill consists of the royal palace itself, home to several museums. The previous castle was destroyed in World War II, but was rebuilt afterward and named the royal palace specifically to house museums. The Castle District has a long history going to pre-Celtic times, but what remains today are the medieval neighborhoods of small, winding streets, circling around Holy Trinity Square (Szentháromság tér), site of the Gothic Church of Our Lady or commonly referred to as St. Matthias Church. There's little traffic on Castle Hill, and the only industry is tourism. Souvenirs, food, and drink tend to be more expensive here than in Pest.

Gellért Hill, to the south of Castle Hill, is named after the martyred Italian bishop who aided King István I (Stephen I) in his conversion of the Hungarian nation to Christianity in the 10th and 11th centuries. A giant statue of Gellért sits on the side of the hill, where legend has it that he was martyred by angry pagans for his efforts. On top of the hill is the Citadella, marked by a 45-foot Liberation Statue of a woman holding a palm leaf to represent victory. It was erected in 1947 and visible from most points along the Danube on the Pest side.

Below Castle Hill, along the Danube, is a long, narrow neighborhood and distract known as **Watertown (Víziváros).** The main street of Watertown is Fő utca (Main St.). One of the original market places is off of Batthyány tér in this district. The famous Király thermal bath from Turkish times is right down the street.

Central Buda, the term used in this guide, is a collection of mostly low-lying neighborhoods below Castle Hill. The main square of Central Buda is **Moszkva tér,** just north of Castle Hill, a hub for trams, buses, and the Red line metro, this area is in serious need of revitalizing. Beyond Central Buda, mainly to the east, are the Buda Hills.

Óbuda is on the left bank of the Danube, north of Buda. Although the greater part of Óbuda is lacking any architectural significance, reminding one of the communist times, the area boasts both a beautiful old city center and the impressive Roman ruins of Aquincum. Unfortunately, the road coming off the Árpád Bridge slices the old city center in half, destroying its integrity. The historic center of the old city is **Fő tér (Main Sq.),** a charming square dotted with little, yet impressive museums. **Óbuda Island (Óbudai-sziget)** is home to an enormous park that swells in size every August when it hosts Hungary's own annual Woodstock music festival, called the Sziget (Island) Festival. This festival has developed an international following. For more on this event, see p. 18.

FINDING AN ADDRESS Locating addresses in Budapest or anywhere in Hungary for that matter can be an exercise in frustration. Not only is strangeness of the Hungarian language confusing, the difference between an *o, ö, ó, or ő,* can make all of the difference and with 14 vowels to choose from, it can be a real puzzle. However, with a little practice and a good map, you should be successful.

Budapest is divided into 23 districts, called *kerülets* (abbreviated as *ker.*). All addresses in Hungary start with a Roman numeral followed by a period signifying the *kerület;* for example, VII. Akácfa u. 18 is in the seventh *kerület*. Many street names are often used repeatedly in different districts, but are not all continuations of the same street. This makes it very important to know which *kerület* a certain address is in. You will also need to pay attention to the type of street. Is it utca, út, tér, or tere? For example, there are streets named Templom (church) in nine different districts with various utca, út, körönd, and so on added to them.

A common mistake made by visitors is to confuse **Váci út,** the heavily trafficked main road that goes from Nyugati Station toward the city of Vác, with **Váci utca,** the pedestrian-only street in the Inner City. Similarly, visitors sometimes mistake Vörösmarty utca, a station on the Yellow metro line, with Vörösmarty tér, the terminus of that same Yellow metro line.

If the address you are hunting for doesn't have a Roman numeral preceding it, look for the postal code for the *kerület*. Postal codes are four digits with the middle two digits representing the *kerület;* thus, Akácfa u.18, 1072 Budapest will be in district VII.

Street signs are posted high up on the corner buildings on a street and on two corners; one showing the even numbers and one with the odd numbers. The information given is the Roman numeral of the *kerület* followed by the name of the district, under this is the name of the street or square, and finally the building numbers found on that block. Look at the arrow on the sign; for example, 29–35 with an arrow pointing to the right tells you that if you walk to the right, the numbers will get higher. You may have to look at all four corners before you see the one you want. Even and odd-numbered buildings are on opposite sides of the street; however, they do not follow any pattern otherwise. You may be in front of number 98 on one side of the street and see number 79 directly across from you. Depending on whether you are looking for an even or odd number on the street, orient yourself with the signs showing the even or odd numbering. Numbers are seldom skipped, but two or more places may share a number; often you'll end up walking longer than you expected to reach a given number. Adding to the "guess where it is" game, many businesses do not have a numeral posted on their doors, so look for other signs.

Many street names were changed following the systemic changes of 1989, reverting for the most part back to their pre–World War II names, aside from a handful of central streets with politically evocative former names, like Lenin körút (now Teréz körút) and Népköztársaság útja ("Road of the People's Republic," now Andrássy út). The one outstanding exception is Moszkva tér.

Floors in buildings are numbered European style, meaning that the floor you enter, is the ground floor *(földszint),* so for the first floor, you have to go up one flight *(első emelet),* and so on. Addresses are usually written with the floor number in Roman numerals and the apartment number in Arabic numerals, following the street name. For example, a full address would be VII. Budapest Akácfa u. 18, IV/24. The district is the seventh in Budapest and the location is on Akácfa u. 18 on the fourth floor, apartment 24.

Read signs carefully and match all of the little marks above those vowels. The Hungarian alphabet has 44 letters, making it very detailed in writing and in speech. Refer to the "Hungarian Address Terms" box above.

STREET MAPS   A good map can save you lots of frustration in Budapest. You can get a good free map at the Tourinform office. Otherwise, maps are sold throughout Budapest, but Cartografia, a Hungarian company, makes two maps that are substantially cheaper and cover Budapest in great detail. The Cartografia foldout map is fine, but if you find its size awkward, you should pick up Cartografia's *Budapest Atlas*. Both maps are available throughout central Pest at kiosks and bookstores. Public transportation lines are shown on the maps, but, in some places, the map is too crowded to make the lines out clearly. The BKV térkép (Budapest Transportation Authority map), is available from metro ticket windows, therefore recommended as a complementary aid (see "Getting Around," below). If you plan on any hiking excursions in the Buda Hills, you should pick up *A Budai Hegység map, no. 6* of the Cartografia Turistatérképe (Touring Map) series.

If you love maps, you will find these **map stores** in Pest a true haven, where you can pick up the maps listed above (except the transit map), maps of other cities in Hungary, the Budapest-by-bike map, and international maps: **Cartographia Térképbolt** (Globe and Map Shop) is the publisher-owned store of the map discussed above. They are located at VI. Bajcsy-Zsilinszky út 37 (© 1/312-6001), and open Monday through Friday from 10am to 6pm (metro: Arany János utca on the Blue line); **Térképkirály (Map King)**, at VI. Bajcsy-Zsilinszky 23 (© 1/472-0505; www.mapking.hu), is open Monday through Friday from 9am to 6pm, and Saturday 9am to 1pm (metro: Arany János). My favorite, due to its location more than its selection, is **Párizsi Udvar Book and Map Shop** at V. Petőfi Sándor utca and Ferenciek tere (in the Párizsi courtyard) which is open Monday through Friday from 9am to 6pm, and Saturday 9am to 1pm. Even if you don't want a map, the courtyard is phenomenally beautiful. You can also find maps in most of the bookstores recommended in chapter 9, "Budapest Shopping."

You'll also find an excellent online Budapest map with great search capabilities at http://tinyurl.com/2r4psn. Enter the street name, and you'll get a detailed map.

NEIGHBORHOODS IN BRIEF

Buda

Castle District (Várnegyed)   This district is the city's most beautiful and historic dating back to the 13th century, with some settlements here even earlier. This is district one, which is a small district that encompasses the plateau where the grand royal palace and grounds fill the southern end above the surrounding neighborhoods and the Danube below. The Castle District is defined by its medieval walls. The northern end is home to small winding streets, with old homes, St. Matthias Church, the Fisherman's Bastion, and the Hilton Hotel.

Watertown (Víziváros)   A long, narrow neighborhood wedged between the Castle District and the Danube, makes up district II. Víziváros is historically a quarter where fishermen and artisans reside. Built on the steep slope of Castle Hill, it has narrow alleys and stairs instead of roads in many places. Its main street, Fő utca, runs the north-south length of the Víziváros, parallel to and a block away from the river. It is a high-rent district for residents and tourists.

Rose Hill (Rózsadomb) This is the part of Buda Hills and still part of district II, closest to the city center and one of the city's most fashionable and luxurious residential neighborhoods.

Buda Hills The Buda Hills are numerous remote neighborhoods that feel as if they're nowhere near, let alone within, a capital city. By and large, the hills are considered a classy place to live. Neighborhoods are generally known by the name of the hill on which they stand. Unless you like to walk neighborhoods, there is nothing more for the traveler in this part of the city.

Óbuda

Óbuda makes up district III and is mostly residential now, though its long Danube coastline was a favorite spot for workers' resorts under the old regime. Most facilities have been privatized, so a large number of hotels are found here. Transportation for the traveler into Pest would be cumbersome, so we do not recommend staying out here. The extensive Roman ruins of Aquincum and the beautifully preserved old-town main square are Óbuda's chief claims to fame.

Pest

Inner City (Belváros) The historic center of Pest, the Belváros, literally meaning "city center" is the area inside the Inner Ring, bound by the Danube to the west. Making up part of district V, it has many of Pest's historic buildings in this area. In addition there are many of the city's showcase luxury hotels and most of its best-known shopping streets here also.

Leopold Town (Lipótváros) The continuation of district V, is just north of the Belváros, making Lipótváros a part of central Pest. Development began here at the end of the 18th

century, and the neighborhood soon emerged as a center of Pest business and government. Parliament, plus a number of government ministries, courthouses, banks, and the former stock exchange, are all found here. Before the war, this was considered a neighborhood of the "high bourgeoisie."

Theresa Town (Terézváros) The character of Terézváros, district VI, is defined by Andrássy út, the great boulevard running the length of the neighborhood from Heroes' Square through Oktogon and down into the Inner City. This grand street has been regaining its reputation of elegance: Andrássy út is once again the "best address" in town, especially since the upper part is now a World Heritage site. The Teréz körút section of the Outer Ring cuts through Terézváros; Oktogon is its major square. The area around Nagymező utca is the city's small theater district.

Elizabeth Town (Erzsébetváros) This is district VII. Directly to the southeast of Terézváros, Erzsébetváros is the historic Jewish neighborhood of Pest. During the German occupation from 1944 to 1945, this district was where the ghettos where established for the Jewish people. This district is still the center of Budapest's Jewish life. Although it had been exceedingly run-down due to the war, in the last couple of years, it has become gentrified and considered one of the up and coming districts to invest in.

Joseph Town (Józsefváros) One of the largest central Pest neighborhoods is the VIII district. Józsefváros is to the southeast of Erzsébetváros. It has had a reputation of being a less than desirable district of Pest, but there are some places in this district worth your time and energy. It should not be dismissed across the board. It is working hard at gentrifying.

Budapest at a Glance

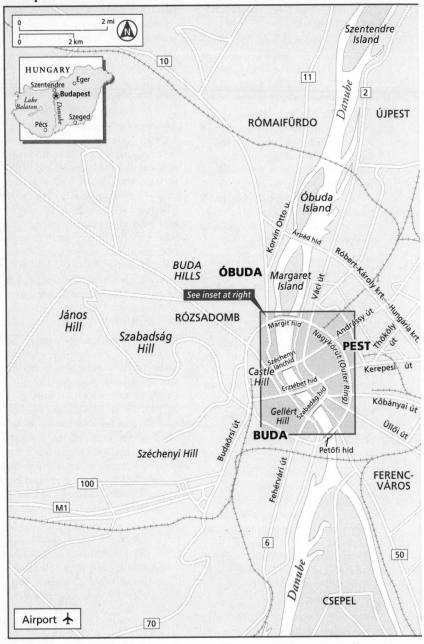

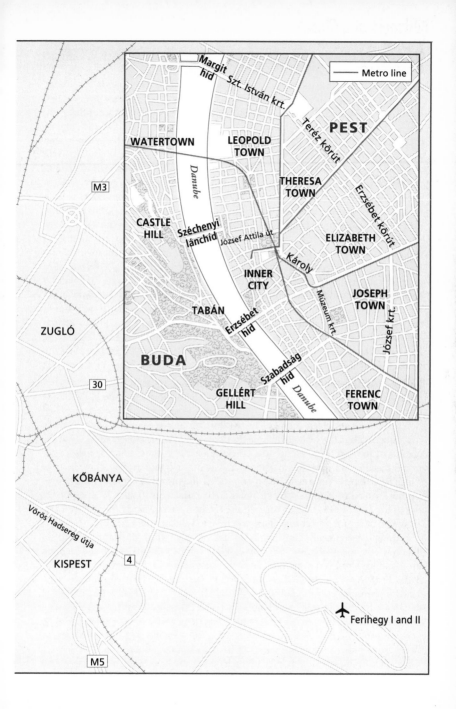

2 Getting Around

BY PUBLIC TRANSPORTATION

Budapest has an extensive, efficient, and inexpensive public transportation system, but locals without global experiences, disagree with this. If you have some patience and minimal skills with reading maps, you can easily learn the system. It is not that difficult to master. Public transportation, however, is not without its drawbacks. Due to the construction of a fourth metro line, there have been interruptions throughout parts of the city at various points in time and this is likely to continue until 2010. In addition, for the last 3 years, remodeling has taken place on the Red metro line in 6-to-8-week increments, sometimes with only 2 weeks warning. They are efficient enough to provide buses to replace the stations being worked on, but it can be confusing. The biggest disadvantage, however, is that metros and tram routes shut down for the night at around 11:30pm (see "Night Service," below). Some areas of the city, most notably the Buda Hills, are beyond the reach of some night bus service making taxi drivers happy to provide those late-night journeys. BKV, the company that runs the whole transportation network, has dramatically increased the night bus service to overcome some of these problems, but it still is not perfect with some long waits at dark and lonely bus stops. During rush hours, all forms of transport are crowded making it best to plan your travel around these times. A disadvantage, mostly pertinent to travelers, is that Castle Hill can be reached in only three ways by public transportation and all of these modes of transportation are quite crowded in the high seasons. Most importantly, crowded public transport is the place where you are most likely to be targeted by Budapest's professional pickpockets (see "Staying Safe," in chapter 2).

FARES All forms of public transportation (metro, bus, tram, trolleybus [an electric bus evident by the connection to wires above], some portions of the HÉV railway lines, and cogwheel railway) in Budapest require the self-validation of prepurchased tickets (*vonaljegy*), which cost 230 Ft ($1.25/65p) apiece (children under 6 travel free); single tickets can be bought at metro ticket windows, newspaper kiosks, and the occasional tobacco shop, though the latter are on the decline. There are also automated machines in most metro stations and at major transportation hubs, most of which have been recently modernized or installed and provide somewhat reliable service, but I wouldn't depend on them. You can also purchase a 10 pack (*tizes csomag*) of tickets for 2,050 Ft ($11/£5.85) or a 20 pack (*huszas csomag*) for 3,900 Ft ($21/£11). However, each time you change lines, you have to validate a new ticket.

I strongly recommend that you buy a transport pass, which does not require validation. They are available for 1 day (*napijegy*) for 1,550 Ft ($8.40/£4.40) and are good until midnight of the day marked. The other pass options are 3 days (*turistajegy*) for 3,400 Ft ($18.40/£14.15), 7 days for 4,000 Ft ($21.60/£16.60) or for longer stays, 14 days (*kéthétibérlet*) for 5,300 Ft ($28.65/£22). The 7- and 14-day passes need to be signed. If your plans are even longer, there is a 30 consecutive day pass (*30 napos bérlet*) at 8,250 Ft ($44.60/£34.30), which requires a photo. If you are going to be here for 4 to 5 days, the 7-day (*hetijegy*) pass is still a savings over individual tickets. Passes are so much more convenient than having a handful of tickets that you have to worry about remembering to validate each time or replenishing your stock at odd hours. Honestly, these will save you money in the long run.

While this standard ticket is valid on the metro, there are other types of optional single-ride metro tickets introduced years ago, making ticket buying a bit more complicated for those who want the exactly appropriate ticket for their journey. Personally, I don't think any traveler should waste time caring about this, but I have met some who do. A metro section ticket *(metrószakaszjegy)*, at 180 Ft (.95¢/50p), is valid for a single metro trip stopping at three stations or less. A metro transfer ticket *(metróátszállójegy)*, at 380 Ft ($2.05/£1.10), allows you to transfer from one metro line to another on the same ticket, without any limit to the number of stations that the train stops at during your journey.

Transportation inspectors are those dreaded people who, like the secret police of yesteryear, whip out a hidden blue or red (the old color, but still sometimes used) armband when approaching you or are standing guard at the top or bottom of an escalator at the metro stops, or hop on the tram or buses after the door has closed. Some are uniformed, so you know you are heading into the lion's den. However, they have become trickier and more covert over the years and are often in plainclothes. It is not until they materialize the dreaded armband and greet you, that you realize you have had a false sense of security about having a peaceful ride. There were horror stories for years about how they treated people, screaming and yelling and causing a scene of hysterics when they caught someone without a ticket or an invalid one. Due to the hundreds of letters of complaints filling volumes, the BKV instituted mandatory (but token) customer service in-services meant to file down the teeth of these overly aggressive warriors of transportation justice. For some it has taken hold. We have actually witnessed the miracle of an inspector who captured two unsuspecting and confused Swedish women without a ticket and rather than a fine, offered to sell them a 3-day pass on the spot. This was a difference of a pass worth 3,100 Ft ($17/£8.80) versus a fine of 5,000 Ft ($27/£14). Since they can appear on trams, trolleybuses, and buses, they are impossible to avoid completely. So notorious are these inspectors, a young Hungarian filmmaker made a movie about them called ***Kontroll*** (2003). Director Antal Niród received special permission to use the metro underground to shoot the film. We highly recommend you view this movie at least twice.

The fines for not having a validated ticket or pass is 5,000 Ft ($27/£14) if paid on the spot or 10,000 Ft ($54/£28) if paid later; this does not include the embarrassment of getting caught.

We don't recommend the **Budapest Card,** which is available for 1 or 3 days. It does include transportation, but the other savings are negligible and it is not a good value. Some museums are free with the card, while others are simply discounted. The other discounts with the card don't make it a plausible savings and it is cheaper to pay as you go after buying a transport pass. Realistically, how many museums on the list are you really interested in?

SCHEDULES & MAPS All public transport operates on approximate schedules, posted at bus and tram shelters and in metro stations. The schedules are a little confusing at first, but you'll figure them out when you realize the time column on the left is weekdays and the list shows the hours of the clock with the list of minutes on the same row. The middle column is usually Saturday's schedule and the right-hand column is Sunday and holidays. Buses and trolleybuses are subject to traffic and traffic lights just like cars are, so expecting them to be exactly on time is never a realistic expectation. Trams are also hostage to traffic lights, which can put them behind too. *Note when the last ride of the night departs, and don't miss it.* Many unlucky travelers have found themselves waiting alone at a bus or tram stop for long periods of time. This is a clue that you have missed the last opportunity for a ride. If you have

Internet service, you can also check the BKV online, which has an excellent English language section (at www.bkv.hu/english/home/index.html) to help you plan your evening accordingly.

The transportation map produced by the Budapest Transport Authority (BKV térkép) is usually available at most metro ticket windows for a small fee. Since transportation routes are extremely difficult to read on most city maps, we suggest that you buy one of these handy maps if you plan to spend more than a few days in the city. In addition, on the map's reverse side is a full listing of routes, including the all-important night-bus routes. Note that there are some popular routes of trams that are being replaced by buses due to construction of metro 4 and these will not be on the maps. Keep your eyes open for signs in English on the tram stops. The Red metro has been closed on and off for reconstruction for the last 3 years and it will continue for the next 2 years at least. Look for signs in English stating that the M2 bus will replace any closed stations.

NIGHT SERVICE   Most of the Budapest transportation system closes down between 11:10pm or midnight and 4:30am. There are, however, 31 night routes, a dramatic increase over years past, due to consumer demand. They're generally quite safe, though you may find a number of loud and inebriated Hungarian youth continuing their party plans or going home to sleep it off. For the most part, they are harmless. Night routes are posted at bus stops if that route has one. The no. 906 night bus follows the route of the no. 6 tram line. All night buses have a 9 as the first of a three digit number. A few of them share the same numbers as buses on daytime routes or they may actually run different routes. Night buses require the standard, self-validated ticket. Many night buses will skip stops if no one signals to stop and if they do not see passengers waiting, so pay attention and press the button for your stop.

UNDERPASSES   Underpasses are found beneath most major boulevards in Budapest. Underpasses are often little underground cities with vendors, shops, and bakeries, some with bars. The most confusing part for a traveler as well as some long-time residents is which exit to use. Many of them have as many as five or six different exits, each letting you out onto a different part of the square or street and can be quite disorienting. Signs direct you to bus, tram, trolleybus, and metro stops, often using the word *fele,* meaning "toward." The signs will also include the street(s) at the top of the stairs. We suggest that before you enter the underground, you take note of the landmarks on the corner of your destination, framing the direction you will need to follow once downstairs. When you think you've found the correct exit, walk halfway up the stairs to see if you recognize the landmarks you want. (I have had so much exercise going up and down stairs needlessly, which has saved a great deal of money on gym membership.) *Note:* Although Budapest is a very safe city, especially when compared to American cities of comparable size, underpasses tend to be among the more suspect places late at night. There have not been any serious problems, but various undesirable types use these as meeting venues and can be loud, drunk, and boisterous, while others use them for their bedroom. Either way, it makes the uninitiated passerby feel uncomfortable.

BY METRO

You may find yourself spending a lot of time in the Budapest metro getting around and time is tight. The system is clean and efficient, with trains running every 3 to 5 minutes on weekdays and 6 to 8 minutes on weekends, from about 4:30am until about 11:10pm. Currently, there are three lines, with only the Red line going under the Danube to Buda. Construction on the long-awaited fourth line has begun, but it will be several years (think 2010) before it becomes functional. In the meanwhile, this construction is causing some chaos in the city at different places and different times. The three existing lines are universally known by colors: Yellow, Red, and Blue. Officially, they have numbers as well (1, 2, and 3, respectively) which is what you will see on maps, but people will refer to them by color, and all signs are color-coded. All three lines converge at **Deák tér,** the only point where any lines meet. Remember that if you change lines here, you need to validate a new ticket if you are not using a pass.

To make sure you are on the correct side of the tracks, each station has the list of stations posted either on a wall, or more modernly in remodeled stations, above the tracks. There is some distinctive mark like a filled circle showing the station where you are. The stations to follow are in a pronounced colored mark, whereas the stations the train has already left are in pale or lighter colors. Some stations enhance this visually by including arrows too. If you don't see the station you want in a prominent color, look on the other side of the tracks.

The **Yellow (1) line** is the oldest metro on the European continent and second oldest in the world, having been built in 1894 as part of the Hungarian millennial celebration. It has been refurbished and restored to its original splendor, making it the most attractive and shortest metro line in the city. For trivia buffs, London has the oldest metro line in the world, built in 1863, followed by Budapest, then surprise, the third is Boston. They built their first metro in 1897, eclipsing New York City. Signs for the Yellow line, are different than those for the Red and Blue lines since they lack the *M* to signify metro. Instead, the stations above ground have large yellow signs above the stairwells with *földalatti* (underground). Most of the stations entryways are painted yellow as a visual clue that this is a metro station. Each station has two separate entrances, one for each direction. What I've found contradictory and confusing is that some of the stairwell entrances are in the opposite direction from the direction the train will be going. The Yellow line runs from Vörösmarty tér, site of Gerbeaud's Cukrászda in the heart of central Pest, out the length of Andrássy út, past the Városliget (City Park), ending at Mexikói út, in a trendy residential part of Pest known as Zugló. So, depending on the direction you're heading, enter either the side marked IRÁNY MEXIKÓI ÚT or IRÁNY VÖRÖSMARTY TÉR. Incidentally, somewhere in the middle of the line is a stop called Vörösmarty utca; this is a small street running off Andrássy út and should not be confused with the terminus, Vörösmarty tér. (However, at each of these stops you will find the traditional coffeehouses, Gerbaud and Lukács, respectively.) It's worth taking a ride on this line, with its distinct 19th-century atmosphere. If you would like to walk it, see the chapter "Strolling Around Budapest" (p. 168).

The **Red (2)** and **Blue (3) lines** are modern metros, though the outside of the cars tend to look old and decrepit; they are clean inside, which is what counts. To reach them you descend long, steep escalators; the Red line has the longest and steepest. If you are prone to vertigo, you may want to take care. The Red line runs from Örs vezér tere in eastern Pest, through the center, and across the Danube to Batthyány tér, Moszkva tér, and finally Déli Station. Keleti Station is also along the Red line. This line has had its stations remodeled over the last 3 years, but in increments, thus causing some disruption in services. However, M2 buses above ground replace any closed station. There is only a short time warning given when this is going to happen, but the signs are in English giving alternate directions. Hopefully, this will all be completed and back to normal by the end of 2008. The Blue line runs from Kőbánya-Kispest, in southeastern Pest, through the center, and out to Újpest-Központ in northern Pest. Nyugati Station is along the Blue line. The Blue line has the ugliest stations of the three lines, but fortunately for travelers, they do not have to use many of them.

On the street above stations of both the Red and Blue lines are distinctive colored *M* signs. Tickets should be validated at automated boxes before you descend the escalator. When changing lines at Deák tér, you're required to validate another ticket (unless you have a special metro transfer ticket). The orange or red validating machines are in the hallways between lines, but are easy to miss, particularly if there are big crowds. Most of the validating machines are being replaced by electric models. If you need to use the manual type (usually on trams or buses), insert your ticket with the number down first and facing you. Then pull the black ticket holder toward you until you hear a paper cutter sound. If you don't see any visible difference on your ticket, the machine is not working, so look for another. When using the electronic type, make sure your ticket is numbers up and first into the machine. You will hear a little tone as the ticket is printed with the date and time. Failure to do this properly is cause for a fine if caught by an inspector. Once validated, your ticket is good for one hour, so don't dally.

Directions given throughout this book use a metro station as a starting point whenever possible. In a case where that's simply not feasible, other major identifiable transportation hubs are used as starting points.

BY BUS

There are almost 175 different bus *(busz)* lines in greater Budapest. Many parts of the city, most notably the Buda Hills, are best accessed by bus. Although buses are the most difficult to use of Budapest's transportation choices, with patience (and a BKV map) you'll be able to get around in no time. With the exception of night buses, most lines are in service from about 4:30am to about 11:30pm. Some bus lines run far less frequently (or not at all) on weekends, while others run far more frequently (or only) on weekends. This information is both on the reverse of the BKV transportation map and on the schedules posted at every bus stop.

Black-numbered local buses constitute the majority of the city's lines. Buses with red numbers are express buses that follow the same routes as local buses with the same number, simply skipping minor stops along the way. Check the list at the stop to see if your destination is one of the stops. If the red number on the bus is followed by an *E* (there are only five routes with an *E*), the bus makes very few stops between terminals and is best avoided, since they also change the stops periodically and only post it in Hungarian. Depending on your destination, an express bus may be a much faster way of traveling. Buses have always been blue, though now some express buses are beginning to appear in red, while others are bowing to commercialism and are covered in advertisements making it difficult to tell if they are a local or express without seeing the sign in front.

Tickets are self-validated onboard the bus by the mechanical or electronic red box found by each door (see above for directions for use). You can board the bus by any door, but manners dictate that you stand to the side of the door to allow disembarking passengers out before you start to board. Each time you change buses, you need a new ticket and have to validate it. Again, this is not necessary with a transport pass. Tickets cannot be purchased from the driver; see "Fares" on p. 54 for information on where to purchase public transportation tickets.

I have a couple of problems with riding the bus. I think the bus drivers are recruited from former carnival ride operators and thus they have had prior training in making abrupt stops when you least expect it. If you were not lucky enough to find a seat, you can expect to have a body slam experience or a case of whiplash before reaching your desired stop. It is common practice for the drivers to bypass stops when no one is waiting to get on and no one has signaled to get off. If you are uncertain and need a moment to orient yourself, press the stop button regardless to give yourself an opportunity to take note of the stop. Most of the modern buses have buttons on the poles by the seats, so it can be done inconspicuously. If it is not your stop, look innocently away from the door. When you know you want to get off at the next stop, press the button to signal again. The older buses only have buttons above the door that light up after being pressed (beware—some drivers open only the doors that have been signaled). Few stops have their names posted; some buses have a list of stops posted inside, but if stops are passed up and you are not aware of it, you will lose track. Chances are, though, that the locals riding a given bus will know exactly where your stop is, and will kindly help you to reach your stop. You can also ask the driver to let you know when he has reached your stop.

Avoid buses in central areas during rush hours, since traffic tends to be quite bad. It pays to go a bit out of your way to use a metro or tram at these times instead, or simply to walk.

BY TRAM

You'll find Budapest's 32 bright-yellow tram lines (known as *villamos* in Hungarian) very useful, particularly nos. 4 and 6, which travel along the Outer Ring (Nagykörút). These tram lines underwent major reconstruction in 2006, modernizing each tram stop with the name of the stop prominently displayed in etched glass at various points on the tram platform. The platforms were also raised 6cm (2.4 in.) to make them compliant with the new combi-tram, the only routes in the city with these trams. The combi-tram is one long continuous car, modern looking, with clean upholstered seats. The major appeal is two-fold: They are wheelchair- and stroller-accessible and they are air-conditioned. However, the city neglected to order the added cost air-conditioning. Within a week of their being put into service, they blew out the electric lines that were in place for the old trams, but all of the kinks seem to have been worked out with one exception. (See the fun fact about these trams on p. 150.) Routes 47 and 49, which run along the Inner Ring were replaced by buses with the same numbers due to construction of the fourth metro line. Beyond the ring, they change back to trams, but generally in areas that travelers are not interested in going. Tram no. 2, which travels along the Danube on the Pest side between Margit híd and Boráros tér, provides an incredible view of the Buda Hills, including the Castle District, and is far better than any sightseeing tour on a bus. We especially recommend this route at night when the castle is lit on the Buda side and Parliament is spotlighted on the Pest side. It is a romantic ride.

Tickets are self-validated onboard (see instructions above for doing this properly). As with buses, tickets are valid for one ride, not for the line itself. Trams stop at every station, and all doors open, regardless of whether anyone is waiting to get on.

Strangely, you will notice Hungarians pressing the green stop buttons to either signal a stop or to make the door magically open faster than it is intended, but neither has any valid results. *Important:* The *red* buttons near the tram doors are for emergency stops, not stop requests.

When a tram line is closed for maintenance, replacement buses are assigned the tram route. They go by the same number as the tram, with a *V* (for *villamos*) preceding the number. See "Fares" on p. 54 for information on where to purchase public transportation tickets.

BY TROLLEYBUS

Trolleybuses are electric buses that receive power from a cable above the street. There are only 16 trolleybus lines in Budapest, all in Pest. Of particular interest to train travelers is no. 73, the fastest route between Keleti Station and within a block of Nyugati Station. All the information in the "By Bus" section above regarding boarding, ticket validation, and stops applies to trolleybuses as well. See "Fares" on p. 54 for information on where to purchase public transportation tickets.

BY HÉV

The HÉV is a suburban railway network that connects Budapest to various points along the city's outskirts. There are four HÉV lines; only two lines, the Szentendre line (see chapter 11, "The Danube Bend") and the Gödöllő line, are of serious interest to visitors.

Most hotels, restaurants, and sights in northern Buda and Óbuda are best reached by the HÉV (so indicated in the directions given throughout this book). To reach Óbuda's Fő tér (Main Sq.), get off at the Árpád híd (Árpád Bridge) stop. For trips within the city limits, the cost is one transit ticket, self-validated as on a bus or tram.

The HÉV suburban railroad connects Budapest's Batthyány tér with Szentendre. On the Pest side, you can catch the HÉV from the Margit Híd, Budai Híd Fő.Trains leave daily, year-round, every 20 minutes or so from 4am to 11:30pm (trip time: 45 min.). The one-way fare is 500 Ft ($2.70/£1.40); subtract 230 Ft ($1.24/65p) if you have a valid Budapest public transportation pass. The trip takes 45 minutes. This HÉV route runs regularly between 4am and 11:30pm.

The HÉV line to Gödöllő begins at Örs vezér tere, the end of the Red metro line. Trains run from 4:30am to 10:00pm. The one-way fare is 830 Ft ($4.50/£2.40); but only 600 Ft ($3.25/£1.70) if you have a valid Budapest public transportation pass. The trip takes 40 minutes.

BY COGWHEEL RAILWAY & FUNICULAR

Budapest's **cogwheel railway** *(fogaskerekű)* began running in 1874, becoming electrified in later years. It runs from Városmajor, across the street from the Hotel Budapest on Szilágyi Erzsébet fasor in Buda, to Széchenyi-hegy, one terminus of the Children's Railway (Gyermek Vasút) and site of Hotel Panoráma in 20 minutes. The cogwheel railway runs from 5am to 11pm, and normal transportation tickets (see "Fares," p. 54; self-validated onboard) are used. The pleasant route twists high into the Buda Hills reaching a height of 327m (1,073 ft.); at 230 Ft ($1.25/65p), it is well worth taking just for the ride and the patches of lovely scenery along the way.

The **cable car** or **funicular** *(sikló)* connects Buda's Clark Ádám tér, at the head of the Széchenyi Chain Bridge, with Dísz tér, just outside the Buda Castle. The funicular is one of only two forms of public transportation serving the Castle District (bus no. 10 and bus no. 16 are the other possibilities; see "By Bus," above). An extremely steep and short ride, but fun view, though like a solarium on sunny days, is the funicular. It runs at frequent intervals from 7:30am to 10pm (closed on the second Mon of the month). Tickets cost 700 Ft ($3.80/£2) to go up, and 1,300 Ft ($7.30/£3.70) for a round-trip for adults, while children get a break at 400 Ft ($2.15/£1.15) up and 750 Ft ($4.05/£2.15]) round-trip. After public protest, the funicular now goes slower than it originally did, as riders wanted to enjoy the scenery longer.

BY TAXI

Budapest taxis fall into two general categories: legitimate and those that are not. There is no sense in wasting your precious research time in discussing the latter, so just pay particular attention to the ones we recommend, if you need to use one. First a rundown on laws regarding taxis that will help you understand the system. All legal taxis must have a yellow license plate and a yellow taxi sign on the roof. The fare to be paid at the destination consists of three basic parts: the base fee, which is not dependent on the distance traveled; the kilometer fare, which is based on the distance traveled; and the waiting tariff, which is used if the taxi has had to stop or fails to move in traffic at a rate of at least 15kmph (9 mph). When you call for a taxi, the dispatcher will ask for the phone number you are calling from and they will get your address from this. They will also ask for a name. By law, the driver has to ask your name to ensure you are the one he is to pick up. If you have a complicated name use one that will be easily understood and remember it for when the driver asks you. Calling for a taxi is less expensive than getting one on the street, but if you cannot call, use the following companies only where their names are clearly displayed on the side. Legally, taxis can charge different rates if requested through the dispatcher than if hailed on the street or taken from a queue. Make sure the driver starts the meter once you are in the taxi. By law, they must provide a written receipt. If you have a problem, write down the name of the driver from his license, his taxi number, and the company name and report it to the **Tourism Office of Budapest** at (C) 1/266-0479. Many travelers scam themselves by giving the taxi driver a bill much larger than needed, feeling rushed and unfamiliar with the currency. Once the taxi is gone, so is the big fat tip you gave the driver. Taxis used to be a bargain, but this is no longer the case. I rarely use them due to the inflated rates and a great public transportation system, but when I do, I use the following.

The best rates are invariably those of the larger fleet companies. I particularly recommend **City Taxi** ((C) 1/211-1111). Other reliable fleets include **Volántaxi** ((C) 1/466-6666), **Rádió Taxi** ((C) 1/377-7777), **Fő Taxi** ((C) 1/222-2222), **Tele5** ((C) 1/355-5555), **6×6** ((C) 1/266-6666), and **Budataxi** ((C) 1/233-3333). You can call one of these companies from your hotel, ask a restaurant person, or ask whomever is in charge to call for you, even if there are other private taxis waiting around outside. You will seldom, if ever, wait more than 5 minutes for a fleet taxi unless you're in an extremely remote neighborhood (or in bad weather).

Finally, you are most likely dealing with a dishonest driver if he asks you to pay for his return trip, asks to be paid in anything but forints, or quotes you a "flat rate" in lieu of running the meter. The chances are slim that you will encounter this with any of the companies above, but there are bad apples everywhere. If you need extra room, request a station wagon by asking for a *kombi* when calling for your taxi and in the summer you can also request an air-conditioned vehicle.

Tipping is usually not more than 10%. Hungarians usually round the bill up. If you think the driver has cheated you, then you certainly should not tip. In fact, it is recommended that you call the company and complain, as most will punish their members for untoward behavior. Report it to the Tourism Office also.

BY CAR

There's no reason to use a car for sightseeing in Budapest and I believe anyone wanting to drive in the city has a death wish. Not only are they crazy drivers, but you will find a serious lack of stop signs on most streets that are not blessed with a traffic light. You may, however, wish to rent a car for trips out of the city (see chapters 11–14). Hertz, Avis, Alamo, National, and Budget have offices that can be found in town and at the airport, but marginally better deals may be found by making arrangements directly and in advance on their website. You are urged to reserve a rental car as early as possible. If you reserve from abroad, ask for written confirmation by fax or e-mail. If you don't receive a confirmation, it's wise to assume that the reservation has not been properly made.

We have sample quoted rates for an economy car currently listed by each of the following agencies with these conditions: The driver must be 21 years old with no upper age limit and is the only authorized driver. The driver's license must be at least one-year-old. One requires an international driver's license.

Budget Car Rental, both Ferihegy airports or at I.Krisztina körút 41–43 in the Hotel Mercure Buda (© **1/214-0420**). A credit card deposit is required equal to twice the amount of the rental terms. A rental is a continuous 24-hour day. The renter is responsible for any damages and repairs needed. A typical economy car, such as a Ford Fiesta rents for 15,000 Ft ($81/£43) a day for a 1-to-3-day rental or 65,000 Ft ($351/£185) for a week. They also require a hold on a credit card of 255,000 Ft ($1,216/£640) as a deposit. This includes insurance, unlimited mileage within Hungary, and VAT.

Fox Auto Rent, XXII. Nagytétényi út 48–50, XXII Budapest (© **1/382-9000;** fax 1/382-9003; www.fox-autorent.com), rents the Fiat Panda for 12,000 Ft ($65/£34) per day for a rental of 1 to 3 days, and 65,000 Ft ($351/£185) for a week, insurance and mileage included. A deposit of 100,000 Ft ($541/£285) on a credit card is required. Though located far from the city center, Fox will deliver the car to you at your hotel without charge between 8am to 6pm, but only if you book it directly through the number above. Rates are more expensive if booked online. Special arrangements need to be made directly with the office listed if you intend to drive outside of Hungary.

Denzel Europcar InterRent (National), VIII. Üllöi út 60–62, 1082 Budapest (© **1/477-1080;** fax 1/477-1099; www.nationalcar.hu), offers the Opel Corza or Fiat Punto for 14,300 Ft ($77/£41) per day with insurance, or 38,000 ($205/£108) for 3 days, including insurance. They also have a rental counter at the airport (© **1/296-6610**), but you will pay an additional 12% airport tax. Booked through the Internet, you receive a 35% discount. Driving outside of Hungary may incur other charges. An international driver's license may be required.

DRIVING TIPS

DRIVING REGULATIONS The speed limit in Hungary is 50kmph (31 mph) in built-up areas, 90kmph (56 mph) on main roads, and 130kmph (81 mph) on motorways. Safety belts must be worn in the front seat and back seat; children under 6 may not sit in the front seat and may not travel without a safety belt. Horns may not be used in built-up areas, except in emergencies. Headlights must be on at all times on all intercity roads and highways. A highway sticker must be bought for using highways M1, M3, M5, and M7. It can be bought at petrol stations near the highways and are available in 4 days, 10 days, and monthly and yearly versions. Always keep the receipt for the sticker as the Highway Control may ask for it. The sticker must be affixed to the front windscreen. It is illegal to use a hand-held mobile phone when driving. On-the-spot fines are issued and must be paid within 30 days at the bank by the yellow bill given. If the police officer requests payment immediately, refuse. They used to be allowed to collect the fine, but are no longer. Credit cards are not accepted. Drunk-driving laws are strictly enforced; any alcohol content in the driver's blood is illegal.

Cars are required to have a first-aid kit and a reflective warning triangle in them at all times. A decal indicating the country of registration is also required. These items should be included in all rental cars, so check or ask when you pick up your car. If you're driving a rental car rented from another country, make sure you have the so-called green card (proof of international insurance), not automatically given by all rental agencies. Rental agencies usually provide authorized permissions to cross international borders, so we recommend that you check your itinerary with the firm before departure. Hungarian police set up random checkpoints where cars are pulled over and drivers are made to present their papers. If all your papers are in order, you'll have no trouble. Still, foreigners residing in Budapest and driving cars with foreign plates, report being routinely stopped by police and fined for rather ridiculous infractions. There are plenty of gas stations along major routes. Newly built sections of the major highways outside Budapest require payment of a toll. *Warning:* Some neighborhoods—notably Buda's Castle District, allow vehicular access only to cars with special resident permits.

BREAKDOWN SERVICES   The **Hungarian Auto Club (Magyar Autóklub)** operates a 24-hour free emergency breakdown service: Call Ⓒ **188** (note, however, that not all operators speak English).

The Autóklub also has an **International Aid Service Center,** at II. Rómer Flóris u. 4/a (Ⓒ **1/345-1744**), which was established specifically for international motorists; however, our attempts to get assistance with information was a bit frustrating. Stay on the line; you will be connected. Services provided include emergency aid, towing, and technical advice, but the center may refer you to the rental company first, which in turn may have to make the contact with the auto club.

PARKING   Parking is very difficult in central Pest and parts of central Buda, but it is easier elsewhere in the city, though still not carefree. People have always parked virtually anywhere that a car will fit—on the sidewalk, in crosswalks, and so on—but the introduction of awkward posts lined up along the curb, fines, and the Denver Boot (placed on the tires), has made this practice less than a desirable option. Cars are regularly ticketed for parking in illegal spots, so don't risk parking illegally. Parking fines are left on the windshield in small red or blue plastic bags. For many years, they were red only and sarcastically referred to by some as a gift from Santa. On practically all central streets, a *fizető* sign indicates that there's a fee for parking in that area. Purchase a ticket from the machine that is centrally located on that block. Some streets have more than one, making it hard to figure out which machine covers which particular parking space. It does make a difference. Once you have your ticket, leave it on the dashboard (visible through the window). In a few cases, a parking fee will be collected by an agent who will approach you as you park. Fees vary with the centrality of the location. There are several parking garages in the Inner City, including those at V. Aránykéz u. 4–6, V. Szervita tér 8, VII. Nyár u. 20, and VII. Akácfa u. 14. The newest and biggest parking lot is located in the heart of the city underground called "The Ditch" (Gödör), in Erzsébet tér. Vacant lots on Pest's Inner City side streets provide some makeshift parking lots; look for the sign with a *P* in white on a blue background. If they are not attended, do not risk parking there. Prices are lower than they are at garages, but the lots are not always as secure, even if an attendant is there to collect your fee, he may not be there all day long. These types of parking lots seem to be disappearing and new apartment or office buildings are taking up the space.

BY BIKE

I have warned people about riding bikes in Budapest for a long time now; even if the city is making an effort to incorporate bike lanes into the city streets, it does not change the attitude or aptitude of the drivers of the cars around you. They disregard all others on the roadways. The many bikers in Budapest are always lobbying for better conditions; the Critical Mass Bicycle Demonstration is held biannually and draws over 50,000 participants. Bicyclists still are sans helmet, which I think is ludicrous, considering the conditions. As it stands, for safety reasons, unless you are living life in a No Care Zone, I repeat: Do not bike.

If you still insist on this activity, you should at least consider a bicycle tour where you are part of a group with an experienced leader who knows the safe paths. Centrally located **Yellow Zebra Bikes,** V. Sütő u. 2 (© **1/266-8777;** www.yellowzebra bikes.com), open daily 8:30am to 8pm in high season, and 10am to 6pm from November to March offers guided bike tours, with optional helmets. Bike rentals cost 1,500 Ft ($8.10/£4.25) for 1–5 hours or 3,500 Ft ($19/£9.95) for 24 hours. Guided tours may be your best option, setting you back 4,500 Ft ($24/£13) for adults, 4,000 Ft ($22/£11) for students with an ID card. The tour price includes the guide, a bike, optional helmet, basket, bungee cords, and a front bag. Just show up at the office before the tour leaves at 11am. In July and August, there is a second tour at 4pm. Yellow Zebra Bikes has a second location with shorter hours, Monday through Friday 9:30am to 7pm and Saturday and Sunday 9:30am to 4pm, at VI. Lázár u. 16 behind the Opera House.

BudapestBike.hu, located at VII. Wesselényi u. 8 (© **061/30-944-5533,** mobile phone), was started in 2005 by six Hungarian bicyclists. From March 1 to October 1 they offer a tour daily at 10am from their location with no minimum people needed; each tour runs 5,000 Ft ($27/£14) and includes a tour guide, the bike rental, a helmet, map, chain lock, and a drink. The rest of the year, they will arrange tours by request and continue to provide bike rentals. They also have tours outside of the city. If you are bound and determined to go it alone, they will rent you a bike for 6 hours for 2,000 Ft ($11/£5.10) or for a full day for 3,000 Ft ($16/£8.55); a tandem will run you 3,000 Ft ($16/£8.55) for 6 hours and 5,000 Ft ($27/£14) for a full day. A helmet, chain lock, and insurance are included in the rental. They also offer a guided evening program, called a pub crawl that takes you to the hottest pubs in Budapest. Priced at 5,000 Ft ($27/£14), it includes a guide for 4 hours, a minimum of four pubs, two beers, and a shot. A group of four people is the minimum for this tour. In the event you need a taxi at the end of the tour, they can call one for you.

Charles Apartment House, I. Hegyalja út 23 (© **1/201-1796**) rents bikes for 2,000 Ft ($11/£5.10) per day. A 20,000 Ft ($108/£57) per bike security deposit is required. In contrast to the rest of Budapest, Margaret Island is closed to cars and, thus, is ideal for casual bike riding. Look for the map titled *Kerékpárral Budapeste* ("Budapest on Bike"), which shows biking trails and streets with bike lanes around the city. A welcome development for cyclists is the bike paths along Lake Balaton. **Bringóhintó** *Kids*, XIII. Hajós A. sétány (© **1/329-2746**), on Margaret Island, rents bikes and more making this the ideal place for those who don't believe that "its just like riding a bike, you never forget how." Here you can rent a Bringóhintó or a Családi Bringóhintó. What are these you ask? They are pedal cars where two adults pedal up to three adults and two small children or the latter, four adults pedal up to six adults and two small children, all safely within the confines of Margit Island. "Occasional" tickets can be purchased for 5, 10, or 15 occasions, and they are valid for 30 minutes or 1 hour. They can be used at any time, and they never expire. This fun loving company also has miniature vehicles for small children. No kids to share the fun? Then make it a romantic stroll around the island with your loved one.

FAST FACTS: Budapest

American Express Budapest's only American Express office closed its doors in 2005. There are still many references to it on the Internet and even when calling American Express Customer Service, which is shameful for a company that prides itself on good service. The office has been replaced with a local toll free number, so if you need assistance, call them at © **06/800-1-7920**.

Area Code The country code for Hungary is 36; the city code for Budapest is **1**.

ATM Before leaving home, check with your financial institution to see what your daily limit for withdrawals is in a 24-hour period. If it is too low, you may want to ask to have it increased temporarily. You may also want to ask if your financial institution partners with any foreign banks that will save you ATM fees if you use their machines. If your PIN code is longer than 4 digits, you will have difficulty using the ATMs here except for OTP Bank, which now allows up to 8-digit PIN codes. For networks see p. 15.

Babysitters Be sure to ask at your hotel about its services before you book. Better hotels, including the Four Seasons Hotel Gresham Palace (p. 75), can offer reliable babysitters for guests within 6 hours of a request.

Business Hours Most stores are open Monday through Friday from 10am to 6pm and Saturday from 9 or 10am to 1 or 2pm. Most stores are closed Sunday, except those in the central tourist areas. Some shop owners and restauranteurs also close for 2 weeks in August. On weekdays, food stores open early, at around 6 or 7am, and close around 6 or 7pm. Convenience stores, called "nonstops," are open 24 hours and just about every neighborhood has at least one.

Banks in general are open Monday through Friday from 8am to 4pm. Some banks open a half-hour later on some days, but stay open an hour later that day too.

Museums in Budapest are usually open Tuesday through Sunday from 10am to 6pm. Almost all of them are closed on Monday, but there are exceptions to the rule.

Computers All modern laptops will convert to European electrical current automatically. It is not necessary to have a transformer; just an adapter for the plug will do fine. You can find adaptors at Oktogon Műszaki és Háztartási (Oktogon Technological Home; © 061/70-335-0505 mobile). It is open Monday through Friday 10am to 6pm and Saturday 9am to 1pm.

Doctors & Dentists For American-type care, we recommend the **First Med Center** (formerly called the American Clinic), I. Hattyu u. 14, 5th floor (© 1/224-9090; www.firstmedcenters.com), a private outpatient clinic with two U.S. board-certified physicians and several English-speaking Hungarian doctors. There is an OBGYN on staff, and an ultrasound machine on the premises; referrals are available for specialists. It does have a growing list of U.S. insurance companies that it has contracts with and may be able to direct bill. Otherwise, payment is expected at the time of service (credit cards accepted), but the office will provide coded invoices in English in a form acceptable to most insurance carriers. The clinic is located in a modern building on the street that ends at the Mammut shopping center, just a few minutes by foot from Moszkva tér (Red metro). Also recommended is the **Rózsakert Medical Center** (© 1/391-5903) located in the Rózsakert Shopping Center, II. Gábor Áron u. 74–78/a. It has the largest pool of American-trained physicians in Hungary with doctors on call 24 hours. Another suitable facility is **IMS**, a private outpatient clinic at XIII. Váci út 184 (© 1/329-8423), with English-speaking doctors; it's reached via the Blue metro line (Gyöngyös utca). The same drill applies with respect to payment and insurance claims. IMS also operates an emergency service after hours and on weekends at III. Vihar u. 29 (© 1/388-8257).

For dental work, Hungary has become somewhat of a European trendsetter. They have had the best-trained dentists for more than a couple of decades. People from neighboring countries come here for dental care for the quality and the low cost, thus creating the niche market of dental tourism. If you are thinking of extensive dental procedures, check out what is available, at Dental-Hungary.hu, XII. Normafa u. 54 (© 061/20-381-3534 mobile; www.dental-hungary.hu). Pasaréti Dental at II. Pasaréti út. 8 (© 1/488-7919) also provides a wide range of services. If you just need some emergency work done, you can also try S.O.S. Dent Kft, a 24-hour emergency dental clinic at VII. Király u. 14 (© 1/269-6010), just a few minutes by foot from Deák tér (all three metro lines); look for the red cross on the building. Not all dentists on staff speak English.

Electricity Hungarian electricity is 220 volts, AC. If you plan to bring any North American electrical appliances, you'll need a 110–220 volt transformer/converter. Transformers are available at electrical supply stores throughout the city, but they tend to be heavy or bulky. If there is a transformer built into the adapter of the appliance that you are bringing, as there are in many laptop computers, you will need only a small adapter to fit the North American flat plugs or the British three-prong plugs into the round holes in the wall. With the exception of the U.K., the same adapter will serve you throughout Europe.

Embassies The embassy of **Australia** is at XII. Királyhágó tér 8–9 (ⓒ **1/457-9777**); the embassy of **Canada** is at II. Ganz u. 12–14 (ⓒ **1/392-3360**); the embassy of the **Republic of Ireland** is at V. Szabadság tér 7 (ⓒ **1/301-4960**); the embassy of the **United Kingdom** is at V. Harmincad u. 6 (ⓒ **1/266-2888**); and the embassy of the **United States** is at V. Szabadság tér 12 (ⓒ **1/475-4400**). New Zealand does not have an embassy in Budapest, but the U.K. embassy can handle matters for New Zealand citizens.

Emergencies Dial ⓒ **104** for an ambulance, ⓒ **105** for the fire department, ⓒ **107** for the police, and ⓒ **188** for car breakdown service. ⓒ **1/438-8080** is a 24-hour hot line in English for reporting crime.

Etiquette & Customs Old-world etiquette is still very much alive in Hungary with older people, but it is not always the same with the young generation. Those taught well hold doors open for women and readily give up their seats on the bus for those who need them. Since older people feel entitled, you may not receive any thanks for your efforts.

Eyeglasses Optika or *ofotért* is the Hungarian name for an optometrist's shop. The word for eyeglasses is *szemüveg*. There are a plethora of shops around the city and you will notice the large selection of eyeglass frames in the windows. If you are a contact lenses wearer, bring ample solutions with you as it is very expensive here. There are not as many Hungarians wearing contact lenses due to the cost, so the solution is not as available.

Internet Access If you have your laptop with you and your hotel does not provide free Wi-Fi access, then treat yourself to a coffee or tea and hang out at any of a number of cafes and restaurants that offer free Wi-Fi access. One drink will allow you to stay as long as you want to crawl the Web. Look for Wi-Fi signs on windows, doors, and standing signs outside the door. **Café Szóda,** VII. Wesselényi u. 18, was the first place in the city to provide free Wi-Fi. It is a funky place to hang out with old seltzer soda bottles lining the windows and at various times, art exhibits on the walls. There are also many outlets so your batteries don't run dry. **Farger,** V. Zoltán u. 18, is another place to enjoy a drink and have a sandwich while enjoying free Wi-Fi. Browse the books or surf the Internet for an hour free, with a cup of fair trade coffee at **Treehugger Dan's Bookstore Café,** VI. Csengery u. 48. If you didn't lug your laptop along, then there are plenty of Internet cafe options. The best place in town is **Kávészünet,** V. Tátra u. 12/b (ⓒ **1/236-0853**). This is a comfortable and friendly place located in between Nyugati Pályaudvar and Jászai Mari tér, and is open Monday to Friday 8am to 10pm and 9am to 8pm on weekends. It serves coffee, sandwiches, and cakes and has rotating exhibitions of young artists, illustrators, or photographers. Minimum time is 15 minutes for just 100 Ft (55¢/28p) with each additional 15 minutes costing 100 Ft. CD burning for 500 Ft ($2.75/£1.40) apiece, and scanning for 200 Ft ($1.10/55p) per page is also available. **Ami Internet Coffee,** V. Váci u. 40 (ⓒ **1/267-1644;** www.amicoffee.hu), near Ferenciek tére (Blue line), is open daily from 9am to midnight. This drab space has more than 20 terminals, and the cost is 200 Ft ($1.10/55p) for up to 15 minutes, with pricing by 15-minute intervals. **Yellow Zebra Bikes,** V. Sütő utca 2 (ⓒ **1/266-8777;** www.yellowzebrabikes.com), a friendly hangout for back-packers, has five computers at the Deák (central) location and four at the other. (See "By Bike," above). Other Wi-Fi hotspots can be found at www.hotspotter.hu. Unfortunately, the site is in Hungarian, but if you click on a green flag (*Ingyenes* meaning free); the name of the establishment and its address will pop up. There are dozens in the city, so keep your eyes open. They are not all listed on Hotspotter.

Language See appendix A, "Help with a Tough Tongue," in the back of this book for more information.

Laundry & Dry Cleaning Self-service launderettes do not exist in Budapest. The Mister Minit chain, a locksmith and shoe-repair service located in all large shopping centers throughout the Inner City area, now offers a laundry service as well. Many hotels and pensions also provide laundry services. Private room hosts usually are happy to make a little extra money doing laundry. I recommend **Shirt Express** © **06/30-966-5480** (mobile only). Pick up and delivery is free and the charges are very reasonable. Chances are this is the service your hotel uses and at a higher rate to you.

Liquor Laws Alcohol is sold everywhere and is available for purchase at all times. The legal drinking age in Hungary is 18. Note that Hungary has a zero-tolerance law for drunk drivers and this is strictly enforced if you are stopped.

Luggage Storage There are left-luggage offices (*csomagmegőrző* or *poggyász*) and lockers at all three major railroad stations. At Keleti, the office is in the main waiting room alongside track 6. It's open 4am to midnight. At Nyugati, the office is in the waiting room behind the international ticket office and is open 24 hours. The lockers are nearby, and the cost is also the same as at Keleti. Déli Station has a new automated locker system in operation in the main ticket-purchasing area; the lockers are very large, and directions for use are provided by a multilingual computer.

Mail & Post Office Budapest will be closing over 300 post offices during the next 2 years. We strongly do not recommend receiving mail here unless you have a regular address to use. Even at that, the postal system is not the most efficient or honest, so take great care with sending or receiving packages. Most post offices are open Monday through Friday from 8am to 6pm. The post offices near Keleti and Nyugati stations have longer hours. The post office near Nyugati is at VI. Teréz krt. 51 (© 1/312-1480), and is open Monday through Saturday 7am to 9pm. Keleti is at VIII. Baross tér 11/c (© 1/322-9013), and is open Monday through Saturday 7am to 9pm and Sunday 8am to 8pm.

Names Hungarians write their names with the family name first, followed by the given name. When mentioning Hungarian names in this book, we have employed the international form of given name followed by family name. The only exception is with street names, where we have used the Hungarian style: hence Ferenc Deák (the man) but Deák Ferenc utca (the street).

Newspapers & Magazines The *International Herald Tribune, USA Today, Guardian, Guardian Weekly,* the *Economist, Financial Times, Times of London, European, Newsweek,* the *Wall Street Journal Europe,* and *Time* are all commonly found in luxury hotels and at kiosks and bookstores in the central Pest neighborhood around Váci utca. At larger newsstands you can also find

People, Vogue, Harper's, and, once in a blue moon, the *New York Times.* On any given day at Sajtó Térkép, with locations at V. Kálvin tér 3 (Blue line) and V. Városház u. 3–5 (Ferenciek tere, Blue line), you might also find such periodicals as *Barron's,* the *Nation, GQ, Architectural Digest,* and *House & Garden,* usually at two to three times the cover price of the magazine.

For English-language articles on current events and politics in Hungary, pick up the **Budapest Sun** or the **Budapest Times,** both weeklies and free at many restaurants, hotels, and the Tourinform offices. The free bimonthly **Funzine** and the monthly **Visitors' Guide** provide listings of cultural events, as does **Where** magazine. All of these publications are widely available.

Passports **For Residents of the United States:** Whether you're applying in person or by mail, you can download passport applications from the U.S. State Department website at http://travel.state.gov. Consider the new digitalized passport since it will be the norm in the future. For general information, call the National Passport Agency (© **202/647-0518**). To find your regional passport office or other location that accepts applications, check the U.S. State Department website or check with your local post office. It often has applications.

For Residents of Canada: Passport applications are available at travel agencies throughout Canada or from the central Passport Office, Department of Foreign Affairs and International Trade, Ottawa, ON K1A 0G3 (© **800/567-6868;** www.ppt.gc.ca). Check the website for the delay time in processing it.

Note: European countries are changing passport rules to meet EU laws and some are initiating the new biometric passports. Use this information as a guide, but check with your own country's passport agency for the most up-to-date changes in the procedures.

For Residents of the United Kingdom: To pick up an application for a standard 10-year passport (5-year passport for children under 16), visit your nearest passport office, major post office, or travel agency or contact the United Kingdom Passport Service at © **0870/521-0410** or search its website at www.ukpa.gov.uk.

For Residents of Ireland: You can get a passport application at the Passport Office, Setanta Centre, Molesworth Street, Dublin 2 (© **01/671-1633;** www.irlgov.ie/iveagh); most post offices; and Garda Stations. With EU changes continuing to take effect, you should check the current information at the site above.

For Residents of Australia: You can pick up an application from your local post office or any branch of Passports Australia, but you must schedule an interview at the passport office or some authorized postal offices to present your application materials. Call the **Australian Passport Information Service** at © **131-232,** or visit the government website at www.passports.gov.au.

For Residents of New Zealand: You can pick up a passport application at any New Zealand Passports Office or download it from their website. Contact the **Passports Office** at © **0800/225-050** in New Zealand or 04/474-8100, or log onto www.passports.govt.nz. Having outstanding fines could stop you from leaving the country.

Pharmacies The Hungarian word for pharmacy is *gyógyszertár,* or occasionally, *patika.* Only pharmacies can carry prescription drugs or anything medically related even if no prescription is needed, for example aspirin or something for a cold. Many pharmacies also carry saline solution for contact lenses, homeopathic remedies, dandruff shampoo, and sun-tan lotions. Some hotels advertise "drugstores," but these are just shops with soap, perfume, and maybe cosmetics. There are a number of 24-hour pharmacies in the city—every pharmacy posts the address of the nearest one in its window. If necessary, ask for a specific address at Tourinform or pick up a copy of the *Budapest Sun,* which lists them. Your best bet for 24-hour service year-round is Oktogon Patika on Teréz körút, next to Hotel Radisson (off Oktogon Square, tram nos. 4 or 6). If you are looking for basics like pantyhose, chapstick, and so on, you'll want to find a drugless-store (Rossman or Scheckler's) rather than a pharmacy. A number of European drugless-store chains have set up shop in Budapest; look for Rossman, Scheckler's or less common now, the Drogerie Mart, known as DM.

Police Dial ⓒ **107** for the police.

Religious Services in English **Roman Catholic** masses are held at 5pm on Saturday in the Jesuit Church of the Sacred Heart, VIII. Mária u. 25 at Lórinc Pap tér (ⓒ 1/318-3479). **Anglican Episcopal** is at St. Margaret's Church, VII. Almássy u. 6 on Sunday at 10:30am. **International Baptist Church** of Budapest holds services at II. Móricz Zsigmond Gymnasium, Törökvesz ut 48 on Sunday at 10:30am. Jewish services for High Holy Days are held in English and Hebrew, call ⓒ **061/20-927-7200** (mobile phone).

Restrooms The word for toilet in Hungarian is *WC* (pronounced vay-tsay), *mosdó,* or *toalett.* You are bound to find one of these names shown somewhere. *Női* means "women's"; *férfi* means "men's." Note that many American-type fast-food restaurants are charging for the use of their bathrooms unless you have your receipt from a purchase made that day.

Smoking Smoking is forbidden in all public places (including on all public transportation), except in most restaurants and pubs, where smoking is considered to be an indispensable part of the ambience. Although a 1999 law requires all restaurants to have a nonsmoking section, the fact is that some still do not comply or do so by setting two tables right next to the smoking section, but not allowing smokers to sit there. Expect many restaurants to be smoky places and bars even worse. *Tilos a dohányzás* or *Dohányozni tilos* means "No Smoking."

Taxes Taxes are included in restaurant and hotel rates, and in shop purchases. International travelers are entitled, upon leaving the country, to a refund of the 25% VAT on certain purchases. See chapter 9, "Budapest Shopping," for details.

Taxis See "Getting Around," earlier in this chapter.

Telephone **To make local phone calls:** MATÁV, the government-owned phone company, not to be confused with Malév, the airline or MÁV, the railroad, is no longer the fashionable or number-one provider of phone services since deregulation. This allowed cable companies into the home and business phone market. Outside of Budapest, there still may be a dependency on MATÁV for phone services.

The **area code** for Budapest is 1, and all phone numbers in Budapest (except mobile phones) have seven digits. Phone numbers in this book are printed with the area code and mobile phone numbers are marked as such. Most other towns in Hungary have a two-digit area code and six-digit telephone numbers.

To make a call from one Hungary area code to another, first dial 06; when you hear a tone, dial the area code and number. Numbers that begin with 06/20, 06/30, or 06/70 followed by a seven-digit number are **mobile phone numbers.** Mobile phones are extremely popular and some businesses use mobile phones as their primary number. Here it gets complicated, since the rates are different depending on whether the company servicing the phone you are using and the one you are calling is the same or different. The latter will be more expensive. Be aware that all phone calls made to a mobile phone from a landline are charged at a higher rate than calls to a landline, regardless of the location of the caller or the receiver. Usually, if the number you are dialing has recently changed, you will get a recording first in Hungarian and then in English, indicating the new number or that it has been disconnected. If further information is needed, dial ℂ **191** for **local directory assistance** in English.

Public **pay phones** for the most part have been taken over by T-Com and are distinguished by their pink booths or pink phones if they are on the wall of a metro station underground. The charges are varying amounts for local calls depending on the time of day that you place your call. It's cheapest to call late in the evenings and on weekends. Public phones operate with 20, 50, and 100 Ft coins or with phone cards (in 50 or 120 units), which can be purchased from post offices, convenience stores, or magazine kiosks. I really do not recommend using a pay phone, especially the booths since they are common places for the homeless to call their *WC.* Hotels typically add a surcharge to all calls (although some allow unlimited free local calls).

To call to Hungary from abroad: Dial the appropriate numbers to get an international dial tone (011 from the U.S.), then dial 36 (Hungary country code), followed by the appropriate city code (for Budapest, 1), followed by the six- or seven-digit telephone number. You will notice that cities outside of Budapest only have a six-digit phone number. Take note of their city code.

To make international calls: To make international calls from Hungary, first dial 00 and then the country code (U.S. or Canada 1, U.K. 44, Ireland 353, Australia 61, New Zealand 64). Next dial the area code and number. For example, if you want to call the British Embassy in Washington, D.C., dial ℂ 00-1-202/588-7800.

For international calls to the U.S., there are several options. If you have your laptop with you, you can go to any Internet cafe or other place with Wi-Fi and use **Skype** (www.skype.com) for all of your family and friends who are also Skype members. The service is free between Skype members, or you can pay a minimal amount for those who are not. A light miniature headset is all that is needed. Similar services are provided by Google with **Gtalk** (www.google.com/talk), but only for those with Gtalk also installed on their computer. If your hotel has a landline phone without an extension number and Wi-Fi, you can register with **Jajah** (www.jajah.com) and call the States or Canada for 3 euro cents a minute. You log in, enter the number you want to call, and the phone rings; your call is connected and no headset is needed. Alternatively, without the aid of a computer, you can use a phone card. There are at least a dozen different names for phone card brands, but their rates are so similar, it would take a mathematician to figure out the differences. The ones I have used are **EZ Phone; Bla, Bla, Bla;** and **Telecard.** All come in prepaid amounts of 500 Ft ($2.70/£1.40), 1,500 Ft

($8.10/£4.25), 3,000 Ft ($16/£8.55), and 5,000 Ft ($27/£14); the advantage being that the larger the amount, the less each call costs. The disadvantage is that most will not work outside of Hungary, even if they claim they do. Use it or lose it!

Hungarian telephone books are scarce, but if you should happen on one, they list the numbers of all countries that can be directly dialed. Failing either of these resources, dial ℂ **199** for international directory assistance.

Those calling the U.S. can reach the **AT&T** operator at ℂ **06/800-01111,** the **MCI Worldcom** operator at ℂ **00/800-01411,** and the **Sprint operator** at ℂ **00/800-01877. Australia Direct** (ℂ **06/800-06111**), **Canada Direct** (ℂ **00/800-01211**), **New Zealand Direct** (ℂ **06/800-06411**), and **U.K. Direct** (ℂ **06/800-04411** [BT], or 06/800-04412 [Mercury]) are direct-access numbers that connect you to operators in the country you're calling, with whom you can arrange your preferred billing.

For directory assistance: Dial ℂ **198** if you're looking for a number inside Hungary, and dial ℂ **199** for numbers to all other countries.

For operator assistance: If you need operator assistance in making a call, dial ℂ 199 if you're trying to make an international call and ℂ **198** if you want to call a number in Hungary.

Time Zone Hungary is on Central European time, 2 hours ahead of Greenwich Mean Time and 6 hours ahead of Eastern Standard Time (EST). Hungary "springs ahead" and "falls back" on the same schedule as the U.S. and is consistently 6 hours ahead of EST and 9 hours ahead of PST.

Tipping The tipping rate is generally 10% to 15% and only higher if the service was above and beyond the call of duty. Among those who welcome tips are waiters, taxi drivers, hotel employees, barbers, cloakroom attendants, toilet attendants, masseuses, and tour guides. With restaurants there is some confusion and we don't want any waitstaff shortchanged; we did that work in our youth. According to reports in the English language papers, there was an unclear law passed that service charges must be added to all restaurant bills; however, like many laws, they are ignored by some restaurants. To add to the mix of confusion, this law was called tax revenue for the city, not for the poor waitstaff that worked so hard at making your meal enjoyable. But yet it gets more complicated. Some restaurant owners divide all of these proceeds among all of the staff, including the chef and kitchen help. Other restaurant owners, on the other hand, pocket the money. See the restaurant section tips for tipping on p. 96.

Useful Phone Numbers U.S. Dept. of State Travel Advisory: ℂ **202/647-5225** (manned 24 hr.)

U.S. Passport Agency: ℂ **202/647-0518**

U.S. Centers for Disease Control and Prevention International Hotline: ℂ **404/332-4559**

Water Tap water in Budapest is safe for drinking. Mineral water, which many Hungarians prefer to tap water since they can take it with them, is called *ásványvíz.* Purified bottled water *(szénsav mentes)* is sold in delicatessens, convenience stores, fast-food restaurants, and grocery stores all over the city. As a rule, all brands that have a pink label for identification are without gas (carbonation), blue is with gas, and yellow has gas, but minimal amounts. There are some rogue brands that just don't follow the color schemes.

5

Where to Stay in Budapest

Budapest's accommodations run the gamut of categories from beautiful, historic gems, those that have sprung from the ground up, and those that have remained the same from the beginning.

A few new hotels such as the **Hotel Zara** and **Atrium** opened in 2006 and 2007, while more hotels are being built as of this writing. The most distinctive of the Budapest hotels include the historic **Gresham Palace Four Seasons, Corinthia Grand Hotel Royal,** and **Castle Hill's Hilton Hotel,** being among the city's most elite lodgings.

Lodging rates in Budapest have risen considerably in the last few years, becoming more comparable to the rates of other European capitals.

With the addition of so many new hotels, Budapest has become much more attractive as an international conference venue, filling properties with conference enrollees. Due to this and the increased accessibility to the city via budget airlines, this has further instigated seasonal rates.

During the high season from April or May to the end of September, it can be difficult to get your first choice of a room in your first choice of hotel. During the Hungarian Formula One weekend or the Sziget Festival both in August, it can be quite difficult to secure a hotel or pension room or even a hostel bed, so make reservations and get written confirmation well in advance of your stay.

When booking, bear in mind that many European standards call a room with two twin beds a double. If you want a double bed, you will need to request it specifically. Extra beds or cots are generally available also. Hungarian hotels often blur the use of the words *apartment* and *suite* to describe bedrooms with a living room in it or connected rooms including a bedroom and living room. Some have a kitchen, while others do not. In these listings, we have specified if there is a separate living room area and/or kitchen facilities.

Air-conditioning can be a major concern during the summer months; the small hotels, pensions, and hostels are less likely to have it than the larger and more expensive places.

BUDGET LODGINGS There are a number of recommendable budget accommodations in Budapest. Travelers have the advantage of choosing from a wealth of perfectly acceptable, options. Small pensions, rooms in private homes, and a number of good youth hostels make the city inviting to travelers on any budget. Remember the realtor phrase: *location, location, location.* The location of your accommodations is a significant factor in cost. Normally, one can expect to pay more for the location, the history, and the reputation of a hotel; being in the center of the city will add to the inflated cost. Note that with construction of the new metro 4 line, many transportation services on the Buda side are being diverted or stopped. This can make it trickier to get to your hotel and make it difficult to get to the tourist places. Returning late in the evening in some parts can be more difficult than in the past. Question the transportation options carefully. There is nothing worse than having to end a pleasant evening early just to catch the last bus back to your room. Remember, time is precious and you don't want to spend too much of it on public transport.

ACCOMMODATIONS AGENCIES

The most established accommodations agencies are the former state-owned travel agents **Ibusz** (see below), **MÁV Tours** (© 1/182-9011), and **Budapest Tourist** (© 1/117-3555). Although newer private agencies continue to bloom, the older agencies tend to have the greatest number of rooms listed. There are agencies at the airport, in all three major train stations, throughout central Pest, and along the main roads into Budapest for travelers arriving by car. You can also reserve online through many of the agencies listed below.

The main **Ibusz reservations office** is at Ferenciek tere 10 (© 1/485-2700; fax 1/318-2805; www.ibusz.hu), accessible by the Blue metro line. This office is open year-round Monday through Friday 9am to 6pm.

SEASONS Many, but not all hotels and pensions in Budapest divide the year into three seasons. **High season** is roughly from March or April through September or October. Easter week and the period of the Budapest Spring Festival (mid- to late Mar) are also considered high season by some hotels. **Special season** includes the weekend of the Hungarian Formula One in August, and New Year's. **Low season** is roughly November through February, with the exceptions above. Some hotels discount as much as 30% in low season, while others offer no winter discounts, so be sure to inquire.

PRICE CATEGORIES Most hotels and pensions in Budapest list their prices in euros. Listing rates in euros is not just intended as a means of transition to the EU currency (Hungary is expected to adopt the euro sometime after 2010), it is also a hedge against forint inflation (though the forint has had its highs and lows over the past few years). All hotels in Budapest accept payment in Hungarian forints as well as in foreign currencies. Where prices are quoted in euros, I provided a dollar and a British pound conversion. The euro exchange rate as this book goes to press is 1€ equals $1.30. Exchange rates fluctuate over time, of course, so the price of a room in dollars will change as the euro-to-dollar exchange rate changes.

All hotels are required to charge a 12% value-added tax (VAT). Most build the tax into their rates, while a few tack it on top of their rates. When booking a room, ask whether the VAT is included in the quoted price. Unless otherwise indicated, prices in this book include the VAT.

Hotels in Hungary are rated by the international five-star system. In our view, however, the ratings are somewhat arbitrary and are not included in our entries for that reason. You can find an explanation of the Frommer's star ratings used throughout this guide in the front matter.

Note: I have discovered that just about every major hotel has some Internet specials or packages on its website. Just like the airlines, hotels continually gauge their occupancy and change rates according to room availability; but they all say that the early bird gets the biggest discount. Unless noted otherwise, the hotels listed have Internet deals, so check their website. Once you have booked, confirm the rate and the room desired and get a confirmation number.

I have found that the websites of smaller hotels and pensions are frequently inaccurate with respect to rates if they don't have online booking capabilities, so make sure to call them to confirm. If you can book online, the rates should be current and accurate.

1 The Inner City & Central Pest

VERY EXPENSIVE

Corinthia Grand Hotel Royal ★★★   One of the grand dames of Budapest, originally built in 1896 by architect Dezső Rey, this hotel reopened in its current grandeur fashion in 2003. It exudes opulence the minute you walk in. There is a staircase to the baroque grand ballroom, where balls and conferences are often held. Paintings of famous Hungarians hang on the walls. The secessionist splendor of the rest of the hotel continues throughout. The guest rooms come in two categories: superior and executive. All are beautifully appointed to meet every need a traveler could have. When you climb into the bed, it caresses your body. The bathrooms are done in marble tiles with separate showers and tubs. Bathrobes and slippers are waiting for you to cozy up in on the sofa with a glass of wine. Executive rooms give access to the exclusive business lounge, breakfast area, and lounge where snacks and drinks are offered complimentarily. This is a place to be pampered.

VII. Erzsébet krt. 43–49. ✆ 1/479-4000. Fax 1/479-4333. www.corinthiahotels.com. 414 units. 140€–230€ ($182–$299/£96–£157) superior; 350€–600€ ($455–$780/£239–£411) deluxe. Executive Club 60€ ($78/£41) superior; included with deluxe. Breakfast 22€ ($29/£15). Children under 12 stay free in parent's room. AE, DC, MC, V. Secure underground parking. Tram: 4 or 6 to Király u. **Amenities:** 3 restaurants; 2 bars; 1 cafe; large indoor heated pool; Jacuzzi; sauna; bikes; concierge; tour desk; business center; salon; room service; in-room massage; babysitting; laundry service; dry cleaning service (same day if in before 9am); nonsmoking rooms; executive-level rooms. *In room:* A/C, TV/DVD, minibar, hair dryer, iron/ironing board, safe, high-speed Internet, Wi-Fi, movie library, bathrobes, slippers, scale, coffee/tea available from housekeeping.

Four Seasons Hotel Gresham Palace ★★★   This hotel is so remarkable, tour buses stop here to allow people to look over the lobby. This Art Nouveau building, one of the most elegant and majestic properties in the city, stands as one of the finest in the world. With the Chain Bridge directly opposite the front doors, it has a picture-perfect view of the Buda Castle making this the most picturesque location of any hotel in the city. Originally built as the Gresham Life Assurance Company in 1906, it awed the world even then with the craftsmanship provided by the most acclaimed craftsmen of the time. Nearly destroyed by World War II and subsequent vandalism, it was restored over 5 years using and matching every single piece of remaining item of decor to bring it back to its original glory, even returning to the original manufacturers when possible. The doors reopened on June 18, 2004. As is Four Seasons tradition, guests are pampered in every way possible. While all rooms are beautifully decorated with mahogany furniture, the most expensive suites are equipped with bedroom sets made of mother-of-pearl and some with fireplaces. Each bathroom of all rooms is fitted with Italian and Spanish marble with deep-soak bathtubs. No detail in design has been overlooked, and each room has been recreated in its original glory.

V. Roosevelt tér 5–6. ✆ 800/819-5053 in North America or 1/268-6000. Fax 1/268-5000. www.four seasons.com/budapest. 179 units. 320€–860€ ($416–$1,118/£219–£588) double; 1,050€–4,800€ ($1,365–$6,240/£718£–£3,284) suite. Rates do not include VAT. Children stay free in parent's room. Breakfast 7,200 Ft ($39/£21). AE, DC, MC, V. Parking 10,000 Ft ($54/£29) per day. Metro: Deák (all lines). **Amenities:** 2 restaurants; bar; indoor swimming pool; exercise room; sauna; concierge; airport transfer; business center; salon; 24-hr. room service; massage; laundry service; dry cleaning. *In room:* A/C, satellite TV, Web TV, minibar, hair dryer, safe, high-speed Internet access (for a fee), robe, slippers, newspapers, fax machine (on request).

Le Meridien Budapest ★★★   Centrally located near Deák tér is Le Meridien, which was originally designed in 1913 for the Italian Adria Insurance Company; the building was completed in 1918. After World War II, the Budapest Police made this

Where to Stay in Central Budapest

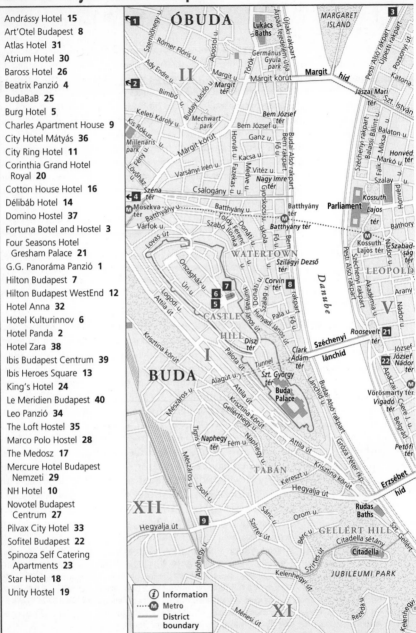

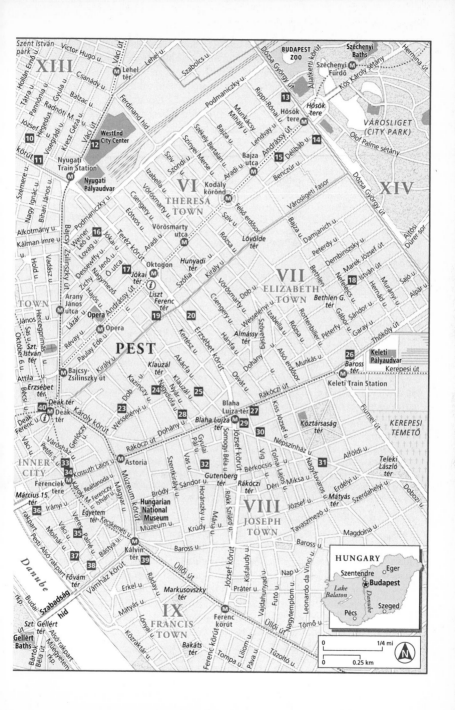

their home until 1997. The original structure is a protected monument, thus still has its austere exterior. The structure was bought by the Duna Plaza Group and after a beautiful renovation reopened at the end of 2002. Elegant architectural details are evident in the lobby as well as the hallways, which are surrounded by wrought-iron railings. These overlook the stained-glass dome topping the breakfast area below. Guest rooms are beautifully appointed with French classical decor with a navy and beige color scheme, luxurious fabrics, and mahogany furniture. The suites are sumptuously grand, some with artificial fireplaces, and range from extra large to huge.

V. Erzsébet tér 9–10. (©) **800/253-0861** in North America, **0845/6000-778** in Britain, or **1/429-5500.** Fax 1/429-5555. www.lemeridien.com/budapest. 218 units. 399€–429€ ($519–$558/£273–£294) double; 499€–3,000€ ($649–$3,900/£341–£2,052) suite. Rates do not include VAT or city tax. Children 12 and under stay free in parent's room. Breakfast 27€ ($35/£19). AE, MC, V. Parking 9,000 Ft ($49/£26) per day. Metro: Deák tér (all lines). **Amenities:** 2 restaurants; bar; indoor swimming pool; exercise room; sauna; steam bath; concierge; tour desk; business center; conference facilities; salon; 24-hr. room service; massage; babysitting; laundry service; wireless Internet on conference floor; currency exchange. *In room:* A/C, TV, minibar, hair dryer, safe, high-speed Internet (for a fee; free in suite), coffee/tea, stereo (in suite), PlayStation (on request).

EXPENSIVE

NH Hotel 🎀🎀   We don't usually associate modern elegance with a homey atmosphere, but this Spanish-owned chain has accomplished this. Built from the ground up in 2003 directly behind the Vigszinház Theater, this hotel has taken a modern, minimalist approach that still has a warm welcoming feeling. The use of textiles in the room decor in shades of browns and tans with rich dark wood, the variety of fabric from the drapes, the bed cover, and the fabric panels on the bed board, add a cozy warmth to the spacious room. Add to this, the mottled brown and tan marble used in the bathroom, the feeling of quiet elegance is carried throughout. Although the exercise room on the eighth floor is limited, it is beautifully executed with the most modern exercise equipment, separate changing rooms for women and men, a solarium (for a fee), and a relaxation room with beautiful lounge chairs. It's eco-friendly to boot.

XIII. Vigszinház u. 3. (©) **1/814-000.** Fax 1/814-0100. www.nh-hotels.com. 160 units. 131€–191€ ($170–$248/£90–£131) double. Breakfast 16€ ($21/£11). AE, DC, MC, V. Secured parking 16€ ($21/£11) per day. Metro: Nyugati (Blue line) or tram 4 or 6. **Amenities:** Restaurant; bar; exercise room; bikes; room service; massage; laundry service; dry cleaning service; free LAN connection. *In room:* A/C, TV, minibar, coffeemaker, hair dryer, iron/ironing board (on request), safe, Wi-Fi (for a fee), LAN connection (cable available), electric adaptors (on request).

Novotel Budapest Centrum 🎀   Originally built in 1911, this is another Art Nouveau example of Budapest's past glory, which reopened in 2002. The fifth floor are the executive rooms, which have an espresso machine, free mineral water, films, Wi-Fi or LAN connection, local calls, a bathrobe, and slippers. These rooms have been redecorated with modern blond furniture, beige on beige print wallpaper, blue drapes, and tangerine-color pillows and chairs. Standard rooms are more dated, but still have the blue and beige color scheme, comfortable, but not luxurious. Bathrooms are tiled and of adequate size. The second floor is a smoking floor, while all others are nonsmoking. All rooms range from 23 to 28sq. m (248–301 sq. ft.).

VIII. Rákczi út 43–45. (©) **1/477-5450.** Fax 1/477-5454. www.novotel.com. 227 units. 130€–165€ ($169–$215/£89–£113) double, 155€–190€ ($202–$247/£106–£130) executive; special season 245€ ($318/£168) double, 270€ ($351/£185) executive. Breakfast 17€ ($22/£12). Children under 16 stay free in parent's room. AE, DC, MC, V. Parking 17€ ($22/£12]) per day. Metro: Blaha Lujza tér (Red line). **Amenities:** Restaurant; bar; Jacuzzi; room service; laundry service. *In room:* A/C, TV, minibar, coffeemaker, hair dryer, ironing board, safe, LAN Internet (for a fee).

Sofitel Budapest ✿✿   Formerly the Hyatt, this hotel was totally transformed into the Sofitel Budapest, the only Sofitel in Hungary. The brand-new lobby has a definite Parisian flare to it with the central elevator and a large, splashy Biblioték area where guests can sit and borrow a book to read. The hallways and rooms have been redecorated with soft beige on beige designs and the beds have luxurious new bedspreads and huge pillows. Bathrooms are a good size with marble tile and countertops of gray and cream. Rooms on floors one to seven have a tub/shower combo, while those on the eighth-floor executive level have separate showers and bathtubs plus access to the executive lounge where snacks, drinks, and a special breakfast is served. Junior suites on several floors have kitchenettes and a combined living room and bedroom. The fitness center is decked out with a large indoor pool, exercise room, massage area, and sauna. One floor is nonsmoking.

V. Roosevelt tér 2. ⓒ 1/266-1234. Fax 1/266-9101. www.sofitel.com. 350 units. 250€–285€ ($325–$370/£171–£195]) double; 300€–335€ ($390–$436/£205–£229) executive floor; 295€–500€ ($384–$650/£202–£342) suites. Rates do not include VAT. Breakfast 24€ ($31/£17). AE, MC, V. Parking 7,000 Ft ($38/£20) per day. Metro: Vörösmarty tér (Yellow line). **Amenities:** 2 restaurants; bar; cafe; pool; exercise room; sauna; concierge; business center; 24-hr. room service; massage; laundry service; wireless Internet throughout hotel; executive lounge. *In room:* A/C, TV, minibar, coffeemaker, hair dryer, iron/ironing board, safe, Lan Internet, robe, slippers.

MODERATE

City Hotel Mátyás ✿   Old world charm lives within this simplistic hotel. It has some rooms with a fantastic view of the Buda Castle District. You should request this view when reserving to assure it. The hotel is located on a street with busy traffic, but I was not disturbed by noise. The rooms are plain, with minimal decor, clean white walls, and comfortable beds and linens. A pie-slice-shaped shower takes up little space, leaving room for a second person to use the sink at the same time. One drawback was an insufficient number of electric outlets. In 2008, there are plans to remodel the front of the building and the rooms, a few at a time. I hope not much is refurbished; it has great character; however, it may draw a younger crowd as it seems to be drawing all 40-somethings and older currently. Breakfast is served in the adjoining famous Mátyás Pince Restaurant (p. 102), a restaurant with outstanding decor. Mellow Moods operates the hotel.

V. Marcius 15 tér. ⓒ 1/338-4711. Fax 1/317-9086. www.cityhotels.hu. 85 units. 25,000 Ft–35,500 Ft ($135–$191/£71–£101) double, 30,000 Ft–42,000 Ft ($162–$227/£85–£120) triple, 35,000 Ft–48,500 Ft ($189–$262/£100–£138) apt (no kitchen) for 4 people; special season 46,500 Ft ($251/£132) double, 59,000 Ft ($319/£168) triple, 71,500 Ft ($387/£204) apt (no kitchen) for 4 people. Rates include full breakfast. AE, MC, V. Limited street parking. Metro: Ferenciek tere (Blue line). **Amenities:** Restaurant; bar; laundry service; dry cleaning; Internet access (for a fee); nonsmoking rooms; safe. *In room:* A/C, TV, minibar, hair dryer (on request), iron (on request).

City Ring Hotel ✿✿✿   Perfectly located for the train traveler coming or going from Nyugati train station, this hotel is only 1 block away, making it ultraconvenient. Situated on the ring road, you have access to transportation, shopping, and restaurants just outside your door. The rooms are a bit overwhelmed by the modern furniture giving it a crowded feeling, but if you are out all day touring, they are more than adequate, impeccably clean, and the beds are great. We could have used thicker pillows, but they were sufficient. One caution is that the shower is on the small side, which may pose a challenge for larger people. Clientele seem to be 30-somethings and over. The staff is incredibly helpful and friendly. The rooms are in a different building than the reception area, so you have to cross a small corridor and go up a short flight of steps before reaching the elevator. The staff will assist with luggage for those in need, but there is no bellhop service per se. The hotel is operated by Mellow Moods.

XIII. Szent István krt. 22. ℭ **1/340-5450.** Fax 1/340-4884. www.cityhotels.hu. 39 units. 19,000 Ft–27,000 Ft ($103–$146/£54–£77) double, 24,000 Ft–33,500 Ft ($130–$181/£68–£95) triple, 21,500 Ft–30,750 Ft ($116–$166/£61–£88) deluxe double; special season 31,500 Ft ($170/£90) double, 40,500 Ft ($219/£115) triple, 37,750 Ft ($204/£107) deluxe double. Rates include full breakfast. AE, MC, V. Metro: Nyugati (Blue line) or tram 4 or 6. **Amenities:** Dry cleaning (next-day service); nonsmoking rooms; safe deposit box. *In room:* A/C, TV, minibar, hair dryer (on request), iron (on request).

Cotton House Hotel ★★★ *Finds* You will see stars at this hotel for sure. As you walk into the lobby, you will feel transported back in time to 1930s Americana. Each room is named for some famous personality and decorated with his or her pictures. All rooms have beautifully replicated '30s furniture, down to the old cradle phone modernized with buttons. Though the beds may look old, the mattresses are modern and comfortable. The bathrooms are definitely 21st century, with lovely tile, some with Jacuzzi tubs, and others with hydro showers. Sink and tub fixtures are brass adding to the authenticity. The Al Capone room is the largest with a sitting area, while Humphrey Bogart did not fare as well, his room is smaller, but still a comfortable size. Liza Minnelli is sized between the two others. Room service is available in the larger rooms where space permits a table. This hotel opened in 2005 with six rooms and has expanded since then. The Cotton Club restaurant (p. 99) and theater downstairs maintain the same motif.

VI. Jókai u. 26. ℭ **1/354-2600.** Fax 1/354-1341. www.cottonhouse.hu. 23 units. 100€–120€ ($130–$156/£68–£82) double; special season (3-night minimum) 130€–150€ ($169–$195/£89–£103) double. Rates include breakfast, city tax, and 1 fitness center visit. AE, MC, V. Limited street parking. Metro: Opera (Yellow line). **Amenities:** Restaurant; bar; exercise area; Jacuzzi; room service; laundry service; nonsmoking rooms; cigar room. *In room:* A/C, TV, minibar; hair dryer, iron (on request), safe, Wi-Fi (for a fee).

Hotel Anna ★ This very cozy in a mundane sort of way, small Hungarian hotel is located on a quiet street. It has been around for a number of years without much remodeling to bring it up-to-date, but this actually adds to its homey charm. To reach the rooms, you need to walk through the lobby and then back outside again where the double rooms use a different entrance then the suites. Although the room decor is unremarkable to the point of being dull, the rooms are comfortably large and sparkling clean. The suites are composed of a living room and bedroom, with no kitchen facilities except a coffeemaker. For breakfast you can choose to sit indoors in the breakfast room or take it to the outside dining area, a covered space with tables and chairs. This also functions as the smoking area since the hotel is all nonsmoking.

VIII. Gyulai Pál u. 14. ℭ **1/327-2000.** Fax 1/327-2001. www.annahotel.hu. 36 units. 72€–108€ ($94–$140/£49–£74) double, 78€–120€ ($101–$156/£53–£82) jr. suite, 82€–136€ ($107–$177/£56–£93) deluxe suite, 18€–29€ ($23–$38/£12–£20) extra bed; special season 140€ ($182/£96) double, 165€ ($215/£113) jr. suite, 190€ ($247/£130) deluxe suite; 30€ ($39/£21) extra bed. Rates include breakfast, and city tax. MC, V. Parking 15€ ($20£11). Metro: Blaha Lujza (Red line). **Amenities:** Bar; laundry service; Wi-Fi in lobby. *In room:* A/C, TV, fridge (in suite), coffeemaker (in suite), safe, high-speed Internet access.

Hotel Zara ★★ Located on a small side street off of Váci utca, the pedestrian shopping street, this hotel is just 2 short blocks from the Great Market. It is a great location. Having opened in 2006, this small boutique hotel is the first of four planned by this company. The decor is a beautifully executed mix of eclectic styles with Murano glass light coverings to Thai designs for the carpeting and drapery, created by Hungarian craftsman. The standard rooms seem small at 18sq. m (194 sq. ft.), since most of them sport a queen-size bed, a rarity in less than a five-star hotel, but roomy enough

to be comfortable. Superior rooms are 23sq. m (248 sq. ft.) giving more room to spread out. The furniture style is Asian modern with a soft pink and chocolate brown theme, while the bathrooms are tiled in browns and beiges, with showers only. Each corridor has only five rooms for an intimate feeling with designated smoking and non-smoking floors. Excellent staff would add to a stay here.

V. Só u. 6. ⓒ 1/577-0700. Fax 1/577-0710. www.zarahotels.com. 74 units. 95€–150€ ($124–$195/£65–£103) standard, 105€–165€ ($137–$215/£72–£113) superior; special season 165€ ($195/£105) standard, 185€ ($241/£127) superior. Children up to 12 stay free in parent's room. Rates include breakfast and city tax. AE, MC, V. Parking 18€ ($23/£12). Metro: Kálvin tér (Blue line). **Amenities:** Restaurant; bar; room service; laundry service; dry cleaning (same day); Wi-Fi in public areas. *In room:* A/C, TV, minibar, safe, high-speed Internet access.

Ibis Budapest Centrum ⓖ

The location of this hotel is ideal, based at the foot of Ráday utca, one of the major dining streets in the city and a street that is becoming a cultural-event hotspot. A 2-minute walk away is the National Museum. Váci utca is 5 minutes away, where shopping and a multitude of dining options are available. The Ibis chain has a 15-minute satisfaction guarantee so if there is something wrong with a room and it is not taken care of in 15 minutes, you get one night free. Rooms are basic, adequately sized, not huge, but impeccably clean. There is a peaceful garden terrace on the first floor where you can sit and relax. If you are very sensitive to sound, you should request a room overlooking the terrace rather than Ráday.

IX. Ráday u. 6. ⓒ 1/456-4100. Fax 1/456-4116. www.ibishotel.com. 126 units. 16,250 Ft–19,550 Ft ($88–$108/£46–£57) double; special season 37,500 Ft ($203/£107). Breakfast 2,000 Ft ($11/£6). AE, DC, MC, V. Parking 20€ ($26/£14). Metro: Kálvin tér (Blue line). **Amenities:** Bar; laundry service (next day); computer in lobby; T-Com mobile Wi-Fi vouchers available; snacks 24 hr.; nonsmoking rooms. *In room:* A/C, TV.

King's Hotel ⓖ *Finds*

The King's Hotel opened for business in 1995 in a beautifully renovated and restored *fin de siècle* building in the heart of Pest's Jewish District. Rooms resonate with a 19th-century atmosphere due to the plainness of the furniture. All of the beds are twins, but they don't mind if you push two together. Many rooms have small balconies overlooking the quiet residential street. The reception is uniformly friendly and helpful. The adjoining restaurant is strictly kosher. Due to its location and the restaurant next door, it is attractive to Orthodox Jewish travelers.

VII. Nagydiófa u. 25–27. ⓒ/fax 1/352-7675. www.kingshotel.hu. 78 units. 80€–100€ ($104–$130/£55–£68) double; 100€–120€ ($130–$156/£68–£82) triple; 120€–140€ ($156–$182/£82–£96) quad. Rates include breakfast. AE, DC, MC, V. Metro: Astoria (Red line). **Amenities:** Restaurant; bar; babysitting; laundry service. *In room:* A/C, TV, safe, high-speed Internet.

Leo Panzió ⓖ *Finds*

This small pension sports a fantastic location in the downtown area of Budapest close to the heart of the business and shopping area, and within a stone's throw of the Blue line metro station. Váci utca and all of the other shopping opportunities are minutes away. The hallway and bedroom walls are decorated with framed antique Budapest postcards. Dark red wood in the bedrooms is accented by the deep red patterned drapes and bedspreads that evoke a feeling of embracing the past, while living in the present. The rooms are on the smallish side with the double bed and desk overpowering the room, but it is adequate, as is the bathroom in each room. If charm and location are more important then living space, then this is the hotel you want, though don't count on the charms of the reception; we would best describe the man who helped us as apathetic, but he may have been having a bad day.

V. Kossuth Lajos u. 2/A. ⓒ 1/266-9041. Fax: 1/266-9042. www.leopanzio.hu. 14 units. 76€–89€ ($99–$116/£52–£61) double; 97€–118€ ($126–$153/£66–£81) triple; special season 119€ ($155/£81) double,

148€ ($192/£101) triple. No Internet deals. Rates include breakfast. DC, MC, V. No parking. Metro: Ferenciek tere (Blue line). **Amenities:** Laundry service; fax. *In room:* A/C, TV, minibar, hair dryer, iron (on request), Wi-Fi.

Mercure Hotel Budapest Nemzeti ★ *(Finds* Formerly the Hotel Nemzeti, this hotel was built specifically for the National Theater on Blaha Lujza tér in the 1900s. The hotel was remodeled the last time in 2000, but the original Art Nouveau elegance has been restored and it is lovely. Each floor is named for an old Hungarian actor or actress. The exterior and the lobby definitely draw attention for their charm, but the rooms have a simple decor of blue, beige, and a nondescript print bedspread. Some doubles include a sofa, though others don't; you might request one for no extra charge. The hotel is very centrally located; it directly overlooks one of the busiest squares in the city. The rooms have high ceilings and some have spacious bathrooms. The original hotel had bathrooms at the end of the corridors, so some rooms have space for only a shower, while others have a tub/shower combo. There are two nonsmoking floors. The hotel's restaurant is topped with a beautifully ornate stained-glass ceiling and the same original accoutrements as the rest of the hotel.

VIII. József krt. 4. ⒸⓉ **1/477-2000.** Fax 1/477-2001. www.mercure-nemzeti.hu. 74 units. 90€–120€ ($117–$156/£62–£82) double; 26€–36€ ($34–$48/£18–£25) extra bed. Breakfast 13€ ($17/£9). Children 12 and under stay free in parent's room. AE, DC, MC, V. Parking available in neighborhood garage for 17€ ($22/£12) per day. Metro: Blaha Lujza tér (Red line). **Amenities:** Restaurant; bar; room service; laundry service; wireless Internet in public areas (for a fee). *In room:* A/C, TV, minibar, hair dryer, iron (on request), safe, Lan Internet (for a fee).

Pilvax City Hotel ★★ The best word to describe this hotel is *charming;* you'll be overcome by a snuggly, comforted feeling as soon as you enter. Located on a pedestrian street, there is only traffic on one small one-way street, keeping noise to a minimum. Having so few rooms has its advantages, and personalized service is excellent. With only two floors the hotel lacks an elevator and instead has a grand winding staircase; a guestbook available on the landing is filled with many wonderful accolades. Each of the rooms is well equipped for the weary traveler, all perfectly quiet for a good night's sleep on an excellent mattress with matching quality pillows. No one should feel cramped in these well-appointed rooms. The bathroom is equally as comfortable, but the quarter-circle shower is a bit small. Adjoining the hotel is the Pilvax Restaurant, an institution in Budapest restaurant culture. Both hotel and restaurant are part of the Mellow Mood chain.

V. Pilvax köz 1-3. ⒸⓉ **1/266-7660.** Fax 1/317-6396. www.cityhotels.hu. 32 units. 20,000 Ft–29,000 Ft ($108–$157/£57–£83) double, 25,000 Ft–35,500 Ft ($135–$192/£71–£101) triple; special season 34,000 Ft ($184/£97) double, 46,500 Ft ($251/£132) triple. Rates include full breakfast. AE, MC, V. No parking. Metro: Deák (all lines). **Amenities:** Restaurant; bar; dry cleaning (next-day service); nonsmoking rooms. *In room:* A/C, TV, minibar.

INEXPENSIVE

Medosz ★ The hotel, formerly a trade-union hotel for agricultural workers, retains its communist utilitarian appearance with tread-worn carpeting and ugly halls. Those staying here certainly do not do it for the decor or the beauty of the rooms; the rooms are simple, on the smallish side, but clean. The location cannot be beat. Jókai tér is less than 1 block from the bustling Oktogon and across from Liszt Ferenc tér with a dozen restaurants. Because of this, it can be noisy at night with the many restaurants and clubs in the area. Courtyard-view rooms are subject to neighbor noise from other apartments, but not nearly as bad as the front of the hotel. The hotel remains a great value given its location. A reader reports that their room had springs popping from the mattress. We advise you to check out the mattresses immediately upon checking in and ask for a room change if needed.

VI. Jókai tér 9. ℂ **1/374-3001**. Fax 1/332-4316. www.medoszhotel.hu. 68 units. 60€–70€ ($78–$91/£41–£48) double; 70€–80€ ($91–$104/£48–£55) triple; 86€–96€ ($112–$125/£59–£66) quad; extra bed 6€ ($8/£4]). 1 night discounted if 3 or more nights booked. Special season and high season rates are the same. Rates include breakfast. DC, MC, V. Metered on-street parking; indoor garage nearby. Metro: Oktogon (Yellow line). **Amenities:** Restaurant; bar; laundry service. *In room:* TV, No phone.

2 Outer Pest

VERY EXPENSIVE

Hilton Budapest WestEnd 🐸🐸   Shop until you drop has new meaning with this hotel conveniently located in West End City Center, one of the largest shopping malls in Central Europe. Situated next to Nyugati train station, it is convenient for train travelers. This Hilton is geared for the business set, but it welcomes leisure travelers as well. Opened in 2000, it was a start-up player in the new group of five-star hotels. Each room is stylishly decorated with extra-large beds and a large ergonomic lounge chair offering luxurious relaxation. The room color scheme of eggplant, dark green, and tans is standardized throughout all rooms. The fourth floor executive lounge (and its panoramic views) makes check-in quick and easy, and it offers snacks and drinks throughout the day. The suites are extremely roomy, with executive suites sporting two rooms. The chic and ultramodern Zita cafe on the ground level attracts many people from the area with their lunch specials.

VI. Váci út 1–3, 1069 Budapest. ℂ **800/445-8667** in North America, 00/800-44-45-8668 in Britain. Fax 1/288-5588. www.hilton.com. 230 units. 200€–280€ ($260–$364/£137–£192) double; 260€–405€ ($338–$527/£178–£277) suite. Lower weekend rates. Rates do not include VAT or city tax. Breakfast 27€ ($35/£19). AE, MC, V. Parking 4,000 Ft ($22/£11) per day. Metro: Nyugati pu (Blue line). **Amenities:** Restaurant; bar; cafe; exercise room; sauna; concierge; car-rental desk; business center; secretary services; 24-hr. room service; babysitting; laundry service; dry cleaning (same day); Wi-Fi (for a fee). *In room:* A/C, TV, dataport w/ISDN, minibar, coffeemaker, hair dryer, iron/ironing board, safe, robe, slippers.

EXPENSIVE

Andrássy Hotel 🐸🐸   The Andrássy Hotel started as the Bauhaus orphanage for Jewish children in 1937, but it has undergone many incarnations since. The hotel has been fully renovated a number of times, the last being the end of 2007. It continues to recreate a fresh image to be fully worthy of its exclusive luxurious boutique-hotel status featured in "Small Luxury Hotels of the World" (www.slh.com); there are only two in Hungary. With each change, it only gets better, which is difficult to imagine of this treasure of a hotel, located in an exclusive embassy neighborhood. It is just a few minute's walk to Heroes' Square and the City Park, and a 1-minute walk to the nearest metro station. The lobby is sleek, spacious, and tasteful, with everything done in shades of orange and etched glass. All of the rooms are newly redecorated in relaxing grays, greens, and browns, with burnt-orange sofas and chairs combined with contemporary design blond wood furniture and modern Asian prints. The holistic mood is a Zen feel for sure making it perfectly relaxing. The spacious suites are worth the splurge. Most rooms come with terraces. No fitness facilities here, but guests can use those at a partner hotel located nearby. *Note:* This hotel also arranges special Budapest/Tokaj packages with Gróf Degenfeld Castle Hotel (another member of the Small Luxurious Hotels of the World) on their vineyard in Tokaj.

VI. Andrássy út 111. ☎ **1/462-2100.** Fax 1/322-9445. www.andrassyhotel.com. 70 units. 109€–229€ ($142–$297/£75–£157) classic; 129€–259€ ($168–$337/£88–£177) superior; 149€–289€ ($194–$376/£102–£198) deluxe; 209€–329€ ($272–$428/£143–£255) jr. suite; 239€–409€ ($311–$532/£164–£280) ambassador suite. AE, DC, MC, V. Parking 16€ ($21/£11) per day. Metro: Bajza u. (Yellow line). **Amenities:** Restaurant; lounge; concierge; 24-hr. room service; in room massage; laundry service; dry cleaning (same day); wireless Internet throughout hotel, Wi-Fi card provided if needed. In room: A/C, satellite TV, VCR (on request), DVD (on request), fax, dataport, minibar, hair dryer, iron/ironing board (on request), safe, bathrobes, slippers, umbrella, 2 phone lines, snacks.

Atrium Hotel ⭐⭐   Reopened in March 2007, this ultramodern hotel part of the Mellow Mood chain is a breath of fresh air to the area, only 1 block from the Red metro. Attention to detail was obvious when this former post office was converted into its current incarnation, a completely nonsmoking hotel. The greenish-gray walls mixed with the blues in the carpeting make the rooms feel airy and roomy, yet they exude a warmth that will welcome even the finicky guest. The extra-large built-in double closet is convenient for a long-term stay, where luggage and clothes can be stored without taking up space in the room. Rooms have soundproof windows. The desk has three outlets at the back, making it convenient for plugging in devices while working. A table lamp uses a low light that's not obtrusively bright. For those who like to read, a comfortable chair is set by the desk with a floor lamp nearby. This is suited to travelers of all ages and all ages were represented during my stay.

VIII. Csokonai u.14. ☎ **1/299-0777.** Fax 1/215-6090. www.hotelatrium.hu. 57 units (22 with double beds; 35 with twin beds). 31,200 Ft–39,000 Ft ($169–$211/£89–£111) double; special season 46,800 Ft ($253/£133) double; 7,000 Ft ($38/£20) extra bed. Rates include full breakfast. AE, MC, V. Parking 4,320 Ft ($23/£13) per day. Metro: Keleti (Red line). **Amenities:** Bar, room service, in-room massage, babysitting, dry cleaning. In room: A/C, TV, minibar, fridge, coffeemaker, hair dryer, safe, Wi-Fi.

MODERATE

Atlas Hotel ⭐   The inside of this hotel has a comfy feel, but the neighborhood is on the sketchy side; though not a dangerous area, it's not winning any beauty contests. The current hotel was opened 2 years ago by Mellow Moods, but it was a hotel prior. Before the reopening, it was repainted in white and refurnished with modern stuffed sofas and chairs in pleasant, but nondescript patterns. The oversize maple-colored wardrobe is generously covered with panels of mirrors on the doors. The rooms will not give anyone claustrophobia; they are generous with space. There are fixed wall lamps for plenty of lighting. We were disappointed that the few electric outlets in the room were being used by other lamps, making it impossible to plug in a laptop at the desk in the room without getting on hands and knees to unplug something. The bathrooms were highly inadequate, lacking large towels or even an outlet. If Keleti train station is in your plan, this is very close and convenient.

VIII. Nepszinhaz u. 39. ☎ **1/340-8585.** Fax 1/299-0255. www.atlashotelbudapest.com. 136 units. 70€–100€ ($91–$130/£48–£68) double, 75€–101€ ($98–$131/£51–£69) deluxe double, 93€–141€ ($121–$183/£64–£97) triple, 110€–176€ ($143–$228/£75–£120) quad; special season 120€–150€ ($156–$195/£82–£103) double, 117€–135€ ($152–$176/£80–£92) double deluxe, 150€–180€ ($195–$234/£103–£123) triple, 192€–200€ ($250–$260/£131–£137) quad. Rates include full breakfast. MC, V. Parking 3,000 Ft ($16/£8.50) per day. Metro: Blaha Lujza tér (Red line). **Amenities:** Bar; dry cleaning (next day); safe. In room: A/C, TV, minibar, hair dryer (on request), iron (on request).

Baross Hotel ⭐   For rail travel convenience, you couldn't ask for a better location; this hotel is located across the street from Keleti train station, literally 1-minute away. To add icing on the cake, the metro Red line is just outside the door, along with four bus lines. On the negative side, Baross tér is one of the less-desirable neighborhoods, not for the crime, but for the decaying buildings in the neighborhood. With that said, this hotel is a little diamond in the rough, and the area is trying hard to clean its face. If you request a room with the courtyard view, you will have plenty of natural light with pleasant flower pots hanging on the railings giving a minigarden effect. The apartments have kitchenettes. The entire building, even the nonhotel floors, has been well maintained. Guests run the gamut from seniors to young travelers in this Mellow Mood hotel. Baross tér is a busy street, so a room on that side may be noisier late at night.

VII. Baross tér 15. (℅) 1/461-3010. Fax 1/343-2770. www.barosshotel.hu. 48 units. 78€–98€ ($101–$127/£53–£67) double, 90€–114€ ($117–$148/£62–£78) triple, 100€–126€ ($130–$164/£68–£86) quad, 125€–200€ ($163–$260/£99–£137) apt; special season 145€ ($189/£99) double, 165€ ($215/£113) triple, 180€ ($234/£123) quad, apt rates same as high season rates. Rates include full breakfast. AE, MC, V. Parking 2,000 Ft ($11/£5.75) per day. Metro: Keleti (Red line). **Amenities:** Internet access (for a fee); safe; nonsmoking rooms. *In room:* A/C, TV, minibar, hair dryer (on request), iron (on request), safe.

Délibáb Hotel 🐾

Once the neo-Renaissance home of the famous Hungarian Eszterházy family, built at the turn of the 20th Century, this small Mellow Mood–owned hotel is ideal for the traveler with a short amount of time in the city. Located 1 short block from Heroes' Square, it provides ready access to the Museum of Fine Arts, City Park, Szechányi thermals, and other museums, not to mention the Yellow metro line. The rooms border on dowdy, not modernized, but plain, simple, and fastidiously clean; they are a little larger than a monk's quarters. If you are impressed with history, this historical place is not a bad place to lay your head at night. I found it perfectly comfortable considering the amount of time I normally spend in a hotel room. If you are interested in a beautiful view, ask for any of these rooms: 210, 211, 212, 310, 311, or 312 for a spectacular panorama of Heroes' Square when it is lit up at night, but take into consideration there isn't a lift and the second floor is really the third floor.

VI. Délibáb u. 35. (℅) 1/342-9301. Fax 1/342-8153. www.hoteldelibab.hu. 34 units. 68€–83€ ($88–$108/£47–£57) double, 85€–100€ ($111–$130/£58–£68) triple, special season 115€ ($150/£79) double, 131€ ($170/£90) triple. Extra bed 15 € ($20/£10) per person per night. Rates include full breakfast. AE, MC, V. Limited parking on grounds, 10€ ($13/£7) a day. Metro: Hősök tér (Yellow line). **Amenities:** Laundry service (next day); nonsmoking rooms; snacks and drinks sold in lobby. *In room:* TV, hair dryer (on request).

Fortuna Botel and Hostel 🐾🐾 (Kids)

Ahoy matey, if you like boats, you'll love this hotel. It is on a ship built in 1967 and it once cruised the Danube as a holiday ship for trade unions. It was retrofitted in 2000 and all of the cabins were enlarged and an English Pub was created in the former engine room. The hotel section has rooms on the upper and main decks each with in-suite bathrooms, including four superior rooms. Some of my older friends have stayed here and gave it a great review. A hostel area is on the lower deck in the hull with shared bathrooms and showers. Each of the rooms is named after a famous sailor or pirate.

XIII. Szent István park, also rakpart. (℅) 1/288-8100. www.fortunahajo.hu. 50 units. Hotel 65€–100€ ($85–$130/£44–£68) double; 80€–120€ ($104–$156/£55–£82) superior. Hotel rates include breakfast. Hostel 30€–35€ ($39–$46/£21–£24) double; 40€–47€ ($52–$61/£27–£32) triple. Breakfast 5€ ($6.50/£3.50). AE, MC, V. Tram: 4 or 6 to Jászai Mari tér. **Amenities:** Restaurant; bar; safe. *In room:* A/C, TV, minibar.

Ibis Heroes Square 🐾🐾

Formerly the Hotel Liget, Ibis Heroes Square is an unusual modern design by the Hungarian architect Jozsef Finta. The location is excellent, across the street from the zoo, the Museum of Fine Arts, and Heroes' Square. Accor bought the property in 2007 and has completely remodeled it in the company's new Accor "poppy" theme. The color scheme is poppy red with beiges and tans throughout the hotel and rooms. Each room is 20 sq. m (215 sq. ft.) furnished with modern sleek furniture and wood floors. The terra-cotta, beige walls and deep red curtains are quietly soothing. Bathrooms are equipped with showers only, no tubs in any of the rooms. Unlike its predecessor, the hotel is focusing on business and leisure travelers, not families. Both smoking and nonsmoking floors are offered. For the best view of the zoo across the street, request room 420.

VI. Dózsa György út 106. (C) 1/269-5300. Fax 1/269-5329. 139 units. 61€–74€ ($79–$96/£42–£51); special season 130€ ($169/£89). Rates do not include city tax. Breakfast 8€ ($11/£5.50). AE, DC, MC, V. Metro: Hősök tere (Yellow line). **Amenities:** Restaurant; bar; bike rental. *In room:* A/C, TV, hair dryer, iron (on request), safe, Internet connection, Wi-Fi (for a fee).

Star Hotel ⟮ This small Mellow Mood hotel opened in 2000, but does not appear to have that 7-year itch to make any changes, nor does it need to. The rooms still have a youthful attraction, while being very roomy and painstakingly clean. Guests run the gamut from seniors to young backpackers, mostly Europeans. The modern furniture is simple, yet functional with the bed in a box frame, so watch your toes. The mattress is firm, but not stone-slab hard and there are extra large pillows. The TV desk has plenty of room to share with a laptop or to just sit and write, though there is a shortage of plugs, something has to be traded out. There are also apartments that can sleep up to four people, but they don't have kitchens. Having a competent multilingual staff adds to the enjoyment of the property. All rooms are nonsmoking. It is a bit out of the city center, but a bus line stops right in front of the hotel, making it very convenient to access.

VII. István u. 14. (C) 1/479-0420. Fax 1/342-4661. www.starhotel.hu. 48 units. 17,500 Ft–21,000 Ft ($95–$114/£48–£60) double, 20,000 Ft–24,000 Ft ($108–$130/£57–£68) triple, 22,500 Ft–30,000 Ft ($122–$162/£64–£85) apt; special season 29,000 Ft ($157/£83) double, 32,500 Ft ($176/£93) triple, 37,000 Ft ($200/£105) apt. Rates include full breakfast. AE, MC, V. Limited street parking. Trolleybus: 74. **Amenities:** Bar; dry cleaning (next day); safe. *In room:* A/C, TV, minibar, hair dryer (on request), iron (on request).

3 Central Buda

VERY EXPENSIVE

Art'Otel Budapest ⟮⟮ Opened in 2000 by the Park Plaza hotel group, this is the first Art'Otel outside of Germany. The distinguishing concept of this chain is that each property spotlights the work of one particular artist, thus you are staying in a gallery of modern art. At this hotel, the artist is Donald Sultan, an American modernist. More than 600 pieces of his work grace the hotel's walls from the lobby to the hallways and guestrooms. He also designed everything from the carpets to the dinnerware. The modern side of the hotel is a seven-story building facing the Danube, with a walkway leading to four 17th-century, two-story, baroque town houses, which now serve as rooms, suites, and the Chelsea Restaurant. Many pieces of the original houses are protected by historical conservation laws, so were incorporated into designs. Somewhere in each room there is a bird on a perch designed by Sultan. Rooms on the top three floors of the new building facing the Danube command the best views, especially rooms ending with 19, 20, and 21 and are called the Danube view rooms, with a higher price tag, while rooms in the old houses have higher ceilings, some unusual doors and locks from their original time, but no view. Suites have a living room in the bedrooms, while the art suites are separate rooms.

I. Bem Rakpart 16–19, Budapest. (C) 800/814-7000 or 1/487-9487 in North America; 800/169-6128 or 1/487-5500 in Britain. Fax 1/487-9488. www.artotel.hu. 164 units. 125€–155€ ($163–$202/£86–£106) double non-Danube view; 25€ ($33/£17) Danube view supplement; 155€–185€ ($202–$241/£107–£127) executive suite; 185€–210€

($241–$273/£127–£144) art suite. Lower weekend and Internet rates. Children 12 and under stay free in parent's room. Breakfast 12€ ($16/£8.25). AE, DC, MC, V. Self-parking or valet parking 15€ ($21/£11) per day. Metro: Batthyány tér (Red line). **Amenities:** Restaurant; bar; exercise room; sauna; concierge; business center; salon; limited room service; wireless Internet in public areas. *In room:* A/C, TV, dataport w/ISDN (for a fee), minibar, coffeemaker (in suite; on request in other rooms), hair dryer, iron/ironing board (on request), safe, Wi-Fi (for a fee), robe, slippers.

MODERATE

Charles Apartment House 𝒢   After opening in 1991, owner Károly Szombati has accumulated 73 apartments in a group of buildings in a less-than-eye-appealing Buda-side neighborhood. The apartments are a 45-minute walk at a good pace or a 15-minute bus ride from downtown Pest. All of the apartments were refurbished in 2006, though they are pleasant enough, they are nothing spectacular. The furnishings are comfortable, clean, and for the most part new with the remodel. All apartments have full bathrooms and kitchens; some kitchens are part of the bedroom, while others have them in a separate room. The kitchens are stocked with dishes, cups, silverware, and other things can be borrowed from reception. Hegyalja út is a very busy street, but only two apartments face out onto it (avoid these); the rest are in the interior or on the side of the building. Also take note that only the deluxe rooms have air-conditioning. A nearby park has tennis courts and a track. There is a new restaurant in the apartment complex. The staff are friendly and speak English. The reception desk is open 24 hours. The clientele are the more sedate who are not interested in the nightlife, therefore, are not concerned with transportation after hours.

I. Hegyalja út 23. ⒸⒸ 1/212-9169. Fax 1/202-2984. www.charleshotel.hu. 73 units. 57€–79 € ($74–$103/£39–£54) double, 72€–89€ ($94–$116/£49–£61) deluxe double, 77€–114€ ($100–$148/£53–£78) triple, 77€–138€ ($100–$179/£53–£94) apt for 1–4 people; special season 100 € ($130/£68) double, 130€ ($169/£89) deluxe double, 130€–160€ ($169–$208/£89–£110) triple and apts. Rates include breakfast. AE, DC, MC, V. Parking 2,500 Ft ($14/£7) per day. Bus: 78 from Keleti pu. to Zsolt u. stop, then a 200m (656-ft.) walk; 8 or 112 stop in front. **Amenities:** Restaurant; bar; bike rental; business center (for fee); babysitting; laundry service; Wi-Fi in building. *In room:* A/C, TV, minibar, hair dryer (in deluxe room; on request for standard room), safe.

4 The Castle District

VERY EXPENSIVE

Hilton Budapest 𝒢𝒢   This Hilton has the most enviable piece of real estate in Budapest, sitting right next door to St. Matthias Church with part of the Fisherman's Bastion behind it. The hotel's award-winning design incorporated both the ruins of a 13th-century Dominican church (the church tower is alongside the hotel) and the baroque facade of a 17th-century Jesuit college, which makes up the hotel's main entrance. The hotel was renovated in 2007; the rooms are now a uniform rose, green, and beige color scheme. The corner suites are beautifully decorated with separate sitting areas, a dining area, and bedroom with oversize windows for a spectacular view of the Bastion and Danube. The elegant Baroque Room is three levels and has a fully equipped kitchen. Two floors are nonsmoking.

I. Hess András tér 1–3. ⒸⒸ 1/899-6600. Fax 1/899-6644. www.hilton.com. 322 units. 90€–160€ ($117–$208/£62–£110) advanced purchase; 100€–170€ ($130–$221/£68–£116) value rate; 120€–220€ ($156–$286/£82–£151) flexible rate; 30€ ($39/£21) Danube view supplement; 60€ ($78/£41) executive floor supplement. Rates do not include VAT or city tax. One child per adult stays free in parent's room. Breakfast 27€ ($35/£19). AE, DC, MC, V. Parking 25€ ($33/£17) per day in public garage. Bus: 10 from Moszkva tér or 16 from Deák tér. **Amenities:** Restaurant; bar; exercise room; concierge; business center; shops; salon; 24-hr. room service; in-room massage; babysitting; laundry service; Wi-Fi in lobby. *In room:* A/C, TV, minibar, coffeemaker, hair dryer, iron/ironing board, safe, Wi-Fi (for a fee in standard room).

MODERATE

Burg Hotel ✦✦✦ *(Finds)*   An overlooked treasure on Castle Hill, this hotel was highly recommended by a friend, so we had to investigate it. Sitting on a corner directly across from St. Matthias Church, it is an excellent location. The multilingual staff is as friendly as they are talented with languages. The rooms are spacious and beautifully decorated in muted greens, rose, and beige with modern comfortable furniture from their last remodel in 2006. The corner rooms are extra large, but any room would be comfortable. The blue-tiled bathrooms are simple, but sizeable. All have a view of Trinity Square. Breakfast is served in a large lovely decorated room with many windows overlooking the square. There is no lift, but it is only two floors above the ground floor entrance.

I. Szentháromság tér 7–8. ℂ **1/212-0269.** Fax 1/212-3970. www.burghotelbudapest.com. 26 units. 99€–115€ ($129–$150/£68–£79) double, 29€–39€ ($38–$51/£20–£27) extra bed; special season 175€ ($228/£120) double, 39€ ($51/£28) extra bed. Children under 14 stay free in parent's room. Rates include breakfast and city tax. AE, DC, MC, V. Parking 25€ ($33/£17) per day in public garage. Bus: 10 from Moszkva tér or 16 from Deák tér. **Amenities:** Bar; laundry service; dry cleaning; Wi-Fi in lobby. *In room:* A/C, TV, minibar, hair dryer, safe.

Hotel Kulturinnov ✦ *(Value)*   For those with cultural interests or a burning desire to stay on Castle Hill, this is a modest alternative. The actual hotel is located on the first floor in the building of the Hungarian Culture Foundation, built in the early 20th century. The foundation's mission is to promote the culture of Hungarians living outside of the country. The building has an impressive entrance. Entering one long hall, the rooms are at the end. A total remodel is planned by March 2008, where the carpets, drapes, and all of the bathroom fixtures will be replaced. The rooms are small, impeccably clean, with very high ceilings. None of the rooms have exceptional views, except perhaps number 10, which overlooks the garden. However, for the location, the price is a bargain. The staff is warm and friendly.

I. Szentháromság tér 6. ℂ **1/224-8100.** Fax 1/375-1886. www.mka.hu. 16 units. 64€–80€ ($83–$104/£44–£55) double; 74€–100€ ($96–$130/£51–£89) triple; 10€–20€ ($13–$26/£7–£14) extra bed. Children under 10 stay free in parent's room. Rates include breakfast and city tax. MC, V. Parking 10€ ($13/£7) per day. Bus: 10 from Moszkva tér or 16 from Deák tér. **Amenities:** Laundry service; dry cleaning; Wi-Fi; safe; snack bar. *In room:* Minibar, hair dryer, iron (on request), fan.

5 The Buda Hills

Unless you have some special reason to want to stay in the Buda Hills, be aware that you will be using precious time to travel to the Pest side where the lion's share of sights are located. These accommodations take two transport connections to reach the center.

MODERATE

Beatrix Panzió   The Beatrix Panzió opened in 1991 as a modern pension with clean, comfortable rooms. The suites have private balconies and full kitchens. Guests are welcome to use the sun deck with the landscaped garden and a goldfish pond; in good weather, breakfast is served in the garden. For a fee, the management offers grill or goulash parties where they cook traditional goulash on the outdoor grill. Staff assists with making tour arrangements and restaurant reservations. Though the pension is located on a small but heavily traveled road instead of a back street (on which most pensions are found), the guest rooms are not noisy. A well-stocked grocery store is conveniently located down the street.

II. Széher út 3, 1021 Budapest. ☎ **1/275-0550.** Fax 1/394-3730. www.beatrixhotel.hu. 22 units. 60€–70 €
($78–$91/£41–£48) double; 70€–80€ ($91–$104/£48–£55) triple; 80€–120€ ($104–$156/£55–£82) suite. Double
and triple room rates include breakfast; 5€ ($6.50/£3.50) for suite. No credit cards. Free parking in secured lot. Tram:
56 from Moszkva tér to the 7th stop. **Amenities:** Bar; 24-hr. room service; laundry service (limited). *In room:* TV,
kitchen (in suite), minibar, safe.

G.G. Panoráma Panzió 🖈   The friendly English-speaking Gabor Gubacsi runs this
small guesthouse in her home. Guest rooms are on the top floor of the house, which
is located on a steep, but quiet street in the lovely Rose Hill (Rózsadomb) section of
Buda. The rooms are small, but furnished tastefully with simple-styled furnishings and
private bathroom with shower. All of the rooms share a common balcony from where
you have a great view of the hills. The common kitchen has full facilities and a dining
area, as well as access to an outdoor garden space where you can relax. It's a casual
place with a bit of class mixed in, and the Gubacsis reportedly take good care of their
guests. There are two bus lines down the hill and fairly close to the neighborhood providing access to the center of the city. Be warned you will need to take a bus and then
either the metro or tram from there to get to the city center.

II. Fullánk u. 7, 1026 Budapest. ☎/fax **1/394-6034** or 1/394-4718. www.ggpanorama.hu. 4 units. 50€–60€
($68–$78/£34–£41) double. Breakfast 5€ ($6.50/£3.50). No credit cards. Parking available on street. Bus: 11 from
Batthyány tér or no. 49 from Moszkva tér. **Amenities:** Common kitchen; phone. *In room:* TV, Wi-Fi, no phone.

Hotel Panda   This hotel sits on Pasaréti Square, a neighborhood with a modern
Catholic Church, grocery store, and other businesses in a very busy little square. The
reception staff are friendly and efficient. Unfortunately, the desirability of the rooms
varies greatly. Rooms facing the front (10 in all) have terraces, with a southern exposure and nice views. Rooms elsewhere in the hotel have smaller windows and no terraces, so they can get a bit stuffy and hot in warm weather. Each bathroom has a
window. While the larger suites are quite big, the smaller ones are identical in size to
normal double rooms.

II. Pasaréti út 133, 1026 Budapest. ☎ **1/394-1392** or 1/394-1395. Fax 1/394-1002. www.budapesthotelpanda.hu.
28 units. 50€–60€ ($65–$78/£34–£41) double; 60€–70 ($78–$91/£41–£48) triple and suite. Rates include breakfast. AE, MC, V. Limited free parking. Bus: 5 from Március 15 tér or Moszkva tér to Pasaréti tér (the last stop). **Amenities:** Restaurant. *In room:* TV, minibar.

6 Alternatives to Hotels

Let me first state that not all hostels are created equal and should not be considered
for young party people only. There are alternatives out there and I have listed a couple of good ones. There is intense competition in Budapest between the leading youth
hostel companies and various privately run hostels since there are over 85 hostels in
the city.

The leading company is **Travellers' Youth Way Youth Hostels,** also known as **Mellow Mood Ltd.** (☎ 1/413-2062; www.mellowmood.hu). It runs three hostels: **Marco
Polo** (☎ 1/413-2555; www.marcopolohostel.com), **Domino Hostel** (☎ 1/235-0492;
www.mellowmoodhostel.com), and **Hostel Fortuna** (☎ 1/215-0600; www.fortuna-
hostel.hu), in addition to six summer-only hostels.

Representatives from the Budapest Tourinform office sometimes board inbound
trains early to pass out tour information and maps. In the past, international trains
arriving in Budapest were also assaulted with people trying to book backpackers into
their property. Some representatives even boarded Budapest-bound international

Value   Staying in Private Rooms or Hostels

It is becoming less and less common, but private rooms in private apartments are definitely an option for budget travelers in Hungary. When you book a private room, you get a room in someone's apartment. You'll usually share the bathroom either with the hosts or with other guests. Breakfast may or may not be included, but the host will often offer a continental spread (bread, butter, jam, coffee or tea) for an extra charge, but it may be cost saving to get your breakfast elsewhere. You may also have limited kitchen privileges (ask in advance to be sure). Some landlords will greet you when you arrive, give you a key, and seemingly disappear; others will want to befriend you, help you change money, show you around, and sometimes provide other services depending on their language skills.

Most rooms are quite adequate; some are even memorable for positive reasons, but any number of reasons may cause you to dislike your accommodations. A location in a noisy or difficult-to-reach neighborhood, a tiny bathroom, or wretched coffee are among the complaints overheard from the occasional displeased traveler. The great majority of guests, though, are satisfied; certainly, staying in a private room provides a window into someone's everyday life in Hungary that you can't really find anywhere else.

You can book rooms through accommodations agencies (for example, **Ibusz** ℰ **1/485-2700**; www.ibusz.hu). Prices vary slightly between agencies, but, generally speaking, an average room will cost between 4,500 Ft and 6,500 Ft ($23–$33/£12–£17) for two people, or 5,000 Ft ($25/£13) for a single, plus a 3% tourism tax. High-end rooms in fashionable neighborhoods can cost significantly more. Most agencies add a 30% surcharge (to the first night only) for stays of less than 4 nights. When booking a room, make sure you know its exact location on a map and that you know how to get there. Although there's scarcely an address in Budapest that cannot be reached by some form of public transportation, some are much more difficult to get to than others.

trains at the Hungarian border crossing so that they could work the backpacking crowd before the train reached Budapest. This is not as common as it once was, but your best bet is to book a bed in advance at one of the recommended hostels. Otherwise you can check with the booking agencies at the trains stations or airport for assistance once you arrive. You can try your luck with a hostel hawker, but for your own safety, it is wise not to. Shop around and don't let yourself be pressured. If they are pushing you, you have to wonder why they need to do so. Most hostels that solicit at the station have a van parked outside. The ride to the hostel is usually free, but you may have to wait a while until the van is full.

Mellow Mood Ltd. operates a youth hostel placement office for their own hostels at Keleti Station (ℰ **1/343-0748**), off to the side of track 9 and track 6, near the international waiting room. This office, open daily 7am to 8pm, can help you book a bed. They also run a useful youth travel agency located at VII. Baross tér 15

(© 1/413-2062; www.mellowmood.hu), which also books hostel stays from its office, usually for their own properties. To reach the agency, get off at Baross utca on tram no. 4 or 6. This agency is open Monday through Friday from 8am to 4pm. For other hostels, check out the website **www.hostelworld.com** for other offerings in the city.

In July and August a number of university dormitories and other empty student lodgings are converted into hostels. Their locations (as well as their condition) change from year to year, so we haven't reviewed any of them in this guide. The youth hostels and budget lodgings listed below are all open year-round. All hostel rates are per person, not per room.

INNER CITY & CENTRAL PEST

BudaBaB ★★ *Value*   Throwing humility to the wind, here is the full disclosure: my partner and I are the owners of this B&B. We are small, but have been open for four years and have had guests from over 17 countries. Be warned that we thrive on the interaction with guests, which was the motivating reason for opening our home. Being small allows us to give individualized attention to meet your needs. Plus, you can tell your friends you stayed with the author of this guide, get it autographed, pick up expert advice along the way, and share your own experiences. Seeing the city through others' eyes refreshes our appreciation for it.

The kitchen has a mural painted by American artist Scott Allen, who is becoming known for his murals around the globe. Each room has been painted and decorated with trinkets from our own travels, providing a relaxed atmosphere. Situated at the edge of the historic Jewish ghetto, we are only two blocks from two tram lines, the red metro, and two bus lines. Keleti train station is one metro stop away. Smoking is allowed in common rooms, but not the bedrooms. Whether you stay here or not, feel free to contact me while you are here.

VII. Akácfa u. 18 © 1/267-5240. www.budabab.com. 2 units. No seasonal changes. Double 40€–50€ ($52–$65, 28£–35£), triple 55€–70€ ($59–$91, 38£–48£), quad 85€ ($111, 58£). Breakfast included. No credit cards. Metro: Blaha Lujza (Red line). **Amenities:** Communal kitchen; Internet access; Wi-Fi; washing machine; hair dryer; and iron available.

Domino Hostel ★★ *Finds*   For a hostel, this location could not be more perfect. This new hostel from Mellow Mood only opened in July 2007 on Váci utca the ideal place for eating, drinking, and shopping, not to mention close to public transportation. The new bunk beds are stainless steel framed for support and comfort. Larger rooms have tables and chairs for guests to work or read. Linens are provided. The place is very clean, and the staff is friendly. Reception is open 24 hours which means you are free to come and go as you please. Each bed has its own locker for safe storage of your goods while you are gone for the day. The large common room is a great place to meet other guests, watch TV, or play some darts. This is a nonsmoking facility. Domino has opened a restaurant and pub that is open 24 hours a day with an entrance right around the corner from the hostel, so you can party all night and not worry about getting back to your bed.

V. Váci u. 77. © 1/235-0492. Fax: 1/216-4733. www.dominohostel.com. 26 units (120 beds). 7,700 Ft ($42/£22) double; 5,500 Ft ($30/£16) quad; 4,950 Ft ($27/£14) 6-bed unit; 4,400 Ft ($24/£13) 8-bed unit. 10% discount for IYHF members or ISIC cardholders. No credit cards. Metro: Kálvin tér (Blue line). **Amenities:** Restaurant; communal kitchen; tours booked at reception; car-rental desk; coin-op washers and dryers; Internet access (for fee); hair dryer (for fee), iron (for fee).

The Loft Hostel *Value*   True to its name, this hostel, which opened in 2007, is on the top floor of a building with dormer loft-type ceilings. It has an elevator, but regrettably, the elevator only goes to the third floor, so there is one short flight to climb. Run by a young Brit and a Hungarian, both are in a band that has just cut its first album. They did the remodeling themselves and did an impressive job of it, with plans to make a chill out space in the attic area. The kitchen area is spacious and well supplied for cooking meals; tea, coffee, and hot chocolate are free at all times. A common room is huge, with sofas, oversized pillows and TV. The rooms have skylights giving an extra airy feeling to them and the ability to air them out. Bed linens and towels are provided at no cost. There are two bathrooms that are shared by all. Both of the owners have hostel experience and want to provide more for less, but they also want to keep their lease, so they try not to make this a late night party place. Tours are also booked at cost, with no commission. Access is 24/7 with a code to the front door and a key.

V. Veres Palne u. 19 IV/6 bell 44. ©/fax **1/328-0916.** www.lofthostel.hu. 3 units (20 beds). 2,500 Ft–4,000 Ft ($14–$22/£7–£11) quad; 2,000 Ft–3,500 Ft ($11–$19/£6£–£10]) 6 bed; 1,500 Ft–3,000 Ft ($8–$16/£4–£9) 8 bed. Special season add 500 Ft ($3/£1.50]) to high season rates. Weekends add 500 Ft ($3/£1.50) to high season rate. Cash only. Limited street parking. Metro: Ferenciek tere (Blue line). **Amenities:** Communal kitchen; tours booked at reception; Wi-Fi; washer/dryer (1,000 Ft [$5.50/£3] per load); hair dryer(on request).

Marco Polo Hostel *Value*   Calling this establishment a youth hostel is a bit of a misnomer, since it closely resembles a hotel. This place is not just for backpackers as just about anyone would be comfortable spending the night here. The central location is great for hopping on a bus or catching the metro. The rooms have clean and attractive linens, and each bed has its own large wardrobe with a lock. The dorm rooms are separated with walls with a bunk bed in each section and a curtain separating it from the narrow common area of the dorm. You can have privacy or sit out and meet others here or in the well-appointed common room. This is a very good deal with no curfew and a 24-hour reception. For party animals, the bar in the basement is open 24 hours, but music stops at 10pm. Open year-round, the hostel is operated by Mellow Mood Ltd. There are safes available at the front desk.

VII. Nyár u. 6. © **1/413-2555.** Fax 1/413-6058. www.marcopolohostel.com. 47 units (156 beds; double, quad, and 12-bed units have shower and toilet within the unit). 9,600 Ft ($52/£27) double; 7,000 Ft ($38/£20) triple; 6,300 Ft ($34/£18) quad; 4,400 Ft ($24/£13) 12-bed dorm. Rates include breakfast. 10% discount for IYHF members. MC, V. Limited street parking. Metro: Blaha Lujza tér (Red line). **Amenities:** Restaurant; bar; tours booked at reception; carrental; Internet access (for fee); coin-op washers and dryers; communal kitchen. *In room:* TV (in double and quad), hair dryer (for fee), iron (for fee).

Spinoza Self-Catering Apartments *Finds*   Located next to the Spinoza cafe, these self-catering apartments just opened in September 2007. They are all fully furnished for filling your everyday needs, including cooking if you wish to do so. Everything is modern and ready to go. They have four apartments, which will accommodate from one to eight people. Rates depend on the apartment and the number of people.

VII. Dob u 15. © **1/413-7489.** www.spinozahaz.hu. 4 units. 40€–120€ ($52–$156/£28–£82) double to 8 people. **Amenities:** Restaurant, washing machine. *In room:* Kitchen; TV; Wi-Fi; linens; towels.

Unity Hostel *Value*   Only 1 year old, this hostel takes quiet time seriously. To stay here you need to sign a statement stating that all loud noise ends at 10pm and the common room should be empty by midnight, making it a perfect place for older travelers or those with children. They happily accommodate all. Located on the third floor of a building with an elevator, all of the rooms are bright and clean. The common room has a TV with cable, a video library, and a computer that is free to use. The kitchen area is fully equipped to prepare meals. One room has a shower with bathrooms outside; the other rooms share a bathroom and showers. Linens are provided and towels can be rented for 500 Ft ($3/£1.50) per stay. Each bed has a security locker and a lock. For sun lovers, there is a rooftop terrace that overlooks the Liszt Music Academy lending itself to free concerts or just a relaxing space. The location is perfectly located with Liszt Ferenc tér less than a minute away and the ring road 1 block away. Access is 24/7. Péter, the owner, has many years in the hospitality business.

VI. Király u. 60. III/15. © 1/413-7377. Fax 1/413-7378. www.unityhostel.com. 5 units. 4,300 Ft ($23/£12) double; 3,400 Ft ($18/£10) triple; 3,100 Ft ($17/£9) quad; 3,000 Ft ($16/£9) dorm. Add 500 Ft ($3/£1.50) for high and special seasons. Cash only. Limited street parking. Tram: 4 or 6: Király u. **Amenities:** Communal kitchen; tour booking at reception; Wi-Fi; laundry service (2,000 Ft [$11/£6] per load); hair dryer (on request).

6

Where to Dine in Budapest

Budapest features an amazingly diverse range of restaurants as well as those more traditional eateries that have stood the test of time. Some ethnic restaurants have appeared on the scene in the last decade and more open regularly; you'll find Japanese, Korean, Indian, Middle Eastern, Greek, and Mexican restaurants in the city. Of course, the best part of travel is sampling the cuisine of the culture and you will have ample opportunities to choose either traditional or nouveau Hungarian recipes. For a list of snacks and meals that should not to be missed in the gastronomic culture, see appendix B, "Hungarian Cuisine," p. 295 for suggestions. If you are here for more than a couple of days, you may need a change of pace and other ethnic restaurants are here for suggestions. Since there are times when you'll want to eat, but not a full meal, I have also included places for a snack.

Something fish-less is going on here: Do take into consideration when ordering fish that this is a landlocked country. Unless it is fish that has come from one of Hungary's rivers or lakes, it is imported and was most likely frozen for shipment. If this is of importance to you, you should question your waiter before ordering. One Hungarian national dish is a particular fish soup, which is also part of the traditional Christmas meal. Most famous among these soup recipes are those of Szeged where fish from the Tisza River are used to prepare it. If you enjoy fish, you will find this item on many traditional restaurant menus.

WHERE TO EAT There are many words used for eateries, while few of them have clear cut boundaries. *Étterem* is the most common Hungarian word for restaurant and is applied to everything from cafeteria-style eateries to first-class restaurants. A *vendéglő*, an inn or guesthouse, is a smaller, more intimate restaurant, often with a Hungarian folk motif; a *csárda* is a countryside *vendéglő* (often built on major motorways and frequently found around Lake Balaton and other holiday areas). An *önkiszolgáló* indicates a self-service cafeteria, which is open for lunch only. *Büfés* (snack counters) are not to be confused with buffets in English. They are found all over the city, including transportation hubs. A *cukrászda* is a bakery for pastries and a coffee, while a *kávéház* is a coffeehouse with usually a limited selection of pastries. Traditionally, many coffeehouses are places to sit for hours to meet with friends, read a book, or just sit and people-watch. Today, some establishments use the word *kávéház* in their name, but really are restaurants that sell food. You will be able to tell the difference if you scope out the tables.

Other establishments that you will come across in your travels are those whose primary function is to serve liquor, but some also serve meals or snacks. A *borozó* is a wine bar; these are downstairs off of the street (they are likely to include in their name the word *pince* [cellar] or *barlang* [cave]), and generally feature a house wine. A *söröző* is a beer bar; these places, too, are often found in downstairs

Tips Hints for a Better Dining Experience

Reserving a table for most Budapest restaurants is almost always necessary. It is not unusual for a table that has been reserved by someone for 9pm to sit empty even if you happen to show up at 6pm. They will not allow you to use that table although there should be ample time to change the linens between guests. Call the restaurant to make your reservation or ask your hotel to do it for you. If you call, speak slowly. To reserve for the half-hour use the phrase "and a half"—for example "seven and a half," not "seven-thirty." You will want to avoid the downstairs restaurants in summer months; they can be brutally hot. Almost no restaurants offer air-conditioning, even if it says so on their window. Mysteriously, it is just not working on the day you show up for dinner. Before you order wine, take a good look at the menu. Glasses of wine are priced by the deciliter (dl) and you should order how many decis you want. If you don't, you may receive a full glass of wine with a surprisingly large bar tab. 1 dl = approximately 3.3 ounces.

locations. Sandwiches are usually available in *borozós* and *sörözős*. Some are wonderful places, while others are dives where cheap drinks are served to the less economically advantaged.

MUSIC Live Gypsy music is often touted in traditional Hungarian restaurants that are marketing to travelers. Most often, this is not authentic Gypsy music but a fair imitation for the unbeknownst traveler who can say they heard Gypsy music. One exception is the **Mátyás Pince** (p. 102). Chances are a member or the whole band will rotate playing a song or two at your table. If you feel uncomfortable or this is disrupting your conversation, politely decline his or her offer to play for you, as soon as they approach your table. If however, you allow them to play, then you have committed yourself to giving them a tip. The appropriate amount varies whether it is one person or more and the price category of the restaurant itself. Giving 1,000 Ft to 2,000 Ft ($5.40–$11/£2.85–£5.70) is an example for a single musician.

PRICE CATEGORIES For the purposes of this book, I have classified restaurants as follows: A restaurant is inexpensive if the average main dish is $10 or under; moderate, between $10 and $20; expensive, between $20 and $30; and very expensive, $30 and over. Restaurant meals are not the bargains they once were and with currency fluctuations, they come with sticker shock to some. For those whose home is not in a large urban city with already expensive restaurant meals, prices may be surprising to you. For this reason, I have tried to provide a wide range of choices to fit any mood and budget. One day you may feel like splurging on a great restaurant, but other days you may want something more moderate.

Credit cards are still not as ingrained in all businesses as they are elsewhere, so check with a restaurant if you need to use a credit card. I have listed the cards accepted at the time of this writing, but things change. Unless otherwise noted in the review, an English-language menu is available in all of the restaurants listed, although it may not be posted outside with the Hungarian menu. Don't hesitate to go in and ask to see a menu before you decide to stay.

Sometimes specials are posted either outside or on an inner wall of offerings, which are not on the menu; if you don't

Tips   Fizetek, kérem! = "Check, Please!" & Other Tipping Tips

One of the glorious holdovers from times past is the ability to sit in any drink or food establishment without concern of being hurried out the door. Unless the doors are closing for the evening, no one will approach you to pay your bill until you signal that you are ready; therefore, you can linger for hours on end. In 6 years, I have only found one exception to this.

Don't be surprised if the person who comes to collect your money is not the person who served you. Many places have a designated cashier who will arrive at your table to collect your money. It may be a few minutes before they arrive, so be patient. Smaller restaurants still have this annoying habit of giving you a small piece of paper with a list of numbers and nothing else to associate them with. If you have questions about it, ask to see a menu to match the charges on the list before you pay or ask the cashier to explain it. If there is a mistake, challenge it and it will be corrected.

Always ask if a service charge is already included. It should show somewhere on the bill, but it is worth asking to make sure. If the service is included, you are not expected to tip. If no service charge is included, **add 10% to the bill (15% for exceptional service in high-priced restaurants only**—though note that the waiter very rarely gets a share of the tip). I like to hand the tip directly to our waiter to make sure he receives it. Never leave the tip on the table and walk out.

The cashier will often remain at your table after delivering the bill, waiting patiently for payment. State the full amount you are paying (bill plus tip), and the waiter will make change on the spot. If the restaurant accepts credit cards and you are using one, then the cashier will bring a portable card reader to your table to swipe the card. If you want to add the tip to the charged amount, you need to say so before the charge is processed; most often it can't be added to the bill later. When I really appreciated our server, I slip some money to him or her privately to make sure the server receives some compensation.

It is rare, the restaurant that will give separate bills to one table. If you ask, they will often say they can until it comes time to pay, then suddenly they can't do it any longer. If you are sharing a bill, you may want to keep note of your charges to make things easier when it comes time to split the bill.

notice one, ask your server about any specials along with their prices before ordering to avoid any embarrassment. If a restaurant doesn't list drinks on the menu, which is rare, feel free to inquire about the price before deciding. Cocktails are extremely costly, while wine and beer are reasonable.

WARNING The U.S. Embassy provides a list of restaurants that engage in unethical business practices such as excessive billing, using physical intimidation to compel payment of excessive bills, and assaulting customers for nonpayment of excessive bills. However, it states that this list is not comprehensive. At all costs, you should avoid these establishments. The list includes **Városközpont** (accessible by outside elevator), Budapest V district, Váci utca 16; **La Dolce Vita,** Október 6. u. 8; **Nirvana Night Club,** Szent István krt. 13; **Ti'Amo Bar,** Budapest IX district, Ferenc körút 19–21; **Diamond Club,** Budapest II district, Bimbó út 3; and **Pigalle Night Club,** Budapest VIII district, Kiss József utca 1–3. If a woman approaches you and asks for directions, but then asks you to buy her a drink, red flags should shoot into the air. The embassy cannot offer too much assistance in these situations due to Hungarian laws that are ineffective. Buyer beware.

You can always check the embassy website for updated information: visit http://hungary.usembassy.gov/tourist_advisory.html.

1 Restaurants by Cuisine

AZERBAIJAN

Marquis de Salade ✶✶✶ (The Inner City & Central Pest, $$, p. 111)

COFFEEHOUSES

Aztek Choxolat Café ✶✶ (The Inner City & Central Pest, p. 129)

Café Alibi ✶ (The Inner City & Central Pest, p. 130)

Café Noé ✶ (The Inner City & Central Pest, p. 130)

Centrál Kávéház ✶✶✶ (The Inner City & Central Pest, p. 127)

Fröhlich Kóser Ckrászda ✶ (The Inner City & Central Pest, p. 130)

Gerbeaud's (The Inner City & Central Pest, p. 128)

Lukács Cukrászda (The Inner City & Central Pest, p. 128)

Művész Kávéház ✶ (The Inner City & Central Pest, p. 128)

Rétesbar ✶✶✶ (The Castle District, p. 128)

Spinoza Étterem ✶✶ (The Inner City & Central Pest, p. 130)

DUTCH

Old Amsterdam ✶✶ (The Inner City & Central Pest, $, p. 119)

Mosselen Belgian Beer Café ✶✶✶ (The Inner City & Central Pest, $$, p. 112)

FRENCH

Le Jardin de Paris ✶✶ (Central Buda, $$$, p. 124)

GREEK

Taverna Dionysos (The Inner City & Central Pest, $$, p. 115)

Zorbas Taverna ✶✶ (The Inner City & Central Pest, $$, p. 116)

HUNGARIAN CONTEMPORARY

Angelika Kávéház és Étterem ✶✶ (Central Buda, $$, p. 124)

Articsóka ✶ (The Inner City & Central Pest, $$, p. 103)

Blue Tomato Pub ✶✶✶ (The Inner City & Central Pest, $$, p. 104)

Buena Vista ✶✶ (The Inner City & Central Pest, $$, p. 104)

Café Eklektika ✶✶ (The Inner City & Central Pest, $$, p. 104)

Café Kör ✶ (The Inner City & Central Pest, $$, p. 105)

Firkász ✶ (The Inner City & Central Pest, $$, p. 107)

Gerlóczy Kávéház ✶✶✶ (The Inner City & Central Pest, $$, p. 107)

Hemingway ✶✶✶ (Central Buda, $$$, p. 124)

Kőleves Vendéglő ✶✶✶ (The Inner City & Central Pest, $, p. 118)

Kossuth Museum Ship Vénhajó ✶✶ (The Inner City & Central Pest, $$, p. 110)

M ✶✶✶ (The Inner City & Central Pest, $$, p. 111)

Menza ✶ (The Inner City & Central Pest, $$, p. 112)

Key to Abbreviations: $$$$ = Very Expensive $$$ = Expensive $$ = Moderate $ = Inexpensive

Red Pepper ☘☘ (The Inner City &
 Central Pest, $, p. 120)
Remiz ☘☘☘ (The Buda Hills, $$,
 p. 126)
Rivalda Café & Restaurant ☘ (The
 Castle District, $$, p. 126)
Vista Café Restaurant (The Inner
 City & Central Pest, $$, p. 116)

HUNGARIAN TRADITIONAL

Alföldi Kisvendéglő ☘☘ (The Inner
 City & Central Pest, $$, p. 103)
Bagolyvár ☘☘ (Beyond Central Pest,
 $$, p. 121)
Bajai Halászcsárda (The Buda Hills,
 $$$, p. 126)
Café Csiga (Beyond Central Pest, $,
 p. 123)
Fészek ☘☘ (The Inner City & Cen-
 tral Pest, $$, p. 106)
Főzelékfalo Ételbar ☘☘ (The Inner
 City & Central Pest, $, p. 117)
Frici Papa Kifőzés ☘ (The Inner City
 & Central Pest, $, p. 117)
Gundel ☘ (Beyond Central Pest,
 $$$$, p. 120)
Kispipa Vendéglő ☘ (The Inner City
 & Central Pest, $$, p. 109)
Kulacs Etterem ☘ (Beyond Central
 Pest, $$, p. 110)
Mátyás Pince ☘☘☘ (The Inner City
 & Central Pest, $$$, p. 102)
Nagyi Nonstop Palacsintázója ☘☘
 (The Inner City & Central Pest, $,
 p. 119)
Paprika Vendéglő ☘☘☘ (Beyond
 Central Pest, $$, p. 121)
Pilvax Restaurant ☘☘ (The Inner
 City & Central Pest, $$, p. 114)
Szent Jupát ☘☘ (Central Buda, $$,
 p. 125)
Szép Ilona ☘ (The Buda Hills, $$,
 p. 127)
Tabáni Terasz ☘☘☘ (Central Buda,
 $$, p. 125)
Trófea Grill Étterem ☘☘☘ (Beyond
 Central Pest, $$, p. 121)

Vörös Postakocsi Étterem ☘☘ (The
 Inner City & Central Pest, $$,
 p. 116)

INDIAN

Bombay Express ☘☘ (The Inner City
 & Central Pest, $, p. 117)
Govinda Vegetariánus Étterem ☘
 (The Inner City & Central Pest, $,
 p. 118)
Shalimar ☘☘☘ (The Inner City &
 Central Pest, $$, p. 115)

ITALIAN

Il Terzo Cerchio ☘☘ (The Inner City
 & Central Pest, $$, p. 108)
Olíva Étterem és Pizzéria ☘☘☘ (The
 Inner City & Central Pest, $$,
 p. 113)
Pink Cadillac ☘☘ (The Inner City &
 Central Pest, $, p. 119)
Pomo D'oro ☘☘ (The Inner City &
 Central Pest, $$, p. 114)

INTERNATIONAL

Cotton Club ☘☘☘ (The Inner City
 & Central Pest, $$$, p. 99)
Crazy Dszungel Café ☘☘☘ (The
 Inner City & Central Pest, $$,
 p. 106)
Cream Restaurant and Music Pub
 ☘☘☘ (The Inner City & Central
 Pest, $$, p. 106)
Gresham Kávéház ☘☘ (The Inner
 City & Central Pest, $$$, p. 99)
Karma (The Inner City & Central
 Pest, $$, p. 108)
Kogart Restaurant ☘☘ (Beyond
 Central Pest, $$$, p. 120)
Leroy Café ☘☘☘ (The Inner City &
 Central Pest, $$, p. 110)
Menta Terasz ☘ (The Inner City &
 Central Pest, $$, p. 111)
Mokka ☘☘ (The Inner City &
 Central Pest, $$$, p. 102)
Soul Café ☘☘ (The Inner City &
 Central Pest, $$, p. 115)

JAPANESE

Momotaro Metélt ★★ (The Inner City & Central Pest, $$, p. 112)

Wasabi Running Wok & Sushi Etterem ★★ (The Inner City & Central Pest, $$$, p. 103)

JEWISH

Carmel Restaurant (The Inner City & Central Pest, $$, p. 105)

KOSHER

Hanna's Orthodox Restaurant (The Inner City & Central Pest, $, p. 118)

Salamon Kosher Restaurant (The Inner City & Central Pest, $$, p. 114)

MEDIEVAL

Sir Lancelot ★★ (The Inner City & Central Pest, $$$, p. 102)

MEXICAN

Iguana Bar & Grill ★ (The Inner City & Central Pest, $$, p. 107)

SCOTTISH

Caledonia Scottish Pub and Restaurant ★★ (The Inner City & Central Pest, $$, p. 105)

SPANISH

Két Szerecsen ★★ (The Inner City & Central Pest, $$, p. 109)

Pata Negra Tapas Bar ★★ (The Inner City & Central Pest, $$, p. 113)

TEAHOUSES

Tea Palota (Tea Hall; The Inner City & Central Pest, $, p. 131)

Teaház a Vörös Oroszlánhoz (The Red Lion Teahouse; The Inner City & Central Pest, $, p. 131)

Zöld Teknős Barlangja (Green Turtle Cave; The Inner City & Central Pest, $, p. 131)

VEGETARIAN

Eden ★ (Central Buda, $, p. 125)

Hummus Bar ★★ (The Inner City & Central Pest, $, p. 118)

Napos Oldal Café ★ (The Inner City & Central Pest, $, p. 119)

2 The Inner City & Central Pest

EXPENSIVE

Cotton Club ★★★ *Finds* INTERNATIONAL   I came across this restaurant when I went to the hotel in the same building (see Cotton House Hotel in chapter 5, "Where to Stay in Budapest"). The restaurant is as beautifully decked out as the hotel in a 1920s and 1930s theme focusing on the music of those eras. The period furniture and lighting has been made especially to keep this hideaway looking like a place of nostalgia. The eating area is all nonsmoking, but you can indulge in the adjoining cigar room. I had the garlic soup, which was strong with the stinking rose, just how I love it. I would have preferred a bowl rather than a cup, but that was not an option. The crispy duck legs were served with red cabbage and potato doughnuts. I could not have asked for better, the legs were meaty and crispy. The waiters could not be more accommodating. It was a lucky stumble upon a place that was well worth the cost. The band starts playing at 8:30pm on weekends and continues through the night with a vocalist who pours out the songs of yesteryear.

VI. Jókai u. 26. © 1/354-0886. www.cottonclub.hu. Reservations recommended. Main courses 2,290Ft–6,990 Ft ($13–$38/£6.50–£20). AE, MC, V. Daily noon–1am. Metro: Opera (Yellow line).

Gresham Kávéház ★★ INTERNATIONAL   Taking its name from the historic coffeehouse from 1906 and situated in the Gresham Palace Four Seasons Hotel, this is not a coffeehouse, but a lovely restaurant. The architectural restoration of the hotel has been carried forth into this restaurant, representing its former and original glory.

Where to Dine in Budapest

Alföldi Vendéglő **69**
Angelika Étterem **8**
Articsóka **35**
Aztek Choxolat Café **62**
Bagolyvár **80**
Bajai Halászcsárda **2**
Blue Tomato Pub **23**
Bombay Express **42**
Buena Vista **45**
Café Alibi **67**
Café Csiga **75**
Café Eklektika **33**
Café Kör **38**
Café Noé **61**
Caledonia Scottish Pub and Restaurant **31**
Carmel Pince Restaurant **57**
Central Kávéház **66**
Cotton Club **29**
Crazy Dszungel Café **28**
Cream Restaurant and Music Pub **60**
Eden **7**
Fészek **50**
Firkász **21**
Főzelékfalo Ételbar **32**
Frici Papa Kifőzés **47**
Fröhlich Kóser Cukrászda **55**
Gerbeaud **15**
Gerlóczy Étterem **63**
Govinda Vegetariánus Étterem **17**
Gresham Kávéház **16**
Gundel **81**
Hanna Orthodox Restaurant **53**
Hemingway **13**
Hummus Bar **49**
Iguana Bar and Grill **20**
Il Terzo Cerchio **58**
Karma **44**
Két Szerecsen **46**
Kispipa Vendéglő **51**
Kogart Restaurant **78**
Kőleves Vendéglő **54**
Kossuth Museum Ship Vénhajó Restaurant **14**
Kulacs Étterem **76**
Le Jardin de Paris **9**
Leroy Café **37**

Lukács Cukrászda **77**
M **48**
Marquis de Salade **34**
Mátyás Pince **65**
Menta Terasz **1**
Menza **43**
Mokka **39**
Momotaro Metélt **19**
Mosselen Beer Café **22**
Művész Kávéház **41**
Nagyi Nonstop Palacsintázója **6**
Napos Oldal Café **30**
Old Amsterdam **68**
Olíva Étterem és Pizzéria **36**
Paprika Vendéglő **79**
Pata Negra Tapas Bar **70**
Pilvax Restaurant **64**
Pink Cadillac **73**

(i) Information
· · · **M** Metro
District boundary

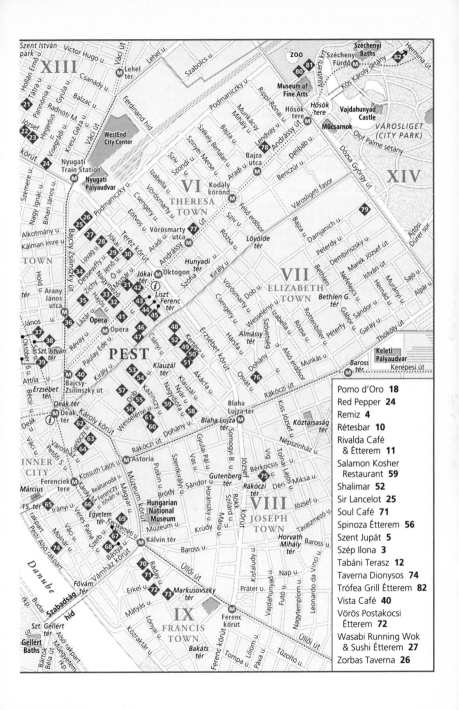

Pomo d'Oro **18**
Red Pepper **24**
Remiz **4**
Rétesbar **10**
Rivalda Café
 & Étterem **11**
Salamon Kosher
 Restaurant **59**
Shalimar **52**
Sir Lancelot **25**
Soul Café **71**
Spinoza Étterem **56**
Szent Jupát **5**
Szép Ilona **3**
Tabáni Terasz **12**
Taverna Dionysos **74**
Trófea Grill Étterem **82**
Vista Café **40**
Vörös Postakocsi
 Étterem **72**
Wasabi Running Wok
 & Sushi Étterem **27**
Zorbas Taverna **26**

It also doubles as the "breakfast room" for hotel guests. We tried the Wiener schnitzel, which is served with potatoes, a tomato and arugula salad. The portions were more than generous for a lunch and cooked to perfection. The Italian chef likes to rotate the menu every 3 months, but they also have a full list of daily special offerings in addition to the regular menu. On our visit, we found a number of seafood offerings. If the decor is not enough, which it should be, the ambience is further enhanced by the view of the Chain Bridge right outside the window. Smart casual attire is required.

V. Roosevelt tér 5–6. ⓒ 1/268-5110. Reservations recommended. Main courses 3,500 Ft–6,200 Ft ($19–$34/ £10–£18). AE, DC, MC, V. Mon–Wed 7:30am–10pm; Thurs–Sat 7:30am–10:30pm; Sun 6:30–10:30pm. Metro: Deák tér (Red line) or tram 2 to Roosevelt tér.

Mátyás Pince ✲✲✲ (Moments) HUNGARIAN TRADITIONAL   Art, history, or music buffs will love this restaurant established in 1904, named for King Mátyás; the myths and legends of his reign grace the walls in magnificent style. The frescoes and stained glass decorating the dining areas were registered as national monuments in 1973. Music is provided by the Lakatos gypsy music dynasty every night but Monday from 7pm until closing, creating an all-around romantic experience. I sampled the cold blackberry soup, rich in creamy fruit flavor. The main entree was King Mátyás's favorite menu of sirloin of beef on a spit, leg of duck, goose liver wrapped in bacon, roast sausage, onion potatoes, steamed cabbage, and letcho. Beautifully presented, every morsel was delectable, and certainly fit for a king or anyone aspiring to eat like one. The service was impeccable. The menu is extensive and the combination of an excellent meal and entertainment makes for a wonderful evening out.

V. Március 15 tér 7-8. ⓒ 1/266-8008. www.cityhotels.hu. Reservations recommended. Main courses 2,700 Ft–7,900 Ft ($15–$43/£7.75–£23). AE, MC, V. Daily 11am–midnight. Metro: Ferenciek tere (Blue line).

Mokka ✲✲ (Moments) INTERNATIONAL   Close to the basilica on Sas utca, Mokka creates a dramatic first impression: dark orange walls, etched bamboo designed glass, masks on the walls, and the horizontal bamboo art over the bar area. Orange glass balls as hanging lights make for a romantic tryst. The menu contains imaginative choices for some of the most interesting combinations of foods I have seen on a Budapest menu. However, the prices reflect all of this and the food doesn't always justify the ambience or the selections offered. I started with the hot paprika cream soup with spinach chips; my friend had the salmon salad. Excellent portions and flavors satisfied us until the entrees. The chicken in lime leaves is served with shitake stew and Thai lasagna, while the other entree was vanilla marinated chicken with chestnut cream and a green apple pancake. The vanilla chicken was overcooked and dry. The pancake was really green, but also dry. The most inviting part of the meal was the dollop of chestnut cream, which had to be used as a moistener for both the chicken and pancake. The menu changes seasonally due to the chef's commitment to using the freshest ingredients available.

V. Sas u. 4. ⓒ 1/328-0081. www.mokkarestaurant.hu. Reservations recommended. Main courses 2,480 Ft–8,580 Ft ($14–$47/£7–£25). AE, MC, V. Daily noon–midnight. Metro: Bajcsy-Zsilinszky út (Blue line) or Deák Ferenc tér (all lines).

Sir Lancelot ✲✲ (Kids) MEDIEVAL   Plan for a knight of excitement when you enter this medieval cellar venue decorated with stone, stained glass, and lion-head fountains. Eat as in times of yore with a knife and spoon, but no fork; eating with your hands is encouraged. Candle lighting and flute music add to the atmosphere as costumed servers place humungous dishes of food such as Saint Grill, Virtue of Womanfolk, or Basket of Merlin before you. As you are eating, don't be surprised if a sword fight breaks out between two rival knights or a fire-eater decides to dine on flames right next to you while a belly dancer is shimmering down the aisle. Set menus are available for three, four, or six people, fixed knight's meals are for one person, and individual menu items are available for your choosing. No matter which you choose, have a big appetite ready and be open for the excitement that follows.

VI. Podmaniczky u. 14. ℂ 1/302-4456. www.sirlancelot.hu. Set menu 15,990 Ft–27,990 Ft ($87–$151/£46–£80); knight's meal 3,990 Ft–4,690 Ft ($22–$25/£11–£13); entree 1,990 Ft–4,290 Ft ($11–$23/£5.75–£12). AE, DC, MC, V. Daily noon–1am.

Wasabi Running Wok & Sushi Etterem 🎄🎄 JAPANESE This is a new and unusual concept for an all-you-can-eat restaurant. The dining area is one long room tastefully set out with one wall of all exposed rock, while the other wall has large windows with Japanese-style amber-simulated paper lantern lights. Tables can seat up to four, so larger parties have to separate; they are placed on either side of the restaurant. Down the center of the room separating the tables is a 25m (82-ft.) two-level, glass-encased, metal conveyer belt. On the upper conveyor, all hot dishes will flow by you, while on the lower level, the cold dishes. Each section is temperature controlled to keep the food the right temperature. By each table, there are sliding doors, so when a tasty morsel gets to you, you open the door and snatch it. You have to be friends with your dining companions, since competition can be fierce for certain selections. In the cold section, every three items is sushi, while the others are a variety of desserts and cold salads. The hot selections include meats and other fish. For the best and first selection, ask to be seated on the right side closest to the kitchen to get first pick of what the chefs are setting out. Sixty wok entrees and eight sushi rolls are offered, but drinks are not included.

VI. Podmaniczky u. 21. ℂ 1/374-0008. Lunch 3,790 Ft ($21/£11); dinner and all day on weekends 4,790 Ft ($26/£14). Children 3–12, 40% off. MC, V. Daily lunch 11:30am–5pm; dinner 5–11:30pm. Tram: 4 or 6 Nyugati.

MODERATE

Alföldi Kisvendéglő 🎄🎄 HUNGARIAN TRADITIONAL Alföldi is named after Hungary's flat plain region and is paneled with horizontal brown wood-stripped walls with assorted old plates above, creating a homey country feel. The dining room offers wooden booths or tables with traditional country hand-embroidered tablecloths and placemats in folk designs. Each table has a basket of spicy homemade *pogácsas* (a type of biscuit), and you will be charged for each one eaten, but worth the nominal charge. The veal Bakony style with gnocchi-like pasta had the same sauce as the chicken paprika, a sour cream sauce with paprika. Both were delicious, served without any flare, in a down-home country manner. The kitchen closes an hour before the restaurant.

V. Kecskeméti u. 4. ℂ 1/267-0224. No reservations needed. Main courses 1,230 Ft–4,100 Ft ($6.65–$22/£3.50–£12). MC, V. Daily 11am–11pm. Metro: Astoria (Red line) or tram 47 or 49 to Kálvin tér.

Articsóka 🎄 HUNGARIAN CONTEMPORARY This establishment looks like it was touched by King Midas; almost everything is painted gold with few visual distractions like the crystal chandeliers in the main room. However, when a restaurant is empty on a Friday night at 8pm, the decor is even more obvious than when crowded with lively diners. Articsóka is a restaurant, a cafe, and a roof terrace. With the moon full, our party of four could not resist eating on the roof terrace, where we where the only diners during our entire visit, making the service of two waiters exemplary. The menu is limited to 11 entrees of Hungarian dishes with a couple of vegetarian dishes included. Our waiter stated they were out of most wines on their list, but would have more the following week. I started with the goat cheese soup with sun-dried tomato ciabatta and my friend started with the pear soup with ginger and lamb-liver dumplings. Both were so mouthwatering delicious, we actually could have screamed from the rooftop. We eagerly anticipated the entrees, but we should have left then and relished the memory of the soup. We had the pasta with smoked beef covered in paprika chili served with aubergine and pepperoni and the polenta with roasted aubergine served with tomato spinach ragout. The entrees were not even close to our expectations promised by the descriptions.

VI. Zichy Jenő u. 17. ℂ 1/302-7757. www.articsoka.hu. Reservations recommended, especially for the roof terrace. Main courses 2,100 Ft–4,400 Ft ($11–$24/£6.00–£13). AE, MC, V. Daily noon–midnight. Metro: Opera (Yellow line).

Blue Tomato Pub ★★★ HUNGARIAN CONTEMPORARY   Don't let the "Pub" in the name fool you, this is a serious place for treating your taste buds with tasty morsels. The dark woody walls are plastered with old Americana and European advertisements, creating a cozy relaxing atmosphere. The smoking section is fully segregated from the nonsmokers, a real plus in Hungary. The corn soup with bacon and almond slivers tempted me for a starter. It gave me a new appreciation for corn. Thick, creamy, and with the chunks of bacon and lots of almonds, it was bowl-licking delicious. Ordering rib steak with fried onions and oven-roasted potatoes turned out to be a pleasant surprise. The steak was pounded thin and covered with a mound of thin crispy onion rings. A fellow diner had walnut-coated, stuffed fried chicken breast. The only thing we regretted was not having come here before now. Fantastic food at reasonable prices with good service is a winning combination.

XIII. Pannónia u. 5–7. ℂ 1/339-8099. www.bluetomato.hu. Reservations recommended. Main courses 1,390 Ft–3,900 Ft ($7.50–$21/£4–£11). MC, V. Mon–Sat 11am–4am; Sun noon–midnight. Tram: 4 or 6 Jászai Mari tér.

Buena Vista ★★ HUNGARIAN CONTEMPORARY   Reportedly this restaurant is named for the famous Buena Vista Social Club that performed at this location before this restaurant opened. Perhaps the success of the band has lent its success to its namesake. This is one of the oldest restaurants on this square (Liszt Ferenc tér), and it has thrived for over 7 years. The interior, brick and stone on multiple levels, is not that memorable; it could be any other restaurant in the city. What makes this restaurant stand out from the crowd is its service and food. The breast of pullet with caramelized peaches (menu states apricots) with rucola mashed potatoes or the breast of turkey stuffed with quince, rolled in almonds and served with saffron raison rice are both winners. In the warm months, the outdoor seating is the only place to be to see or be seen by the many people walking up and down the tér, plus there is no air-conditioning inside. Due to its longevity and outstanding reputation, this is one of the most popular hotspots in the area.

VI. Liszt Ferenc tér 4–5. ℂ 1/344-6303. www.buena-vista.hu. Reservations recommended. Main courses 1,650 Ft–4,400 Ft ($8.90–$24/£4.70–£13). AE, MC, V. Daily 10am–11pm. Metro: Opera (Yellow line).

Café Eklektika ★★ 𝘝𝘢𝘭𝘶𝘦 HUNGARIAN CONTEMPORARY   When a beloved restaurant moves from one location to another, but along the way changes from a funky, zany, but comfortable interior to one of a more traditional style, you have to wonder if the romance is over. Well, for this restaurant, it did not happen; the loyal diners followed, accepted the new do, and got over it, because the food is as good as ever. With tables and booths, no longer sofas and overstuffed chairs, the mellow mood is still created by the soothing vocals with a cabaret feel serenading in the background, the monthly changing artwork on the walls, and the dependably excellent service. We return for the chicken breaded in hazelnuts with the almond potato balls and wine steamed pears. Sometimes we are seduced by the rosé duck breast with mashed potatoes and cinnamon plum ragout. Besides the menu offerings, there are weekly specials on a blackboard. Outside seating is available in good weather, but inside you will be treated to free unlimited Wi-Fi, for the price of a coffee. No one will rush you out; this is a place to call home away from home.

V. Nagymező 30. (C) **1/266-1226.** Reservations for dinner recommended. Main courses 1,390 Ft–2,890 Ft ($7.50–$16/£3.95–£8.20). Cash only. Mon–Fri 10am–midnight; Sat–Sun noon–midnight.

Café Kör ⊛ HUNGARIAN CONTEMPORARY
This centrally located restaurant around the corner from the basilica, transforms Hungarian cuisine into au courant recipes. Though it is very popular, we attribute this to location and marketing rather than to the atmosphere or food. The decor is simplistic with stucco-colored walls and low lighting, situated within one large room; the tables and chairs can get cramped when the dining room is full, which is often. The waitstaff is extensive, so service is excellent, regardless of the size of the crowd. We ordered the apple soup for a starter. It was refreshing on a balmy evening, but not overly exciting; it tasted like apple juice with cream added. Our entrees were worthy of some praise. We ordered the chicken breast in hot caramel sauce with sesame seeds and potato croquettes and salmon in Compari sauce. Both the chicken and the salmon were moist and full of flavor. The apricots on the chicken looked too perfect to be fresh, which for the prices and the season, one would expect. Nevertheless, the food was tasty and satisfying, to the point that there was no room for dessert.

V. Sas u. 17. (C) **1/311-0053.** Reservations recommended. Main courses 1,880 Ft–4,190 Ft ($10–$23/£5.35–£12). No credit cards. Mon–Sat 10am–10pm. Metro: Bajcsy-Zsilinszky út (Blue line) or Deák Ferenc tér (all lines).

Caledonia Scottish Pub and Restaurant ⊛⊛ SCOTTISH
If whiskey comes to mind when you think of Scotland, this pub will not disappoint with its 40 varieties of the finest malts. The wood-paneled walls and soft lighting provide a relaxing atmosphere to enjoy a drop or to have a fine meal. We especially enjoy their all-day Scottish breakfast featuring a fried egg, sausages, fried mushrooms, gammon steak, beans, tomatoes, black pudding, and toast. Okay, we leave the black pudding on the plate, but the rest makes for a great brunch outing. Other selections are available, like the Scottish salmon salad or for the real adventurer, haggis. With the large screen televisions, this is a most popular place to watch soccer games and have rowdy fun times, so if this is not your thing, avoid it during these times. For a larger group, reserve a table on the mezzanine to eat and enjoy a lofty feel overlooking the main dining room and the goings-on below. If this has not convinced you, there is also free Wi-Fi and a small Scottish gift shop.

VI. Mozsar u. 9. (C) **1/311-7611.** Reservations recommended. Main courses 1,090 Ft–2,990 Ft ($5.90–$16/£3.10–£8.50). AE, DC, MC, V. Sun–Thurs 11am–midnight; Fri and Sat 11am–1am; kitchen closes at 10pm. Free Wi-Fi. Metro: Oktogon (Yellow line).

Carmel Restaurant JEWISH
Though this establishment is not kosher, they have Jewish and international cuisine on the menu. When you enter, go down the stairs to find the restaurant as no one will greet you to direct you. The restaurant, which opened in 1987, is a long room with an outdated motif, probably the original and in dire need of renovations. However, all of the smiling faces of the diners who were leaving as we entered gave the impression that decor is secondary to being well fed. The

Jewish meals are marked by numbers on the menu, with vegetarian options as well. During the summer on Thursday nights, you can be entertained by the Klezmer concerts held here; there is an entrance fee, but you can deduct 5% from your meal. This is one of the popular dining spots for Jewish tours in the city.

VII. Kazinczy u. 31. *C* 1/322-1834. Fax 1/461-0024. www.carmel.hu. Reservation recommended. Main courses 1,400 Ft–4,000 Ft ($7.60–$22/£4–£11). Daily noon–11pm; closed Sat in summer. AE, MC, V. Metro: Astoria (Red line) or Deák (all lines).

Crazy Dszungel Café ★★★ (Kids) INTERNATIONAL

It may be perfect for kids, but this restaurant packs in the adults. It consists of several rooms, each with its own identity and decor. There is the jungle room, the savannah room, the ocean room, and even a pirates' room. Throughout, there is a glass walkway with different objects to set the mood of the room. Seashells and sand are used in the ocean room for example. The pirates' room has life-size pirate dolls climbing ship's ropes and locked in the brig. The menu is equally inventive with a page devoted to each theme and menu items named accordingly. With all of this fun, we really thought the food would be a letdown, but we could not be more wrong. The food was excellent and plentiful; two of us had doggie bags when we left filled with enough for a full lunch the next day. We highly recommend the Yellow Threat, a creamy garlic soup and Slouch Dromedary, roast ostrich in King Bolete sauce with puff pastry. Why dromedary for an ostrich? Beats us. The pork stuffed with feta cheese and prune was also outstanding.

VI. Jókai u. 30. *C* 1/302-4003. Reservations recommended. Main courses 1,250 Ft–3,290 Ft ($6.75–$18/ £3.55–£9.35). AE, MC, V. Daily noon–1am. Tram: 4 or 6 to Nyugati.

Cream Restaurant and Music Pub ★★★ (Finds) INTERNATIONAL

We were pleasantly shocked when entering here. The wide circular staircase leading up to a mezzanine with cafe-style chairs separates the smoking from the nonsmoking sections of the main floor of this elegantly decorated restaurant. The cream-colored walls are trimmed in white, but giving color and character to the dining rooms are the high columns with burnt orange fiber and the wooden finials on top. The walls are decorated with original art by international artists on a rotating basis. Downstairs is a huge music pub and dance floor with different music genres on different nights, but it doesn't intrude in the dining area. Soft jazz plays in the background allowing conversation or a romantic dinner. Our dish of beef steak with spiced butter and polenta in a sage merlot sauce, served with sautéed vegetables was artistically presented and mouthwateringly tasty. The lemon sorbet with pink grapefruit looked picture-perfect with fresh lemony zest. The menu has a generous selection for all tastes including vegetarians. A cigar and pipe room is also available for those who just want to relax with a good smoke.

VII. Dohány u. 28. *C* 1/413-6997. Reservations recommended. Main courses 1,690 Ft–3,890 Ft ($9.15–$21/£4.80–£11). AE, MC, V. Restaurant daily 11am–midnight; pub 11am–4am. Free Wi-Fi. Metro: Blaha Lujza (Red line).

Fészek ★★ (Value) HUNGARIAN TRADITIONAL

We walked past this restaurant dozens of times, before realizing it was a dining place. Fészek, which means nest is situated in the center of an old grand building that has seen better days. The building's exterior entry courtyard displays photos of famous Hungarian entertainers; this historic building has been popular with artists of all types for the last century. Once you traipse through a rundown lobby and enter the interior courtyard do you realize there is a restaurant here. The inner ring has tables both in a covered circular terrace area as well as the center exposed courtyard, where 100-year-old chestnut trees canopy the tables. Meals are plentiful in the Hungarian tradition. The corn soup is excellent with a thin layer of toasted cheese covering the top. The veal paprika is creamy and delicious served with homemade Hungarian cheese noodles. In the winter, portable heaters are used to make the dining experience a year-round dining adventure. Because of the quality and quantity, it is often filled with Hungarian diners, so be sure to reserve a table.

VII. Kertész u. 36 (corner of Dob u.). ⓒ **1/322-6043.** Reservations recommended. Main courses 1,550 Ft–3,950 Ft ($8.40–$21/£4.40–£11). No credit cards. Daily noon–midnight. Tram: 4 or 6 to Király utca.

Firkász ⚑ HUNGARIAN CONTEMPORARY   The name means scribbler in English and based on the decor and speaking with the waiter, it refers to journalists who scribble their notes. The walls are wallpapers with old newspapers from the early 20th century and these are accented with old typewriters; clocks; shadowboxes of old pens, erasers, and pencil sharpeners; and other memorabilia of yesteryear. Wine bottles litter the shelves all around, which is appropriate for the vast menu selection of vino. We tried the cheese soup and the crispy pork with cabbage. The soup was limp with some cheese flavor, and we have had much better at half the cost. A potato side was extra, so we settled for the entree only. The pork slices were plentiful, but dry. The cabbage was the saving grace for swallowing. A fellow diner ordered the steak, which was tough and difficult to cut. Though a third diner ordered the pork medallions and was extremely satisfied. There were more tourists than locals during our visit, which with these prices is understandable. Seated close to the piano player made it difficult to carry on a conversation, but with the room being small, there were no other options at the time.

XIII. Tátra u. 18. ⓒ **1/450-1118.** Reservations recommended. Main courses 1,890 Ft–4,900 Ft ($10–$27/£5.40–£14). MC, V. Daily noon–midnight. Tram: 4 or 6 to Jászai Mari tér.

Gerlóczy Kávéház ⚑⚑⚑ *Value* HUNGARIAN CONTEMPORARY   Two of us had coffee here once by accident, when caught unexpectedly in a sudden summer storm. Enjoying the atmosphere, we vowed to return. When we did return, we did so without reservations. The tables in front were occupied, and the host noticed our dilemma; he appeared with another table and set it with two chairs. This was the start of a perfect dinner, which included a half portion of two different ciabattas: pepperoni and walnuts. To accompany this, we had a plate of sliced tomatoes with mozzarella cheese. The smoked sheep cheese slices with grilled peppers and garlic were enormous, think slices grilled to a crusty coat, but soft on the inside. They left little room for the salad that came with it. The five huge pieces of grilled filet mignon of pork, was served with boiled potatoes, cut into chunks and formed into a ball with Swiss chard interlaced. Both dishes had us nabbing at each other's plate with sounds of pleasure in between, neither were overly spiced, allowing the natural flavors to express their character, making it sumptuous. The waiter returned to check on us enough times to provide great service, but not enough to be disruptive. Thank goodness for sudden storms.

V. Gerlóczy u. 1. ⓒ **1/235-0953.** Reservations recommended. Cold main courses 890 Ft–1,980 Ft ($4.80–$11/£2.55–£5.65); hot main courses 1,680 Ft–4,200 Ft ($9.10–$23/£4.80–£12). MC, V. Mon–Fri 7am–11pm; Sat–Sun 8am–11pm. Metro: Deák tér (Red line).

Iguana Bar & Grill ⚑ *Kids* MEXICAN   Colorfully decorated and always buzzing with activity, this is a popular restaurant where you might have trouble finding a seat. Opened in 1997, Iguana continues to attract those who are looking for good Mexican food, though this is closer to Tex-Mex than authentic Mexican. Over the years, the quality of the food has sometimes faltered, but if you have a hunger for Mexican food

---

Fun Fact Cows and Pigs on the Menu

Hungary has its own breed of cows and pigs that you will see on some menus. Magyar *szürke szarvasmarha* or grey cow is a breed that was brought to the Carpathian basin in the 9th century. The Hungarian Mangalica pig breed, characterized by its long curly hair was developed in the 19th century. It doesn't need any special breeding or feeding, but has fatty meat making it ideal for sausage and salami, but sometimes it is served in cooked dishes. The other pork you will find served in restaurants is wild boar, a little gamier tasting than domestic pork.

---

like we do, it will fill the bill. This dining spot is a real hangout for Budapest expatriates, and also acts as a place to meet for the younger crowd. It is family-friendly, but families with young children are better off going in the earlier hours. The decor includes old Mexican posters and Diego Rivera reproductions. The menu consists of Mexican classics, including a selection of quesadillas, chilies, fajitas, burritos, and enchiladas. Jenö's Quesadilla is my favorite. The enticing fajitas made of marinated strips of tenderloin, chicken, or shrimp are grilled on a sizzling hot iron platter with onions and peppers. If you are a mole aficionado, you will be disappointed, so stick with other choices. The ample selection of vegetarian dishes offered will not make anyone feel left out. The restaurant does have special parties for Mexican holidays. Try the Iguana Beer, made especially for the restaurant by a small Csepel Island brewery.

V. Zóltán u. 16 ⓒ 1/331-4352. www.iguana.hu. Reservations recommended. Main courses 1,590 Ft–3,990 Ft ($8.60–$22/£4.50–£11) AE, MC, V. Daily 11:30am–midnight. Metro: Kossuth tér (Red line).

Il Terzo Cerchio 🖈🖈 ITALIAN   The restaurant's name, which means the third circle, has this inside the menu: "In the 3rd level of Dante's Inferno, gluttony was punished with acid rain. In our hell, tasty and fresh food is the punishment." If this is punishment, punish us on a regular basis. The oversize windows, the whitewashed walls, the brick concave ceiling, and the exposed kitchen creates a real Tuscanny feel, making you want to cozy up with some comfort food. We especially love the gnocchi with gorgonzola, pecorino, and cream sauce; the pizzas have the wonderful thin crusts of our childhood, and the spinach cooked with garlic and olive oil will get any kid to eat their veggies. But we have to confess: We have been here a number of times and have not had a bad meal yet. Pizzas are cooked in a brick oven and some of the cooks are imported from Italy along with the ingredients they use. No matter how crowded it happens to be, you still feel the intimacy of those you are with; the ceilings absorb the sound from those around you. The waitstaff are attentive without being overbearing and they all help each other, so you may have three or four people delivering your drinks, food, or the replacement fork you dropped.

VII. Dohány u. 40. ⓒ 1/354-0788. Reservation recommended. Main courses 1,750 Ft–4,400 Ft ($9.45–$24/£5–£13); pizza 1,750 Ft–2,400 Ft ($9.45–$13/£5–£6.85). MC, V. Daily noon–11:30pm. Metro: Blaha Lujza (Red line).

Karma INTERNATIONAL   Trying to create a space of peace and tranquility that this restaurant suggests in its menu, is difficult to accomplish when there is contemporary music blasting from the speakers, not the soft Mediterranean music promised. The interior is beautifully decorated in a mix of Indian and Asian styles, with Buddha looking over the serving of meals. They have a large patio where every table is full in clement weather, but not always with diners, but with those drinking. We made the mistake of trying to get a table without a reservation, only to be met with rudeness by the host and the server. Seated right inside by the door under the speakers was traumatic, not relaxing. Our cream of corn soup with tortillas and chili cream cheese was smooth and rich in flavor as was the veal ragout soup with asparagus and fussili. However, the duck breast in cognac cherries served with cabbage mixed with bacon was beyond disappointing, being dry, with no sauce and not a cherry to be found. The Indian turkey stew served with Nan bread did get rave reviews, being extra spicy and served piping hot. However, the ambience is lost if the service is poor and the music is not in harmony with the atmosphere.

VI. Liszt Ferenc tér 11. ℂ 1/413-6764. www.karmabudapest.com. Reservations recommended, especially for outdoor seating. Main courses 1,650 Ft–2,950 Ft ($8.90–$16/£4.70–£8.40). MC, V. Daily 10am–1am. Metro: Oktogon (Yellow line).

Két Szerecsen (Two Brothers) ★★ (Kids) SPANISH

This restaurant opened in 2000, and only gets better with time. In 2006, it underwent a dramatic remodel and expansion of the interior. Now with an equally large smoking and nonsmoking room, each is beautifully decorated with deep orange walls and pounded metal lamps with multicolored glass pieces dangling. What may be disturbing are the many old advertisement signs and posters with two black men. We learned that two black men from Africa had a coffeeshop here over 100 years ago, thus the restaurant's name and decor is a tribute to them. If you are in the mood for tapas, there are 13 choices. Just a couple of choices could make a complete meal. The regular menu is not extensive, but there are a number of daily specials that are imaginative. One example is the lasagna with peach and duck ragout, which we tried. The pasta layers were filled with julienned carrots, peach chunks, and leaf spinach, covered with a light duck sauce. Our other choice was the chicken breast with pesto and mozzarella with safron risotto. The chicken was moist and the risotto was al dente with flecks of parsley. The portions are very generous. We were impressed with the child special, a small portion of a menu item and a dessert. Sitting outdoors under the huge tree is relaxing and although it is on a trolleybus route, there are no fumes and little noise from the electric buses.

VI. Nagymező u. 14. ℂ 1/343-1984. www.ketszerecsen.hu. Reservations recommended. Main courses 1,390 Ft–3,990 Ft ($7.50–$22/£3.95–£11); tapas 670 Ft–1,590 Ft ($3.60–$8.60£1.90–£4.50); child menu 1,100 Ft ($5.95/£3.15). AE, DC, MC, V. Daily 8am–1am. Metro: Opera (Yellow line).

Kispipa Vendéglő ★ (Value) HUNGARIAN TRADITIONAL

Located on a residential street in Erzsébetváros, at the far edge of the old Jewish district, Kispipa (Little Pipe) is a cozy, well-lit establishment. Vintage Hungarian poster advertisements, which were probably new when hung up, decorate the cream-colored walls. A pianist played vintage Cole Porter melodies and other familiar tunes. Zsolnay china graces the tables as do fresh flowers, and paper napkins. Go figure. The cold lemon soup with a dollop of whipped cream was refreshingly tart and chilled for a hot evening in a hotter restaurant with no air-conditioning. The menu is extensive, with wild-game dishes the house specialty; vegetarians will find it lacking. We chose the stuffed cabbage with pork chops (which was actually minced pork with cabbage and tomato sauce), and the duck breast, which was lean and grilled to perfection with generous portions of quince and three saucer-size potato pancakes. At the end of the delightful evening, we were told the credit card machine wasn't functioning; running to the ATM did not even work off the soup, the portions are so generous. At lunch, they have six fixed-meal selections and all are priced at 4,220 Ft ($22/£12), a bit much for lunch.

VII. Akácfa u. 38. ⓒ **1/342-2587.** Reservations recommended. Main courses 1,160 Ft–4,560 Ft ($6.30–$25/ £3.30–£13). AE, MC, V. Mon–Sat noon–1am. Metro: Oktogon (Yellow line).

Kossuth Museum Ship Vénhajó (Old Ship) ✮✮ *Kids* HUNGARIAN CONTEM-PORARY   One hundred years old and one of the last remaining paddle boats in Hungary, this old ship serves as both a museum (opened in 1986) and a restaurant (added during 2004 remodeling). Docked on the Pest side directly across from the Castle and facing the Széchenyi Chain Bridge, it has the most romantic and spectacular view when the sun goes down and the castle and bridge are lit. Of the boat restaurants docked along the same waterway, this one is at the forefront of the three—giving it a better view—and it is not nearly as expensive. In good weather, request a table on the outer and upper deck. The turkey breast was smothered in delicious camembert cheese, but the chicken Caesar with iceberg lettuce was a disappointment. Eating while the boat is swaying from side to side may not be for everyone, but we found it added to the charm of being onboard a historic boat. It does come out of dock at times for dinner cruises.

V. Vigadó 2. ⓒ **1/411-0942.** www.europahajo.hu. Reservations recommended, especially for outdoor seating. Main courses 1,350 Ft–4,350 Ft ($7.30–$24/£3.85–£12). MC, V. Daily 11am–11pm. Tram 2: Eötvös.

Kulacs Etterem ✮ HUNGARIAN TRADITIONAL   If you don't have sensory overload after being seated, you will enjoy the food at this old-fashioned restaurant. They have filled all nooks and crannies with decor that resembles an old-fashioned country home. The back wall behind the Rezsö Seres Gypsy band has a large mural. Our young waiter was a little pushy trying to get us to order more than we wanted, but I settled on the chicken pie with oven-roasted potatoes. The pie was really two layers of fried cheese with a piece of chicken between, not what was expected, but delicious nevertheless. The band plays nightly, but they seemed to wait for more than our group of four to start. Once they do, they roam to the tables, so we asked them to leave. When it was time to pay, the credit card machine was not working, but became operational after we claimed not to have the cash to cover the bill. In spite of the games, the food is well worth repeated visits.

VII. Osváth u. 11. ⓒ **1/322-3611.** Reservations recommended. Main courses 1,100 Ft–4,300 Ft ($6–$23/£3–£12). AE, MC, V. Daily noon–midnight. Metro: Blaha Lujza (Red line).

Leroy Café ✮✮✮ *Moments* INTERNATIONAL   When a restaurant can have six satisfied patrons at one table, it's a sign they're doing something right. We highly recommend the lobster cream soup with spinach gnocchi and asparagus. Chicken breast on eggplant with goat cheese was moistened by the Dijon-saffron mustard dressing. The lasagna also received rave reviews as did every other dish. The cafe's six separate locations are decorated differently, giving a unique touch to each, though the menus are similar. The restaurant at the basilica has most unusual lighting; large candelabras of metal with reflector lights shining on them to make yet larger shadows on the deep green walls and ceiling. Lighting was sufficient, yet warm and romantic at the same time. High-back carved wooden chairs added a touch of charm to the overall surroundings. With excellent service from a very attentive waiter, the evening was an excellent way to spend time with friends.

V. Sas u. 11. ⓒ **1/266-5248.** www.leroy.hu. Reservations recommended. Main courses 2,480Ft–5,400Ft ($13–$29/ £7.05–£15). AE, MC, V. Daily 11am–midnight. Metro: Bajcsy-Zsilinszky út (Blue line) or Deák Ferenc tér (all lines).

M ⭐⭐⭐ HUNGARIAN CONTEMPORARY   This quiet and unassuming restaurant can be easily overlooked, especially with the simple name that does not require a large display and only two tables at the street entrance. Once inside the door, there are only three more tables, but others are upstairs. Within minutes of being seated, you will be welcomed with glasses of fresh lemonade and a basket of potato bread with sunflower seeds. The menu is handwritten on white butcher paper, which is practical since the menu changes completely every Tuesday. It would be sinful to whet your appetite with the choices available, because they may not reappear in the future, but the chef does prefer poultry dishes. The chef and waitstaff stop by the table to make conversation and offer suggestions, and they will modify any menu item to one's liking if possible. The decor grabs your attention and holds it until the meal is served. Every inch of the walls and ceiling are covered with brown wrapping paper with black line drawings of furnishings found in a home. There are piles of books, lamps, a parrot in a cage, vases, a phone on a stand, and the ceiling even has a drawing of a fan with a real cord hanging from it. This place has a warm, creative atmosphere to simulate being in someone's home and the hospitality was excellent, as was the food. You can check the website for the week's menu. Reserve for outside or on the main level in warm weather; upstairs is hot.

VII. Kertész 48. ② **1/342-8991.** Reservations recommended. Main courses 1,550 Ft–2,450 Ft ($8.35–$13/ £4.40–£6.90). No credit cards. Daily noon–midnight. Tram: 4 or 6 Király u.

Marquis de Salade ⭐⭐⭐ (Moments) AZERBAIJAN   We discovered this restaurant on our first trip to Budapest in 1998 and loved it then. After 10 years, it has only improved. The entrance is on the street level, but the restaurant is downstairs in a cavelike atmosphere, decorated with Asian rugs on the walls and ceiling. Beyond the first dining area, there is another room for a group of six and yet another room in the back suitable for two for a romantic interlude. The latter is more like a Pasha's den with low seating and lots of cushions. Our group started with the Marquis's salads, which is a sampler platter of six different salads. Along with the bread, this about constituted a diversely sumptuous meal, but we plunged forward with entrees; the Adajab sandal, a luscious lamb stew cooked with eggplant, tomato, and potato cooked in a clay pot was excellent. Another entree, eggplant stuffed with walnuts and other spices had all of us savoring the flavors and begging for more. This is a small intimate restaurant so the service is impeccable.

VI. Hajós u. 43. ② **1/302-4086.** www.marquisdesalade.hu. Reservations recommended. Main courses 2,500 Ft–3,900 Ft ($14–$21/£7.10–£11). No credit cards. Daily 11am–1am. Metro: Arany János (Blue line); bus: 70 or 78 to Bajcsy-Zsilinszky út.

Menta Terasz ⭐ INTERNATIONAL   A multisensory experience for sure, hot on the food scene, and as they claim, it is like visiting the eccentric relative's bizarre villa home, but this is a good thing. The dining room is done up in classy wallpaper with unusual dangly lamps creating a New Orleans feel. The garden has beautiful handmade wooden chairs and tables with Italian mosaic panels gracing the walls. Downstairs is the music area where live performances are held, until the DJ takes over at 10pm. On the rooftop, there are the colonial gardens with water lilies and lounge chairs for relaxing under the bamboo roof. It is a shame that all of this engaging decor is undermined by mediocre food. The cream of broccoli soup tasted like mushroom and though it was green, there was no hit of a green veggie in it. The asparagus soup was too salty to eat. Bravo to the waiter who showed concern about why it was untouched, a first in Budapest. The entrees were enjoyable, not served hot, and not something that will necessarily draw us back.

II. Margit krt. 14. ✆ 1/336-1250. Reservations recommended. Main courses 1,290 Ft–3,200 Ft ($7–$17/£3.70–£9.10). AE, MC, V. Sun–Wed 11am–2am; Thurs–Sat 11am–4am. Tram: 4 or 6 Margit Híd, Budai Hídfő, then walk around the corner.

Menza ✿ HUNGARIAN CONTEMPORARY   Rumors have it that this restaurant is supposed to be reminiscent of cafeterias of yesteryear. Decorated in a '60s and '70s retro style, the orange, green, and brown decor, with emphasis on orange, takes some getting used to, especially the walls that are covered with the pale brown and green oversize flowers. The outdoor seating is the most popular, perhaps to avoid the decor; even in colder months, there are heaters to utilize the space. Menu choices are varied, so all diners will have choices, plus there is a daily menu that changes weekly. We started with the cream corn soup; the pureed corn was slightly sweet and delicious. The *gulyás* soup was prepared traditionally with nice chunks of beef and vegetables in the broth. Steak wrapped in bacon with eggs seemed more appealing than the steak with two fried eggs sitting on top that appeared, but it was an interesting and tasty mix of flavors due to the accompaniment of the stewed tomatoes served with it. The Chicken a la Menza was a casserole-type dish mixing large slices of chicken with mushrooms, french fries, and cheese, all topped with a broiled camembert cheese crust on top. The servers are exceptionally attentive and aware of guest needs, without hovering. Considered a yuppie hangout, this restaurant has continued to be popular with all types of people in all age groups.

VI. Liszt Ferenc tér 2. ✆ 1/413-1482. www.menza.co.hu. Reservations recommended. Main courses 1,290 Ft–3,390 Ft ($7–$18/£3.70–£9.65). AE, MC, V. Daily 10am–midnight. Metro: Oktogon (Yellow line).

Momotaro Metélt ✿✿ JAPANESE   Metélt means noodle, but the waiter at this restaurant told us that the name is Japanese for the peach boy, based on a Japanese legend. According to our server, the menu is a combination of Japanese and Chinese. Regardless of its name, this once huge restaurant has shrunk in size, reserving its large banquet hall for special groups only. Now it is cozy and simple with plain wooden tables and stools in a nonsmoking environment. The tangy steamed pork dumplings, two in a serving, are large enough to share without feeling cheated. Shanghai pork rolls are hot and greasy, but with fresh oil, so you can taste the combined flavors of the meat and vegetables stuffed inside. Entrees like the Eight Delicacies combine chicken, pork, and tofu, with vegetables and peanuts. Beef with broccoli in oyster sauce has generous portions of beef and broccoli. The fried rice was cooked with shredded cabbage, not at all greasy, but light and an excellent side dish. No one will leave here hungry; the portions were sufficient to ask for a take-away container. The telling tale is the number of Asian diners during our meal; we were among the minority. There are many selections available at the lower end of the price range with specialty items at the higher end of the range.

V. Széchenyi u. 16 near Nádor u. ✆ 1/269-3802. Main courses 1,500 Ft–4,500 Ft ($8–$24/£4.30–£13). No credit cards. Daily 11am–10pm. Metro: Kossuth Lajos tér (Red line).

Mosselen Belgian Beer Café ✿✿✿ *Finds* DUTCH   Mosselen means mussel in Flemish, but before you push the door open, you cannot help but notice the names of different famous beer brands etched into the glass panels on the doors. What also will not escape your attention are the number of "Best of Budapest" award stickers on the other glass panels. Once you step into this L-shaped restaurant, the world around you changes to a Belgium feeling. The dark wood bar has to be huge to accommodate the 10 different beers on tap, plus the further selection of over 50 others. Each beer is distinctively served in a glass appropriate for the brand, with a coaster to match and the prices widely range from 790 Ft to 5,300 Ft ($4.30–$29/£2.25–£15) for an 11 oz glass. This restaurant takes a serious view of beer. The wainscoted walls of similarly deep rich wood continuing around the bar continue the motif above. The beige wallpaper complements the wood, but was aged for a distressed look. The numerous old metal advertisements, bottles, pictures, and stenciled words are reminiscent of an old-time pub. Cabinets of old beer bottles and an antiques store, add to the homey atmosphere. The menu has an interesting selection of fish dishes from tuna steak to prawns, but meat and vegetarian options are also available. One warm starter that could substitute for dessert is the hot raisin creme soup with cinnamon and an almond cookie. Entrees have fun names, such as Thanks I'm Fine, which is grilled strips of pork filet with chives, ricotta cheese, bolete mushrooms served over homemade pasta noodles.

XIII Pannónia u. 14. (C) 1/452-0535. Reservations recommended. Main courses 2,790 Ft–4,590 Ft ($15–$25/£7.95–£13); beer 790 Ft–5,300 Ft ($4.30–$29/£2.25–£15). AE, DC, MC, V. Daily noon–midnight. Tram 4 or 6 to Jászai Mari tér.

Olíva Étterem és Pizzéria ★★★ ITALIAN

When a restaurant serves excellent Italian food, but also has Hungarian items on the menu, it makes it difficult to pigeonhole it into a category. Walking into Olíva is like entering an old-fashioned Italian country farmhouse, with country-style plates and knickknacks in shadowboxes decorating the walls and the red-checked tablecloths adding to the country charm. In spite of the busy large room, there is still a sense of coziness that envelopes each table, blocking out the rest of the surroundings. We ventured here as a group of eight, which did not inhibit the very competent staff. The service was quick and efficient throughout the evening. We started with the meat soup with spinach tortilla strips, a flavorful broth with an abundant amount of chewy stripes floating in it. The chicken with feta cheese was served as two extra-large pounded chicken breasts with thick slices of feta cheese roasted on top and a large bowl of Hungarian-style cucumber salad, where the cucumber is julienned and swimming in a sour cream sauce. At the end of the meal, we were given Limoncello, the Italian lemon liqueur, to end the evening.

VI. Lázár u. 1. (C) 1/312-0080. Reservations recommended. Main courses 1,290 Ft–2,590 Ft ($7–$14/£3.70–£7.40). MC, V. Daily noon–midnight. Metro: Arany János (Blue line).

Pata Negra Tapas Bar ★★ Value SPANISH

We are not certain how the name black foot or paw fits this establishment, but the food is too good to care about Spanish semantics. The space's *au courant* brick ceiling complements the colorful Spanish tiles that cover the wall behind the bar, along with rows and rows of wine bottles, like vino soldiers; each row is one type of wine. Other walls are graced with Spanish prints between the oversize windows; Spanish ballads play softly in the background. However, the main attraction here is the menu; it is primarily a tapa restaurant for which you will not be disappointed. Tapas are appetizers, but many make them a full meal, which we did by ordering six: garlic spinach with cream and chorizo; white beans with spinach and chorizo; lentil croquettes; fried eggplant with cheese; Spanish meatballs with spicy tomato sauce; and baked vegetables with chorizo and Serrano ham. The garlic spinach was so delectable, we ordered a second. The white beans were bland as were the lentil croquettes. The others were repeats for sure. The waiter smiled so much, we questioned his nationality; the service was exemplary. Due to the construction of the metro four line, which will continue for some years, this restaurant is hidden from view from the street, but is worth hunting for. There are many choices at the low end of the price range, but they also have some full meals also.

IX. Kálvin tér 8 (where Ráday starts). © 1/215-5616. www.patanegra.hu. Reservations recommended. Main courses 2,000 Ft–4,900 Ft ($11–$27/£5.70–£14); tapas 300 Ft–1,900 Ft ($1.60–$10/85p–£5.40). No credit cards. Daily 11am–midnight. Metro: Kálvin tér (Blue line).

Pilvax Restaurant 🎔🎔 HUNGARIAN TRADITIONAL   History permeates this city; this restaurant is no exception. First opened in 1848, it has had its openings and closings due to political regime changes, but since 1989, it has been open continuously and associated with the Pilvax City Hotel (p. 82). The large dining room is decorated in renovated Biedermeier style with old Hungarian prints on the walls and crystal chandeliers. It is like being in your Hungarian granny's dining room, except granny did not have strolling musicians playing during a meal like they do here. Musicians play from 7 to 11pm Tuesday through Saturday. The outdoor terrace is covered, situated on a pedestrian street; it is a relaxing place to enjoy a meal, which you will do. The menu has a scarce 21 entrees, but four are vegetarian. We sampled the spinach strudel, flaky layers of pastry stuffed with spinach and cheese and a Caesar salad loaded with chicken for starters. We could have stopped here, but we went forward in the name of research with the roasted duck with letcho and filet mignon of pork stuffed with goose liver, both dishes perfectly cooked. The meal as well as the service was worthy of applause.

V. Pilvax köz 1-3. © 1/266-7660. www.cityhotels.hu. Reservations recommended. Main courses 2,100 Ft–5,000 Ft ($11–$27/£6–£14). MC, V. Daily noon–midnight. Metro: Deák (all lines).

Pomo D'oro 🎔🎔 ITALIAN   All palates lead to the power of the tomato in this restaurant. The menu insert treats us to the legend that goes like this: In the 16th and 17th centuries the tomato was thought to be an aphrodisiac used by alchemists in various curative potions. We started with the half moon pie with squaquarone cream cheese, arugula, and Buffalo mozzarella. The pie was a type of bread for soaking up the delicately sweet and creamy pool of squaquarone pooled around the greens and firmer cheese; a gallon of this to go would have satisfied us. The other starter that was exceptional was the spinach soufflé served in a shallow lake of cheese sauce. We did continue on with main courses with eager anticipation. Tortelloni stuffed with parmesan-pumpkin cream served with spinach and cream was delectable, perfectly cooked with an exciting mix of flavors, while the Priest Strangler pasta dish of homemade noodles was a disappointment; the al dente pasta was closer to hard, making it too chewy to be enjoyable. The two-level restaurant itself is massive and impressively made of walls of stone, divided into four sections. We were seated in the loft area and although they supposedly have air-conditioning, we were medium rare by the end of the starter and well done at the end of the meal. The loft is above the pizza oven. The atmosphere is quiet and intimate in the upper levels, but the nonsmoking section is right at the entrance and may not be as engaging.

V. Arany János u. 9. © 1/302-6473. www.pomodorobudapest.com. Reservations recommended. Main courses 1,750 Ft–5,990 Ft ($9.70–$32/£5.10–£17). MC, V. Mon–Fri 11am–midnight; Sat–Sun noon–midnight. Metro: Arany János u. (Blue line).

Salamon Kosher Restaurant KOSHER   Located next door to the only Jewish hotel, King's Hotel, this 10-year-old restaurant offers two large, but mundane dining rooms. The emphasis is on their meals, both Hungarian and international selections being kosher with their certificate of authenticity by the entrance; the decor is obviously not a concern. Kashrut is ensured by the rabbi of the orthodox community. They close at various hours on Friday depending on the time of sunset, but they do offer Shabbes meals if prearranged. The menu is limited, but upon our visit, we could see that they were healthy portions.

VII. Nagydiófa u. 27. 🕐 **1/413-1484.** www.kosherrestaurant.hu. Main courses 1,960 Ft–3,960 Ft ($11–$21/£5.60–£11). Mon–Thurs noon–10pm; Fri variable; Sat noon–11pm. Cash only. Metro: Blaha Lujza tér.

Shalimar 🕐🕐🕐 INDIAN   Many have walked right by this unpretentious, downstairs restaurant due to its small outdoor sign. Being among the first Indian restaurants in the city, it has reinvented itself a number of times, but it remains a perpetual award winner in Budapest culinary competitions. What you find on the menu are typical items from Mughlai cuisine, from northern India. They are typically rich meat dishes in various sauces, grilled meats using an enormous array of spices cooked in a tandoor along with different breads. Newly redecorated with false backlit stenciled windows, it has a fresh new appearance. We have been here so often over the years that we have sampled almost everything on the very extensive menu. Pork Vindiloo is served in lavish red gravy made with a coconut milk base. Shahi beef korma cooked in a cashew and almond cream gravy is excellent. Order different nan breads to enrich your meal; they are baked in a tandoori clay oven, fired with charcoal. For awhile the portions shrunk, but they are doggie-bag size once again. Fixed business lunch specials are now available.

VII. Dob u. 50. 🕐 **1/352-0305.** Reservations recommended. Main courses 1,680 Ft–4,150 Ft ($9.10–$22/£4.80–£12); business lunch special 1,100 Ft–1,300 Ft ($5.95–$7.05/£3.15–£3.70). AE, MC, V. Daily noon–4pm lunch; 6pm–midnight dinner. Tram: 4 or 6 to Király u.

Soul Café 🕐🕐 INTERNATIONAL   During the summer months, this restaurant not only has tables along the side of the building, but also a massive area across the street as well. Not realizing this, we went inside to a large room filled with tables, with low lighting to the point it was difficult to read the menu and warm-colored walls with carpet weavings in frames. We tried the duck breast with blackberry sauce and truffles in potatoes. The duck was a good-size portion and moist on its own, no blackberry sauce; instead there was a tiny burrito-type wrap with some type of berry inside. The potatoes were flavored with truffle, but none were added in. It often makes us wonder if it is an issue with translation. Although we had a large group, the service was quick efficient and everyone was satisfied with their choices. I would return here again.

IX. Ráday u. 11–13. 🕐 **1/217-6986.** www.soulcafe.hu. Reservations recommended. Main courses 1,600 Ft–4,490 Ft ($8.65–$25/£4.55–£13). AE, MC, V. Daily noon–1am. Metro Kálvin tér (Blue line).

Taverna Dionysos GREEK   You will feel like you have been transported to Greece at this authentic looking Greek tavern, located on Pest's Danube embankment. It serves all of the typical Greek specialties you would expect if you were sitting at a tavern in a Greek village. The menu comprises an extensive fish selection, shrimp, lobster, as well as souvlakia, and other delicacies all in a Mediterranean environment. The restaurant is located in a typical Greek whitewashed building, and you are served on blue-and-white tablecloths. We have found the food here to be on par with what we had in Greece, but our only complaint is that the servings seem to get smaller as the years go by while the prices are going up. Weather permitting, sidewalk dining overlooking the Danube is available, but call in advance to reserve.

V. Belgrád rakpart 16. 🕐 **1/318-1222.** Reservations recommended. Main courses 2,800 Ft–12,100 Ft ($15–$65/£8–£34). MC, V. Daily noon–midnight. Metro: Ferenciek tere (Blue line).

Vista Café Restaurant HUNGARIAN CONTEMPORARY   This place is so convenient it is usually full at lunchtime, since it is right in the center of town. It serves hardy meals and is associated with the popular Vista travel agency across the street. The restaurant's manager is László Gulyás, who returned to Hungary, homesick, after working in the service sector in Graz and Munich. The restaurant is airy, with high ceilings and the works of local artists and special themes like World Cup soccer championship artifacts hanging on the walls. The nonsmoking section is far enough away from the smoking room to make a difference, something unusual in Hungary. The menu includes dishes like duck steak topped with asparagus and bundled in bacon, beef roasted in Guinness beer with mashed potatoes, and the dish that we had: breast of turkey filled with feta cheese, ham, and leeks, served with gnocchi. For some strange reason, the days and hours of operation change without notice, which is frustrating when you are all set for their great brunch choices. A pianist entertains nightly and there are also Internet-connected computers to check your e-mail.

VI. Paulay Ede 7. ⓒ 1/268-0888. www.vistacafe.hu. Reservations recommended. Main courses 1,080 Ft–3,350 Ft ($5.85–$19/£3.10–£10). MC, V. Daily 11am–midnight. Metro: Deák tér (Red line).

Vörös Postakocsi Étterem ✫✫ HUNGARIAN TRADITIONAL   The eclectic building on the very busy Ráday utca was built in 1876, where it once served as a coffeehouse. The restaurant opened in 1970, named after the Hungarian writer Gyula Krudy's book *The Red Post Coach,* which is on display in the entry. The restaurant reflects the tone of the novel with an early-20th-century feel inside with heavy dark furniture and old-fashioned wallpaper; it is like eating in a history lesson. Food selections embrace traditional as well as modern Hungarian recipes. As a starter, the *gulyás* soup is spicy and filled with meat, carrots, and potatoes; the bean soup is thick, but not as flavorful, lacking something. Those who appreciate turkey will love the breast steak stuffed with dried tomatoes and bacon topped with mozzarella served with steak fries. The Caesar salad with tenderloin was the first salad we have had with Romaine lettuce in Hungary. This type of lettuce is a rarity, often replaced with the iceberg variety. The tenderloin was cooked perfectly to enhance the flavor of the salad without overwhelming it. The dressing was close to a true Caesar dressing, but needed some lemon, which the server brought after we asked. Live music is provided daily, but Monday. They will serenade you while you eat indoors or outside, thanks to the oversize windows that signal no air-conditioning inside. We found the service somewhat tenuous; we waited for menus, then for a lengthy time to order, while three servers stood close by and chatted with each other.

IX. Ráday u. 15. ⓒ 1/217-6756. Main courses 1,290 Ft–4,990 Ft ($7–$27/£3.70–£14). AE, DC, MC, V. Daily 11:30am–11pm. Metro Kálvin tér (Blue line).

Zorbas Taverna ✫✫ GREEK   Although this Greek restaurant does not have a Danube view, you will feel like you are in a Greek village once inside. Typical rough whitewashed walls are heavily decorated in Greek regalia to transport you to the Mediterranean. This place is large enough to hold the population of a small island, but the service was quick and efficient. The food was excellent and the portions were more than we could finish. The tarragon scented turkey ragout soup served in a bread bowl was filled with chunks of turkey and vegetables. The pork stuffed with pistachios and feta cheese was a bit dry, but they do not skimp on the nuts and cheese. The choices here are not your typical Greek fare; they are original offerings. If you are looking for the usual selections, you will not find them here. There are a number of choices of seafood, lamb, poultry, and pork, but the beef is neglected and is not missed. Most main dishes are entrees only, but the sides are reasonably priced. Friday nights there is Greek dancing and entertainment.

VI. Podmaniczky u. 18. (©) 1/332-7900. www.zorbastaverna.hu. Main courses 1,420 Ft–4,390 Ft ($7.70–$24/£4.05–£13). Mon–Thurs noon–midnight; Fri–Sat noon–1am; Sun noon–10pm. Tram: 4 or 6 Nyugati.

INEXPENSIVE

Bombay Express ★★ INDIAN   At one time, there was a very expensive, but beautiful Indian restaurant on this site that closed down for remodeling. When it reopened, no one was prepared for the Indian fast-food restaurant that it now is. Almost a year later, this cafeteria-style restaurant has successfully found its niche. Owned by the people who run Salaam Bombay, the food is excellent and the portions are extra large. With your tray in hand, you have choices of tandoori wraps with chicken, mincemeat, or vegetables. There are express meals with chicken, beef, lamb, or vegetables and they come with rice and nan bread. Samosas and potato bombas are also available. Nothing is overly spicy, so ask for hot sauce if you want some fire in your food. We have tried everything on the menu and still return for more. You won't leave here hungry or broke.

VI. Andrássy út 44. (©) 1/332-8363. Main courses 650 Ft–1,400 Ft ($3.50–$7.60/£1.85–£4). Daily noon–midnight. Metro: Oktogon (Yellow line).

Főzelékfalo Ételbar ★★ (Value HUNGARIAN TRADITIONAL   Although this is not a dining place, as in sit down and be served, this little restaurant is so popular with Hungarians there is a line out the door at lunchtime. Főzelék is a cross between a soup and a stew, though it is puréed and this wisp of a restaurant has been voted the best in the city by all who have been polled. Főzelék is a national dish and treasure, so if you have not tried it, you have not officially been to Hungary. Inside there are only bar tables and stools, but if the weather is good, the sidewalk will be packed with tables. Take it to go if you have to. They will give you a spoon. The stew comes in a number of varieties, but green pea and potato are the most popular. If you want something more hearty, they sell fried chicken too. This is the cheapest, filling meal you will find in the city. If you still want some dessert, they serve *palacsinta* (Hungarian crepes).

VI. Nagymező 18. No phone. Main courses 320 Ft–480 Ft ($1.75–$2.60/90p–£1.40). Cash only. Mon–Fri 9am–10pm; Sat 10am–9pm; Sun 11am–6pm. Metro: Opera (Yellow line).

Frici Papa Kifőzés ★ (Value HUNGARIAN TRADITIONAL   This is a restaurant with attitude, not for the decor, but from the staff. At times they can be downright surly, but it does not keep the customers away; we think it actually makes for entertainment with the meal if you know in advance. This is a plain, down-home place with no frills and the prices reflect it. The daily offerings from soup to desserts and everything in between are posted with signs hanging on a Pegboard near the front windows. Everything is al a carte, even catsup for the French fries will cost you extra. If you want to see the surly waiter, ask for something again after he has delivered your meal and before you ask for your check. The portions are humongous and when something runs out, that is the end of it. We love the chicken with the bleu cheese sauce and the mashed potatoes are the real deal. Lunch or an early dinner is best for the full day's selection. After 7pm, you are taking your chances. Now take a deep breath and order everything you think you want.

VI. Király u. 55. No phone. Main courses 559 Ft–600 Ft ($3.00–$3.25/£1.60–£1.70). Cash only. Mon–Sat 11am–9pm. Tram 4 or 6 Király u.

Govinda Vegetariánus Étterem *INDIAN* Once you descend the steep steps to enter this restaurant, you will find a simply decorated ultraclean restaurant that is run by the local Hari Krishna–type group here in the city. Eliminate any negative thoughts since the proceeds from this restaurant help support their efforts in feeding the homeless of the city through a monthly food giveaway. They serve delicious vegetarian food in a tranquil, smoke-free environment with Indian gods and goddesses looking over your shoulder. The operation is on a self-service system where you can choose from different dishes, each at a set price. You can also choose from two daily menu options written on a blackboard or a small or large sampler platter. Choices might include stuffed squash with Indian ragout and brown rice; or a potato-pumpkin casserole with garlic Roquefort sauce, steamed cabbage, and spinach soufflé. Or you can simply go for a soup (cream of cauliflower perhaps, or lentil) and the salad bar. Unless you have a really healthy appetite, we recommend the small sampler which is ample. Seating is plentiful, but this place can be packed at lunchtime on weekdays, so you may have to wait in line. The staff speaks English and will explain each dish. There is a small shop in back, stocked with New Age and Eastern literature, clothes, candles and incense. For those inclined, there is a meditation room also.

V. Vigyázó Ferenc u. 4. *(*) 1/269-1625. Main courses 620 Ft ($3.25/£1.70); small sampler meal 1,450 Ft ($7.80/£4.10); large sampler meal 1,750 Ft ($9.45/£5); student menu 720 Ft ($3.95/£2.05). Cash only. Mon–Sat noon–9pm. Metro: Kossuth Lajos tér (Red line).

Hanna's Orthodox Restaurant KOSHER If you happen to be at the Orthodox Kazinczy Synagogue, you will see signs for this restaurant next to two oversize metal doors with a buzzer to push to be let into the courtyard. You can enter this way, but this is the back entrance. One of two kosher restaurants in the city, this one has a large room with simple tables and chairs that lack any decoration. Serving good kosher meals at low prices is the utmost concern, not making this a place to linger about. On the wall is a framed certificate of kosher authenticity. The menu changes daily, but the price range stays the same. We could not help but overhear very satisfied tourists praising the food while we were here. The other positive is that the cashier will try to get someone to open the synagogue for viewing in the afternoons if it is not already open—an added benefit to having a meal here.

VII. Dob u. 35. *(*) 1/342-1072. Main courses 1,100 Ft–1,900 Ft ($6–$10/£3.15–£5.40). Sun–Mon 11:30am–10pm, Sat 11am–3:30pm. Cash only. Bus: 74 to Kazinczy Synagogue.

Hummus Bar *Value* VEGETARIAN This is the most popular hummus and falafel bar in the city. You can eat in, seating is upstairs, or you can take it with you. Either way, the food is delicious and very inexpensive. Several varieties of hummus and salads are offered to go with the falafel. While you are waiting, don't be surprised if you are offered some tea or samples of other items. All of the limited choices are made fresh.

VII. Kertesz u.39. *(*) 1/321-7477. Menu items 200 Ft–1,000 Ft ($1.10–$5.40/60p–£2.85). No credit cards. Daily noon–midnight. Tram 4 or 6 Király u.

Kőleves Vendéglő (Stone Soup) *Finds* HUNGARIAN CONTEMPORARY If you remember the story of *Stone Soup,* the playfulness of the little drawings on the menu, the light fixtures made of inverted glasses and cheese graters, the pieces of modern art that grace the walls, and the soup bowls adorning the bar will amuse you. But the real delight comes with the food, made from preservative-free ingredients. The matzo ball soup had shredded chicken with a baseball-size matzo ball, appealingly spiced. We could not resist trying the tenderloin steak in black pepper coated with chili and chocolate, which was mouth-watering from the first bite to the last. Each entree a la carte has a suggested side dish that is extra, but at 360 Ft to 400 Ft ($1.95–$2.15/£1–£1.10) for a side, it is still a bargain for such delicious treats. The line of people waiting to get in as we were leaving is a testament to the success of this relative newcomer.

VII. Kazinczy u. 35. (C) 1/322-1011. www.koleves.com. Reservations recommended. Main courses 1,280 Ft–1,780 Ft ($6.90–$9.60/£3.65–£5.10). AE, MC, V. Daily 11am–midnight. Close to Dohány Synagogue on the corner of Kazinczy u. and Dob u.

Nagyi Nonstop Palacsintázója 👁👁 (Value) HUNGARIAN TRADITIONAL

Whether you are having a snack attack at 3am, craving something sweet, or wanting a full inexpensive meal, this is your place. *Palacsintá* is the Hungarian version of crepes. At this restaurant, you can find fixed menus of three or four crepes as well as individual crepes in savory or sweet categories. Crepes are made within the hour and are prepared in front of you. It is a great place to refuel after leaving the clubs. There are multiple locations; the two most popular are on Batthyány tér and Petófi Sandor utca.

I. Batthyány tér 5 and V. Petófi Sandor u. 17–19. No phone. 175 Ft–890 Ft (95¢–$4.80/50p–£2.55). No credit cards. Daily 24 hr. Metro: Batthyány (Red line) and Deák tér (Yellow line).

Napos Oldal Café 👁 VEGETARIAN

This shop has attracted my attention for a couple of years, but I never stopped in. Writing this book was a good enough reason to satisfy my curiosity and step into this combo bioproduct store, small restaurant, and tea and coffees cafe all lumped into one cute shop. The biostore section sells a range of goods from soap to shampoo on the right side of the store, while on the left, the display case of fresh salads and baked goods, including organic and sugar–free pastries will grab your attention. Do some shopping, have a bite to eat, and relax over a cup of tea, coffee, freshly squeezed juice, or homemade ginger ale, before continuing on with your day. The staff here is friendly and warm adding to the general-store feeling of the place. You all come back now, ya hear?

VI. Jókai u. 7. (C) 1/354-0048. Daily menu 800 Ft–1,100 Ft ($4.35–$5.95/£2.30–£3.15); salads 230 Ft–290 Ft ($1.25–$1.60/65p–85p) per10dg (3.5 oz.); drinks 250 Ft–450 Ft ($1.35–$2.45/70p–£1.30). Mon–Fri 11am–9pm, Sat 10am–1:30pm; biostore Mon–Thurs 10:30am–6pm, Fri 10:30am–5pm, Sat 10am–1pm. Metro: Opera (Yellow line).

Old Amsterdam 👁👁 DUTCH

When we arrived here, armed with a half-off offer for Sunday dining, we found an outside table available on the quiet street and it was thoroughly relaxing. In keeping with its name, Old Amsterdam offers over 20 beers of Dutch and Hungarian labels. The cafe quality has improved with more ambience; lovely Dutch-style ornaments and pictures grace the walls to create the illusion of the city of canals. The menu is not extensive, but satisfying. Each of us had an incredible dish and we were all satisfied. When the check came, there was no sign of a discount. When we questioned the waiter, we were told the restaurant had a new owner as of the week prior. The offer was no longer valid, but with the quality and quantity of the food and service, we did not mind.

Királyi Pál u. 14. (C) 1/266-3649. Reservations recommended. Main courses 950 Ft–1,950 Ft ($5.25–$11/£2.75–£5.50). Daily noon–midnight. Metro: Kálvin tér (Blue line).

Pink Cadillac 👁👁 ITALIAN

Who would have thought to name an Italian restaurant Pink Cadillac? But it seems to have worked. This is one of the longest-surviving restaurants of the increasingly trendy Ráday utca. After a number of remodels, it looks more modern, but retains some '50s flare of tackiness with the half pink Cadillac crashing through the wall. The tiled areas on the walls also add that yesteryear flavor. The inside seating is now large enough to make reservations not needed most of the time. In summer, you will want to sit outside, where mists of water are lightly sprayed into the air to cool down the temperature. We love the table-side buzzer for calling the waitstaff, who responds almost instantly. What has not changed over the course of time is the quality of the food, which is wonderful. Pizza is the specialty, but a full range of Italian selections are also excellent choices. We love their penne pasta al gamberini pomodoro, shrimp fried in garlic oil with tomato sauce. Their motto is "good mood food" and it is.

IX. Ráday u. 22. ✆ 1/216-1412. www.pinkcadillac.hu. Main courses 990 Ft–1,680 Ft ($5.35–$9.10/£2.80–£4.80); pizza 790 Ft–2,490 Ft ($4.30–$14/£2.25–£7.10). AE, MC, V. Mon–Fri 11am–midnight; Sat–Sun noon–midnight. Metro: Kálvin tér (Blue line).

Red Pepper ✶✶ HUNGARIAN CONTEMPORARY   This long, semibarrel-shaped basement restaurant with rounded brick ceilings continuing for half of the wall on one side, is minimally decorated. The large curved windows on the street side, allow light to pour in during the day, and the modern lights, sometimes too bright illuminate the rest of the time. Intimate space is not what this restaurant is known for, so they have to rely heavily on their food offerings, and this is where they excel. Chicken paprika with cottage noodles and the pork stuffed with cheese pepper sauce and mushrooms are a pleasant marriage of flavors. The food was equally appealing both visually and in taste. The service people are exceptionally friendly, but being a cellar restaurant, you will want to avoid it in the hot months. There is no air-conditioning and it gets hot and stuffy.

XIII. Visegrádi u. 2. ✆ 1/352-1394. www.redpepper.cjb.hu. Reservations recommended. Main courses 1,050 Ft–2,790 Ft ($5.70–$15/£3.00–£7.95). MC, V. Daily noon–midnight. Metro: Nyugati (Blue line).

3 Beyond Central Pest

VERY EXPENSIVE

Gundel ✶ *Overrated* HUNGARIAN TRADITIONAL   Budapest's fanciest, most famous, probably most expensive, and most overrated restaurant, Gundel reopened in 1992. The restaurant is the place for the Hungarian elite and other dignitaries to see and be seen dining in the opulent dining room adorned with 19th-century paintings. Lamb and wild-game entrees are house specialties. The Gundel menu also includes four sets of gourmet choices with fixed prices. There are many other choices in the city for excellent meals at a lower cost. Jacket required for men.

XIV. Állatkerti út 2. ✆ 1/468-4040. www.gundel.hu. Reservations highly recommended; jackets required for men in the evening. Main courses 3,990 Ft–10,620 Ft ($22–$57/£11–£30); dinner prix-fixe menu 11,890 Ft–39,200 Ft ($64–$212/£34–£112); lunch prix-fixe menu 3,500 Ft–4,700 Ft ($19–$25/£9.95–£13); Sun brunch buffet 5,800 Ft ($31/£17); children 5–15 2,900 Ft ($16/£8.25); children under 5 free. AE, DC, MC, V. Mon–Sat noon–4pm and 6:30–11pm; Sun 11:30am–3pm (brunch) and 6:30–11pm. Metro: Hősök tere (Yellow line).

EXPENSIVE

Kogart Restaurant ✶✶ INTERNATIONAL   Situated in the lower level of the **Kogart Art Gallery,** this restaurant emits an understated elegance. The walls are decorated with paintings on a rotating basis; the chairs are covered with beautiful print covers, the linens elegantly draped over the tables. One corner has a sitting area with leather sofas to wait for the rest of your party or relax with a drink. In summer, there

is a terrace where the food is cooked on a grill. The sommelier assists with wine choices from the extensive list. Surprisingly, the menu is limited, but has a number of fish choices. The chicken with lasagna and the scampi with salad were excellent choices. The cranberry crème brulée turned out to be blueberry, but mouth-watering nevertheless. Although the restaurant is elegant, dress is sporty casual to more formal.

VI. Andrássy ut. 112. ⓒ 1/354-3830. www.kogart.hu. Reservations recommended. Main courses 2,390 Ft–5,590 Ft ($13–$30/£6.80–£16). AE, MC, V. Daily 10am–midnight. Metro: Bajza (Yellow line).

MODERATE

Bagolyvár (Owl Castle) ✶✶ *Kids* HUNGARIAN TRADITIONAL   Bagolyvár is a budget alternative to Gundel as it has the same owners, but the prices are much more reasonable. Housed in a lovely Transylvanian manor house, the idea, as sexist as it may be is that you are dining in your mother or grandmother's place; therefore, you are served only by women who care for your needs. The size of the room defeats the romantic notions of family-style intimacy, but the female waitstaff does provide excellent service; the female kitchen people do produce excellent cooking. The only male in attendance was the one playing the cimbalom by the entry. The Bagolyvár menu is limited to a dozen main courses (supplemented by daily fixed-menu three-course meals). We had the sweet and spicy spare ribs with cabbage salad wrapped in corn omelet. The ribs were meaty, dripping with a great sauce, but there were only three small ones, when our mouths were craving more. The cabbage salad was actually wrapped in corn tortillas, a mix up in translation, but nevertheless, enjoyable. For dessert, the turos palachinta was perfectly tasty with the vanilla sauce to top it with. Our only complaint was the noise level; the place was filled on a Thursday night and it was difficult to carry on a conversation among the four of us.

XIV. Állatkerti út 2. ⓒ 1/468-3110. Reservations recommended. Main courses 1,930 Ft–3,990 Ft ($11–$22/ £5.50–£11). AE, DC, MC, V. Daily noon–11pm. Metro: Hősök tere (Yellow line).

Paprika Vendéglő ✶✶✶ *Finds* HUNGARIAN TRADITIONAL   If you want to escape to the Hungarian countryside to sample the cuisine without leaving the city, this is the place. The old-fashioned earthen oven, the oversize cooking utensils, and the log-cabin interior will mellow you in rustic comfort. The chairs and benches are also made of logs adding to the country ambience. Let yourself go hog wild and try the roasted wild boar with brandy or saddle of deer. My personal favorite is the leg of goose Vadazsdi style, oven roasted served with red cabbage and parsley potatoes. Not feeling so adventurous? No problem, they have other poultry, beef, and pork dishes to choose from on a liberal menu. No matter what you order, the portion will be generous; don't hesitate to ask to have leftovers wrapped to take home. The wine list has a wide selection of Hungarian wines. Sometimes the service can be a bit slow, but this is a minor inconvenience. Menus are in English. There are separate dining areas for smoking and nonsmoking.

VII. Dozsa Gyorgy 72. ⓒ 06/70-574-6508 mobile phone. Reservations recommended. Main courses 1,650 Ft–3,200 Ft. ($8.90–$17/£4.70–£9.10). No credit cards. Daily 11am–11pm. Metro: H_s_k tere (Yellow line) 4½ blocks from Heroes' Square.

Trófea Grill Étterem ✶✶✶ *Finds* HUNGARIAN TRADITIONAL   Prepare to starve yourself the whole day before heading off to this restaurant and you will not be sorry you did. The interior is decorated like an old hunting lodge, with cozy booths and tables in between. This is the best all-you-can-eat restaurant in the city where you

Uncork, Swirl, Sniff, Taste: Hungarian Wine Culture

The wines of Spain, South Africa, and Hungary have one thing in common. Governmental changes thwarted their production and development for periods of time. Before communist times, Hungarian wines were developing into a mature market, but one that never reached much beyond its borders. During the politically difficult times, winemakers' efforts were stomped and trampled and only the cheapest and most insignificant wines could be produced and mostly sold only to other Soviet bloc countries. The few wines that did make the export list were the insignificant offerings that did nothing to put Hungary on the winemaking radar for vintners to keep an eye on. When the climate changed in the early 1990s, the winemakers found themselves starting from the beginning once again, not only creating new varieties of grapes, but developing their wines, and struggling for international recognition to abolish the reputation of the past.

One of the major achievements of the industry was the creation of an annual festival to bring attention to the wines of the country. If you are a wine buff or if you just like to drink it, you will surely want to plan your trip around the first week of September when Budapest celebrates the first wheat harvest and the largest wine festival of the year is held atop Castle Hill. The celebration begins with the Harvest Parade, and people from different regions of the country (dressed in traditional clothing) dance, play folk music, and sell their crafts. Each year, a celebrated wine-producing country is invited to share the spotlight with Hungarian winegrowers and their many varieties of wines. In 2007, at the 16th annual festival, it was South Africa that held this honor.

The winemakers created the foundation Hungarian Viti- and Vini-cultural Public Benefit Company, a trade group to market their wines by bringing wineries to international competitions as well as hosting them. In June 2007, they hosted the 30th Congress and 5th General Assembly of the Organisation of Internationale de la Vigne et du Vin (OIV), where 500 member

get to select from over 100 different dishes. Once the waiter brings your drinks, you are on your own, but he will return to clear all dirty dishes or replenish the drinks. Start with a choice of five soups, and then work your way over to the numerous salads, followed by a choice of six different entrees and the vegetable bar. If the prepared entrees are not to your liking, move on over to the section of marinated meats and bring them to the grill to be cooked while you wait. Save some room though, because there are about 15 desserts waiting to be sampled. There is more: It is all you can drink, too. You have choices of tap beer, house wine, champagne, sodas, coffee, espresso drinks, and tea. Everything is included in one price if you don't order wine off the wine list. Each Sunday, a playroom is set up for children with qualified kindergarten teachers supervising. Note that there are four locations with the same name, but they are owned by different companies. This location is the only one we recommend.

XIV. Erzsébet Királyné útja 5. ✆ 1/251-6377. www.trofeagrill.com. Reservations recommended. Lunch 2,499 Ft ($14/£7.10); dinner Mon–Thurs 3,699 Ft ($20/£11); dinner Fri–Sun and holidays 4,199 Ft ($23/£12). Half-price for organizations converged on the city. This and other international events bring further exposure of Hungarian wines to international audiences.

For a Hungarian wine education, be sure to visit the **House of Hungarian Wines** on Castle Hill at Szenthóromság tér 6 across from the Hilton hotel, any time of the year. After purchasing your ticket, you are free to roam the cellars where over 50 varieties are available for tasting within a 2-hour period. There is a concise, but dated wine region primer on their website at www.magyarborokhaza.hu with a link for various languages.

Wine Primer: Hungary has 22 wine regions and cultivates more than 93 varieties of wine grapes, producing the full spectrum of reds, whites, roses, and sparkling wines. Serious wine enthusiasts will know that varietals indigenous to Hungary are referred to as Hungaricum and are only grown here. Some such varieties are Budai Zöld, Furmint, Juhfark, Hárslevelű, Kadarka, Kéknyelu, and Királyleányka.

Best Regions for Whites: White wine is still the major product of Hungarian wineries with each region producing its own distinctive variety. Somló produces some of the country's best whites, which are usually acidic. Tokaj produces world-famous dessert wines under the name "Tokaj." Tokaj's vineyard area is strictly delimited, less than 5,463 hectares (13,500 acres) in 26 villages with well-defined regulations going back to the 16th century. It was declared a UNESCO World Heritage Site in 2002. The Balaton regions, particularly Badacsony, make excellent whites, as does Gyöngyös in the Mátraalja region.

Best Regions for Reds: Hungary has been producing increasingly greater amounts of reds due to international demands. Villány has achieved recognition as the Bordeaux of Hungary. Szekszárd, Sopron, and Eger also produce fine reds. But great reds also come from regions better known for their whites, like Balatonlelle.

children up to 150cm (59 in.). MC, V. Mon–Fri noon–midnight; Sat 11:30am–midnight; Sun 11:30am–8:30pm. Playroom Sun 11:30am–5pm. Metro: Mexikói (Yellow line).

INEXPENSIVE

Café Csiga *Finds* HUNGARIAN TRADITIONAL   Owned by an Irish expat, this small cafe is the perfect hiding place for a relaxing cafe latte or an unhurried lunch, where you can sit with your book for hours. Set back on a corner off of a square, it is a bit difficult to find at the moment, as a metro 4 station is under construction close to it. However, the laidback atmosphere, the country-style tables and chairs, and the funky artwork on the walls make us return for more. We have eaten the cook's food that he prepared for a banquet, and it was excellent. But the menu changes continually, so we hesitate to make suggestions. The daily offerings are written on the blackboard. The coffee is served hot, which is a plus in our book and the staff actually smiles at you.

VIII. Vásár u. 2. © **1/210-0885.** Menu items 500 Ft–1,200 Ft ($2.70–$6.50/£1.40–£3.40). Mon–Sat 11am–1am; Sun 4pm–1am. Kitchen closed at 11pm and all day Sun. Tram: 4 or 6.

4 Central Buda

EXPENSIVE

Hemingway ⭐⭐⭐ *Moments* HUNGARIAN CONTEMPOARY   You will feel like you are escaping the city when visiting this restaurant next to a small lake with plenty of trees. Opened seven years ago, it has never lost its popularity. The interior of the venue made us feel like we have joined Hemingway in one of his favorite getaways; the room is open and airy. Most of the tables sit on a platform, with the nonsmoking section in another room. The piano and bass duo adds to the relaxing Casablanca atmosphere. We started with one order of the grilled ewe cheese over a mixed olive-oil salad. Fortunately, it was the only starter we chose as it was large enough for two. The thick slice of cheese was golden and the salad dressing excellent. For main courses, we recommend highly the Glenn Close pasta, spinach linguine with garlic, red peppers, cream sauce, and a touch of anise. The Mangalica pork was perfectly prepared with a tomato-brown sauce over mounds of fresh mashed potatoes. The white chocolate mousse was presented beautifully, but it was a little more sugary than chocolate. The waiter service was superior. In clement weather, eat outside on the terrace overlooking the water.

XI. Kosztolányi D. tér 2, Feneketlen tó. ☎ 1/381-0522. www.hemingway-etterem.hu. Reservations recommended. Main courses 2,390 Ft–5,990 Ft ($13–$32/£6.80–£17). AE, DC, MC, V. Daily noon–midnight. Bus: 7 toward Buda from Ferenciek tér to Feneketlen tó, a small "lake."

Le Jardin de Paris ⭐⭐ FRENCH   Appropriately, this little jewel of a restaurant is located across the street from the Institut Français. It is celebrating its 18th year, so it is an established fixture in this Watertown district. From May to September, the restaurant is completely outdoors, wrought-iron patio furniture under enormous umbrellas protected by shade trees, all on gravel ground, acts as the dining room. As unadorned as it is, it is relaxing. The rest of the year, the cozy indoor restaurant, which seats only 40, is the winter alternative. Decorated with a collection of Hungarian posters, French antiques, and bentwood chairs, it has a definite bistro feel to it. The menu features variety such as hare, venison, and lobster, as well as more mundane meats and fish. The wine choices are both French and Hungarian varieties. The service is impeccable, the plates are beautifully presented, and the food is very good. We tried the French soup, which was overloaded with onions, the soup thick and pungent. The turkey ragout with pineapple and curry was bland in color, but not in taste. The bite-size chunks of turkey were splendidly enhanced by the fresh pineapple bits and the mild curry. The skewered grill was a mix of beef, pork, and chicken with a side salad and yogurt dressing. As you eat by lantern light outside, a keyboardist plays both American and French tunes.

I. Fő u. 20. ☎ 1/201-0047. Reservations recommended. Main courses 1,950 Ft–8,500 Ft ($11–$46/£5.55–£24). AE, MC, V. Daily noon–midnight. Metro: Batthyány tér (Red line).

MODERATE

Angelika Kaveház és Étterem ⭐⭐ HUNGARIAN CONTEMPORARY   Angelika is housed in a historic building next to St. Anne's Church and was once part of the church's ministerial buildings on Buda's Batthyány tér. Better known as a place for drinks and pastries on a summer's day, their multilevel terrace has perfect views of Parliament across the Danube. Inside you will find extra-large rooms where smokers and nonsmokers are truly segregated. Each room has Art Deco love seats and well-padded individual chairs to match in blue, maroon, and beige. The rest of the decoration is simple, but appealing creating a pleasant atmosphere for dinner. The menu is not extensive, but our entree of pork wrapped in bacon with oven-baked potatoes was excellent. Surprisingly, we were served four full baked potatoes as well as two thick boneless chops. The pork was grilled coated in spices, keeping it moist and very flavorful. With little sectioned off areas, this restaurant has an intimate feeling for dining and enjoying a meal.

I. Batthyány tér 7. ℂ **1/201–0668.** Main courses 1,990 Ft–3,290 Ft ($11–$18/£5.70–£9.35). No credit cards. Mon–Sat 9am–midnight; Sun and holidays 9am–11pm. Metro: Batthyány tér (Red line).

Szent Jupát ⭐⭐ (Finds) HUNGARIAN TRADITIONAL   We are guessing that St. Jupát has something to do with fishermen, but we could not find a server who could tell us for sure. Along with the rustic wood booths with tables, there stands a life-size wood-carved statue bringing back childhood memories of the boxes of frozen fish sticks. That and the number of fish dishes was yet another clue to the restaurant's namesake. The menu is extensive with food served on wooden trenchers, which can be purchased new if you are so inclined. The portions were huge in our minds, but others have said the restaurant has cut down on them; we cannot imagine being able to eat more than what we were served. After finishing off the hot and perfectly prepared bowl of bean soup that would have sufficed as a meal, we forged ahead for the leg of pork Dubury style, two large slabs of pork with cauliflower, smothered in cheese sauce. To top it off, they serve new potatoes and rice as sides. This was the only restaurant in Budapest that has given us our check before we asked for it, though the restaurant was not full; chalk it up to speedy service or a waiter annoyed by a barrage of our questions.

II. Dékán u. 3 (corner of Retek u.). ℂ **1/212-2923.** Reservations recommended. Main courses 1,290 Ft–2,890 Ft ($7–$16/£3.70–£8.25). No credit cards. Thurs–Mon noon–6am. Metro: Moszkva tér (Red line).

Tabáni Terasz ⭐⭐⭐ HUNGARIAN TRADITIONAL   We had to sneak a peek at the inside of this restaurant since we sat outside on the large terrace shaded by umbrellas. The dishes are all prepared with a nice variety of vegetables, which is unusual for Hungarian cuisine. The dishes were the traditional fare, heavy on the portions. The ewe cheese salad had the nondescript iceberg lettuce, but the dressing was mild and tasty; the portions of cheese were generous enough to share. Chicken breast rolled around asparagus with Hollandaise sauce and tarragon potatoes was an incredible three large pieces of chicken. The turkey breast with cheese sauce, an eggplant salad, and jasmine rice, was beautifully presented, but the turkey was a thin, yet large slice. In the off season the interior dining is cozy and intimate. The inside is made up of small rooms with tables and chairs and gives the feel of entering someone's home, being decorated with wall hangings, some paintings, and other regional touches. It is a bit difficult to get to from the Pest side, but worth the effort.

I. Apród utca 10. ℂ **1/201-1086.** www.tabaniterasz.hu. Main courses 1,990 Ft–4,300 Ft ($11–$23/£5.70–£12). AE, MC, V. Daily noon–midnight. Bus: 86 to Döbrentei tér.

INEXPENSIVE

Eden ⭐ (Finds) VEGETARIAN   Vegans can celebrate for this historic building houses the first and only vegan restaurant in Buda. The building was restored in 2001 and this vegan buffet restaurant opened. All ingredients are natural and fresh without any coloring, additives, or preservatives. After making your selection, you have the choice of sitting in the charming country-cozy dining room or in the atrium garden. Their selection of 12 juices freshly squeezed from fruits or vegetables will quench anyone's thirst. When you order, take note that the price for salad is by weight and the drinks are by volume.

I. Iskola street 31, Batthyányi sq. ℂ **06/20-337-7575** mobile phone. www.edenetterem.hu. 290 Ft–590 Ft ($1.55–$3.20/80p–£1.70). Cash only. Sun 11am–9pm; Mon–Thurs 7am–9pm; Fri 7am–6pm; Sat closed. Metro: Batthyányi (Red line).

5 The Castle District

MODERATE

Rivalda Café & Restaurant ⍟ HUNGARIAN CONTEMPORARY   The building has much history to tell, once being a monastery and later a theater with a casino in the 17th century. In the summer months, you will be pleased to be seated in the huge courtyard with wicker tables and chairs, hurricane lights, and a pianist serenading diners while the stars shine in the sky. Peeking inside, we found the interior to be pleasingly decorated with Impressionist scenes from theater productions, actual theater lighting directed at the small stage at the end of the room, and gossamer hanging lucidly from the ceiling. Rivalda has a simple, but varied menu, so we started with the pear ginger soup and the lemon chicken soup. We followed these with an Argentinean steak served with a baked potato and green beans and rosé duck breast accompanied by couscous and mixed vegetables. The food was excellently prepared, the vegetables were al dente, but the menu was not as imaginative as we had been led to believe. Unfortunately, the surroundings are more theatrical then the dinner options.

I. Szinház u. 5–9. ✆ 1/489-0236. www.rivalda.net. Reservations recommended. Main courses 2,300 Ft–4,950 Ft ($12–$27/£6.55–£14). AE, MC, V. Daily 11:30am–11:30pm. Bus: 16 from Deák or Várbusz from Moszkva tér.

6 The Buda Hills

EXPENSIVE

Bajai Halászcsárda HUNGARIAN TRADITIONAL   Csárda means a restaurant near a major traffic area and this one is right next to a Cogwheel and bus stop, making it easy to access. Halász means fisherman and the interior is country style with heavy woods and fishing decor tastefully ornamenting the walls. However, in the Buda Hills, one would not expect to find a restaurant with an extensive fish menu, but here it is. The specialty is the traditional Bajai type of fish soup, which has a special pastry in it. But we bypassed anything fishy for the turkey stuffed with cheese and French fries. The five exceptionally large pieces of fried turkey were overflowing with cheese. It was moist and flavorful, but not exceptional. If you have a desire for fish dishes, this would be the place to go and other diners seemingly were enjoying their fresh-from-the-river tasty treats. There is a pianist and violinist serenading with American and Hungarian oldies. Every few songs, the pianist would belt out a song a la Piaf with a hauntingly romantic voice. The resident parrot's whistling in the background was a mix of humor and annoyance.

XII. Hollós u. 2. ✆ 1/275-5245. www.bajaihalaszcsarda.com. Reservations recommended. Main courses 2,900 Ft–5,400 Ft ($16–$29/£8.25–£15). AE, MC, V. Daily 11:30am–10pm. Bus: 21 from Moszkva tér.

MODERATE

Remiz ⍟⍟⍟ ⍟alue HUNGARIAN CONTEMPORARY   A remiz is literally the place where trams spend the night, and such is the location of this restaurant. It can be an adventure to get to from the city center, but you will be well rewarded, especially in summer. This is when they crank up the barbecue outside in the gazebo for their ultimate special dish, spare ribs. Unlike any we have ever tasted, the two extra large racks of ribs, sans any sauce were incredibly meaty and flavorful. This dish unique to Hungarian menus has been perfected here. A sea of diners on the tree-and-umbrella-covered terrace with plates of ribs in front of them is a common occurance during the summer months. The Italian garlic soup starter was excellent as was the breaded eggplant Caesar salad with chicken ordered by a fellow diner. During the rest of the year, the tram-shaped restaurant, which is decorated with early-20th-century posters is the setting for delicious meals.

II. Budakeszi út 5. (€) **1/275-1396.** www.remiz.hu. Reservations recommended. Main courses 1,980 Ft–3,980 Ft ($11–$22/£5.65–£11). AE, DC, MC, V. Mon–Fri 11am–11pm, Sat–Sun 9am–11pm. Bus: 158 from Moszkva tér (departs from Csaba ú., at the top of the stairs, near the stop from which bus 10 departs for the Castle District).

Szép Ilona ✿ HUNGARIAN TRADITIONAL   If you remember the wonderful fountain on the castle with King Matthias from the 15th century, who came across a maiden in the woods and they fell in love, you will recognize Ilona as the maiden. Szép meaning beautiful and as legend has it, this love tryst happened where this restaurant is now located. The interior is simplistic to the point of being Socialist outdated, but since it has a 150-year-old history, and the food is served in hearty, delicious portions, who can complain about decor. When weather permits, sit on the terrace. If you feel something furry pass by your legs, it is the restaurant cat. Some selections are cooked on lava stones and the barbecue pork cooked this way is moist and tender. We strongly suggest the Hortobagy pancakes, which are meat wrapped in a thin crepe with a creamy sauce poured over the top and a dollop of sour cream. Though located in a Buda neighborhood that is a bit of a trek to reach, the food is great and sitting under the trees is relaxing.

II. Budakeszi út 1–3. (€) **1/275-1392.** Main courses 1,200 Ft–3,000 Ft ($6.50–$16/£3.40–£8.55). MC, V. Daily 11am–10pm. Bus: 22 from Moszkva tér.

7 Coffeehouses: Historic & Traditional

As part of the Austro-Hungarian Empire, Budapest (just as in Vienna) developed a coffeehouse culture where people of like minds met to discuss politics, literature, or music. Each coffeehouse has its own story as to which literary movement or political circles favored their establishment. More than one claims the legend that someone stole the keys to the front door to keep their favorite cafe from ever closing. During communist times, these traditions evaporated into history, though a few of the coffeehouses did survive those strained times. With full freedoms returned, some coffeehouses have been restored to their previous glory. Other more modern coffeehouses have sprung up to create a new legacy of java traditions; see "Coffeehouses: Modern & Fun," below.

All of the classic coffeehouses offer a variety of traditional pastries and coffee, with pastries displayed in a glass case. Some also serve ice cream, while others offer bar drinks. As in restaurants, there is no need to rush; no one will push you out the door when you finish your drink or pastry.

Centrál Kávéház ✿✿✿   Coffeehouse culture is ingrained in Budapest history; this coffeehouse is one of the historic places where writers and artists gathered. Today it is a perfect replica of the original establishment, which opened in 1887. Although there is a superb restaurant here as well, the menu is limited, making it best known as a coffeehouse. Restored by one of Hungary's own millionaires, Imre Somodyt, to its former richness, it is a hotspot, not only for tourists, but also for locals. With its perfect location, it is always busy with a mix of tourists, businessmen, locals, and local celebrities coming in for a pastry or meal. In the room at the right, at the right-hand corner of the smoking section, there is a table perpetually reserved for local writer Géza Csemer. He happened to be there on our visit, and it was confirmed by the waitstaff. While mellowing in this coffeehouse's calm green interior with lavishly attractive ceilings, and brass hanging lamps with glass shades, you can browse the free copies of various newspapers over a coffee and a fresh croissant. A simple espresso at Centrál costs 420 Ft ($1.83/95p), but for the ambience it is worth the price. If you order a torta, a piece of cake after 10pm, you will receive a 30% discount on it.

V. Károlyi Mihály u. 9. ℂ 1/266-2110. www.centralkavehaz.hu. Main courses 1,490 Ft–3,790 Ft ($8.05–$21/£4.25–£11). AE, MC, V. Daily 8am–midnight. Metro: Ferenciek tere (Blue line).

Gerbeaud's *Overrated*   Perhaps the most famous of the Budapest coffeehouses, Gerbeaud's is most likely the most overrated also. Founded in 1858, it has stood on its current spot since 1870. There is no denying that the exterior and interior are lovely, but the pastries and coffee are no better than any other shop in the city. The extravagant prices are for the window dressing, not the goods. If you are interested in the decor of the late 19th century, go in and take a look and then go to another pastry shop for your snack.

V. Vörösmarty tér 7. ℂ 1/429-9000. www.gerbeaud.hu. AE, DC, DISC, MC, V. Daily 9am–9pm. Metro: Vörösmarty tér (Yellow line).

Lukács Cukrászda *Overrated*   After a hefty and lengthy remodeling, Lukács Cukrászda is now a faithful reproduction of a vintage coffeehouse. It opened its doors on the wings of fame of the former coffeehouse by the same name, which closed years ago. Located in the World Heritage area of Andrássy Boulevard, it is just a few minutes' walk from Oktogon, and not far away from the House of Terror. This is appropriate since the prices are frightfully high, thus less frequented than most traditional coffeehouses. They refuse to offer tap water as a side to the coffees ordered, stating that water must be ordered from the menu. A small bottle of water is 1,100 Ft ($5.95/£3.15), while a latte or a lemonade runs 690 Ft ($3.75/£2) each. The surroundings are lovely, but obviously recently remodeled and historically unoriginal, so the prices are to pay for the decor, not the quality of the drinks. The pastries are the usual that are found in many other cukrászdas, but also at highly inflated prices. Our suggestion is to have your coffee at Oktogon and bypass this establishment.

VI. Andrássy út 70. ℂ 1/302-8747. DC, MC, V. Mon–Fri 9am–8pm; Sat–Sun 10am–8pm. Metro: Vörösmarty u. (Yellow line and not to be confused with Vörösmarty tér, both are on this line).

Művész Kávéház ⋆   Just diagonally across Andrássy út from the Opera House, Művész (artist) was one of Budapest's finer traditional coffeehouses; it dates back to 1898. The lush interior of the long-gone past still reflects the elegance of the time with marble tabletops, crystal chandeliers, and mirrored walls. Regardless of its appearance of opulence, Művész is still a casual place to just unwind. They have many of the traditional desserts such as somlói galuska, which is considered a national dessert, plus pastries, and an ice cream bar. Everything is on display behind glass, so after you decide, take a seat and tell the waitstaff your choice. The inside back room can get quite smoky at times, so the tables in the front room or on the street, weather permitting are a pleasant alternative.

VI. Andrássy út 29. ℂ 1/352-1337. No credit cards. Daily 9am–11:45pm. Metro: Opera (Yellow line).

THE CASTLE DISTRICT

Rétesbar ⋆⋆⋆ *Finds*   To say that this little bakery has the absolute *rétes* (strudel) we have ever had is no exaggeration. Warm out of the oven, the flaky pastry was just enough to hold the warm cheese filling inside. It is melt-in-your-mouth scrumptious. They have a variety of other *rétes* and some other savory small pizza-type pastries. The place is small, though there are benches outside to sit and enjoy. It is a bit difficult to find; it is directly across from the Tourinform office, right past the woman fountain in the brick alleyway (köz).

I. Balta köz 4. No phone. No credit cards. Daily 9am–8pm. Bus: 10 from Moszkva tér or no. 16 from Deák tér to Castle Hill. Funicular: From Clark Ádám tér to Castle Hill.

Our Favorite Sweets

Hungarians love their sweets as you will discover by all of the pastry shops and bakeries everywhere. There will be some type of confectionary to satisfy everyone. The cakes are much drier than what most people are used to and they seem stale at first, but they aren't. Only the pastries with fruit or creams are going to be moist.

Flódni is a Central European layered pastry of apples, poppy seeds, and walnuts only found at **Café Noé**, Wesselényi u. 13 (© **1/321-7145**) as far as we have found. They also have a nice selection of diabetic pastries.

Found only in Hungary, **Dobos torta** is a light chocolate layer cake with a caramelized frosting. Take the topping off before cutting into the cake and then eat the topping separately. **Ischler** dates back to Viennese times. It is two shortbread cookies with apricot jam filling, sometimes dipped in dark chocolate.

Meggyes rétes (rétes is a strudel) is with sour cherries and is a traditional favorite as is the **Mákos rétes, Alma rétes** (apple), or our favorite **Szilva rétes** (plum) when in season. All of them have flaky pastry and are delicious snacks. The best we have had is from **Rétesbar** ★★★ at Balta köz 4 in the Castle Hill District.

Somlói galuska is a national treasure in the dessert world. See appendix B, "Hungarian Cuisine."

Kürtőskalács is an interestingly different honey bread. You can watch them wrap the dough around a cylindrical piece of wood shaped like an oversized rolling pin and bake them in an extremely hot oven. It's not available in regular shops or cafes, but readily available at festivals and craft fairs.

If you like cinnamon, Hungarian **cinnamon ice cream** (fahej) is unbeatable for flavor. And if you come across the rarest of its varieties, cinnamon rice ice cream (fahejes rizs), by all means try it. **Rizs** alone is also common in the summertime.

8 Coffeehouses: Modern & Fun

THE INNER CITY & CENTRAL PEST

Aztek Choxolat Café ★★ (Finds   If you have seen the movie *Chocolat* and dreamed of finding a cafe where you could indulge in the hot chocolate served in the movie, you are in for one extraordinary treat. Being such a small place, you would never expect it to be a chocoholics fantasyland, with a hot chocolate called Secret of the Mayas with a blend of six herbs and spices mixed in hot molten chocolate, our personal favorite. For the less adventurous there is chocolate with sour cherry and coriander; chocolate with amaretto, ginger, and nutmeg; and 10 other combinations. If your taste buds run more to java than chocolate, there are treats in store for you also. The coffees come in 20 combinations, many that the big chains have not yet discovered, but also in three sizes. If you super size it here, you will be floating out. In agreeable weather, they have four tables in the passageway; otherwise, you will have to scramble for one of the three tables inside. And did I mention that all of their spices can be bought mixed for 400 Ft ($2.15/£1.15) a bag to be added to your own cocoa when you return home? They also sell pralines in imaginative flavors, beautiful designs, and placed in a lovely box ready for gift giving. You can enter the short passageway from either street, but keep your eyes open, it is sometimes easily missed.

V. Karoly korut 22 or Semmelweiss u. 19. © **1/266-7113.** Hot chocolate 400 Ft–750 Ft ($2.15–$4.05/£1.15–£2.15); coffee 280 Ft–750 Ft ($1.50–$4.05/79p–£2.15). Mon–Fri 7am–7pm; Sat 9am–2pm. Metro: Deák Ferenc tér.

Café Alibi ⊛ (Finds Sitting on a corner across from the university for law is this little pearl of a cafe with its limited food menu. Inside is cozy and meant to have an old-cafe feel with the old-fashioned chairs, the streetlamp lighting, and the prints hanging on the wall. The antique cash register adds to the flavor of the place. Personally run by the owner, Laszlo Vagi with an efficient staff, it continues to thrive by accommodating guest wishes whenever possible. We stopped by for the Café Alibi scrambled eggs with mushrooms, tomatoes, and grated cheese melted on top. Breakfast is served until noon, and then the lunch menu starts. Best of all, if you sign up for their newsletter on their website, you can get a code for a free coffee. Special wine dinners for a fixed price are also available different times; check the website for specifics.

V. Egyetem tér 4. © **1/317-4209.** www.cafealibi.hu. Breakfast 690 Ft–1,490 Ft ($3.75–$8.05/£2–£4.25); main courses 1,190 Ft–1,490 Ft ($6.45–$8.05/£3.40–£4.25). No credit cards. Mon–Wed 8am–9pm; Thurs–Fri 8am–10pm; Sat 9am–9pm; Sun 9am–5pm. Metro: Kálvin tér (Blue line).

Café Noé ⊛ For a delectable pastry treat called *flódni* this small pastry shop is the only place to find it. *Flódni* is a layered pastry with apple, poppy seed, walnuts, and plum jam; it is an old Eastern European traditional pastry, we have only found here. Every pastry we sampled has been fresh and delectable. They have diabetic pastry selections also. Order a coffee and wander upstairs to their funky cafe area and bring your laptop, the Wi-Fi is free here. They just started featuring local Hungarian artists creating a gallery atmosphere. If it catches on, they will do a rotating art show. They have a second location called the **Bulldog Cukrászda.** You can also order a custom cake from their website and have it delivered in to someone special in Budapest.

VII. Wesselényi u. 13. © **1/321-7145.** www.torta.hu. AE, MC, V. Mon–Fri 10am–6pm. Or Bulldog Cukrászda V. Veres Pálne u. 31.

Fröhlich Kóser Ckrászda ⊛ KOSHER If you want your baked goods kosher or you just want tasty baked goods, this is the place to go. This is a basic type of bakery, where atmosphere is not high on the priority list, but good baked goods are sold. There are a couple of not-too-comfortable tables to sit for a coffee and pastry, but take-away is the best option, enjoying your goods in a park. The staff does not speak English, so you have to point to your selection.

VII. Holló u. 1. © **1/267-2851.** Cash only. Sun–Fri 9am–6pm. A short walk from Dohány Synagogue.

Spinoza Étterem ⊛⊛ Opened by a Hungarian woman who had spent many years in The Netherlands and who, after returning to Budapest, wanted to combine the Dutch and Jewish philosophical cultures for her restaurant located in the historic Jewish quarter. With a limited menu, it is more a cafe than a restaurant, but the kitchen will be remodeled to make it a full restaurant by the end of 2007. As a cafe, it is one of my favorites in the city. With a small cabaret theater in the back, musical events are offered on a regular basis. The schedule is posted in the window of the cafe.

VII. Dob u. 15. © **1/413-7488.** www.spinoza.hu. AE, MC, V. Daily 11am–11pm. Bus: 74 to Dohány Synagogue.

9 Teahouses

Tea drinkers are finally being recognized with their own places to sit, relax, and savor a pot a tea of their choosing. In these teahouses, there is no limit to the variety of teas available. Just like the coffeehouses, you are welcome to unwind as long as you wish without concern of overstaying your welcome. This is just a sample of teahouses; they are cropping up all over the city.

Tea Palota (Tea Hall) Come here if you want to free Tibet or even just feel free in Tibet. Entering this tea shop, you'll find a huge mural of a Tibetan mountain on the wall; you can use your imagination to feel the cool mountain air in summer, since they don't have air-conditioning. They do have relaxing ambience in a Zen-like atmosphere. For larger groups with good backs, you can venture upstairs to a room full of pillows and Japanese-style tables for lounging while sipping your tea. At the top of the stairs is a smoking room for those who like to mix their tea with nicotine. Teas are available in a wide range, but sadly the menu is in Hungarian only. If you describe your desires to the waitstaff, they will make recommendations.

VI. Jókai u. 20. ℭ 1/354-1453. MC, V. Mon–Sat 10am–11pm; Sun 2–11pm.

Teaház a Vörös Oroszlánhoz (The Red Lion Teahouse) This is a place to hide from the tourists running around and with multiple locations, you have choices too. You can choose from various "atmospheres": business-talk-like chairs and tables, friendly bean-bags, or intimate private rooms with mattresses. Within the shop, a small yet fitting bookstore features a nice selection of exoteric, literary books in English as well. Tea lovers will be amazed at the countless high-quality tea offerings from Indian green teas and Chinese black teas to Healing teas.

IX. Ráday u. 9 ℭ 1/215-2101; VI. Jókai tér 8. ℭ 1/269-0579; XI. Villányi u. 12. ℭ 1/279-1133. MC, V. Mon–Sat 11am–11pm; Sun 3–11pm at all locations.

Zöld Teknős Barlangja (Green Turtle Cave) 🎈🎈 *Kids* A Native American tea house seems out of place in Budapest, but it's still fun to see how other cultures interpret some aspects of Hungarian culture. It looks overwhelmingly like a tourist trap, but step downstairs for the real fun. Down in the nonsmoking section, the room is decorated in a rustic, log-cabin style—a comfy spot for a pot of tea. Even better: To the left of the staircase are intimate little nooks for two, and behind those doors you'll find little rooms with comfortable chairs and a fake fireplace for small inviting tea parties. Smokers can head to the first floor (one up from the street), where Native American motifs add to the ambience—right down to the chief sitting with his hollowed out log fire as an ashtray. Pressing a silent bell button will call the waitstaff to take your order for a pot of tea from over 50 different choices, all with Native American names.

VI. Jókai u. 14. ℭ 1/302-0024. AE, MC, V. Mon–Thurs 11am–11pm; Fri–Sat 11am–midnight; Sun 1–11pm. Metro: Opera (Yellow line).

7

Exploring Budapest

Historic Budapest is smaller than people realize when they first arrive. Since this is a great walking city, many attractions listed in this chapter are easily reached by foot from the city center or if you would rather save some time, public transport will get you there too. As you stroll from one place to the next, look up at the buildings even if you have to stop a minute. There are so many missed treasures above normal views that go underappreciated by many.

Regardless of a building's decay, take into consideration it probably has a long and interesting history associated with it. Many people have commented to me, about how nice a building would be if it were restored, but they forget that this city was heavily bombed during World War II. That rubble falling from the facade most likely has a story to tell. Clean and pretty buildings are nice to look at, but what historical secrets are they keeping?

1 The Top Attractions on the Pest Side

MUSEUMS

Museums are closed on Monday, except where noted. Museums sometimes offer senior discounts for EU citizens or student discounts with an international ID; however, if it is not posted, ask anyway. If a senior discount is posted, there are times when a cashier is willing to bend the rules in your favor. A few museums offer a family rate. All rates are usually posted next to the ticket window. All museums have coat-check rooms. You are expected to check your coat and bags, but women can keep their purse. This is a fairly standard rule. Unlike many countries, museums in Hungary allow photos and videotaping, which thrills a shutterbug like me, but they charge for the privilege. In the listing details, I have included the cost of a photo and video ticket if they offer it so you can determine if it is worth your while to carry the equipment. Where photos or video are not allowed, there are no ticket prices.

Holokauszt Emlékközpont (Budapest Holocaust Memorial Center) ★★★

Opened in 2004 to coincide with the 60th anniversary of the Holocaust, this is the first government-funded Holocaust memorial center in central Europe. Architecturally, it is a combination of classical and modern creating asymmetrical lines. All of the distorted symmetry is intentionally symbolic of the warped, perverse history of the Holocaust. In the center is a refurbished eclectic-style synagogue that was originally designed by Leopold Baumhorn, a famous architect of synagogues at the turn of the 20th century. The space has a permanent exhibition, a research center, and an excellent bookshop with many English selections. Temporary exhibitions are local and international. A large wall surrounds the courtyard serving as remembrance for the Hungarian victims of the Holocaust. The names of the victims are engraved onto the glass wall

IX. Páva u. 39. ⓒ 1/455–3333. www.hdke.hu. Admission 1,000 Ft ($5.50/£3) adults, free for students with ID. Tues–Sun 10am–6pm. Metro: Ferenc krt. (Blue line).

Nemzeti Múzeum (Hungarian National Museum) 🎟🎟

The Hungarian National Museum was founded in 1802 thanks to the numismatic, book, and document collections of Count Ferenc Szénchényi. One of my favorite buildings in Budapest, this enormous neoclassical structure was finished in 1846. It was here that the poet Sándor Petőfi and others of like mind are said to have roused the emotions of the people of Pest to revolt against the Habsburgs on March 15, 1848. If you look carefully, you will find a column on a plinth on the left side of the entrance that was given to Hungary by Mussolini. The column was from the Forum in Rome. Due to its negative history, the plague now states: "A gift from the Italian nation."

The permanent exhibit holds over one million pieces of Hungarian historical artifacts, including the main attraction, a replica of the so-called crown of King St. Stephen. Stephen was the first king of Hungary and brought Christianity to the land, thus he made it to sainthood upon his death in 1000. The original of what is referred to as King St. Stephen's crown is in the Parliament building. It was stored in the Pentagon in the U.S. after World War II and returned in 1978. Hungarian historians state that the crown was not St. Stephen's; its lower part is believed to have been a gift to King Géza I (1074–77), and its upper part was built for Stephen V, who reigned almost 250 years after the first Stephen's death. The permanent exhibition is the History of Hungary from the Foundation of the State to 1990. Featured are various objects and documents illustrating the migratory history of the early Hungarians from Siberia to the area now known as Hungary, and other displays of their military and social history up to the freedoms regained in 1990. A second permanent exhibit is Lapidarium Roman Stone Finds located in the basement.

VIII. Múzeum krt. 14. ⓒ 1/338–2122. www.hnm.hu. Free admission for permanent exhibits; temporary exhibits vary. Photo 3,000 Ft ($16/£8.50); video 5,000 Ft ($27/£14). Tues–Sun 10am–6pm. Metro: Kálvin tér (Blue line).

Néprajzi Múzeum (Museum of Ethnography) 🎟🎟 *Kids*

One of the largest specialist museums in Europe, it contains over 139,000 Hungarian and 53,000 international art objects. Housed in the former Hungarian Supreme Court building, directly across Kossuth tér from the House of Parliament, the museum has the pleasure of being in a Renaissance, baroque, and neoclassical building. The lavish interior alone is worth a visit. A ceiling fresco of Justitia, the goddess of justice, by the well-known artist Károly Lotz, dominates the lobby. The permanent exhibition named From Primitive Cultures to Civilization needs a good dusting, but nevertheless, it is fascinating and holds my attention on each visit. It features dioramas with articles from all periods of early Hungarian history. Temporary exhibits rotate often and have varied admission prices. Even if you are only going to the permanent exhibit, you need to get your free ticket from the cashier.

V. Kossuth tér 12. ⓒ 1/473-2400. www.neprajz.hu. Free admission for permanent exhibits; temporary exhibits vary. Photo 300 Ft ($1.50/85p); video 1,000 Ft ($5.50/£3) Tues–Sun 10am–6pm. Metro: Kossuth tér (Red line).

Szépművészeti Múzeum (Museum of Fine Arts) 🎟🎟🎟

During the 1896 millennial celebration of the Magyars settling and forming a nation in 896, the plans were proposed for the Museum of Fine Arts. Ten years later in the presence of Franz Josef, the king and emperor of Austria and Hungary, the Museum of Fine Arts was opened at the left side of Heroes' Square. This was the last great monument to be built during the most

Central Budapest Attractions

ATTRACTIONS

Belvárosi Plébániatemplom
(Inner-City Parish) **47**

Bélyegmúzeum
(Postal Stamp Museum) **42**

Buda Palace **14**

Budapest Holocaust Memorial
Center **51**

Budapesti Történeti Múzeum
(Budapest History Museum) **16**

Csodák Palotája
(Palace of Wonders) **4**

Dohány Synagogue **41**

Fővárosi Állat és Növénykert
(Zoo and Botanical Gardens) **25**

Füvészkert (Botanical Garden) **52**

Gellért Hegy (Gellért Hill) **18**

Gül Baba Türbéje
(Tomb of Gül Baba) **3**

Gyermekvasút
(Children's Railroad) **6**

Hadtörténeti Múzeum (Museum
of the History of Warfare) **9**

Halászbástya
(Fisherman's Bastion) **12**

Hősök tere (Heroes' Square) **31**

Iparművészeti Múzeum
(Museum of Applied Arts) **50**

János-hegy Libegő
(János Hill Chairlift) **5**

Kerepesi Cemetery **44**

Kozma Cemetery **45**

Középkori Zsidó Imaház
(Medieval Jewish Prayer
House) **11**

Közlekedési Múzeum
(Transport Museum) **28**

Liszt Ferenc Emlékmúzeum
(Franz Liszt Memorial House) **32**

Ludwig Museum of
Contemporary Art **49**

Magyar Állami Operaház
(Hungarian State
Opera House) **35**

Mátyás Templom
(Matthias Church) **13**

Miksa Róth Memorial House **43**

Millenáris Park **4**

Művészetek Palotája
(Palace of Arts) **49**

Nagy Cirkusz (Great Circus) **26**

Nemzeti Galéria (Hungarian
National Gallery) **15**

Nemzeti Múzeum (Hungarian
National Museum) **46**

Nemzeti Zsidó Múzeum és
Levéltár (National Jewish
Museum and Archives) **40**

Néprajzi Múzeum
(Ethnographical Museum) **23**

Parliament **22**

Postamúzeum
(Post Office Museum) **37**

St. Stephen's Bazilika **36**

Semmelweis Orvostörténeti
Múzeum (Semmelweis Museum
of Medical History) **17**

Széchenyi Lánchíd
(The Chain Bridge) **21**

Szépművészeti Múzeum (Museum
of Fine Arts) **30**

Természettudományi Múzeum
(Museum of Natural History) **53**

Terror Háza (House of Terror) **33**

Vajdahunyad Castle **29**

Vasúttörténetipark (Hungarian
Railway Museum) **24**

Vidám Park (Amusement Park) **26**

Zenetörténeti Múzeum
(Museum of Music History) **10**

INFORMATION
Tourinform **34, 39**

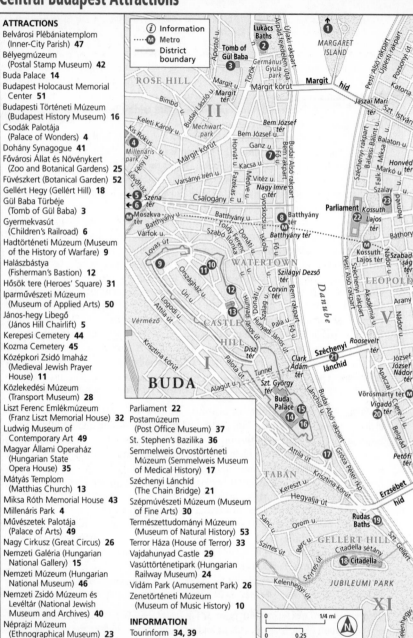

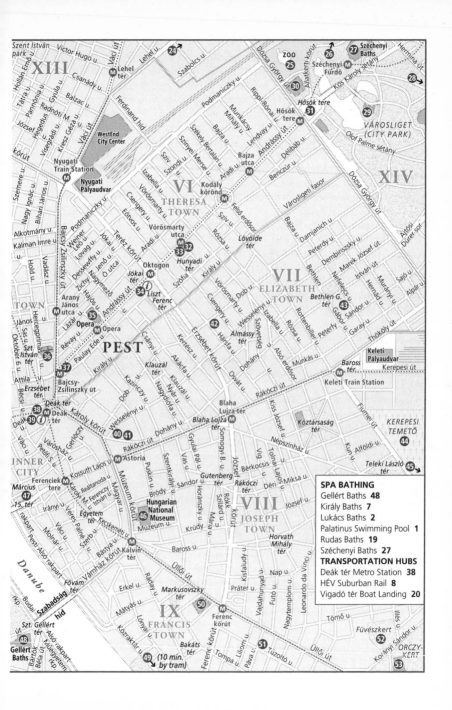

SPA BATHING
Gellért Baths **48**
Király Baths **7**
Lukács Baths **2**
Palatinus Swimming Pool **1**
Rudas Baths **19**
Széchenyi Baths **27**
TRANSPORTATION HUBS
Deák tér Metro Station **38**
HÉV Suburban Rail **8**
Vigadó tér Boat Landing **20**

prosperous period of Hungary's history. Designed in the Beaux Arts style, the main facade has three classical Greek temples connected by colonnades. The temples represent the grove of muses, a place of relaxation. The Greek influence is further incorporated with the Corinthian columns and sculpture in the pediment: the Battle of the Lapiths and the Centaurs from the Temple of Zeus at Olympia. The museum is the main repository of foreign art in Hungary and it houses one of central Europe's major collections of such works. The initial collection was donated by Count Széchenyi who presented a number of portraits. A significant part of the collection was acquired in 1871 from the Esterházy collection, an enormously wealthy noble family who spent centuries amassing great art. There are eight sections in the museum: Egyptian art, antiquities, baroque sculpture, old masters, drawings and prints, 19th-century masters, 20th-century masters, and modern sculpture. Most great names associated with the old masters: Tiepolo, Tintoretto, Veronese, Titian, Raphael, Van Dyck, Brueghel, Rembrandt, Rubens, Hals, Hogarth, Dürer, Cranach, Holbein, Goya, Velázquez, El Greco, and others are represented here. Delacroix, Corot, and Manet are the best-represented 19th-century French artists in the museum. The overall collection consists of over 3,000 paintings, 10,000 drawings, and 100,000 prints. Trained docents offer a 1-hour guided tour in English, free of charge. Go to the cashier's desk close to the starting time and a docent will announce the tour. They are offered Tuesday through Friday at 11am and 2pm and Saturday at 11am.

XIV. Hősök tere. © 1/469-7100. www.szepmuveszeti.hu. Free admission for permanent collection; temporary exhibits vary. Photo 300 Ft ($1.50/85p); video 1,500 Ft ($8/£4). Tues–Sun 10am–5:30pm. Metro: Hősök tere (Yellow line).

2 More Pest Museums & Sights

PEST

Bélyegmúzeum (Postal Stamp Museum) ⟨★⟩   When I had the personal mission to visit every museum in Budapest one summer, I thought this would be one I could spend 10 minutes in and check it off of my list. Almost 3 hours later, I left in awe. Beyond the unappealing entry, the museum itself is modern, bright, and air-conditioned. Admittedly this is my first stamp museum ever, but the displays were ingenious with rack after rack of the country's finest stamps starting from the first stamps ever ordered by royalty to almost current times totaling over twelve million. The Madonna with Child in **Rack 49,** which was mistakenly printed upside-down, is said to be Hungary's most valuable stamp. Variations on Lenin and Stalin can be seen in **Racks 68 to 77,** and **Racks 70 to 80** ⟨★★⟩ contain numerous brilliant examples of Socialist Realism. Aside from Hungarian stamps, stamps from around the world are just as impressive, though obviously not as complete. Make sure you go into the little dark room with the audio in English that plays while you view a U.S. stamp with a magnifying glass. The staff seldom sees visitors so they are extremely friendly and welcoming. My only regret was that photos are not allowed.

VII. Hársfa u. 47. © 1/341-5526. www.belyegmuzeum.hu. Admission 200 Ft ($1.10/55p). Apr–Oct Tues–Sun 10am–6pm; Nov–Mar Tues–Sun 10am–4pm. Tram: 4 or 6 to Wesselényi u.

Füvészkert Botanical Garden ⟨★★⟩   This is the botanical garden of Eötvös Loránd University, containing a plethora of flora with over 7,000 species including over 800 varieties of cactus. It was established here in 1847 after being started by Cardinal Péter Pázmány in 1635, in what is now Slovakia. The garden was uprooted and replanted a few times, before finding its Budapest home. The gardens also contain a palm house and Japanese garden complete with pond and goldfish.

VIII. Illés u. 25 (entrance is on the corner of Illés u. and Korányi Sándor u.). No phone. Admission 500 Ft ($2.70/£1.40) adults, 250 Ft ($1.35/70p) students and children. English audio CD rental 500 Ft ($2.70/£1.40) with a 5,000 Ft ($27/£14) deposit. Daily 9am–5pm; greenhouses 9am–noon and 1–4pm.

Iparművészeti Múzeum (Museum of Applied Arts) 🎔🎔   You have to see this building and not just from the outside. Even if you are not interested in the collections, walk into the lobby and take a peak. It makes me think of what being inside a wedding cake must be like. Architect Ödön Lechner was the designer of the museum along with Gyula Pártos in what is called Secessionist or Hungarian Art Nouveau in the 1890s. The roof is done in Zsolnay ceramic tiles (for more on Zsolnay, see p. 196). Lechner left his stamp in other parts of the city as well as the country. If you like this building, visit the former Post Office Savings Bank on Hold utca. Permanent exhibits, which are made up of antique decorative arts from all over Europe, are divided into five sections: furniture; textiles; metalwork; ceramics, porcelain, and glass; and an eclectic display of books, leather, and ivory. I find the temporary exhibits far more interesting than the permanent ones, which are fortunately given more space. Unlike the other museums, you have to pay the special exhibit price when there is one to enter the regular collection. Regardless, you have to see the interior.

IX. Üllői út 33–37. © 1/456-5100. www.imm.hu. Admission 800 Ft–2,000 Ft ($4.25–$11/£2.25–£5.75) depending on exhibit. Photo 500 Ft ($2.75/£1.50); video 1,500 Ft ($8/£4) Tues–Sun 10am–6pm. Metro: Ferenc krt. (Blue line).

Miksa Róth Memorial House 🎔🎔🎔   This museum is in the artist's last home, making is sometimes difficult to find, but well worth hunting for. Róth was a mosaic and stained-glass artist who gained worldwide acclaim for his work. He has pieces in the Parliament, on public buildings, and in Mexico and other countries. His stained glass is breathtaking, as is the method of painting on glass that he developed. Once you have been to this museum, you will become aware of how prolific an artist he was. This is one of my favorite museums of the small variety.

VII. Nefelejc u. 26. © 1/341-6789. www.rothmuzeum.hu. Admission 500 Ft ($2.75/£1.40) adult, 250 Ft ($1.40/70p) student. Photo 1,000 Ft ($5.50/£2.80). Tram 4 or 6 Wesselényi.

Nemzeti Zsidó Múzeum és Levéltár (National Jewish Museum and Archives) 🎔🎔   Sitting to the left of the Dohány Synagogue (p. 141), the museum contains an excellent collection of Judaica, which survived the war by being housed in the basement of the National Museum. The permanent collection contains devotional objects for Jewish holiday celebrations, everyday objects, and a special room with the History of the Hungarian Holocaust exhibit. Outside there is a plaque stating that Theodor Herzl, the founder of Zionism, was born on this spot. The museum is only four rooms, but it is a powerful display. Note that admission to the synagogue includes the museum.

VII. Dohány u. 2–8. © 1/342-8942. Admission 1,400 Ft ($7.50/£4) adult, 700 Ft ($3.75/£2) student. Photo 500 Ft ($2.70/£1.40) synagogue, free for museum. Mon–Thurs 10am–4:30pm; Fri 10am–2:30pm; Sun 10am–5:30pm, except Jewish holidays. Closed ½ hour earlier every day in winter. Metro: Astoria (Red line) or Deák tér (all lines); bus: 74.

Postamúzeum (Post Office Museum) 🎔🎔 *(Finds)*   This museum is often overlooked, but like the Museum of Applied Arts, you should come here to see the historic building interior. The stained glass in the entryway is only the beginning of the razzle-dazzle to follow. It surprised me how interesting the collection was once I was immersed in the grandeur of my surroundings. There are explanation sheets in English, so you self-tour around the pieces of post, communications, and program broadcasting historical pieces. The collection of objects consists of 20,000 items, but don't fear, you can do this museum in an hour or less if you rush through. The apartment and furnishings were owned by the Sexlehner family who obviously were a prosperous clan. Chandeliers hang royally from the frescoed ceilings, and intricately carved wood moldings trim the walls, making this a must for anyone interested in history, design, or antiques.

VI. Andrássy út 3. (C) 1/269-6838. www.postamuzeum.hu. Admission 400 Ft ($2.25/£1.25) adult, 200 Ft ($1/55p) student, free admission Sun. Photo free. Tues–Sun 10am–6pm. Metro: Bajcsy-Zsilinszky út (Yellow line) or Deák tér (all lines).

Terror Háza (House of Terror) ★★   You will have to brace yourself before going into this historical building. Also bring your reading glasses; all of the information in English is on copious sheets of paper in each room. This is the former headquarters of the ÁVH secret police. This building is witness to some of the darkest days of 20th-century Hungary and is now a chilling museum. The goal was to create a memorial to the victims of both fascism and communism, the successive oppressive regimes in Hungary, but according to critics, it misses the mark by putting more energy into the communist times. The Nazis headquartered here in 1944 used the basement for torture and murder of suspected traitors and others they thought were undesirables. The communist secret police wasted no time at all in taking over the building and continuing the reputation the fascists started. The fact that it is now a museum has caused much debate amongst locals who feel it is glorifying the evil past. The artsy roof that overhangs its stenciled letters onto the street doesn't help the cause with Andrássy út being a World Heritage site.

VI. Andrássy út 60. (C) 1/374-2600. www.houseofterror.hu. Admission 1,500 Ft ($8/£4.25) adult, 750 ($4/£2) student. Tues–Fri 10am–6pm; Sat–Sun 10am–7:30pm. Metro: Oktogon (Yellow line).

Vajdahunyad Castle ★★ (Kids)   Many refer to this castle as a replica of a Transylvanian castle, but actually, it was built for the 1896 Millennium celebration. The purpose was to highlight the different architectural styles of the past with detailed replicas of historic buildings in Hungary incorporated into the design. The main section is a copy of the Vajdahunyad Tower, giving it its name. Interestingly, the original made for the celebration was made of cardboard, and of course disintegrated. Now the building houses the Museum of Agriculture, a surprisingly interesting place to visit, not only for seeing the interior of the building, but also for the exhibits. The permanent exhibit is free.

XIV. City Park–Városliget. (C) 1/422-0765. Admission 750 Ft ($4/2) adult, 650 ($3.50/£1.75) student. Photo free. Sun–Fri 9am–5pm; Sat 9am–6pm. Metro: Széchenyi fürdő (Yellow line).

Vasuttortentipark (Hungarian Railway Museum) ★★ (Kids)   Occupying the former site of the Budapest North Depot of the Hungarian State Railways, this is the first European interactive railroad museum, which opened in July 2000. With a roundhouse and 34 bays, there is plenty of room to keep the vintage railroad engines and cars including a steam engine from 1840. The pride of the vintage fleet is the elegant teak dining car built for the Orient Express in 1912. Not only can you admire the old machines, but you can also try them out. You can drive a steam engine, travel in a car converted for rails, operate a handcart, and ride on the turntable or the horse drawn tram. For the really serious railroad buff, Hungary has a wide assortment of seasonal vintage and narrow-gauge railroad excursions. Check the website for dates and times or contact Tourinform (p. 45).

XIV. Tatai út 95. (C) 1/450-1497. www.vasuttortenetipark.hu. Admission 900 Ft ($4.75/£2.50) adult, 300 Ft ($1.50/75p) children, 1,800 Ft ($9.75/£5.25) family. Photo 200 Ft ($1/50p); video 800 Ft ($4.25/£2.25). Apr–Oct

---

Fun Fact Pucker Up!

Hungarians made history once again on June 9, 2007, when 6,637 Hungarian couples gathered to make Hungary the world's record-holding country for simultaneous kissing. All of the kissing you see everywhere else is just a warm-up for the next go round. In September 2007, the Bosnians claimed to have beat the record with 7,000 smackers. Paris could not get more than 1,500 participants.

Tues–Sun 10am–6pm. Bus: 30 from Keleti Station; tram: 14 from Lehel tér, both to Rokolya u. stop; a vintage rail diesel runs from Nyugati Station to the museum during the season.

HISTORIC SQUARES & BUILDINGS

Hősök tere (Heroes' Square) ᚷᚷ *Kids*   If you want a really dramatic experience, come up from the yellow metro station at Hősök tere from the city center at night. When Hősök tere is lit it is majestic in its splendor, not to say that it is not stunning during the day too. Located at the end of the grand World Heritage Boulevard, Andrássy út, the square is the entryway into the best-known park in the city, City Park (Városliget). Like so many other things in the city, the square and the park were planned and built to celebrate the arrival and settling of the Magyars' forming a nation in 896. The tricky part at the time was that Hungary was part of the Austrian Empire and was beholden to the emperor while celebrating their independence as a nation. The monument as it is seen today was not completed until 1929, which had the collapse of the empire precede it.

In the center of the monument is a column 37m (120 ft.) high, topped by a large statue of Gabriel, the Archangel. The sculptor György Zala won a prize for his work at the World Exhibition in Paris after it had been shipped where it waited out testing of the strength of the column to support it. If you look at Gabriel's hands, he is holding a crown. Legend has it that Stephen, the first king, had a dream where Gabriel appeared to him and prompted him to continue his efforts to convert his people to Christianity.

At the base of the column are statues of the conquerors on horseback. The one in the forefront is Árpád the leading chieftain who led the six other Magyar tribal leaders in conquering the land. To the sides of the column in a colonnade, are seven heroes of Hungarian history on each side. Starting from the far left you will find King Stephen I, the country's first Christian king, followed by six other kings who followed him. On the right side, only the second statue is a royal; King Matthias Corvinus, who presided over Buda's golden age in the 15th century (sixth from right). Other statues found atop the colonnade are immediately to the left and right of the column, the chariots of peace and war. At the forefront top on the left and right sides are statues representing work and welfare, while on the other side glory and knowledge.

Heroes' Square is a popular place with kids who come with their parents, but also local kids and teens who generally arrive with their skateboards after the throngs of tourist buses leave the area. Many concerts, fairs, and political demonstrations are held on this plaza throughout the year.

Two of Budapest's major museums, the Museum of Fine Arts and the Exhibition Hall, flank Heroes' Square.

Metro: to Hősök tere (Yellow line).

Magyar Állami Operaház (Hungarian State Opera House) ✰✰✰   Built in a neo-Renaissance style, this is the most beautiful building of this style on Andrassy út. The architect was Miklós Ybl, the most successful and prolific architect of his time. He created what many agree is one of the most beautiful opera houses in Europe. It was completed in 1884. It is Budapest's and Hungary's most celebrated performance hall; the opera house boasts a fantastically ornate interior featuring frescoes by two of the best-known Hungarian artists of the day, Bertalan Székely and Károly Lotz. Both inside and outside are dozens of statues of such greats as Beethoven, Mozart, Verdi, Wagner, Smetana, Tchaikovsky, and Monteverdi. In corner niches you will find the muses Terpsichore, Erato, Thalia, and Melpomene representing dance, love poetry, comedy, and tragedy. Home to the State Opera and the State Ballet, the opera house has a rich and evocative history, which is related on the guided tours given daily at 3 and 4pm (these can be arranged in English). A minimum of 10 people is required for a tour to begin and the tour costs 2,500 Ft ($14/£7) for adults and 1,300 Ft ($7/£3.75) for students with an international ID card. If 10 people do not show up, there is no tour for that time period. Well-known directors of the opera house include Gustav Mahler and Ferenc Erkel, the composer of the Hungarian national anthem. See p. 222 for information on performances. You may enter the lobby where the ticket office is located without charge, but the only way to tour the interior is with the guided tour.

VI. Andrássy út 22. ✆ 1/331-2550. www.opera.hu. Tour 2,500 Ft ($14/£7) adults, 1,300 Ft ($7/£3.75) students. Photo 500 Ft ($2.75/£1.40); video (with small camera) 500 Ft ($2.75/£1.40). Tours daily 3 and 4pm. Metro: Opera (Yellow line).

Parliament ✰✰✰   Budapest's great Parliament, the second largest in Europe after London, is an eclectic design mixing the predominant Gothic revival style with a neo-Renaissance dome. Construction began in 1884, 16 years after Westminster and was completed in 1902. Standing proudly on the Danube bank, visible from almost any riverside point, it has from the outset been one of Budapest's proud symbols, though until 1989 a democratically elected government had convened here only once (just after World War II, before the communist takeover). Before entering, take note that the top of the building is 29m (96-ft.) high at its peak, commemorating the 896 conquest. St. Stephen's Basilica is the same height.

It used to be a bicameral parliament with an upper and lower house, but now is unicameral with coalitions having to be formed. As you walk up the imposing staircase, you are led under the dome along a 16-sided hallway with 16 statues of rulers. In the center floor under the dome is a glass case with the legendary jeweled crown and scepter of King St. Stephen. Historical records have shown that the crown is of two parts and from two different eras, neither from King St. Stephen's time, but Hungarians want to believe it was Stephen's. Nevertheless, it is one of the oldest royal crowns in history. You will notice the bent cross on the top; although there are many legends as to why it is bent, no one knows for sure. In St. Matthias Church on Castle Hill, there is a small, but impressive museum dedicated to the crown (p. 145).

V. Kossuth tér. ✆ 1/441-4415. Tourist.office@parliament.hu. Admission (by guided tour only) 50 min. tour in English 2,300 Ft ($12/£6) adults, 1,150 Ft ($6.20/£3.25) students, free admission EU Passport holders with passport. Photo free. Tickets available at gate X; pre-book by e-mail or phone ✆ 1/441-4904 or 1/441-4415. Tours year-round Wed–Sun 10am, noon, 1pm, and 2pm. Closed when Parliament is in session, usually Mon and Thurs. Metro: Kossuth tér (Red line); tram 2 or 2A Szalay u.

CHURCHES & SYNAGOGUES

Belvárosi Plébániatemplom (Inner City Parish Church) ✴   The Inner City Parish Church dates back to the 12th century and is built in the Romanesque style, on the site of the grave of Bishop Gellért, the martyr who was said to have been killed by angry pagans. This is the oldest church in Pest. Nothing from the original building exists any longer having been built over through the centuries with Gothic features. In the 17th century, the Turkish invaders turned it into a mosque. After a fire destroyed part of the church in 1723 the rebuilding included the baroque style with an interior of neoclassical features. From the outside, it looks rather dilapidated, but inside, the attractive features are the Gothic chapel, the neo-Gothic carved pulpit, the 15th century Italian frescoes, and the 20th-century main altar. Daily mass is held at 6:30am and 6pm; Sunday mass is at 9am, 10am, noon, and 6pm.

V. Március 15 tér. ℂ 1/318-3108. Free admission. Mon–Sat 6am–7pm; Sun 8am–7pm. Metro: Ferenciek tere (Blue line).

Dohány Synagogue ✴✴✴   Built in 1859, this is the second-largest working synagogue in the world (the largest is in New York City), and the second-oldest large building of those still standing. The oldest is the National Museum. The architect was non-Jewish Lajos Förster who designed it with Romantic, Moorish, and Byzantine elements. The synagogue's interior is a mix of Orthodox and Reformed Judaism for the Hungarian Neolog Jewish denomination, which seems to exist only in Hungary. Due to this, many are surprised to see an organ in the loft. They had to and still have to have a non-Jewish organist to play it. The synagogue has a rich, but tragic history; it was one of many detention areas for Jews during the Holocaust. There's a Jewish museum next door that traces the origins of Hungarian Judaism and features exhibits of ceremonial Judaica throughout the centuries. The museum periodically puts on excellent temporary exhibitions. The Holocaust Memorial and Heroes' Temple in the courtyard are well worth visiting. Note that the Holocaust Memorial Museum is at a different location.

VII. Dohány u. 2–8. ℂ 1/342-8942. Admission 1,400 Ft ($7.50/£4) adult, 700 Ft ($3.75/£2) student. Photo 500 Ft ($2.70/£1.40) for synagogue, free for museum. Mon–Thurs 10am–4:30pm; Fri 10am–2:30pm; Sun 10am–5:30pm, except Jewish holidays. Closes ½ hour earlier every day in winter. Metro: Astoria (Red line) or Deák tér (all lines); bus: 74.

Szent István Bazilika (St. Stephen's Church) ✴✴   The country's largest church, this basilica took more than 50 years to build (the 1868 collapse of the dome caused significant delay) and was finally completed in 1906, which explains the differences in architectural designs. Szent István Square, a once-sleepy square in front of the church, was elegantly renovated in the autumn of 2002 and the entire church was given a good cleaning in 2003. The plaza area was converted along with several neighboring streets into a pedestrian-only zone, now surrounded with restaurants. As you wander into the church and to the left in the back chapel you can view St. Stephen's mummified hand or you can wait until August 20, his feast day and see it for free when it is paraded around the city. To get the box to light up to actually see it, you will have to spring for 100 Ft (55¢/30p).

V. Szent István tér 33. ℂ 1/318-9159. www.basilica.hu. Church free admission; treasury 400 Ft ($2.15/£1.15); panorama tower 500 Ft ($2.70/£1.40). Photos free. Tour 12,000 Ft ($11/£5.70). Church daily 9am–7pm, except during services; treasury daily 9am–5pm; Szent Jobb Chapel Mon–Sat 9am–5pm, Sun 1–5pm; panorama tower daily 10am–5pm. Metro: Arany János u. (Blue line) or Bajcsy-Zsilinszky út (Yellow line).

CEMETERIES OF HISTORICAL INTEREST

Kerepesi Cemetary ✴✴✴   You may find visiting a cemetery a strange place to visit for a vacation, but this one will not be disappointing. Here you will find the final resting place of Hungary's richest and most prominent men and women. The sculptured monuments are often suggestive of the deceased life's work and are scattered among many chestnut trees giving the place a unique, almost classical air. The most extraordinary or egotistical personages are in huge mausoleums, while alongside you find memorials to communists of a previous era. Many who died in the 1956 uprising can be found in plot 21. My favorite is the Blaha Lujza, the Sarah Bernhardt actress of Hungary. Her reclining full-figured body is surrounded by small angels. One chess master has a chessboard headstone and an author has a distinguished chair with his hat and coat draped over it. The gravestones make it a walk through an art gallery. Right after All Saints' Day, the graves are covered with flowers. Half of the streets in Hungary are named after people buried here. You can get a map at the gate.

VIII. Fiumei út. Free admission. Mon–Fri 8am–8pm; Sat–Sun 9am–5pm. Closes 1 hr. earlier in winter. Metro: Keleti Station (Red line).

Kozma Cemetery ★★ The city's largest Jewish cemetery dates back to 1868, when the land was given to the Jewish community. The cemetery was designed by architect Freud Vilmos and the building was completed in 1896. More than a half-million Jews are buried here. Those memorialized include the 10,000 Hungarian Jews who fought in World War I and those who are victims of the Holocaust. Alfréd Hajós the Hungarian Olympic champion and architect (the first Hungarian to win a gold medal) made the memorial possible. A set of nine large walls with pillars are inscribed with the names of victims with family and friends having hand-filled in others. About 6,500 names appear including the 2,000 victims of the Klauzál tér ghetto, who perished during the last months of the war. The cemetery is still in use today, and the many monuments and orate headstones are worth visiting as a reminder of man's injustice to man. Situated in the eastern end of the Kőbánya District, it is a tram ride away from the center of town.

X. Kozma u. 6. Free admission. Mon–Thurs 8am–4pm; Fri and Sun 8am–2pm. Tram: 37 from Blaha Lujza tér to the next to last stop.

3 Sites of Jewish Interest
MEMORIALS
Along the Danube, on the embankment between the Chain Bridge and the Parliament building is a row of 60 pairs of bronze shoes that look suddenly abandoned. The memorial was created by sculptor Gyula Pauer. He named it ***Shoes on the Danube Promenade*** to commemorate those who were shot to death on the riverbank as the Allies were approaching the city. On the sidewalk, you will find a mosaic monument not far from the shoes. The inscription is in Hungarian, and states: "In the memory of the Hungarians who fell victim to the Arrow Cross terror in the winter of 1944–45."

There are a number of memorials to **Raoul Wallenberg,** the Swedish diplomat who saved the lives of so many Jews. *Snake Killer* is a statue created by sculptor Pátzay Pál as a tribute to Wallenberg's work and it is in XIII. St. István Park. It was completed in 1949 and destroyed, but renewed and erected in 1999. You can get there by tram 4 or 6. Raoul Wallenberg utca is named in his honor and is where he established the "Swedish houses." There is a relief of Wallenberg on a wall with an inscription that translated says: "Raoul Wallenberg, The Deputy of the Swedish Nation. From the beginning of July 1944 until January 1945 he coordinated the brave and noble humanitarian activity of the Royal

Swedish Embassy in Budapest. He became a legendary hero in that dark period of destruction. May this monument announce our imperishable gratitude in the middle of the city, which people were protected by his persistent humanity in an inhumane era's night." Another Raoul Wallenberg memorial created by Imre Varga is in Erzsébet Szilá-gyi Fasor a park in the second district consisting of a statue of the hero between two large rose-colored blocks of stone. Inscribed on the back of the stones is an imprint of the *Snake Killer* statue with the Latin phrase: "Donec eris felix multos numerabis amicos tempora si fuerint nubila solus eris." Translated it says: "When you are lucky, many friends you have, once the sky turns cloudy, alone you remain." Unfortunately, the park itself is not well maintained.

In district V. at Vadász u. 29, where the "Glass House" is located there is a memo-rial room with a plague to commemorate the deeds of **Carl Lutz,** the Swiss diplomat who created safe houses for the Jews under Swiss protection. The Glass House (Üveg-ház) was the headquarters of the Zionist youth movement. If you take Walking Tour 4: The Jewish District (p. 185), you will see the memorial honoring him.

Stolpersteine or Stumble Stones *★★★* in English was the inspiration of Cologne-based artist Gunter Demmig. He started making stone plaques with Holocaust vic-tims' individual names on them and placing them in the pavement in front of the last-known address for the victim. They have already appeared in Italy, The Nether-lands, and Austria, but as of April 2007, the first ones were placed in Budapest. Pri-vately funded at 95€ ($124/£65) each, the first three stones have been placed on **Ráday utca.** Each stone reads: "Here lived" followed by the person's name, date of birth, and fate. The first three are for Béla Rónai, an unemployed public official at Ráday u. 5; Oszkár Vidor Weisz, a textile dealer and shoe repair person at Ráday u. 25; and Imre Pollák, a spice dealer at Ráday u. 31. Throughout the summer of 2007, 50 more stones were to be placed throughout Hungary. One criterion for selecting those to be remembered is that they have no surviving relatives, thus keeping their memory alive when no one else is available to commemorate them. For more infor-mation, see www.stolpersteine.com. I accidently came across the first one on Ráday utca after learning about these, but had not had it on my mind at the time. I later found all three. It was a heartwarming experience.

OTHER SITES OF NOTE

Kazinczy utca Synagogue located in the middle of the historically Jewish VII Dis-trict is the center of traditional Orthodox Jewish life. Enclosed by residential build-ings there is the synagogue, prayer room, kosher restaurant, school, and nearby is the only mikveh of Budapest. Admission is 800 Ft ($4.25/£2.25).

Vasvári Pál utca Synagogue, VI. Vasvári Pál u. 5 just off of Király u (tram: Király u.), is operated by the Shas Chevra Lubavitch Shul and the Budapest Yeshiva. The synagogue entrance is through the courtyard.

Rumbach Synagogue, Rumbach u. off Dob u (no phone), was built in a roman-tic-Moorish style in 1872. It was closed for years due to it being so dilapidated. How-ever, it reopened in 2006, though its interior and exterior condition is still in a devastated state. When I went to visit in October 2007, it was open, but I was told that it will be closed yet again for renovation. No one knew when and for how long; this "Nem tudom" (I don't know!) is a typical response in Hungary. My best advice is to stop by and check on its status when you are here.

The **Leo Frankel Synagogue,** II. Frankel Léo u. 49 (② **1/326-1445;** Tram: 17), was built in 1928, but houses were built surrounding the shul to hide its appearance from outsiders passing by. The Germans used the shul as a stable during the Holocaust. It has recently been restored and is in use by members of the local Buda community. Suggested admission is 600 Ft ($3/£1.55), but any donation is gratefully accepted. Open Monday through Friday 9am to 1pm by prior arrangement. Services are Friday nights and Saturday mornings.

The Rabbinical Seminary at Gutenberg tér has been open since the early 1900s and was one of the few seminaries open during the communist period. It houses a huge library of more than 150,000 priceless volumes of Jewish literature. You will need to make an appointment to visit, but they did not want their number published.

Gozsdu Udvar (Gojdu Courtyard) was a unique part of the Jewish District at one time connecting Dob u. 16 and Király u. 13 by six courtyards and seven attached buildings that were 240m (787-ft.) long. The pavilion-structured houses served as a passageway between the two streets, with apartments on the top floors with 45 shops and workshops on the ground floor. It was this courtyard that served as a Jewish ghetto during the Holocaust. Thousands of Jews were locked in the courtyard by heavy gates. See "Walking Tour 4: The Jewish District" (p. 185).

BUDA
MUSEUMS
Budapesti Történeti Múzeum (Budapest History Museum) ☆ This museum, also referred to as the Castle Museum, is easily overlooked since it is tucked in the back courtyard behind the palace. Once you approach it, there are no lavish signs advertising it either. If you are interested in the history of this great city as well as the whole Carpathian basin from medieval times, you will love this museum. When I went, I was not expecting much and was more than surprised at how enjoyable it was. The exhibit descriptions detail (in English) the palace's repeated construction and destruction.

What you should not miss is the 3rd floor exhibit where you will find historic maps of battle plans and weapons used in the liberation from the Turkish occupation. At the back of the main floor, you will find a statue area that has an outstanding collection of Roman and medieval-era pieces. The highlight is the lowest level; it is actually part of the old palace and hidden back there is a chapel. With the museum atop of Castle Hill, the courtyard garden and tower (accessible only through the museum) have amazing views and there are benches to sit and relax with refreshments bought from the small stand.

I. In Buda Palace, Wing E., on Castle Hill. ✆ 1/224-3700. Admission 1,100 Ft ($6/£3). Photo 800 Ft ($4.25/£2.25); video 1,600 Ft ($8.75/£4.50). Audio-guided tours 850 Ft ($4.50/£2.50). May 15–Sept 15 daily 10am–6pm; Nov 1–Feb 28 Wed–Mon 10am–6pm. Bus: 10 from Moszkva tér or 16 from Deák tér to Castle Hill. Funicular: From Clark Ádám tér to Castle Hill.

Ludwig Múzeum (Ludwig Museum of Contemporary Art) This museum is located in the Palace of Arts (Mûvészetek Palotája), which opened in 2005, overlooking the Danube. It has the most important collection of contemporary Hungarian and international art. The collection includes American, German, Russian, and French artists from the last 50 years and central European contemporary works from the 1990s. It includes several late Picassos, Andy Warhol's *Single Elvis*, as well as an eclectic mix of Hungarian works by artists like Imre Bukta, Beáta Veszely, and Imre Bak. Like the Kunsthalle in Vienna, this museum is worth visiting for the various temporary exhibitions of contemporary works, mostly by alternative European artists. Art experts have told us that this museum uses its funding to bring exhibitions here, depleting their funds to add to the permanent collections.

IX. Komor Marcell u. 1. ℂ 1/555-3444. www.ludwigmuseum.hu. Free admission for permanent collection; special exhibits vary. Tues–Sun 10am–8pm; last Sat of the month 10am–10pm. Tram: 2 or 2A.

Nemzeti Galéria (Hungarian National Gallery) 🏛 With a collection of over 10,000 art objects, this museum is not for the cultural faint of heart. The works cover the period from the beginning of Hungary as a nation to the present day. I have yet to see the entire collection even with subsequent visits as it is so easy to succumb to sensory overload and not everything is labeled in English. Hungarian artists have produced some outstanding work, particularly the period for which they are most famous, the late 19th century. Permanent exhibitions include: medieval and Renaissance lapidariums, Gothic woodcarvings, Gothic winged altars, Renaissance and baroque art and the Hungarian celebrities Mihály Munkácsy, László Paál, Károly Ferenczy, and Pál Szinyei Merse. Some other pieces to look for are sculptures by Isván Ferenczy and Miklós Izsó. József Rippl-Rónai's canvases are premier examples of Hungarian post-Impressionism and Art Nouveau (see *Father and Uncle Piacsek Drinking Red Wine* and *My Grandmother*), while Tivadar Csontváry Kosztka's *Rousseau of the Danube* is considered by some critics to be a genius of early modern art.

I. In Buda Palace, Wings B, C, and D, on Castle Hill. ℂ 1/375-5567. Free admission to permanent collection; temporary exhibits vary. Dome 300 Ft ($1.50/85p). Photo 1,500 Ft ($8/£4.25); video 2,000 Ft ($11/£5.75). Tues–Sun 10am–6pm. Bus: 10 from Moszkva tér or 16 from Deák tér to Castle Hill. Funicular: From Clark Ádám tér to Castle Hill.

A FAMOUS CHURCH

Mátyás Templom (Matthias Church) 🏛🏛🏛 Originally founded by King Béla IV in the 13th century, this church is officially named the Church of Our Lady and is a symbol of Buda's Castle District. It is popularly referred to as Matthias Church after the 15th-century king Matthias Corvinus who added a royal oratory and was twice married here. The original church was built in stages that spanned from the 13th to the 15th century. Like other old churches in Budapest it has a history of destruction and reconstruction, always being refashioned in the architectural style in vogue at the time. Renovation has been an ongoing process as financial considerations allow and it is currently half-covered with scaffolding. When I went in to see how long this would continue, I was shocked to hear it was planned until 2012. Regardless, it is a church not to be missed and this one too has Zsolnay ceramic tiles. Do not miss the museum upstairs; often overlooked by travelers who do not realize it is there, it has an interesting history of the royal crown and a wonderful view of the church.

I. Szentháromság tér 2. ℂ 1/355-5657. www.matyas-templom.hu. Admission 650 Ft ($3.50/£1.85) adults, 400 Ft ($2.15/£1.15) students. Photos free. Mon–Fri 9am–5pm; Sat depends on weddings; Sun 1–5pm. Metro: Moszkva tér, then bus no. 10; or Deák tér, then bus 16. Funicular: From Clark Ádám tér to Castle Hill.

SPECTACULAR VIEWS

Gellért Hegy (Gellért Hill) 🏛🏛 Towering 235m (750 ft.) above the Danube, Gellért Hegy offers the city's best panorama on a clear day (bus 27 from Móricz Zsigmond körtér). It's named after the Italian bishop Gellért, who assisted Hungary's first Christian king, Stephen I, in converting the Magyars. Gellért became a martyr when vengeful pagans, according to legend, outraged at the forced and violent nature of Stephen's proselytism, rolled Gellért in a nail-studded barrel to his death from the side of the hill. An enormous statue now stands on the hill to celebrate his history. On top of Gellért Hill you'll find the **Liberation Monument,** built in 1947 to commemorate the Red Army's liberation of Budapest from Nazi occupation. The 14m (45ft.) statue of the woman holding the palm leaf of victory can be seen from just about any viewpoint along the river. To her sides are statues representing progress and destruction. Following the first election in 1990, there was much discussion as to whether the statue should be removed since the Soviet troops were more occupiers than liberators. Also atop the hill is the **Citadella,** built by the Austrians shortly after they crushed the Hungarian uprising from 1848 to 1849. Views of the city from both vistas are excellent, but the Citadella is spectacular. Don't bother paying the extra to traipse up to the upper part; the view is not that much higher, so don't waste your money.

Halászbástya (Fisherman's Bastion) 🎔🎔 The neo-Romanesque Fisherman's Bastion, behind Matthias Church and the Hilton Hotel has a spectacular panorama of the river and Pest beyond it. Built at the turn of the 20th century, it was included as part of the refurbishing of the church area. Local legend states that this stretch of medieval parapets was a protected area by the fishermen's guild, but the area was once a fish market area, so either could be true. The local city council imposed a fee of 3€ ($3.90/£2) to pass through the turnstile allowing you to climb to the top lookout points. If you happen to be in the area after 6pm, it is no longer manned and you can go up for free. An overpriced cafe is open in the warm months, but don't let the tables intimidate you from going to the railing and looking at the view over the Danube to Pest, you can see (from left to right): Margaret Island and the Margaret Bridge, Parliament, St. Stephen's Basilica, the Chain Bridge with the Hungarian Academy of Sciences and the Gresham Palace behind it, the Vigadó Concert Hall, the Inner City Parish Church, the Erzsébet Bridge, and the Szabadság Bridge. To get here, take the no. 10 bus from Moszkva tér or bus no. 16 from Deák tér, or the funicular from Clark Ádám tér to Castle Hill.

ÓBUDA
ROMAN RUINS

Aquincum (Roman Ruins) 🎔🎔 When thinking of the conquests of the Roman Empire, rarely does Hungary pop into anyone's mind, but if you enjoy Roman history or ruins, this is a must. One of the largest archaeological parks in the country, this area was the capital of the Lower Pannonian province in the 2nd century where the Romans flourished for over 110 years. At the time it was an important city in the Roman Empire, now named Óbuda. When you arrive by HÉV, the suburban train to the stop by the same name, you will see the ruined **Amphitheater of the Civilian Town** alongside the HÉV stop. It is open all of the time, but it is often home to homeless people, so you may want to view it from the fence, rather than wander among the ruins. Just a little farther down the road is the **Aquincum** park with the **Aquincum Museum.** Don't be fooled by outside appearances; at first glance the park looks small, but once you enter you will realize you need a good half-day here to do justice to the 2,000-year-old history that is still intact. Each section has its own map of the buildings in that section and the maps are in English. Chronoscopes have been installed to give the full effect of what the buildings originally looked like. There are shelters around the park that seem to be out of place, but these house additional ruins that are being protected from the elements. The small museum has limited English explanations, but the visuals are still worth your time to view. There are many special events, some recreating Roman history.

III. Szentendrei út 139. 🕐 1/454-0438. www.aquincum.hu. Admission 900 Ft ($4.85/£2.55) adults, 450 Ft ($2.45/£1.30) students. Photo for garden free; photo for exhibitions 500 Ft ($2.70/£1.40); video for exhibitions 1,500 Ft ($8/£4.25). Apr 15–30 and Oct 1–31 10am–5pm; May 1–Sep 30 9am–6pm; closed Nov 1–Apr 14 and on Mon. HÉV: Aquincum (direction Szentendre from Batthyány tér).

BRIDGING PEST & BUDA

Széchenyi Lánchíd (The Chain Bridge) ⭐ *Moments*   Prior to the building of this bridge, people relied on a structure on the water that had to be dismantled when ships passed and that easily wrecked in stormy weather. The Széchenyi Chain Bridge was named for the man who financed it in its original form, Count István Széchenyi. Széchenyi reportedly funded the bridge while his father was dying because he was not able to cross the river by ferry for medical assistance; bad weather delayed the ferry for 8 days, and his father died in the meantime. He came from one of the wealthiest families of the time and was intent on bringing Hungary into the modern times by funding a number of projects.. He wanted to not only unite Buda with Pest for the first time, but also to unite the country as well. After successive trips to London to view bridge construction, he commissioned Tierney Clark to design the bridge. The bridge was an exact copy of the bridge Clark designed at Marlowe for crossing the Thames. Ádám Clark, no relation to the designer, was hired as the chief engineer. He is responsible for the tunnel that runs under Castle Hill and the square at the foot of the bridge is named for him.

During the war with Austria in May 1849, the Austrians planned on blowing up the yet-to-be-completed bridge. Ádám Clark had the anchoring chambers flooded to foil their plans and the bridge was completed later that year. In January 1945, the Germans destroyed the bridge as well as all of the others that were in existence by that time. The Széchenyi Chain Bridge was rebuilt and reopened in November 1949.

With its advantageous location in the city center, it is most beautiful at night when thousands of lights adorning it are lit up like a chandelier until midnight. In summer, when festivals are held on it on weekends and traffic is diverted, it is a place to stroll while stopping at the booths set up by artists, craftspeople, vendors, and musicians who entertain the locals and tourists alike. At other times, there are pedestrian lanes on either side, to make a walk across for a view of the Danube a pleasant experience and an excellent photo opportunity.

4 More Museums & Sights

BUDA

Arany Sas (Golden Eagle) Pharmacy Museum   If you have any interest in medicine, allopathic, or homeopathic, this little museum will fascinate you. The back area has all of the concoctions in lovely old bottles that were once used to create remedies. There is even a replica of the fireplace and cooking area to show how it was done. If old ceramics get your attention, then that is another reason to explore here. There are only four small rooms, but you will leave with tidbits of curious information. There is no set fee for photos, but a donation is accepted.

I. Tárnok u. 18. ℰ 1/375-9772. www.semmelweis.museum.hu. Free admission; donations accepted. Mar–Oct Tues–Sun 10:30am–5:30pm; Nov–Feb Tues–Sun 10:30am–3:30pm. Bus: 10 bus from Moszkva tér or 16 from Deák tér to Castle Hill. Funicular: From Clark Ádám tér to Castle Hill.

Hadtörténeti Múzeum (Museum of the History of Warfare)   Housed in a former barracks in the northwestern corner of the Castle District, this museum has a collection of many weapons from the days before the Turkish invasion to the 20th century. There is also a large display of uniforms, flags, models, weapons, maps, photographs, and 28,000 coins. All of the displays' distributive notes are in Hungarian only.

I. Tóth Árpád sétány 40. © 1/325-1600. www.militaria.hu. Free admission. Photo 200 Ft ($1.10/55p); video 500 Ft ($2.75/£1.50). Apr–Sept Tues–Sun 10am–6pm; Oct–Mar Tues–Sun 10am–4pm. Bus: 10 bus from Moszkva tér or 16 from Deák tér to Castle Hill. Funicular: From Clark Ádám tér to Castle Hill.

Kőzépkori Zsidó Imaház (Medieval Jewish Prayer House) *Finds* You could walk past this tiny medieval Sephardic synagogue without realizing it is here. The door is not well marked. This prayer house was built at the end of the 14th century and was excavated accidentally in 1964; no one knew it was here. What was found were Jewish decorations on the walls of a chapel from the 17th century. One picture shows a bow pointing to heaven with statements from Hanna's prayer: "The bows of the mighty men are broken, and they that stumbled are girded with strength." Another is a Star of David with Aaron's blessing: "The LORD bless thee, and keep thee: The LORD make his face shine upon thee, and be gracious unto thee," as translated in the King James Bible. In the entry chamber there is a medieval grave with headstones on display demonstrating the life and history of the early Jews in the area. For more information on Jewish history, see appendix C, p. 300. The English-speaking caretaker will give you a free informal tour; he is more than pleased to have visitors. You can pretty much see the whole place from the entry; consider your admission fee a contribution to the museum.

I. Táncsics Mihály u. 26. No phone. Admission 400 Ft ($2.25/£1). Photos outside free. May–Oct Tues–Sun 10am–6pm. Bus: 10 from Moszkva tér or 16 from Deák tér to Castle Hill. Funicular: From Clark Ádám tér to Castle Hill.

Semmelweis Orvostörténeti Múzeum (Semmelweis Museum of Medical History) This museum, which traces the history of medicine from ancient times to the modern era, is located in the former home of Ignác Semmelweis, Hungary's leading 19th-century physician. Semmelweis is hailed as the "savior of mothers" for his role in identifying the cause of puerperal (childbed) fever and preventing it by advocating that physicians wash their hands between patients, an uncommon practice at the time. The museum, spread over four rooms, displays everything from early medical instruments to anatomical models to old medical textbooks. There's also a faithfully reconstructed 19th-century pharmacy. Descriptions are in Hungarian only, but many exhibits are self-explanatory.

I. Apród u. 1–3. © 1/375-3533. Free admission. Photo 600 Ft ($3.25/£1.75); video 1,500 Ft ($8/£4.25). Tues–Sun 10:30am–5:30pm. Take any bus or tram to Döbrentei tér (for example, bus 8 from Március 15 tér).

A MUSLIM SHRINE
Gül Baba Türbéje (Tomb of Gül Baba) *Finds* Celebrating the conquest of Buda with festivities and dinner in 1541, the ill-fated Turkish dervish Gül Baba fell over dead. Gül Baba belonged to a group of Turkish religious who worked with horticulture, specifically on developing new species of roses. His tomb is located in the steep, twisting neighborhood of the Hill of Roses (Rózsadomb) District. The Turkish government maintains it as a Muslim shrine. The descriptions of the religious items and rugs on display are in Hungarian and Turkish, but an English-language pamphlet is available on request.

II. Mecset u. 14. © 1/326-0062. Admission 500 Ft ($2.75/£1.50). Tues–Sun 10am–6pm. Tram: 4 or 6 to the Buda side of Margaret Bridge; the most direct route to Gül Baba tér is via Mecset u., off Margaret u.

ÓBUDA
Varga Imre Gyűjtemény (Imre Varga Collection) *Finds* Imre Varga is Hungary's best-known contemporary sculptor. As you walk to the small museum, just off Óbuda's Fő tér, you will run into some ladies holding umbrellas regardless of the

Statues, Which Statues?

By now, most people have forgotten that the city was littered with statues to Lenin, Marx, Engels, and the other representations of the communist times. If you have some recollection of them and are wondering where they have disappeared to, here is your answer. In the aftermath of 1989, they were not wanted any longer being constant reminders of difficult times. A plan was conceived for a **Socialist Statue Park (Szoborpark Múzeum).** The park is inconveniently located outside of the city and to call it a park is bordering on a misnomer. From the outside, it looks like an old American fort, but as you enter Socialist marching music is playing on the loud speaker. The large unkempt plot of dusty land has a circular exhibit of the statutes. What little information is available on or near each statue is in Hungarian only, which is confusing; the majority of visitors are tourists and not Hungarians.

Located in the XXII district (extreme Southern Buda) on Balatoni út (© **1/424-7500;** www.szoborpark.hu), the park is a memorial to an era, to despotism, and to hatred. The tiny museum gift kiosk sells communist-era memorabilia, such as T-shirts with flamboyantly modern sayings, medals, and cassettes of Red Army marching songs. The park is open daily from 10am to dusk and admission is 600 Ft ($3.25/£1.75). To get to the park, take the black-lettered bus no. 7 from Ferenciek tere to Etele tér. Buy a separate ticket for the yellow Volán bus (to Érd) for a 20-minute ride to the park; ask the driver where to get off. It is not easily marked and the stop is just a roadside stop. The Volán bus is not a city bus; passes and transit tickets are not valid. Or, for a premium, you can take the new and convenient direct bus service from Deák tér for 3,950 Ft ($22/£11) or 2,450 Ft ($13/£7) for students (admission ticket to the park included). The timetable varies by season, but the 11am departure remains constant with an additional run at 3pm in July and August.

Other statues have replaced some of the old while others are in spaces not formerly graced with artwork. One statue that just about every tourist sees is *The Little Princess,* but without a plaque, it is often mistaken for a jester. It sits on the railing on Vigadó tér, a straight shot down to the river from Vörösmarty tér. You will see by her knees that she has been rubbed in admiration for some time. The sculptor is László Marton, who also created the incredible statue of Attila József, the famous Hungarian poet, as he gazes toward the Danube by Parliament. Sculptor Imre Varga created the statue you will find on the tiny Vértanúk tér across from Parliament. The man on the bridge is **Imre Nagy,** Hungary's prime minister during the '56 revolution, who tried to build a democratic Hungary by negotiating with the Soviets and gaining Western support. His place on the bridge is a metaphor for being caught in the middle. He was later taken prisoner by the Soviets and executed. Varga is also the artist who created the *Weeping Willow* in the courtyard of the Great Synagogue. And back again to Vigadó tér, you will find the fairly new *Girl with a Dog,* a playful statue of a child playing ball with her canine friend, by artist Dávid Raffay. All of these artists are contemporary and still living and working at their craft.

Fun Fact **Did You Know. . . ?**

- A network consisting of 10km (6¼ miles) of tunnels, built in the Middle Ages for military purposes, lies underneath Buda's Castle District.

- Budapest did not become a unified city until 1873, when Pest, Buda, and Óbuda merged. A bridge crossing the Danube prompted this momentous decision.

- Budapest is the site of the European continent's first underground metro line, which you can still ride today (the Yellow line). It was built for, you guessed it, the Millennium celebration. So where was the very first metro built? London.

- The Swedish diplomat Raoul Wallenberg, stationed in Budapest, saved thousands of Jews from Nazi deportation by issuing fake passports and setting up safe houses, only to disappear himself into the Soviet gulag after the city's liberation. He was never heard from again. Petitions sent to the Soviet government requesting the opening of their secret records regarding Wallenberg's fate, have fallen on deaf ears. Others who helped the Jews are discussed in appendix C, p. 300.

- The retreating Nazis blew up all of Budapest's bridges in the final days of World War II. They have all been reconstructed since then as close to their original designs as possible.

- The Red Army liberated Pest from Nazi occupation on January 18, 1945, but did not manage to liberate Buda until February 13.

- The longest "basket handle" bridge was opened in Dunaújváros, Hungary, in 2007. Being 308m (1,010-ft.) long, beating out the previous record holder, Osaka, Japan by 60m (197 ft.).

- On St. Stephan's feast day and national holiday, Sunday, August 20, 2006, a major storm came from nowhere and destroyed trees and cars and caused five deaths. On Sunday, August 19, 2007, another major storm whipped up the city, but a worse storm came through on Monday, August 20, 2007.

- If you ride either the 4 or 6 tram from beginning to end in either direction, you will have ridden the longest tram route in the world.

weather, one of his works on display outside. Inside the museum, a varied cross section of Varga's work will have you alternating smiles with winces At the back of the museum is a garden with more pieces; people are portrayed without embellished glory, while the museum's cats play in and out of the garden. For an example of the sculptor's work in a different public context, see the statue of Imre Nagy near Parliament. Have small currency ready; they rarely have change.

III. Laktanya u. 7. (✆) 1/250-0274. Admission 500 Ft ($2.75/£1.50) adults, 250 Ft ($1.25/75p) students. Tues–Sun 10am–6pm. Train: HÉV suburban railroad from Batthyány tér to Árpád híd.

Victor Vasarely Museum   Often referred to as the father of op-art, Vasarely was born in Pécs, lived in Budapest, but left for Paris where he died in 1997. This museum was opened in 1987 after the artist donated 400 pieces of his work to the country. Downstairs you will find a number of his earlier graphic artist pieces and upstairs are the larger op-art works of colorful, geometric art. If this leaves you wanting more, there is also a museum with his work in Pécs, see chapter 14, p. 278.

III. Szentlélek tér 6. ⓒ **1/250-1540.** Free for permanent collection; special exhibits 300 Ft ($1.50/75p). Photo 300 Ft ($1.50/75p); video 1,500 Ft ($8/£4.25). Tues–Sun 10am–5:30pm; call in advance, since the museum closes occasionally for private events. Train: HÉV suburban railroad from Batthyány tér to Árpád híd.

5 Parks, Gardens & Playgrounds

Spending time in a park or any green space is a wonderful escape for many of the city dwellers who cannot actually retreat from the city for some countryside getaway to recharge their mental batteries.

Popular **Margaret Island (Margit-sziget)** ⭐⭐⭐ has an interesting royalty related history going back to King Béla. He vowed that if he were successful in the Mongol invasion from 1242 to 1244, his daughter Margaret would be brought up as a nun. Well he was, so when she was ten, she was brought to the island to live a life of pious chastity. On the island, there are the ruins attesting to the religious who lived here. You can walk around what is left of the Dominican Convent where you will find signs mentioning St. Margaret, a 13th-century Franciscan church. The island was once called Rabbit Island since it seemed to be infested with them. No bunny was able to leave without a bridge connecting the island to shore at the time. The island has been open to the public since 1908, but visitors were charged a fee, double on Sunday. It was not until 1945 when it was declared free for all. The long, narrow island is a wonderful escape from the hectic city.

In the summertime, you will find the large fountain plays classical music every 20 minutes and all of the selections are posted on a pole nearby. The flower gardens are well-kept, so it is not unusual to find crowds gathered on the lawn or benches surrounding it.

Connected to both Buda and Pest via the Margaret and Árpád bridges all but local buses are banned from the island with few other exceptions. The island holds many attractions including the Palatinus Strand open-air baths (p. 166), the Alfréd Hajós Sport Pool, and the Open-Air Theater. In the warm season, there is a restaurant called the Holdudvar, which serves good food at reasonable prices. It features outdoor movies and is very popular with the university set.

Sunbathers line the steep embankments along the river, and bikes are available for rent (see "By Bike," under "Getting Around" in chapter 4). There is a small petting zoo, many walking trails, and lots of green areas for spreading a blanket out. Several snack vendors and even clubs can fulfill your hunger or thirst needs. With what may seem like a near overload of options, Margaret Island remains a tranquil place for a city break within the city. Margaret Island is best reached by tram no. 4 or 6, which stops at the entrance to the island midway across the Margaret Bridge or bus no. 26 from Nyugati tér, which continues through the length of the island. *Warning:* Be aware of pickpockets. See "Staying Safe," in chapter 2.

City Park (Városliget) ⭐ sits behind Heroes' Square and is just as popular as Margaret Island for lazy walks, picnics in the grass, and the many attractions located in and around the park. It was built in stages, but the first stage started in the mid-1800s. The famous Hungarian poet János Arany (Arany János u. fame) wrote a poem called "Song of the City Park" in 1877. The park along with Heroes' Square has been privy to many

---

Tips **Instant Picnic**

Before heading off on a hike, taking a leisurely stroll in a park, or going to Margaret Island, make the trip extra special and plan to have a picnic. Head over to the **Plus** grocery store at the Wesselényi utca tram stop on either the 4 or 6 tram. Inside the door to the right are delicious oven-roasted whole chickens for 790 Ft ($4.30/£2.25). If you only want half, ask for *fél* (pronounced fail). To the left of this counter is the deli, which sells all types of salads and the clerk will give you plastic ware to eat it with. Directly across from the deli on the other side of the lobby is a bakery. Pick up some dessert. You can go into the grocery section to buy drinks or pick them up at one of the kiosks at or near the park. Viola! Instant picnic with disposable waste, so there is nothing to carry when you are done.

---

demonstrations as well as celebrations during their long histories. The **Vajdahunyad Castle** (p. 138) located by the lake is stunning when lit at night. The lake is used for small boat rides in the summer. Near the lake, an area is flooded to provide a frozen surface for ice skating in winter (p. 167). The park also embraces **Animal Garden Boulevard (Állatkerti körút),** where the zoo, the circus, and the amusement park are all found (see "Especially for Kids," p. 154). You will also find Széchenyi Baths (p. 166) on one outer rim of the park. The **Transport Museum** is off at the southern end of City Park which is considerably less crowded, but also less landscaped making it less attractive as a relaxation area. The nearby **Petőfi Csarnok** is the venue for a variety of popular cultural events, concerts, and the weekly flea market (p. 215). The Yellow metro line makes stops at Hősök tere (Heroes' Square), at the edge of the park, and at Széchenyi fürdő, in the middle of the park.

There are numerous parks and nature reserves in the **Buda Hills.** You can ride the Children's Railroad through the hills or take the János Hill chairlift to its highest point (p. 156).

The Buda Hills are a great place to explore on your own; but depending on where you go, you may want to spot a bus or tram line to return to. Moszkva tér is the best place to start an excursion into the hills. Pick up tram no. 56 or bus no. 21, 22, or 28; get off when you see an area you like.

If you have time to meander through Budapest, there are some well-maintained parks that are worth taking a seat in for a few moments rest. The Hungarian word for playground is *játszótér* (or *játszó kert*) or just *kert* for garden. **Károly kert** ★★ is a wonderful little enclosed park in the city, just a couple of blocks from the Hungarian National Museum. It is bordered by Ferenczy István utca, Magyar utca, and Henszlmann Imre utca. Enter the park through a wrought-iron gate. Once inside, you'll find swings and seesaws, a sandbox with a slide, and a nice stretch of green grass to run on. In the middle of all this is a fountain surrounded by flowers. This is a busy and popular park for mothers with their children and for seniors who like to sit and watch the youthful action. Indeed, it once belonged to the adjacent Károlyi mansion, which was the home of Mihály Károlyi, who served briefly as Hungarian prime minister in 1918. The mansion functions as the Petőfi Museum of Hungarian Literature (© **1/317-3611,** ext. 203). Its location in the Inner City makes it a convenient destination. Admission is 400 Ft ($1.25/50p) and it is open Tuesday through Sunday 10am to 6pm.

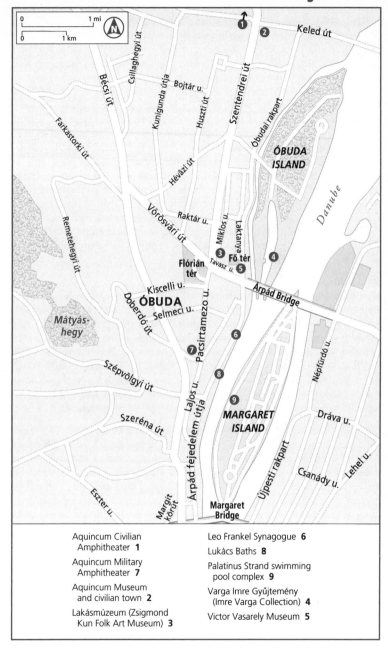

Aquincum Civilian
Amphitheater **1**

Aquincum Military
Amphitheater **7**

Aquincum Museum
and civilian town **2**

Lakásmúzeum (Zsigmond
Kun Folk Art Museum) **3**

Leo Frankel Synagogue **6**

Lukács Baths **8**

Palatinus Strand swimming
pool complex **9**

Varga Imre Gyűjtemény
(Imre Varga Collection) **4**

Victor Vasarely Museum **5**

6 Especially for Kids

Just because this section is geared toward children, you don't have to have children with you to visit the places mentioned here. Everyone has a child inside waiting for the chance to escape. When you are in a foreign country where no one knows you, it is a wonderful opportunity to be playful, so let loose.

Directly behind the Mammut Shopping Mall in Buda's Széna tér is the **Millenáris Park** Zöld Péter playground where all of the toys are based on the fairy tale. Besides the large wooden house to climb in, there are wooden toys, a giant fish, a smaller house, and a cable glider. Within the Millenáris park is a fishpond and food court next to the Place of Miracles (see below). Parents can sit and watch their kids playing in this safe and creative playground from the shade of trees.

Three attractions below are the zoo, the amusement park, and the circus. They are located in City Park (Városliget), along the famed Animal Garden Boulevard (Állatkerti körút). You could easily spend a whole child-oriented day here. In addition to the information below, see the information on the Palatinus Strand outdoor swimming-pool complex (p. 166) and horse and pony riding in the Buda Hills (p. 167). Also see the latter half of the section, "Parks, Gardens & Playgrounds," above for the lowdown on the best of Budapest's playgrounds.

MUSEUMS

Jövő Háza (House of the Future) *Kids*   The House of the Future is an interactive exhibition in a 1,300sq. m (13,990 sq. ft.) science playground that is renewed annually to be current. Inside, kids are certain to learn as they play. The House of the Future is an interactive science center featuring dozens of fun, educational exhibits, including laser displays, optical puzzles, and mazes in one large room. This place is best for kids over 3 years old. Note that the **Palace of Wonders** (Csodák Palotája) shares the space with the House of the Future, so admission is for combined tickets.

II. Fény u. 20–22. © 1/336-4000. www.jovohaz.hu. Admission 1,790 Ft ($9.75/£5) adults, 1,190 Ft ($6.50/£3.50) students. Photos free. Tues–Sun 9am–6pm. Metro: Moszkva tér (Red line), behind Mammut Mall.

Természettudományi Múzeum (Museum of Natural History) *Kids*   During my days of discovery, visiting all of the museums in Budapest, I found this museum delightful for children. It is child user-friendly with a number of interactive modules to keep a child entertained and informed at the same time. Through the natural history of the Carpathian Basin and the exhibits, a child can learn about human development from the earliest times to present. The museum is nicely situated next to Orczy Kert (Orczy Garden), a large park featuring over 100 different species of trees

---

Tips City Guide for Children

A family from The Netherlands who moved to Budapest has created an outstanding children's guidebook with the cooperation of children from 12 schools adding their drawings to bring it alive. **Benjamin in Budapest** *Kids* is a phenomenal book for family trips; kids will love the chance to help plan the trip. It is available at most bookstores in the city including the Alexandra chain and Tourinform offices and will make a memorable souvenir.

and a small lake. Until after World War II, the park belonged to the Hungarian Military School; the museum is in the more modern building to the left of the old school.

VIII. Ludovika tér 2–6. ℂ 1/210-1085. www.nhmus.hu. Admission 1,300 Ft ($7/£3.75) adults, 800 Ft ($4.25/£2.25) students. Photos 200 Ft ($1/50p). Wed–Mon 10am–6pm; closes 1 hr. earlier in winter. Metro: Nagyvárad tér (Blue line).

FAMILY FUN IN CITY PARK

Fővárosi Állat és Növénykert Zoo and Botanical Gardens *(Kids)*   Opened in 1866, the zoo houses animals in some beautiful Art Noveau– and national-style buildings designed by the best Hungarian architects of the time. It is located near the circus and the amusement park on City Park's famous Animal Garden Boulevard, a favorite spot for Hungarians for 140 years. The entry is stunning and other parts of the zoo have been modernized several times attempting to create a contemporary and humane environment for their 2,000 animal residents. A polar bear exhibit has been built to show the frolicking of the bears when they are in the water or lazying on the ice. The elephant house has also been restructured giving the animals more space. The petting zoo is a favorite attraction within the zoo. Two renovated greenhouses, the largest of their kind in central Europe, contain spectacular tropical plants. During the summer, the zoo hosts special concerts.

XIV. Állatkerti krt. 6–12. ℂ 1/273-4900. www.zoobudapest.com. Admission 1,400 Ft ($7.50/£4) adults, 950 Ft ($5.25/£2.75) children 2–14, free for children under 2. Children under 14 must be accompanied by a parent. Mon–Thurs 9am–5pm; Fri–Sun 9am–7pm; hr. vary by month, verify on website. Metro: Hősök tere or Széchenyi fürdő (Yellow line).

Közlekedési Múzeum (Transport Museum) *(Kids)*   Located near the Petőfi Csarnok in the little-visited southeastern corner of City Park, this wonderful museum, which celebrated its 100th anniversary in 1999, features large-scale 1:5 models of various kinds of historic vehicles, especially trains. The museum also exhibits vintage motorcycles and bicycles, early model cars, and antique horse buggies. A model train set runs every 15 minutes on the mezzanine level; follow the crowds. On weekends a film on aviation history is shown at 11am. The gift shop features all sorts of transportation-related trinkets. An aviation exhibit is housed in the Petőfi Csarnok, an all-purpose community center nearby.

XIV. Városligeti krt. 11. ℂ 1/273-3840. Free admission for permanent collection; temporary exhibits 800 Ft ($4.25/£2.25)adults, 400 Ft ($2/£1) students. Photo 1,000 Ft ($5.50/£2.75). Tues–Fri 10am–5pm, Sat–Sun 10am–6pm; Oct–Mar closes 1 hr. earlier. Trolleybus: 74 from Károly krt. (pick it up on Dohány u., across the street from Dohány Synagogue) or 72 from Podmaniczky u., near Nyugati Station.

Vidám Park (Amusement Park) *(Kids)*   This is a must if you're traveling with kids or are a child at heart. Some rides in particular aren't to be missed. The 100-year-old **Merry-Go-Round** *(Körhinta),* constructed almost entirely of wood, has been restored to its original grandeur, though it still creaks mightily as it spins. The riders must actively pump to keep the horses rocking, and authentic Würlitzer music plays. The **Roller Coaster,** operating since 1926, has a wooden frame and is listed as a historic monument. You will rush over nine waves before finishing the ride. The **Ikarus** will tickle your senses with its 30m (98-ft.) height and 30kmph (18 mph) speed making for a titillating 3-minute ride.

XIV. Állatkerti krt. 14–16. ℂ 1/343-9810. www.vidampark.hu. Admission 3,100 Ft ($17/£8.80) adults, 2,100 Ft ($11/£6) children 100–140 cm (39–55in) tall. Admission includes all rides with the wristband provided. Apr–Sept Mon–Fri 11am–7pm, Sat–Sun 10am–8pm; Oct–Mar Mon–Fri noon–6pm, Sat–Sun 10am–6:30pm. Metro: Széchenyi fürdő.

(Kids) The Buda-Triangle

Are you ready to head for the hills? No matter your age, you can enjoy the triple-transport triangular trip on the slopes of the Buda Hills. From Moszkva ter, hop on tram 56 for two stops to the **Cogwheel Railway (Fogaskereku)**, which clicks its way up a steep grade to the **Children's Train**on Szechenyi-hegy (hill). Uniformed children, true to the original model of the Soviet Pioneer Scouts, assist in ticketing and boarding the open-air cars. Enjoy the short ride across the wooded ridge. Get off at the fourth stop, Janos-hegy, where you will find the path to a terrace bufe (cafe) for refreshments, a playground, and toilet facilities. Nearby, the Erzsebet Look-out Tower, four-stories high and on the highest point of Budapest (529m/1,736 ft.), is worth the climb. There is no fee. When ready to return to Danube area, take your seats on the gently descending **Chair Lift (Libego)**, and marvel at the spectacular views of the city. Just outside the exit, bus 158 will take you back to Moszkva ter. The whole triangle can be done in reverse too. For those who may want more outdoor action, check with Tourinform for hiking trails atop the Buda Hills.

A RAILROAD & CHAIRLIFT

Gyermekvasút (Children's Railroad) ✮✮✮ (Kids)   Built in the 1940s, this railroad is a throw back to communist times when the Young Pioneers, the youth movement of the Communist Party ran the operation. Today, it is only specially trained children learning and having fun under adult supervision. The scenery along this narrow-gauge rail journey is lovely, especially in spring and fall. The youthful staff dresses in miniature versions of the official MÁV (Hungarian State Railways) uniforms, with all the appropriate paraphernalia. The train slowly winds 11km (6.8 miles) through the Buda Hills, providing numerous panoramas along the way.

To get to the Széchenyi-hegy terminus, take the same no. 56 tram from Moszkva tér two stations to the railroad (*fogaskerekű vasút*) station (the railroad station is called Városmajor, and it is across the street from the Hotel Budapest, on Szilágyi Erzsébet fasor in Buda). One-way travel time on the railway is 45 minutes.

Call the Széchenyi hegy terminus. ✆ **1/395-5420.** www.gyermekvasut.com. One-way trip 450 Ft ($2.50/£1.50) adults, 300 Ft ($1.50/75p) children 6–14 yr., free for children under 6; round-trip 600 Ft ($3.25/£1.75) adults, 250 Ft ($1.25/75p) children 6–14 yr., round trip family ticket 3,000 Ft ($16/£8.50). Summer daily 10am–5pm, Winter daily 9am–4pm. Trains run every hour or so.

János-Hegy Libegő (János Hill Chairlift) ✮✮ (Kids)   An old-fashioned chairlift lifts you over the tree tops to János Hill. From here you can take a steep 10 to 15 minute walk to Budapest's highest point. At the top is the neo-Romanesque ***Erzsébet Kiláto* (Lookout Tower)**, built in 1910. When I went there was no charge, but others have claimed there was a nominal fee to climb the tower. It is well worth it for the view. The tower is open daily from 8am to 5pm. You'll find a nondescript snack bar at the tower, but be careful of bees in the warm weather. You can ride the chair back down, hike back down to the no. 158 bus, or, if you like try the **Buda Triangle** above.

XII. Zugligeti út 93. ✆ **1/394-3764.** Chairlift trip each way 500 Ft ($2.75/£1.50) adults, 400 Ft ($2/£1) children. Daily 10am–4pm; in summer to as late as 7pm, depending on demand. Bus: 158 from Moszkva tér to the last stop.

Kids Bábszínházak (Puppet Theaters)

Kids from around the world love **Hungarian puppet theater** ⓐ. The shows are all in Hungarian, but with such standard fare as Hungarian versions of *Cinderella, Peter and the Wolf,* and local favorites *Misi Mókus, Marcipán cica,* and *János Vitéz,* no one seems to have trouble following the plot. The audience is an important part of the show: For instance, Hungarian children shriek "Rossz farkas!" ("Bad wolf!") at every appearance of the villain in *Peter and the Wolf.*

Budapest has two puppet theaters, with the season running from October to mid-June. Tickets are extremely cheap, usually in the 600-Ft-to-1,100-Ft ($3–$5.50/£1.55–£2.90) range. The **Budapest Puppet Theater (Budapesti Bábszínház)** is at VI. Andrássy út 69 (© 1/321-5200); the nearest metro station is Oktogon (Yellow line). The **Kolibri Puppet Theater (Kolibri Bábszínház)** is at VI. Jókai tér 10 (© 1/353-4633); Jókai tér is halfway between the Oktogon and Opera stations of the Yellow metro line. Shows start at various times throughout the day (days vary, so call in advance) with the first show usually at 10am and the last at 5pm, and tickets are available all day at the box offices.

A CIRCUS

Nagy Cirkusz (Great Circus) *Kids*   The building which is the venue for the circus is the only stone circus in central Europe and seats 1,850. It is open year-round. This is a traditional circus, with clowns, animals, jugglers, acrobats, and so on. When buying tickets, it's helpful to know that *porond* means "ring level" and *erkély* means "balcony." Check the website (it has an English link) to verify times, as the schedule was not confirmed as of this writing. The box office is open daily from 10am to 7pm.

XIV. Állatkerti krt. 7. © 1/343-9630. www.maciva.hu. 1,300 Ft–2,400 Ft ($7–$13/£3.75–£7) adults, 1,200 Ft–2,000 Ft ($6.25–$11/£3.30–£5.65) children, free for children under 4. Performances Wed–Fri 3pm; Sat 10:30am, 3pm, and 7pm; Sun 10:30am and 3pm. Metro: Hősök tere or Széchenyi fürdő (Yellow line).

7 For the Music Lover

Three museums in Budapest celebrate the contributions of great Hungarian musicians.

The greatest Hungarian composer of the 19th century, and one of the country's most famous sons, is undoubtedly **Ferenc (Franz) Liszt** (1811–96). Although Liszt spent most of his life abroad, he maintained a deep interest in Hungarian culture and musical traditions, as evidenced by his well-known "Hungarian Rhapsodies." Liszt is well-known for creating the musical idiom known as the symphonic poem with his *Les Preludes* (1848). He served as the first president of Budapest's Academy of Music, which is named after him. To top it all off, Liszt was also one of the great virtuoso pianists of his century.

If Liszt was the towering figure of 19th-century Hungarian music, **Béla Bartók** (1881–1945) and **Zoltán Kodály** (1882–1967) were the giants of the early 20th century. The founders of Hungarian ethnomusicology, Bartók and Kodály traveled the back roads of the country in the early 1900s, systematically recording not only Hungarian and Gypsy folk music, but also music of the whole Carpathian Basin region. Peasant folk music had been an important part of the region's rural culture for hundreds of years, but by the early 20th century, there were not many musicians playing and the music was in danger of being lost. In addition to saving a wealth of music from oblivion, Bartók and Kodály made some important discoveries in their research, noting both the differences and the interrelationships between Hungarian and other folk-music traditions (especially Gypsy music), which had fused considerably over time. Both men were composers, and the influence of the folk music they so cherished can easily be heard in their compositions. Kodály established the internationally acclaimed Kodály method of musical education and lived to become the grand old man of Hungarian music, while Bartók died relatively young in the United States, an impoverished, embittered refugee from fascism.

Concerts are given at the museums below; see the Budapest's free bimonthly *Koncert Kalendárium,* available at most four- and five-star hotels, and tourist information centers or online at www.koncertkalendarium.hu.

Bartók Béla Emlékház (Béla Bartók Memorial House) This little museum, high in the Buda Hills, occupies Béla Bartók's final Hungarian home and exhibits artifacts from Bartók's career as well as some of the composer's original furniture. The house has been decorated to reflect the time period and atmosphere in which the composer lived, and is run by the composer's heirs. At the time of this writing, the museum was undergoing extensive renovations that will extend the museum. Every year on September 26, the date of Bartók's death, the Bartók String Quartet performs in the museum. Concerts are also given on Friday evenings in spring and autumn, and occasionally on Sunday as well. Concerts are also offered on occasion, but they are only scheduled 3 months in advance and prices vary.

II. Csalán u. 29. ⟨© 1/394-2100. www.bartokmuseum.hu. 700 Ft ($3.75/£2) adults, 400 Ft ($2.25/£1.25) students. Tues–Sun 10am–5pm. Bus: 5 from Március 15 tér or Moszkva tér to Pasaréti tér (the last stop).

Károlyi Palace A renovated gem of the inner Budapest, this palace is an intimate courtyard with a strong stay-a-while atmosphere while the Sándor Petőri Literary Museum occupies the bulk of the building. On a stage set up in the garden with seating capacity of 500, concerts of classical, jazz, and folk music fulfill the magic of a summer evening's entertainment. The upcoming schedule of events is only posted 1 month before the season, so call for current concert information.

V. Károlyi Mihály u. 16. ⟨© 1/317-3450. Check performance schedule for dates/hours. Metro: Ferenciek tere or Kálvin tér (Blue line).

Kiscelli Museum Sitting at the top of Remetehegy (Hermit's Hill) in Óbuda, the Trinitarians first built this baroque castle as a monastery in the 18th century. What is left is an intriguing shell of a church hall, a bare courtyard, a baroque sculpture hall, and an enormous, mysterious crypt. During the summer months concerts are sporadically scheduled, which are worth attending just to see the building. Check the bimonthly *Koncert Kalendárium* or the other calendar resources given above for current offerings, if any. At other times, the hall is host to an art gallery and special art exhibitions.

III. Kiscelli út 108. ⟨© 1/388-7817. www.btmfk.iif.hu. 600 Ft ($3.25/£1.75) adults, 300 Ft ($1.50/85p) students. Photos 500 Ft ($2.75/£1.50); video 1,500 Ft ($8.25/£4.50). Tues–Sun 10am–6pm. Tram: 17 from Margit Bridge.

Liszt Ferenc Emlékmúzeum (Ferenc Liszt Memorial Museum) Located in the apartment in which Liszt spent his last years, this modest museum features several of the composer's pianos, including a child's Bachmann piano and two Chickering & Sons grand pianos. Also noteworthy are the many portraits of Liszt done by the leading Austrian and Hungarian artists of his time and two busts by the Hungarian sculptor Alajos Stróbl. Concerts are performed here on Saturday at 11am.

VI. Vörösmarty u. 35. (©) **1/322-9804**. 500 Ft ($2.75/£1.50) adults, 250 Ft ($1.25/75p) students. Photo 800 Ft $4.25/£2.25); video 1,600 Ft ($8.75/£4.50). Mon–Fri 10am–6pm; Sat 9am–5pm. Metro: Vörösmarty u. (Yellow line).

8 Organized Tours: Traditional

BUS TOURS

EUrama Travel Agency ((©) **1/327-6690;** www.eurama.hu) offers a bus tour called the Budapest City Circle Sightseeing Tour. Their red double-decker bus can be seen rolling through the streets of the city. They also offer a variety of other tours including walking tours of the Jewish District and Parliament. The duration of the City Circle Tour is 3 hours with the usual stops around the city. They will pick you up free at your hotel, otherwise there is a meeting point for alternative accommodations. In summer, they have three tours at 10am, 11am, and 2:30pm. In winter, the tours are offered at 10am and 2:30pm only. The price is 6,500 Ft ($35/£19) per person. The office is located at V. Apáczai Csere János u. 12–14 in the Intercontinental Hotel. You can book by phone, through your hotel, or online.

Ibusz ((©) **06/40-428-794;** www.ibusz.hu), has been around for a long time, but that does not always equal quality. They have 11 different boat and bus tours, ranging from basic city tours to special folklore-oriented tours. Unfortunately, the tours are pretty sterile and boring. (If you want a bus tour, try one of the alternative tours listed below.) Ibusz operates year-round, with an abbreviated schedule in the off season. All buses are air-conditioned, and all guides speak English. Some sample offerings are a 3-hour **Budapest City Tour** for 26€ ($34/£18) in high season and 13€–26€ ($17–$34/£9–£18) in low season, with the 1-hour Parliament Tour included it is 20€–40€ ($26–$52/£14–£27). There's a free hotel pickup service that will pick you up 30 minutes before departure time. For a full list of tours, pick up the Ibusz *Budapest Sightseeing* catalog, available at all Ibusz offices, Tourinform, and most hotels. Tours can be booked at any Ibusz office and at most major hotels, or by calling Ibusz directly at the toll-free number above. All major credit cards are accepted.

We highly recommend **Budapest Tour** ★★★ ((©) **06/70-455-0356** mobile only; www.seebudapest.hu) for its personal service. You receive a 3-hour tour in a small-group comfortable minivan (min. 1 or max. 12 people), with a live guide who is energetic about touring. The tours are done in English only, so there is no time delay waiting to hear the same information in various languages. The tour has 5 stops with explanations: Heroes' Square, St. Stephen's Basilica, Royal Castle Quarter, the Citadel, and finishing in downtown Pest. Being small groups, they do not rush you, allowing you time to take pictures or to stroll, depending on the group's wishes. The tour is rich in historical details, interesting stories, and practical information. The guides have a great knowledge of the city and welcome questions. The same company has a variety of other tours, custom tours for groups, and tours in other languages as well. Pick up anywhere in Budapest is free. The office is located at V. Molnar u. 3. The price for adults is 6,500 Ft ($35/£19), for children under 12, 3,250 Ft ($18/£9.25), and students with ISIC or Hostelling International cards receive 15% discount. Tours are offered daily 10am and 2:30pm.

9 Organized Tours: Untraditional

BIKE TOURS

Budapest Bike   Budapest Bike was started in 2005, by six Hungarian bicyclists. They offer the coolest bike tours downtown, starting at 10am daily for as few as one person. The tour costs 5,000 Ft ($27/£14). It includes a tour guide, the bike rental, a helmet, a map, a chain lock, and a drink. They also have tours outside of the city. If you are bound and determined to go it alone, they will rent you a bike for 6 hours for 2,000 Ft ($11/£5.75) or for a full day at 3,000 Ft ($16/£8.50); a tandem will run you 3,000 Ft ($16/£8.50) for 6 hours and 5,000 Ft ($27/£14) for a full day. A helmet, chain lock, and insurance are all included in the rental. They also offer a guided evening program, called a pub crawl, which will take you to the hottest pubs in Budapest for a mere 5,000 Ft ($27/£14). Included in this tour is a guide for 4 hours, a minimum of four pubs, two beers, and a shot. A minimum group of four people is needed.

VII. Wesselényi u. 13 © **06/30-944-5533** mobile only. www.budapestbike.hu. High season daily 9am–7pm; Nov–Mar daily 10am–6pm. Metro: Astoria (Red line) or Deák (all lines).

Yellow Zebra Bikes   Centrally and soon to be all over the city, Yellow Zebra Bikes offers bike rentals and guided bike tours, with optional helmets. Bike rentals cost 1,500 Ft ($8.10/£4.25) for 1 to 5 hours or 3,500 ($19£9.95) for 24 hours. Guided tours may be your best option, setting you back 4,500 Ft ($24/£13) for adults, 4,000 Ft ($22/£11) for students with an ID card. The tour price includes the guide, a bike, optional helmets, baskets, bungee cords, and a front bag. Just show up at the office before the tour leaves at 11am. In July and August, there is a second tour at 4pm. Yellow Zebra Bikes will be expanding to seven locations by the end of March 2008. You can find all of them on their website.

V. Sütő u. 2 © **1/266-8777**. www.yellowzebrabikes.com. High season daily 8:30am–8pm; Nov–Mar daily 10am–6pm. Metro: Deák (all lines). VI. Lázár u. 16. Same phone. Mon–Fri 9:30am–7pm; Sat–Sun 9:30am–4pm. Metro: Opera (Yellow line).

BOAT TOURS

EUrama Travel   The bus tour people now have extended their offerings to boat tours as well. Sailing up and down the river on a boat to tour the city is a wonderful way to see the major sites along the river's edge. The discount bus tour company has extended their services to the waters of the Danube, offering 1-hour sightseeing tours by boat. It is able to accommodate up to 100 passengers with roof and side decks for good weather viewing. Boats depart frequently from Vigadó tér (on the Pest waterfront, between the Erzsébet Bridge and the Chain Bridge, near the Budapest Marriott hotel). In winter, the inside is heated, making this a year-round tour option. The tour is in English and German, passing Parliament, turning at Margaret Island, and passing many popular sights along the way. The price for adults is 3,500 Ft ($19/£10) with pickup or 3,000 Ft ($16/£8.50) at the dock, and for students the price at the dock is 2,500 Ft ($14/£7). From June 1 to October 31, eight tours are offered daily. From November 1 to 29, and in February, there are two tours daily and in March there are four tours daily.

V. Vigadó tér pier 8. © **1/327-6690**. www.eurama.hu. Call for times and reservations. Tram: 2.

Legenda Tours   This private company was founded in 1990 and offers several boat tours on the Danube, using two-story steamboats. The daytime tour, called "Duna Bella," operates daily at 2:30pm, year-round, with additional daily trips during the summer. The 2-hour ride includes a stop at Margaret Island, with a walk on the island.

Tickets cost 3,800 Ft ($21/£11). The nighttime tour, departing daily at 8:15pm, is called "Danube Legend" and is less than impressive. Take a day tour and then the no. 2 tram for the lit-up view of the river attractions. Danube Legend tickets cost 4,700 Ft ($26/£14). On both trips your ticket entitles you to two free glasses of wine, beer, or soft drinks. A shorter variation of the daytime tour, without the stop on the island, runs from mid-April to mid-October. All boats leave from the Vigadó tér port, Pier 7. Tickets are available through most major hotels, at the dock, and through the Legenda website where they will give you a CD if you book two tickets online.

V. Vigadó tér Pier 7. © 1/317-2203. www.legenda.hu. Daily 2:30 and 8:15pm year-round. Tram: 2.

MAHART The Hungarian state company operates a daily 2-hour daytime sightseeing cruise on the Danube, using two-story steamboats. Boats depart frequently from Vigadó tér (on the Pest waterfront, between the Erzsébet Bridge and the Chain Bridge, near the Budapest Marriott hotel) on weekends and holidays in the spring and every day in summer. In the low season, it sails October 1 to November 4 and March 30 to April 29. Rates are 2,990 Ft ($16/£8.50) for adults, 2,490 Ft ($14/£7) for students with ISIC card, and 1,490 Ft ($8/£4.25) for children 6 to 15. For something different, MAHART also offers evening cruises with and without dinner included. If this floats your boat, they sail daily during high season; sailings are Friday, Saturday, and Sunday in low season. Buffet dinner and cruise is 5,990 Ft ($32/£17) or cruise only 2,990 Ft ($16/£8.50).

V. Belgrád rakpart. © 1/318-1704. www.mahartpassnave.hu. Call for times and reservations. Tram: 2.

Operetta Ship If you are an opera buff, you just may enjoy this unique candlelit boat tour that includes performers singing famous operas, operettas, Italian and Spanish songs, musicals, instrumental solos, and Hungarian folklore. During the tours, you will hear famous excerpts from Strauss, Mozart, Lehar, Gershwin, Puccini, and others. The boat tour with a dinner included costs 12,800 Ft ($70/£37), or 8,700 Ft ($47/£25) without the meal. There is also a music sightseeing tour guided in English, German, or Hungarian, that costs 4,000 Ft ($22/£12). This is more for the music enthusiast since you will not be paying much attention to the sights and the singing; so choose one or the other.

Vigadó tér 9 at Március 15 tér. © 06/20-332-9116. www.operetthajo.hu. Apr–Oct Mon, Wed, Fri, and Sun 8–10pm. Tram: 2.

CAVE TOUR

Barlangaszat *(Kids)* If you have a craving for caving, then this tour company will fill that hole in your life. They have been providing this tour since 1994. Spend 3 to 3½ hours traipsing through the second-longest cave of Hungary, the Pál-völgyi–Mátyáshegyi cave system. Most of it is situated under Budapest. Following a professional caving guide, you will explore the natural untouched cave system. The guides explain the formation of the Budai Mountains, the cave formations, and fossils along the way. All the necessary equipment is provided with the tour: overalls, helmet, and headlamp. A changing room is available at the cave entrance. Crawling, scrambling, and hunkering down will be done many times during the tour, but no previous experience in caving is needed. Minimum age is 6 years, but no upper age limit. It is not recommended for those who are claustrophobic or unable to squeeze through tight places. Three English tours a week or a special tour for a minimum of five people are offered.

No office. © 06/20-928-4969 mobile only. www.barlangaszat.hu. 3,800 Ft ($16/£8.50). Meet at 3:45pm at Nyugati tér. Reservations mandatory by phone, Internet, or Yellow Zebra Bikes at V. Sütő u. 2 location only.

JEWISH HISTORY TOUR

Chosen Tours   This tour company has been operating since 1990 and specializes in tours showing the city through the Jewish life and heritage in Budapest. All of their guides are from the Jewish community and speak excellent English. The Special City Tour is by coach lasting 3 hours with stops and adds the focus of the Jewish connections with the usual history. The Jewish Heritage Tour is 3 hours as a combined coach and walking tour taking you to Buda's extraordinary Jewish landmarks followed by a walk in Pest's Jewish quarter where you visit and enter all the highlights and the hidden treasures. Each of the tours runs 9,250 Ft ($50/£26). The walking portion can be done separately at 6,500 Ft ($35/£19) per person. To combine both 3-hour tours over 2 days, the cost is 14,800 Ft ($80/£42). For private tours for a minimum group of four, add 1,850 Ft ($10/£5.25) to the rates above per person. They also have a tour to Szentendre with Jewish sights pointed out.

No office. ℭ/fax **1/355-2202**. chosentours@yahoo.com. Reservations mandatory.

SEGWAY TOUR

Segway Tour 🕮🕮   How about a tour while riding a Segway? Ride a Segway (a stand up scooter) through the city getting an overview in a unique mode of transportation offered by Discover Hungary/Yellow Zebra. Riders must be a minimum of 12 years old. Reservations are necessary and they advise that you book a month ahead of time. You can combine a unique ride and a tour. Each of the tours begin with a 30- to 45-minute orientation session in the plaza and park next to their office, where you will practice on the Segway so you feel comfortable and ready to go out and conquer Budapest. The Segway is appropriate for virtually anyone 12 and older. Unfortunately, pregnant women are not able to participate. Helmets are required to be worn at all times. An insurance damage and liability waiver will also be required for all riders.

VI. Lázár u. 16. ℭ **1/269-3843**. www.citysegwaytours.com. Apr–Oct 10am and 6:30pm; Nov–Mar 10am. 55€ ($72/£38). Metro: Opera-Yellow line.

WALKING TOURS

Several companies offer walking tours of historic Budapest. One that I would recommend is the Absolute Walking Tour in Budapest offered by **Absolute Walking Tours,** part of the Discover Hungary/Yellow Zebra group (ℭ **1/266-8777;** www.discover hungary.com). The tours are conducted by energetic, friendly, and knowledgeable guides who meet you at the pickup point outside the Evangelical Church on Deák tér (all metro lines) at 9:30am and 1:30pm from mid-May through September. From October through mid-May, tours start daily at 10:30am only, from the same departure point that is listed above. No tours on December 24, 25, or January 1. Tickets are 4,000 Ft ($22/£12) for adults and 3,500 Ft ($19/£10) for students with ID and children 15 years and younger with a paying adult. Buy your ticket from the tour guide at the start of the tour. Tours last 3½ hours taking you throughout both central Pest and central Buda. Wear your best walking shoes and leave the heavy knapsack at your hotel. This company also offers other popular tours such as the **Pub Crawl** and **Hammer and Sickle,** but they are dependent on registration, so call ahead for information and a reservation.

   Underguide Tours 🕮🕮🕮 (ℭ **06/30-908-1597** mobile only; golocal@underguide) may sound ominous, but you can relax. These tours are geared for those who don't expect the usual and this is what you will experience when you take this half- or full-day tour. These are fully organized around your needs, so when you meet your Underguide tour guide, he or she forms the tour based on your ideas and then takes you to off-the-beaten-path places that the guide thinks you will like the best. It is fully customizable based on your interests and they strive to meet any requests. You can go it alone or with your own group, but never with strangers. If you book by Internet, you need to give them 3 days advance notice, but by phone, the prior day is fine. A half-day will run you 15€ ($20/£10) or 25€ ($33/£17) for a full day. All rates are per person, but children under 14 are free. A private tour with an Underguide is 64€ ($83/£44) for a half-day or 110€ ($143/£75) for a full day.

10 Budapest's Most Popular Thermal Baths

The baths of Budapest have a long history, stretching back to Roman times. The thermal baths were popularized by the Turks who started building them in 1565 giving them a place to bath in case of a siege on the city. Budapest and other parts of Hungary are built over hot springs making this a natural way of acquiring the mineral rich waters for bathing. Hungarians and other Europeans are great believers in the medicinal powers of thermal bathing with all of the thermals being medical clinics as well for the treatment of skin, muscular, and bone ailments. Even if you are not in need of the health benefits, time spent in thermal baths will lift your spirits. The Király's construction was started by Arslan, Pasha of Buda in 1565, but was completed by his successor. The Rudas, also built in the 16th century by the Turks, still functions today. Both are among the architectural achievements of the Turkish period. The Rudas boasts a 10m (33-ft.) diameter dome, sustained by eight pillars with an octagonal pool. From 1936 until 2007, it was only for men. Today, women are allowed on Tuesday. In the late 19th and early 20th centuries—Budapest's "golden age"—several fabulous bathhouses were built: the extravagant and eclectic Széchenyi Baths in City Park, the largest spa complex in Europe; the secessionist-style Gellért Baths; and the solid neoclassical Lukács Baths. All of these bathhouses are still in use and are worthy of visiting. Most baths in Budapest have recently instituted a complicated new pricing system (dubbed the "refund system") that charges according to the time that you have spent in the baths. Previously, a single admission ticket bought you an unlimited visit. Now, you are generally required to pay for the longest possible duration (4 hr. or more) when you enter the bathhouse and you are refunded on the basis of the actual time that you spent on the premises when you exit. You are given a chip card upon entry; keep careful track of the card because if you lose it you are assumed to have stayed for the maximum time and you will not receive a refund. The exception is the Király, which is still a set fee for entry and you are allowed 1½ hours and then are expected to leave. On Saturday, it is limited to 1 hour.

THE BEST & WORST BATHHOUSES

Gellért Baths *Overrated*   Once one of Budapest's most spectacular bathhouses, the Gellért Baths are located in Buda's Hotel Gellért, the oldest Hungarian spa hotel and a secessionist-style hotel. Over the years, the baths have lost their luster and some of the tile work. For the cost of entry, I do not recommend this bath at all and it is mostly frequented by foreigners, usually those staying at the hotel, due to the fees. Most of the pictures you will see in tour books are very outdated and you will be disappointed with the current condition. The staff is churlish, which I don't appreciate with the hefty fee. If you go, enter the baths through the side entrance. The exterior of the building is in need of restoration, but once inside the lobby, the details are lovely, but

Tips Thermal Bathing 101

Thermal bathing is a social activity deep within the Hungarian culture and each bath has its own set of rules, which can change without notice. Bathhouse employees tend to be unfriendly holdovers of the old system, who still have a civil service position since most baths are owned by the city. They do not speak English, and have little patience. Many foreigners find a trip to the baths stressful or intimidating in the beginning, but plunge forth, it is a cultural experience and they are not pinpointing you for their woes. Try to spot a resident and follow their example of what to do. Explore once inside and you'll find you will feel comfortable and confident within minutes. The best advice is to try to enjoy the foreignness of the experience, because after all, this is the reason you are here.

The most inhibiting may well be approaching the ticket window, with the long list of services and prices, often without English translations. Chances are you're coming to use one of the following facilities or services: *uszoda* (pool); *termál* (thermal pool); *fürdő* (bath); *gőzfürdő* (steam bath); massage; and/or sauna. There is no particular order in which people move from one facility to the next; do whatever feels most comfortable. Most of the thermals are also medical clinics; therefore, many services will not apply to you. Towel rental is *törülköző* or *lepedő*. Few places will provide a towel or sheet for drying off; if you don't want to rent one, bring your own. An entry ticket generally entitles you to a free locker in the locker room *(öltöző)*; or, at some bathhouses, you can opt to pay an additional fee for a private cabin *(kabin)*.

Remember to pack a bathing suit and a bathing cap if you wish to swim in the pools so you won't have to rent vintage 1970 models. Lukács requires a bathing cap for both sexes and for all thermals and pools. Long hair must

most of it stops here. The unisex indoor pool has marble columns, majolica tiles, and stone lion heads spouting water. The two single-sex Turkish-style thermal baths, off to either side of the pool through badly marked doors, are in dire need of restoration. In the summer months, the outdoor roof pool attracts a lot of attention for 10 minutes every hour on the hour, when the artificial wave machine is turned on. In general, you need patience to navigate this place and the staff is not helpful to foreigners.

XI. Kelenhegyi út 4. ℂ **1/466-6166.** Thermal bath 3,100 Ft ($16/£8.80) for 4 hr. or more; massage 2,500 Ft ($14/£7.10) for 15 min. Prices include a locker or cabin. Pools and baths 2,800 Ft ($15/£8) for 3 hr. or more. Price includes communal dressing rooms. Prices and the lengthy list of services, including the complicated refund system, are posted in English. Apr 30–Sep 30 daily 6am–7pm; winter Mon–Sat 6am–7pm, Sun 6am–5pm, with the last entrance an hr. before closing. Tram: 47 or 49 from Deák tér to Szent Gellért tér.

Király Baths ✦✦ This is one of the oldest baths in Hungary, dating back to around 1563, when the Turkish built the baths so they could bathe and be ready for battle readily. Other legends say this was the way the Turks got the Hungarians to bathe. Regardless of the reason, the Király Baths are still one of Budapest's most important architectural tributes associated with Turkish rule. Bathing under the octagonal domed roof with sunlight filtering through small round windows in the ceiling, gives the water a special glow. In winter, late afternoons you can look at the night sky watching the stars be capped when bathing at the other facilities. In the single-sex baths, Rudas, Lukács, and Gellért, men are provided with a loin cloth; bathing suits are not permitted. At the Király, bathing suits are now required. You may want to bring your own towel with you into the bathing areas in a plastic grocery bag. Flip-flops are also a good idea. Shower before getting into a thermal or pool. Soap and shampoo are only allowed in the showers, but you should bring everything you will need from the locker or cabin to avoid multiple trips and having to hunt down the attendant to unlock the locker. Some of the waters are high in mineral content, so you will most likely want to shower well and shampoo your hair before leaving. Depending on the pool, you may find a strong sulphur smell, but remember it will do glorious things for your skin. If it is possible to see without them, leave your eye-glasses in your locker as they will get fogged up in the baths.

Generally, extra services (massage, pedicure) are received after a bath. Locker room attendants appreciate tips, especially if you plan on returning. A tip of 200 Ft ($1.10/55p) is typical, unless you have repeatedly returned to the locker, then make it a bit more. Masseurs and manicurists expect a tip in the 400-Ft-to-600-Ft range ($2.15–$3.25/£1.15–£1.70).

There are drinking fountains in the bath areas, and it's a good idea to drink plenty of water before, during, and after a bath. Bathing on an empty stomach can cause nausea and light headedness for those unaccustomed to the baths. Most bathhouses have snack bars in the lobbies where you can pick up a cold juice or sandwich on your way in or out, but you must eat it there. Stay hydrated.

hanging in the distance. Either way, it is a relaxing experience. In addition to the thermal baths, there are sauna and steam room facilities. If you so desire, you can get a massage while you are there. This bath is time limited; Monday through Friday, you are only allowed to stay for 1½ hours and on Saturday, only 1 hour, before being expected to leave. Bathing suits are required for both sexes and take a towel with you. Women can use the baths on Monday, Wednesday, and Friday from 7am to 6pm. Men are welcome on Tuesday, Thursday, and Saturday from 9am to 8pm. You can enter up to 1 hour before closing, but it is not worth the effort since everyone is required to head to the lockers ½ hour before closing time.

I. Fő u. 84. ✆ 1/201-4392. Admission to baths 1,300 Ft ($7/£3.75). Metro: Batthyány tér (Red line).

Rudas Baths ✶✶   Near the Erzsébet Bridge, on the Buda side of the city, is the second oldest of Budapest's classic Turkish baths, built in the 16th century. These baths are for men only every day except Tuesday during the day or Friday and Saturday nights. This is a new phenomenon, which was started after the bath reopened after a year's remodeling. The centerpiece is an octagonal pool under a 10m (33-ft.) domed roof with some of the small window holes in the cupola filled with stained glass, while others are open to the sky, allowing diffused light to stream in. Along the sides, there are four corner pools of varying degrees of temperature. During early mornings the crowd is predominantly composed of older men. You'll find the same services and facilities here that you would at Király: thermal baths of varying degrees, a sauna, and a steam bath.

I. Döbrentei tér 9. ((*) 1/356-1322.Thermal baths 2,200 Ft ($12/£6.25) refunds available up to 3 hr.; swimming pool with locker 1,200 Ft ($6.50/£3.40). Weekdays 6am–8pm; weekends pool only 6am–2pm. Bus: 7, not express stops right in front on the Buda side.

Széchenyi Baths *Kids* One of the largest spa complexes in Europe, it was also the first thermal on the Pest side. Located in the City Park, the Széchenyi Baths are the most popular with locals and travelers alike. From the outside, you'd never believe its enormity, but once inside it is humungous with a variety of water temperature pools including a whirlpool that spins you around. Crowds of bathers including many families and tourists visit the palatial unisex outdoor swimming pool, but due to its size, it never feels overcrowded. Turkish-style thermal baths are segregated and are located off to the sides of the pool. In warm weather, there is segregated nude sunbathing on the roof. Any tourist photo of older gentlemen playing chess on floating chess boards while half-immersed in water is a photo of this bath. Prices are all posted in English, and the refund system is described.

XIV. Állatkerti út 11–14, in City Park. ((*) 1/363-3210. www.spasbudapest.com.Thermal baths 2,400 Ft ($13/£6.80); dressing cabins 400 Ft ($2.15/£1.15); massage 3,500 Ft ($19/£9.95) for 30 min. Daily 6am–10pm, some pools close earlier on Sat–Sun. Metro: Széchenyi fürdő (Yellow line).

AN OUTDOOR POOL COMPLEX

Palatinus Strand *Kids* In the middle of Margaret Island is Budapest's best-located *strand* (literally "beach," but in reality a water park). The huge complex is fed by the Margaret Island thermal springs and consists of three thermal pools, an extra-large swimming pool, a smaller artificial wave pool, a water slide, a grassy area, and segregated nude-sunbathing decks on top of the building. Other facilities include Ping-Pong tables, pool tables, trampolines, and dozens of snack bars. The waters of the thermal pools are as relaxing as those at any of the other bathhouses (but the older bathhouses offer a much more memorable experience). Rates include either a locker or a cabin.

XIII. Margit-sziget. ((*) 1/340-4505. 1,800 Ft–2,200 Ft ($9.75–$12/£5–£6)adults, 200 Ft ($1.10/55p) children. Discount Mon–Fri. Prices include either a locker or cabin. May to mid-Aug daily 9am–7pm. Last entry at 6pm. Bus: 26 from Nyugati pu.

11 Outdoor Activities & Sports

BIKING We don't generally recommend biking in Budapest due to crazed drivers and erratic-moving traffic. That said, see "Getting Around," in chapter 4, "Getting to Know Budapest," or earlier in this chapter for some biking options.

GOLF You will not find much in the way of golf in the city, which means you are in for a drive if you want to practice your drives. For information, contact the **Hungarian Golf Club,** V. Bécsi út 5 (((*) 1/317-6025; www.golfhungary.hu). The nearest course is located on Szentendre Island, 25 minutes north of Budapest by car. Call the course directly at ((*) 26/392-465. For putting practice, the **19th Hole Golf Driving Range** is located at II. Adyliget, Feketefej u. 6 (((*) 1/354-1720) or e-mail them at golfcentrum@golfcentrum.hu. The Budapest Central Golf Club is located at X. Fehér út 7 (www.golfrange.hu). Two golf stores have opened in Budapest, one on each side of the river. On the Pest side is **Golf Centrum** at VI. Nagymez_ u. 52 (℃ **1/354-1510**) or on the Buda side, **Swing** at II. Szilágyi Erzsébet fasor 121, floor I, no. 43 (℃ **1/275-0855**).

HORSEBACK RIDING Riding remains a popular activity in Hungary, land of the widely feared Magyar horsemen of a bygone era. A good place to mount up is the **Petneházy Lovasiskola (Riding School),** at II. Feketefej u. 2 (℃ **06/20-567-1616** mobile only). Far, far out in the Buda Hills, the school is located in open country, with trails in the hills. Open riding with a guide is 6,000 Ft ($33/£17). There are also pony rides for children at 2,500 Ft ($14/£7) for 15 minutes, and the 30-minute horse-cart rides for 10 people is 25,000 Ft ($135/£71). The stable is open year-round, but only on Friday, Saturday, and Sunday from 9am to 5pm. Take bus no. 56 (56E is fastest) from Moszkva tér to the last stop, then bus no. 63 to Feketefej utca, followed by a 10-minute walk.

The **Hungarian Equestrian Tourism Association,** located at V. Ferenciek tere 4 (℃ **1/317-1644;** fax 1/267-0171; www.equi.hu), may be of interest to you if you are interested in horses in general, but every number they gave me for other leisure horseback riding information was out of order as was those from Tourinform.

ICE SKATING Ice rinks in Budapest are very kid-friendly. The oldest and most popular ice rink is in Városliget, on the lake next to Vajdahunyad Castle. Being an open-air facility, it is open only from mid-November till the end of February. Hours are Monday through Friday 9am to 1pm and 4 to 8pm; Saturday and Sunday 10am to 8pm. The fee is 600 Ft ($3.25/£1.75) on weekdays and 900 Ft ($4.75/£2.50) on weekends. Skates rent for 600 Ft ($3.25/£1.75) an hour. International visitors should also have their passports for ID when renting. Adults and children can rent in-line and ice skates at all the rinks.

SQUASH City Squash Courts (Országos Fallabda Központ), at II. Marczibányi tér 13 (℃ **1/336-0408**), has four courts, which are an easy walk from Moszkva tér (Red metro line). The hourly rates vary during the day: 7 to 9am and 3 to 5pm, 3,000 Ft ($16/£8.50); 9am to 3pm, 2,200 Ft ($12/£6.25; and 5 to 10pm, 4,200 Ft ($23/£12) for 1 hour of play. Racquets can be rented for 500 Ft ($2.75/£1.50); balls can be purchased. The courts are open daily from 7am to midnight.

TENNIS If you plan to play tennis in Budapest, bring your own racket along since most courts don't rent equipment; when it is available, it's usually primitive. Many of Budapest's luxury hotels, particularly those removed from the city center, have tennis courts that nonguests can rent.

8

Strolling Around Budapest

Budapest is a walking city. There is nothing I like better than to meander around the streets to see what I can discover or rediscover. The walking tours included here are intended to give you a sense of the vibrancy that radiates from the city's history. On these walking tours, I have made a special effort to bring things to your attention that you may otherwise miss. In so saying, you can certainly pick and choose parts of the tour that appeal to you most and hit those spots without doing the full tour. Many of the city's top attractions such as the Buda Palace, Parliament, the National Gallery, and the National Museum are included on these tours, but dozens of minor sites—vintage pharmacies and quiet courtyards, market halls and medieval walls—are included as well.

See chapter 3, "Suggested Budapest & Hungary Itineraries," for ways to incorporate these walking tours into a 1- or 2-day visit.

WALKING TOUR 1	THE MILLENNIUM TOUR

Start:	Vörösmarty tér.
Finish:	Mexikói út.
Time:	2 to 3 hours (at a slow pace excluding restaurant or museum stops).
Best Times:	Any time, but preferably mid-afternoon.
Worst Times:	Early morning.

When have you ever heard of a crowned monarch riding a subway, if ever? This tour will follow the historic metro line of the Millennium metro, where over 110 years ago, the Austrian emperor and Hungarian king Ferenc József (Franz Josef) boarded the first subway in continental Europe. At the time, London was the only city in Europe to have a subway. It had just been completed in time for the 1896 millennium celebrations that would be held in Budapest. Galas and gatherings were planned all over the city, but the most important was held in Városliget. Andrássy út was the most direct link to the park; however, even then, it was a grand boulevard. Authorities had refused permission for a tram line that was either horse drawn or electrified, for fear of ruining the elegance of the street. It was not until 1893 that permission was given for the underground to be built to solve the logistics problem of moving huge gatherings of people from place to place. Bureaucracy being what it is, they only had 20 months to complete the entire 3.7km (2.3 mile) long line. What helped their work was the fact that at the time, Andrássy was paved with wooden blocks making digging the tunnel that much easier. With a tight deadline, they built the metro to be ready in time. The white and burgundy tiles, the cast iron pillars, and the wooden accessories create a distinctive atmosphere that is still maintained today. After Franz Josef completed the first ride, he agreed to allow it to be named after him. The following tour is above ground, stopping at each of the metro's stops, so if you are so inclined, you can hop on the metro to skip from one stop to another, but if you do, you will be missing much above ground.

Begin at Vörösmarty tér, where the Yellow metro 1 line begins.

❶ Vörösmarty tér

In 1896, this square was named Gizella tér when it was not the hub of activity it is today. In the center is an enormous Carrara marble statue made of 19th-century poet, Mihály Vörösmarty. Vörösmarty wrote *Szózat,* the second most important hymn in Hungarian history after the national anthem. This is the site of many holiday markets and celebrations.

The famous **Gerbeaud** coffeehouse is here as it was in 1858. The founder came from Switzerland with his pastry recipes to set up shop on this square. These recipes are still used today.

Today, this is where the Christmas Market is held and where the Spring Festival Parade starts from. In recent years, this square has had some major transformations with some old historic buildings being torn down to make way for the new and modern.

If you want to view a bit of art before we leave this square, the street to the left of Gerbeaud's has the **Dorottya Gallery.** The windows are so large there is no need to walk in to see everything they offer.

If you need a coffee and a pastry to fortify you, now is your chance to get them. From here, we go to Deák Ferenc tér past the statue and to the left.

❷ Deák Ferenc tér

Politico Ferenc Deák was named the "sage of the nation" for having worked on the Compromise of 1867 between Austria and Hungary when Austria refused to recognize Hungary's independence.

On one corner of the square is the Lutheran Museum and Church at Deák Ferenc tér 4. To the side of the church is a gold memorial tablet that states "Sándor Petôfi, the romantic poet, was educated here." The church gains attention through its plain structure and its lack of a spire. The original church did have a spire, but when the roof had to be reconstructed, there was not enough money to stabilize the roof properly to hold the spire, so it was left off. The church is extremely simple inside, even by Lutheran standards according to my Lutheran friends. The church is only open for services or concerts; the concert schedule is posted outside.

The square has changed considerably since the first metro was built. This square is the only place where all three metros connect and in a few years four metros will connect here. In the station, if you descend the correct set of stairs among the number of ways to get down there, you will find the **Underground Railway Museum.** Outfitted like an old subway station, the museum features a beautifully preserved train from the European continent's first underground system, built in Budapest in 1896. Appropriately, the cost of admission is one transport ticket. If you wish to go in, the museum is small, so ½ hour is about all you need.

When you ascend again, you cannot help but notice the **Anker Palace** across the street from the Le Meridian Hotel. This impressive building was built at the turn of the 19th century. The towers and bastion-looking architecture represent the romantic style. The antique marble columns on the second level and the triangle at the top, gives the building the name "palace." This square is the most frequented tourist destination.

Walking Tour 1: The Millennium Tour

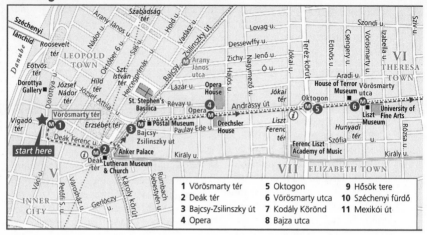

1 Vörösmarty tér	5 Oktogon	9 Hősök tere
2 Deák tér	6 Vörösmarty utca	10 Széchenyi fürdő
3 Bajcsy-Zsilinszky út	7 Kodály Körönd	11 Mexikói út
4 Opera	8 Bajza utca	

On the other corner, is **Erzsébet tér.** This was where the National Theater was originally going to be constructed. However, with a political election and a change in power, the location was changed. The argument was that the final construction would block fresh air coming from the river to the inner city, so the idea was abandoned, but only after the underground parking had been built. Now you can find a serene fountain pond, attractive flower beds, and benches to relax on along the way.

Using the underground, you will cross under the street until you are in front of the Anker Palace and walk toward the basilica. You will see its steeple ahead of you.

❸ Bajcsy-Zsilinszky út

This is the start of Andrássy út. If you see a red mailbox, that is the **Postal Museum** (p. 137), sitting at Andrássy út 3 on the first floor. The building was built for Andreas Saxlehner; you can still see his initials in the ironwork. It is worth visiting the museum to see the interior stained glass and frescoes created by Károly Lotz. The museum was originally the private home of Saxlehner, consisting of seven rooms. As you walk through the flat, you may notice his initials all over the flat as well as the building.

When you reach Andrássy út 9, you are in front of the former **Dutch Insurance Company** headquarters. What is not visible from the street level is the huge "drop" left on top after a 1990s reconstruction for the board of directors. However, the view from the street is impressive. As you walk to the next stop, notice the architecture of the buildings and please be sure to look up. Most people miss some wonderful pieces by never looking above eye level.

Right before our next stop, you will cross the theater district of the city on Paulay Ede utca. It is here that you will find the Thalia Theater, the New Theater, and the Moulin Rouge. Closely located to the Opera House, this is the most concentrated area of cultural events in the city.

Continue down Andrássy to our next stop:

❹ Opera

When the metro was built, each station had an ornate entrance building covering it. They have long since been torn down, but this station still has the marble balustrade. The station does not take away from the glorious neo-Renaissance styled **Opera House** (p. 140). Built by Miklós Ybl, it was completed in 1884.

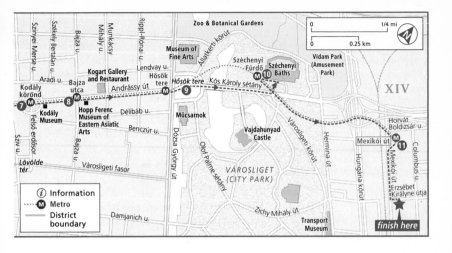

Stop back for a tour or to buy tickets for a performance.

Across from the Opera House is a large building built by Ödön Lechner and Gyula Pártos in1882. It was named the Drechsler House, because it once housed a large cafe by the same name on the street level and apartments occupied the upper floors. The building has a tainted history as six consecutive owners went bankrupt or committed suicide. The National Ballet Institute occupied the building for decades, but they abandoned it also.

For the movie *Munich,* the Paris scenes were filmed using the Opera house and the old Drechsler House, which was transformed by movie magic into a lamp store with a cafe on the left side of it.

Proving that Budapest is once again a sophisticated destination, a Louis Vuitton shop is on one side of Andrássy, while a Chanel store is on the other. Many upscale home interior design stores have opened for business on this street and more are in the planning stages, making this an upscale haven for the shopping maven.

On the opposite side of the street from the Opera House is the **Mûvész Confectionery** at Andrássy út 29 (p. 128). Although it has become touristy, it still has the old-fashioned feeling of the coffeehouse culture that is ingrained in Budapest.

If you have a snack attack and did not stop for a pastry, you are in luck. On the left is **Bombay Express,** a fast-food Indian restaurant with low prices and excellent quality food. If you walk a little farther, you will find Liszt Ferenc tér on one side of the street with the famous music academy of the same name at the very end of the tér. There is also a Tourinform office here in addition to a choice of over 10 restaurants. The center park has been refurbished as a winding and undulating garden area with benches; it is quite lovely with the humongous and commanding statue of Liszt in the center.

Opposite Liszt Ferenc tér is Jokai tér. In the back of the square is one of the two puppet theaters in the city (p. 157). Walking down Jokai, you will see a number of teahouses of various styles.

Walk down Andrássy to our next stop:

❺ Oktogon

When you come to the intersection of Andrássy út and the Nagykörút (large ring road), the buildings form an octagonal square providing its name. For 40-some years, this intersection was known as November 7 Square. It is one of the busiest intersections in the city. Sadly, over the years, it has become more commercialized now being home to what is supposed to be the world's largest Burger King on one corner and a T.G.I. Friday's on the opposite corner. The huge billboards and electric signs atop of the buildings for various companies have depleted the charm. After crossing through Oktogon, Andrássy starts to widen. It is this section of Andrássy, past Oktogon that is a World Heritage site.

Now cross over the körut as we continue up Andrássy.

⑥ Vörösmarty utca

Don't confuse this with Vörösmarty tér, the pedestrian street. Notice how much wider the boulevard is from here on up to Heroes' Square. The street is lined with chestnut trees (chestnuts are often used in Hungarian pastries) giving a fresh feeling of leaving the city behind.

At this stop, you will find Franz Liszt's last home at Andrássy út 67 where he lived on and off in a first floor apartment for the last 5 years of his life. Today it is a museum displaying his pianos and other memorabilia dedicated to his life and work. During some months, there are free concerts on Saturday mornings, a tradition started when Liszt was alive. This building was where the Academy of Music originated with Liszt being a founding member.

Across the street almost in a different dimension is the House of Terror Museum at Andrássy út 60, the place were both the Nazis and communists headquartered and tortured people. For more information, see chapter 7, p. 138.

The University of Fine Arts is located at Andrássy út 69–71. The central building was built in 1876 and refurbished in 1978. The exterior has sgrafitto (decoration created by cutting away parts of a surface layer to expose a different-colored background) portraits of Bramante, Michelangelo, and Leonardo da Vinci.

Students study here for 5 years in a selection of media to earn a master's of fine arts degree upon successful completion.

In the same building as the University of Fine Arts, you will also find the second puppet theater of Budapest at Andrássy út 69. Over 57 years old, this theater has presented puppet shows of high standards for adults and children alike, but only in Hungarian.

Continuing onward, we reach:

⑦ Kodály körönd

A körönd is a circle; here being a broad traffic circle where turns are not permitted, so the circle is cut into four pie slices to making turns. On each corner of the "pie" you will find a statue of someone famous. You will see Szondy György. He was the commander who with his troops, stood firm against Ali Pasha and his Turkish troops when they invaded in 1552. Bálint Balassi was a poet who is considered the first to bring poetry in the Hungarian language to world-class standards. He was a creator of new poetic forms in his writing. Combining love lyrics into the experiences of the fight against the Turkish conquerors, he has a lose association with Szondy György. Next is Zrinyi Miklós, another defender of the nation from the Ottoman rule, but he did much of it from his castle in what is now part of Croatia. Well educated in languages and warfare, he was a strong commander who lost the backing of the Habsburgs and went back to his home in disgust. Vak Bottyán or "Blind Bottyán," the popular nickname of Bottyán János, he fought for Buda against the Ottomans, but later fought for liberation from the Habsburgs.

The circle is named after Zoltan Kodály, who was one of the first persons to give special attention to folk music. He was one of the most significant contributors to early ethnomusicology, later becoming the mentor to Béla Bartók, another famous Hungarian musician. Although the Kodaly Method of teaching music is associated with him, he influenced it with his work, but did not actually create it. His former apartment at Andrássy út 89 houses the museum dedicated to Kodály and his work. The building it is in has been undergoing renovations for more than a year, so if you see scaffolding, it still is not open yet.

Lofty mansions are situated on this ring; they were originally built for the Austro-Hungarian aristocracy. Peeking past the lavishly created wrought-iron gates, attached to stone pillars, you will notice that these frescoed beauties need a well-deserved makeover. Historical values not being the same to all, some of these lovelies nearby are being torn now to create new and modern apartment buildings in their place.

Continue straight onward to:

❽ Bajza utca

As you have walked to this stop, you may have noticed that the boulevard has widened even more and that the houses are changing in style. These personal palaces have a sense of serenity to them with personal parks spread between the entrance gates and the front doors of the houses. In this area different countries have taken over the former private homes to create their embassies.

There is a lovely museum and also a private gallery/restaurant at this stop. On one side of the street, there is the Kogart Gallery and Restaurant at Andrássy út 112. The gallery has rotating exhibitions of Hungarian art upstairs and a lovely restaurant downstairs (See p. 120 in chapter 6, "Where to Dine in Budapest."").

At Andrássy út 103, you will find the Hopp Ferenc Museum of Eastern Asiatic Arts. Hopp was a business owner and a world traveler, which stimulated his collecting as well as being a patron of art. He bequeathed his entire collection of 4,000 pieces to the government to create a museum. If you need a rest, you can enter the Zen garden for free to relax. The

museum is open Tuesday through Sunday from 10am to 5pm. Along this section of Andrássy, the house styles include Art Deco, baroque, and communist boring. However, this is the most desirable stretch of real estate in Budapest.

Continue down to:

❾ Hősök tere

Usually when people emerge from the metro station at this stop, they are in awe at the beauty of Heroes' Square with its arcade of statues (p. 139). It is even more stunning in the evening. Since you have been walking up to it, you have had the opportunity to see its glory get larger as you get closer.

On this square to the left is the Museum of Fine Arts (p. 133). If you are in this area at 11am or 2pm Tuesday to Friday or 11am on Saturday, I strongly encourage you to use this opportunity to take the free tour of one gallery by highly trained docents.

On the right of the square is the Műcsarnok (art hall) or just the Exhibition Hall. Prompted by the Hungarian National Fine Arts Association, it was founded in 1877. Originally, it was located at 69–71 Andrássy út where the University of Fine Arts is now located. As many other buildings were built specifically for the millennium celebrations so was the exhibition hall. Albert Schikedanz was the designer and the outside design is magnificent. Today the hall operates on the pattern of the German Kunsthalle: It is an institution run by artists, but does not maintain its own collection. Light enters through the roof by a three-bayed, semicircular apse. After a full renovation in 1995 the Műcsarnok opened to the public, displaying the work of leading Hungarian and international contemporary artists. It is open Tuesday to Sunday from 10am to 6pm and admission is 1,500 Ft ($8/£4.25).

If you walk over the bridge behind the colonnade, on the right is a small pond area, usually empty until wintertime when it is filled with water to freeze for ice skating. You can rent skates here (p. 167) and partake in the action or you can just admire the view from the bridge. Once over the bridge, to the right, you will already have noticed the castle known as Vajdahunyad Castle. It was originally built from cardboard for the millennium celebrations, but was so popular; it was rebuilt with more durable materials. Some call it a mishmash of styles, but it is intended to be this way, showing all of the different architectural styles of Hungary.

If you have time to visit the castle area, you will see small boats floating around the lake in the summer time. It is a popular place for celebrations and weddings.

Cross the street from the path that would lead to the castle and walk across the park to the:

⑩ Széchenyi fürdő

When you see pictures of men playing chess on floating chessboards while floating in water, they are enjoying the thermal waters of the Széchenyi Baths. A bath existed here as early as 1881, but being a temporary one, it started to lose favor. Gyozo Czigler came up with the plans to create a more permanent structure in 1913 and it was expanded in 1927 with public bathing for men and women. By the middle of the 1960s, it was time to bring further improvements to the facility by adding a group thermal section and an outpatient clinic. All of the thermals treat muscular, bone, and some respiratory ailments. A fancy bath was installed, which

is a whirling pool that twirls you around like an amusement ride. Effervescent devices, neck showers, and water beam back massages were installed in the sitting bank areas. This is one of the largest spa complexes in Europe.

At one time, this was the last stop on the Millennium metro, but in 1973 that changed and one more stop was added.

From here, I suggest you hop on the metro for a ride to the end of the line, which is the next and last stop on this tour. If you want to see more of the park first, you could venture to the far end to visit the Transport Museum at Vajdahunyad-vár with permanent exhibits that include History of the Railway, History of Urban Transport, and the History of Shipping and Road Traffic in Hungary in addition to others.

⑪ Mexikói út

Although there is noting of note at this stop of a historic nature, it is the stop where my most favorite restaurant in the city is located. If you ambled along on this tour, then I presume you will have built up an appetite and will appreciate this last stop. When you reach the top of the stairs of the metro station, turn right. You will see tram tracks and turn left after crossing them. At the end of the block you will see Trófea Grill Étterem at XIV. Erzsébet Királyné útja 5. This is the best all-you-can-eat restaurant in the city. There are others with the same name, but this is the only location I recommend. Enjoy!

Now that you are full and too tired to walk back, hop back on the Millennium metro and enjoy the old-fashioned stations you will pass by on your way back.

WALKING TOUR 2   THE CASTLE DISTRICT

Start:	Roosevelt tér, Pest side of Chain Bridge or alternatively take bus 16 from in front of the Le Meridian Hotel.
Finish:	Tóth Árpád sétány, Castle District.
Time:	3 to 4 hours (excluding museum visits).
Best Times:	Tuesday through Sunday.
Worst Time:	Monday, when museums are closed.

Castle Hill was not always the focal point of Hungarian rule and authority. The original capital was in Esztergom, where King Stephen was crowned and where the seat of the Hungarian Catholic Church is located. It was not until King Béla IV, who built a fortress on this hill, did it become something more than a hill. During the reigns of Kings Charles Robert and Louis the Great (1342–82), a castle was built. Holy Roman Emperor Sigismund of Luxembourg, who was also king of Hungary, built a large Gothic palace and strong fortifications against attack, making this the permanent seat of royal power. It was King Matthias who transformed the castle and decorated the hill with Italian Renaissance due to the influence of his Italian queen from Naples. This district has had its share of devastation, the last time being the 1945 Soviet bombing of Nazi forces. With each reconstruction, the prevailing style shifted from Gothic to baroque to Renaissance. Castle Hill, a UNESCO World Cultural Heritage site, consists of two parts: the Royal Palace (no longer a castle) and the associated Castle District, which is now a mostly reconstructed city reflecting a former time in history. The Royal Palace is home to a number of museums, including the Hungarian National Gallery and the Budapest Museum. The National Archives, the equivalent to the Hungarian Library of Congress is an attached building in the back. The rest of the Castle District is a small tapered neighborhood with cobblestone streets and twisting alleys; with the exception of buses, most traffic is prohibited, making the streets pedestrian-friendly enhancing the tranquility and the old-world feel. Prime examples of every type of Hungarian architecture, from early Gothic to neo-Romanesque, can be seen. A leisurely walk in the Castle District will be a historical and memorable experience. When you see *SZ* on a sign followed by Roman numerals, it is indicating the century of the building. HELYÉN gives the name of the building that was on this site prior to the current building.

Views of Castle Hill can be see from all points on the riverbank, but we will start from Pest's Roosevelt tér just past the Gresham Four Seasons Hotel and walk on the:

❶ Széchenyi Chain Bridge

Originally funded by Count Széchenyi after weather prevented his getting across the river to be with his dying father, the bridge was built in 1849. During World War II, the Nazis destroyed all of the bridges in the city to hold off the Allied forces. The bridge was rebuilt and in 1949 the opening ceremony was held 100 years to the day after its original inauguration.

Walk across the bridge. Arriving in Buda, you're now in:

❷ Clark Ádám tér

Ádám Clark was a Scotsman engineer commissioned to build the bridge. After doing so, he stayed here with the Hungarian wife he met and married. This square was named for him.

From Clark Ádám tér, take the:

❸ Funicular *(sikló)*

The funicular, an almost vertical elevator will transport you up the 100m (328-ft.) long track to the entryway of the Royal Palace. (see "Getting Around," in chapter 4, "Getting to Know Budapest"). It was originally put into service in 1870 to provide cheap transport to workers in the district, and it was run by a steam engine. It was destroyed during World War II and not rebuilt until 1986. The new funicular was built to be powered by electricity. At the time, it went up and down much faster than it does now making the trip in 1 to 2 minutes, but the public petitioned for it to be slowed down, so the view could be enjoyed longer. If you are feeling energetic, you can also walk up the steep stairs to Castle Hill or take the winding trail.

Whichever method of ascent you choose, when you arrive at the top, turn and look left at the statue of the:

❹ Turul

The oversized bird you see perched on the top of the wall looking out is often mistaken for an eagle, but it is in fact a turul. The turul is the Hungarian mythical bird that legends say appeared to Emese telling her she was pregnant with a great leader of the nation, Álmos, the future father of Árpád. It is supposed to be the largest bird statue in the world with a 15m (49-ft.) wingspan. From here you enter:

The main courtyard of the palace. The entrance to the Hungarian National Gallery is located farther down the path, but first go down the nearby stairs to see the statue of the fisherboys and past them to the:

❺ Equestrian Statue of Prince Jenő (Eugene) Savoyai

On September 11, 1697, Prince Eugene and his 50,000 men caught the Turks while they were crossing the river Tiza and annihilated the Ottoman army. You might want to visit the National Gallery now or return after the walking tour.

The first museum is the:

❻ Hungarian National Gallery

This museum houses much of the greatest art ever produced by Hungarians. Be warned, it seems to go on forever and not much is in English, though it is worth a look. If you are an art lover, you will be in heaven. The most important era in Hungarian art was the 19th century and the artists of that period are Mihály Munkácsy, László Paál, Károly Ferenczy, Pál Szinyei Merse, Gyula Benczúr, and Károly Lotz. József Rippl-Rónai was a great Art Nouveau painter of the turn-of-the-20th-century period. You will also find pieces from medieval times, and the 18th, 19th, and 20th centuries as well.

Proceed through the courtyard to the:

❼ Matthias's Well or Fountain

This is one of my favorite fountains in the city. Legend has it that King Matthias

was on a hunting expedition when a fair maiden came across him by chance. She, Ilona, not knowing he was the king, fell in love with him instantly and him with her. He has the deer he has just killed, his hunting dogs, and his servants with him. This is most likely the most photographed statue in the city.

If you continue around the fountain and into the large courtyard, directly in front of you is the:

❽ Budapest History Museum

Boasting four floors, the museum offers exhibits containing pre-historic, ancient, Roman, pre-Hungarian and modern-day pieces. The highlights here are the Gothic rooms and statues that were uncovered by surprise when reconstruction and rebuilding of the Royal Palace was taking place. The rooms and all their contents, dating back as far as the 14th century, were buried for hundreds of years. From the downstairs, you can venture out on the grounds and you should do so to see some of the ancient architecture that has been preserved.

Next as we turn to leave the courtyard again, on our left we have the:

❾ Széchenyi National Library

The library was started through the initiative of Ferenc Széchenyi, the father of István, who had the Chain Bridge named for him. It was founded in 1802. It now houses the world's greatest collection of "Hungarica," with some four million holdings. Any print matter that receives an ISBN number in Hungary has to have four copies sent here. It is the Hungarian Library of Congress.

Now proceed up the path, where you'll find the:

❿ Csikós (Cowboy) Statue

The horse wrangler is taming a wild horse. This statue originally stood in front of the Riding School in the former Újvilág terrace. It was moved here after being repaired in 1983.

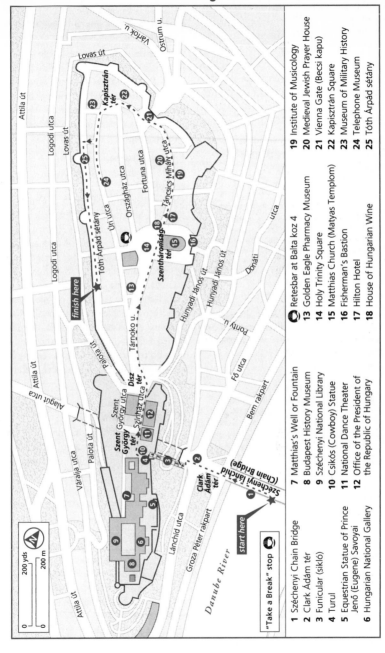

"Take a Break" stop 🍴

1 Széchenyi Chain Bridge
2 Clark Ádám tér
3 Funicular (sikló)
4 Turul
5 Equestrian Statue of Prince
  Jenő (Eugene) Savoyai
6 Hungarian National Gallery
7 Matthias's Well or Fountain
8 Budapest History Museum
9 Széchenyi National Library
10 Csikós (Cowboy) Statue
11 National Dance Theater
12 Office of the President of
  the Republic of Hungary

🍴 Retesbar at Balta koz 4
13 Golden Eagle Pharmacy Museum
14 Holy Trinity Square
15 Matthias Church (Matyas Templom)
16 Fisherman's Bastion
17 Hilton Hotel
18 House of Hungarian Wine

19 Institute of Musicology
20 Medieval Jewish Prayer House
21 Vienna Gate (Becsi kapu)
22 Kapisztrán Square
23 Museum of Military History
24 Telephone Museum
25 Tóth Árpád sétány

As you continue walking past the funicular, you will find the:

⓫ National Dance Theater

First built as a cloister and church by an order of Carmelites in 1736, this building was turned into a theater when the order disbanded in 1787. It was turned into a theater then and today continues as the National Dance Theater.

Right next to the theater you will see:

⓬ Office of the President of the Republic of Hungary

The classicist palace next to the theater was ordered by Count Vincent Móric engaging the services of architects János Ámon and Mihály Pollack. It was the head office of the prime minister from 1887 to 1945. Now it is the Office of the President of the Republic of Hungary. Across from this in the grassy field, you can see the remains of a medieval church.

Continue walking away from the palace area, you will pass an open-air tourist area with crafts and folk goods for sale, but I don't recommend that you buy here. Instead:

TAKE A BREAK
The Rétesbar at Balta köz 4 (p. 128) has the best strudels I have eaten in Budapest. You can have a coffee or tea with a sumptuous pastry. They also have savory snacks. Sit on the bench in the köz and enjoy the rest.

Now that you are rested, we come to the:

⓭ Golden Eagle Pharmacy Museum (Arany Sas Patikamúzeum)

I love this museum, because admission is free. The Renaissance and baroque pharmacy relics displayed are really interesting, but what I like most is the display in the back room that shows how medications and remedies were created before the onslaught of modern-day medicines.

Just ahead on Tárnok utca is:

⓮ Holy Trinity Square (Szentháromság tér)

This central square of the Castle District is the highest point on the hill and where you'll find the Holy Trinity Column, or Plague Column. At 14m (46-ft.) high, it was under construction from 1710 to 1713. It was hoped that it would fend off another plague.

Sitting near it is the:

⓯ Matthias Church (Mátyás templom)

Officially called the Church of Our Lady, this symbol of the Castle District is universally known as Matthias Church because the Renaissance monarch, Matthias Corvinus, one of Hungary's most revered kings, was the major donor of the church and was married twice inside it. There's an ecclesiastical art collection on the second floor. Most people never notice the stairs and miss out. King Béla and his queen are buried here and you can see their tombs through the wrought-iron gates on the left side of the church. The church has frequent concerts.

As we leave the church, to our left is the:

⓰ Main Customs House

Now a university economics building (pop into the lobby to admire the statue of Karl Marx), the house overlooks the Danube—from here, normally you would be able to admire the full span of the Szabadság Bridge, but it is being retrofitted and this is expected to continue through 2010.

Walk around the church once again to come to the:

⓱ Hilton Hotel

The Castle District's only major name hotel, the Hilton, through the work of architect Béla Pintér, incorporated one wall of the old Jesuit cloister built in late rococo and decorated in plaits along with the Gothic remains of a Dominican church dating back to the 13th century into the modern hotel. The baroque facade of the 17th-century Jesuit college makes up the hotel's main entrance. The hotel has frequent art gallery shows in areas that demonstrate the melding of the old and the new. Admission is free. Summer concerts are held in the Dominican Courtyard.

Across from the Hilton is the:

⑱ House of Hungarian Wine

If you like or love wine you will want to come back to this place. For a set fee, you are set loose to try 60 different Hungarian wines from all regions of the country. You are given 2 hours to taste with snacks for palate cleaning along the way.

Now we head a few feet for a:

LUNCH BREAK:
If you would like some down-home Hungarian cooking, stop at the Fortuna passage, just a short way from the House of Wine. Turn into the passage, but pass the first door, which goes to the Fortuna Restaurant and look for the next door with a wooden sign that says önkiszolgáló vendéglő. If you see stairs up, you are in the right place. This is a cafeteria that is only open until 2pm. The food is great and inexpensive.

Because the entire length of each of the Castle District's north-south streets is worth seeing, the tour will now take you back and forth between the immediate area of Szentháromság tér and the northern end of the district. First, head down Táncsics Mihály utca, to Táncsics Mihály u. 7, to the:

⑲ Institute of Musicology

Built by Count György Erdődy in 1730, the building has the count's coat of arms over the ornamented door and the balcony. The building is now used by the Hungarian Academy of Sciences Department of Musicology; the museum portion was closed indefinitely as of fall 2007. If the museum is still closed when you visit, you can at least see the outside and the inner court. If it happens to have reopened, then you are in luck. The musical archives of the famous Hungarian composer Béla Bartók are on display. This courtyard has a plague stating that Táncsics Mihály u. 9, was used as a prison at one time. Two of the famous prisoners were Mihály Táncsics, the 19th-Century champion of free press after whom the street is named, and Lajos Kossuth, the leader of the 1848 to 1849 anti-Habsburg revolution. Buda's medieval Jewish community was centered on Táncsics utca. During excavation and reconstruction work done in the 1960s, the remains of several synagogues were uncovered.

Continue walking down the street to Táncsics Mihály u. 26, where you'll find the:

⑳ Medieval Jewish Prayer House

This building dates from the 14th century. In the 15th and 16th centuries, the Jews of Buda thrived under Turkish rule. This building belonged to the Jewish Prefect. The synagogue was built in his home in the 16th century. The 1686 Christian reconquest of Buda was soon followed by a massacre of Jews. Many survivors fled Buda; this tiny Sephardic synagogue was turned into an apartment.

After exiting the synagogue, retrace your steps about 9m (30 ft.) back on Táncsics Mihály utca, turn left onto Babits Mihály köz, and then turn left onto Babits Mihály sétány. This path will take you onto the top of the:

㉑ Bécsi kapu (Vienna Gate)

This is one of the main entrances to the Castle District. If you have come from or are going to Moszkva tér by bus, you will use this gateway. The enormous neo-Romanesque building towering above Bécsi kapu tér houses the National Archives. Bécsi kapu tér is also home to a lovely row of houses (nos. 5–8).

From here, it is a 1-minute walk to:

㉒ Kapisztrán Square

Named for a companion of the Turkish conqueror János Hunyadi, Kapisztrán Square is where you will see the ruins of a Gothic church, which was erected in 1276 honoring Magdalen. During the Turkish invasion it was alternately used by Catholics and Protestants, only to become a Turkish djami. The church was destroyed during World War II, leaving only the base walls, the tower, and one window of the sanctuary left to memorialize it.

You don't have to venture far. On the northwest corner of the square is the:

㉓ Museum of Military History

On the northwest side of the square, you can't miss noticing the Museum of Military History (Hadtörténeti múzeum). Besides a large collection of flags, military uniforms, and other military memorabilia, it has a collection of items from Hungary's involvement in various wars. Admission is free.

Now take Úri utca back in the direction of the Royal Palace. In a corner of the courtyard of Úri u. 49, a vast former cloister, stands the small:

㉔ Telephone Museum

Sometimes the entrance to the courtyard changes from one side to the other, meaning it will be on the street parallel to Úri u.

Press the bell for the attendant to open the door. The museum's prime attractions are the collection of old phones, the actual telephone exchange (7A1-type rotary system) that was in use in the city from 1928 to 1985, and the phone line cable system. I find it fascinating.

Walk back down Úri utca toward the tower and make the first left turn to bring you to the:

㉕ Tóth Arpád sétany

This promenade runs the length of the western rampart of the Castle District. This is a shady road with numerous benches. If you walk to the right, you will run into the Museum of Military History again, but it is worth the view over the wall to see the panorama of Buda's Rózsadomb (Rose Hill) district, Géllert Hill, and the small neighborhood of Krisztinaváros (Christine Town) situated just west of Castle Hill. Krisztinaváros is named after Princess Christine the daughter of Maria Theresa, who interceded for buildings to be erected in this area. Walking away from the museum along the wall, you'll find your way to Korona Cukrászda, a pastry shop.

The walking tour ends here, where you can take the no. 16 bus down to Deák tér or if you go around the corner, the no. 10 bus will take you down to Moszkva tér.

WALKING TOUR 3	LEOPOLD TOWN & THERESA TOWN

Start:	Kossuth tér, site of Parliament.
Finish:	Művész Coffeehouse, near the Opera House.
Time:	About 2 hours (excluding museum visits and the Opera House tour).
Best Times:	Tuesday through Sunday. Note that if you want to visit the Parliament building, you should secure your ticket in advance.
Worst Time:	Monday, when museums are closed.

In 1790 the new region developing just to the north of the medieval town walls of Pest was dubbed Leopold Town (Lipótváros) in honor of the emperor, Leopold II. Over the next 100 years or so, the neighborhood developed into an integral part of Pest, housing numerous governmental and commercial buildings: Parliament, government ministries, courthouses, the Stock Exchange, and the National Bank were all built here. This tour will take you through the main squares of Leopold Town. You'll also

Walking Tour 3: Leopold Town & Theresa Town

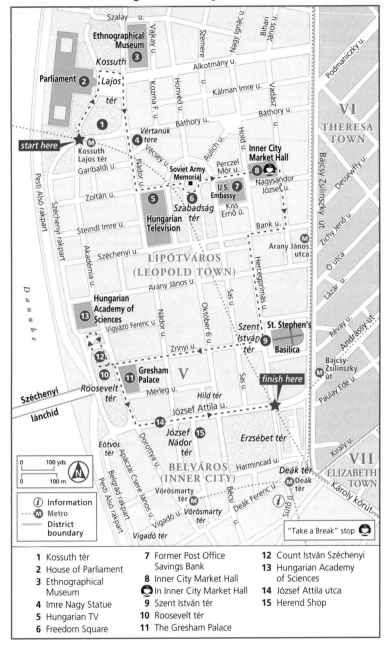

1 Kossuth tér
2 House of Parliament
3 Ethnographical Museum
4 Imre Nagy Statue
5 Hungarian TV
6 Freedom Square

7 Former Post Office Savings Bank
8 Inner City Market Hall
   In Inner City Market Hall
9 Szent István tér
10 Roosevelt tér
11 The Gresham Palace

12 Count István Széchenyi
13 Hungarian Academy of Sciences
14 József Attila utca
15 Herend Shop

walk briefly along the Danube and visit a historic market hall. Along the way, you can stop to admire some of Pest's most fabulous examples of Art Nouveau architecture, as well as the city's largest church.

Exiting the Kossuth tér metro (Red line), turn to the left at the top of the escalator and you'll find yourself on the southern end of:

❶ Kossuth tér

Walk toward Parliament where you will see the equestrian statue of Ferenc Rákóczi II the Transylvanian prince who led the revolt against the Habsburgs that turned into the War of Independence. At one time loyal to the Habsburgs, he grew disenchanted with their lack of interest in the Hungarian nobility. He was imprisoned for conspiring against them, but escaped and sought refuge in Poland. On the northern lawn, you will find a statue of Lajos Kossuth for whom the square is named. He was the political leader of the 1848 Hungarian War of Independence from the Habsburgs. Both men fought for the independence of Hungary and both were defeated in their efforts.

Sitting gloriously on your left is one of the most important symbols of Budapest, the neo-Gothic:

❷ House of Parliament

Work on the Parliament building began in 1884, but was not completed until 16 years later. The similarities to the Westminster in London is due to them both having the same architect, Imre Steindl. Since 2000, besides its government functions, the Parliament building has also been home to the fabled Hungarian crown jewels. Many protests have been held in front of the building including, the uprising in October 2006, when tapes were leaked that the prime minister had lied to the public about the state of the economy. Unfortunately, you can enter only on guided tours (the ¾ hr. tour is worthwhile for the chance to go inside). It is a magnificent building inside as well as outside, being one of the largest parliament buildings in the world. See p. 140

for tour times and information. Minor protests still occur in front sometimes disrupting the tour schedule.

Here, you have an option. If you are feeling fearless and are without children, go down the stairs behind the back of Parliament, and dodge the traffic on the busy two-lane road to the river embankment. Walk to your left toward the Chain Bridge. You will see dark bronzed shoes of various sizes and styles lined up along the river. This is a respectful remembrance of the Jews who were lined up along the river and shot by the Germans, during the last days of the Holocaust. The Germans knew they did not have time or access to continue sending train cars to detention camps.

When you return to Parliament and ascend the stairs again, head across the street to the eclectic-style building that now houses the:

❸ Ethnographical Museum

This museum boasts more than 150,000 objects in its collection. The From Ancient Times to Civilization exhibition contains many fascinating relics of Hungarian life. See p. 133 for more information.

Continue walking past the front of Parliament, and walk past the statue of 1848 revolutionary hero Lajos Kossuth, mentioned earlier.

As you get to the corner with the Parliament Café turn left and continue through Vértanúk tere (Square of Martyrs). Here stands:

❹ Imre Varga's statue of Imre Nagy

The Nagy statue *Witnesses to Blood* was erected in 1996 portraying the former prime minister in a realistic manner of dress, but slimmer than he was in life crossing a symbolic bridge. Although he was a reformist communist who was made prime minister with the backing of the Soviets, he attempted to create a solution for Hungarian independence. It was he who led the failed 1956 Hungarian Uprising. He was executed in 1958, 2 years after the Soviet-led invasion.

Now walk a few blocks down Nádor utca and turn left onto Zoltán utca. The massive yellow building on the right side of Zoltán utca is the former Stock Exchange, now headquarters of:

⑤ Hungarian Television

There have been plans to move the television headquarters to a new building, but these plans constantly fail due to financial reasons. The significance of this building now is that this is where the riots of September 2006 started. Angry demonstrators bombarded the stations' doors, destroyed equipment, and set fires inside, while setting cars on fire in the front of the building.

The front of the television building is on:

⑥ Freedom Square (Szabadság tér)

Directly in front of you and barricaded is the Soviet Army Memorial, built in 1945 to honor the Soviet-led liberation of Budapest and topped by the last Soviet Star remaining in post-communist Budapest. The monument has been vandalized several times, but after the riots occurred, the barriers were fortified. The American Embassy is at Szabadság tér 12, also surrounded by gates, barriers, and guards. The embassy is famous, but not for its architecture. During World War II, the Swiss governed over U.S. interests in Budapest. This was the official base of operations for Carl Lutz, the diplomat who saved thousands of Jews. Lutz later moved his safe house to 29 Vadász utca, the Glass House as it was called. On the wall of the embassy, if you can get close enough to see it, there is a plague for Cardinal Mindszenty, who spent 15 years in internal exile within the embassy after being badly mistreated following the 1956 uprising.

Walk to the left of the U.S. Embassy to Hold utca and turn right onto Hold utca (Moon St.), formerly known as Rosenberg házaspár utca, for Ethel and Julius Rosenberg. Here you will find the spectacular and restored:

⑦ Former Post Office Savings Bank (Posta Takarékpénztár)

Stand across the street and look up for the best view, but if the trees are in bloom, you may have to risk standing in the street. One of the most unusual and one of my favorite buildings, it was designed by Ödön Lechner, the architect who in 1900, attempted to fuse Hungarian folk elements with the Art Nouveau style, which was popular at this time. I love the bees crawling up to the beehive as a metaphor for saving your money. At the top are winged dragons and serpents, but you need binoculars to best view them.

⑧ Inner City Market Hall (Belvárosi Vásárcsarnok)

Built at the end of the 1800s, this is one of the five cavernous market halls around the city that all opened on the same day. It has been newly restored, but with limited light during parts of the day, so it seems cavelike at times. In this market, you will find fresh fruits, vegetables, and an assortment of spices. The bakery has some excellent selections of unusual and delicious varieties of bread.

TAKE A BREAK
When in the market, there is a *lángos* stand in the side corner. Treat yourself to a Hungarian favorite snack, but don't be tempted to spoil it by getting the tourist variety like Mexican or Italian. Get the real thing with cheese, sour cream, and garlic juice.

Emerge from the Market Hall onto Vadász utca and turn right. Passing Nagysándor József utca, look right for a great view of the colorful tiled roof of the former Post Office Savings Bank you recently passed. Turn right on Bank utca (the metro station you see on your left is Arany János utca; Blue line) and left on Hercegprímás utca. After a few blocks, you'll find yourself in:

⑨ Szent István tér

It would be impossible to miss the most famous church in Budapest, St. Stephen's Basilica. It is the largest church in the city and second largest in the country, after Esztergom's cathedral. With seating for 8,500 people, it can really pack them in. The first architect, József Hild, designed the neoclassical church, and construction started in 1851. However, he died before it was completed and Miklós Ybl reworked the plans creating a neo-Renaissance style, but he also died before it was completed. The third architect was József Krauser, who completed it in 1906. In the Szent Jobb Kápolna, behind the main altar to the left of the church, you can see an extraordinary and gruesome holy relic: Stephen's preserved right hand, but it will cost you 100 Ft (55¢/30p) to light up the box to get a good look. It is paraded around the city annually on St. Stephen's Day, August 20. Monday-night organ concerts are held in the church courtyard in summer. The square in front of the church has been completely refurbished and is now a great place to spend some time. See p. 141 for more information.

Walk down Zrínyi utca, straight across the square from the church entrance. You may want to stop at the corner of Zrínyi utca and Nádor utca and walk into the building of the Central European University; downstairs you will find its bookstore, which has an academic stock of works by central and east European scholars, including works on the political, economic, and cultural changes in the region. Returning now to the Danube, you'll find yourself emerging into:

⑩ Roosevelt tér

This square is lovely and lies at the beginning of the famous Chain Bridge. Crossing the street to get to the grassy area can be dangerous to your health. When plans were made to destroy this park and cut the trees down to create a parking garage, a group of environmental activists chained themselves to the 100-year-old trees, defeating the plan to cut them down and transform the graceful park.

Surrounding the square are several important and lovely buildings, including:

⑪ The Gresham Palace

This Art Nouveau building was built in 1907 and is one of Budapest's best-known and most exclusive hotels: the Hotel Four Seasons Gresham Palace. During tediously detailed renovations, the hotel chain spared no expense to make sure every detail was as close to the original work as possible. It is absolutely magnificent inside. The staff are very used to having travelers venture in to have a look around and they are proud of their hotel.

To your right, as you face the river, is the statue of the Greatest Hungarian:

⑫ Count István Széchenyi

Accompanying the statue of Széchenyi are four secondary figures representing the Great Hungarian's four areas of interest: Minerva (trade); Neptune (navigation); Vulcan (industry); and Ceres (agriculture).

Sitting behind the statue is the neo-Renaissance facade of the:

⑬ Hungarian Academy of Sciences

Széchenyi being a patriot through and through, funded the Academy of Sciences just as he did with the Chain Bridge. After offering a tender for the design, the committee responsible rejected those of some of Hungary's most famous architects of the day. The tender was re-opened and finally awarded to Freidrich August Stüler, the architect who designed the Stockholm National Museum and the Berlin National Gallery. Some Hungarians were upset that a foreigner was chosen to design a national building, but Stüler won out and the building was inaugurated in 1865. Guards prevent access beyond the academy's lobby, but it's worth sneaking a peek over their shoulder.

Turn left away from the river onto bustling:

⑭ József Attila utca

This street was named for the poet whose statue embellishes Kossuth tér. You're now walking along a portion of the Inner Ring (Kiskörút), which separates the Inner City (Belváros), on your right, from Leopold Town (Lipótváros), on your left.

At József nádor tér, you may want to stop in at the:

⑮ Herend Shop

Herend china is perhaps Hungary's most famous product, and this museum-like shop is definitely worth a look.

If you pass this, you will arrive at Erzsébet tér and Deák to the right of it.

WALKING TOUR 4   THE JEWISH DISTRICT

Start:	Dohány Synagogue.
Finish:	Wesselényi utca.
Time:	About 2 hours (excluding museum visit).
Best Times:	Sunday through Friday.
Worst Time:	Saturday, when the museum and most shops are closed.

Jews and their Jewish District in Pest have had a long and ultimately tragic history. There is an additional, although condensed, Jewish history within Budapest; see Appendix C for more information. The impressive synagogues we will walk to on this tour will give you a sense of the vibrancy of the Jewish community prior to World War II. Under German occupation during the war, the district became a walled ghetto, with 220,000 Jews crowded inside; almost half perished during the war. Sadly, the neighborhood is now more or less in a state of decay. Buildings are either crumbling or are being bought by corporations to be destroyed and rebuilt into modern buildings that will house stores, restaurants, offices, and apartments. Much of the compacted little neighborhood is rapidly changing, with history being ripped away, but there are sill some wonderful sights to see.

Halfway between the Astoria metro (Red line) and Deák tér (all metro lines) is the:

❶ Dohány Synagogue

This striking Byzantine building, Europe's largest synagogue and the world's second largest, was built in 1859. It was built before most of the other important buildings of Pest, including the Academy of Sciences (1867), the Opera House (1884), Parliament (1904) and the basilica (1905), just to mention a few. It has a capacity of 2,964 seats (1,492 for men and 1,472 for women). Being a Neolog synagogue, it is still used by Budapest's Jewish community. Neolog is a combined form of Conservative and Reformed Judaism. See p. 141 for more details.

The small, free-standing brick wall inside the courtyard, to the left of the synagogue's entrance, is a piece of the original:

❷ Ghetto Wall

This brick wall is symbolic of the one that kept Budapest's Jews inside this district during World War II. This is not actually the wall, since the real wall was built out of wood planks.

To the left of the wall, on the spot marked as the birthplace of Theodor Herzl, the founder of modern Zionism, is the:

❸ National Jewish Museum

On display are artifacts and art from the long history of Hungarian Jewry. Admission to the synagogue includes the museum, and courtyard. The courtyard can be entered through the rear of the complex on Wesselényi utca. Between Wesselényi utca and the synagogue are many gravestones. Most of these are for the people who were held in the synagogue or surrounding area and died. By Jewish law, the dead need to be buried within 24 hours, yet another law is that the dead are not to be buried on synagogue grounds. Due to the circumstances during the war, one law had to give way to the other.

Inside the courtyard is the still-expanding:

❹ Holocaust Memorial

Designed by Imre Varga, a wonderful contemporary Hungarian sculptor, the memorial is in the form of a weeping willow tree and an inverted menorah with seven branches. An inscription above it is from the bible and reads "Whose pain can be greater than mine?" Nearly 600,000 thin metal leaves are inscribed with the names of the Hungarian Jews killed in the Holocaust. A broken brick has the single word *Remember* on it. The courtyard behind the memorial is dedicated to the "righteous Gentiles" who saved thousands of Jewish lives in wartime Budapest. The more famous amongst them are Raoul Wallenberg from Sweden, Carl Lutz from Switzerland, and Angel Sanz Briz from Spain: all diplomats from their country. For more information see Appendix C.

Walk up Wesselényi. Now turn left on Rumbach utca. On the right, against a cement wall near the corner of Rumbach utca at Dob utca 10, is the unusual:

❺ Memorial to Carl Lutz

Lutz was the Swiss consul who set up the safe house he declared as Swiss property. His heroic attempts are attributed with saving 62,000 of Budapest's Jews from the Nazi death camps. The inscription from the Talmud reads: "Saving one soul is the same as saving the whole world." The rest of the inscription states "In memory of those who in 1944 under the leadership of

the Swiss Consul Carl Lutz (1895–1975) rescued thousands from National Socialist persecution." This somewhat abstract wall memorial is interesting but awkward; perhaps the artist, Tamás Szabó had a specific purpose when this was installed in 1991. However, when the tree in front of it is in full foliage, one can pass the monument without noticing it is there.

Half a block farther on Rumbach utca is the:

❻ Rumbach Synagogue

Built in 1872 by the Vienna architect Otto Wagner, this handsome but decrepit yellow-and-rust-colored building is, in its own way, as impressive as the Dohány Synagogue. Be warned that this Orthodox synagogue occasionally closes for repairs. See p. 143 for more information.

Continue down Rumbach utca and make a left on Madách út to look at the giant archway of:

❼ Madách tér

This is the area where the original old city was located in medieval times. Plans in the 1930s were to create a great boulevard similar in form and style to Andrássy út, but World War II put an end to that idea. Madách tér leads only to itself now. Looking through the arch on a clear day, you get an unusual view of Gellért Hill, crowned by the Liberation Monument.

Head back to Rumbach utca and proceed down that street. Take a right onto Király utca, which forms the northern border of the historic Jewish District. At Király u. 13, you will see what used to be a long series of:

❽ Connected Courtyards

These historically significant courtyards once emerged onto Dob utca, back in the times of the Jewish District (which thrived in the 18th and 19th centuries) and until 2006. This kind of complex with residential buildings connected by a series of courtyards is typical of the Jewish District. During the war, these courtyards became ghettos with thousands of Jews locked within a courtyard.

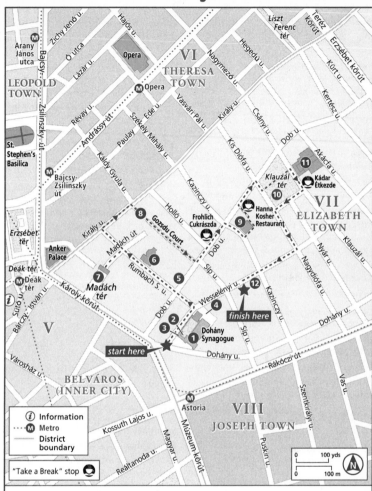

1 Dohány Synagogue

2 Ghetto Wall

3 National Jewish Museum

4 Holocaust Memorial

5 Memorial to Charles Lutz

6 Rumbach Synagogue

7 Madách tér

8 Connected courtyards

🍮 Frohlich Cukrászda

9 Orthodox Kazinczy Synagogue

10 Klauzál tér

11 District Market Hall

🍮 Kádar Étkezde, or
   Hanna Kosher Restaurant

12 Judaica Art Gallery

TAKE A BREAK
Frohlich Cukrászda, Dob u. 22, is the only functioning kosher *cukrászda* (sweet shop) left in the district. Here, you can find pastries, rolls, and ice cream. There are two unadorned tables to sit at while you eat. (Be aware that the shop is closed on Sat, and for 2 weeks at the end of Aug.)

Half a block to the left off Dob utca on Kazinczy u. 29 is the:

⑨ Orthodox Kazinczy Synagogue

Built in 1913 and still active, this synagogue is being slowly and beautifully restored. It has a well-maintained and lively courtyard in its center. There are a number of apartments in which members of the Orthodox community live. While hundreds of travelers visit the Dohány each day, far fewer make the trip here.

Go all the way through the courtyard, emerge onto Dob utca, turn right, and head into:

⑩ Klauzál tér

This is the district's largest square and its historic center. A dusty park and renovated, but still unappealing playground fill the interior of the square.

At Klauzál tér 11, you'll find the:

⑪ District Market Hall (Vásárcsarnok)

One of the five great steel-girdered market halls built in Budapest in the 1890s, they all opened on the same day. This one looks like it has had better days. Age has

not been kind. It now houses a Kaiser grocery store with small kiosk vendors surrounding the perimeter as well as outside. The entrance area is filled with vendors selling fruits, vegetables, candies, shoes, and other surprises from time to time. On Saturdays, from early morning until 1pm, there is a farmers' market in the street.

TAKE A BREAK
You have two lunch options in Klauzál tér and its immediate vicinity, each with a markedly different character. **Hanna Kosher Restaurant,** back at the Kazinczy Synagogue, is one of the city's two strictly kosher restaurants. It's open daily for lunch and offers a limited selection. Wash your hands at the sink on the way in. Men should keep their heads covered inside. (**Note:** Meals can't be purchased on Sat—they have to be prepaid the day before, though they can be eaten on Sat.) **Kádár Étkezde,** at Klauzál tér 9, is a simple local lunchroom with bargain prices (Tues–Sat 11:30am–3:30pm) serving a regular clientele ranging from young paint-spattered workers to elderly Jews and the occasional tourist.

Now head back out on Nagydiófa utca to Wesselényi utca, where you can end the walking tour at Wesselényi u. 13, the:

⑫ Judaica Art Gallery

Here you'll find Jewish-oriented books, both new and secondhand (some are in English). Clothing, ceramics, art, and religious articles are also for sale.

WALKING TOUR 5   TABÁN & WATERTOWN (VÍZIVÁROS)

Start:	The Pest side of the Erzsébet Bridge.
Finish:	The Buda side of the Margaret (Margít) Bridge.
Time:	About 2 to 3 hours (excluding museum visits).
Best Time:	Any time.
Worst Time:	There is no bad time to visit.

This tour will take you through a narrow, twisting neighborhood along the Buda side of the Danube. Tabán, the area between Gellért Hill and Castle Hill, was once a vibrant but very poor workers' neighborhood. The neighborhood was razed in the

Walking Tour 5: Tabán & Watertown (Víziváros)

1 Erzsébet Bridge
2 Tabán Parish Church
3 Berlin Wall
4 Semmelweis Medical
   History Museum
5 Ybl Miklós tér
6 Öntőház utca
7 Clark Ádám tér
8 Funicular *(sikló)*
9 Tunnel
10 Fő utca (Main Street)
11 Jégverem utca
12 Hunyádi János út
13 Institut Français
🍴 Horgásztanya
   Vendeglő/
   Le Jardin de Paris
14 Capuchin Church
15 Corvin tér
16 Iskola utca
   (School Street)
17 Bem rakpart
18 Szilágyi Dezső tér
19 Batthyány tér
20 St. Anne's Church
21 The Vásárcsarnok
   (Market Hall)
🍴 Angelika Cukrászda
22 St. Elizabeth's Church
23 Nagy Imre tér
24 Király Baths
25 Chapel of St. Florian
26 Öntödei (Foundry)
   Museum
27 Bem József tér
28 The Buda side of the
   Margaret Bridge

Overpass or Bridge
Tunnel
Medieval Wall
🍴 "Take a Break" stop

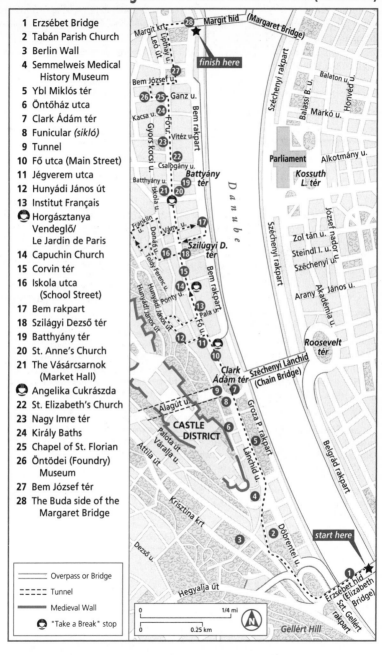

early 20th century for sanitary reasons; only a handful of Tabán buildings still stand below the green expanse of parks where the rest of Tabán once was. The neighborhood directly beneath Castle Hill, opposite the Inner City of Pest, has been called Víziváros (Watertown) since the Middle Ages. Historically home to fishermen who made a living on the Danube, Víziváros was surrounded by walls in Turkish times. The neighborhood still retains a quiet integrity; above busy Fő utca (Main St.), which runs one street up from and parallel to the river along the length of Watertown, you'll wander along aged, peaceful lanes.

Begin the walking tour on the Pest side of the:

❶ Erzsébet Bridge

The nearest metro stations are Ferenciek tere (Blue line) and Vörösmarty tér (Yellow line). The Erzsébet was named for the most-loved queen of Hungary. The bridge was completed in 1903 and sits at the most narrow part of the Danube. All of the city's bridges were destroyed by the Germans in World War II. The bridge you are walking over was reconstructed from 1961 to 1964. The bridge starts at Marcius 15 tér at one of the oldest churches in Pest, the Inner City Parish Church, which dates to the 12th century. Cross the bridge on the right side with the flow of traffic. In order to do this, you'll need to be in front of the church; there's a staircase opposite, leading up to the bridge.

You are walking toward Gellért Hill with the statue of Bishop Gellért. Remember he was killed by the vengeful 11th-century pagans, who were forced with cruelty to convert to Christianity. Bishop Gellért was an Italian bishop, who assisted King Stephen's crusade and suffered by being put to death in a spike embedded barrel and rolled in the river far below.

Upon reaching Buda, going down the steps you will pass the statue of Queen Erzsébet, the queen who the bridge was named for. There is a tablet here to commemorate the anti-fascist revolutionaries who destroyed the statue of Gyula Gömbös, which was located here. Gömbös was a leading Hungarian fascist politician between the wars. You're now at the bottom of the historic Tabán District. Walk away from the bridge, toward the yellow church whose steeple is visible above the trees. Your first stop here in Buda is the:

❷ Tabán Parish Church

Tabáni plébánia templom is a baroque church with one steeple. It was dedicated to St Catherine of Alexandria, built between 1728 and 1740 to replace a medieval church which, during the Turkish occupation, was known as the Mustafa Mosque. You can enter this church. Inside, you'll find a copy of a 12th-century carving called the *Tabán Christ.* The original is in the Budapest History Museum (inside the Buda Palace; p. 144).

When you leave the church, you will see in front of and above you the southern end of the Buda Palace. Watertown is the long, narrow strip of Buda that lies on a slope between Castle Hill and the Danube. Before proceeding to it, note the tile-roofed Gold Stag Restaurant on Szarvas tér, diagonally across the street. Cross to the side of the street that the Gold Stag is on. From here, you can see across busy Attila út (the street that runs behind Castle Hill) two graffiti-covered pillarlike chunks of the:

❸ Berlin Wall

Pieces of the wall here represent the pivotal role that Hungary played in the fall of East German communism. Thousands of East German vacationers crossed the border from Hungary into Austria after Hungary opened the iron curtain in August of 1989. This exodus helped spark the popular movement that led ultimately to the collapse of the East German regime and the breaching of the Berlin Wall.

Continue now down Apród út. The rust-and-white building at Apród út 1–3 is the:

❹ Semmelweis Medical History Museum

Named for Ignác Semmelweis (1818–1865) the obstetrician and "savior of mothers," was born and is buried in this house. He was the first to discover that puerperal fever could be prevented by hand washing with chlorinated lime solution. The exhibition follows the history of healing and medicines and has exhibits related to a variety of medical fields and contains furnishings from the 19th-century Szentlélek Pharmacy.

Proceed down the street to:

❺ Ybl Miklós tér

This narrow square on the Danube is named for one of Europe's leading architects and Hungarian son, born in Székesfehérvár. The lovely building at the square's southern end is the former Várkert (Castle Garden) Kiosk; it's now a casino. The patio ceiling here is covered with sgraffito, a decoration created by carving into a coating of glaze to reveal the color below. Directly across the street from Miklós Ybl's statue is the Várkert Bazaar. Once a beautiful place that went into ruin, it is now designated for gentrifying. The goal is to have it completed by 2010, but there has been a problem with finding investors.

Walk the length of the old Bazaar to Lánchíd utca (Chain Bridge St.), so named because it leads into Clark Ádám tér, the Buda head of the Chain Bridge. Walking away from the river, take the steep set of stairs on your left up to quiet, canyonlike:

❻ Öntőház utca

In summer the terrace gardens of these residential buildings thrive. Flowers, small trees and shrubs, ivy, and grape vines are cultivated with care. Number 5 on this street was the site of the main Jewish temple of the Buda side. The temple

was designed by Ignác Knabe in the Moorish style in 1865. Sitting directly under the castle on the Danube, it was visible from the Pest side.

Turn right, winding back down to Lánchíd utca toward:

❼ Clark Ádám tér

This is a busy traffic circle named for the Scottish engineer who supervised the building of the Chain Bridge in 1848 and 1849. Clark fell in love with a Hungarian woman, married and stayed in Budapest until his death at the very early age of 55 years old. Clark Ádám tér was one of the few streets named after a foreigner that was not renamed during communism.

Immediately to your left is the:

❽ Funicular (sikló)

The funicular opened for business on March 2, 1870. It was destroyed in World War II, but was reopened in 1986. It climbs a length of 95m (312 ft.) at a grade of 48% using two cars, one for each direction at 3m (10 ft.) per second. It carries passengers to the Buda Palace. In front of the funicular is the Zero Kilometer Stone, the marker from which all highway distances to and from Budapest are measured. The original marker was at the threshold of the Royal Palace, but changed to its current location in 1849.

Straight across the square from the Chain Bridge is:

❾ The Tunnel

Built between 1853 and 1857, the tunnel connects Watertown with Christina Town (Krisztinaváros) on the other side of Castle Hill. The old joke was that the tunnel was built so that the precious Chain Bridge could be placed inside when it rained. Just across the street from the tunnel, a set of stairs marks the beginning of the long climb up to Castle Hill. Adam Clark was also the builder of this project.

Passing straight through the square, you'll find yourself at the head of Watertown's:

⑩ Fő utca (Main St.)

You'll be either on or near this long, straight street for the remainder of this walking tour.

Now head left on:

⑪ Jégverem utca (Ice House St.)

At Kapucinus utca, you'll get a marvelous view of the steep old tile rooftops down the street.

Proceed up the stairs to the next street:

⑫ Hunyadi János út

Notice the absurdly tall, narrow doorway of Hunyadi János út 9.

At the intersection with Szalag utca, turn right and then right again on Szőnyeg utca, back toward Fő utca. Bear left on Pala utca. Crossing Kapucinus utca, continue down the steps. Here are the rooftops you viewed from a distance a short while ago. Emerge onto Fő utca, where you'll see the site of the monstrous:

⑬ Institut Français

Note also the reconstructed remains of a medieval house across the street from this French cultural center.

> **TAKE A BREAK**
> Stop for a coffee and snack at the **French Institute** or have lunch or an early dinner at **Le Jardin de Paris** (p. 124), I. Fő u. 20, a delightful French bistro.

Across the street from Horgásztanya is the former:

⑭ Capuchin Church

This church dates back to medieval times; it was built by the Capuchin order of monks. When it was refurbished, it was built into the hillside and in romantic style. Note the Turkish door and window frames on the church's southern wall.

Just past this church is:

⑮ Corvin tér

Several interesting buildings, including the home of the Hungarian Heritage House

that houses the Hungarian Folk Ensemble, the Folks Arts Department, and the Folklore Documentation Center are at number 8 on this square. If the timing is right, you might hear a rehearsal through the open windows. Note the row of very old baroque houses at the top of the square. If you look up, you can see the spires of Fisherman's Bastian from here.

Head above Corvin tér to:

⑯ Iskola utca (School St.)

Turn right on Iskola utca and left up the Donáti *lépcső* (stairs) to Donáti utca; a clay frieze of two horsemen adorns the residential building to the left, opposite the stair landing. Turn right and walk to the next set of stairs, Toldy *lépcső*. Turn left up the stairs and right onto Toldy Ferenc utca, a residential street lined with old-fashioned gas lampposts. This street is so tranquil that the only other travelers are likely to be following this very walking tour. Notice the gorgeous brick secondary school on your right (Toldy Ferenc Gimnázium); a plaque notes "itt tanított Antall József" ("József Antall [first post-communist prime minister] taught here").

Now turn right on Iskola utca, then left onto Vám utca. Cross Fő utca, heading to the:

⑰ Bem rakpart

This is the Danube embankment. In pleasant weather, it can be a nice walk along the river's edge, but below the wall to the river is a highway, which can distract any relaxing thoughts. Directly across the river is Parliament; the view is lovely during the day, but exceptional at night. The next bridge on your left is the Margaret Bridge, where this walking tour will end.

Turn right now and you'll immediately find yourself in:

⑱ Szilágyi Dezső tér

The architect, Samu Pecz, who designed this church, used the same type of brick that was used in the Great Market, but in a neo-Gothic style for this Calvinist Church. It dates from the end of the 19th century. Composer Béla Bartók lived at Szilágyi Dezsó tér 4 in the 1920s. The Danube bank near this square is the site of a piece of Hungary's darkest history: Here, the Arrow Cross (Nyilas), the Hungarian Nazis, massacred thousands of Jews in 1944 and 1945, during the last bitter winter of World War II. Many were tied together into small groups and thrown alive into the freezing river.

Returning now to Fő utca, turn right and continue on toward Watertown's main square, Batthyány tér. You may want to stop in at the Herend Village Pottery shop at Bem rakpart 37, on the ground floor of the housing block. You'll find several attractions along:

⑲ Batthyány tér

One of this area's principal sights is the 18th-century:

⑳ St. Anne's Church

One of Budapest's finest baroque churches, St. Anne's was started by Kristóf Hamon in 1740, but completed by Mátyás Nepauer in 1761. It was almost destroyed in the early 1950s because the Hungarian dictator Mátyás Rákosi (known as "Stalin's most loyal disciple") thought that when Stalin visited him at his office in Parliament, he would be loath to look across the Danube at a Buda skyline dominated by churches. Fortunately, Rákosi's demented plan was never realized. It has been threatened by floods and earthquakes and even the construction of the metro, but it still survives.

Also on the square is:

㉑ The Vásárcsarnok (Market Hall)

One of the markets built in 1897 to improve sanitation of meats and vegetables, this building now houses a grocery store which really drains the charm from the building. The interior is worth a look. Two doors down is the former White Cross Inn with a mix of rococo and baroque ironwork on the balconies. Joseph II (1780–1790) stayed here twice as did the legendary womanizer, Casanova. This is where the ground-floor nightclub acquired its name. To the left of the back gate is where trademen enter the market hall.

Continue along Fő utca. The next church on your right is:

㉒ St. Elizabeth's Church

This church has a fine baroque interior if you can ever get in to see it. As with most churches here, when there is no mass, you can only enter the foyer and peek in the glass windows to the church's interior. The frescoes date from the 19th century.

Continue along Fő utca. You're now approaching the northern border of Watertown where the streets get larger, such as Batthyány utca and Csalogány utca, which bisect Fő utca. You can no longer see Castle Hill. The next square is:

㉓ Nagy Imre tér

A small park hidden behind a Total gas station, this square is named for the reform communist leader who played a leading, if slightly reluctant, role in the 1956 Hungarian Revolution. The prisonlike building on the corner is the Military Court of Justice, where Nagy was secretly tried and condemned to death in 1958, thus providing Hungary with yet another martyr. Nagy's reburial in June 1989 was a moment of great national unity, and a statue of Nagy was later erected near Parliament (p. 149). The main entrance to the Military Court of Justice is on Fő utca.

Two blocks farther up Fő utca, at Fő u. 82–86, are the:

㉔ Király Baths

This 16th-century bathhouse is one of the city's major positive reminders of Turkish rule. Most people walk right past it even when purposefully looking for it, since from the street, it does not look like much at all. Inside, the gorgeous interior dome over the baths has holes in the ceiling that let in rays of light. You won't get to see it unless you pay the entry fee and use the thermal's waters. The baths are open on different days for men and women (p. 164).

Next door, at the corner of Fő utca and Ganz utca, is the baroque:

㉕ Chapel of St. Florian

A baker had this chapel commissioned in the 18th century. Due to flooding before the protective wall was built on the river, the church had to be lifted 1.4m (4½ ft.) in 1938. The contemporary painter Jenő Medveczky painted all of the frescoes. Now it is home to the Greek Orthodox community in Buda.

Turn left on Ganz utca, passing through the small park between the baths and the church. At the end of Ganz utca is the:

㉖ Öntödei (Foundry) Museum

This museum is housed inside the original structure of the famed Abraham Ganz Foundry (started in 1845). From the exterior, painted a creamy yellow with a rusty-red trim, it's hard to imagine the vast barnlike interior. The collection of antique cast-iron stoves is the highlight of the exhibits.

Turn right onto Bem József utca, a street with several small fishing and army-navy-type supply stores, and head back down toward the Danube. You'll find yourself in:

㉗ Bem József tér

Józef Bem was of Polish origin, and a hero in the War of Independence of 1848. He commanded the Hungarian troops against the Habsburgs. On October 23, 1956, the square hosted a rally in support of the reform efforts in Poland. The rally, and the subsequent march across the Margaret Bridge to Parliament, marked the beginning of the famous 1956 Hungarian Uprising.

Turn left onto Lipthay utca, which is parallel to the river. Always remember to admire the buildings as you make your way to the end of the tour at:

㉘ The Buda Side of the Margaret Bridge

Here, you can pick up the no. 4 or 6 tram and head to either Buda's Moszkva tér (Red metro line) or across the river to Pest's Outer Ring Boulevard.

9

Budapest Shopping

The world of fashion and commercialization has bombarded the capital with a silent invasion. Each week, COMING SOON signs appear on storefront windows promising yet another piece of globalized fashionable items, but you can rest assured they are not for the average Hungarian. From famous designer labels like Louis Vuitton and Chanel to brand-name items, stylish secondhand shops, and, sad to say, "as seen on TV" stores, Budapest offers a far wider array of shopping experiences than just a few years ago.

Budapest has become a metropolitan shopping city. At one time, the streets were cluttered with store after store of small unappealing shops and boutiques with window displays that looked like someone's junk closet; everything was tossed in without order or separation. The offerings were a scanty selection of goods and oftentimes, they were all behind a counter where no customer dares to tread. You were at the mercy of the sales clerk to decide whether or not you were worthy of examining the goods. But today, local Budapest shoppers and tourists alike have the opportunity to actually touch the goods before making a decision. The crowds still flock to the ever-growing number of gigantic malls and shopping centers for comparison shopping.

Still, buyer beware: Quality and value do not always go hand in hand with a hefty price tag. As you wander through the megamalls, as crowded as they may be, you still don't see dozens of shopping bags filled with purchases, which makes one wonder where the locals are shopping. A number of fashion-driven, retro-loving, or economically suppressed shoppers are still shopping at the small shops where they can seek out a bargain. Overcoming bankruptcy due to the influx of the megamalls, these shops—stylish, modern, and cool—have become the center of attention once again. To add to the mix, secondhand clothing stores have started to pop up like mushrooms after a good rain.

Vásárló utca is a street of shops underground off Váci utca near Haris köz. You will recognize it by the escalator going down to it. We do not recommend that you go down there, especially at night. It is easy to get trapped down there by an unsavory type, particularly business ladies who may have brawny friends at the top of the escalator to convince you to use unwanted services.

FOLKLORE Travelers seeking folklore objects do not have to look far. First check out the second floor of the great market for a wide selection of popular items that include pillowcases, embroidered tablecloths, pottery, porcelain, intricately painted and carved eggs, dolls, dresses, skirts, and sheepskin vests. The vendors here are willing to bargain, but in the stores, they are not. Antiques shops, running along Falk Miksa utca in downtown Budapest, feature a broad selection of vintage furniture, ceramics, carpets, jewelry, and accessories, but over the years, it has become more expensive with less bargaining going on, for tourists.

Transylvania was once part of Hungary before the Trianon Treaty of World War I. Most of the residents in the area are ethnic Hungarians. These women come to Budapest with bags full of handmade craftwork selling their goods to Hungarians and tourists alike. Keep your eyes open for these vendors, who sell their goods on the street or in the metro plazas. They are unmistakable in their characteristic black boots and dark-red skirts, with red or white kerchiefs tied around their heads. Their prices are generally quite reasonable, and bargaining is customary. If they spot the police, they may disappear fast, but often return when the coast is clear again.

PORCELAIN   Another popular Hungarian item is porcelain, particularly from the country's two best-known producers, Herend and Zsolnay. Although both brands are available in the West, you'll find a better selection and lower prices in Hungary. We have heard from collectors that they now have to really hunt much more for substantial bargains than they did in the past.

HUNGARIAN FOOD   Typical Hungarian foods also make great gifts. Hungarian salami is world famous. Connoisseurs generally agree that Pick Salami, produced in the southeastern city of Szeged, is the best brand. Herz Salami, produced locally in Budapest, is also a very popular product (though not as popular as Pick). You should be aware that some people have reported difficulty in clearing U.S. Customs with salami; bring it home at your own risk. Another typical Hungarian food product is chestnut paste *(gesztenye püré)*, available in a tin or block wrapped in foil; it's used primarily as a pastry filling but can also top desserts and ice cream. Paprika paste *(pirosarany)* is another product that's tough to find outside Hungary. It usually comes in a bright-red tube. Three types are available: hot *(csípős)*, deli-style *(csemege)*, and sweet

(édes). Powdered paprika is also a popular gift and also comes in the same three varieties as the paste. All of these items can be purchased at grocery stores *(élelmiszer)*, delicatessens *(csemege)*, and usually any little convenience store. In the great market, you will find the powdered version in little decorated cloth bags, making it ready for gift giving. Another product to look for is Szamos brand marzipan. Szamos Confectioners, a recently reestablished family business that was originally founded in 1935, is also said to make the best ice cream in the country. They're based in Szentendre, with a shop in Budapest at V. Párisi u. 3 (© 1/317-3643). See appendix B, "Hungarian Cuisine" for more food information.

WINES   Illustrious local traditional wines and spirits have matured. The sweet white Tokaji Aszú, Tokaji Eszenzia, and Tokaji Szamorodni, and the mouthwatering Egri Bikavér, Villányi Cuvée, Szekszárdi Bikavér, and Kékfrankos are the most representative. The infamous Palinka is a strong fruit brandy that is a Hungarian treasure. Unless you indulge in an expensive brand, you may get a bottle that seems to have had the fruit waved over the top of the bottle without ever really touching the drink. If someone offers you schnapps, this is what you are getting; chances are it is homemade and usually much better than the less-expensive commercial brands. Visit the House of Palinka to learn about the different types and qualities of the drink. Every European culture has its herbal digestive drink that they swear will cure what ails you. For the Germans it is Jagermeister; for Hungarians, it is the black spirit made of 40 different herbs, Unicum, the trademark product of Zwack. It is a bitter liqueur and an acquired taste. In the last couple of years, they tried their hand at a carbonated Unicum called Unicum Next to lure the youth market; it has been a success.

MARKETS   If you love markets, you're in for a treat. There are numerous markets here: flea markets *(használtáru piac)*, filled not only with every conceivable kind of junk and the occasional relic of communism, but also with great quantities of mostly low-quality new items like clothing, cassettes, and shoes; and food markets *(vásárcsarnok, csarnok,* or *piac)*, which sell row after row of succulent, but limited varieties of fruits and vegetables, much of it freshly picked and driven in from the surrounding countryside. You can find saffron and several varieties of dried mushrooms for surprisingly low prices at these markets.

1 The Shopping Scene

MAIN SHOPPING STREETS   The hub of the tourist-packed capital is the first pedestrian shopping street in Budapest, Váci utca. It runs from the stately Vörösmarty tér in the center of Pest, across Kossuth Lajos utca, all the way to Vámház körút. This is the area for the Hungarian elite and travelers alike who stroll Váci utca as well as the boutique- and shop-filled roads bisecting pedestrian streets and courtyards. Váci utca was formerly known throughout the country as *the* street for good bookshops. Sadly, only one remains, but don't fret. We have other bookstore recommendations to follow that will satisfy your needs. The street is now largely occupied by Euro-fashion chain stores that flood every major city with their European-style prices. There are an overwhelming number of folklore/souvenir shops, which might be nice to window-shop, but unless we have recommended them below, you may be paying more than you should for that souvenir. This area is home to many cafes and bars, but it, like Castle Hill, is notorious for tourist traps.

Another popular shopping area for travelers is the **Castle District** in Buda, with its abundance of overpriced folk-art boutiques and art galleries. This is where tour buses drop off travelers with minimal time to shop, thus forcing them into unwise choices. A healthy selection of Hungarian wines and wine tasting from historical local viticulture regions can be found in the intimate labyrinthine cellar of the **House of Hungarian Wines.**

While Hungarians might browse or people-watch in these two neighborhoods, they tend to do their serious shopping elsewhere. One of the favorite shopping streets is Pest's **Outer Ring (Nagykörút),** which extends into **West End Center,** central Europe's largest multifunction shopping mall, located just behind the Nyugati Railway Station. This designation may not last for much longer as larger malls are on the architects' drafting tables. Another bustling shopping street is Pest's **Kossuth Lajos utca,** off the Erzsébet Bridge, and its continuation, **Rákóczi út,** which extends all the way out to Keleti Railway Station. **Király utca** has gentrified and is becoming known for its small boutiques of home decor. **Andrássy út,** from Deák tér to Oktogon, is also a popular, though more upscale. Designer stores have recently opened and more are in various stages of being created. Together with the adjacent **Liszt Ferenc tér** and **Nagymező utca,** Andrássy út is where evenings comes alive, with numerous cafes and restaurants. Intermingled with the plethora of cafes and restaurants of the revitalized **Ráday utca,** a few small shops offer unique ceramic, glass, and other brick-a-brack that may be exactly what you are missing in your life. In Buda, Hungarian crowds visit the shops at Fehérvári út, the end of the number four tram line. You can often pay by credit card in the most popular shopping areas.

HOURS   Most stores are open Monday through Friday from 10am to 6pm and Saturday from 9 or 10am to 1 or sometimes 2pm. Some stores stay open an hour or two later on Thursday or Friday. Most shops are closed on Sunday, except for those on Váci utca. Shopping malls are open on weekends, sometimes as late as 9pm.

TAXES & REFUNDS Refunds on the 5% to 16.5% **value-added tax (VAT),** which is built into all prices, are available for most consumer goods purchases of more than 45,000 Ft ($243/£128) purchased in one store, in 1 day (look for stores with the "Tax-Free" logo in the window). The refund process, however, is elaborate and confusing. In most shops, the salesperson can provide you with the necessary documents: the store receipt, a separate receipt indicating the VAT amount on your purchase, the VAT reclaims form, and the mailing envelope. The salesperson should also be able to help you fill out the paperwork. Use a separate claim form for each applicable purchase. If you are departing Hungary by plane, you can collect your refund at the **IBUSZ Agency** at Ferihegy Airport. You have to do this right after checking in but *before* you pass security control. Otherwise, hold on to the full packet until you leave Hungary and get your forms certified by Customs when you land. Then, mail in your envelope and wait forever for your refund. Two wrinkles: You must get your forms certified by Customs within 90 days of the purchase showing that it is leaving the country, and you must mail in your forms within 183 days of the date of export certification on the refund claim form. We have never found this to be any significant savings since there is a service charge for the service. Unless you are making grandiose purchases, you may want to save your time and energy for other things. For further information, contact **Global Refund (Innova-Invest Pénzügyi Rt.)** at IV. Ferenciek tere 10, 1053 Budapest (*©* **1/411-0157;** fax 1/411-0159; www.globalrefund.com).

SHIPPING & CUSTOMS You can ship a box to yourself from any post office, but the rules on packing boxes are as strict as they are arcane. The Hungarian postal authorities prefer that you use one of their official shipping boxes, for sale at all post offices. They're quite flimsy, however, and have been known to break open in transit. The Hungarian post does not have a five-star rating for service, but they do rank four stars for misappropriating packages coming and going from the country.

Very few shops will organize shipping for you. Exceptions to this rule include most Herend and Zsolnay porcelain shops, Ajka crystal shops, and certain art galleries, which employ the services of a packing-and-shipping company, Touristpost. Touristpost offers three kinds of delivery: express, air mail, and surface. The service is not available directly to the public, but functions only through participating contracted shops. You need to consider whether the cost of shipping will still save you money by purchasing your fine porcelain and crystal in Hungary than at home.

Hungarian customs regulations do not limit the export of noncommercial quantities of most goods, except collectibles. However, the export of some perishable food is regulated, but allowed if acceptable to the receiving country. The limit on wine and spirits is not limited at export if shipped, but may be limited by Customs at your destination. Shipping wine can be prohibitively expensive. For more on customs, see p. 12.

2 Shopping A to Z

ANTIQUES

Just about everywhere a traveler will venture, one will find shops carrying antique artifacts from keys to heirloom furniture; Budapest antiques shops have something to please every shopping buff.

Maria Theresa approved the establishment of pawn shops in 1773 with the goal of preventing predatory lending of money. These pawn shops have evolved into today's antiques stores. Many of them still function as a pawn shop as well as an antiques store, selling what people have not returned to claim. During the communist times, art collecting or trading was illegal, so couldn't be done openly. Dealers and collectors made their covert deals around the pawnbroker shops on this street. When the laws changed, news agents, grocers, and repair shops changed hands and became antiques shops.

Nevertheless, when shopping for antiques, you should know that Hungary forbids the export of items that are designated "cultural treasures." All antiques over 50 years old need to follow a process. First the antique must be shown to an expert for valuation purposes. To receive the valuation certificate, you will need to present the object or a minimum of five photographs of it and the charge of valuation is a percentage of the item's price. After you have the valuation certificate, you must then receive a permit issued by the appropriate official government office: For paintings, it is the Hungarian National Gallery; for furniture, the Museum of Applied Arts; and all other objects, the Cultural Inheritance Office. The entire process can take up to 4 weeks to complete. Unless noted otherwise, the antiques shops and galleries below have standard Monday to Friday hours of 10am to 6pm and Saturday from 10am to 2pm. The most celebrated street for art and antiques is Falk Miksa utca where more than 20 shops and galleries are filled to the brim with collectables of all varieties; some shops specialize in particular items, while others are generalists. As you stroll through the city, you will no doubt find other isolated antiques shops as well.

The **Ecseri Flea Market** (see "Markets," later in this chapter) also deserves mention here, as numerous private antiques dealers operate booths at this one-of-a-kind open-air market. As with all flea markets, the quality and selection are never consistent, so it is just luck of timing in finding a real bargain. Take your chances for the fun of it; it may be your lucky day.

Anna Antiques   Carefully packed from wall-to-wall, this beautiful shop presents a nice selection of furniture and pottery while also excelling in hand-embroidered textiles. Take your time and find out more about the objects on display from the charming shop owner. Hours are Monday through Friday 10am to 6pm and Saturday from 10am to 2pm. V. Falk Miksa u. 18–20. ℂ **1/302-5461.** Tram: 4 or 6 Jászai Mari tér.

Bardoni Eurostyle Antiques   With its stay-a-while atmosphere, the store is decorated as a chic but congested living room. Bardoni carries characteristic Art Nouveau, Bauhaus, and Art Deco furniture and decorative items. Hours are Monday through Friday 10am to 6pm and Saturday from 10am to 2pm. V. Falk Miksa u. 12. ℂ **1/269-0090.** Tram: 4 or 6 Jászai Mari tér.

BÁV (Bizományi Kereskedőház és Záloghitel Rt   Although it no longer has a monopoly on the sale of antiques, this state-owned trading house continues to control the lion's share of the antiques market in Hungary. BÁV people will tell you where to take an item for valuation, however, once it is purchased, they will only refund 60% of the paid price if their permission to export is denied, so it is best to take photographs first and then only purchase the item after receiving permission to export certificates. Hours are Monday through Friday 10am to 6pm and Saturday from 10am to 2pm. V. Bécsi u. 1. ℂ **1/277-2590.** Deák tér. V. Ferenciek tere 10. ℂ **1/318-3733.** Metro: Ferenciek (Blue line). II. Franken Leo u. 13. ℂ **1/315-0417.**

Dunaparti Auction House and Gallery   One of the largest galleries with a wide range of antiques, paintings, porcelains, furniture, rugs, and lamps with something for collectors and souvenirs hunters as well. Hours are Monday through Friday 10am to 6pm and Saturday from 10am to 2pm. V. Váci ut 36. ℂ **1/267-3539.** Metro: Vörösmarty (Yellow line).

Ecclesia Szövetkezet   Next door to the Franciscan church, this store has authentic hand-painted icons from Russia, Bulgaria, and Ukraine, starting at around 12,000 Ft ($65/£34); contemporary hand-painted copies start as low as 7,000 Ft ($38/£20). Hours are Monday through Friday 10am to 6pm and Saturday from 10am to 2pm. V. Ferenciek tere 7. ℂ **1/317-3754.** Metro: Ferenciek (Blue line).

Empire Antique Gallery   A family-owned treasure chest operating shops in Lima, Peru, and Ecuador, this gallery is located in the lush environment of the Budapest Marriott Hotel's foyer, so call the hotel to be connected. Showcased are valuable porcelain, jewelry, silverware, numismatic medals, and paintings. Hours are Monday through Friday 10am to 6pm and Saturday from 10am to 2pm. V. Apáczai Csere János u. 4. ℂ **1/486-5000.** Metro: Deák (all lines).

Mihálka Gallery   In this centrally located cramped gallery you'll find a wide array of 18th- and 19th-century vintage furniture, paintings, objets d'art, and interior decorative items. Hours are Monday through Friday 10am to 6pm and Saturday from 10am to 2pm. V. Markó u. 3. ℂ **1/30-951-4652** mobile. Tram: 2 Szalay.

Pintér Antik Diszkont   This shop stocks a widespread selection of vintage furniture, porcelain and decorative in its daedal interior, a small post–bomb shelter salon, while the **Pintér Szonja Contemporary Gallery** is located within the antiques shop, which also displays groundbreaking contemporary Hungarian artworks. Hours are Monday through Friday 10am to 6pm and Saturday from 10am to 2pm. V. Falk Miksa u. 10. ℂ **1/311-3030.** Tram: 4 or 6 Jászai Mari tér.

ART GALLERIES

Budapest is home to a developing, yet often economically turbulent art gallery scene. Many galleries open; seem to generate public enthusiasm, then just as quickly are vacant storefronts. Uniquely, some art galleries are also auction houses, and vice versa, but dedicated art galleries are trying their hand at independence. Many galleries are antique and contemporary hybrid ventures that feature anything from fine art to vintage books. A new generation of Hungarian collectors has developed, and significant interest from European and international collectors has really fueled the development of the Hungarian modern-art market. The market for antiques has also been on the rise as long forgotten objects from the communist era have been removed from storage and are once again entering the market. Contemporary artists have made less headway in the past, but in the last few years they are starting to get recognized and rewarded for their efforts.

Export rules apply to all works of art as well as antiques that are considered Hungarian cultural treasures, although that list has become less expensive than it once was. Before completing a purchase, confirm that you'll be allowed to take the work out of the country; gallery proprietors should have the requisite documentation on hand. See the information above about documentation needed.

The new galleries are breaking with tradition regarding their opening hours. Some are open daily, while others are closed on Monday, like museums. Still others are open until early evening on Saturday, really deviating from all norms. Two areas of concentration are the Inner City of Pest and Buda's Castle District. However, breaking out of the crowd, means breaking out of the neighborhood too. If you want to power browse in a concentrated area, then head to the art and antiques area of Budapest along Falk Miksa, from Jászai Mari tér down to the parliament. A host of art galleries and antiques shops can be found along this route.

ACB A contemporary art-oriented gallery, ACB was founded in 2003 by a group with a business-in-art mentality and it hosts frequently changing exhibitions of Hungarian and international artists. The gallery also features the eclectic, dynamic paintings, digital prints, photos, and videos collected by the founders, now described as the Irokéz Collection. It is open Tuesday through Friday 2 to 6pm and Saturday by appointment. VI. Király u. 76. ⊘ **1/413-7608.** Tram: 4 or 6 to Király.

Art Factory Gallery and Studio I just discovered this gallery and though it is small, you can arrange to visit the studio and the artists while they are working. Their work is varied and exceptional. Meeting the artist really gives a new dimension to the work. Even hanging on your wall at home, it will speak of a memorable experience. Organized and run by an American, Dianne Brown, you can call her for a studio tour, but the gallery is in a public building Open Monday through Friday 10am to 6pm and Saturday from 10am to 2pm. XIII. Váci út 152–156 (ABB Building). ⊘ **06/20-954-9941** mobile only. Metro: Forgách u. (Blue line).

Csók István Galéria One of my favorites for browsing, this gallery has it all and sells it all too. There is a fine collection of paintings, ceramics, glassware, and other artful objects by Hungarian artists who are trying to break into the art scene. Open daily from 10am to 8pm. V. Váci u. 25. ⊘ **1/318-2592.** Metro: Vörösmarty tér (Yellow line).

Dorottya Gallery Albeit oppressively austere and small to some, this one-room gallery is associated with the Ernst Museum and compiles excellent contemporary installations, photographs, and media art. You don't even need to go in, you can see it all from the windows. It is open Monday through Saturday 10am to 6pm. V. Dorottya u. 8. ⊘ **1/266-0223.** Metro: Vörösmarty tér (Yellow line).

Ernst Gallery The gallery features fine and applied arts from Hungary and around Europe. The Ernst Gallery, the most posh gallery in town, is run by a dynamic duo of the Austrian-born Ernst Wastl and his Greek-born wife, Eleni Korani. They put together exhibitions, discover "unknown" Hungarian artists, and whatever they put their hands onto ends up being the talk of the town. The gallery also exhibits and sells fine furniture and a wealthy collection of rarities including vintage art books, posters, and other curiosities. Hours are Monday through Friday 10am to 6pm and Saturday from 10am to 2pm. V. Irányi u. 27. ⊘ **1/266-4016** or 1/266-4017. Metro: Ferenciek tér (Blue line).

Godot Gallery Located beside the cafe of the same name, Godot opened its door to the arty crowd in 1999 in order to present a new, dynamic space for contemporary Hungarian art. Exhibitions follow distinctly different themes, which makes it a gallery worth returning to, to see the works displayed. Hours are Monday through Friday 10am to 6pm. It is closed on weekends. VII. Madách I. u. 8. ⊘ **1/322-5272.** Metro: Deák tér (all lines).

Impresszio Art Gallery This gallery features four Hungarian contemporary artists at the moment. They are impressive enough to have kept this little gallery open, so it is worth a look. Hours are Monday through Friday 10am to 6pm and Saturday from 10am to 2pm. XIII. Pozsonyi u. 11. ⊘ **061/30-397-0251** mobile phone only. Tram: 4 or 6 Jászai Mari tér.

kArton Gallery Run by the art institution kArton, kArton and its sister **raktArt** gallery feature a colorful segment of contemporary visual art: underappreciated genres

Finds Contemporary Hungarian Art Lights the Spark

Sometimes a foreigner can make a difference in the country they adopt as a home, and this is what Dianne C. Brown has done. After moving here in 1994 when her husband was transferred to Budapest, Dianne founded the **Friends of the Fine Arts Museum,** the first museum docent program in Europe. At the time, the museum was a place for research, but not an amicable place for visitors. Many of the holdings of the museum were shipped to Germany during the war, and returned at the end of the war with the help of repatriated Hungarians who raised money and awareness of the importance of the pieces. The newly founded Friends organization sponsored events such as Open Day, allowing a behind-the-scenes look at the holdings which were not on display and how paintings were restored. Dianne continued to work with the organization for 6 years acting as its first president and continuing as a member of the board.

With her 14-year commitment to working with Hungarian art, she has been inspirational in renewing interest in the country's contemporary artists and their work. Dianne founded the **Sparks Gallery;** she opened the **Art Factory** in 2005 and continues as its director.

The Art Factory was created with the mission of highlighting some of Hungary's most promising young artists while promoting their work abroad and establishing their place in the international art world. To achieve this, the Art Factory is planning to be an active participant in international art fairs. In 2007, Sparks Gallery and the Art Gallery were combined to create the Art Factory Gallery. Up to this point, the most important period of Hungarian art was from the late 19th and early 20th century, but with all of those pieces off of the market, new interest has developed in contemporary pieces.

like comics, illustrations, and cartoons. The opening hours are out of sync with other galleries hours, Monday through Friday 1 to 6pm and Saturday 10am to 2pm. V. Alkotmány u. 18. ☎ 1/472-0000. Metro: Ferenciek tere (Blue line).

Kieselbach Gallery and Auction House   Established and directed by art historian Tamás Kieselbach in 1994, the Kieselbach Gallery functions as a gallery and auction house. It also puts on museum-type shows that present artworks from private collections at biannual nonselling exhibitions. The gallery specializes in paintings by Hungarian artists dating from the 19th and 20th centuries, which are becoming short in supply. Most are now off of the market. The gallery has a reputation for the documentation and display of artworks previously unknown to the public. Hours are Monday through Friday 10am to 6pm and Saturday from 10am to 2pm. V. Szent István körút 5. ☎ 1/269-3148. Tram: 4 or 6 Jászai Mari tér.

Koller Gallery   This is the oldest private gallery in Hungary. Since 1953, it has been representing internationally known sculptures and artists. Hours are Monday through Friday 10am to 6pm and Saturday from 10am to 2pm. I. Táncsics Mihály u. 5. ☎ 1/356-9208. Tram 19.

Delia Vekony, the gallery curator, oversees a rigorous exhibition schedule in several venues, including galleries, institutions and museums abroad. Miami-based associate Ileana Bravo is the chief U.S. adviser. Ed Mocsi of InterUrban Art and art dealer Keith Jacomine are associates in New York. In Hungary, these four have formed alliances with both Várfok and Virag Judit, two of the leading galleries in Budapest.

The studio is located in a Socialist-era industrial complex near the center of Budapest; a tremendously large space where artists can develop their style and their career simultaneously. While the artists work in all mediums and styles, the common thread is a distinctly Eastern European emotional expressionism. Artists in residence are Zsolt Bodoni, Levente Herman, Dora Juhasz, Marta Kucsora, Mamikon Yengibarian, Ágnes Verebics, Krisztián Horváth, and Luca Korodi. Their work can be viewed at the Gresham Four Seasons Hotel, which has purchased work from the studio's artistic pool.

In addition to the Art Factory Gallery's vast studio and exhibition space, the facility also houses a newly built micro-gallery for photography, video, and works on paper. A small gallery and photo gallery are also at this location, but viewing is by appointment only along with a studio tour. Contact Dianne C. Brown at (C) **06/20-954-9941** (mobile phone) or e-mail her at dcbrown@starkingnet.hu. She welcomes visitors.

The **Art Factory Gallery** itself is located in public space in the mezzanine of the ABB Office Building, XIII. Vaci ut 152–156 (just past the Arpad Bridge; www.budapestartfactory.com). Admission is free when the building is open, which is Sunday through Friday 10am to 6pm and Saturday 11am to 2pm. Since this is a public space, the gallery is unattended, but the studio is nearby, making a tour convenient if arranged ahead.

Liget Gallery   Curator and art critic Tibor Várnagy has run this gallery since 1983. The Liget (grove) gallery in the City Park features nonprofit exhibitions and an open, easygoing artistic space for performances, film screenings, and concerts. Highlights are the socially conscious artwork of local talents. Open Wednesday through Monday 2 to 6pm. XIV. Ajtósi Dürer sor 5. (C) **1/351-4924.** Metro: Hősök tere (Yellow line).

Mû-terem Gallery and Auction House   Established and directed by art historian Judit Virág and her husband, István Törö, this gallery also functions as an auction house. Similar to its main competitor, the Kieselbach Gallery, this gallery also puts on museum-type shows presenting artworks from private collections. Paintings by 19th- and 20th-century Hungarian artists are found here, a gallery that regularly produces record-setting prices for artists. Auctions are held twice a year. Hours are Monday through Friday 10am to 6pm and Saturday from 10am to 2pm. V. Falk Miksa u. 30. (C) **1/269-3148** or 1/269-2210. Tram: 4 or 6 to Jászai Mari tér.

Nagyházi Galéria és Aukcióház   Works by Hungarian and international artists, furniture, and classical European artworks are found in this gallery and auction house.

Up to 10 auctions are held yearly. Hours are Monday through Friday 10am to 6pm and Saturday from 10am to 2pm. V. Balaton u. 8. ✆ 1/475-6000. Tram: 4 or 6 to Jászai Mari tér.

Stúdió Gallery   The frequently changing exhibitions in this gallery feature the works of Hungarian art students. If you're looking for the zest of the newest artsy trend, don't miss out on this studio. Open Monday through Friday 4 to 8pm and Saturday noon to 4pm. V. Képíró u. 6. ✆ 1/267-2033. Metro: Kálvin tér (Blue line).

Várfok Gallery   An art dealer by the name of Károly Szalóky has an ambitious plan to transform Várfok utca in the Castle District into a street of contemporary Hungarian art galleries. He has already opened two new galleries on the street, **Spiritusz** and **XO Gallery.** The main gallery, Várfok, features a fine mix of old and novel Hungarian artwork. Open Tuesday through Saturday 11am to 6pm. I. Várfok u. 14. ✆ 1/213-5155. Bus: 10 from Moszkva tér.

Virag Judit Gallery   This is the second oldest gallery in the city after the change in government having opened in 1997. It specializes in Hungarian artists of the 19th and 20th century. Hours are Monday through Friday 10am to 6pm and Saturday from 10am to 2pm. V. Falk Miksa u. 30. ✆ 1/312-2071. Tram: 4 or 6 Jászai Mari tér.

ART SUPPLIES

Kenderkó   Serving and boosting creative ideas, this store features wooden boxes and other wooden pieces for collage as well as the tools needed for carving. It also has a selection of fiber art supplies. Hours are Monday through Friday 10am to 6pm and Saturday from 10am to 2pm. VII. Ertzsébet krt. 10–12. ✆ 1/351-9620. Tram: 4 or 6 Királyi.

Művészellátó Szakáruház   If you are feeling a need to get your hands on some craft items, this store will most likely fill the bill for what you need. From scrapbook supplies to oil paints, it has it all and a helpful staff. Perhaps you can make a scrapbook of your visit while you are here. There are three convenient locations in the city. Hours are Monday through Friday 10am to 6pm and Saturday from 10am to 2pm. II. Margit körút 3. ✆ 1/212-2807. Tram: 4–6. Two other shops in the city center are at VIII. Üllői út 36. ✆ 1/212-1938. Metro: Üllői (Blue line), and VI. Nagymező u. 45–47, ✆ 1/311-7040. Metro: Opera (Yellow line).

Neoart   For the amateur and professional artist, Neoart offers a wide selection of watercolors, oil paints, and acrylic paints, as well as brushes, drawing materials, canvas, and paper. Open weekdays 9am to 5pm. I. Zách u. 6B. ✆ 1/353-3750.

BEAUTY & HEALTH

Before you happen to have the need for an aspirin, but realize you forgot to pack it, it is best to know that anything remotely related to medication from pain relievers to stomach upset remedies, can only be purchased in a pharmacy. Conversely, personal products for ladies and condoms can be found everywhere (see "Pharmacies," p. 69).

Bio-ABC   Bio-ABC started as a little hole-in-the-wall health food store, but due to popular demand and the closure of all of the Bio chain stores, this one has flourished. It is now like a health supermarket with everything from organic produce to soy cheeses, and vitamins, plus everything in between. The staff speaks limited English, but they are always willing to try to be of assistance. Hours are Monday through Friday 10am to 6pm and Saturday from 10am to 2pm. V. Múzeum krt. 19. ✆ 1/317-3043. Metro: Astoria (Red line) or Kálvin tér (Blue line).

Bio-Mania 🐾🐾   Combatting chemically "infected" products and unhealthy lifestyles, this store features bioproduced medicinal and health-supportive products in addition to cosmetics. Hours are Monday through Friday 10am to 6pm and Saturday from 10am to 2pm. XIII. Pannónia u. 57/b. ℭ **06/30-489-0717** mobile phone. Metro: Lehel tér (Blue line).

Black Tulip for Men ✶✶   Beauty treatments abound for women in every city, but what about men? Now men can be pampered in masculine privacy in a men's emporium of revolutionary procedures to maintain youthful and supple looks. Popular choices include the Huber machine, which encourages complete exercise for all the body's major muscle groups, improves posture, and eliminates back pain and Oxy-Life, which aids the deepest layers of the skin using pure oxygen to leave it restored and regenerated. Hours are Monday through Friday 10am to 6pm and Saturday from 10am to 2pm. VI. Révay u 14. ℭ **1/302-5577**. Metro: Bajcsy-Zsilinszky (Blue line).

Ilcsi Beautifying Herbs   Everyone wants beautiful skin; some have it and some know how to "create" it. Mrs. Daniel Molnár and son, Ferenc Molnár are creators of Ilcsi. Over 130 products made from 65 to 70 herbs, fruits, vegetables, and water, build the base of this enterprise, one that strengthens the legend of the beauty of Hungarians. Try the tomato suntan lotion to block those nasty rays, but still get a perfect tan. Only licensed beauty salons are allowed to carry their products. They are listed at **www.ilcsi.com**. One option is Health Island (*Egészségsziget*). Open Monday, Wednesday, and Friday 1pm to 8pm, and Tuesday and Thursday 9am to 2pm. VII. Dohány u. 16-18. ℭ 1/269-6088. www.kozmetikati.hu.

Long-Time Liner   If you want to return home a bit more glamorous than when you left, then this cosmetic salon will provide you with permanent make-up. Trained professionals can provide permanent eyeliner, augment your existing eyebrows to make them look lush, or do lip contouring all with a microprocessor. V. Váci u. 8, félem 1 (in courtyard). ℭ **1/318-4951**. Metro: Vörösmarty tér (Yellow line).

Lush ✶✶✶   Lush creates outstanding, environmentally friendly soaps, lotions, creams, and more out of purely organic materials such as pine, lavender, orange, avocado, or banana. Take a long, relaxing balmy bubble bath in French Kiss or Blue Skies aroma bars. The citrusy shower gel Slammer will open your eyes, but my favorite is Pied de Pepper for tired dry feet. Other Lush stores can be found in MOM Park and Árkád shopping malls. V. Szent István krt. 1. ℭ **1/472-0530**. Tram: 4 or 6 to Jászai Mari tér.

Rossmann   A mainstream brand of cosmetics, perfumery, and personal essentials, Rossmann operates 150 outlets around the country. It carries more than your ordinary drugstore-type store, but no medicines other than herbal remedies. You can find quick birthday gifts like cheap CDs, home decor, and even munchies for your favorite pet. Outlets are all over the city and recognizable by their signs with the name in red letters on a white background.

Scheckler's ✶✶✶   This is another store chain similar to Rossmann where you can get simple needed items in a hurry. They too are all over the city and have dark blue and white signs. Forgot your toothbrush? This is where you head.

BOOKSTORES

There is never a moment when we are without a book, so browsing in a bookstore is an avocation. If you are time limited, want a book fast, but don't want to splurge on a new book, Bookstation, Red Bus and Treehugger Dan's are the best for used English-language books.

Bestsellers   Bestsellers is Budapest's first English-language bookstore (opened in 1992). With its spacious and bright interior, the shop is popular with the expat crowd and English-speaking travelers who need the latest best-selling title before returning home. The store has a wide selection of fiction, science fiction, travel, and children's books, including books on Hungary. Half of the store is devoted to French-language books. A wide selection of newspapers and magazines is also available. Open Monday through Friday 9am to 6:30pm, Saturday 10am to 5pm, and Sunday 10am to 4pm. V. Október 6 u. 11. ✆ 1/312-1295. Metro: Arany János utca (Blue line).

Bookstation ★★★ *Kids*   This is a great store. It's a bit difficult to find, but worth the effort. The staff will happily check their in-stock inventory for a book by title, author, or subject. The focus is fiction, nonfiction, cookbooks, and many other genres, including a large selection of children's books, all in English. It is located in an udvar (courtyard). Cross the street from Keleti Station and about a half a block up, look for the Thököly udvar sign on the top of the building. Walk into the courtyard and the store is at the back. Hours are 10am to 7pm daily. VII. Thököly út. 18–Thököly Udvar. ✆ 1/413-1158.

Central European University Bookstore ★   This store features books covering a wide variety of disciplines. The selection of books on central and eastern European politics and history is particularly notable since the Central European University Press publishes a great variety of books on all topics central European. It has a nice selection of academic texts since it is associated with the university, but the texts are expensive. Open weekdays 10am to 6pm. V. Nádor utca 9. ✆ 1/327-3097. Metro: Kossuth tér (Red line) or Arany János u. (Blue line).

Honterus Antikvárium és Aukciós Ház Kft.   Located near the Központi Antikvárium, across the street from the Hungarian National Museum (Nemzeti Múzeum), this shop has more prints and maps on display than any other *antikvárium* in town, which is suitable; the shop was named after János Honter, a renowned Transylvanian map master. There's a shelf of mostly arcane, outdated English-language academic books as well as a stack of *National Geographic* magazines. Broadening its activity, the shop hosts auctions specializing in Hungarian literary curios. Hours are Monday through Friday 10am to 6pm and Saturday from 10am to 2pm. V. Múzeum krt. 35. ✆ 1/267-2642. Metro: Astoria (Red line) or Kálvin tér (Blue line).

Írók Boltja ★   *Írók Boltja* means "Writers' Bookshop," and this shop is truly a literary center with a rich history, first-rate literary events, and inspired window displays, making it a mecca for writers, readers, and curious bystanders. In the first half of the 20th century the store was the popular Japanese Coffee House, a popular literary coffeeshop, then became the Spark Bookstore around 1955, during the communist era. The shop's name was changed around 1958, and was state run until 1991, when 14 employees became the co-owners during the privatization of state-owned business. It is now practically an institution, and Hungarian authors such as Péter Nádas, Péter Eszterházy, and Nobel Prize–winner Imre Kertész have read here. Almost all events are held in Hungarian, but the store has a cozy in-store coffee corner. Hours are Monday through Friday 10am to 6pm and Saturday from 10am to 2pm. VI. Andrássy út 45. ✆ 1/322-1645. Metro: Oktogon (Yellow line).

Központi Antikvárium   Central Antikvárium is the city's oldest and largest old-and-rare book bookstore. Indeed, it is said to be the largest of its type in all of central Europe. Opened in 1885 across the street from the Hungarian National Museum on "Antikvárium Row" (Múzeum krt. was the antikvárium u. during the pre–World War I era, home to 37 different shops at that time), this shop has books, prints, maps, and a shelf of assorted really junky and dusty knickknacks. The staff are fluent in English but can be abrupt with English speakers. Hours are Monday through Friday 10am to 6pm and Saturday from 10am to 2pm. V. Múzeum krt. 13–15. © 1/317-3514. Metro: Astoria (Red line) or Kálvin tér (Blue line).

Libri Studium Könyvesbolt   This is one of the few bookstores left on Váci utca, which was formerly home to dozens of bookstores. This is a good option for those in search of English-language books published by Corvina about Budapest or Hungary. Coffee-table books, guidebooks, fiction and poetry in translation, and scholarly works are available. There's also a good selection of maps, including the hard-to-find Cartographia trail map of the Buda Hills *(A Budai Hegység)*. Hours are Monday through Friday 10am to 6pm and Saturday from 10am to 2pm. V. Váci u. 22. © 1/318-5680. Metro: Vörösmarty tér (Yellow line) or Deák tér (all lines).

Litea: Literature & Tea Bookshop   Situated in the Fortuna courtyard, opposite the Hilton Hotel, this bookshop/tea house stocks a wide range of books on Hungary; CDs and cassettes of the works of Hungarian composers; and cards, maps, and other quality souvenirs for serious enthusiasts of Hungarian culture. Take your time browsing, order a cup of tea, sit, and have a closer look at the books that interest you. This calm, no-obligation-to-buy atmosphere along with friendly staff is a rare find. Hours are Monday through Friday 10am to 6pm and Saturday from 10am to 2pm. I. Hess András tér 4. © 1/375-6987. Bus: 10 from Moszkva tér or 16 from Deák tér; funicular: from Clark Ádám tér to Castle Hill.

Pagony and Kispagony Children's Bookstores *(Kids*   A bookstore devoted to children in my opinion is an exceptional idea. Not only will kids find books here, mostly in Hungarian, but they will also discover toys, presents, CDs, and DVDs. The children's reading area with the huge tree, lots of pillows, and other child-safe items, make this an ideal place for kids to unwind. What better memory of their trip and something to show off to their friends than a Hungarian alphabet book? It just might inspire a future linguist. Open Monday through Friday 10am to 7pm and Saturday 10am to 2pm. A second location, Kispagony, is open the same weekday hours, plus Saturday and Sunday, 10am to 6pm. XIII. Pozsonyi út 26. © 1/239-0285 and II. Lövöház utca 17. © 1/336-0384.

Red Bus Bookstore *(*   This is a paperback sanctuary with a large selection of classical literature, thrillers, and fiction by more British authors than the other bookstores. For as small as this shop is, they have stuffed an incredible amount of books into it, forcing the serious browser to spend considerable time here, especially since it doesn't have a computerized inventory. Nevertheless, the staff is helpful. It is open Monday through Friday 11am to 7pm and Saturday 10am to 2pm. V. Semmelweis u. 14. © 1/337-7453. Metro: Astoria or Deák (Red line).

Treehugger Dan's Bookstore Café *(Finds*   Treehugger Dan's is another tiny giant of a bookstore and now at two locations. Run by a former American, these wisps of a store are loaded to the rafters with over 4,000 books, all in English. The extensive collection includes a wonderful travel guide selection including Frommer's. How can you not love this place? Have a cup of fair trade organic coffee or tea while shopping and receive a free hour of Wi-Fi Internet service besides. Dan has a computerized inventory and the staff is very helpful finding particular items. He will also do a book exchange if you want to lighten your load of that last novel you just finished. Two locations below: Open Monday through Friday 10am to 7pm and Saturday 10am to

5pm; or Monday through Friday 9:30am to 6:30pm and weekends 10am to 6pm, respectively. VI. Csengery u. 48. (℃ **1/322-0774** and VI. Lazar u. 16 (in Yellow Zebra Bike Rentals office) (℃ **1/269-3843**.

COINS

Nuismatica Érembolt   Conveniently located on the famous square, this store has a wide selection in a clean well-lit shop with normal weekday hours. V. Vörösmarty tér 6. (℃ **1/3374908**. Metro: Vörösmarty (Yellow line).

DEPARTMENT STORES & MALLS

As everywhere else in the world, Budapest has a lion's share of American-style malls, which like many other places is putting a drain on the small stores' financial health. Although they are immensely popular to Budapesters, they also lament the closing of the local stores that were once their only shopping opportunity.

Árkád   Opened in 2002, Árkád is the youngest mall in the city at the moment. The spacious, but not immense mall is German owned and contains some of the most trendy stores including Marks & Spencer, C&A, Mexx, Nike, and Zara. The large circular cafe/restaurants in the heart of the mall tend to rapidly fill up in the afternoon. X. Örs vezér tere 25. (℃ **1/433-1400**. Metro: Örs Vezér tér (Red line).

Asia Center   Built in the proximity of the Polus Center, the Asia Center opened its doors in 2003 to myriad Asian-produced products from clothing to furniture, replacing a huge outdoor Asian market that had been popular for years. The second wing of the mall is scheduled to be completed by 2008. XV. Szentmihályi út 167–169. ((℃ **1/688-8888**. Bus: 73 (red-lettered) or Polus mall shuttle departing from Keleti train station.

Duna Plaza   This was the first mall built and boasts 120 different shops, a nine-screen Hollywood Multiplex, snack bars and pubs, and a bowling alley. Duna Plaza is open daily 10am to 9pm; the entertainment complex closes later than the rest of the mall. XII. Váci út 178. (℃ **1/465-1600**. Metro: Gyöngyösi (Blue line).

IKEA   IKEA sprawls out over Örs vezér tere, the eastern terminus of the Red metro line. It is the first of two Budapest branches of the internationally known Swedish furniture store. Remodeled and enlarged in 2005, the other location, which is only accessible by car, is even larger. XIV. Örs vezer tere. (℃ **1/460-3100**. Metro: Örs vezer tere (Red line).

Mammut   Mammut is really a two-part mall, with Mammut I and Mammut II connected by a glass passageway connecting the two wings. The mall was extended in 2001, and thus comprises over 300 shops, though when you see the immense open courtyard in one wing, you will wonder where they are hiding all of the stores. Along corridors, you will see parts of mammoth remains found while excavating the mall, hence its name. This is the mall where the bowling alley is filled with English speakers, an expat hang out. At the back of the mall, on the outside ramp, you will find the Fény utca market selling produce and flowers. II. Lövőház u. 2–6. (℃ **1/345-8024**. Metro: Moszkva tér (Red line).

MOM Park   Located near the Budapest Congress Center, MOM Park is among the most recent malls in the spacious, sophisticated new conglomerate. Home to one of three Palace Cinemas (operating the first digital multiplex in central Europe), plus a chic interior design boutique called Goa and a trendy Italian shoe shop by designer Alberto Zago. XII. Alkotás utca 53 (℃ **1/487-5500**. Tram: 61 or 59 from Moszkva tér.

Pólus Center   The Pólus Center is home to **TESCO,** the British supermarket chain, as well as to countless other shops. Wings in the mall have flashy American street names: Rodeo Drive, Sunset Boulevard, Wall Street. In spite of the street names, the shops are less than interesting and the quality of the merchandise is less than stellar. Open weekdays 10am to 8pm, weekends 10am to 6pm. XV. Szentmihályi út 131. ℂ 1/415-2114. Bus: 73 (red-lettered) or Polus mall shuttle no. 173 departing from Keleti train station.

WestEnd City Center   This behemoth mall opened in 2000 right behind Nyugati Railway Station, giving it the auspicious title of being the largest mall in central Europe. This will be changing with the construction of yet more malls. It has generated much concern about the future of downtown shops and boutiques, and has led to the demise of numerous small businesses in the immediate area of the Outer Ring boulevard. Within its 400 or so shops, however, it has a rich selection of stores. There is a lovely fountain on the ground floor that reaches one story up that was donated from Canada. Take a breather from shopping and relax on the open-air garden roof terrace with a cafe in the summer and an ice-skating rink in the winter, but lovely statues all year-around. VI. Váci út 1–3. ℂ 1/238-7777. Metro: Nygati (Blue line).

FASHION FOR WOMEN & MEN

We list some options, assuming that you'll discover new ones on your own, but to start you off, we suggest you begin on Haris köz, an alleyway that is actually just a small street that starts at Váci utca. There is a large and diverse selection of fashionable shops there. For discount clothes, see "Markets," later in this chapter.

Alberto Guardiani   Alberto Guardiani offers shoes in the latest fashion trends for the sophisticated man or woman who demands excellent craftsmanship as well as style in a high-end selection of shoes. Accessories are sold also. VI. Andrássy ut 34. ℂ 1/354-0054. Metro: Opera (Yellow line).

Alessandro & Co.   This store offers made-to-measure suits characterized by taste and quality of the finest Italian tradition. Casual wear, dress shirts, neckwear, shoes, and accessories are also available. I. Lánchíd u. 5. ℂ 1/201-5526. On the Buda side, just off of the Chain Bridge. Metro: Batthyány tér (Red line).

Bagaria (★★★   I don't carry a purse, but if these handbags and purses make a man take notice of them, they will certainly attract your attention. Venconi, a Hungarian designer makes up 50% of the collection, while the rest are Italian designs. The colors and styles were bright, exciting, and original. The shop is back in the courtyard, so don't miss it. V. Váci utca 10. ℂ 1/318-5768. Metro: Vörösmarty tér (Yellow line).

Best Cipő   Best Cipő sells men's and women's fashionable shoes. The men's shoes are especially interesting with unusual designs, yet fun and comfortable. VII. Erzsébet krt. 32. ℂ 1/322-6916. Tram: 4 or 6. Király.

Chantal Boutique   If shoes are your thing, don't pound the pavement looking until you see the offerings at this shoe boutique, where you are sure to find some innovative designs. V. Haris köz 2. ℂ 1/318-3812. Metro: Vörösmarty tér (Yellow line).

Emilia Anda   Made of mixed organic materials like silk with plastic or paper, the noted young designer Emilia Anda's clothes make heads turn. Her studies in architecture paved the way for creating her inimitable lustrous get-ups, one that stands out in the Hungarian fashion world. V. Váci u. 16/b. No phone. Metro: Vörösmarty tér (Yellow line).

Enrico   Enrico offers elegant and sporty clothing for men with designer labels that include Gianfranco Ferre, Roberto Cavalli, Dolce & Gabbana, and of course, Enrico. VI. West End Shopping Mall Váci út 1–3. ✆ 1/238-7693. Metro: Nyugati pu (Blue line).

Eventuell ★★★ *(Finds*   A young American friend came upon this store and has made this her store of choice on each visit to the city. Among the unusual textiles used in clothing, she swears by the felt jacket she purchased. It looks terrific. The scarves and other clothes, jewelry, and other accessories are unique. V. Nyálry Pál u. 7. ✆ 1/318-6926. Metro: Ferenciek tere (Blude line).

Iguana   Looking for some sparkling oversize grandma glasses or perhaps crazy '60s or '70s cult accessories? A shrine for retro rats, the shop stocks rows of peace jackets, trousers, bags, and jewelry. Listen to or purchase some of their all-star euphoric second-hand CDs. Don't confuse this store with the restaurant of the same name. No nachos here. VIII. Krúdy Gyula u. 9. No phone. www.iguanaretro.hu. Metro: Kálvin tér (Blue line). Tram: 4 or 6.

Intvita Art Gallery ★★★   You will also find this gallery listed under home decor below, because they have two locations with the same name, but very different products. This shop is filled with textiles; clothing, scarves, handbags, hats, and jewelry all made by Hungarian designers filling the shelves and racks. Notice the artistic wood walls and shelves while you are there. The owner handcrafted them himself and they are superb. This is at the end of the pedestrian street closer to the great market. V. Váci u. 61. ✆ 1/337-1248. Tram: 47 or 49.

Katalin Hampel ★★★   This Hungarian designer has her own unique designs blending traditional Hungarian clothing with a modern flair. Katalin Hampel designs women's clothing marked by delicate precision of handmade embroidery creating a new chic style. V. Váci u. 8. ✆ 1/318-9741. Metro: Vörösmarty tér (Yellow line).

Katti Zoób   Celebrated Hungarian fashion-designer Zoób's high-end couture ranges from slick, eccentric, yet harmonious businesswomen's outfits to smart and naughty on-the-go wear and accessories. The shop, located in the capacious MOM Park, is open Monday through Saturday 10am to 8pm and Sunday 10am to 6pm. V. Szent István körút 17. ✆ 1/312-1865. Tram: 4 or 6.

Kis Royal Férfi Ruházat   This is a men's clothing store with some designer labels such as Pierre Cardin. VII. Erzsébet krt. 34. ✆ 1/342-6538. Tram: 4 or 6. Király.

La Boutique   Showcasing the products of significant high-end shoe designers, the shop specializes in men's and women's shoes and accessories, but the prices match Western designer-label prices. VI. Andrássy út 16. ✆ 1/302-5646. Metro: Opera (Yellow line).

Látomás ★★★   Run by 25 suave, creative designers, the shop is a fashion statement to the young Hungarians who want to break all the molds of the past and caste their own impression on the fashion world. The colors and designs to spice up your life and your wardrobe can be found in their collection of chic and unique hats, handbags, clothing, jewelry, and accessories. Browse through their saucy selection of secondhand clothing upstairs to find some fashion bargains. VII. Dohány u. 20. ✆ 1/266-5052. Tram: 4 or 6.

Louis Vuitton   View the latest handbags, purses, and accessories by this famous designer at his own store directly across the street from the opera house. VI. Andrássy ut 24 ✆ 1/373-0487. Metro: Opera (Yellow line).

Manu-Art   Handmade by local designers, these warm clothes are likely to cheer up those who work in the cool outdoors. Odd fluffy sheep, crazy snails, or curlicue

Budapest's Youthful Designers

WAMP (WAsárnapi Művész Piac) is the Hungarian designers association that follows the example of the London and New York markets. Their main objective is to establish a regular forum for design and applied-art products. Secondly, they want to create a more intense relationship between artists and potential buyers through interaction. Success has come for many artists in this organization when they have improved their craft through interactions with buyers or direct feedback from visitors.

Not every artist or craftsperson can get into WAMP; first you have to present a portfolio of your work and have it judged for quality of workmanship, design, and unique appeal. After passing that round, the artist is allowed to register in the WAMP database and sell at their sponsored functions.

The number of Hungarian designers associated with **WAMP** is quickly growing with more than 90 artists exhibiting and selling their products after only 1 year of the organization's existence. Artists are realizing the uniqueness of the sponsored events as a seal of approval of their work. A wide range of design objects, such as jewelry, textiles, clothing, ceramics, glassware, children's toys, games, and cake design are routinely presented. WAMP opens its market, usually on the first Sunday of the month. During the warm months, it is held at Erzsébet tér (a former bus station) across from Le Meridian Hotel from 11am to 8pm. During the winter, the locations change, so check their website (**www.wamp.hu**) for current information.

For more information on the Budapest designer and fashion scene, you may want to try your luck with the Hungarian-only sites of the Budapest fashion scene, **www.bpfashion.hu**, **www.budapestfashionweek.com**.

---

non-figurative designs suit all ages. You'll find a second store in the busy Mammut mall (same phone number). V. Károly krt. 10 ✆ **1/266-8136.** Metro: Astoria (Red line).

Náray Tamás   Situated in the posh Ybl Palace, across from the Central Kávéház, this elegant and spacious shop sells the creations of one of Hungary's most celebrated designers, Tamás Náray. The clothes are tasteful, but expensive. V. Károlyi Mihály u. 12. ✆ **1/266-2473.** Metro: Ferenciek tere (Blue line).

Retrock   A group of young contemporary designers display their modern, exclusive, entrancing clothes and accessories for women and men in a nostalgic atmosphere of the last century. I call this a den of discovery for those fashion aficionados who like living on the edge. Very popular with college students. V. Heinszlmann Imre u. 1. ✆ **06/30-556-2814** mobile phone. Metro: Astoria (Red line).

Tisza Cipő   A former Soviet-era brand, Tisza Shoes has been smartly resuscitated into a retro-shoe brand that shot up on the must-have shoe list in Hungary and is steadily moving into the international market. It is now enjoying its laid-back high-end segment market position. VII. Károly krt 1. ✆ **1/266-3055.** Metro: Astoria (Red line).

Vakondgyár   Hungarian youth fashion, this T-shirt boutique chain features outrageous shirts designed by a whimsical young artist. Starting with the mole figure, the cute key character that gave the brand its name, the shirts' self-indulgent designs include fanciful insects, goofy Hungarian cartoon characters, and other New Age logolike creations in a cacophony of color. V. Magyar u. 52. ⓒ No phone. Metro: Kálvin tér (Blue line).

V50 Design Art Studio ⍟   Fashion designer Valeria Fazekas has an eye for clothes that are both eye-catching and elegant. Her hats are works of art. Prices are reasonable, and she now accepts credit cards. She has a second shop at V. Belgrád rakpart 16, where she can often be found working late into the night in the upstairs studio. V. Váci u. 50. ⓒ 1/337-5320. Metro: Ferenciek tere (Blue line).

Za-Za   Za-Za offers the imaginative creations of the hot young Hungarian designers of Magenta Clothing Company, who brag that they have a new line every 2 weeks. I cannot attest to this, but their display of clothes did get my attention. V. Váci u. 12. ⓒ 1/267-0280. Metro: Vörösmarty tér (Yellow line).

FOLK CRAFTS

Hungary's famous folkloric objects are the most popular souvenirs among foreign visitors. The mushrooming number of folk-art shops *(Népművészeti Háziipar)* have a great selection of handmade goods. Popular items include pillowcases, embroidered tablecloths, runners, wine cozies, pottery, porcelain, dolls, intricately painted or carved eggs, dresses, skirts, and sheepskin vests. The main store, **Folkart Centrum,** is at V. Váci u. 58 (ⓒ 1/318-5840), and is open daily from 10am to 7pm. One shop that has a wide selection and helpful staff is **Folkart Craftman's House** (ⓒ 1/318-5143) on the side street, Régiposta u. 12 right off of Váci utca and open daily 10am to 7pm. One outstanding private shop on Váci utca is **Vali Folklór,** in the courtyard of Váci u. 23 (ⓒ 1/337-6301) open weekdays 10am to 5pm. A soft-spoken man named Bálint Ács, who travels the villages of Hungary and neighboring countries in search of authentic folk items, communist-era badges, pins, and medals, runs this cluttered shop. His sales staff does not speak English, so don't try to ask questions.

Holló Folkart Gallery, at V. Vitkovics Mihály u. 12 (ⓒ 1/317-8103), is an unusual gallery selling handcrafted reproductions of folk-art pieces from various regions of the country. It is open weekdays from 10am to 6pm; Saturday 10am to 2pm. **Csók István Galéria,** located at V. Váci u. 25 (ⓒ 1/318-2592) is the perfect place for something a little more upscale and unique, but still affordable, so don't miss browsing. Although it is called a *képcsarnok* (picture gallery), it has a wonderful and exciting selection of ceramics, glass work, and other artistic media as well as pictures from some of Hungary's current artistic talent pool. Csók István Galéria is open daily10am to 8pm.

FOR KIDS

Baby Planet Baby Store   This store carries everything for the baby from clothes to booties. They also have car seats, strollers, feeding supplies, playtime diversions, and gift ideas for the little ones. Hours are Monday through Friday 10am to 6pm and Saturday from 10am to 2pm. IV. Aradi u.16. ⓒ 1/272-1230. Metro: Újpest-városkapu (Blue line).

Kenguru Kuckó   Providing a holistic supply of mandatory kids' gear, this shop has an extensive selection of clothing, toys, books, and accessories. Choose and schedule one of their entertaining children's events for the weekend. Open weekdays 10am to 6pm. II. Margit krt. 34. ⓒ 1/212-4780. Metro: Nyugati Pályaudvar (Blue line).

> ### *Fun Fact* Penning a Name in History
>
> László József Biró was born in Budapest, Hungary, in 1899. In the 1930s he worked as a journalist, and he noticed the ink printed on newspapers dried immediately. He tried using this ink in fountain pens, but it clogged the nib. Working with his brother, a chemist, they invented a roller-ball fit at the bottom of the pen to pull the ink from the cartridge, thus inventing the ballpoint pen. They patented it in Paris in 1938, after escaping anti-Jewish laws in Hungary. They later sold the patent to Marcel Bich, and the pen is now known as the Bic pen. Biró also invented the automatic gearbox for automobiles.

Kis Herceg Gyermekdivat (Little Prince Children's Fashion)   Infant and children's clothes and shoes are sold here. You'll find everything from swimsuits to ski jackets in bright sunny colors and adorable prints. Hours are Monday through Friday 10am to 6pm and Saturday from 10am to 2pm. VI. Andrássy u. 55. ℂ 1/342-9268. Metro: Oktogon (Yellow line).

Mammina   Here you'll find clothes for children and young mothers with a fashionable collection of comfortable clothes. Hours are Monday through Friday 10am to 6pm and Saturday from 10am to 2pm. VII. Nagydiófa u. 30–32. ℂ 1/321-9866. Metro: Blaha (Red line).

GIFTS & HOME DECOR

Ban Sabai   Assisting in creating a sensual and warm home, Ban Sabai, which means calm, perfect home, features various lush gift and interior design objects brought from mystical Thailand. Hours are Monday through Friday 10am to 6pm and Saturday from 10am to 2pm. VI. Jókai u. 5. ℂ 1/707-6564. Metro: Oktogon (Yellow line).

Bedő Paper Antiques   As the name implies, this shop specializes in antique paper goods such as old postcards, letters, and banknotes, making it a find for collectors. Hours are Monday through Friday 10am to 6pm and Saturday from 10am to 2pm. I. Corvin tér 3. ℂ 1/201-9770. Metro: Batthyány tér (Red line).

BomoArt   This jampacked shop stocks unique handmade paper "artworks" of boxes, stationery, and diaries. Seductive nature-inspired decorative accessories further stimulate visitors to set the inner creator free. Hours are Monday through Friday 10am to 6pm and Saturday from 10am to 2pm. V. Régiposta u. 14. ℂ 1/318-7280. Metro: Deák tér (all lines).

Demko Feder   Here you'll find bedding, furniture, and home comforts, all in natural materials. Demko Feder's line of pure wool and nonallergenic bedding is sure to please the most temperamental sleeper. Hours are Monday through Friday 10am to 6pm and Saturday from 10am to 2pm. V. József Attila u. 20. ℂ 1/212-4408. Metro: Deák tér (all lines).

Goa Love   Featuring furnishings for the home in the spirit of Provence, this charming interior decorating and design shop specializes in singular wedding presents and Japan ceramics. Hours are Monday through Friday 10am to 6pm and Saturday from 10am to 2pm. VII. Király u. 19. ℂ 1/352-8449. Metro: Deák tér (all lines).

Hephaistos Háza   Having contacts with many of the interior designers in Hungary as well as abroad, this shop either has what you want or can get it for you. Hours are

Monday through Friday 10am to 6pm and Saturday from 10am to 2pm. V. Molnár u. 27. ℰ 1/266-1550. Tram 2: Szabadság tér.

Intvita Art Gallery   This innovative, little, four-year-old shop features unusual ceramic ware, leather-crafted books, sculpted glasses, and leather game boards with ceramic pieces featuring Aquincum designs. The enameled jewelry pieces are also pieces of art to wear. Hours are Monday through Friday 10am to 6pm and Saturday from 10am to 2pm. V. Váci u. 67. ℰ 1/266-5864. Tram: 47 or 49.

Roomba Home Culture   Created by talented brothers Oszkár and Bence Vági, this novel furniture and design shop offers sizzling trendy yet reasonably priced designs, decorations, and accessories. Hours are Monday through Friday 10am to 6pm and Saturday from 10am to 2pm. V. Arany János u. 29. ℰ 1/374-0570. Metro: Arany János u. (Blue line).

Sós Antikvárium   This store has a splendid selection of prints and antique maps that would dress up any wall adding a sophisticated air to the room. The shop is small, but the selection is extensive. Hours are Monday through Friday 10am to 6pm and Saturday from 10am to 2pm. V. Váci u. 73. 1/266-3204. Tram: 47 or 49.

JEWERLY

Varga Design   A wide and individualized handcrafted selection of jewelry is available in this shop by Miklos Varga, who after perfecting gold jewelry turned to silver and semiprecious stones. Each design is available in a complete set of necklace, earrings, and other pieces. Open Monday through Friday 10am to 6pm and Saturday 10am to 2pm. V. Harias köz 6. ℰ 1/318-4089. Metro: Vörösmarty tér (Yellow line).

MARKETS

Markets in Budapest are very crowded, bustling places. Beware of pickpockets; carry your valuables under your clothing in a money belt rather than in a wallet (see "Staying Safe," on p. 22 in chapter 2, "Planning Your Trip to Budapest").

OPEN MARKETS *(PIAC)*

Ecseri Flea Market   According to locals you can find anything at this busy flea market—from the glorious to the kitsch, old soda siphons to antique violins, and more. Well, if you are not prone to sensory overload, you can see for yourself. Row after row of wooden tables are overflowing with old dishes, toys, linens, old watches, paintings, and bric-a-brac. From the tiny cubicles in the narrow corridors, serious dealers market their wares: Herend and Zsolnay porcelain, Bulgarian and Russian icons, silverware, furniture, clocks, rugs, prewar dolls and stuffed animals, antique clothing, and jewelry. Due to all the tourist attention, mostly weekend shoppers, the prices of the market have increased severely. Some bargains can still be made, but sellers are less willing to seriously bargain with tourists. Haggle over the price, but in some instances, you will not budge the seller too far from the original price. Antiques buyers: Be aware that you'll need permission from the Museum of Applied Arts to take your purchases out of the country (p. 199). Only cash is accepted for purchases. The market runs weekdays 8am to 4pm, Saturday 6am to 3pm, and Sunday 8am to 1pm. XIX. Nagykörösi út. ℰ 1/280-8840. Bus: 54 from Boráros tér.

Józsefvárosi Piac   The market closest to the city center, the Józsefvárosi piac is informally known as "Four Tigers," an allusion to the tremendous presence of Chinese vendors. The piac, situated on the side of a railroad yard, near the Józsefváros Station, is not really a flea market, since most of the goods are not secondhand. But you'll find bargains aplenty: Chinese silk, Turkish dresses, Russian caviar and vodka, the occasional piece of Stalinist memorabilia, toy tanks, Romanian socks, slippers, and chalky tasting chocolate. Also for sale are dishes, clocks, pens, combs, clothes, tea, and east European condoms. All prices are negotiable. Dozens of languages are spoken in the tightly packed, crowded lanes of this outdoor market, which operates daily from 6am to 6pm. Feel free to flex your bargaining muscles here. VIII. Kőbányai út. ⓒ 1/313-8890. Tram: 28 from Blaha Lujza tér (Red line metro) or 36 from Baross tér (Keleti Station, Red line metro), and get off at Orczy tér.

PECSA Flea Market   Located in the area of the open-air stage at Petáfi Csarnok, this market is little known by travelers. In the midst of the enchanting Városliget (City Park), this market features a wide array of offerings, from vintage to brand-new bric-a-brac, antique jewelry, books, clothing, and electronic equipment. This place is where you can find a bargain, where few tourists have ventured to date. Open on weekends from 7am to 2pm, but the earliest bird gets the goodies. XIV. Zichy Mihály út 14. ⓒ 1/363-3730. www.pecsa.hu. A short walk in the park from Hősök tere (Heroes' Square; Yellow line).

FRUIT & VEGETABLE MARKETS (*CSARNOK* OR *PIAC*)

There are five vintage market halls *(vásárcsarnok)* in Budapest. These vast cavernous spaces, architectural wonders of steel and glass, were built in the 1890s in the ambitious grandiose style of the time. Three are still in use as markets and provide a measure of local color you certainly won't find in the grocery store. Hungarian produce in season is sensational, and you'll seldom go wrong with a kilo of strawberries, a cup of raspberries, or a couple of peaches.

The **Központi Vásárcsarnok (Central Market Hall)**, IX. Vámház krt 1–3 (ⓒ 1/217-6067; Metro: Kálvin tér on Blue line), is the largest and most spectacular market hall. Located on the Inner Ring (Kiskörút), just on the Pest side of the Szabadság Bridge, it was impeccably reconstructed in 1995. This bright, three-level market hall is a pleasure to visit. Fresh produce, meat, and cheese vendors dominate the space. Keep your eyes open for inexpensive saffron and dried mushrooms. We have had French guests who found truffles for very little money. The mezzanine level features folk-art booths, coffee and drink bars, and fast-food booths. The basement level houses fishmongers, pickled goods, a complete selection of spices, and Asian import foods, along with a large grocery store. Open Monday 6am to 5pm, Tuesday through Friday 6am to 6pm, and Saturday 6am to 2pm.

The recently restored **Belvárosi Vásárcsarnok (Inner City Market Hall)**, V. Hold u. 13 (ⓒ 1/476-3952; Metro: Kossuth tér on Red line or Arany János utca on Blue line), is located in central Pest in the heart of the Lipótváros (Leopold Town), behind the Hungarian National Bank at Szabadság tér. It houses a large supermarket and several cheesy discount clothing shops, in addition to a handful of independent fruit-and-vegetable vendors. Open Monday 6:30am to 5pm, Tuesday through Friday 6:30am to 6pm, and Saturday 6:30am to 2pm.

The **Rákóczi tér Vásárcsarnok**, VIII. Rákóczi tér 7–9 (ⓒ 1/313-8442; Tram: 4 or 6 to Rákóczi tér), was badly damaged by fire in 1988 but was restored to its original splendor and reopened in 1991. There's only a small area of private vendors; the rest of the hall is filled with retail booths. Open Monday 6am to 4pm, Tuesday through Friday 6am to 6pm, and Saturday 6am to 1pm.

In addition to these three large classic market halls, Budapest has a number of neighborhood produce markets. The **Fehérvári úti Vásárcsarnok**, at XI. Kőrösi J. u. 7–9 (ⓒ 1/385-6563), in front of the Buda Skála department store, is the latest classic food market in Budapest to be renovated. Some of the charm is lost, but such is progress. Just a block from the Móricz Zsigmond körtér transportation hub, it's open Monday 6:30am to 5pm, Tuesday through Friday 6:30am to 6pm, and Saturday 6:30am to 1pm. To get there take tram 47 from Deák tér to Fehérvári út, or any tram or bus to Móricz Zsigmond körtér.

The **Fény utca Piac** is on the Buda side behind the Mammut Mall at II. Fény utca (Metro: Moszkva tér on Red line). Formerly a nondescript neighborhood market, it underwent an ambitious reconstruction in 1998 in connection with the building of the Mammut shopping mall, to which it is now attached. Unfortunately, the renovation has meant higher rental fees, which have driven out most of the small independent vendors. Except for a small area on the first floor designated for vendors, the new market retains little of the old atmosphere. Open Monday 6am to 5pm, Tuesday through Friday 6am to 6pm, and Saturday 6:30am to 1pm.

Lehel tér Piac (VI. Lehel tér; ✆ 1/288-6898; Metro: Lehel tér on Blue line), is another neighborhood market, whose reconstruction was completed in 2003, making it look like a beached ship. The market features a wide selection of fresh food and meats, cheap Hungarian trademark products as well as rinky-dink clothing, kitchen appliances, and flowers. Open weekdays 6am to 6pm and Saturday 6am to 2pm.

MUSIC

Akt.Records Once known as Afrofilia, this cozy shop in the heart of Budapest stocks an impressive collection of minimal, hip-hop, electro, jazz, and folklore records. Hours are Monday through Friday 10am to 6pm and Saturday from 10am to 2pm. V. Múzeum krt 7. ✆ 1/266-3080. Metro: Astoria (Red line).

Fonó Budai Zeneház The Fonó Budai Zeneház entertainment complex is your source for Hungarian folk music. The complex features a folk-music store and an auditorium for live folk performances *(táncház)*. It's open Monday and Tuesday 2 to 5pm, Wednesday through Friday 2 to 10pm, and Saturday 7 to 10pm. It has a summer camp for children and Argentine tango on Monday in July, otherwise it is closed July and August. XI. Sztregova u. 3. ✆ 1/206-5300. Bus: 49V from Deák tér (5 stops past Móricz Zsigmond körtér).

Hungaroton The factory outlet of the Hungarian record company of the same name, this is definitely *the* place for classical-music buffs looking for Hungarian composers' recordings by contemporary Hungarian artists such as Zoltán Kocsis, Dezső Ránki, and András Schiff. Reasonable CD prices keep the Hungarian music alive. Open Monday through Friday 8am to 3:30pm. XII. Nagy Jenőu. 12. ✆ 1/202-2088. Metro: Gyöngyösi utca (Blue line).

Liszt Ferenc Zeneműbolt (Ferenc Liszt Music Shop) Budapest's musical crowd frequents this shop, located near both the opera house and the Ferenc Liszt Academy of Music. Sheet music, scores, records, tapes, CDs, and books are available. The store carries an excellent selection of classical music, composed and performed by Hungarian artists. It has expanded the collections to include jazz recordings. Open Monday through Friday 10am to 6pm and Saturday 10am to 1pm. VI. Andrássy út 45. ✆ 1/322-4091. Metro: Oktogon (Yellow line).

Selekta Located behind the impressive opera house, this shop—with an enticing chill-out interior—presents a broad spectrum of rhythmic Jamaican music, current dance-hall, ska, hip-hop, and roots grooves. Open weekdays noon to 8pm and Saturday noon to 4pm. VI. Lázár u. 7. No phone. Metro: Opera (Yellow line).

Wave On a small side street off Bajcsy-Zsilinszky út, directly across the street from the rear of St. Stephen's Basilica, Wave is a popular spot among young Hungarians looking for acid rock, rap, techno, and world music. Révay u. 4. © 1/331-0718. Metro: Arany János u. (Blue line).

PORCELAIN, POTTERY & CRYSTAL

Ajka Crystal Hungary's renowned crystal producer from the Lake Balaton region sells fine stemware and other crystal at great prices. Founded by Bernát Neumann in 1878, the company was privatized by FOTEX Rt. in 1990. Showcased are the company's brilliant yet simple crystal glasses, chalices, and crystal artwork. Hours are Monday through Friday 10am to 6pm and Saturday from 10am to 2pm. V. József Attila u. 7. © 1/317-8133. Metro: Deák tér (All lines).

Herend Shop Hand-painted Herend porcelain, first produced in 1826 in the town of Herend near Veszprém in western Hungary, is world renowned (check it out at www.herend.com). This shop, the oldest and largest Herend shop in Budapest, has the widest selection in the capital. It can arrange shipping through Touristpost. Even if you aren't a collector, it is interesting to come here to see some of Hungary's most famous products. The store is located in Pest's Inner City, on a quiet street just a few minutes' walk from Vörösmarty tér. All locations are open Monday through Friday10am to 6pm and Saturday10am to 2pm. József nádor tér 11. © 1/317-2622; VI. Andrássy u. 16 © 1/374-0006; I. Szentháromság u. 5 © 1/225-1051.

Herend Village Pottery Some find the formal Herend porcelain styles stuffy or overly decorative. This is an alternative. Casually designed pottery may be the alternative, but know that this is not associated with the Herend porcelain company. The majolika (village pottery) is a hand-painted folklore-inspired way of making pottery. Choose from a wide variety of colors and patterns or have custom pieces made with names added, such as for a baby's first plate. All pieces are dishwasher and oven safe. Prices are reasonable here and reorders are welcome. The owners are very knowledgeable and eager to assist, but not pushy. Open Tuesday through Friday 9am to 5pm and Saturday 9am to 2pm. II. Bem rakpart 37. © 1/356-7899. Metro: Batthyány tér (Red line).

TOYS

Apróságok Boltja (Small Fry Shop) *Kids*   While many toy stores have been driven out of business, this store has survived. It specializes in wooden toys, but also carries games, puppets, and other toys for young children. Hours are Monday through Friday 10am to 6pm and Saturday from 10am to 2pm. VII. Erzsébet krt. 23. No phone. Tram: 4 or 6 Wesselényi u.

Sárkányvár *Kids*   This enchanting castle is staffed with playful teachers and offers state-of-the-art creative games to educate children and keep them occupied. It functions as a sort of child depository in the Campona mall, and the toys can be bought and borrowed, a unique idea that's worth visiting for. It is located next to the Tropicaquarium. Check out the quality kids' program list. Hours are Monday through Friday 10am to 6pm and Saturday from 10am to 2pm. XXII. Nagytétényi út 35–47. © 1/424-3140. Bus: 3.

Toys Anno Part museum, part specialty shop, Toys Anno might be of more interest to toy collectors than to kids. The shop sells exact replicas of antique toys from around the world. The tin toys are exceptional, especially the monkeys on bicycles, the Ferris wheels, and the Soviet rockets that prepare themselves for launch. There are also

---

---

old-fashioned dolls and puzzles. Items are behind glass and tagged with serial numbers. Though you have to request prices and ask to see the toys that interest you, the clerk is more than happy to oblige. Hours are Monday through Friday 10am to 6pm and Saturday from 10am to 2pm. VI. Teréz krt. 54. ✆ 1/302-6234. Metro: Nyugati pu. (Blue line).

WINE & SPIRITS

Wine store hours are Monday to Friday 10am to 6pm and Saturday 10am to 3pm, unless noted otherwise in the description.

Budapest Wine Society   Truly among the experts in wine, the Wine Society operates in four shops in Budapest. Founded by Tom Howells and Attila Tálos, the shop sells an immense amount of wines produced by over 50 local winegrowers. Drop in for free samples on Saturday at the Batthyány utca location, which is a much larger store with a wider selection. I. Batthyány u. 59. ✆ 1/212-2569. Metro: Batthyány tér (Red line).

In Vino Veritas 𝒳𝒳   Like a wine supermarket, this store carries a vast assortment of wines and wine accessories from all over the country. You will notice its logo in many restaurant wine lists as the supplier of the wine and the list. The gentleman who runs this store speaks English well. Hours are weekdays 9am to 8pm and Saturday 10am to 6pm. VII. Dohány u. 58–62. ✆ 1/341-0646 or 1/341-3174. Metro: Blaha Lujza (Red line).

The House of Hungarian Pálinka   Locals say that good Palinka (a traditional form of brandy) should warm the stomach, not burn the throat, a common side effect of strong brandy. This shop offers the finest selection of Palinka distilled from everything from plums, pears, apples, and walnuts to honey paprika. Watch out for the after-drink kick effect. Unfortunately, you cannot taste before buying. VIII. Rákóczi St. 17. ✆ 1/338-4219. Metro: Blaha Lujza tér (Red line); Bus: 7.

House of Hungarian Wines 𝒳𝒳   Taste your way through Hungary's 22 winegrowing regions in the convenience of one wine cellar. Upon payment of the entry fee, you are given a wine glass and a map of the cellar where more than 50 wines are waiting to be tasted within a 2-hour time allotment. Snacks along the way are freely available to cleanse your palate and if you need assistance, cellar masters are there to answer questions. Each month a different region is highlighted with growers from that area presenting their selections. The House of Hungarian Wines also arranges wine tours. It is open daily noon to 8pm. I. Szentháromság tér 6. ✆ 1/212-1030 or 1/212-1031. www.wine house.hu. Admission 4,000 Ft ($22/£11). Castle District directly across from Hilton hotel.

Le Boutique des Vins   Sophisticated, classy, and welcoming, this wine shop is a cut above the others. This is a great place to learn about and purchase Hungarian wines. The longtime manager of the shop, Ferenc Hering, speaks excellent English and is extremely well versed in his merchandise. Try the excellent Villány reds (some from the shop's own vineyard) or the fine whites from the Balaton region. You can pick up a fine bottle for as little as 1,500 Ft to 15,000 Ft ($8.10–$81/£4.25–£43). A wide range of Hungary's famous Tokaj dessert wines, in the general price range of 5,000 Ft to 25,000 Ft ($27–$135/£14–£71), is also available. Shipping can be arranged, but at a steep price. V. József Attila u. 12 (behind the Jaguar dealership). ⓒ 1/317-5919 or 1/266-4397. Metro: Deák tér (any line).

Pántlika Borház ★★ Not only does this store carry a vast selection of wines from all over Hungary, but the owner's knowledge of them is just as impressive. His English is good and he willing to help you make the right choice of wine for any occasion. Also in the store, you will find a nice selection of wine glasses, decanters, and other vino enthusiast accessories. Open weekdays 10am to 6pm. VII. Dohány u. 30A. ⓒ 1/328-0115. Metro: Astoria (Red line).

Présház This tasteful wine store—named after the press room, or the room where the grapes are rammed to extract the sweet nectar—is located in the Inner City area. It offers over 300 types of Hungarian wine and has a knowledgeable staff who are fluent in English. You can have your order delivered within Budapest if you purchase a crate. V. Váci u. 10. ⓒ 1/266-1100. Metro: Vörösmarty tér (Yellow line).

Unicum Unicum is a beloved digestive bittersweet liqueur that is said to cure all ills especially aching stomachs. Made with over 40 herbs and spices, Unicum is the trademark product of Zwack, the best-known spirit brand in Hungary. With its memorable bomb-shaped bottle, emergency-cross logo, and unforgettable taste, it has to be Uniqum. Try it at the Zwack Museum, but if you don't get there, it is available in all grocery stores. Hours are Monday through Friday 1pm to 5pm, but by compulsory reservation only. IX. Dandár u. 1. ⓒ 1/476-2383. Tram: 2.

Wine & Arts Decanter Borszaküzlet This shop features elegant wines from hidden provincial Hungarian winegrowers, top-notch award-wining wine masters in addition to Italian and Spanish wines. Open Tuesday through Friday 10am to 8pm and Saturday 10am to 2pm. MOM Park, XII. Kléh István u. 3. ⓒ 1/201-9029. Tram: 59 or 61.

ASSORTED FOODSTUFFS

Culinaris Missing a taste of home while traveling and cannot find it in the markets? Well then, you will not want to miss a visit to **Culinaris**. It stocks everything from American Cheerios to Australian Vegemite. Its goal is to be the prime location for food from around the world at two locations. The Pest store is open Monday noon to 7pm and Tuesday through Saturday 9am to 7pm. The Buda store is open Monday noon to 8pm and Tuesday through Saturday 9am to 8pm. VI. Hunyadi tér 3. ⓒ 1/341-7001 and III. Perc u. 8 ⓒ 1/345-0780.

Szega Camembert If you are a lover of cheeses, this vendor at the Fény utca market is worth knowing about. Located on the first floor of the recently renovated market hall (p. 216), Szega Camembert offers a huge selection of domestic and imported cheeses. You can also buy delicious homemade butter and sour cream here, as well as wholesome breads. II. Fény u. ⓒ 1/345-4259. Metro: Moszkva tér (Red line).

T. Nagy Tamás Sajtkereskedése (Thomas T. Nagy's Cheese Shop) Opened in 1994, this shop deals exclusively in cheese, selling more than 300 types of hard and soft cheeses, including Hungarian, as well as imported French, Italian, Dutch, and English varieties. Open Monday 10am to 5pm, Tuesday through Friday 9am to 6pm, and Saturday 8am to 1pm. V. Gerlóczy u. 3. ⓒ 1/317-4268. Metro: Deák tér (all lines).

10

Budapest After Dark

B udapest is definitely a cosmopolitan city with a tremendous variety of varied cultural events all throughout the year. There is no event that is unaffordable to the average tourist if you don't have your heart set on a particular section of a theater, but even then, seats are bargains as compared to New York, San Francisco, or London. At the opera house, one of Europe's finest, tickets generally range from 300 Ft ($1.60/85p) for the nose-bleed balcony to the ultraluxurious royal box once used by the Habsburgs for 10,900 Ft ($59/£31) Almost all of the city's theaters and concert halls, with the exception of those hosting internationally touring rock groups, offer tickets for 1,000 Ft to 5,000 Ft ($5.40–$27/£2.85–£14). Of course, higher-priced seats are available also at the same venue if you want a closer view. In some cases, it is wise to choose performances based on the venue. For example, you may not particularly be a fan of ballet, but if that is all that is offered during your stay, you may want to consider less expensive tickets just to see the opera house up close and personal. You won't regret it; its splendor is superlative and it can be appreciated with any performance.

The opera, ballet, and theater seasons run from September through May with some sporadic events in June, but most theaters and halls also host performances during the summer festivals. Bear in mind that none of them are air-conditioned and heat rises. If you are sitting in a balcony on a hot evening, you may be miserable. A number of the better-known churches and stunning halls offer concerts exclusively in the summer. While classical music is ingrained into the culture in Budapest, the country, jazz, blues, rock, disco, and every other variation you left at home is here also. Stylish and unique new clubs and bars open and close regularly. The bar and club scene starts late and lasts until morning; sometimes until the last patron leaves. Only the bars in residential areas have strict closing times. Restaurants and bars in these areas in the summer have to bring in their tables at 10pm by district law in consideration of the neighbors. So whether you have dancing feet or a taste for opera, whatever your entertainment preference, Budapest nights offer plenty to choose from.

PROGRAM LISTINGS For the most up-to-date information, go to www.jegymester.hu and click on the English link. This site includes information for the opera house as well as the major theaters in the city. A complete schedule of mainstream performing arts is found in the free bimonthly *Koncert Kalendárium,* available at any of the Tourinform offices or you can check it online at www.koncertkalendarium.hu; there is a link for English. The *Budapest Sun* and *Funzine* (see "Fast Facts: Budapest," in chapter 4, "Getting to Know Budapest") also have comprehensive events calendars; the weekly *Budapest Times* includes cultural listings. *Budapest Panorama,* a free monthly tourist booklet, offers only partial entertainment listings, featuring what the editors consider the monthly highlights. All of the publications mentioned above are in English.

TICKET OFFICES   If you are looking for the easy way out, you can look at ticket availability online for purchasing opera, ballet, theater, or concert tickets for a number of different venues at www.jegymester.hu. It shows how many tickets are available with a seating chart to help you decide how much you want to spend for what seat. Its secure server allows you to make your purchase online. You can also prepurchase special museum exhibitions on this site also, but it may require your printing an e-ticket. If you don't have Internet access, you can save time by going to the **Cultur-Comfort Ticket Office (Cultur-Comfort Központi Jegyiroda),** VI. Paulay Ede u. 31 (✆ **1/322-0000).** The office is open Monday through Friday 9am to 6pm. It is easier than going to the individual box offices. They sell tickets to just about everything, from theater and operettas to sports events and rock concerts. Schedules are posted for a variety of choices and they will show you a seating chart. If none of the cashiers speaks English, find a helpful customer who can translate for you. For last minute tickets or performances that are looking like they are sold out, try the venue box office for no-show tickets about 30 minutes before the performance. For **opera and ballet,** go to the **Hungarian State Opera Ticket Office (Magyar Állami Opera Jegyiroda),** VI. Andrássy út 22 (✆ **1/353-0170),** open Monday through Friday 11am to 5pm. Try **Concert & Media,** XI. Üllői út 11–13 (✆ **1/455-9000;** www.jegyelado.hu), for classical performances as well as pop, jazz, and rock concerts. For just about everything from rock and jazz concerts to opera, ballet performances, and theater tickets, try **Ticket Express,** VI. Jókai u. 40 (✆ **1/353-0692;** www.tex.hu), open Monday through Saturday from 10am to 7pm. Further Ticket Express offices can be found at V. Deák Ferenc u. 19 (✆ **1/266-7070**), open Monday through Saturday from 10am to 9pm; VI. Andrássy út 18 (✆ **1/312-0000**), open Monday through Friday 9:30am to 6:30pm; and VIII. József krt. 50 (✆ **1/344-0369**), open Monday through Friday 9:30am to 6:30pm.

Note: For cheaper tickets, look online at one of the sites above and then try going to the actual box office of the venue. Some of the ticket agencies only carry the higher-end price range of tickets. You may also find that agencies charge a commission (usually about 4%), especially for hit shows or international performers.

1 The Performing Arts

The major symphony orchestras in Budapest are the Budapest Festival Orchestra, the Philharmonic Society Orchestra, the Hungarian State Symphony Orchestra, the Budapest Symphony Orchestra, and the Hungarian Railway Workers' (MÁV) Symphony Orchestra. The major chamber orchestras include the Hungarian Chamber Orchestra, the Ferenc Liszt Chamber Orchestra, the Budapest String Players, and the Hungarian Virtuosi. Major choirs include the Budapest Chorus, the Hungarian State Choir, the Hungarian Radio and Television Choir, the Budapest Madrigal Choir, and the University Choir.

Budapest is now on the touring route of dozens of major European ensembles and virtuosos. Keep your eyes open for well-known touring artists.

Note: Most Budapesters tend to dress more formally than casually when attending performances. However, the location of your seat determines your dress code. If you are on the lower level, you should dress from smart casual to more semiformal. In the upper regions, you can get away with jeans and a sweater. In wintertime, you are expected to check your coat and any bags. There is no getting around this, so don't try to argue with the attendant.

OPERA, OPERETTA & BALLET

Budapesti Operettszínház (Budapest Operetta Theatre)　What is known as the Operetta Theatre was designed by the famous Viennese architects Fellner and Helmer in 1894. When it was built, the giant stage of the auditorium faced two levels of intimate boxes arranged in a semicircle. A dance floor was included to provide a space adequately large enough for the waltz, polka, mazurka, and the galop. Between 1999 and 2001, the theater was fully restored. The 100-year-old chandelier presides above the auditorium. The original lamp statues and supporting columns blend in with the newly added colored glass windows, mirrors, and the period-style furnishings of the snack counter. The original ornamentation was restored, a row of boxes in the circle was rebuilt, and the most advanced European stage machinery was installed. Today the theater not only boasts having 917 seats, but it also has air-conditioning in the auditorium. A highlight among Art Nouveau style buildings, the Operetta Theatre hosts exquisite banquettes and balls—among which is the opulent Operetta Ball. Performances of *Romeo and Juliet* are among the rotating standards. The off season is mid-July to mid-August. The box office is open Monday through Friday 10am to 2:30pm and 3 to 7pm and Saturday 1 to 7pm. VI. Nagymező u. 17. ⓒ 1/312-4866. www.operettszinhaz. hu. Tickets 2,250 Ft–8,000 Ft ($12–$43/£6.40–£23). Metro: Opera or Oktogon (Yellow line).

Erkel Színház (Erkel Theater)　This theater was closed as of May 31, 2007, but we felt it should stay as a listing here as a historical note. Coincidently, we were at the very last performance, a dance event, and had no idea at the time that it would be our last to visit. It seems it is in such a state of disrepair that tearing it down is far more cost-effective than remodeling it. Named the "People's Opera," the Erkel Theater was the second home of the State Opera and Ballet. It was the largest theater in Hungary seating up to 2,400 people. Originally, it was built in Art Nouveau style in 1911; various renovations made it look like another Soviet-era monstrosity. If you want to see a token of Budapest history while it lasts, go for a visit. It most likely will be there through 2009 according to the last word published. VIII. Köztársaság tér 30. Metro: Keleti pu. (Red line).

Magyar Állami Operaház (Hungarian State Opera House)　One of the most important buildings in Budapest, this opera house was designed by famous Hungarian architect Miklós Ybl. He was also the designer of the basilica and the original Parliament (now the Italian Institute). The opera house was completed in 1884 and is considered one of the most beautiful in Europe. When standing outside, on the first level, you can see the muses of opera: Erato, Thalia, Melpomene, and Terpsichore. There are also statues of Franz Liszt and Hungary's father of opera, Ferenc Erkel. The second level has statues of famous composers. The lobby is adorned with Bertalan Székely's frescoes; the ceiling frescoes in the concert hall itself are by Károly Lotz. Hungarians are great opera fans and many tickets are sold as season tickets. Regardless, if you don't wait until the last minute, you often will have a wide range of seats to choose from. The season runs from mid-September to mid-June. During the regular season, there are often matinees on Saturday and Sunday at 11am. Regular performances start at 7pm, not the customary 8pm starting time. Summer visitors, however, can take in the approximately 10 performances (both opera and ballet) during the Summer Operafest, in July or August.

Tips   Bistros: For the Sophisticated Night Owl

If you're looking for a late-night cocktail but want to avoid the typical bar and club scene, try **Cream Restaurant** (p. 106). It is drawing a crowd with their eye-opening decorating scheme and varied music styles to suit any mood. Being centrally located close to either the körút or Astoria, a bar/bistro, it draws a mixed crowd. **Paris, Texas** on the popular Ráday utca, is a pleasant place to sit down and talk or eat after a concert, but their food comes from the **Pink Cadillac** (p. 119).

Seating capacity is 1,289. The box office is open Tuesday through Saturday from 11am until the beginning of the performance, or to 5pm and Sunday from 11am to 1pm and 4pm until the beginning of the performance. **Guided tours** of the opera house leave daily at 3 and 4pm; the cost is 2,000 Ft ($11/£5.70). VI. Andrássy út 22. ℂ 1/335-0170. www.opera.hu. Tickets 300 Ft–10,900 Ft ($1.60–$59/85p–£31). Metro: Opera (Yellow line).

CLASSICAL MUSIC

Bartók Béla Emlékház (Béla Bartók Memorial House)   This charming little hall is in Béla Bartók's last Budapest residence, and in addition to hosting concerts and exhibitions, it is the site of a Bartók museum (p. 158). Concerts are organized and performed from the end of September through December independently of the museum. The museum rents out its concert hall for performing musical artists. Getting to the English pages on their website (www.bartokmuseum.hu) can sometimes be a exercise in frustration. Your best bet is to check the schedule information in the bimonthly *Koncert Kalendárium* or the other calendar resources given above. Open Tuesday through Sunday 10am to 5pm, but closed August 1 to 20. Ticket prices depend on the function. II. Csalán út 29. ℂ 1/394-2100. Bus: 5 from Március 15 tér or Moszkva tér to Pasaréti tér (the last stop).

Matthias Church   In my opinion, this is one of the most beautiful churches in Budapest, an icon in the center of the historic Castle District. This church is a neo-Gothic classic, named after Matthias Corvinus, the Renaissance king who was married here. King Béla and his queen are buried here. Much to the dismay of many, the church is undergoing major renovations, which will last incredibly until 2012. Much of it is under scaffolding at all times. However, the church is a key location for excellent organ recitals, sacred music concerts for a cappella choir, orchestras, and at times folk concerts throughout the year. Ticket prices vary widely based on the offering, so the prices here are just a guideline. The ticket office is open Wednesday through Sunday 1 to 5:30pm. I. Szentháromság tér 2. ℂ 1/355-5657. Tickets 1,000 Ft–7,000 Ft ($5–$35/£2.65–£18). Bus: 16 from Deák across from the Le Meridian Hotel or 10 bus from Moszkva tér (Metro: Red line).

Óbudai Társaskör (Óbuda Social Circle)   In an island within Óbuda's residences, a building dating back to the turn of the century has been restored to its original appeal. Temporary exhibitions, music workshops, and theatrical performances on the open-air stage during the summertime all elevate this tiny venue to compete with its larger rivals. Since 1995, it has hosted *Art Salon in Óbuda* where art in many forms, such as music, literature and the visual arts, coexist to be available for those interested in a particular subject or period in history, a school of art or, occasionally, a taste in gastronomy. Proudly, it is also home to the Budapest Ragtime Band, a prominent venue of the Budapest Spring Festival, and also presents up-to-par chamber music concerts. Ticket prices vary from program to program, but each has its own set price. The box office is open daily 10am to 6pm. III. Korona u. 7. ℭ 1/250-0288. www.obudaitarsaskor. hu. Tickets 1,000 Ft–2,800 Ft ($5.40–$15/£2.85–£8). Tram: 1 from Árpád Híd (Metro: Blue line) over the bridge to Szentlélek tér or the HÉV to Árpád-híd.

Palace of Arts 👁👁 The Palace of Arts' National Concert Hall and Festival Theater concert and performing arts venues opened in 2005. For the first few years, the locals either loved the building or they hated it, but all have come to at least accept it. Originally scheduled to be at Deák tér, a change in government after an election turned the original space into underground parking and a park. The Palace of Arts was awarded the FIABCI Prix d'Excellence 2006 in the specialized category, which is the equivalent of an Academy Award for construction and real estate development. The main concert hall is the finest contemporary classical music venue in Budapest, and now hosts concerts from the most important orchestras from around the world. The scheduled events run the gamut and are not only classical music; the website has been beautifully created to be user-friendly. IX. Komor Marcell u. 1. ℭ 1/555-3001. www.mupa.hu. Tram: 2 from downtown toward the Lágymányos bridge.

Pesti Vigadó (Pest Concert Hall) Located right in the middle of the famed riverside Danube Promenade (Dunakorzó), the Vigadó is one of the city's oldest concert halls, dating to 1864. It is a magnificent building from the outside and I cannot wait to see the inside after the remodel. A remodel was planned for completion by 2006, but like most things in Hungary, scheduled times can vary by years. As of this writing, it has not yet reopened, so we suggest you stroll by for a look at the exterior and see if it has reopened. V. Vigadó tér 2. ℭ 1/318-9903. www.vigado.hu. Metro: Vörösmarty tér (Yellow line).

Saint Michael's Church in the City This church is the venue for summer concerts. Built in 1765, with the original frescoes still intact, it has one of the oldest organs in Budapest dating to 1893. Summer concerts are held on Friday and Saturday nights in the coolness of the church. There is another concert series in October also. Tickets can be purchased at the church shop or at Libri Bookstores. V. Váci u. 67–68. No phone. Daily 10am–6pm for visits.

Stefánia Palace Cultural Center The eclectic-style 19th-century palace hosts a number of entertainment options by renting out their space for different groups to hold their events. In addition, they provide theater and music-dance performances in the new building. This was the cultural center during the communist times for the armed forces. I would recommend checking one of the events calendars in the English papers for current ticket prices since they vary considerably from event to event depending on who is sponsoring it. XIV. Stefánia u. 34. ℭ 1/273-4132. Bus: 7 or 73 to Stefánia u.

Zeneakadémia (Ferenc Liszt Academy of Music) Once known as the Royal National Hungarian Academy of Music, the academy has five buildings around the city, but the primary one is at this location. With a seating capacity of 1,000, it is Budapest's leading center of musical education and students come from around the world to study here. The academy was built in 1907 in its present form; the building's interior is decorated in lavish Art Nouveau style. The people are friendly, so don't hesitate to wander in just to look around at the extravagant decoration. Unfortunately, the Great Hall is not used in the summer months; the smaller Kisterem, also a fine hall, is used at that time. Student recitals are usually open to the public and are often

The Millennium City Center

The **Millennium City Center** is situated on what was the last large available parcel of riverfront land in Budapest. On the 10 hectares (25 acres) of land, the plans have been to build a convention center in the southern section to include a 10,000-seat center for hosting conventions and sporting events, a casino, and a medicinal and recreational spa. A multifunctional exhibition hall will be adjacent to the Convention Complex while two international hotels will be built on the north side.

With the opening of the **Palace of Arts** 𝒜𝒜 in early 2005, the latest cultural complex created in the Hungarian capital includes a **National Concert Hall**, the **Ludwig Museum of Contemporary Art**, and the smaller **Festival Theater**. However, the plans for the rest of the center have not yet been realized, still sitting on the architects' tables.

---

free; however, major productions are the Hungarian and international performances. A weekly schedule is posted outside the Király utca entrance to the academy. The box office is open Monday through Friday from 10am to 8pm, and weekends 2 to 8pm. Performances are frequent. VI. Liszt Ferenc tér 8. © 1/462-4600. www.lfze.hu. Tickets 2,000 Ft–10,000 Ft ($11–$54/£6–£28). Metro: Oktogon (Yellow line).

FOLK PERFORMANCES

Budai Vigadó (Buda Concert Hall)   The Budai Vigadó is the home stage of the Hungarian State Folk Ensemble (Állami Népi Együttes Székháza). The ensemble is the oldest in the country, having started in 1951 with the goal of keeping Hungarian traditional dance and music alive. The group has toured over 44 countries and consists of 30 dancers, a Gypsy orchestra of 14, and a five-member folk orchestra. Tickets can be reserved by telephone. The box office is open 10am to 6pm daily. Performances usually start at 8pm on Tuesday, Thursday, and Sunday. I. Corvin tér 8. © 1/317-2754. Tickets 3,300 Ft–5,600 Ft ($18–$30/£9.25–£16) adults; 3,000 Ft–5,100 Ft ($16–$28/£8.50–£15) students. Bus: 86 till Szilágyi Dezső tér or tram 19 till Halász u. stop.

Fonó Budai Music Hall   Fonó means spinning in English; it also refers to a social custom of country life. The hall was created with the mission published on their original pamphlet: "We wanted there to be a place where people could get together; get to know each other's joys, torments, thoughts, music, dance, words." Besides performances of prominent local folk-old-boys like Félix Lajkó, Kálmán Balogh, and the Ghymes Ensemble, the Fonó makes way in presenting the current folk trends, hosting theaters, dance houses, and exhibitions. They have expanded their scope to younger artists who are expanding the scope of music. The box office opens an hour before the start of the performance. XI. Sztregova u. 3. © 1/206-5300. www.fono.hu. Tickets 800 Ft–2,000 Ft($4.50–$11/£2.25–£5.75). Tram: 41 or 47 from Móricz Zsigmond körtér.

Hungarian Heritage House   In the same building as Budai Vigadó, the Heritage House is comprised of three divisions: the Hungarian State Folk Ensemble, the Folklore Documentation Centre, and the Folk Arts Department. Revival of folk dance for stage performances did not come about until the beginning of the 1970s; they reproduce the dances in the precise manner and interpretation they were originally intended. I. Corvin tér 8. © **1/201-5017.** www.heritagehouse.hu. Tickets 2,000 Ft–5,000 Ft ($14–$27/£7–£14).Bus: 86 till Szilágyi Dezső tér or tram 19 till Halász u. stop.

Petőfi Csarnok   Located in the tree-lined surroundings of the Városliget (City Park), this old-style no-frills hall has stages used for some of the best folk performances in the city. The venue hosts folk dance events, various national folk performances, and festivals in addition to jazz, blues, pop, and rock concerts; exhibitions; workshops; and a weekend-only flee market. The main folk event is the annual Csángó Bál, which presents the colorful culture of this small, Moldavian-born community, and is a must-see event for folk dance and tradition seekers. The box office is open 2 to 7pm. XIV. Zichy Mihály út 14. © **1/363-3730.** www.pecsa.hu. Tickets 1,500 Ft–8,500 Ft ($8–$46/£4.25–£24). Metro: Hősök tere (Yellow line).

THEATER & DANCE

Budapest has a varied and vivacious theater season from September through June, but most plays are in Hungarian only. The **Merlin Theater,** V. Gerlóczy u. 4 (© **1/317-9338** or © 1/318-9844; www.merlinszinhaz.hu), used to be the mainstay for English speakers who wanted to indulge in good theater productions, but the theater had a falling out with their resident English theater troupe, and now the options are slim and rare. Located on a quiet street in the heart of the Inner City, the Merlin now programs less than 20% English-language shows. During the unusual times when they do have an English show, tickets cost 1,000 Ft to 2,500 Ft ($5.50–$14/£2.75£7); the box office is open daily 2 to 7pm. Take the metro to Astoria (Red line) or Deák tér (all lines).

For international or Hungarian dance, music, or theater of the contemporary sort, the **Trafó House of Contemporary Art,** IX. Liliom u. 41 (© **1/215-1600** or © 1/456-2040; www.trafo.hu) is the place to go. Having opened in 1998, this venue has offered a wide range of events that are extremely different and experimental, definitely not for the traditional thinker. Regardless, there have been performances I could have seen repeatedly and those I wanted to demand a refund, but it all equalizes in the end. If you happen to be here for any length of time, a season ticket of five performances is only 7,000 Ft ($38/£20). The beauty is that you can get two tickets for the same performance deducted from your five, to take a friend along. Prepare to get there early and stand close to the doors to the theater. It is open seating and like a cattle call when the doors open. We especially recommend some of the dance works by groups such as the French-Hungarian **Compagnie Pál Frenák** (www.ciefrenak.hu); their men on ropes were unbelievably well done. Tickets cost 1,500 Ft to 2,000 Ft ($8–$11/£4.25–£5.75); the box office is open Monday through Friday from 2 to 8pm and weekends 5 to 8pm. Reserve or purchase tickets in advance on the website. Take tram no. 4 or 6 or the metro to Ferenc Körut (Blue line).

One theater company that has been brought to my attention is the **Katona József Theater** at V. Petőfi Sándor u. 6. (© **1/318-6599;** www.katonaj.hu). As a public theater, its main support is provided by the City of Budapest. An independent company was created here in 1982, after seceding of the National Theatre of Budapest. The troupe has extensive international connections, which are enhanced by its being a founding member of the Union of European Theatres. The company regularly embarks on international tours and to date has performed in more than 60 cities of the world. The productions as well as the artists have received numerous national and international awards.

For musical productions, especially those by Andrew Lloyd Webber, go to the **Madách Theater,** VII. Erzsébet krt. 29–33 (© **1/478-2041;** www.madachszinhaz.hu). However, I find it disconcerting to hear all of the songs redefined to accommodate the Hungarian language, so brace yourself for the experience. The theater was built in 1961 on the site of the famous Royal Orpheum Theater and has been restored to its former elegance. Its hit production since spring 2003 is *The Phantom of the Opera.* The theater has a love affair with the plays by Tim Rice and Andrew Lloyd Webber. You will find many of the plays rotating for years into 2008–09 with a few other American classics thrown into the mix. Ticket prices are 500 Ft to 10,000 Ft ($2.75–$54/£1.50–£29), but if you value your legs, do not sit in the balcony where leg room is nonexistent. The box office is open daily from 3 to 7pm; performances are usually at 7pm. Take tram no. 4 or 6 to Wesselényi utca. Affectionately called the wedding cake, the very ornate and striking theater is the **Vígszínház (Comedy Theatre of Budapest),** XIII. Szent István krt. 14 (© **1/329-2340;** www.vigszinhaz.hu). Here you will again only find productions in Hungarian, usually by Hungarians, but at times there will be international playwrights. The Vígszínház operates in the traditional repertory system, which is incredible to most foreigners; almost every evening a different performance is given with the technical staff having to build and strike down the sets each day. The theater has a repertoire of actors who appear in numerous shows over the course of the month, having to learn the roles for each show. The repertory consists of 10 to 12 plays on the stages of the Víg's 1,100 seats. With a show almost every night, the theater stages numerous plays that pull in delighted audiences. The box office is open daily 11am to 7pm. Ticket prices are 900 Ft to 3,200 Ft ($4.75–$17/£2.50–£9). Take the metro to Nyugati pu. (Blue line).

An important venue of the world of contemporary performing arts in Budapest is the **MU Theatre,** XI. Körösy József u. 17 (© **1/209-4014;** www.mu.hu). Offering the work of contemporary choreographers and young dancers, this venue has similar events as the Trafó above. The box office is open Monday through Thursday 6pm to the beginning of the performance, and Friday through Sunday from 1pm until the start of the performance. Tickets cost 1,500 Ft to 2,000 Ft ($8–$11/£4.25–£5.75). Take bus no. 86, or tram no. 4 to Moricz Zsigmond körtér.

The first children's and family theater in Budapest, the **Kolibri Pince** (Hummingbird Cellar), VI. Andrássy út 77 (© **1/351-3348**), is a small theater with seating for 60. It offers entertainment for all age groups, but children are its main focus. The repertoire includes adaptations and story-musicals as well as one-man shows and small theater pieces. Other theater locations include the **Kolibri Fészek** (Hummingbird Nest), VI. Andrássy út 74, a room-theater where 50 to 70 children view the show sitting on pillows and chairs. The largest is the **Kolibri Színház** (Hummingbird Theater), VI. Jókai tér 10, with a stage where puppet performances are usually held seating 220. Tickets cost 500 Ft to 2,000 Ft ($2.75–$11/£1.50–£5.75). Metro: Oktogon (Yellow line).

2 Dance Clubs

Budapest has a hot club scene, but what is offered at any given time is apt to change often depending on the current trend at any given time. To find out what is happening when you are ready to explore the nightlife, it is best to pick up a copy of *Funzine,* the English-language guide, published every 2 weeks for up-to-date information. Other English-language publications the ***Budapest Sun*** (www.budapestsun.com) and

Budapest Times (www.budapesttimes.hu) also list highlights; however, they are less likely to list the bar scene venues unless a well-known name is performing. You can pick up a copy of *Pesti Est,* the largest free weekly program magazine, but it is in Hungarian only and difficult to navigate. In order to help define the different categories of nightlife, we have tried to define an "average-age" guideline for the venues. Opening hours vary, but most clubs start dancing around 11pm and stay lively until closing time which could be as late as 5am. There are no laws stating when traditional bars or clubs have to close, but those with outside seating may be restricted by district laws to move things inside after 10 or 11pm in consideration of the neighbors.

Acapulco 77   This lounge and club brings a sexy Mexican flare to the scene, exotic for Budapest, with House, Electron, Salsa, and other Latin music to spin your feet to the beat. Open Tuesday to Saturday 4pm to 2am and Sunday 4pm to midnight for those in their 20s and 30s. VI. Lövölde tér 3. ℂ **06/30-606-4018** mobile only. Metro: Kodály Körönd (Yellow line).

Barokko Club and Lounge   Currently one of the hot spots on Liszt Ferenc tér, where seeing and being seen is of the utmost importance for those in their 20s and 30s when it really matters. Don't be fooled by the restaurant above, the club itself rocks. Open Sunday through Tuesday noon to 2am and Wednesday through Saturday noon to 3am. VI. Liszt Ferenc tér 5. ℂ **1/322-0700**. www.barokko.hu. Metro: Oktogon (Yellow line).

Cactus Juice Pub   If you miss that Old West feeling, head here for a large drink selection with over 50 whisky blends and a real party atmosphere. Light shows and special events are held on the weekends, with a DJ at other times. Open Monday through Thursday noon to 2am and Friday and Saturday noon to 4am for those in their 20s, 30s, and pushing it a little older. VI. Jókai tér 5. ℂ **1/302-2116**. www.cactusjuice.hu. Metro: Oktogon (Yellow line).

E-Klub   Meeting Hungarian guys or the young fashionable ladies is not a problem at this huge and hedonistic disco oozing with popularity. At one time, it was the "E" building of Polytechnic University, hence the name. It has since moved to its current location and has been remodeled a number of times to stay current. It offers different special events for the party animals around the city. Guys have to pay 800 Ft ($4.30/£2.25) on Friday and 900 Ft ($4.85/£2.55) on Saturday for entry, but the ladies are always free. Drinks are cheap. Open for those in their teens to 20s on Friday and Saturday 10pm to 5am. X. Népligeti u. 2. ℂ **1/263-1614**. www.e-klub.hu. Metro: Népliget (Blue line).

Fat Mo's Music Club ★★   A restaurant with an American Prohibition speak-easy theme, it has live jazz, blues, and R&B concerts that start at 9pm, but the dancing doesn't begin until 11pm. Open Monday through Wednesday noon to 2am, Thursday and Friday noon to 4am, Saturday 6pm to 4am, and Sunday 6pm to 2am. The music crowd includes those in their 30s. V. Nyári Pál u. 11. ℂ **1/267-3199**. Metro: Kálvin tér (Blue line).

School Club Közgáz   Touted as the biggest and most famous of the university pubs, this party place is located in the basement of Corvinus University. The disco floors are packed solid during weekends. Cheap drinks, all mix music, and the chance to test your singing with a karaoke tune, all add up for a ton of fun. Open Tuesday through Saturday 10pm to 5am. Crowd: 20s and 30s. IX. Fővám tér 8. ℂ **1/215-4359**. Cover: 500 Ft ($2.50/£1.30) for men, free for women. Metro: Kálvin tér (Blue line) or tram 2.

3 Live Music

A38 Boat 👁️👁️   This is a former Ukrainian stone-carrying ship anchored at the Buda-side foot of the Petőfi Bridge. On the lower deck, you can get your fill of the city's best range of jazz, world, electronic, hip-hop, and rock music bands. The terrace is open only in the summer while the concert hall downstairs is open year-round. Open daily 11am to 4am, with crowds generally in their 20s and 30s. XI. Pázmány Péter sétány. ☎ 1/464-3940. www.a38.hu. Cover varies for different events. Tram: 4 or 6 to the Buda side of Petőfi bridge.

Alcatraz   Themed like its San Francisco namesake, the bar has a prison motif with waitstaff in prisoner uniforms. Sometimes their attitude is similar to a prisoner's. Drinks are pricey, but the music is good. Open Monday through Wednesday 6pm to 2am and Thursday through Saturday 6pm to 4am. Crowd: 30s. VII. Nyár u. 1. ☎ 1/478-6010. www.alcatraz.hu. Metro: Blaha Lujza tér (Red line).

Bitch Lounge 👁️👁️   It calls itself the best chill-out lounge in the city and from the reviews I have heard, I have to agree. The one thing that sets it apart from the crowd is the "Happy Hour," which is rare in Hungary. Free snacks and DJs playing music are offered, while at other times, classic movies are shown. The feel is old Hollywood. Open Wednesday and Thursday 5 to 9pm and Friday 5pm to midnight. IX Üllői út 47. No phone. Metro: Kőbánya-Kispest (Blue line).

Columbus Jazz Klub   Discover the world of music on the Columbus ship without leaving port. Besides being a restaurant, this is where bands of the Society of Hungarian Jazz Artists and other guests take to the stage nightly at 8pm. Concerts last for 2¾ hours for those who have reserved seats. All ages are welcome. V. Vigadó tér dock 4. ☎ 1/266-9013. www.columbuspub.hu. Cover 1,500 Ft ($8.10/£4.25); students with ID 950 Ft ($5.10/£2.70). Metro: Vörösmarty tér (Yellow line).

Cream Restaurant & Music Pub   New to the music scene, this rocking basement pub made a name for itself on the music scene in 2006. It features live bands with Hungarian and international talents including African and Baltic music. With over 30 types of beer, a good time is in store for all. Start with dinner in the excellent restaurant upstairs (See chapter 6, "Where to Dine in Budapest," p. 94). From 20-somethings upward are welcome. VII. Dohány u. 28. ☎ 1/413-6997. www.creammusiccafe.hu. Metro: Blaha Lujza (Red line).

Gödör Club   Located right in the middle of the city, Gödör (Pothole) was built in/under a park, where the main bus station used to be and was until an election and change of administration. This versatile space is sometimes an art gallery and sometimes a music lounge or outdoor movie theater. Outside of the summer months, events seem to be sporadic. You are bound to be at Deák, so you may want to check it out to see if there is anything going on. The park is a popular hangout for skateboarders in the evening and other alterative-lifestyle youth. Prices depend on the event. V. Erzsébet tér. No phone. www.godorklub.hu. Metro: Deák (all lines).

Living Room 👁️   A real hotspot for the 20s and 30s crowd, this club has two halls with different music. It plays Hungarian and international songs from the current list of hits. It is very popular with the university set, especially on students' nights. Open Wednesday through Saturday 10pm to 5am. V. Kossuth Lajos u. 17. ☎ 061/70-277-7576. Cover varies for different events. Metro: Astoria (Red line).

Macskafogó   This dynamic, jampacked cellar club was named after the cult Hungarian animation movie (roughly translated as *Cat City*). Mainstream disco tunes and pop classics draw a vast crowd of easygoing dance fanatics. Open Friday and Saturday 9pm to 4am. Crowd: 20s and 30s. V. Nádor u. 29. ⓒ 1/473-0123. Metro: Kossuth tér (Red line).

Old Man's Music Pub ⭐⭐   Old Man's offers the best jazz and blues in Hungary. Hobo and his blues band are regulars here. Hobo was a friend of Alan Ginsberg and he broke new ground in Hungary by writing his master's thesis on rock 'n' roll in the 1960s. The pub has an ever-changing menu of music from rock to blues and jazz in between. If you are in the neighborhood, see the list of current entertainment posted inside the door. This pub created its own Hard Rock version of Hungarian music artists. Be cautioned, it is downstairs with only one visible exit and it gets very crowded. Music is daily, but only from 9 to 11pm. Open daily 3pm till the crowd leaves. Crowd: 30s and up. Akácfa u. 13. ⓒ 1/322-7645. www.oldmans.hu. Metro: Blaha Lujza tér (Red line).

Piaf   Named after the French torch chanteuse, Piaf is infamous for its very late-night, after-hours parties. Some have said that you need a woman on your arm to gain entrance beyond the bouncer at the door, while others say they have heard people banging on the other side of the door to get out. Decked out like a brothel in red velvet furnishings and low lights, part of its mystique is what happens once you are in and if you can survive the experience. On the downstairs dance floor the spinning of oldies can get pretty heated, and the crowd can be quite wild. Open Sunday through Thursday 10pm to 6am and Friday and Saturday 10pm to 7am. Crowd: varied. VI. Nagymező u. 25. ⓒ 1/312-3823. Metro: Oktogon or Opera (Yellow line).

Spinoza Étterem ⭐⭐ (Finds)   A small restaurant is in front, but in back there is a small cabaret where nightly music performances are offered from Klezmer to classical. Monthly programs are posted in the window or you can check the website. VII. Dob u. 15. ⓒ 1/413-7488. www.spinozahaz.hu. Performances range 1,800 Ft–2,000 Ft ($9.75–$11/£5–£5.75). Bus: 74 to Dohány Synagogue.

Trafó Bar Tango   Associated with the dance venue by the same name and location, this club is housed in the basement. Trafó has a reputation for hosting the best of the best in alternative artists, from reggae to classic Indian music. The dance floor is not a reason to come here, but the small bar area is only the way station before heading to the relaxed, easygoing lounge where you can chill out with friends. Open daily 6pm to 4am or later depending on performances. Crowd: varied. IX. Liliom u. 41. ⓒ 1/215-1600. www.trafo.hu. Cover: 500 Ft–2,000 Ft ($2.75–$11/£1.50–£5.75). Metro: Ferenc krt. (Blue line); tram: 4 or 6 to Üllöi út.

Underground   An oldie among clubs, Underground has had more rebirths than someone with really bad karma. For a brief time, it was a gay bar, but it transformed yet again. The entry is a small room and the bar is downstairs. With its many openings and closings, you may want to make sure it is open before planning a night out there. A minimalist selection of homemade-style specialties is served during the day. It is open daily when it is open at all from 3pm to 3am. Crowd: 20s and 30s. VI. Teréz krt. 30. ⓒ 1/269-5566. Metro: Oktogon (Yellow line); tram: 4 or 6.

4 Pubs & Cafe Bars

Balettcipő   The "Ballet Shoe" is a lovely, cheerful coffeehouse/bar on the street to the side of the opera house. We found it the best when it first opened since we did not

Bar Warning

The **Longford Irish Pub**, V. Fehérhajó u. 5 (℃ **1/267-2766**), has been reportedly gouging both tourists and Hungarians alike. Due to numerous complaints sent to the *Budapest Times*, the paper did an "undercover" investigation and reported their findings in the June 18–24, 2007, issue. What they reported was that the bill received at the end of the meal was illegible and incomplete in details, thus allowing the bar to include higher-priced items or items that had not been ordered at all. Although this practice has been reported at some restaurants in the Castle District, this is the first experience with an establishment in Pest. See p. 96 for other U.S. Embassy warnings.

have to share the space. When weather does not permit outdoor seating, the place fills quickly with a local crowd. The cafe-style menu is widely eclectic in offerings, but the food is good regardless of what you choose. We love the Greek mural inside. Open daily 10am to midnight. VI. Hajós u. 14. ℃ **1/269-3114**. Metro: Opera (Yellow line).

Café Aloe   This sizzling bar is filled with long-legged lovelies with warm brown eyes, and powerful yet remarkably cheap drinks prepared by attentive bar staff. This place is known among locals as the temple of good, inexpensive cocktails. Open daily 5pm to 2am. VI. Zichy Jenő u. 37. ℃ **1/269-4536**. Metro: Nyugati pu. (Blue line).

Café Bobek   Named for a communist rabbit, this is a cute little cafe bar where you can go for a quiet drink with friends. It also offers free Wi-Fi. Open Monday through Thursday 8am to 1am, Friday 8am to 3am, Saturday 11am to 3am, and Sunday 11am to 1am. VII. Kazinczy u. 51. ℃ **061/372-9158**. www.bobek.hu. Tram: 4 or 6 Király u.

Fehér Gyűrű   Described as an unpretentious place for having a beer and a *pogácsa* (biscuit) where the university youth to the young working crowd like to hang out to talk without overloud music drowning out conversation. Benches and plastic chairs provide extra seating if your crowd happens to grow as others join you. Open Monday through Thursday 1pm to midnight, Friday and Saturday 1pm to 1am, and Sunday 4pm to midnight. V. Balassi Bálint u. 27. ℃ **1/312-1863**. Tram: 4 or 6 to Jászai Mari tér.

Fregatt   This was the first English-style pub in Hungary, though depending on the day you go, it could be overcrowded or dead; it goes both ways. Locals make up the better half of the clientele, but English-speaking expats manage to find it also. Though the name refers to a ship theme, it does not deliver on that count, but the atmosphere is amicable and that is what matters. Guinness stout is on draft. Live jazz is offered on various nights, but it starts and ends early. Open Sunday through Friday 4pm to 1am and Saturday 5pm to 1am. V. Molnár u. 26. ℃ **1/318-9997**. Metro: Ferenciek tere (Blue line); tram: 2, 47, or 49.

Irish Cat Pub   This was the first Irish-style pub in Budapest; there's Guinness on tap along with other beer favorites in addition to the great selection of whiskies. It's a popular meeting place for expats and travelers. It serves food and has special events, especially around March 17. Open daily 11am to 2am. V. Múzeum krt. 41. ℃ **1/266-4085**. www.irishcat.hu. Metro: Kálvin tér (Blue line).

Finds   Budapest's Underground Courtyard Parties

One of the strangest things I have come across is the underground nightlife scene in Budapest. Entrepreneurs take over the space of an abandoned building or courtyard and create a pub there until they are evicted or the building is torn down. Often found inside dark **abandoned building courtyards** not visible from the street, these squatters' pubs, ruins pubs, or *kerts* (gardens) as they are known here, are mysterious and exciting to visit. If you were merely strolling by, you would have no idea of the party scene shaking the interior walls, just a few feet away behind what on the outside is a dilapidated facade or an overly abused door.

How do these parties get started? Here is the generic explanation we have been able to filter out, but we are still searching for the full story: Organizers seek out the properties, which are in a bureaucratic quagmire; usually they are buildings with no tenants, and the ownership of the property is questionable, making renovations impossible. As in all real estate deals, location is the prime ingredient for success. They peruse the notices for abandoned properties ripe for squatting. These are the places that have fallen from the radar of the bureaucratic. Add this situation to a bit of rebelliousness, and the desire to make money and before you know it, a star is born on the party scene. However, to stay undercover, these party places are generally advertised by word of mouth only, so you have to ask around to find the current hotspots. When the wrecking ball is looming above, the party is over and then it is on to the next spot.

One *kert* success story is the bustling bar known as **Szimpla Kert.** Colorful paintings hung on the walled-up doors, a bar and jukebox occupied the empty courtyard, and paper lanterns and strange sculptures were hung from above. The party was eventually shut down, but the "Szimpla Kert" party moved on to other venues with a dark cloud hanging over it waiting

Janis Pub   Named after the legendary Janis Joplin, this easygoing pub has an Irish theme with Guinness on tap, a selection of alcohol, live music nightly, and Janis Joplin artifacts for you fans out there. Open Monday through Thursday 4pm to 2am, Friday and Saturday 4pm to 3am, and Sunday 6pm to 2am. V. Királyi Pál u. 8. © **1/266-2619.** www.janispub.hu. Metro: Kálvin tér or Ferenciek tere (Blue line).

Karma Point   With all of the bamboo and grass decor you may feel you have wandered into a tropical dive with a Buddhist flare. This is an underground emporium for the easygoing, young, booze-loving crowd. Open daily 3pm to 2am. VI. Zichy Jenő u. 41. No phone. Metro: Nyugati pu. (Blue line).

Kuplung   Located in a former motorcycle repair shop, Kuplung (Clutch) packs a lively, young crowd in its gardenlike interior. In the squatters-pub atmosphere you will find table football *(csocsó)* fans spinning away on one of the many tables, while loud groovy sounds fill this vast hangar. Cheap drinks might just make you "clutch" onto your chair, but clutch your purse instead. Bag theft happens. Don't look for a sign, you for the swan song to announce the end of a decade. However, that did not happen. Szimpla Kert is still going strong and is more vibrant than ever before. With an actual roof covering it now, it is no longer the *kert* of days past, but still a hot, hot spot to be with the in crowd.

Corvin kert, the very first rooftop *kert* opened in 2007 atop the **Corvin** shopping complex at Blaha Lujza tér right on the square, so you cannot miss it, but don't confuse it with the Corvin movie complex. Unusual in two ways, the stores below are still operational and the *kert* is a rooftop, the first in the city. Though doomsayers have said this will not last, it seems to have become popular and whispers are that it will last a few years, until the building below is sold off, which could take years. Speaking of Corvin theaters, right behind it is the **West Balkan** (VIII. Futó u. 46). It is open from 2pm to very late until the developers continue with their plans to make this a complex of shops, apartment buildings, and offices. Until then West Balkan is playing funk, ska, and any other splinter genre imaginable. Look for the false front of a beachfront cafe.

Túz (Fire)Tate will heat up your night. After 3 years of occupying an old laboratory, this place is still going strong, though the name has changed more than once. The main action is in the inner courtyard where the music is spun out by DJs while light paintings are projected on the four-story high walls. If you are feeling adventurous, explore the interior of the abandoned building in the dark. Careful, there are piles of rubble in the rooms. This is the most ruined of the ruin pubs.

Although Budapest's courtyards seem to disappear one after the other, there are always one or two open somewhere in the city, but the seventh, eighth, and ninth districts seem to be the popular places of choice, perhaps due to the number of vacated buildings.

won't find it, so take note of the address before venturing out. Open daily 4pm to 2am. VI. Király u. 46. (C) **061/30-986-8856.** Tram: 4 or 6 to Király u.

Paris, Texas   Paris, Texas has the distinction of being the first nightlife spot with the foresight to have opened up on the now-buzzing Ráday utca, the partial pedestrian-only street now lined with bars and cafes. The clientele runs the gamut during tourist season, but other times it is mainly a student-aged clientele who linger into the morning. This is a cozy place to drink and talk, but any food ordered comes from the Pink Cadillac nearby. The walls of three adjacent rooms are lined with old photographs, providing a window into the local culture of the 1910s and 1920s. In the summer there is limited outdoor seating. It is open Monday through Friday 10am to 3am and Saturday and Sunday 1pm to 3am. IX. Ráday u. 22. (C) **1/218-0570.** Metro: Kálvin tér (Blue line).

Picasso Point   This cafe-bar is a warm spot to hang out. It offers a limited selection of pizzas and sandwiches. Others find pleasure in the basement party-arena during their short evening hours. Open Tuesday through Thursday 6pm to midnight and Friday and Saturday 6pm to 2am. VI. Hajós u. 31. (C) **1/312-1727.** Metro: Nyugati pu. (Blue line).

The Budapest Klezmer Music Scene

The word *Klezmer* is derived from two Hebrew words, *clay* and *zimmer,* denoting a vessel of music or song with the idea being that an instrument personifies human characteristics such as joyous laughter or mournful crying. Originally it was part of the Eastern European Yiddish culture.

Klezmer musicians were wanderers who went from village to village playing traditional songs, folk songs, dances, and solemn hymns before prayer time. Rarely did they read music; there was no one in the *shtetl* to teach them. They had to travel in order to make a living, earning little money as they played. Typically, a group consisted of three to six musicians playing various instruments: trumpets, bugles, flutes, clarinets, fifes, violins, cellos, and drums.

The music of the klezmorim, the players of klezmer, was influenced by other cultures as the Jewish people traveled throughout Central and Eastern Europe. Thus the music has strong Middle Eastern influences, which are heard in Jewish liturgical music with other influences coming from Romania, Russia, and the Ukraine.

In the late 1800s, the clarinet gained popularity as the most important instrument of klezmer replacing the violin. Brass instruments were introduced at the end of the 19th century.

When Jews immigrated en masse to the U.S. between 1880 and 1920, it happened to be the time that commercial recording devices were being developed. Those recordings of klezmer produced between 1912 and 1940 survived as the primary source material for the current revival of klezmer music. Klezmer fell out of favor after World War II with Jews assimilating into mainstream society; however, in the 1970s, it was discovered yet again.

Pótkulcs   A bohemian bar, Pótkulcs (Spare Key) draws an artsy-looking crowd of travelers and locals alike. My students took me here my first year and I believe the bar's motto: "Pótkulcs is difficult to find and hard to leave." Beyond the rusty metal entrance, this large pub is filled with rickety chairs, couches, and tables—a great place to socialize. The friendly yet crazy-looking chef prepares tasty and ample meals. Presenting the local artists-to-be, the pub features an eclectic mix of temporary art exhibitions and unique concerts. Open Sunday through Wednesday 5pm to 1:30am and Thursday through Saturday 5pm to 2:30am. VI. Csengery u. 65/b. (C) 1/269-1050. www. potkulcs.hu. Metro: Nyugati pu. (Blue line).

Szilvuplé   This is a lounge, cafe, restaurant, and bar all rolled into one large party place. Szilvuplé's attractiveness lies in its steady, calm, welcoming atmosphere. The secession-style indoor design, colorful cocktail bar, attentive staff, moderate prices, and talented DJs set the tone with rock and indie music; it also features karaoke nights and dance lessons during the week. Open Thursday through Saturday 6pm to 4am and Sunday through Wednesday 6pm to 2am. VI. Ó u. 33. (C) 1/302-2499. www.szilvuple.hu. Metro: Opera (Yellow line).

Szimpla Kert (★★)   For cultural experiences, you cannot pass up Szimpla Kert. It is a beer garden, alternative culture Mecca. Located in an abandoned apartment

Today, it is more popular than ever and is played by bands around the world. The popular bands are touring the world as well as recording CDs. The Budapest Klezmer Band, organized in 1990, was responsible for the revival of klezmer in Hungary, and it is the first Klezmer band to form in Hungary since World War II.

The Budapest Klezmer Band is just one of many Klezmer bands that have come into existence over the years, getting their start in Budapest. Klezmer no longer has a strictly Jewish fan base or a Budapest one either. Due to this, the bands are touring around the world, and when they do land back in Budapest, they are playing at larger venues than in years past, to sell out audiences. This makes it difficult to point the direction for finding a klezmer concert. The locations of the past are not as reliable as they once were. Therefore, I direct you to the website of two of the popular bands to check their concert schedules for the time of your visit. The **Budapest Klezmer Band's** schedule is on their website at www.budapestklezmer.hu and the **Chagall Klezmer Band** at www.chagallband.hu. Both have an English-language link. Alternatives are to look for listings for performances by the **Pannonia Klezmer Band, Sabbathsong, Klezmer Band,** or **Klezmereszek.** A few of these groups play at **Spinoza Etterem** (p. 230) or contact the Fonó Music Hall at XI. Sztregova u. 3. (© **1/206-5300;** www.fono.hu). It produces many of the klezmer CDs. Lastly, you can check with Tourinform for concert information. If you happen to be here at the end of August to the beginning of September, you will find klezmer concerts at the annual Jewish Festival.

courtyard that has not seen the wrecking ball, Szimpla Kert mixes junkyard aesthetics with such modernisms as Wi-Fi, a daytime cafe, and evenings of live music and indie film screenings. Dimly lit, couch-packed, with little open to the sky rooms off of the courtyard, it is a relaxing, pleasant place to unwind. Check your reality at the door. Open weekdays 10am to 2am and weekends noon to 2am. VII. Kertész u. 48. © 1/342-1034. Metro: Oktogon (Yellow line); tram: 4 or 6 to Király u.

Szóda   When I need a Wi-Fi and caffeine fix at the same time, this is my favorite hangout. Redesigned a few times, it seems to look the same each time, with retro-futuristic leather bench seats and '50s style chairs. The windows are filled with empty fashions spritzzer soda bottles. The underground bar and dance floor is shelter for the whacky all-night dance-rats. Open daily 8am to 5pm. VII. Wesselényi u. 18. © 1/461-0007. www.szoda.com. Tram: 4 or 6 to Wesselényi u.

Vittula   Hidden and small, this new-wave cellar bar looks like someone's basement that has not been cleaned of old storage items for 10 years. Yet it seems to be a busy and popular place for youthful travelers, expatriates, and locals alike who come to listen to retro-funky vibes or live music by local youth talents. Some say there should be a warning label on the front door due to the unbearable smoke. Open daily 6pm to dawn. VII. Kertész u. 4. No phone. Metro: Blaha Lujza tér (Red line).

5 Hungarian Folk-Dance Houses

Hungarian folk music has many styles, sounds, and instruments with some music associated with dances, while others are autonomous. Hand in hand with national identity, folk music has had a revival via the *táncház* (dance house). An evening of folk music and folk dancing can be a wonderful cultural experience during your stay here. The events in a neighborhood community center certainly come with a higher recommendation than those offered as tourist events. When an American choreography student was studying here, she pointed out that many of the dances were male centered with the ladies as window dressing. Perhaps some are, but others are definitely mixed equally. Listed below are a few of the best-known dance houses. The offering is dance instruction for an hour and then several hours of dancing accompanied by a live band. You just might hear some of Hungary's best folk musicians in these simple dance houses. If you have two left feet, just come to watch and listen. Every festival has some folk dancing included, so if you are too inhibited to try these places, try to arrange your trip around some festival time. Most dance houses are open from September to June and are closed for the summer.

Authentic folk-music workshops are held at least once a week at several locations around the city. The leading Hungarian folk band is **Muzsikás,** the name given to musicians playing traditional folk music in Hungarian villages. They have toured the U.S., playing to great acclaim, but may not always be available at the **táncház,** but music is every Thursday (Sept–May only) from 8pm to midnight (500 Ft/$2.75/£1.50) at the **Marczibányi Square Cultural House (Marczibányi tér Művelődési Ház),** II. Marczibányi tér 5/a (© 1/212-2820). Take the Red line metro to Moszkva tér. Also try the **Municipal Cultural House (Fővárosi Művelődési Ház),** at XI. Fehérvári út 47 (© 1/203-3868). At the **Kalamajka Dance House,** Belvárosi Ifjúsági Művelődési Ház, V. Molnár u. 9 (© 1/371-5928), reachable by M3 Ferenciek tere, is the biggest weekend dance, with dancing and instruction on the second floor, while jam sessions and serious palinka drinking take place on the fourth. The Kalamajka band is led by Béla Halmos, who started the dance-house movement in the 1970s. Usually traditional villagers give guest performances. Open Saturday from 8pm to 1am for 500 Ft ($2.75/£1.50), you can dance until you drop.

An important heritage-preserving center, the **Almássy Square Culture Center (Almássy téri Művelődési Központ),** VII. Almássy tér 6 (© 1/352-1572), from 6 to 10pm hosts the folk dances to the music of the electric Greeks Sirtos in the main hall. Upstairs is a bit crazier with the small fanatic band of Magyar dancers who twirl to the Kalotaszeg sounds of the Berkó Band until midnight. A short walk from Blaha Lujza tér (Blue line or tram no. 4 or 6) gets you to this folk center. Entrance fees vary from 500 Ft to 1,000 Ft ($2.75–$5.50/£1.50–£2.75).

Most people who come to a *táncház* evening do so to learn the folk dances and the music that accompanies them, not for touristy reasons. However, this does not mean that tourists are not welcome to also learn the dances or sit and observe while hearing musicians practicing and partake in a local scene at next to no expense. You have the opportunity to become part of the program instead of merely watching others perform.

Every Monday, Friday, and Saturday from May to mid-October at 8.30pm, the touristier Folklór Centrum presents a program of Hungarian dancing accompanied by a Gypsy orchestra at the Municipal Cultural House. This performance is one of the best of its kind in Budapest.

6 Gay & Lesbian Bars

The bar scene regardless of orientation is volatile, most likely due to the low wages of the local working stiffs regardless of their profession. There is not much discretionary income to spend in bars. Gay bars open and close in the blink of an eye. The gay bar scene in Budapest is largely male-oriented though progress is being made for women; it comes and goes even faster than the regular scene. For reliable and up-to-date information, visit **www.budapestgaycity.net**, **www.gayguide.net**, or subscribe to the free Yahoo **Gay Budapest Information** group by sending an e-mail to gaybudapestinfo-subscribe@yahoogroups.com.

Action Bar   This is a well-hidden bar and can easily be overlooked. The hanging sidewalk sign is usually not even close to the entrance. Look for a large yellow *A* sign and this is the entrance to this dark, often-crowded basement bar. Most of the group consists of other tourists with a few locals mixed in, but exclusively men. You will receive a drink card which obligates you to drink the minimum of 1,300 Ft ($7/ £3.70) or pay the difference when you leave. Make sure the bartender marks your card with every drink you order. There is a hefty fine for "lost" cards. Highlights are the spicy strip shows and go-go shows at 12:30 and 1:45am, the busy dark video rooms, and the sizzling hot atmosphere, but it is empty until 11pm. Open daily 9pm to 5am. V. Magyar u. 42. ✆ 1/266-9148. www.action.gay.hu. Metro: Kálvin tér (Blue line).

AlterEgo   Another new club to make its way to the gay scene in 2007, this is regaled as a hip jumping club for the younger set. Men and women are welcomed to their different events each night. Besides karaoke on Thursday, it has guest singers and transvestite shows. Open Wednesday to Saturday 10pm until the sun rises again. VI. Dessewffy u. 33. ✆ 06/70-345-4302 mobile only. Metro: Oktogon (Yellow line).

Árkádia   In the city center, this small, intimate sometimes packed bar with a popular backroom is the perfect place to meet, dance, or get cozy with an attractive stranger. There is no cover or minimum consumption charge, but this place attracts the rent boys. Open daily 8pm to 5am. V. Türr István u. 5. No phone. www.arkadiagaybar.hu. Metro: Vörösmarty tér (Yellow line).

Bamboo Music Club   This new gay disco made its way onto the club scene in 2007. It hosts lesbian parties once a month and has a backroom. It is open only on Friday and Saturday 9pm to 4am. VI. Dessewffy u. 44 ✆ 1/428-2225. Minimum consumption 1,500 Ft ($8/£4.25) Metro: Oktogon (Yellow line).

Capella   Although labeled a gay club, with a cross-dressing bar staff, this club draws a large nongay crowd. It offers cabaret-style shows and extravagant drag shows which is a draw for the curious heterosexuals at midnight and 1am. There are three levels to the bar. Some have reported that the cover charge changes sporadically and some customers have been overcharged, so proceed with caution and count your change carefully. Open Monday to Saturday 9pm to 5am. V. Belgrád rkp. 23. ✆ 1/328-6231. Metro: Fereciek tere (Blue line).

Club Bohemian Alibi   Sexual orientation is mixed at this club/restaurant combo; desire and lust fuel up during the evening hours as the Bohemian Transvestite team takes center stage performing a brilliant drag show. Shows start at 11pm on Monday and Tuesday and at midnight Wednesday to Sunday with additional shows at 2am on Friday and Saturday. Open Monday through Thursday 9pm to 3am and Friday and Saturday 9pm to 5am. You charge drinks with a consumption card that you pay for on the way out. Beware, the penalty for losing the card is 10,000 Ft ($54/£29). IX. Üllő út 45. No phone. www.clubbohemian.hu. Minimum consumption 800 Ft ($4.30/£2.25) Sun–Thurs; 1,200 Ft ($6.50/£3.40) Fri–Sat. Metro: Ferenc krt. (Blue line).

CoXx Club   Once known as Chaos, this is a modern, metallic bar for sizzling gay men in the underground shelter. The entry level has an overpriced Internet cafe and a small art gallery, where you will be greeted and given your consumption card. In the winter, coat check is mandatory. Nothing happens here until midnight at the earliest. Open daily 9pm to 4am. VII. Dohány u. 38. (℃ 1/344-4884. www.coxx.hu. Minimum consumption 1,000 Ft ($5.40/£2.85). Metro: Astoria or Blaha Lujza tér (Red line).

Habrolo Bisztro   This is a small gay bar where locals hang out, so you can practice your Hungarian skills here. The staff from the former Angyal's bar has been here since its opening in 2006. Open Tuesday through Sunday 5pm to 5am. V. Szep u. 1/b. No phone. Metro: Astoria (Red line).

Le Café M   Formerly the Mystery Bar, which was the first gay bar in the city, it changed its name for unknown reasons. It is a very tiny, but friendly place that draws a large foreign clientele making it a great place to strike up a conversation and meet new people. Open Monday through Friday 4pm to 4am and Saturday and Sunday 6pm to 4am. V. Nagysándor József u. 3. (℃ 1/312-1436. Metro: Arany János u. (Blue line).

UpSide Down   Formerly operated as a public bathroom, this bar's clientele is mostly nongay. Rather pricey, its laid-back loungelike stylish decor is a suitable place to wind down at the end of the day. Monday and Wednesday nights feature gay and lesbian karaoke, though the word is that the bartenders can become homophobic at the drop of a hairpin. Entrance fees are only for special events. Open daily 5pm to 5am. V. Podmaniczky tér 1. No phone. Metro: Arany János u. (Blue line).

7 More Entertainment

CASINOS   Budapest has a couple dozen casinos. Many are located in luxury hotels: **Casino Budapest Hilton,** I. Hess András tér 1–3 (℃ 1/375-1001); **Las Vegas Casino,** in the Atrium Hyatt Hotel, V. Roosevelt tér 2 (℃ 1/317-6022; www.lasvegas casino.hu); and **Orfeum Casino,** in the Hotel Béke Radisson, VI. Teréz krt. 43 (℃ 1/301-1600). Formal dress is required. Other popular casinos include: **Grand Casino Budapest,** V. Deák Ferenc u. 13 (℃ 1/483-0170), **Tropicana Casino,** V. Vigadó u. 2 (℃ 1/327-7250; www.tropicanacasino.hu), and the most elegant **Várkert Casino** on the Danube side, Ybl Miklós tér 9 (℃ 1/202-4244; www.varkert.hu). There are a number of smaller independent casinos around the city, but we do not recommend patronizing them.

MOVIES   A healthy number of English-language movies are always playing in Budapest. The best source of listings is the ***Budapest Sun*** or online at www.budapest sun.com. Movies labeled *szinkronizált, m.b.,* or *magyarul beszél* mean that the movie has been dubbed into Hungarian; *feliratos* means subtitled. Tickets cost around 800 Ft to 1,800 Ft ($4.30–$9.75/£2.30–£5.15). Most multiplexes provide the option of seeing movies in their original language even if the movie itself was dubbed, but they are the most expensive theaters. For their addresses, check the *Budapest Sun* when checking the schedule. The art cinemas where English-language movies are commonly found are **Corvin,** VIII. köz 1 (℃ 1/459-5050; tram no. 4 or 6 to Ferenc krt.); **Európa,** VII. Rákóczi út 82 (℃ 1/322-5419; no. 7 bus to Berzsenyi u.); **Hunnia,** VII.

Erzsébet krt. 26 (📞 1/322-3471; tram no. 4 or 6 to Wesselényi u.); **Művész,** VI. Teréz krt. 30 (📞 1/332-6726; tram no. 4 or 6 to Oktogon); **Puskin,** V. Kossuth L. u. 18 (📞 1/429-6080; metro to Astoria, Red line); and **Uránia,** VIII. Rákócxi út 2 (📞 1/318-8955; metro to Blaha Lujza tér, Red line).

Going to a movie at one of the cinemas above can be a cultural experience in and of itself. Some theaters are smaller than most people's living rooms. Seats are assigned in all of the theaters. *Jobb* means right and *Bal* means left. First, find the sign to see if that theater uses right and left as you face the seats or as you are facing the stage; it is not a uniform custom. Then find your row number *Sor,* and finally your numbered "chair" *Szék.* If you do not sit in your assigned seat, you may find an upset Hungarian hovering over you telling you that the seat is theirs. As a throwback to earlier times, you will find a half-empty theater with people insisting they have to sit in their assigned seat when better seats are freely available. If popcorn is sold in the theater, don't expect any butter or other topping. As much as the Hungarian diet is made up of fats, they don't use any for their movie munchies.

11

The Danube Bend

The Danube Bend (Dunakanyar), a string of small riverside towns just north of Budapest, is a popular excursion spot for both Hungarians and international travelers. The name "Danube Bend" is actually a misnomer. It should be the Danube twist, turn, and twist again. The river doesn't actually change direction at the designated bend. The Danube enters Hungary from the northwest flowing southeasterly forming the border with Hungary's northern neighbor, Slovakia. Just after Esztergom, about 40km (25 miles) north of Budapest, the river changes abruptly to the south. This is the start of the Danube Bend region. From here the river then sharply twists north again just before Visegrád, before going south yet again before reaching Vác. From Vác, it flows more or less directly south, through Budapest on toward the country's borders with Serbia and Croatia. When looking at it on a map, it looks like a long snake after a seizure.

The small, but historic towns along the snaking Bend, in particular, Szentendre, Vác, Visegrád, and Esztergom, are easy day trips from Budapest since they're all within a half-hour to a couple of hours from the city. The great natural beauty of the area, where forested hills loom over the river, makes it a welcome haven for those weary of the city. Travelers with more time in Budapest can easily make a long weekend out of a visit to the Bend.

1 Railing through the Danube Bend

GETTING THERE

BY BOAT From April to September, boats run between Budapest and the towns of the Danube Bend. A leisurely boat ride through the countryside is one of the highlights of a boat excursion. All boats depart Budapest's Vigadó tér boat landing, which is located in Pest between Erzsébet Bridge and Szabadság Bridge, stopping to pick up passengers 5 minutes later at Buda's Batthyány tér landing, which is in Buda and is also a Red line metro stop, before it continues up the river.

Schedules and towns served are complicated and change sometimes due to water levels of the river, so contact **MAHART,** the state shipping company, at the Vigadó tér landing (© 1/318-1704; www.mahartpassnave.hu; click on the British flag) for information. You can also get MAHART information from Tourinform.

Round-trip prices are 2,085 Ft ($11/£6) to Szentendre, 2,235 Ft ($12/£6.35) to Visegrád, and 1,460 Ft ($7.90/£4.15) to Esztergom. Children under 6 ride for free, children ages 6 to 15 receive a 50% discount, and students receive a 25% discount with the ISIC card.

The approximate travel time from Budapest is 2 hours to Szentendre, 3½ hours to Visegrád, and 5 hours to Esztergom. If time is tight, consider the train or bus (both of which are also considerably cheaper).

The Danube Bend

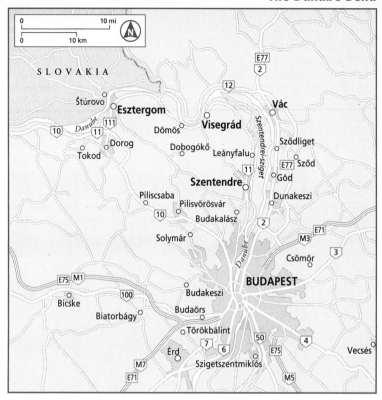

BY TRAIN For information and details on traveling by Budapest rail, see p. 44.

To Szentendre The HÉV suburban railroad connects Budapest's Batthyány tér station with Szentendre. On the Pest side, you can catch the HÉV from the Margit Híd, Budai Híd Fő stop on trams 4 or 6. Trains leave daily, year-round, every 20 minutes or so from 4am to 11:30pm. The one-way fare is 500 Ft ($2.75/£1.50); subtract 230 Ft ($1.25/75p) if you have a valid Budapest public transportation pass. The trip is 45 minutes.

To Vác An incredible 85 trains leave from Nyugati Station during the week and 58 on weekends giving you lots of freedom on time of day to go. However, shoot for the train that leaves 5 minutes to the hour, since the trip is only 25 minutes. Other trains can take 45 minutes to 1½ hour for unknown reasons. The one-way fare is 525 Ft ($2.75/£1.50) each way. All of the trains are locals, so no reservation is needed.

To Visegrád There's no direct train service to Visegrád. Instead you can take 1 of 28 daily trains departing from Nyugati Station for Nagymaros (trip time: 40 min.–1 hr.). From Nagymaros, take a ferry across the river to Visegrád. The ferry dock (RÉV ✆ 26/398-344) is a 5-minute walk from the train station. A ferry leaves every hour throughout the day. The train ticket to Nagymaros costs 900 Ft ($4.75/£2.50); the ferryboat ticket to Visegrád costs 200 Ft ($1.10/55p) for adults and 100 Ft (55¢/30p) for students.

To Esztergom Twenty-five trains make the run daily between Budapest's Nyugati Station and Esztergom (trip time: 1½ hr.); IC trains are not available on this route. Train tickets cost 900 Ft ($4.85/£2.55).

BY BUS Approximately 30 daily buses travel the same route to Szentendre, Visegrád, and Esztergom, departing from **Budapest's Árpád híd bus station (© 1/329-1450;** at the Blue line metro station of the same name). The one-way fare to Szentendre is 375 Ft ($2/£1.10); the trip takes about 45 minutes. The fare to Visegrád is 750 Ft ($4.05/£2.15), and the trip takes 1¼ hours. To Esztergom, take the bus that travels via a town called Dorog; it costs 675 Ft ($3.65/£1.90) and takes 1¼ hours. The bus going to Esztergom via Visegrád takes 2 hours and costs 750 Ft ($4.05/£2.15; fare is determined by number of kilometers of travel, and this is a longer route). Keep in mind, of course, that all travel by bus is subject to traffic delays, especially during rush hour.

BY CAR From Budapest, Route 11 hugs the west bank of the Danube, taking you to Szentendre, Vác, Visegrád, and Esztergom. Alternatively, you could head "overland" to Esztergom by Route 10, switching to Route 111 at Dorog.

2 Szentendre ★★★

21km (13 miles) N. of Budapest

Szentendre (pronounced *Sen*-ten-dreh, St. Andrew), 21km (13 miles) north of Budapest has been populated since the Stone Age by Illyrians, the Celtic Eraviscus tribe, Romans, Lombards, Avars, and naturally, Hungarians. Serbians settled here in the 17th century, embellishing the town with their unique characteristics. Szentendre, counts half a dozen Serbian churches among its rich collection of historical buildings.

Since the turn of the 20th century, Szentendre has been home to an artist's colony, where today, about 100 artists live and work. The town boasts of its selection of 48 museums and monuments, but few people come here to visit the museums, distracted perhaps by the shopping opportunities. It could also be that the times and hours posted are just a loose guide. Museums do not have stable hours, even when posted on the door; there is oftentimes a sign posted stating that the museum is closed for "technical reasons," but no future reopening date is given. Think of a museum as icing on the cake; if it is open take the opportunity to visit it.

The town is an extremely popular tourist destination, with tour buses pouring tourists into the town for a few hours of exploring. This is sometimes a turn-off for other visitors, but the town really is a treasure to be explored. To appreciate the rich flavor of the town, we recommend that you look beyond the touristy shops and wander the streets looking at the architecture, the galleries, and the churches if only from the outside. Dare to wander off the main streets to find hidden shops, beautiful old homes, and quiet little green spaces. Almost all of the streets are cobblestones, so choose comfortable footwear.

At the top of the hill, you will find the Roman Catholic churchyard, with lovely views of the red-tile rooftops and one surprise from here is the winged blue man on a rooftop a couple of blocks away. I could not find anyone to tell me what its purpose was other than frivolity. If you take the steps down from the courtyard, you will come across, in my opinion, the best *lángos* vendor (see below) in Hungary. If you wander down the hill on the side streets, the palinka shop has been known to give a free sample in hopes of making a sale. Szentendre is too small for you to get lost in and too

Szentendre

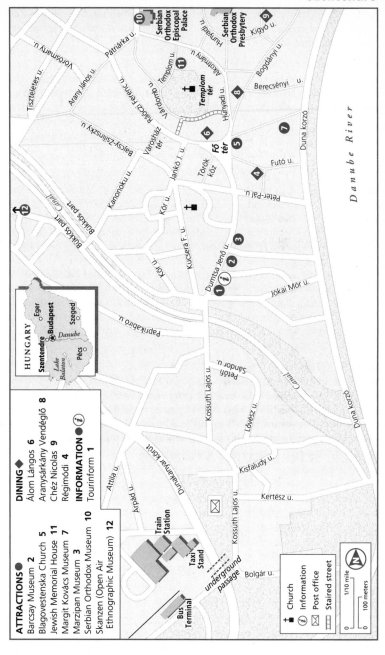

ATTRACTIONS ●
Barcsay Museum **2**
Blagovestenska Church **5**
Jewish Memorial House **11**
Margit Kovács Museum **7**
Marzipan Museum **3**
Serbian Orthodox Museum **10**
Skanzen (Open Air Ethnographic Museum) **12**

DINING ◆
Álom Lángos **6**
Aranysárkány Vendéglő **8**
Chéz Nicolas **9**
Régimódi **4**

INFORMATION ● ⓘ
Tourinform **1**

Legend:
✠ Church
ⓘ Information
⊠ Post office
░░░ Staired street

1/10 mile
0 — 100 meters

beautiful for a less-than-thorough exploration, so make the most of a day, but don't miss walking along the river for a lovely and blissful view of the river and the tree-lined bank on the other side.

ESSENTIALS

For information on getting to Szentendre, see "Railing through the Danube Bend," above. One of Szentendre's information offices, **Tourinform,** is at Dumtsa Jenő u. 22 (© **26/317-965**), with maps of Szentendre (and the region), as well as concert and exhibition schedules. The office can also provide hotel information. The office is open April through October Monday to Wednesday from 9:30am to 6:00pm and Thursday to Sunday 9:30am to 7:30pm; in the off season it's open Monday to Friday from 9:30am to 5:00pm. To get here, just follow the flow of pedestrian traffic into town on Kossuth Lajos utca. Like all things in this town, the office marches to the beat of its own drummer, not always keeping with the schedule it gives. If you arrive by boat, you may find the **Ibusz** office sooner, located on the corner of Bogdányi út and Gőzhajó utca (© **26/310-181**). This office is open April to October, Monday through Friday from 10am to 6pm and weekends 10am to 3pm. From November to March, it's open weekdays only, 10am to 5pm.

Another good source of information, particularly if you are planning to stay in the region more than a day, is **Jági Utazás,** at Kucsera F. u. 15 (©/fax **26/310-030**). The staff here is extremely knowledgeable and dedicated. From planning hunting or horse-back-riding excursions to helping you find the right pension room to recommending the best *palacsinta* (crepe) place in town, they seem to know it all. The office is open weekdays 9am to 5pm and Saturday from 9am to 1pm in summer and weekdays only from 9am to 5pm in winter.

WHERE TO STAY

Róz Panzió ⊕, located at Pannónia utca 6/b (© **26/311-737;** fax 26/310-979; www. hotelrozszentendre.hu), has 10 units and a nice garden overlooking the Danube where you can eat breakfast when weather permits. Rooms are 12,000 Ft ($65/£34) for a double during off season and 13,000 Ft ($70/£37) in high season; breakfast is included. With its new website, you can book online and view videos. Parking is available.

EXPLORING THE MUSEUMS & CHURCHES

Barcsay Museum ⊕   The conservative Socialist dictates of the day restricted the work of artist Jenő Barcsay (1900–88). Nevertheless, in his anatomical drawings, etchings, and charcoal and ink drawings, Barcsay's genius shines through. I particularly like his pastel drawings of Szentendre street scenes.

Dumtsa Jenő u. 10. © **26/310-244.** Admission 400 Ft ($2.15/£1.15). Wed–Sun 9am–5pm.

Blagovestenska Church ⊕   The Blagovestenska Church at Fő tér 4 is the only one of the town's several Serbian Orthodox churches that you can be fairly sure to find open. The tiny church, dating from 1752, was built on the site of a wooden church from the Serbian migration of 1690. A rococo iconostasis features paintings by Mihailo Zivkovic; notice that the eyes of all the icons are upon you.

Fő tér 4. No phone. Admission 250 Ft ($1.35/70p). Tues–Sun 10am–5pm.

Margit Kovács Museum ⊕⊕   This expansive museum features the work of Hungary's best-known ceramic artist, Margit Kovács, who died in 1977. This museum displays the breadth of Kovács' talents. Many appreciate her sculptures of elderly women and her folk-art interpretations of village life. When the museum is full, people are required to wait outside before entering.

Vastagh György u. 1. ✆ **26/310-244**. Admission 700 Ft ($3.80/£2). Mar–Sept Tues–Sun 9am–5pm; Oct–Feb Tues–Sun 10am–4pm. Walk east from Fő tér on Görög utca.

Marzipan Museum ✷✷ *Kids*　Interestingly, this is the most widely known museum in this village, claiming to be the only museum of its type in the world. Who could pass up this chance to see the 1.5m (5-ft.) long Hungarian Parliament made entirely in marzipan? Kids will love the Disney characters and the 1.8m (6 ft.) Michael Jackson, made of white chocolate. What they can create in marzipan and chocolate is amazing.

Dumsta Jeno u. 12 ✆ **26/311-931**. Admission 400 Ft ($2.15/£1.15). May–Sept daily 10am–7pm; Oct–Apr daily 10am–6pm.

Serbian Orthodox Museum ✷✷　The Serbian Orthodox Museum is housed next door to a Serbian Orthodox Church (services are at 10am Sun) in one of the buildings of the former episcopate, just north of Fő tér. The collection here—one of the most extensive of its kind in predominantly Catholic Hungary—features exceptional 16th- through 19th-century icons, liturgical vessels, scrolls in Arabic from the Ottoman period, and other types of ecclesiastical art. Informative labels are in Hungarian and English. Entrance to the museum entitles you to visit the church, but a museum attendant unlocks the door for you and waits for you to leave again.

Pátriárka u. 5. ✆ **26/312-399**. Admission 500 Ft ($2.70/£1.50). May–Sept Tues–Sun 10am–6pm; Oct–Apr Tues–Sun 10am–4pm. Walk north from Fő tér on Alkotmány utca.

Szántó Jewish Memorial House and Temple ✷✷✷ *Moments*　This is the first temple built in Hungary after World War II as a memorial to those from this area who died in the Holocaust. It is probably the smallest Jewish temple in the world. It was dedicated on May 17, 1998, by Professor József Sweitzer, the chief rabbi of Hungary. Men are given a yamaka to wear when entering.

Albotmány u. 4. No phone. Donations accepted. Tues–Sun 11am–5pm.

SIGHTS OUTSIDE TOWN

Pap-sziget (Priest's Island)　This island at the northern end of town provides a place to rest and relax, with thermal waters in the outdoor bathing pools. Bring a bathing suit and towel or rent towels there.

Facilities include basic locker rooms. No entrance fee. Buses for Leányfalu and Visegrád pass the bridge to Pap-sziget.

Skanzen (Open-Air Ethnographical Museum) ✷✷ *Kids*　About 3km (2 miles) northwest of Szentendre is one of Hungary's better *skanzens,* or reproduction peasant villages. This ambitious *skanzen,* the largest in the country, represents rural life from all regions of the country. There are several reconstructed 18th- and 19th-century villages, with thatch-roofed houses, blacksmith and weaving shops, working mills, and churches. You can purchase a guidebook in English at the gate.

Szentendre's bus station is behind the HÉV terminal. Take the bus from bay 7 and get off at the Szabadság-forrás stop. The bus will not stop automatically, so you must press the stop request button. A more convenient way is to go to the boat landing and take a taxi. If you're driving, follow Route 10 N. Turn left on Sztaravodai út.

Sztaravodai út. ✆ **26/502-500**. www.skanzen.hu. Admission 1,000 Ft ($5.40/£2.85); student ticket 500 Ft ($2.70/ £1.50). Apr–Oct Tues–Sun 9am–5pm; Nov 3–Dec 9 Sat–Sun 10am–3pm; Jan 16–Mar 31 9am–4pm; Nov 1, 2 and Dec 10–Jan 15 closed. See directions above.

WHERE TO DINE

Aranysárkány Vendéglő (Golden Dragon Inn) 🔒 HUNGARIAN   Located just east of Fő tér on Hunyadi utca, which leads into Alkotmány utca, the Golden Dragon is always filled to capacity. The crowd includes a good percentage of Hungarians, definitely a good sign in a heavily visited town like Szentendre.

Long wooden tables set with sterling cutlery provide a relaxed but tasteful atmosphere in this air-conditioned restaurant. You can choose from such enticing offerings as alpine lamb, roast leg of goose, Székely-style stuffed cabbage (the Székely are a Hungarian ethnic group native to Transylvania), spinach cream, and venison steak. Vegetarians can order the vegetable plate, a respectable presentation of grilled and steamed vegetables in season. The cheese dumplings do a good job of rounding out the meal. Various traditional Hungarian beers are on draft, and the wine list features selections from 22 regions of the country.

Alkotmány u. 1/a. ⓒ **26/301-479.** www.aranysarkany.hu. Reservations recommended. Main courses 2,400 Ft–3,600 Ft ($13–$20/£6.75–£10); special tourist menus 3,300 Ft ($18/£9.50). AE, MC, V. Daily noon–10pm.

Chez Nicolas ★★★ FRENCH/HUNGARIAN   Set away from the bustle of the square, this charming restaurant has intimate romantic dining with an outdoor terrace looking out to the river. For a more romantic experience, request the single balcony table. You can choose from Hungarian or French dishes. The owner, Tamás Horváth, will be happy to explain the ingredients of each dish in his excellent English. We recommend the Pork Brasso with choice chunks of pork cooked smothered in paprika, oil, and potatoes. This restaurant is a favorite of local residents.

Kígyó utca 10. ⓒ **26/311-288.** Reservations recommended. Main courses 1,790 Ft–3,800 Ft ($9.75–$21/£5–£11). MC, V. Tues–Sun noon–10pm.

Régimódi 🔒 HUNGARIAN   If you walk directly south from Fő tér, you'll find this excellent choice for dining. An elegant restaurant in a former private home, Régimódi is furnished with antique Hungarian carpets and chandeliers. Original artworks decorate the walls. Limited terrace dining is available and in the summer, you will appreciate the outside seating. The menu offers a wide range of Hungarian specialties, with an emphasis on game dishes. There are also numerous salad options, with specials each day on the board. Whatever you choose, the portions are hearty. There's an extensive wine list. It does get crowded with tour groups.

Futó u. 3. ⓒ **26/311-105.** Reservations recommended. Main courses 1,850 Ft–5,800 Ft ($10–$32/£5.25–£17). DC, MC, V. Daily 9am–10pm.

SHOPPING

Blue Land Folklor ★★★ *Finds*   The lady who owns and runs this store is a wealth of information on Hungarian folklore. She is really chatty and will give you the history of everything she sells that has some folk significance. I sometimes wonder if these stories are true or just good selling, but either way, they are entertaining. What is certain is that this store carries decorated eggs from 38 different regions of Hungary, plus some from the ethnic Hungarian areas prior to the Trianon Treaty's loss of land. They are all labeled and custom boxing is provided to ensure safe transport back home.

Alkotmány u. 8. ⓒ **26/313-610.** Daily 10am–5pm.

Handpets ★★★ *Kids*   Being a teacher, formerly elementary and now university, I cannot pass up sharing this information. If you want to find a unique shop while in Hungary, this is it. Handpets are the most creative hand puppets I have ever seen.

> ### (Finds Best *Lángos* Ever
>
> If you get a snack attack, you will find the best *lángos* in Hungary, here in Szentendre at **Álom Lángos** ★★★ at Fő tér 8 (© **06/20-970-7827** mobile), an unassuming little stand. Sometimes the long waiting lines are attesting to this fact, since most will be Hungarians in the know. *Lángos* is the Hungarian version of fried dough, with toppings (see appendix B, "Hungarian Cuisine," p. 295). When standing in Fő tér, there are yellow signs near an alley with LÁNGOS written on them. Halfway up the alley is a gate for the little shed where for very little money, you can have the Hungarian favorite snack: *lángos* with sour cream, ham, and shredded cheese. Garlic and hot sauces are on the counter for you to add. For me, this is worth a trip to Szentendre alone. The stand is only open March through November Tuesday through Saturday 10am to 6pm and a *lángos* will run you 350 Ft to 500 Ft ($1.90–$2.70/£1–£1.50).

They are made for three or five fingers and for child or adult hands. Designed by Kati Szili, they are handmade of high-quality material and are sure to delight children of all ages. This is the only exclusive shop where the entire collection is available, though limited designs and poor imitations are sold elsewhere.

Dumsta Jeno u. 15 © 26/373-746. www.handpets.hu. Daily 10am–5pm.

Mana Ékszer Galéria ★★ *(Finds*   Five young Hungarian designers and jewelry makers open their workshop as a showroom where you will find contemporary works of fashionable pieces of accessories that are unlike any others you will see. Open by appointment.

Bogdányi u. 40. © 061/30-971-4894 mobile.

3 Vác ★★★

34km (21 miles) N. of Budapest

Just past Szendendre along the Danube, sits this historic and lovely little town full of trees and wonderful little streets to explore. It dates back 9 centuries, but I have to admit, that it took me 6 years and the writing of this book to explore this little beauty outside of Budapest. According to legend, there was a monk hermit, Laszlo, who lived in the forest in what is now known as Vác. He prophesied that Prince Géza would win the battle against King Soloman. The prince and the monk came upon a wondrous sight, a deer with candles on its horns. After seeing this, Géza decided to establish a church on this site making it a bishopric, Vác.

ESSENTIALS

For information on getting to **Vác,** see "Railing through the Danube Bend," earlier in this chapter. When you leave the train station, you will find that there is only one street leading away from it. Do not be disheartened by the mundane architecture of the little shops that fill the street, thinking you got off at the wrong station. Walk straight down Széchenyi utca for about 15 minutes until you run into Március 15 tér, where you will find a number of interesting buildings with history to share. Tourinform is located at 17 Március 15 tér (© **27/316-160;** www.tourinformvac.hu). It is open 8am to 5:30pm daily. I will not cover places to stay since the town is small and conveniently located to Budapest. If you have a desire to stay overnight, check with Tourinform for information on accommodations.

EXPLORING THE TOWN

The beauty of this city is that you can see quite a bit for very little money at all. Starting with the main square at **Március 15 tér** ★★★, the center promenade was completely renovated in 2006 according to the design of architect László Sáros, a Ybl Miklos (architectural) Award winner. The huge square is a lovely area with places to sit and relax by the peaceful fountain, and glass flooring that looks down into the most important museum in the city. The square was an important commerce center way back to the Middle Ages. The dominant building on the square now is **White Friar's Church** ★★ at Március 15 tér 24. It was built in the 18th century, in baroque-rococo style, but the inside is highly decorated in bright colors. However, the statues are white. What makes this church extra special is what was found underneath it. In 1995, when doing reconstruction work, workers found a secret crypt with several mummies inside. Final excavations found that walling up the entrance created an ideal climate to maintain the integrity of 262 coffins and their inhabitants. The exhibition is available to view at the **Memento Mori** ★★★ (© **27/500-750**) in the cellar of the house at Március 15 tér 19. The museum is open Tuesday through Sunday 10am to 6pm, but closed in the winter. Admission is 700 Ft ($3.75/£2), 350 Ft ($1.75/£1) for students with an ID. On the side of the church is a statue of **St. Hedwig** with a three-stage fountain at her feet. St. Hedwig is the patron saint of the Danube and Vác is at the heart of it. St. Hedwig was born in 1373, the third and youngest daughter of the Hungarian-Polish king Louis the Great. She had a passion for helping the poor, the ill, the orphaned, and the widowed.

As you approach Március 15 tér 20, you will see the medieval building was once a private residence, renovated in baroque style and from 1170 operated as a hotel. The front is an eclectic style and from September 2006, the **Wine Museum** was established here. It is open 10am to 5pm Monday through Friday. But what caught my attention was the **Chocloteria** in the same building. Operating as a cafe, it has a large selection of chocolates, pastries, coffees, and teas. It is open Monday through Thursday 9am to 8:30pm, Friday through Saturday 9am to 9:30pm, and Sunday 10am to 8:30pm. The building also houses a public gallery free to the public. Outside is the **Bell Pavilion** with a glockenspiel that plays every hour.

Walking down the square first you will come to **City Hall** located at Március 15 tér 11, considered the nicest baroque building in Vác. Above the front door is a wrought iron balcony. On the frontage is a coat of arms of the town. Three statues sit above this with the Greek goddess of Justice in the center with two reclining women on either side; one holds the nation while the other holds the family crest of an important family. Strolling farther you will see the **Hospital of Mercy** and the **Greek Catholic Chapel** at Március 15 tér 7–9. The small chapel is worth a peek. Although you cannot enter it, you can view it through the glass windows. Next at Március 15 tér 6, you will find the **András Chazár Education Institute for Deaf-Mutes.** This was the first school of its kind in Hungary, established in 1802. Before that, the building housed a bishopric palace, a school for religious orders, a cloister, and then a girls' school. Across from this you will find the former **Palace of the Great Provost** at Március 15 tér 4, a medieval house that was rebuilt in baroque style in the second half of the 18th century. The front is decorated with ionic offsets, and a triangular frontal piece at the top. It houses the clerical art collection of the former owner. If you continue down the square you will come to the **Vienna Town Gate,** a modern stone structure closing off the square.

Leave the square to find other treasures in this little town. The **Triumphal Arch** ★★, the oldest baroque arch in Europe outside of France sits at Köztáraság utca.

The **Cathedral of the Assumption** on Konstantin tér has an elegant facade designed by Isidore Canevale. It is the only building in Hungary that was inspired by Parisian revolutionary architecture. The interior is decorated with the paintings of F. A. Maulbertsch. At Géza Király tér is the **Franciscan or "Brown" Church,** which sits next to the castle, the oldest building in Vác, which faces the Danube waterfront park. The synagogue on Eötvös utca is a special building in the town. It was built by Abbis Cacciari an Italian architect, in 1864 in romantic style. It was renovated in 2006.

A walk along the Danube will be a delightful peaceful time. The entire riverside is lined with trees and an extremely wide promenade; it boasts separate winding walking paths intertwined with resting areas, all along the side of sidewalks next to the street for a different stroll under the chestnut trees. Garden patches are dotted here and there where the flowers add color and beauty to the large boulevard. For children, there are a number of play areas that include swings and playhouses, where they can work off extra energy.

WHERE TO DINE

Nosztalgia Cukrászda ★ Located right on the square, this is a nice place to people-watch or relax at a table by the fountain in good weather. The selection of desserts is mouth-watering, though the waitresses are not the friendliest. Inside is decorated like an old-fashioned cafe with old pictures on walls with flocked wallpaper. Sit outside if possible.

Széchenyi u. 2. ⓒ **27/313–539.** Pastries 300 Ft–600 Ft ($1.60–$3.25/£0.85–£1.70). No credit cards. Mon–Sat 8am–5pm.

Vácz Remete Pince ★★★ HUNGARIAN CONTEMPORARY On a warm sunny autumn day, my friend and I sat on the terrace outside of this restaurant next to the hill-sloped garden filled with flowers. The menu was plentiful with choices and the food was creatively presented in a beautiful manner. Many Budapest restaurants could take a lesson. Be warned though that the portions are huge. We ordered side salad to share and could barely finish it with the entrees presented to us. Peeking inside, the two large rooms are decorated in dark wood furniture, with artificial greenery around the arched doorways, giving them a cozy, homey feel.

Fürdő lépcső 3. ⓒ **27/302-199.** Reservations recommended in summer. Main courses 1,290 Ft–2,490 Ft ($7–$14/£3.75–£7). MC, V. Daily noon–10pm.

4 Visegrád ★

45km (28 miles) NW of Budapest

Halfway between Szentendre and Esztergom, Visegrád (pronounced *Vee*-sheh-grod) is a sparsely populated, sleepy riverside village, which makes its history all the more fascinating and hard to believe. The Romans built a fort here, which was still standing when Slovak settlers gave the town its present name in the 9th or 10th century. It means "High Castle." After the Mongol invasion (1241–42), construction began on both the present ruined hilltop citadel and the former riverside palace. Eventually, Visegrád boasted one of the finest royal palaces ever built in Hungary. Only one king, Charles Robert (1307–42), actually used it as his primary residence, but monarchs from Béla IV in the 13th century through Matthias Corvinus in the late 15th century

---

Kids An Annual Festival

Each summer on the second weekend in July, Visegrád hosts the **International Palace Tournament** ⋆⋆, an authentic medieval festival replete with dueling knights on horseback, medieval music, and dance. If you cannot make it to this fabulous event, you can enjoy a tournament on a smaller scale combined with a medieval dinner at 6pm on Thursday in July and August. For more information, contact Visegrád Tours at ✆ **26/398-160.**

---

spent time in Visegrád and contributed to its development. Corvinus expanded the palace into a great Renaissance center known throughout Europe.

ESSENTIALS

For information on getting to **Visegrád,** see "Railing through the Danube Bend," earlier in this chapter. **Visegrád Tours,** RÉV u. 15 (✆ **26/398-160**), is located across the road from the RÉV ferryboat landing. It is open daily 8am to 5:30pm; from November through March, but conduct business from the associated hotel next door.

WHERE TO STAY

Good accommodations can be found at **Honti Panzió and Hotel,** Fő utca 66 (✆ **26/398-120;** www.hotels.hu/honti). Double rooms run 11,000 Ft to 12,000 Ft ($60–$65/ £31–£34) for the *panzio* and 13,000 Ft to 15,000 Ft ($70–$81/£37–£43) in the hotel. All rates include breakfast and VAT, but a 300 Ft ($1.60/85p) tax per person per night is not; parking is provided.

EXPLORING THE PALACE & THE CITADEL

Once covering much of the area where the boat landing and Fő utca (Main St.) are now found, the ruins of the Royal Palace and the Salamon Tower are all that remain today for visitors to explore. The entrance to the open-air ruins, the **King Matthias Museum** ⋆⋆, is at Fő u. 27 (✆ **26/398-026**). Admission is free. The museum is open Tuesday to Sunday from 9am to 5pm. The buried ruins of the palace, having achieved a near-mythical status, were not discovered until the 21st century. The Salamon Tower is open Tuesday to Sunday from 9am to 5pm, May through September.

The **Cloud Castle (Fellegvár)** ⋆⋆⋆ (✆ **26/398-101**), a mountaintop citadel above Visegrád, affords one of the finest views you'll find over the Danube. Admission to the citadel is 800 Ft ($4.30/£2.25). It is open daily from 9:30am to 5:30pm. The "City Bus," a van taxi that awaits passengers outside Visegrád Tours, takes people up the steep hill for a steep fare of 2,000 Ft ($11/£5.70) apiece for the ride up. If you stay less than 30 minutes, you can ride down again for 1,000 Ft ($5.40/£2.85), otherwise, it is again 2,000 Ft ($11/£5.70). Note that it is not a casual walk to the citadel; consider it a day hike and pack accordingly with bottled water.

WHERE TO DINE

Nagyvillám Vadászcsárda (Big Lightning Hunter's Inn) HUNGARIAN   This restaurant is set on a hilltop featuring one of the finest views of the Danube bend, Fekete-hegy, infusing a leafy, countryside dinner with an elegant and warm atmosphere. Although vegetarians may struggle with a menu comprised mainly of meat and game dishes, it is nevertheless an extensive menu combining Mediterranean influences with

Hungarian recipes using 12 varieties of wild forest mushrooms. If you can, reserve a window table to maximize the glorious view and make this a unique dining experience.

Fekete-hegy ⓒ **26/398-070.** Main courses 1,700 Ft–4,500 Ft ($9.50–$24/£4.75–£13). MC, V. Daily noon–11pm.

Renaissance Restaurant *Kids* HUNGARIAN   This restaurant specializes in authentic medieval cuisine. Food is served in clay crockery without silverware, only a wooden spoon. Guests are offered Burger King–like paper crowns to wear. The decor and the lyre music enhance the fun, albeit openly kitschy atmosphere. This is perhaps the only restaurant in the whole country where you won't find something on the menu spiced with paprika, since the spice wasn't around in medieval Hungary. If you're big on the medieval theme, come for dinner on a Thursday (July–Aug), when a six-course "Royal Feast" (not so vegetarian-friendly) is served following a 45-minute duel between knights. It is available for groups of not less than 30 people. However, if you call, they will include you in a group if one is scheduled. It's open daily, from noon to 10pm. Tickets for this special evening are handled by Visegrád Tours (p. 250). The duel gets underway at 6pm sharp.

Fő u. 11 (across the street from the MAHART boat landing). ⓒ **26/398-081.** Set menu 4,500 Ft ($24/£13). V. Daily noon–10pm.

5 Esztergom

46km (29 miles) NW of Budapest

Formerly a Roman settlement, **Esztergom** (pronounced *Ess*-tair-gome), 46km (29 miles) northwest of Budapest, was the seat of the Hungarian kingdom for 300 years. Hungary's first king, István I (Stephen I) renamed from Vajk by German priests, received the crown from the pope in A.D. 1000. He converted Hungary to Catholicism, and Esztergom became the country's center of the early church. Although its glory days are long gone due to invasions from the Mongols and later the Turks, it was rebuilt once again in the 18th and 19th centuries. This quiet town remains the seat of the archbishop primate, known as the "Hungarian Rome."

From Esztergom west all the way to the Austrian border, the Danube marks the border between Hungary and Slovakia. There's an international ferry crossing at Esztergom. There is not much to entice anyone to stay overnight with Budapest so close by, so I strongly recommend making this a day trip returning to Budapest at the end of the day.

ESSENTIALS

Gran Tours, Széchenyi tér 25 (ⓒ **33/502-001**), is the best source of information. Summer hours are from Monday to Friday 8am to 4pm and Saturday 9am to noon; winter hours are from Monday to Friday 8am to 4pm. The station is on the outskirts of town, while the tourist info center is in the city center. Take bus no. 1 or 6 to Széchenyi tér. Local buses depart from outside the train station.

EXPLORING THE TOWN

Castle Museum   This museum is next door to the cathedral, in the reconstructed Royal Palace. The palace, vacated by Hungarian royalty in the 13th century, was used thereafter by the archbishop. Though it was one of only two fortresses in Hungary that was able to withstand the Mongol onslaught in 1241 and 1242, it fell into disrepair under the Turkish occupation. The museum has an extensive collection of weapons, coins, pottery, stove tiles, and fragments of old stone columns; unfortunately, the descriptions are in Hungarian only. Outside the palace, sections of the fortified walls have been reconstructed.

Szent István tér. ⓒ **33/415-986.** Admission 350 Ft ($2/£1.05); special exhibits 350 Ft–500 Ft ($1.60–$2.25/ 85p–£1.20). Summer Tues–Sun 10am–6pm; winter Tues–Sun 9am–5pm.

Esztergom Cathedral ⟨ꞏ⟩ *Kids*   This massive, neoclassical cathedral on Szent István tér on Castle Hill, is the largest church in Hungary. It is Esztergom's most popular attraction and one of Hungary's most impressive buildings. Built in the last century, it was to replace the cathedral ruined during the Turkish occupation. The blue and red marble coloring in the church and chapel is stunning. It claims the world's largest altarpiece painted on one continuous piece of canvas. The crypt, built in old Egyptian style with a magnificent statue of an angel, is also the last resting place of bishops. The cathedral **treasury** *(kincstár)* ⟨ꞏ⟩ contains a stunning array of ecclesiastical jewels and gold works. If you brave the ascent of the cupola, you're rewarded at the top with unparalleled views of Esztergom and the surrounding Hungarian and Slovakian countryside. To get here, take bus 6 from the train station and get off at the cathedral or in good weather, it is a nice walk. If you happen to be in town during the first week of August, don't miss out on one of the classical guitar concerts performed in the cathedral. The acoustics are sublime. The concerts are part of Esztergom's annual **International Guitar Festival** ⟨ꞏ⟩⟨ꞏ⟩.

Szent István tér. ⓒ **33/411-895.** Cathedral admission free; treasury 350 Ft ($2/£1); cupola 250 Ft ($1.25/75p); crypt 100 Ft (55¢/30p). Cathedral summer daily 8am–7pm, winter daily 8am–4pm; treasury and crypt summer daily 9am–4pm, winter Tues–Sun noon–4pm, cupola summer daily 9am–4pm, closed in winter.

Keresztény Múzeum (Christian Museum)   This museum, in the neoclassical former primate's palace, houses Hungary's largest collection of religious art and the largest collection of medieval art outside the National Gallery in Budapest. The Lord's Coffin of Garamszentbenedek is probably the museum's most famous piece; the ornately carved, gilded coffin on wheels was originally used in Easter celebrations.

To get to the museum, continue past the Watertown Parish Church on Berényi Zsigmond utca. Even if you don't plan on visiting this museum, it's definitely worth it to take a break from the crowds at the cathedral and take a stroll through the quiet, cobblestone streets of Esztergom's Víziváros (Watertown).

Mindszenty tér 2. ⓒ **33/413-880.** www.keresztenymuzeum.hu. Admission 600 Ft ($3.25/£1.75) adults; 300 Ft ($1.50/75p) children. Mid-March to Oct 28 10am–6pm; Oct 30–Jan 1 11am–3pm. Closed all other dates.

WHERE TO DINE

Anonim Vendéglő HUNGARIAN   National specialties abound at this intimate restaurant housed in an ancient monument near the Basilica. Well-prepared meat dishes coupled with outstanding vegetarian dishes are combined with attentive service.

Berényi u. 4. ⓒ **33/411-880.** Main courses 1,200 Ft–3,000 Ft ($6.50–$16/£3.50–£8.50). No credit cards. Tues–Sun noon–midnight.

Szalma Csárda ⟨ꞏ⟩⟨ꞏ⟩⟨ꞏ⟩   The food at this remodeled and enlarged restaurant is absolutely first-rate, with everything made to order and served piping hot. The excellent house soups—fish soup *(halászlé)*, goulash *(gulyásleves)*, and bean soup *(babgulyás)* are all large enough to constitute meals in themselves. For main courses, the stuffed cabbage *(töltött káposzta)* and the stuffed pepper *(töltött paprika)* are both outstanding, though not always offered. Finish off your meal with a dish of sweet chestnut purée *(gesztenyepüré)*, a Hungarian specialty prepared here to perfection. There are outdoor tables as well as seating in two dining rooms.

Nagy-Duna sétány 2. ⓒ **33/315-336.** Main courses 950 Ft–9,000 Ft ($5.25–$49/£2.75–£26). No credit cards. Daily 11am–10pm.

12

The Lake Balaton Region

First settled in the Iron Age, the Balaton region has been a recreation spot since at least Roman times. From the 18th century onward, the upper classes erected spas and villas along the shoreline. Not until the post–World War II communist era did the lake open up to a wider tourist base. Many large hotels along the lake are former trade union resorts built under the previous regime.

Lake Balaton may not be the Mediterranean, but it is the largest freshwater lake in Europe. For many years, it has attracted German and British tourists in droves as well as other Europeans, but in smaller numbers, who filled the lake's beaches to worship the sun. In the past few years, though, the love affair has faded, and the beaches of Croatia are now considered the best choice for water resorts. Hungary has instituted a fierce marketing campaign to redevelop the lake's regional favor with tourists, since many of the small towns depend on tourism for their survival. One company is developing a large water sports center, a three-star hotel, and a wellness center in **Balatonfenyves** scheduled to be completed sometime in 2008.

Hungarians naturally are proud of their resort and will defend this spot as one of the best in Europe; many city dwellers own summer homes there. With that said, there are still many other places to see and enjoy, even if you are not a sun and water person. We do caution you to check the health of the lake's waters near the time of your planned trip. Some years, the water level has been too low to support the many water sports it has become famous for and at other times, there have been outbreaks of algae covering the water's surface in many tourist areas.

In the best of times, throughout the long summer, swimmers, windsurfers, sailboats, kayaks, and cruisers fill the warm and silky smooth lake. It is 80km (50 miles) long and 15km (9 miles) wide at its broadest stretch. Around the lake's 197km (122 miles) of shoreline, vacationers cast their reels for pike; play tennis, soccer, and volleyball; ride horses; and hike in the hills.

On the south shore, Siófok was established as a resort in 1891. It is considered to be one of the most important tourist centers in the region, and it is frequented mostly by the youthful generation or those who love to party. Beachside hotels overflow all summer long with youthful party people playing disco music that pulsates into the early morning hours. My students have warned me about having people stop here if they are post-college age. Even for some of them, it is too rowdy to be enjoyable. The most popular venue is the Coca–Cola House where there is nonstop music and dancing until dawn, making it the popular choice for the party animal who really doesn't care about the water adventures. According to my students, Budapest youth take the train to **Siófok,** party until the very wee hours, and then return to Budapest the first train the next morning.

On a positive note, the town itself has an open-air exhibition with sculptures and monuments on public squares including the work of the contemporary Hungarian sculptor, Imre Varga who was born here.

For those of us who are post college and post party until the morning light, and families, the better choice may be the graceful north shore, and it's the region we cover in this section. *Note:* Here and there you will find little villages neatly tucked away in the rolling countryside, where the grapes of the popular Balaton wines ripen in the strong sun. Due to the needs of tourism, the area is becoming more and more commercialized with the small food vendors being pushed aside by modern restaurants.

The best way to see the area is to move westward along the coast, passing from one lakeside settlement to the next, and making the occasional forays inland into the rolling hills of the Balaton wine country.

You'll discover the **Tihany Peninsula,** a protected area whose 12 sq. km (4¾ sq. miles) jut out into the lake like a knob. The city of **Keszthely,** sitting at the lake's western edge, marks the end of the northern shore area.

An annual cultural event called the Valley of Arts is held on the northern side of the lake, near **Kapolcs,** attracting thousands of local and international artists and travelers. It was started as a local project by a handful of Hungarian contemporary artists who settled down in Kapolcs, the center of six little adjacent villages in the gorgeous Káli valley. The 10-day-long arts event includes film, music, theater, visual art exhibits, and literature readings, and is held at the end of July, running through the beginning of August. Visit www.kapolcs.hu for information on exact dates from year to year. For general information on programs and services of just about any area of Balaton, see www.balaton-tourism.hu.

1 Exploring the Lake Balaton Region

GETTING THERE & GETTING AROUND

BY TRAIN   From Budapest, trains to the various towns along the lake depart from Déli Station. A few express trains run from Keleti Station and hook around the southern shore to Keszthely only. All towns on the lake are within 1½ to 4 hours of Budapest by a *gyors* (fast) train, though the trip will take much longer on a *sebes* (local). The *sebes* trains are interminably slow, stopping at each village along the lake. Unless you're going to one of these little villages (sometimes a good idea, though we cover only the major towns in this section), try to get on a *gyors*.

BY CAR   From Budapest, take the M7 motorway south through Székesfehérvár until you hit the lake. Route 71 circles the lake.

If you're planning to visit Lake Balaton for more than a day or two, you should consider renting a car, which will give you much greater mobility. The various towns differ enough from one another that you may want to keep driving until you find a place that really sparks your interest. Without a car, this is obviously more difficult. Also, wherever you go in the region, you'll find that private rooms are both cheaper and easier to get if you travel a few miles off the lake. Driving directly to the lake from Budapest will take approximately an hour and 30 minutes depending on where along the lake you start out and of course traffic. During the summer season, traffic can be congested.

BY BOAT & FERRY   Passenger boats on Lake Balaton let you travel across the lake as well as between towns on the same shore. The boat routes are extensive, and the rates are cheap, but the boats are considerably slower than surface transportation. All major towns have docks with departures and arrivals. Children 3 and under travel free, and those 13 and under get half-price tickets. A single ferry *(komp)* running between Tihany and Szántód lets you transport a car across the width of the lake.

All boat and ferry information is available from the **BAHART** office in Siófok (*©* **84/310-050** or 84/312-144). Local tourist offices all along the lake (several listed below) also have schedules and other information.

BY BUS   Once at the lake, you might find that buses are the best way of getting around locally. Buses will be indispensable, of course, if you take private-room lodging a few miles away from the lake.

WHERE TO STAY IN THE AREA

Because hotel prices are unusually high (especially for Hungary) in the Balaton region, and because many local families rent out a room or two in summer, I especially recommend **private rooms** as the lodging of choice in this area. Most are clean and will give you the opportunity to get to know the local population. You can reserve a room through a local tourist office (addresses are listed below under each town) or you can just look for the ever-present SZOBA KIADÓ (OR ZIMMER FREI) signs hanging on most front gates in the region. When you take a room without using a tourist agency as the intermediary, prices are generally negotiable. In the height of the season, you shouldn't have to pay more than 8,000 Ft ($43/£23) for a double room within reasonable proximity of the lake.

Many budget travelers pitch their tents in **lakeside campgrounds** all around the lake. Campgrounds are generally quite inexpensive, and their locations are well marked on maps. All the campgrounds have working facilities, but are probably not as clean as many people are accustomed to.

2 En Route to Lake Balaton: Veszprém ⭐/⭐

116km (72 miles) SW of Budapest

Just 16km (10 miles) from Lake Balaton, **Veszprém** (pronounced *Vess*-praym) surely ranks as one of Hungary's most charming and vibrant small cities, and it's the ideal starting point for a rail tour of Lake Balaton's northern shore. History and modern living are delightfully combined in this little city. The self-contained and well-preserved 18th-century baroque Castle District spills effortlessly into a typically modern city center, distinguished by lively wide-open, pedestrian-only plazas.

The history of Veszprém, like the scenic Bakony countryside that surrounds it, is full of peaks and valleys. According to local legend, Veszprém was founded on seven hills, like Rome. The seven hills are: Várhegy (Castle Hill), Benedek-hegy (St. Benedict Hill), Jeruzsálem-hegy (Jerusalem Hill), Temet_hegy (Cemetery Hill), Gulyadomb (Herd Hill), Kálvária-domb (Calvary Hill), and Cserhát (no translation).

King Stephen I defeated the armies of his chief opponent, Koppány, near Veszprém in an effort to make Hungary a Christian nation. Hence, Veszprém became the seat of the first Episcopal See in 1009. This was the favorite city of King Stephen's queen, Gizella. The city is often called the City of Queens. It was completely destroyed during the course of the long Turkish occupation, the Habsburg-Turkish battles, and the subsequent Hungarian-Austrian independence skirmishes. The reconstruction of Veszprém commenced in the early 18th century, though the castle itself, blown up by the Austrians in 1702, was never rebuilt. The baroque character of that era today attracts thousands of visitors who pass through each year.

Lake Balaton Region

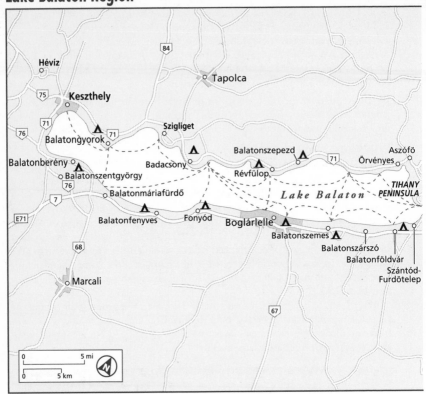

ESSENTIALS

GETTING THERE   Seventeen trains depart Budapest's Déli Station daily for Veszprém with some taking as little as 1 hour and 45 minutes on one of the two IC trains. (It's a 2½ hr. trip if you take a regular train.) Tickets cost 2,160 Ft ($12/£6.15) for an IC train including the supplement, while on other trains the fare is 1,770 Ft ($9.55/£5.05) and the trip is longer. If you're **driving** take the M7 to the lake, then take Route 71 to Route 72 leading into the city.

VISITOR INFORMATION   **Tourinform,** Vár u. 4 (© **88/404-548**), is open in summer weekdays from 9am to 6pm and weekends 10am to 4pm; in winter, weekdays 9am to 5pm, and closed weekends. **Ibusz,** Rákoczi u. 6 (© **88/565-540**), is open Monday through Friday from 8:30am to 4:30pm. Both offices provide information, sell city maps, and help with hotel and private-room bookings.

EXPLORING THE CITY

Most of Veszprém's main sights are clustered along Vár utca, the street that runs the length of the city's small, but lovely Castle District.

Housed inside the 18th-century canon's house, the **Queen Gizella Museum,** Vár u. 35, has a fine collection of religious (Roman Catholic) art. Admission is 300 Ft

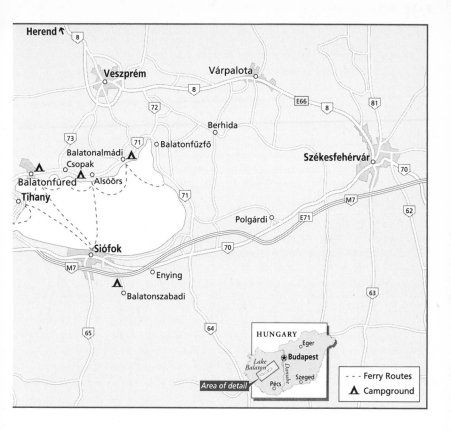

Map showing the Lake Balaton region of Hungary, with locations including Herend, Veszprém, Várpalota, Berhida, Balatonalmádi, Csopak, Balatonfűzfő, Székesfehérvár, Balatonfüred, Alsóörs, Tihany, Polgárdi, Siófok, Enying, Balatonszabadi. Highways marked include 8, 72, 73, 71, E66, 81, 70, M7, 62, E71, 63, 64, 65. Inset map of HUNGARY showing Eger, Budapest, Lake Balaton, Danube, Pécs, Szeged, with "Area of detail." Legend: Ferry Routes (dashed line), Campground (triangle).

($1.60/85p) for adults, and 150 Ft (80¢/45p) for students. It is open daily from 10am to 5pm, May 1 through October 15.

At Vár u. 16, the vaulted **Gizella Chapel,** named for King Stephen's wife, was unearthed during the construction of the adjoining Bishop's Palace in the 18th century. Today, it houses a modest collection of ecclesiastical art, but is best known for the 13th-century frescoes that, in various states of restoration, decorate its walls. Admission is 200 Ft ($1.10/55p) for adults, 100 Ft (55¢/30p) for students. It is open Tuesday through Sunday 10am to 5pm from May 2 through October 15.

For a wonderful view of the surrounding Bakony region, climb the steps to the narrow observation deck at the top of the **Fire Tower** at Óváros tér. Though the foundations of the tower are medieval, the structure itself was built in the early 19th century. Enter via the courtyard of Vár u. 9, behind Óváros tér. Admission is 300 Ft ($1.60/85p) for adults, 250 Ft ($1.35/70p) for students. It is open daily from 10am to 6pm, March 15 through September 30.

In addition to Roman relics uncovered in the surrounding area, the **Laczkó Dezső Museum** (© 88/564-310), near Megyeház tér, features local folk exhibits (art, costumes, tools, utensils, and so on). There are also exhibits about the legendary highwaymen of the region, celebrated figures from 19th-century Bakony who share some characteristics with the legendary outlaws of the American West. Admission is 670 Ft

Herend: Home of Hungary's Finest Porcelain

About 16km (10 miles) west of Veszprém lies the sleepy village of Herend. What distinguishes this village from other villages in the area is the presence of the Herend porcelain factory, where Hungary's finest porcelain has been made since 1826.

Herend porcelain began to establish its international reputation as far back as 1851, when a dinner set was displayed at the Great Exhibition in London. Artists hand paint every piece, from tableware to decorative accessories. Patterns include delicate flowers, butterflies, and birds.

The **Porcelanium Visitors Center** features the newly expanded **Herend Museum** (© 8/826-1801; www.museum.herend.com), which displays a dazzling collection of Herend porcelain. It is open daily from April to October, 9am to 4:30pm and Tuesday through Saturday from November to March, 9:30am to 3:30pm. Admission is 1,500 Ft ($8.10/£4.25) for adults and 500 Ft ($2.70/£1.40) for students. The Porcelanium Visitors Center also has a coffeehouse and upscale restaurant. Food is, naturally, served on Herend china.

At the **factory store** (© 8/852-3223), you might find patterns that are unavailable in Budapest's Herend Shop. The factory store is open October to May, Monday through Friday, 9:30am to 4pm and Saturday 9:30am to 2:00pm. In summer, it's open Monday through Friday 9:30am to 6pm and Saturday and Sunday 9:30am to 4pm. Herend is easily accessible via bus from the Veszprém bus station—the destination "Herend" should be indicated on the front of the bus you want. The ride takes 15 minutes and costs 300 Ft ($1.60/85p); the bus leaves every 15 minutes.

($3.60/£1.90) for adults and 340 Ft ($1.83/96p) for children. From mid-March through October 14, it is open 10am to 6pm, otherwise noon to 4pm. To get to the museum, walk directly south from Szabadság tér, where the old and new towns converge.

The **Veszprém Zoo (Kittenberger Kálmán Növény és Vadaspark)** is located at Kittenberger u. 15 (© **88/566-140**). It's open daily in summer 9am to 6pm until September 30, and in winter daily from 9am to 4pm until the end of February. Admission is 1,100 Ft ($5.95/£3.15) for adults, 750 Ft ($4.05/£2.15) for children. The zoo is set in a small wooded valley at the edge of the city center and boasts 550 animals from 130 species.

WHERE TO STAY

You'll pay some 2,500 Ft ($13/£6.85) for a double room in a private home in Veszprém, and you can find a list of accommodations at www.veszpreminfo.hu. The room price usually does not include breakfast. You can book a private room through either of the tourist offices mentioned on p. 11.

Péter-Pál Panzió ⭐⭐ (© 8/832-8091; www.hotels.hu/peter_pal_panzio), is conveniently located on Dózsa György u. 3; it's a 5-minute walk from the center of town. Don't be put off by the grungy building facade. Inside are 12 tidy but very small rooms, all with twin beds, a shower-only bathroom, and a TV. Insist on a room in the rear of the building, as the pension sits close to the busy road. The rates is 8,900 ($48/£25) for a double. Breakfast is included and is served in the garden in summer. Call ahead for reservations.

Hotel Villa Medici ★★ (©/fax **8/859-0070;** www.villamedici.hu), at Kittenberger u. 11, is a modern, full-service hotel set in a small gorge on the edge of the city, next to Veszprém's zoo-park. There are 24 double rooms and two suites; each has a bathroom with shower and the usual hotel amenities. Rates are 24,300 Ft ($131/£69) for a double room and 32,900 Ft ($178/£94) for a suite. Breakfast is included. The hotel also features a sauna, a small indoor swimming pool, and a salon. Check the website for package deals. The reception staff speaks English and will make tour arrangements for you. Major credit cards are accepted. Take bus no. 4 from the train station to the stop in front of Veszprém Hotel, and then change to bus no. 3, 5, or 10. These buses will take you as far as the bridge overlooking the gorge. You can walk from there.

WHERE TO DINE

Veszprém does not have many dining options, but you should be able to find a satisfying meal at the following places:

Cserhát Étterem ★ (© **8/842-5441**), housed in the huge structure at Kossuth u. 6, is an old-style *önkiszólgáló* (self-service cafeteria). You'll find this very popular cafeteria behind some clothing stores; go up the winding staircase inside the building. Hearty traditional meals are available for less than 500 Ft ($2.70/£1.40). The menu changes daily; it's posted on a bulletin board on the wall inside the restaurant upstairs. It is open Monday through Friday from 10am to 6pm and Saturday 10am to 3pm.

For something more upscale, **Villa Medici Étterem** (owned by the same people who own the hotel), at Kittenberger u. 11 (© **8/859-0072**), is *the* place. It's expensive for Hungary but worth it. Main courses here are between 3,250 Ft and 5,200 Ft ($18–$28/£9.25–£15). Villa Medici serves Hungarian/continental cuisine daily from noon to 11pm.

3 Keszthely ★★

187km (117 miles) SW of Budapest

KESZTHELY

Keszthely (pronounced *Kest*-hay), which sits at the western edge of Lake Balaton, is one of the largest towns on the lake, and is easily reached by rail from both Budapest and other lake towns. Though Keszthely was largely destroyed during the Turkish wars, the town was rebuilt in the 18th century by the Festetics family, an aristocratic family that made Keszthely their home during World War II. The town's main sites all date from the days of the wealthy Festetics clan.

GETTING THERE   Eleven daily trains depart Budapest's Déli Station and six from Keletin Station for Keszthely; five intercity trains also make the journey each week. If the only city you plan to visit on Lake Balaton is Keszthely, take the IC. They are no longer as quick as in the past, but they are air-conditioned and cleaner (trip time: 3½ hrs.). A reserved seat is required. The trip costs 3,420 Ft to 4,420 Ft ($19–$24/£9.70–£13), depending on time of day. Other trains take about 4 hours and 10 minutes.

If you're heading to Keszthely Station out of Szigliget, you can hop on any of the eight daily trains in normal hours or others in the wee hours. Make sure, however, to consult a timetable before leaving, as there's no direct service and where you choose to transfer can seriously affect your journey time from a very reasonable 47 minutes to a ridiculous 2 hours and 20 minutes. Tickets run 525 Ft ($2.85/£1.50).

The train station is on the southeastern edge of the town, but it's a scenic walk that takes about 10 minutes. You can also take a taxi from the main square to the station for about 800 Ft ($4.30/£2.25).

VISITOR INFORMATION   For information, stop in at **Tourinform,** at Kossuth u. 28 (©/fax **8/331-4144;** www.keszthely.hu), in the city's former town hall. From the train station, walk up Mártírok utca and then turn right onto Kossuth utca and walk north until you get to the city's Main Square. It's open Monday through Friday from 9am to 5pm and Saturday and Sunday in high season only from 9am to 1pm.

TOP ATTRACTIONS & SPECIAL MOMENTS

The highlight of a visit to Keszthely is the splendid **Festetics Mansion** ⨉, at Szabadság u. 1 (© **8/331-2190** or 83/312-191), in the center of the city, a short walk north of the Tourinform office. The baroque 18th-century mansion (with 19th-century additions) was the home of generations of the Festetics family. Part of the mansion (16 rooms in total) is now open as a museum. The main attraction is the ornate **Helikon library,** which features magnificent floor-to-ceiling oak bookcases, which were hand carved by a local master, János Kerbl. The museum also features hunting gear and trophies of a bygone era. The museum is open July and August daily 9am to 6pm; the rest of the year it is open Tuesday through Sunday from 10am to 5pm. Admission is 1,300 Ft ($7/£3.70) for foreigners, and 700 Ft ($3.80/£2.00) for students.

The mansion's lovely concert hall, the Mirror Gallery, is the site of **classical music concerts** almost every night throughout the summer (just two or three times a month Sept–May). Concerts usually start at 8pm; tickets, ranging all the way from 1,000 Ft to 5,000 Ft ($5.40–$27/£2.85–£14) apiece, are available at the door or earlier in the day at the museum cashier.

Another Keszthely museum worth a visit is the **Balaton Museum** ⨉, on the opposite side of the town center from the Festetics Mansion, at Múzeum u. 2 (© **8/331-2351;** www.museum.hu). This museum features exhibits on the geological, archaeological, and natural history of the Balaton region. It's open from May through October Tuesday through Sunday from 10am to 6pm and November through April, Tuesday through Saturday from 9am to 5pm. Admission is 340 Ft ($1.85/95p), and students pay 170 Ft (90¢/50p).

Located down the hill from Fő tér (Main Sq.), off Bem utca, is Keszthely's **open-air market.** The major selling days are Wednesday and Saturday. While dawn to 1pm, is the busiest time, some vendors stay open into the later afternoon. You'll find fruit and vegetables, spices, preserves, and honey, as well as household appliances, handmade baskets, and children's clothing.

WHERE TO STAY & DINE

The center of Keszthely's summer scene, just like that of every other settlement on Lake Balaton, is down by the water on the "strand." Keszthely's **beachfront** is dominated by several large hotels. Regardless of whether or not you're a guest, you can rent windsurfers, boats, and other water-related equipment from these hotels.

A good hotel bet is the 232-room **Danubius Hotel Helikon** (© **8/388-9600;** www.danubiusgroup.com). The small but comfortable guest rooms offer balconies overlooking Lake Balaton and have all the necessary amenities. The resort also has an indoor swimming pool, sauna, massage parlor, and outdoor sun deck. Rates run from 17,000 Ft to 30,000 Ft ($92–$162/£48–£85) for a double, including breakfast. Numerous special packages and off-season rates are available.

Oázis Reform Restaurant, at Rákóczi tér 3 (© 8/331-1023), is a self-service salad bar featuring adequate (if uninspired) vegetarian fare. There are cold and hot options and you can combine any salads you want. Go at lunchtime, when the food is freshest. Oázis is open Monday through Friday, 10am to 4pm. All food items cost 2,000 Ft ($11/£5.70 per kilogram.

4 Badacsony & Szigliget ✶

160km (99 miles) SW of Budapest

BADACSONY

Nestled in one of the most picturesque corners of Lake Balaton is Badacsony, an area which includes four villages noted for their beautiful vistas and some of the best wines of Hungary. The Badacsony area is dotted with wine cellars, and the tradition of viticulture and winegrowing dates back to the Celtic and Roman times. Other than wine tasting, Badacsony boasts walking trails where you can study the diverse basalt forms and the former quarry walls. You'll also find a 4km (2.5-mile) long circular trail, starting from the Kisfaludy House on the southern side of Badacsony Hill. Contact **Botanikai tanösvény Badacsony** (© 87/461-069; www.bfnpi.hu) for guided tours.

One of the better-known vintners in Hungary is Huba Szeremley, whose Badacsony wines have consistently been winners in Italy, France, and Hungary. The best way to find out about Szeremley's regular wine tastings is to visit his restaurant, **Szent Orbán Borház és Étterem,** Badacsonytomaj, Kisfaludy S. u. 5 (© 87/432-382; www.szeremley.com). It is open daily from noon to 10pm.

The **Borbarátok Panzió** ✶✶, Badacsonytomaj, Római út. 78 (© 87/471-000; www.borbaratok.hu), is a family-owned and -operated restaurant and hotel. It serves traditional Hungarian fare and also offers a wide variety of programs including wine tasting, harvest, fishing, and walking tours. During the summer months, different music programs are offered each night of the week. Main courses at the restaurant run from 1,700 Ft to 3,200 Ft ($9.20–$17/£4.85–£9.10). The restaurant is open daily 11:30am to 11pm in high season, and daily 11:30am to 10pm in low season.

SZIGLIGET

Halfway between the Tihany peninsula and Keszthely is the lovely tiny village of Szigliget (pronounced *Sig*-lee-get), a picturesque Hungarian lake village with some magnificent castle ruins and an easy stopover point for rail travelers.

GETTING THERE   Five daily trains leave from Veszprém's rail station that will get you to **Badacsonytördemic-Szigliget Station.** The trip can take as little as 2¾ hours or as much as 4½ hours depending on the train you catch and how many connections you need to make (there is no direct train service). Intercity trains (you must make a reservation!) are available for at least part of the route, but, in this case, won't get you to Szigliget any faster than some of the *gyors* trains because you have to make a number of connections.

It is a 20-minute bus ride to Szigliget from the train station. Each arriving train is met by a bus, which stops on the platform right outside the station building. The destination of the buses is Tapolca. You get off the bus at the stop near the beach in the village center (the village itself is tiny and easily traversed on foot).

VISITOR INFORMATION   **Natur Tourist** (© 8/334-6063), in the village center, is open daily from April 15 to September 15 only, 9:30am to 6pm and can help book private rooms. There are also ZIMMER FREI signs along the roads.

Kids   **An Excursion to the Thermal Lake in Hévíz**

If you think the water of Lake Balaton is warm, just wait until you jump into the lake at **Hévíz** ★★ *Kids* (pronounced *Hay*-veez), a resort town about 8km (5 miles) northwest of Keszthely. Here, you'll find the largest thermal lake in Europe and the second largest in the world (the largest is in New Zealand), covering 16,723sq. m (180,005 sq. ft.).

The lake's water temperature seldom dips below 85°F (29°C), even in the most bitter spell of winter. Consequently, people swim in the lake year-round. Hévíz has been one of Hungary's leading spa resorts for over 100 years, and it retains a distinct 19th-century atmosphere.

While the lakeside area is suitable for ambling, no visit to Hévíz would be complete without a swim. An enclosed causeway leads out into the center of the lake where locker rooms and the requisite services, including massage, float rental, and a *palacsinta* (crepe) bar are housed. **Note:** There is no shallow water in the lake, so take care.

Hévíz is an easy 10 minutes by bus from Keszthely (there's no train service), which costs 200 Ft ($1.10/55p). Buses (labeled "Hévíz") depart every half-hour or so from the bus station adjacent to the train station (conveniently stopping to pick up passengers in front of the church on Fő tér). The entrance to the lake is just opposite the bus station. You'll see a whimsical wooden facade and the words "tó fürdó" (Bathing Lake). Your day ticket costs 2,800 Ft ($15/£8), but less for stays from 3 to 6 hours, and entitles you to a locker; insert the ticket into the slot in the locker and the key will come out of the lock. Keep the ticket until exiting, as the attendant needs to see it to determine how long you've stayed.

TOP ATTRACTION & SPECIAL MOMENTS

Szigliget is marked by the fantastic ruins of the 13th-century **Szigliget Castle,** which stand above the town on **Várhegy (Castle Hill).** In the days of the Turkish invasions, the Hungarian Balaton fleet, protected by the high castle, called Szigliget home. You can hike up to the ruins for a splendid view of the lake and the surrounding countryside; look for the path behind the white 18th-century church, which stands on the highest spot in the village.

If you really enjoy hiking, you might take a local bus from Szigliget (the station is in the village center) to the nondescript nearby village of **Hegymagas,** about 4.8km (3 miles) to the north along the Szigliget-Tapolca bus route. The town's name means Tall Hill, and from here you can hike up **Szent György-hegy (St. George Hill).** This marvelous vineyard-covered hill has several hiking trails, the most strenuous of which goes up and over the rocky summit.

The lively **beach** at Szigliget provides a striking contrast to the quiet village. In summer, buses from neighboring towns drop off hordes of beachgoers. The beach area is crowded with fried-food and beer stands, ice-cream vendors, a swing set, and a volleyball court.

Szigliget is also home to the **Eszterházy Wine Cellar,** the largest wine cellar in the region. After a hike in the hills or a day in the sun, a little wine tasting just might be in order. Natur Tourist (see above) can provide you with the best directions, as getting here can be a bit confusing. Tours of the cellar are offered only for organized groups; others can drop in and sample the wares. It's open Monday through Friday noon to 8pm and Saturday 3 to 10pm. There's no admission charge.

WHERE TO STAY

Szőlőskert Panzió (© 8/746-1264) on Vadrózsa utca, might be the best option for a stay, given its close proximity to the beach, which is just 387m (1,270 ft.) away. Situated on the hillside amid lush terraces of grapes, the pension is open only in summer. A double is 8,500 Ft ($46/£24) and includes breakfast.

SIDE EXCURSION TO SÜMEG

If you are staying in either Keszthely or Hévíz and have lots of time, you may want to take an excursion to the small town of Sümeg, a half-hour drive north of Balaton. The main attraction here is the **Fortress of Sümeg** (© 87/352-598; www.sumegvar.hu). Originally constructed in the 13th century, it was subsequently rebuilt 300 years later. The fortress fended away the Turks, but was set ablaze in the 18th century by the Habsburgs. Today, perched high on the hilltop, the fortress hosts performances that take you to the Middle-Ages, with horse shows, folk dances, and reenactments of knightly tournaments with period weaponry. At the foot of the hill is the **Hotel Kapitány** at Tóth Tivadar u. 19 (© 87/550-166; www.hotelkapitany.hu), a hotel and wellness center which includes saunas, fitness areas, and massage. The complex also includes a Turkish bath, restaurants, and a conference room. Note that the town is also known for F. A. Maulbertsch's beautiful 18th-century frescos, located in the baroque **Church of the Ascension,** at Szent Imre tér.

GETTING THERE   Some local hotels and travel agencies offer day trips to Sümeg, including a medieval dinner and show, for an average of 10,000 Ft ($54/£29).

5 Lake Balaton's Southern Shore

If you're in that youthful energy category of spending long days in the sand and surf and then want to follow it up by spending long nights being the party animal, then the town of Siófok at the southern shore of Lake Balaton is where it is at. After all, a million Hungarian students can't be wrong. Or could they?

Siófok, located at the lake's southeastern end is known as the capital of Lake Balaton; it is also the largest resort town on Lake Balaton. Siófok's railway station was completed in 1863, thus 1863 is considered to be the year of Siófok's birth as a holiday resort, with Budapest now connected by rail to the resort town. In 1865 Siófok, a settlement of not more than 200 houses with 1,500 inhabitants was permitted to attain the status of market-town. As the saying goes, the rest is history. It started to become overrun with holiday-makers during the summer season.

Siófok is the star attraction for the young, active crowd of mostly students and teenagers who flood the town's beaches from sunrise to sunset and then move en masse to the town's discos until the sun rises yet again. Large, modern, expensive hotels line the shore in Siófok and more are being developed. If you are looking for a quiet beach experience, you will not find it here, but you will find windsurfing, tennis, and boating. English will be at a premium. Though many younger Hungarians may speak English to some degree, they are not as tempted to indulge when surrounded by their fellow native speakers. This could be an isolating experience and difficult within the town itself once you leave the hotel.

While this city is no cultural capital, the architecture of some of the older buildings is impressive. Note the old railway station, and the many villas around the Gold Coast (Aranypart). You will also find some important contemporary buildings, notably the Evangelical Church, designed by one of Hungary's most appreciated architects, **Imre Makovecz**—who is known for his use of wood and light in his structures that dot the country. Most of the wood used for the building was imported from Finland.

Siófok has also partaken in the major marketing campaign that includes all of the popular resorts of Lake Balaton. It is trying to bring back the throngs of visitors that have abandoned the lake for rediscovered beaches along Croatia's coastline. Due to the development of tourism, the prices have made this destination less of a bargain. Ironically, Siófok is being rejuvenated by constructing new wellness centers that cater to rejuvenations procedures, and by the allure of the warm-water springs of Hungarian fame. These facilities will be year-round operations in an attempt to stimulate the economy of the region.

For more information on the southern shore, contact the **Tourinform** (℗/fax **84/ 310-117;** www.siofokportal.com) office in Siófok, right below the immense water tower in the center of town. Another site that can help you plan your trip is www.siofok.com.

WHERE TO STAY

Siófok is wall-to-wall with tourists during the summer months, mostly Hungarians. You will find a wide variety of lodging options including large hotels and resorts from the Gold Coast to the east of the center of town, and from the Silver Coast (Ezüstpart) to the west. Additional accommodations can be found on the city's website at www.siofokportal.com.

We recommend pampering yourself at a "wellness center" for a few days. The **Hotel Azúr** ⨳⨳, Vitorlás u. 11 (℗ **84/501-400;** www.hotelazur.hu) is one of the most comfortable, plush, and welcoming hotel and wellness centers in town at the moment, but heavy competition is being built continually. They have 222 air-conditioned rooms, many with balconies. The pools are large, and it has a nice fitness room, sauna, massage club, Finnish saunas, beauty salon, and thermal pools. The whole complex is extremely tasteful. Rates are 140€ ($182/£96) in summer and 88€ ($115/£60) in winter for a double room. Breakfast and all taxes are included.

The **Hotel Residence** ⨳, Erkel Ferenc u. 49 (℗ **84/506-840;** with its 56 rooms also has an extensive list of services, including massages, gyms, baths, and aromatherapy. It is located 150m (492 ft.) from the beach. Rates are 125€ ($163/£86) in summer and 105€ ($137/£72) in winter for a double room with breakfast included. Note that the room rate has a 15% additional fee for Friday and Saturday night during high season. The hotel has a good-size indoor swimming pool, a sauna, a massage club, Finnish saunas, a beauty salon, and thermal pools.

WHERE TO DINE

Try the **Sándor Restaurant** (℗ **84/312-829;** www.sandorrestaurant.hu), on Erkel F. u. 30, popular with locals for large portions of contemporary Hungarian food. If you're looking for more traditional Hungarian fare, in the springtime, with live Gypsy music, try the **Csárdás Restaurant,** at Fő u. 105 (℗ **84/310-642**). The menu contains Hungarian fish and meat dishes, but they also have international and vegetarian options as well.

13

Northeastern Hungary: Traveling into the Hills

Northeast of the Danube Bend is Hungary's hilliest region with the country's highest mountain, Matra Hill rising to 998m (3,274 ft). It also contains the country's smallest village, the place where the first Hungarian language bible was written, and the oldest railway from the 19th century. Here you can visit the preserved medieval village of Hollókő; see remnants of the country's Turkish heritage in Eger, also known for its regional wines and the region of the famous Tokaji aszú wines; and explore the 23km (14-mile) cave system in Aggtelek.

1 Hollókő: A Preserved Palóc Village ★

102km (63 miles) NE of Budapest

The village of Hollókő (pronounced *Ho*-low-koo, meaning raven stone) is one of the most charming spots in Hungary hidden in the Cserhát hills. Legend has it that the lord of a castle kidnapped a beautiful maiden, whose nurse was a witch. The nurse made a pact with the devil for the girl's return. The devil's servants disguised themselves as ravens who took the stones of the castle away. The castle of Hollókő was built on top of the rock. Village history dates back to the 13th century; after the invasion by the Monguls, the castle was built on Szár Hill. This UNESCO World Heritage Site is a perfectly preserved, but still vibrant Palóc village with only 400 residents. The rural Palóc people speak an unusual Hungarian dialect, and they have some of the more colorful folk customs and costumes still used for daily wear. They have been able to preserve their folkways partially due to their isolation. When you see people in traditional dress, they are genuine, not a troupe of actors, dressing for tourists. If you're in Hungary at Easter time, by all means consider spending the holiday in Hollókő. Hollókő's traditional Easter celebration features townspeople in traditional dress and masses in the town church.

ESSENTIALS

GETTING THERE   There is only one direct **bus** to Hollókő, which departs from Budapest's central bus station, Stadionok Bus Station (© 1/382-0888). It departs weekends only at 8:30am and takes about 2½ hours to reach the town if there is no traffic, but be warned, it could take as much as 3½ if there is. They do not stop for bathroom breaks either. The one-way fare is 1,750 Ft ($9.50/£5). Alternatively, you can take a bus from Árpád híd bus station in Budapest (© 1/412-2597) to Szécsény or Pásztó, where you switch to a local bus to Hollókő; there are four daily, but the trip will be longer. From Budapest, take the motorway M3 as far as Hatvan, then along the main road turn off onto Route 21 in the direction of Salgótarján until you come to the junction for Hollókő. From here, it is a 17km (11-mile) drive.

VISITOR INFORMATION   The best information office is the **Foundation of Hollókő**, at Kossuth Lajos út. 68 (© **32/579-010;** www.holloko.hu). It's open in summer Monday to Friday 8am to 8pm and weekends 10am to 6pm; in winter, it's open Monday to Friday 8am to 5pm and weekends 10am to 4pm. You can also get information through **Nograd Tourist** in Salgótarján (© **32/310-660**) or through **Tourinform** in Szécsény, at Ady Endre u. 12 (© **32/370-777;** www.szecseny.hu).

SEASONAL EVENTS

At Easter, everyone in the village puts on ornamented folk clothes and during the 2-day celebration (Easter Monday is a holiday), the old Easter traditions of the village are revived. Folklore programs fill the day with displays of folk articles for purchase, artisans' presentations, food specialties, and games for children. On the last weekend in July, folk groups of Nógrád county and from other countries gather to perform on the open-air stage of the village for the **Palóc Szőttes Festival** ✿. On the second Sunday of October for the **Vintage Parade,** the young people of the village walk along the main street in ornamented folk clothes, demonstrating that grape picking is over, celebrating that there will be wine in the next year, too.

EXPLORING THE VILLAGE

A one-street town, Hollókő is idyllically set in a quiet, green valley, with **hiking trails** all around. A restored 14th-century castle is perched on a hilltop over the village. In the village itself you can admire the 14th-century wooden-towered church and the sturdy, traditional peasant architecture (normally seen only in stylized open-air museums, such as the one near Szentendre, p. 245), and observe the elderly women at work on their embroidery (samples are for sale). You can also visit the **Village Museum** at Kossuth Lajos u. 82, where exhibits detail everyday Palóc life starting in the early 20th century. Official hours are Tuesday through Sunday from 10am to 4pm, but it is closed in winter. Like everything else in town, though, the museum's hours are up to the whims of the caretakers. Entry is 150 Ft (80¢/45p).

WHERE TO STAY

If you miss the only direct bus back to Budapest, you will need a place to stay. In Hollókő, traditionally furnished thatch-roofed **peasant houses** are available for rent on a nightly or longer basis. You can rent a **room in a shared house** (with shared facilities), or rent an **entire house.** The prices vary depending on the size of the room or house and the number of people in your party, but 9,000 Ft ($49/£26) for a double room is average. Standard **private rooms** are also available in Hollókő. All accommodations can be booked in advance through the tourist offices in Hollókő or Salgótarján (see "Essentials," above). If you arrive without reservations (which is not advised), the address and phone number of a room finder are posted on the door of the **Foundation of Hollókő.**

WHERE TO DINE

Dining options are limited in tiny Hollókő. The **Vár Étterem** (© **32/379-029**) at Kossuth Lajos u. 95 serves decent Hungarian food at very low prices. Try a dish prepared with the "treasure of the local forests," porcini mushrooms. There is indoor and outdoor seating. The menu is available in English, and the waiters are patient. The restaurant is open daily noon to 8pm, except Christmas Day.

2 Eger ★★

126km (78 miles) NE of Budapest

Eger (pronounced *Egg*-air) is the third-most visited city in the country and the most visited of Northern Hungary. It is a small baroque valley city between the Matra and Bükk mountains. Eger's fame is based on three things: its castle, its wine, and the brave struggle of its 16th-century women. When the Turkish army attacked in 1552, there were only 500 equestrians and an equal number of soldiers inside the fortress. The battle against 80,000 Turks was a little imbalanced to say the least. Those in the fortress, including the girls and women, stood up to the Turks to defend themselves and were remarkably victorious. The exuberant triumph is documented with golden letters in Hungarian history. Today, you can visit the exhibitions of the István Dobó Fortress Museum within the walls of the castle.

From the fortress, you can see a number of church towers defining Eger as a once-important church center for centuries, starting with an archbishopric since 1804. But alas, the Turks eventually succeeded in occupying the town and the minaret, 40m (131–ft.) high with 14 sides, is a reminder of their 100 years of Turkish rule from 1596. The view from the top of the minaret will delight you with a wonderful vista of the town's surroundings.

Today Eger's landscape presents a harmonious blend of old and new. The ruined castle, one of Hungary's proudest symbols, dominates the skyline. Eger is convincingly known as the city of baroque. In its historic city center many beautiful and valuable baroque and late-baroque buildings fill each street. If you wander beyond the confines of the old section, you'll find a small modern city.

One of the most widely known and prestigious wines produced in this city is the claret, Eger Bull's Blood. Its distinctive traits are spiciness, fieriness, and relatively high acidity. In the Valley of the Beautiful Women, the most important outer part of town, wine producers are always ready to receive travelers to offer and sell them wine. Many of the wineries are out of the center of town, making it difficult to access without a car.

If you don't want to rent a car, but want to enjoy the wines of the region, another option may be one of the festivals. Festivals include: Eger Spring Festival, an art festival of all mediums in late March to early April; The Feast of Eger Bikavér, a wine and food extravaganza in July; Wine Tasting, when wine producers present the wines of Northeastern Hungary in August; Agria International Folk Dance Festival, a convention of folk dance troupes in August; The Benediction of Wine on the day of St. John, the traditional celebration of new wine and wine exhibitions in late December.

ESSENTIALS

GETTING THERE   Eger is a 2-hour direct **train** ride from Budapest. Daily trains depart Budapest's Keleti Station every hour. Tickets cost 2,810 Ft ($15/£8).

If you're **driving** from Budapest, take the M3 motorway east to Kerecsend, where you pick up Route 25 north to Eger. There is a toll and toll tickets will be going up in price in the near future, so check at all MOL Petrol stations.

VISITOR INFORMATION   For information, visit or contact **Tourinform,** at Bajcsy-Zsilinszky u. 9 (© **36/517-715**). The office is open in summer Monday through Friday from 9am to 6pm and on weekends from 9am to 1pm; during off season, the office closes an hour earlier on weekdays and is closed on Sunday. For private-room booking, try Eger Hotels at www.egerhotels.com or **Egertourist,** at Bajcsy-Zsilinszky u. 9 (© **36/510-270**). The office is open Monday through Saturday from 10am to 6pm.

Note that the telephone city code for Eger is 36, the same as the country code for Hungary. To call from abroad, you would use 36/36 and then the local 6 digit number.

EXPLORING OLD EGER

Eger's main sites are fairly concentrated making them within easy walking distance of each other and of **Dobó István tér** 𝒜𝒜. Like many European cities and villages, life revolves around the town square. This one is particularly lovely in the center of old Eger. The **Minorite Church** sits on Dobó István tér with many believing it to be one of the most beautiful baroque churches in Europe. It is in razor-sharp contrast to the nearby solemn edifice of the friary. One of the greatest masters of European baroque, Kilian Ignaz Dientzenhofer, designed the church.

In the center of the square, there is an impressive statue of the town defender Dobó, flanked by a knight and a woman. Erected in the 1960s, it was created by Alajos Strobl, one of the country's leading turn-of-the-20th-century sculptors. Strobl's execution of the work did not hold back on his feelings about the battle against the Turks. Strobl's other works include the statue of King Stephen on Buda's Castle Hill and the statue of poet János Arany in front of the National Museum in Pest.

The reconstructed ruins of **Eger Castle,** visible from just about anywhere in the city, are easily reached by walking northeast out of the square; take the path out of Dózsa György tér. You can wander around the grounds free of charge daily from 8am to 8pm in summer and daily 8am to 6pm in winter. You can also explore the two museums on the premises. Walking the ramparts is a lovely stroll in warm weather and provides a nice view of the old town area. The **István Dobó Castle Museum** (ⓒ **36/ 312-744**), as the name implies, offers the castle's history along with displays of some Turkish artifacts. The **Eger Picture Gallery** display pieces from the same 19th-century Hungarian artists who are featured in the Budapest museum. The museums are open Tuesday through Sunday from 10am to 5pm, and until 4pm in winter. Admission to each separate museum is 1,000 Ft ($5.50/£2.75).

Just to the west of the castle, on Harangöntő utca, is Eger's most visible reminder of the Turkish period, its **Minaret** at Knézich u. 1 (ⓒ **36/410-233**). The minaret survived, though the mosque under it was destroyed in 1841. The minaret is 14-sided, 33m (108-ft.) tall, and in good enough condition that for an admission charge of 200 Ft ($1/50p), you can climb to the narrow top. It is open from April to the end of October, Tuesday to Sunday 10am to 6pm. If you suffer from claustrophobia, I warn against it. The scramble up is steep, on a cramped spiral staircase, but because the space is so narrow, you can't turn back if anyone is behind you. Those who are successful, however, are justly rewarded with a spectacular view.

You can't miss the massive **basilica** (ⓒ **30/337-2398**), it is the second-largest church in Hungary, the largest being Esztergom's basilica and it competes in size with the basilica in Pest. You just need to walk a few blocks south on Eszterhazy tér. It is the only classicist building in Eger. Ordered by Archbishop Pyrker József, it was designed by architect József Hild, who was one of the architects of St. Stephen's Basilica in Pest. He completed this church in 1837 in the grandiose neoclassical style of the time. It's open daily from 6am to 7pm. If you are visiting in the high season, wander in at 11:30am Monday through Saturday or at 12:45pm on Sunday for a free organ presentation. Admission is free to the church at other times.

Next you will find the **Lyceum** at Eszterházy Square 1 (ⓒ **36/325-211**) built in late baroque style. Count Eszterházy Károly ordered it to be built as a university at the end of the 18th century. It is now a college. (Colleges in Hungary generally offer 4-year degrees,

Eger

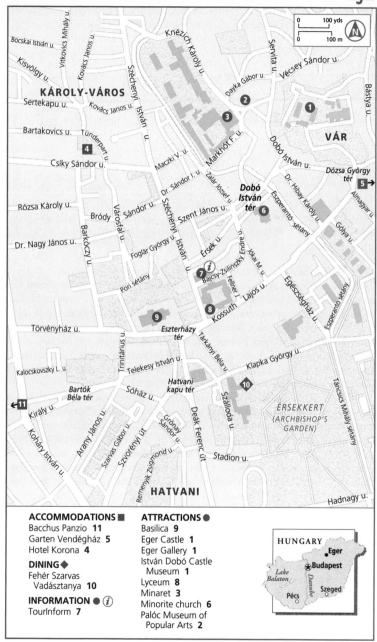

while universities require 4 to 6 years of more specialized study.) The Lyceum houses the nationally famous diocesan library *(kö nyvtár)* on the first floor with an impressive ceiling fresco of the Council of Trent by Johann Lukas Kracker and József Zach. The only original letter written by Mozart, in Hungary, is on display here. You can visit March 1 to September 30 Tuesday through Sunday 9am to 3pm, the rest of the year, on Saturday and Sunday only from 9am to 1pm. Admission is 350 Ft ($2/£1). Entrance to the balcony is free. Concerts are frequently performed in the yard of the Lyceum during July and August, so ask at Tourinform for the schedule and ticket information.

The **Palóc Museum of Popular Arts,** Dobó u. 12 (© **36/312-744**) presents exhibitions of the folk arts of the Palóc, inhabitants of Northeastern Hungary. Wood carvings made by shepherds, including crooksand drinking spoons, and hand-woven fabrics of mainly household textiles, tent sheets, shawls, haversacks, male and female clothing, and ceramics, are displayed. The museum is open April 15 through September 30 Tuesday through Sunday 9am to 5pm. Admission is 100 Ft (55¢/30p).

If you missed visiting a spa or bathhouse in Budapest, check them out in Eger. Northeastern Hungary is rich in thermal waters; ask at Tourinform for a list of spas in the region. The one on Klapa utca is under reconstruction until 2009, but the Tourinform can direct you to other options.

WHERE TO STAY

Eger has some lovely places to stay right in the center of the town. The **Hotel Korona** , Tündérpart 5 (© **36/310-287;** fax 36/310-261), is a clean, cozy establishment on an extremely quiet residential street just a few blocks west of Dobó István tér. The hotel has a wine cellar and a shaded patio where breakfast is served in good weather. There are 40 rooms, all with private bathrooms. A double room goes for 80€ to 110€ ($104–$143/£55–£75). Rates include breakfast and the sauna. Credit cards are accepted. Bus no. 11, 12, or 14 will get you there from the train station; get off at Csiky Sándor utca and you're practically at the doorstep.

Another guesthouse is near the beginning of the Valley of Beautiful Women and only a 15-minute walk from the historical center of the town. The **Bacchus Panzio** , is located at Szépasszony völgy u. 29 (© **36/428-950;** www.bacchuspanzio.hu). This hotel offers double rooms for 43€ to 54€ ($56–$70/£30–£37) in high season and 37€ to 43€ ($48–$56/£25–£30) in low season. Breakfast is 5€ ($6.50/£3.50).

For something peacefully removed from the downtown, try the **Garten Vendégház,** Legányi u. 6 (© **36/320-371;** www.gartenvendeghaz.hu). Operated by the Zsemlye family, this guesthouse is located on a quiet residential street in the hills overlooking the city. The view from the gorgeous garden is splendid. The price of a double room is 40€ ($52/£28) in high season and 30€ ($39/£21) in low season. Rates include breakfast in high season only, otherwise it is 5€ ($6.50/£3.50).

Travelers on a tighter budget should consider renting a private room through **Egertourist** (see above) or **Tourinform.** Rates in Eger are as low as 5,500 Ft ($30/£16) for a bed with a shared bathroom and as high as 11,000 Ft ($60/£31) for an apartment with bathroom and kitchen.

WHERE TO DINE

The **Fehér Szarvas Vadásztanya (White Stag Hunting Inn)** , located next door to the Park Hotel at Klapka u. 8 (© **36/411-129**), a few blocks south of Dobó István tér, is one of Eger's best-known and best-loved restaurants. The menu offers a full range of Hungarian wild-game specialties. Award-winning regional wines are featured. A piano

An Excursion to Bükk National Park

Just to the northeast of Eger lies the Bükk mountain range, a lush, rugged terrain of cliffs and forest land. Established in 1976 this region encompasses the **Bükki Nemzeti Park (Bükk National Park; ✆ 36/411-581)**. This mountainous national park presents a different persona with each season. If you visit in the spring, the palate of colors from countless wildflowers covering the backdrop will be your reward. The park is 43,200 hectares (106,750 acres) of which 97% is covered with forest. There are several unique and rare wildlife species in the mountains; more than 900 caves are known to exist. There are also numerous hiking trails. In the village of Szilvásvárad, you will discover where the world-famous Lippizaner horses are bred. The Lippizaners have more than 400 years of history in this area. You are able to discover the area by horseback. On the Szilvásváradi rail line, you can take a narrow gauge train along a 5km (3-mile) railway line through the mountains going through trout ponds and ending at Veil Waterfall, where the water falls 17m (56 ft.) and resembles a gauzy veil. From here, you can hike to the prehistoric Istállóskö Cave or to the Bükk Plateau.

A public bus from Eger stops here. The area has several pensions and hotels, as well as private-room accommodations. Egertourist or Tourinform (in Eger) will be able to help you book a room. Cartografia publishes the best area map, called *Bükk hegység* (Bükk Hills); it shows all the area hiking trails in good detail. You can find the map in most area bookstores and map stores, including the map stores listed on p. 206 in chapter 9, "Budapest Shopping."

and bass duet plays nightly amid the kitschy hunting lodge decor. The restaurant is open daily from noon to 11pm, and reservations are recommended. Credit cards are accepted.

WHERE TO SAMPLE LOCAL WINE

The best place to sample local wines is in the vineyard country just west of Eger, in the wine cellars of the **Szépasszony-völgy (Valley of the Beautiful Women).** More than 200 wine cellars are located here, each offering its own vintage. Some cellars have live music. Although the wine cellars don't serve food, you can grab a meal at one of the local restaurants. Generally, the cellars open at 10am and close by 9 or 10pm.

The easiest way to get to the Szépasszony-völgy is by taxi, though you can also walk there from the center of town in 30 or 40 minutes. You could also take bus no. 13 to the Hatvani Temető (Hatvan Cemetery) and walk from there; it's a 10- to 15-minute walk.

3 Tokaji: Wine of Kings, King of Wines ✶

200km (125 miles) NE of Budapest

TOKAJ-HEGYALJA

Also in the northern regions of Hungary, you can find the world-famous wine called Tokaji. Its fame and reputation transcends centuries of the history of the area, identifying it as a famous wine region of Hungary. Grapes were found growing in a 43km (27-mile) area when the first Hungarian conquerors appeared on the scene. The uniqueness of the wine is attributed to the growing conditions of the grapes. Starting with a volcanic soil, the area is protected by the Carpathian Mountains. They have a southern exposure with the autumn weather promoting the grapes turning to *aszu* (raisin). Other important grape varieties of the area are the Furmint, Hárslevelű or Linden Leaf, Yellow Muscatel, and Oremus.

Legend has it that a wine grower abandoned his harvest when there was a threat of a Turkish invasion. When it was safe to return to his fields, he feared his harvest had been ruined since the grapes had stayed on the vine too long, but he used them anyway to make wine. The product was Tokaji. The wine has a long history with royalty as well as with poets and writers. As poet Miklós Szemere from the 19th century exemplifies with his short verse:

Blessed Tokaji wine, how good you are,
your mere fragrance is enough to send death running;
for many ill people have been cured by drinking you,
though they were about to be taken away.
Drink of the gods, immortal nectar,
the land is blest where you grow!

The Tokaji wine was well established and popular as early as the 12th century. Admirers of the wine were King Louis XIV, Cromwell, Tsar Alexander the Great, and Tsarina Catherine. The Russians even stationed a small garrison in the surroundings of Tokaj to ensure continuous supply. Believing the wine had curative power, the doctors of Pope Pius I ordered him to drink Tokaj wines regularly to protect his health. The French king Louis XIV called it "the king of wines and the wine of kings."

ESSENTIALS
GETTING THERE   Tokaj is only accessible by car or by taking a tour to the region. If you are driving, take the M3 motorway from Budapest to Miskolc then to Route 37, following the signs, turn onto Route 38. Unfortunately, all tourist information is in Hungarian only. I suggest you take a guided tour to the region, but make sure the tour will have an English guide. If you decide to venture there on your own with a car, then the Tourinform office can be of some assistance. You can contact them at Tokaj 3910, Serház u. 1 (© **47/552-070;** fax 47/352-259).

WHERE TO STAY
The **Tokaj Hotel and Restaurant** at Rákóczi u. 5 (© **47/352-344;** fax 47/352-759; www.hoteltokaj.hu) is found at the foot of Tokaj Mountain, at the fork of rivers Tisza and Bodrog. The hotel has 30 double rooms with a full bathroom and 12 double rooms with a shower that are modern and comfortable. Rates are 15€ to 29€ ($20–$38/£11–£20) per person, not per room.

The **Sos Tavern and Pension** looks like a large converted barn on Tokaj-Hegyalja Route 37 situated between Szerencs and Tokaj and with no specific address. Surrounded by vineyards, the pension has 11 rooms with showers and a restaurant, a sauna, and a traditional wine cellar for guests. The nearby Mádi Lake and the forests of Hegyalja are rich in game and offer excellent fishing facilities. For more specific driving directions, contact István Novák (© **47/369-139;** www.sosborhaz.hu).

WHERE TO DINE
The restaurant at the Tokaj Hotel has many regional specialties and offers special food programs as well. In summertime, the balcony overlooking the river is open and it offers a delightful view. The pension above also has a restaurant for guests.

4 Aggtelek: An Entrance to the Caves ⊛

224km (139 miles) NE of Budapest

Swaddled in the most northern part of Hungary to the Slovak border, about 80km (50 miles) north of Eger is the **Aggtelek National Park (Aggteleki Nemzeti Park)** established as a park in 1985 primarily to protect inorganic natural treasures, surface formations, and caves. A deciduous forest covers 75% of the park inhabited by over 220 species of birds, rare plants, and a rich collection of varied insects. Most fascinating to many is that it also has over 200 caves of various sizes, creating Central Europe's largest cave system. The **Baradla Cave** is the longest with a total length of 25km (16 miles), including side branches. One 5.6km (3.5-mile) section runs into Slovakia and is called by its Slovak name, Domica. The cave is a youthful 2 million years old according to geologists. Water from streams entered through cracks, dissolving and eroding the limestone, eventually widening the water's entry and formed the current passages. The lime content of the dripping water forms stalactites and stalagmites in a range of sizes, colors, and shapes embellishing the passages, inspiring those who discovered them to give them names such as Dragon's Head, Tiger, Mother in Law's Tongue, the Hall of Columns, and the Hall of Giants. Prehistoric people inhabited the caves according to archaeological excavations

Guided daily tours are available lasting 1 to 2 hours *(roved)* covering roughly 1km (½ mile). The more rigorous 5-hour *(közép)*, or 7-hour *(hosszú)* tours cover a range of 7km (about 4½ miles) and include scaling, climbing ladders, and crossing water-filled gullies. They are available from the villages of Aggtelek or Jósvafő from April 1 to September 30 between 8am and 5pm and from October 1 to March 31 between 8am and 3pm. First-time cave visitors will be flabbergasted by the miraculous subterranean world of stalactites, stalagmites, and other bizarre formations that Mother Nature has created.

Classical and other music concerts are held in the beautiful Concert Hall of the Baradla Cave because of its wonderful acoustics; it provides a very special experience for visitors. For more information, call the Aggtelek National Park Jósvafő, Tengerszem oldal 1 (© **48/506-000;** www.anp.hu) for tour information.

The **Hotel Cseppkő** (© **48/343-075**), in the village of Aggtelek, is a popular place to crash after a day in the caves. Double rooms start at 13,000 Ft ($70/£37) and a triple is 18,000 Ft ($97/£51), breakfast included. Though it's very plain, it is clean and conveniently located. Camping is also popular in the area.

Travelers without cars can get to Aggtelek by bus from Eger. The trip takes 3 hours. From Miskolc, the trip takes 2 hours. Ask about transportation at the local tourist office (such as Eger's Tourinform or Egertourist), where you can also ask for help booking a room at the Hotel Cseppkő. Off season there is no need to book in advance.

⌒Tips Cool Caves

Remember, no matter how hot it is outside, the Baradla caves are always damp and chilly (a constant 50°–52°F/10°–11°C), so take a couple of layers of clothes to add as the temperature decreases.

14

Southern Hungary: The Mecsek Hills & the Great Plain

In southwestern Hungary, you will find the fertile Mecsek Hills; the city of Pécs is the major city of this hilly region. Pécs has been named a European Capital of Culture for 2010, when the spotlight will be highlighting its history and cultural life. On the other side of the Danube River to the south and east, lies the mainly agricultural region of the Alföld (Great Plain), which begins not far outside of Budapest; this is the farmland of wheat and orchards. This is a broad, bleak, but yet dramatic land mass that covers almost half of the country. The last remains of the Puszta are in this region, where Hungarian folk legends have sprung from and the land of the Hungarian cowboys or *csikós*. It is similar to the great prairies of the U.S. This is also the home of the famous Nonius horse, a powerful equine breed developed in Hungary in the 19th century, which won the title "Ideal Horse" at the Paris world exhibition in 1900. The main cities here are Kecskemét and Szeged. The Great Plain comprises approximately 51,800 sq. km (20,000 sq. miles).

1 Pécs: A City with a 2,000-Year Past ★★★

197km (122 miles) SW of Budapest

Pécs (pronounced *Paych*) is the largest and most beautiful city in the Mecsek Hill region. Although far from the Mediterranean Sea, it has a Mediterranean feel to it due to its generally warm and arid climate. Due to this, the hills in the region produce some of the country's premium fruit. Pécs is located just 32km (20 miles) from the Croatian border.

Sopiane, as the Romans named it, has over 2,000 years of history still visible to speak of its past. Still in evidence are remnants of the Roman era which date back to around A.D. 350–400. The early Christian burial chamber dating back to the 4th century is the most noteworthy remains.

The later period of the Turkish rule and their structures are even more evident. They occupied the city for over 140 years from 1543. The Inner City Parish Church is an incredibly beautiful place of worship, with an interesting history. It is located at the top of Szechenyi Square in the city center and you may not recognize it as a church, because it looks like a mosque. The Turks used the stones from St. Bartholomew's Church at the other end of the square, to build the mosque of Pasha Gazi Kassim. When the Turks were eradicated from the city in 1686, the mosque was occupied by Jesuits who restored it to a Catholic church.

It was in Pécs that the first university in the country was founded in 1367 while under the rule of King Louis the Great. While that university no longer exists, Pécs is still a university city with the present university. The current University of Pécs was

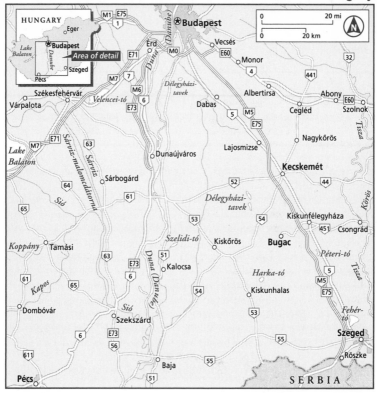

founded on January 1, 2000, the merger of three institutions of higher learning: Janus Pannonius University, the Medical University of Pécs, and the Illyés Gyula Teacher Training College of Szekszárd.

Pécs continued to be a vibrant city through the 143-year Turkish occupation, in part due to the fact that the greatest ruler of the Ottoman Empire, Suleiman II, made this his home. The Turks introduced a new culture with baths, decorative fountains, and drinking fountains. Some of the most important Turkish remains in the country are landmark reminders of this historic time in the city life, such as the Mosque of Pasha Gazi Kassim.

The first public library in the country was created here by Bishop György Klimó in 1774. Maria Theresa, empress of the Austro-Hungarian Empire gave the city the rank of Free Royal City in 1780. During the 19th century, four major companies opened factories: Littke (champagne), Hamerli (gloves), Angster (organs), and later in the century, Zsolnay (porcelain).

Those who live in Pécs declare it is the best city in the country. Pécs is a lovely city that is growing. The people do not exhibit the inertia you might notice on a hot summer afternoon in Great Plain towns like Kecskemét or Szeged.

Walking up Janus Pannonius utca toward Széchenyi tér, about a block up the street, you cannot help but notice a small wrought-iron fence covered with padlocks. There are even padlocks hanging from padlocks in chains. The story goes that one young couple in love placed a padlock there as a token of their love. Others followed and now the fence is at risk from toppling from the weight. Someone started the same tradition on yet another fence just a minute's walk away from the original. If you look closely at the locks, you'll see names and dates engraved on them.

ESSENTIALS

GETTING THERE   Ten **trains** depart daily from Budapest's Keleti Station; seven of these are intercity trains, which are much faster than others. The fare is 3,750 Ft ($20/£11) for a one-way or 6,450 Ft ($35/£18) for a return. You will need a reservation for an IC train and this will be an additional 520 Ft ($2.80/£1.45). An intercity train will get you there in 3 hours. The "fast" train *(gyors)* leaves from Deli Station; the trip is at least 3¾ hours, but you don't need a reservation and the train is not as nice.

If you are **driving** from Budapest, take the M6 south for approximately 3 hours (the distance is 210km/130 miles).

VISITOR INFORMATION   Once you leave Budapest, English speakers are harder to find except in hotels and some restaurants. The best source of information in Pécs is **Tourinform,** at Széchenyi tér 9 (© **72/213-315;** www.tourinform.hu). Tourinform is open April through October, Monday through Friday from 9am to 7pm and on weekends from 9am to 6pm; in winter it is open Monday through Friday from 8am to 4pm. Tourinform can provide a list of local private-room accommodations, though you'll have to reserve the room yourself.

If you want to have a room reserved for you, visit **Mecsek Tourist,** at Ferenciek u. 41 (© **72/513-370;** www.mecsektours.hu). The office is open Monday through Friday from 9am to 5pm; and Saturday in summer from 9am to 1pm.

You can also get city information online at **www.pecs.hu**. Look for the English link at the top.

EXPLORING OLD PÉCS

The old section of Pécs is really awe inspiring with the differences in architecture side by side; there is lots of eye candy to satisfy anyone. One of Hungary's most incredible central squares is **Széchenyi tér** ✶✶✶. Starting with the mosque at the top of minor hill, it descends on down to St. Sebastian's Catholic Church, where there is an unusual fountain made of Zsolnay porcelain sitting in front. Walking down the square, make sure you stroll slowly and look up. The variety of architectural styles and colors within such a short area is just amazing. Grand pastel-colored buildings line the cobblestone streets that border the square.

Old Pécs has a reputation for its many museums and galleries; after Budapest, Pécs comes in second as a cultural center in Hungary. Many of the museums are relatively small, unlike the many grand ones in Budapest, so you can conceivably visit three or four in a day without feeling overstimulated.

MUSEUMS

Most of the museums are under the directorship of the Baranya County Museum's Directorate and therefore, the phone number is a central one while opening hours and admission are uniform throughout. As in Budapest, these museums charge you extra if you're taking photos or video; see p. 132 for more.

Pécs

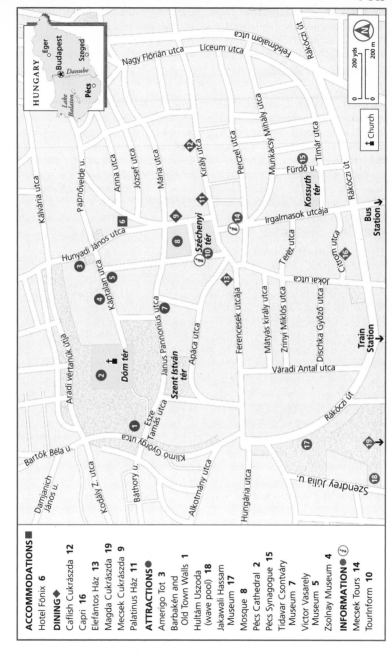

ACCOMMODATIONS ■

Hotel Főnix **6**

DINING ◆

Caflish Cukrászda **12**

Capri **16**

Elefántos Ház **13**

Magda Cukrászda **19**

Mecsek Cukrászda **9**

Palatinus Ház **11**

ATTRACTIONS ●

Amerigo Tot **3**

Barbakén and
Old Town Walls **1**

Hullám Uszoda
(wave pool) **18**

Jakawali Hassam
Museum **17**

Mosque **8**

Pécs Cathedral **2**

Pécs Synagogue **15**

Tidavar Csontváry
Museum **7**

Victor Vasarely
Museum **5**

Zsolnay Museum **4**

INFORMATION ● ⓘ

Mecsek Tours **14**

Tourinform **10**

Amerigo Tot Exhibition 🎯 This displays the work of Hungarian sculptor Americo Tot who moved to Italy in 1937. He presented Pécs with his works *Baptism* (1938), *Madonna of Csurgó* (1968/1980), *Cross as Protest* (1969), and *Still Life in Transylvania* (1980), all of which are beautiful pieces.

Kaptalan u. 2. 🅲 **72/324-822.** Admission 700 Ft ($3.80/£2). Photo 300 Ft ($1.60/85p); video 600 Ft ($3.20/£1.70). Apr 1–Oct 31 Tues–Sat 10am–6pm, Sun 10am–4pm; Nov 1–Mar 31 Tues–Sat 10am–4pm, Sun 10am–4pm.

Jakawali Hassan Museum This museum is housed inside a 16th-century mosque; the most complete Turkish temple in Hungary. The mosque stands with its minaret still intact (though, unfortunately, you can't ascend the minaret). At one time there was a religious house of the Dervishes and a religious college next door. Like the much larger mosque up in Széchenyi tér, this mosque was converted to a church after the Turks were driven from Pécs; however, in the 1950s the mosque was restored to its original form. The museum's main attraction is the building itself, although various Muslim religious artifacts are on display as well.

Rákóczi út 2. 🅲 **72/313-853.** Admission 250 Ft ($1.35/70p). Apr–Sept Thurs–Sun 10am–1pm and 2–6pm. Closed Oct–Mar.

Tivadar Csontváry Museum 🎯 This small museum has a fine collection of the work of Tivadar Csontváry Kosztka (1853–1919), who claimed he had a mystic revelation wherein God told him to paint. He worked 20 years preparing himself financially by opening a pharmacy, then did not start painting until he was 41 years old. His revelation was attributed to the fact he suffered from schizophrenia, which most likely also influenced his art. He is considered the first post-Impressionist artist of Hungary, thus shunned from the artistic community. He remained unknown during his lifetime and when he died, his family wanted to sell his paintings for the value of their canvases, not the work itself. Someone who realized their potential value bought the selection that is now on exhibit (which initially angered wagon makers who wanted the large canvas for their wagon making). Supposedly, Picasso once saw an exhibition of Csontváry's work and said, "I did not know there was another artistic genius in this century, beside me."

Janus Pannonius u. 11. 🅲 **72/310-544.** Admission 700 Ft ($3.80/£2). Photo 300 Ft ($1.60/85p); video 600 Ft ($3.20/£1.70). Apr 1–Oct 31 Tues–Sat 10am–6pm, Sun 10am–4pm; Nov 1–Mar 31 Tues–Sat 10am–4pm, Sun 10am–4pm.

Victor Vasarely Museum 🎯 The late Victor Vasarely, internationally known father of op art, was born in the house that this museum now occupies, though he left early on for France. This is one of two museums in the country devoted solely to Vasarely's work (the other is in Óbuda, p. 150). While Vasarely's fame was achieved abroad, Pécs proudly considers him as a native son. In addition to Vasarely's pieces the museum also displays the work of a few significant Hungarian artists whose work of geometric and kinetic styles are from the second part of the 20th century. Some international artists are also on display at different times.

Kaptalan u. 3. 🅲 **72/324-822.** Admission 700 Ft ($3.80/£2). Photo 300 Ft ($1.60/85p); video 600 Ft ($3.20/£1.70). Apr 1–Oct 31 Tues–Sat 10am–6pm, Sun 10am–4pm; Nov 1–Mar 31 Tues–Sat 10am–4pm, Sun 10am–4pm.

Zsolnay Museum 🎯🎯🎯 This is one of a number of the small museums on Kaptalan utca, Pécs's "street of museums," and you shouldn't miss it. The Zsolnay Museum displays some of the best examples of Zsolnay porcelain, produced locally since 1852. There are vases, plates, cups, figurines, and even ceramic paintings. Once you've seen the museum, check out the Zsolnay fountain at the lower end of Széchenyi tér in front of St. Sebastian's Church.

Kaptalan u. 2. ☎ **72/324-822**. Admission 700 Ft ($3.80/£2.00). Photo 300 Ft ($1.60/85p); video 600 Ft ($3.20/ £1.70). Apr 1–Oct 31 Tues–Sat 10am–6pm, Sun 10am–4pm; Nov 1–Mar 31 Tues–Sat 10am–4pm, Sun 10am–4pm.

HOUSES OF WORSHIP

Mosque of Pasha Gazi Kassim ☆☆   The largest Turkish structure still standing in Hungary was once a mosque and it now houses a Catholic church. It was built in the late 16th century, during the Turkish occupation, on the site of an earlier church. The mix of religious traditions is evident everywhere you look, and the effect is rather pleasing. An English-language description of the building's history is posted on a bulletin board on the left-hand wall.

At the top of Széchenyi tér. ☎ **72/227-166**. Free admission. Apr 16–Oct 14 Mon–Sat 10am–4pm, Sun 11:30am– 3pm; Oct 15–Apr 15 Mon–Sat 10am–noon, Sun 11:30am–1:30pm.

Pécs Cathedral ☆   Originally built in the 11th century by Bishop St. Maurice, this four-towered cathedral has been destroyed and rebuilt more than once like many buildings during wars. The Turkish used it as a mosque and embellished it with a minaret (spire). At the end of the 19th century, the present neo-Romanesque exterior was added. The interior remains primarily Gothic, with some baroque additions and furnishings. The frescoes by leading 19th-century artists Károly Lotz and Bertalan Székely are inside. Organ concerts are performed in the cathedral throughout the year; inquire at the cathedral (no English spoken) or at Tourinform for the schedule.

The square in front of the cathedral and the beautifully landscaped park with a magnificent fountain beneath it is a popular gathering place, and occasionally the site of folk concerts, dances, and fairs.

On Dóm tér. ☎ **72/513-030**. Cathedral admission (includes treasury and crypt) 1,000 Ft ($5.40/£2.85). Apr 1–Oct 31 Mon–Sat 9am–5pm, Sun 1–5pm; Nov 1–Mar 31 Mon–Sat 10am–4pm, Sun 1–4pm. The church is not open to the public during weddings, which are often on Sat afternoon.

Pécs Synagogue ☆   Pécs's grand old synagogue is incongruously situated in what is now one of the city's busiest shopping squares, Kossuth tér. The gentleman at the door speaks excellent English and is warm and inviting. Once inside, you will forget the outside world. Built in 1865 and consecrated in 1869, the synagogue has the original rich oak interior to this day. It was the third synagogue built in the city in Hungarian romantic style for a Neolog Jewish community. Sadly, it is the only surviving synagogue in the city after World War II. Prior to World War II, the synagogue had over 4,000 members, of whom only 464 survived the Holocaust. Every year, Pécs's small and aging Jewish community commemorates the 1944 deportations to Auschwitz on the first Sunday after July 4.

Regular services are held in the smaller temple next door at Fürdő 1 (there isn't a sign; go through the building into the courtyard and cross diagonally to the right) on Friday at 6:30pm.

Kossuth tér. 1–3. ☎ **72/315-881**. Admission 500 Ft ($2.70/£1.40). May–Oct and Mar–Apr Sun–Fri 10am–noon and 1–5pm. Closed Nov–Feb.

SHOPPING

As you stroll through the city, you will be surprised at the number of pedestrian-only streets there are making shopping in Pécs a pleasurable activity. Many of the stores are standard shops that you will have found in Budapest or any other large city, for that matter, thanks to globalization. For a more exotic shopping experience, visit the **Pécsi Vásár (Pécs Flea Market)** *. At this crowded, bustling, open-air market you can find everything from antique china and silver to Turkish T-shirts and Chinese baby booties. The market is open the first Sunday of the month and the previous Friday and Saturday. Take a special bus, marked VÁSÁRTÉR, which departs from the Konsum downtown shopping center. You need two standard city bus tickets for this bus; these are available at newsstands and kiosks or ask the bus driver, but the prices are higher. You can also take the no. 3 bus from the Konsum (only one ticket required), but you'll have to walk some distance from the stop to the entrance of the flea market.

OUTDOOR ACTIVITIES

If you visit Pécs in the summer, plan for the heat. Air-conditioning is not common here, so cool off in the waves at **Hullám uszoda (Wave Swimming Pool)** on Szendrey Júlia utca (© **72/512-936**). Admission is 800 Ft ($4.30/£2.30). The pool is open daily from 6am to 10pm from May 1 to September 30. There is also an indoor pool that is open all year. Another swimming pool complex, which belongs to the university, is at Ifjúság útja 6 (© **72/501-519**, ext. 4195). There is a wading pool for kids as well as a 25m (82-ft.) lap pool. Admission is 600 Ft ($3.25/£1.70). It is only open to the public July to September 6 to 8am and 4 to 8pm.

Pécs is home to perhaps one of the most appealing neighborhood playgrounds in all of Hungary. **Napsugár Játszókert (Sunshine Playground)** is on Vadász utca, a short bus ride from the city center. Built in 1997 by a foundation and with donations from the community, this small grassy playground has a quaint, friendly appeal. There are chunky wooden climbing structures, slides, seesaws, swings (including an infant swing), a sandbox, and picnic tables. To get there, take bus no. 27 from the Konsum to the Ledina stop.

WHERE TO STAY

You can book a private room through **Mecsek Tourist** (see "Essentials," above) or **Ibusz,** Király u. 11. (© **72/212-157;** www.ibusz.hu).

For the best little hotel right in the center of town, try the popular **Hotel Fönix** **, at Hunyadi út 2 (© **72/311-682**). This unique hotel's structure is reminiscent of a building from a children's fairy tale. It sits just off the top of Széchenyi tér across from the mosque. With only 14 rooms and three apartments, this adds to its charm as does the fact that each room has oddly angled walls and partial dormer-type ceilings. Some of the rooms are a bit cramped, but all are clean with refrigerators and TVs and the common facilities are well maintained. The three apartments have full facilities and their own entrance off the street. The staff is incredibly helpful and friendly. Double rooms run 9,590 Ft to 11,590 Ft ($52–$63/£27–£33), triples are 12,990 Ft to 14,990 Ft ($70–$81/£37–£43), and apartments range from 19,990 Ft to 29,990 Ft ($105–$162/£57–£85). Rates include breakfast, but not tourism tax of 200 Ft ($1.10/ 55p) per night per person. Call several days ahead to reserve a room. Credit cards are accepted.

If the Hotel Fönix is full, the management can book a room for you at a pension that they operate called **Kertész Panzió,** at Sáfrány u. 42 (© **72/327-551**).

WHERE TO DINE

Elefántos Ház ** ITALIAN   Given its Mediterranean feel, this Italian restaurant is perfect for downtown patio dining in the warm months. The pasta and pizzas are excellently prepared and the portions are generous. My travel companion and I sampled one of each and were very pleased with our choices.

Jókai tér 6. ℭ **72/216-055.** Reservations recommended in summer. Pizza 1,000 Ft–1,400 Ft ($5.40–$7.55/£2.85–£4) Main courses 1,200 Ft–2,500 Ft ($6.50–$14/£3.40–£7.10). MC, V. Daily 11am–midnight. Off of main square.

Palatinus Hotel Restaurant ✶✶ HUNGARIAN   The interior of this restaurant is incredibly decorated with a combination of Art Nouveau and other styles with Zsolnay porcelain tossed in here and there. The peacock Zsolnay fountain will have you wondering whether to eat or stare at the colors and design of the building. Eat though, the food is excellent and so is the staff. Try the filet mignon slices with potato pancakes and stewed plums. I found it delectable.

Király u. 5. ℭ **72/889-400.** Reservations recommended. Main courses 1,700 Ft–3,500 Ft ($9.20–$19/£4.85–£9.95). AE, DC, MC, V. Daily 11am–11pm. Off of main square.

COFFEEHOUSES & ICE-CREAM PARLORS

If you have a sweet tooth, there are opportunities to satisfy it all over town. Pécs offers numerous places to enjoy coffee and sweets. Try **Mecsek Cukrászda,** on Széchenyi tér 16 (ℭ **72/315-444**), for a quick jolt of espresso and any number of luscious looking and inexpensive pastries. For people-watching on the pedestrian street, try **Caflisch Cukrászda** at Király 32 u. They also have a large selection of ice cream flavors. **Capri,** a very popular shop at Citrom u. 7 (ℭ **72/333-658**), 3 blocks south of Széchenyi tér, serves up various sundaes as well as cones, but their choice of pastries is limited. Another place for sweets and ice cream is **Magda Cukrászda** ✶✶, at Kandó Kálmán u. 4 (ℭ **72/511-055**). It's out of the way but worth the walk. It is open daily 10am to 8pm and to 7pm in winter.

2 Kecskemét ✶

85km (53 miles) SE of Budapest

Kecskemét (pronounced *Ketch*-keh-mate), a city of just over 100,000 people in the western portion of the Great Hungarian Plain, definitely has a village feel. A quiet, sun-baked city with wide, open squares and broad avenues, Kecskemét is blessed with some of the most interesting architecture in the Great Plain region. The town's dizzyingly colorful Art Nouveau buildings may be the equal of any in the country outside Budapest.

Kecskemét was the birthplace of Zoltán Kodály, the early-20th-century musicologist, teacher, and composer who, along with his friend and colleague Béla Bartók, achieved worldwide renown for his studies of Hungarian folk songs and for his compositions. Kodály also developed a method of teaching music that is used worldwide. Today, a music school in town bears Kodály's name. Kecskemét is also famous throughout the country for its many varieties of apricot brandy *(barack Pálinka).*

ESSENTIALS

GETTING THERE   Over 30 daily **trains** depart Budapest's Nyugati Station; 12 of them are intercity trains. The fare on IC trains is 2,120 Ft ($11/£6.05) one-way and you are required to pay an additional seat reservation fee of about 770 Ft ($4.20/£2.20). IC trains take 1½ hours. On a regular train, tickets are 1,770 Ft ($9.60/£5.05) and the journey takes 1¾ hours, with no reservations or reservation fees required. For 15 minutes, you can save some money.

If you're driving from Budapest, take the M5 motorway south. You will have to pay a highway toll each way.

VISITOR INFORMATION   The best source of information is **Tourinform,** at Kossuth tér 1 (©/fax **76/481-065;** www.kecskemet.hu). In summer the office is open Monday through Friday 8am to 5pm and Saturday 9am to 1pm; from July to August, it is open Sunday 9am to 1pm as well. In winter the office is open weekdays 8am to 5pm. **Pusztatourist,** at Szabadság tér 2 (© **76/483-493**), will be useful if you're planning a side trip to Bugac. It is open Monday through Friday 9am to 5pm and Saturday 9:30am to 12:30pm.

EXPLORING KECSKEMÉT

The museums mentioned here are in the immediate vicinity of Kossuth tér, Kecskemét's main square, a beautiful area with gorgeous buildings.

Photography lovers will not want to miss the excellent **Hungarian Photography Museum,** Katona József tér 12 (© **76/483-221;** www.fotomuzeum.hu), featuring the works of contemporary Hungarian photographers, including foreign photographers of Hungarian ethnicity. It is open March 17 through October 31 Wednesday to Sunday 10am to 5pm, and November 1 through March 16 Wednesday to Sunday 10am to 4pm. Admission is 200 Ft ($1.10/55p).

Visit the **Bozsó Collection,** Klapka u. 34. (© **76/324-625**). Open Friday through Sunday 10am to 6pm. The Impressionist paintings of this native son are hauntingly beautiful. Admission is 300 Ft ($1.60/85p).

Explore the work of the country people and the history of their work at the **Museum of Hungarian Folk Art and Handicrafts** at Serfőző utca 19. (© **76/327-203**). It is open 10am to 5pm Tuesday through Saturday January 15 through December 15. Admission is 300 Ft ($1.60/85p).

Hungary's largest toy collection can be found at the **Toy Museum (Játék-műhely és Múzeum)** ✸, at Gáspár András u. and Hosszú u. (© **76/481-469**). This quaint museum has exhibits on toy design and manufacturing, as well as exhibits featuring actual toys. Families with children should try to come on the weekend, when youngsters are allowed to play with some of the goods. Admission is 450 Ft ($2.45£1.30) for adults, free for children under 6; free for everyone on Sun. Open Tuesday through Sunday 10am to 12:30pm and 1 to 5pm. Closes 1 hr. earlier in winter.

City Hall ✸, Kossuth tér 1 (© **76/513-513**), built in 1893 by Ödön Lechner and Gyula Pártos, is a delightful Art Nouveau structure and a must see for aficionados of Lechner's later Budapest buildings: the former Post Office Savings Bank (p. 137) and the Applied Arts Museum (p. 137). Like the buildings in the capital, Lechner's Kecskemét masterpiece is generously decorated with colorful Zsolnay majolica tiles. The council chamber *(dísz terem)* contains ceiling frescoes by the artist Bertalan Székely, whose work is on exhibit in Buda's National Gallery. If the building is closed when you arrive, admire it from the outside while you listen to the bells playing music by Kodály and others throughout the day (usually on the hr.). Admission is 400 Ft ($2/£1.05), by appointment only. Open Monday through Friday 8am to 4pm.

WHERE TO STAY

Fábián Panzió ✸, Kápolna u. 14 (© **76/477-677**), a small family-run guesthouse, is situated in the center of Kecskemét. Six rooms are located in the garden building and four smaller rooms are in the main building, all with private bathrooms. Doubles range from 8,800 Ft ($48/£25) to 10,800 Ft ($58/£31), and rates include breakfast and taxes.

WHERE TO DINE

Háry Restaurant is located at Kodály Zoltán tér 9. (*©* **76/480-400**). Serving traditional Hungarian meals, it also offers occasional live concerts and performances on its
small stage. Their wine list has over 100 choices from all of the wine regions of Hungary. Enjoy the outdoor terrace for summer dining. Main courses cost 800 Ft to 2,600
Ft ($4.30–$14/£2.25–£7.40). It is open daily 7am to 11pm.

Another good dining option is **Liberté,** Szabadság tér 2 (*©* **76/328-636**). The
restaurant serves Hungarian cuisine for 900 Ft to 2,500 Ft ($4.85–$14/£2.55–£7.10).
There's outdoor terrace seating in summer. It is open daily 9am to 11pm.

3 Szeged: Hungary's Spice Capital (★(★)

168km (104 miles) SE of Budapest

Historically, Szeged (pronounced *Seh*-ged), was destroyed on March 12, 1879, when
a distant dyke collapsed and flooded the city. Locals were given financial aid that was
collected in other European countries and sent to Szeged to help the rebuilding;
hence, there are streets named Rome, Brussels, Berlin, Paris, London, Moscow, and
Vienna honoring their contributions. After the catastrophic flood, Szeged was
redesigned with the engineer's precision of a compass and ruler to become the most
modern town of Hungary. Its broad avenues and boulevards along with its extravagant
center won the **Europa Nostra Award,** which is granted annually to outstanding heritage achievements.

It is the proud capital of the Great Plain in Csongrád County; an interesting little,
but hospitable city, large by Hungarian standards with a population of 177,000.
World famous for its paprika and salami *(Pick Szalami),* Szeged is also home to one of
Hungary's major universities, the University of Szeged as it was renamed in 2003.
From 1962 until its renaming in 2003, the university was József Attila University,
named for a poet who did not gain fame until after his death. His statue stands in
front of the university's main building on Dugonics tér. There is another statue of him
next to the Parliament building in Budapest on Kossuth tér, sitting on the steps of the
embankment.

The people of Szegend, many of whom are students, love to stroll along the riverside, sit in cafes, and window-shop on the just reconstructed elegant **Karász utca** (★(★,
the town's main pedestrian-only street. Dóm tér, a beautiful, wide square, is home to
the **Szeged Open Air Drama Festival** (★, which celebrated its 75th year in 2007. It
is a popular summer-long series of cultural events, with the majority in Hungarian,
but they have opened competition to the festival, so other languages may be represented in the future. **THEALTER,** an association of artists was founded in 1991 with
the mission to introduce and support the work of experimenting, innovative artistic
communities. They bring the best artists from minority-marginal positions to Szeged
to perform during their festival. There is an emphasis on introducing well-known
groups from Western Europe as well as local artists to create progressive schemes and
ways of viewing artistic performances. Over the last 16 years, the Old Synagogue has
become synonymous with THEALTER forming a close alliance. THEALTER has presented more than 130 groups from 27 countries to Szeged; some of them making their
premier performance in Hungary, here in the town of Szeged. For more information
about these festivals, contact **Tourinform.** This small city is a delightful travel destination for a day or two of visiting.

ESSENTIALS

GETTING THERE   Over 30 **trains** depart daily from Budapest's Nyugati Station, of which 14 are intercity. The fare for an IC train is 3,130 Ft ($17/£8.90) plus an additional fee for a seat reservation. All other trains cost 2,780 Ft ($15/£7.90). On all trains, the travel time is the same 2½ hours, so the only advantage of an IC train is perhaps cleanliness, but not cost effectiveness.

If you're **driving** from Budapest, take the M5 motorway south through Kecskemét and Kiskunfélegyháza.

VISITOR INFORMATION   The best source of information, as usual, is **Tourinform,** at Dugonics tér 2 (© 62/488-699; www.szegedvaros.hu), located in the renovated 19th-century courtyard of the fine pastry shop Z. Nagy Cukrászda (see below). The office is open Monday through Friday from 9am to 5pm. For private accommodations, stop in at Ibusz at Oroszlán u. 4 or call © 62/471-177.

MAHART, the Hungarian ferry-line company, organizes boat tours up and down the Tisza River from April 1 through mid-October. For information, contact the MAHART boat station in Szeged at Felső-Tisza part or call © 62/425-834.

EXPLORING THE TOWN

In addition to the listings below, you might wander past the **Gróf Palace** ★★ (© 47/580-400; www.hotelgrofdegenfeld.hu), a piece of architecture worthy of a look. Located at the corner of Lajos Tisza körut and Takarektar utca, the building was designed by Ferenc J. Raichl and was built in 1912 for citizens who could afford "higher rent"; it's not a hotel. Nearby, see the **Reök Palace** in Gaudian style at Lajos Tisza körut and Kölcsey utca.

Móra Ferenc Museum   As the name suggests, paintings of Ferenc Lucs are the main attraction here, but also on display are the History of Chemists (a natural sciences exhibition), Avars (an archaeological exhibition), and folk art of Csongrad county (an ethnical exhibition). Temporary exhibits are also displayed throughout the year.

Roosevelt tér 1–3. © 62/549-040. www.mfm.u-szeged.hu. Admission 1,000 Ft ($5.40/£2.85). Tues–Sun 10am–5pm, closes 6pm in summer.

Pick Museum ★★   This is a must for anyone interested in food or cooking. The museum contains the history of Pick brand salami and Szeged paprika, both world famous as Hungarian products that developed from this city. Follow the history and evolution of salami production from 1869 to today. On the first floor, follow the history of paprika production, all with puppets in period dress.

Felső Tisza-part 10. © 06/20-468-9185 mobile only. www.pickmuzeum.hu. Admission 480 Ft ($2.60/£1.40). Tues–Sat 3–6pm.

Synagogue ★   A tribute to the once-thriving Jewish community in Szeged, this synagogue was built in 1907. Created in a number of architectural styles, it is a monumental 49m (161-ft.) tall moorish Art Nouveau building. Its ornamented space between the right or left exterior curve of the arch and the enclosing right angle is the riblike wall above the organ in Gothic style. Roman columns support the galleries. The most beautiful part is the dome, but everywhere you look is awe inspiring. This is considered the masterpiece of architect Lipot Baumhorn, who was a disciple of Ödön Lechner and the most prolific and renowned synagogue architect in modern Europe. It occupies a full block, making it the second largest synagogue in Hungary. The synagogue is fully functioning and holds services at 6pm every Friday.

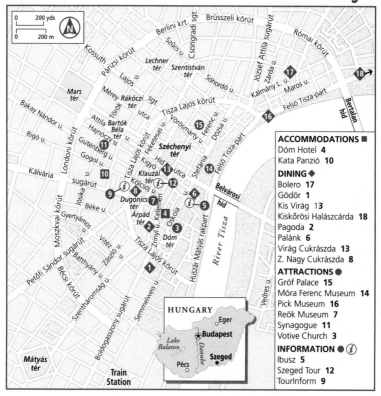

ACCOMMODATIONS ■
Dóm Hotel **4**
Kata Panzió **10**

DINING ◆
Bolero **17**
Gödör **1**
Kis Virág **13**
Kiskőrösi Halászcárda **18**
Pagoda **2**
Palánk **6**
Virág Cukrászda **13**
Z. Nagy Cukrászda **8**

ATTRACTIONS ●
Gróf Palace **15**
Móra Ferenc Museum **14**
Pick Museum **16**
Reök Museum **7**
Synagogue **11**
Votive Church **3**

INFORMATION ● ⓘ
Ibusz **5**
Szeged Tour **12**
TourInform **9**

If you find the synagogue closed when it should be open, go to the address that's posted near the entrance and the caretaker will open the synagogue for you.

Jósika utca. ℂ **62/423-849.** www.zsinagoga.szeged.hu. Admission 300 Ft ($1.60/85p). Summer Sun–Fri 9am–noon and 1–5pm; winter Sun–Fri 10am–2pm. Services Fri 6pm. Closed for Jewish holidays. From Dugonics tér, walk right on Tisza Lajos krt., and turn left on Gutenberg u.

Votive Church   Built by the residents after the flood that destroyed the city, this church sits in a square that is exactly the same size as Saint Mark Square in Venice. In the church is an unusual representation of the Madonna created in mosaic by Ferenc Márton over the baldachin of the high altar. Nicknamed the "Madonna in a fur coat," because she is depicted wearing a richly decorated fur coat, typical of this region, with red slippers typical of Szeged. There are many magnificent pieces of artwork throughout the church. It houses Europe's third largest church organ with 9,040 pipes. Mass is held here at 6:30am, 7:30am, and 6pm every day.

Also on the square is the oldest historic monument of the city: the Saint Demetrius Tower with a foundation dating back to the 11th century. The lower, squared roman styled section and early gothic upper sections are dated to the 13th century.

On Dóm tér. Free admission. Mon–Sat 9am–6pm; Sun 9:30–10am, 11–11:30am, and 12:30–6pm. Mass daily 6:30am, 7:30am, and 6pm.

WHERE TO STAY

Private rooms can be booked through **Ibusz** at Oroszlán u. 3 (© **62/471-177**).

Dóm Hotel   Located on the square near the cathedral, this hotel opened in 2004 offering lovely modern rooms with easy access to all major tourist sights. Two apartments with a separated living room and bedroom are available for two to four people.

Bajza u. 3–6. © 62/423-750. Fax 62/423-750. www.domhotel.hu. 15 units. 20,500 Ft ($111/£58) double; 30,500 Ft–33,900 Ft ($165–$183/£87–£96) apt. Rates include breakfast but not VAT or tourist tax. AE, V. Free parking. Amenities: Sauna; safe. In room: A/C, TV, minibar.

Kata Panzió 🎖   This lovely little pension opened in 1995 and is in a quiet residential neighborhood, just a short walk from central Klauzál tér. It features plenty of common space and sunny balconies on each floor. Four double rooms, one triple, and one quad are available; all have private bathrooms.

Bolyai János u. 15 (between Gogol u. and Kálvária sgt.). © 62/311-258. 6 units. 14,800 Ft ($80/£42) double; 20,500 FT ($111/£58) deluxe double or quad. 300 Ft ($1.65/85p) tourist tax per person per night. Rates include breakfast. No credit cards. Free parking. In room: A/C, TV.

WHERE TO DINE

Bolero HUNGARIAN   The menu starts with overtures for starters and sequels for the entrees. This is a place for elegant dining and for a town this size, the prices reflect it.

Zárda u. 7. © 62/540-656. Main courses 2,280 Ft–4,990 Ft ($12–$27/£6.50–£14). AE, MC, V. Mon–Thurs 11am–10pm; Fri–Sat 11am–2am; Sun 11am–5pm.

Gödör 🎖 HUNGARIAN   Located next to the Hero's Arch right in the center of the city is where you will find this little restaurant. It is frequented by university students, teachers, and tourists alike. From spring to late summer you can enjoy your meal on the terrace.

Tisza Lajos krt. 103. © 62/420-130. Main courses 750 Ft–1,800 Ft ($4.05–$9.70/£2.15–£5.15). No credit cards. Mon–Sat 11am–10pm; Sun 11am–4pm.

Göry 🎖 HUNGARIAN   A varied menu offers something for everyone at this old-fashioned Hungarian restaurant.

Liszt u. 9. © 62/422-157. Main dishes 1,950 Ft–2,990 Ft ($11–$16/£5.55–£8.55). No credit cards. Daily 11am–11pm.

Kiskőrösi Halászcsárda 🎖 HUNGARIAN   You'd do well to sample local fish and the famous Szeged fish soup at this authentic riverside restaurant. Paprika and onions are the spices of choice for hearty fish stews and bisques alike.

Felső Tisza-part 336. © 62/495-698. Reservations recommended. Main courses 700 Ft–1,200 Ft ($3.80–$6.50/ £2–£3.40). MC, V. Sun–Thurs 11am–midnight; Fri–Sat 11am–2am.

Pagoda Étterem 🎖 CHINESE   A favorite Chinese restaurant of the locals, this place will not overwhelm your dining with kitsch decor. The menu is extensive and the dishes are reportedly delicious.

Zrinyi u. 5. © 62/312-490. Main courses 840 Ft–2,800 Ft ($4.55–$15/£2.40–£8). AE, V. Tues–Sat noon–midnight; Sun–Mon noon–11pm.

COFFEEHOUSES & ICE CREAM PARLORS

Sándor Árvay and his son Kálmán created a patisserie, which became famous by the end of the 19th century because of the quality of their goods. It was nicknamed the Gerbaud of Szeged. The Virágh brothers bought it in 1922 continuing the quality reputation and renaming it **Virág Cukrászda,** located on Klauzál tér. It is open daily from 8am to 10pm. This square has more than its share of pastry shops with the **Kis Virág (Little Flower)** 🍴🍴, across the square, where you can get your pastries to go. The prices are slightly cheaper for takeout. Some say this is the best ice cream in town, in winter you can find it inside the Kis Virág. Their specialty is *rakott rétes* (layered strudle), which is the divine local version of the traditional Jewish pastry *flodni.* Kis Virág is open daily from 8am to 8pm. There are other smaller shops on or near the square vying for attention, but these two are the main attractions.

Z. Nagy Cukrászda 🍴 on Dugonics tér, just off Karász utca (the pedestrian-only street) is yet another rivaling pastry shop. With its terrace in the courtyard, it makes a pleasant place to stop and relax. One cookie you might try is *Erzsi kocka,* walnut paste sandwiched between two shortbread cookies, dipped in dark chocolate. When the summer heat is beating down, head for the line of people waiting to be served at the most popular ice cream shop, **Palánk** on the corner of Tömörkény utca and Oskola utca.

SZEGED AFTER DARK

Átrium Music Cafe at Kárász u. 9 (🕾 **06/30-289-4466** mobile only) is a lively place with a variety of different music styles each night including jazz, funk, and soul with specific ladies nights. **Szote Klub** found at Dóm tér 13 (🕾 **62/545-773**) is a definite disco with DJs knocking out the tunes, but the action doesn't start until 9:30pm and goes into the wee hours, whenever the action slows down. The famous **Jate Klub** of the university opened its doors in 1973. Originally it was an air-raid shelter located in the basement of the main building of the university. During the day, it operates as a cafe and in the evening it hosts parties, concerts, and cultural, theatrical, and literary events. It is open Monday to Friday 10am to the end of the program, Saturday 10pm to the end of the program, and closed on Sunday.

Appendix A:
Help with a Tough Tongue

Many travelers are leery to enter a land where the language is so incomprehensible, and they cannot make any connection to their mother tongue. This is certainly true of Hungary and the complex and unusual language of the Hungarians, Magyar. There are only an estimated 15 million people worldwide who use Hungarian as their mother tongue, so if you don't, you are still in the majority. For years, it has been lumped in the Finno-Uric language family with only two other distant cousins: Finnish and Estonian. Finns and Estonians have as much trouble with Hungarian as anyone else, having less than a handful of words in common. The grammar is still very different. Recent scholarship, however, is questioning the theory of where Hungarian really has its leaf on the tree of world languages. Magyar originated on the eastern side of the Ural Mountains, but where is still uncertain.

The Hungarian language has long been one of the country's greatest obstacles and continues to be as many business and tour websites, especially for smaller cities and villages, are in Hungarian only. Nevertheless, the Hungarian people are intensely proud of their language to the point of creating laws to keep foreign language business names at bay whenever possible. Our transcription of Hungarian pronunciations is of necessity approximate. Stress is always on the first syllable of any word, and all letters are pronounced, but there are no Q, X, or Y in Hungarian unless the word has been borrowed from another language. With that said, you will find Y, but it is a consonant combination letter like *gy*, *ly*, or *ny*, making the two letters, one letter unto themselves. Hungarian has 44 letters and 14 of them are vowels.

Fortunately, for the modern-day traveler and Hungary's ascension into the European Union, many Hungarian young people have taken their foreign language studies much more seriously than ever before. Many young people speak English and most people in tourism venues do to some extent. Do not be daunted if you attempt some polite words and find a confused Hungarian staring at you. The difference between an *o* and *ó* can not only change the meaning of the word, but since the Magdar people are so unaccustomed to hearing strangers attempt their language, they are also a bit befuddled to the point of not understanding. At the least, try to learn the polite words and stick with them.

One more thing: Both "hello" and "goodbye" in Hungarian is *hallo* (sounds the same in English) or *szia* (sounds like see-ya). You will often see people saying goodbye to each other and saying "*hallo, szia*" as they depart. They often do the same on the phone before ending a call.

A printable phrase book is available at www.single-serving.com/Hungarian/print.php.

PRONUNCIATION GUIDE
Vowels

a	t*au*t	ó	same as above but held longer
á	b*ahh*	ö	s*u*b
e	*e*ver	ő	same as above but held longer
é	d*ay*	u	l*oo*k
i	m*i*tt	ú	b*oo*t
í	t*ee*n	ü	d*o*ve
o	b*o*ne	ű	same as above but held longer

Consonants

Most Hungarian consonants are pronounced approximately as they are in English, including the following: *b, d, f, h, k, l, m, n, p, t, v,* and *y.* There are some differences, however, particularly in the consonant combinations, as follows:

c	ge*ts*	r	slightly rolled
cs	*ch*ill	s	*sh*eet
g	*g*ill	sz	*s*ix
gy	he*dg*e	z	*z*ero
j	*y*outh	zs	a*z*ure, plea*s*ure
ny	as in Russian *ny*et		

1 Menu Terms

GENERAL TERMS

Bors black pepper
Fóételek main courses
Fózelék vegetable purée
Gyümölcs fruits
Halak fish
Húsételek meat dishes
Italok beverages
Kenyér bread
Leves(ek) soup(s)

Paprika red pepper/paprika
Sajt cheese
Saláták salads
Só salt
Tészták pasta/dessert
Tojás eggs
Vaj butter
Zöldság vegetables

COOKING TERMS

Csípős hot (peppery)
Forró hot (in temperature)
Főtt boiled
Friss fresh
Fuszerezve spiced
Hideg cold
Párolt steamed

Pirított toasted
Pörkölt stew
Rántott fried
Roston sült broiled
Sült roasted/baked
Sútve baked/fried
Töltött stuffed

SOUPS *(LEVESEK)*

Gombaleves   mushroom soup

Gulyásleves   goulash soup

Húsleves   bouillon

Karfioleves   cauliflower soup

Krémleves   cream of whatever is before it

Lencseleves   lentil soup

Paradicsomkrémleves   cream of tomato soup

Zöldborsöleves   pea soup

Zöldségleves   vegetable soup

EGGS *(TOJÁS)*

Kolbásszal   with sausage

Rántotta   scrambled eggs

Sonkával   with ham

Szalonnával   with bacon

Tükörtojás   fried eggs

MEAT & POULTRY *(HÚS ÉS BAROMFI)*

Agyonsütve   well done

Bárány   lamb

Bécsi szelet   Wiener schnitzel

Borjú   veal

Csirke   chicken

Félig nyersen   rare

Gulyás   goulash

Kacsa   duck

Kotlett   cutlet

Közepesen kisütve   medium

Liba   goose

Marha   beef

Pulyka   turkey

Sertés   pork

Tokány   ragout

FISH *(HALAK)*

Csuka   pike

Fogas Balaton   pikeperch

Halászlé   fish stew

Pisztráng   trout

Ponty   carp

Tonhal   tuna

VEGETABLES *(ZÖLDSÁG)*

Bab   beans

Burgonya   potato

Fokhagyma   garlic

Gomba   mushrooms

Hagyma   onion

Káposzta   cabbage

Paradicsom   tomato

Sóska   sorrel

Spenót   spinach

Tök   squash

Zöldbab   green beans

SALADS *(SALÁTÁK)*

Fejes saláta   green salad

Lecsó   stewed pepper, tomatoes, and onion

Paprikasaláta   pickled-pepper salad

Uborkasaláta   cucumber salad

Vegyes saláta   mixed salad

FRUITS *(GYÜLMÖLCS)*

Alma   apple

Barack   apricot

Narancs   orange

Ószibarack   peach

Cseresznye	cherry	Sargadinnye	cantaloupe
Dinnye	watermelon	Szeder	blackberry
Körte	pear	Szilva	plum
Málna	raspberry	Szóló	grapes
Meggy	sour cherry		

DESSERTS

Almás rétes   apple strudel

Dobos torta   layer cake with caramel candied frosting

Fagylalt   ice cream

Ischler   chocolate-dipped shortbread cookie sandwich

Lekváros palacsinta   crepe filled with preserves

Meggyes rétes   sour-cherry strudel

Túrós rétes   cheese strudel

BEVERAGES

Barna sör	dark beer	Sör	beer
Fehér bor	white wine	Tej	milk
Kávé	coffee	Víz	water
Koktél	cocktail	Vörös bor	red wine
Narancslé	orange juice		

2 Basic Phrases & Vocabulary

QUESTION WORDS (IN THE NOMINATIVE)

English	Hungarian	Pronunciation
Where	Hol	hole
When	Mikor	*mee*-kor
What	Mi	mee
Why	Miert	*mee*-ayrt
Who	Ki	kee
How	Hogy	hohdge

USEFUL PHRASES

English	Hungarian	Pronunciation
Good day/Hello	Jó napot	*yoh* napoht
Good morning	Jó reggelt	*yoh* reg-gelt
Good evening	Jó estét	*yoh* esh-tayt
Goodbye	Viszontlátásra	*vee*-sont-lah-tahsh-ra
My name is . . .	Vagyok . . .	*vodge*-yohk
Thank you	Köszönöm	*kuh*-suh-nuhm
You're welcome	Kérem	*kay*-rem
Please	Legyen szíves	*ledge*-yen see-vesh
Yes	Igen	*ee*-gen

No	**Nem**	*nem*
Good/Okay	**Jó**	*yo*
Excuse me	**Bocsánat**	*boh*-chahnat
How much does it cost?	**Mennyi bekerül?**	*men*-yee *beh*-keh-roohl?
I don't understand	**Nem értem**	*nem* ayr-tem
I don't know	**Nem tudom**	*nem too*-dum
Where is the . . . ?	**Hol van a . . . ?**	*hohl* von a . . . ?
bus station	**busz állomás**	*boos ahh*-loh-mahsh
train station	**vonatállomás**	*vah*-not-*ahh*-loh-mahsh
bank	**bank**	*bahnk*
museum	**múzeum**	*moo*-zeh-oom
pharmacy	**patiká**	*paw*-tee-kah
theater	**színház**	*seen*-hahz
tourist office	**turista iroda**	*too*-reesh-ta *eer*-ohda
embassy	**nagykövetség**	*nahdge koo*-vet-shayg
restaurant	**étterem**	*ayt*-teh-rehm
restroom	**wc**	*vayt*-say
Right	**job/jobbra**	*yobl yob*-ra
Left	**bal/balra**	*ball bal*-ra

RESTAURANT SERVICE

English	**Hungarian**	**Pronunciation**
Breakfast	**Reggeli**	*rehg*-geh-lee
Lunch	**Ebéd**	*eh*-bayd
Dinner	**Vacsora**	*vah*-choh-rah
I would like . . .	**Kérnék . . .**	*kayr*-nayk . . .
a table	**egy asztalot**	edge *ah*-stah-lot
a menu	**egy étlapot**	edge *ayt*-lah-poht
a glass (of water)	**egy pohár (vizet)**	edge poh-har (*vee*-zet)
to pay	**fizetni**	*ee*-zeht-nee
I have a reservation	**Foglaltam már**	*fohg*-lawl-tahm mahr

TRAIN TRAVEL

English	**Hungarian**	**Pronunciation**
A ticket, please	**Egy jegyet kérek**	*Edge ye*-dget *kay*-rek
Seat reservation	**helyjegy**	*heyh*-yedge
One-way only	**csak oda**	*chalk oh*-da
Round-trip	**oda-vissza**	*oh*-dah-*vees*-sah
First class	**elsó osztály**	*ell*-shooh *oh*-stahy
Arrive	**érkezik**	*ayr*-kez-eek
Depart	**indul**	*inn*-doohl
Track	**Vagány**	*vah*-ghine

POST OFFICE

English	Hungarian	Pronunciation
Airmail	**Légiposta**	*lay*-ghee-posh-ta
A stamp, please	**Egy bélyeget kérek**	Edge *bay*-yeh-get *kay*-rek
A postcard . . .	**Egy képeslapot . . .**	Edge *kay*-pesh-law-poht
An envelope . . .	**Egy borítéket . . .**	Edge *bohr*-ree-tay-ket

USEFUL WORDS

English	Hungarian	Pronunciation
Map	**térkép**	*tayr*-kayp
Police	**rendórség**	*ren*-du(r)r-shayg
Hospital	**korhéz**	*kohr*-hahhz
Emergency	**szükséghelyzet**	*soohk*-shayg-hey-zet
Theft	**lopás**	*loh*-pahsh
Passport	**útlevél**	*oot*-leh-vayhl
Pillow	**parna**	*par*-na
Window	**ablak**	*ab*-lock
Man/Men	**férfi**	fear-fe
Woman/Women	**nőI**	*noy*

SIGNS

Bejárat Entrance

Érkezések Arrivals

Indulások Departures

Információ Information

Kijárat Exit

Tilos a dohányzás No Smoking

Toalettek Toilets

Veszélyes Danger

Vigyázat Beware

NUMBERS

English	Hungarian	Pronunciation
1	**egy**	edge
2	**kettó**	*ket*-tu[r]
3	*három*	*hahh*-rohm
4	**négy**	*naydge*
5	**öt**	*u*[r]*t*
6	**hat**	*hawt*
7	**hét**	*hayt*
8	**nyolc**	*nyohlts*
9	**kilenc**	*kee*-lents
10	**tíz**	*teez*
11	**tizenegy**	*teez*-en-edge
12	**tizenkettó**	*teez*-en-ket-tu[r]
13	**tizenhárom**	*teez*-en-hahh-rohm
14	**tizennégy**	*teez*-en-naydge
15	**tizenöt**	*teez*-en-u[r]t

16	**tizenhat**	*teez*-en-hawt
17	**tizenhét**	*teez*-en-hayt
18	**tizennyolc**	*teez*-en-nyohlts
19	**tizenkilenc**	*teez*-en-kee-lents
20	**húsz**	*hoos*
30	**harminc**	*hahr*-mints
40	**negyven**	*nedge*-vehn
50	**ötven**	*u[r]t*-vehn
60	**hatvan**	*hawt*-vahn
70	**hetven**	*het*-vehn
80	**nyolcvan**	*nyohlts*-vahn
90	**kilencven**	*kee*-lents-vehn
100	**száz**	*sahhz*
500	**ötszáz**	*u[r]t*-sahhz
1,000	**ezer**	*eh*-zayr

DAYS OF THE WEEK

English	Hungarian	Pronunciation
Monday	**hétfő**	hait-fo
Tuesday	**kedd**	kedd
Wednesday	**szerda**	ser-dah
Thursday	**csütörtök**	chew-tor-tuk
Friday	**péntek**	pain-tek
Saturday	**szombat**	sahm-bat
Sunday	**vasárnap**	vasha-ar-nap

Days of the week are not capitalized as in English.

Appendix B:
Hungarian Cuisine

Traditional Hungarian cuisine reflects the rich and varied flavors of many international influences. Since the first Magyars were nomadic people, they learned from the Turkish and other cultures they came into contact with. Soup was an important staple of their lifestyle. They used a bogrács, a large cast-iron pot that hung on an iron rod over the fire, for cooking soups. It was easily transported with the soup sitting in the pot as the Magyars moved from place to place, and the soup was consumed over days. The bogrács is a very popular cooking utensil even today and soup continues to be an important part of a meal.

Once the Magyars settled in the Carpathian Basin, pork was introduced into the diet with each family raising its own pigs. Culinary transformations occurred through marriage also. After King Matthias and Beatrice of Italy married, she introduced Italian influences into the cooking culture, including turkey, pasta, cheeses, garlic, and onions.

The Turkish may have had the greatest influence on gastronomy as they introduced paprika to the culture. Hungary's climate is perfect for growing the red peppers that are ground up to create the spice. At first, the elite only grew paprika peppers for their decorative value, but the peasants grew it and used it for cooking. At one point in the 19th century, the rising cost of black pepper convinced the masses to switch to paprika, thus dubbing paprika *török bors* or Turkish pepper. Paprika comes in different varieties, which is important for cooking. It ranges from spicy hot *(csípős)* to sweet *(édes)* with other varieties in between, depending on the peppers used.

Another way the Turks influenced the food habits of the early Hungarians was by taking all of the domestic animals with them only leaving the pigs. Due to their religion, they did not care about these lowly animals, making pork an important meat for the Magyars, influencing their cooking culture. Turks are also responsible for introducing strudel, pilaf, lángos, and stuffed vegetables. They also introduced plants such as the tomato, sour cherry, corn, and tobacco.

When the Turks gave Hungarians coffee, it changed the culture in astonishing ways. In the late 1800s, there were over 500 coffeehouses in Budapest alone. Many of the famous ones are where writers, artists, musicians, and other intellectuals gathered to share their passions, network, and create camaraderie.

The Hungarian upper class adopted the French fashion of cooking as did the Austrian aristocrats. Perhaps this is where the love affair with goose liver originated. Middle-class Hungarians incorporated Austrian dishes in their everyday meals, adopting schnitzel, sausages, potatoes, and vegetable stews thickened with flour and lard. Today this thickened vegetable stew is called *főzelék* and is a traditional favorite food.

Different parts of Hungary have their regional traditions and favorite recipes, but any good Hungarian restaurant in Budapest incorporates some from each on their menu. Some restaurants specialize in the more exotic fare such as deer, wild boar, or other nondomesticated animals. Often, when deer is on the menu, it is translated as deer and not venison and it will be saddle of deer. This is the breast meat. Regardless of what is on the menu, if it is a traditional Hungarian menu, you are guaranteed that the food will be plentiful and heavy. Hungarian cooking uses a great deal of pork or goose fat, which adds incredible flavors to dishes that would not be possible without them. Sour cream, potatoes, or a form of pasta are also added to enrich a dish, adding to that gluttony feeling after you finish. Just so you do not miss out on any gastronomical experiences, we have put all of the food items you should sample while here in a box at the end of this chapter. Some are discussed within this chapter also.

Lunch, an important meal of the day, begins with soup. *Gulyás,* often mispronounced as "goulash," is a meat soup usually made with beef or pork, carrots, and potatoes in a rich broth. Travelers often have the misconception that *gulyás* is a stew. *Babgulyás* is a hearty and delicious bean soup similar to *gulyás.* Hungary is famous for its *gyümölcs leves,* a cold fruit soup, which can be made from sour cherry, peaches, or apricots. Usually it is only served in summertime, making it an excellent refreshing way to start a meal. *Sargaborsoleves,* a split pea soup that is a good winter seasonal choice, and *halaszle,* a fish soup, constitute meals in themselves.

Main courses are generally some type of meat dish. Try the *paprikás csirke,* chicken cooked in a savory paprika sauce. It's especially good with galuska, a pasta dumpling. *Pulykamell,* turkey breast roasted with various fruits and/or sauces, is also delicious. Another great choice is *Pörkölt,* a stewed meat dish that comes in many varieties. *Töltött káposzta,* whole cabbage leaves stuffed with rice, meat, and spices, is another favorite. Cabbage is a winter staple food and appears in pastry also. Remember the word *káposzta* (cabbage) if you don't want it as your savory little pastry filling.

Vegetarianism is slowly, ever so slowly being recognized in Hungarian restaurants; many establishments now offer a vegetable plate entree, usually consisting of seasonal steamed and grilled vegetables, or cheese plates. Hungarians look on vegetarians with suspicion, regardless of their nationality. Otherwise, vegetarians would do well to order *lecsó tojással* (eggs scrambled in a thick tomato-onion-paprika sauce), *rántott sajt* (batter-fried cheese with tartar sauce), or *túros csusza tepertó nélkul* (a type of noodle with cottage cheese dish). The kitchen should be able to prepare any of these dishes to order, even if they don't appear on the menu.

Snack foods include *lángos,* a piece of dough pulled into a small pizza shape and served with your choice of toppings: Cheese, ham, and garlic sauce are the most popular, but you can also have powdered sugar and whipped cream. *Palacsinta,* a paper-thin crepe stuffed with a multitude of offerings for either a sweet or savory light bite, is another excellent choice. *Kürtős kalács,* a hollow, tubular honey cake, is an old-fashioned pastry cooked on a wooden bolt; it is sometimes available in metro stations and at outdoor markets and fairs, but is best when freshly baked. *Fagylalt* (ice cream) is the national street food, especially in warm months. Scoops are tiny, so order more than one or you will have more cone than ice cream. Fresh fruit flavors are seasonal: Summer flavors include *eper* (strawberry) and *meggy* (sour cherry) and in the fall flavors include *szilva* (plum) and *körte* (pear). Summer regulars are delicious *fahéj* (cinnamon), *mák* (poppy seed), and *rizs* (rice).

Hungarian pastries are delicious, but many travelers are surprised that the cakes are not as sweet or moist as other countries' offerings. For the first two years, we thought we were being sold stale cakes since we were foreigners. If you like your pastry with some moisture, choose one of the creamy types. The light, flaky *rétes* are filled with fruit (apple, plum, cherry), poppy seeds, or cheese. *Csoki torta* is a decadent chocolate layer cake, and a Dobos torta is a layered cake topped with a shiny hard caramel crust. (Hint: Take the crust off first and eat it separately). *Mákos* pastry, made with poppy seeds, is a Hungarian specialty. *Gesztenye* (chestnuts) are another popular ingredient in desserts; some are chestnut cream with whipped cream on top or chestnut cream in a pastry. *Béigli*, a traditional Christmas holiday pastry, appears everywhere during the season. A log-shaped pastry with crushed walnuts or poppy seeds baked in it like a jelly roll, it is sliced into bite-sized portions.

Picnickers should pick up a loaf of Hungarian bread and sample any of Hungary's world-famous salamis. Before you decide to pack some to take home, check the Customs regulations (p. 12). A number of tasty cheeses are produced in Hungary as well: *Karaván füstölt* (a smoked cheese), *Edami* (Dutch cheese), *márvány* (similar to bleu cheese), and *juhtúró* (a soft, spreadable sheep's cheese similar in flavor to feta). In season, fresh produce is cheap and high quality, but variety is limited compared to many other countries. In the winter, fresh fruits and vegetables are slim pickings with apples, pears, cabbage, potatoes, and carrots being the most common choices. In summer, you'll be amazed at the abundance of fresh produce and the low cost, but again limited varieties at the wonderful markets. Strawberries *(eper)* in May, raspberries *(málna)*, blueberries *(fekete áfonya)*, blackberries *(szeder)*, and sour cherries *(meggy)* start hitting the market with most one type of berry or another continuing throughout the summer.

BEER, WINE & SPIRITS   Hungary never developed a beer culture; as a result, its beer is unremarkable, but don't tell a Hungarian this. They are staunchly proud of anything Hungarian. A number of European beers are now produced under license in Hungary. Among them are German beers, Austrian beers, a Danish beer, a Dutch beer, and a Belgian beer. To our taste, however, all these beers tend to be inferior to those under whose license they are sold and are only marginally better than the best Hungarian beer—Dreher. Your best bet in Hungary is Czech beer, such as Budvar, Staropramen, or Pilsner Urquell, which are not produced in Hungary under license; they are the real thing.

Hungarian wines are excellent. The most renowned red wines come from the region around Villány, a town to the south of Pécs near the Croatian border. As a result of an aggressive marketing campaign mounted by the former Communist regime, many travelers are familiar with the red wines from Eger, especially *Egri Bikavér* (Eger Bull's Blood). However, Eger wines, though rich and fruity, are markedly inferior to Villányi reds. The country's best white wines are generally believed to be those from the Lake Balaton region, though some Hungarians insist that white wines from the Somló region (northeast of Lake Balaton) are better. *Tokaj* wines—*száraz* (dry) or *édes* (sweet)—are popular as aperitifs and dessert wines. Travelers seeking advice on Hungarian wines are encouraged to visit one of the full-service wine stores in Budapest (see p. 218 for shopping suggestions). You can also pick up the free pamphlet *Wine Regions in Hungary* at Tourinform (see p. 45 in chapter 4, "Getting to Know Budapest").

Unikum is the Hungarian national liqueur similar to Germany's Jagermeister or Italy's Fernet Branca. This aromatic bitter liquid is a taste worth acquiring. It is still produced according to the original recipe owned by the Zwack family (the current owner of the company, a Zwack family member, was Hungary's first ambassador to the U.S. after the fall of communism). The distilled fruit brandy Palinka is another variety of Hungarian firewater that is often referred to as schnapps. It is a liqueur with

You Haven't Been to Hungary if You Haven't Tried . . .

Főzelék This hearty dish is somewhere between a soup and a stew in consistency, but without any chunks of meat or vegetables. There are a number of varieties, but green pea, potato, and chicken are the most popular. The vegetable varieties sometimes contain animal fat, so vegetarians should ask ahead of time. One of the most popular főzelék restaurants is listed in chapter 6, "Where to Dine in Budapest."

Lángos Many cultures have their own variety of this. This is dough that is deep-fried in fat, and then topped with shredded cheese and/or ham, finally sprinkled with garlic juice. Due to tourist demand, there are now many types of toppings, but a Mexikói (Mexico) is not really authentic. The best place to sample these is in the Central Market Hall Központi Vásárcsarnok at IX. Vámház körút upstairs on the right-hand wall of food booths.

Halászlé This is fish soup, usually made with carp, pike, or perch, but sometimes with a couple of different fish. Widely available in restaurants.

Palacsinta The French call these crepes. The Hungarians call them a national treasure. There are a number of fillings to make these a complete meal. Some palacsinta restaurants have complete menus of entrees and desserts consisting of three to five crepes for a fixed price usually under 800 Ft ($4.30/£2.30). If you just want to sample one, they are on many restaurant menus.

Somlói Galuska A rich and treasured dessert, this will satisfy a chocolate lover's sweet tooth. Served in a bowl, cubes of spongy cake are sprinkled with a rum flavoring, and then vanilla sauce is poured over the moist cubes followed by a topping of chocolate sauce, which is finished off with whipped cream. A dieter's nightmare and often on restaurant dessert menus.

Turós táska (sweet cheese bag) A cheese filled strudel-type dessert and available in most bakeries.

Túró Rudi This is so Hungarian, you will not find it outside of the country. Many returning visitors look for it on their first day back. Shaped like a small log, it is a cheese called quark, which is thinly coated with chocolate. The most famous is the "natur" flavor, though there are others with fruit added. The original is in a white, red-dotted wrapper. You will not find this on any menu, but if you venture into any convenience store or supermarket, they will be plentiful in the refrigerator case. They are welcomed sweets by Hungarian parents for their nutritional value and low cost, about 80 Ft (45¢/2p]).

high alcohol content and some fruit or honey flavor. Palinka is traditionally brewed at home where apricots, plums, pears, or honey are plentiful; folk wisdom claims it has medicinal value. Only the better brands have much fruit flavor at all.

COFFEE & TEA   Hungarians drink *kávé* (coffee) throughout the day, either in coffeehouses or less seldom in standup coffee bars. With the vast popularity of cappuccinos, lattes, and other specialized coffee drinks, various coffee brands have infiltrated the market trying to stake their claim. The menus in a number of coffee shops have expanded greatly. In general, when ordering coffee in Hungary, you are still ordering espresso. An "American" coffee called *hosszú kávé* (long coffee) will be an espresso with additional hot water added, nothing close to filtered coffee. Cappuccino and its variants with chocolate shavings, cinnamon, or vanilla dust on top are now available in most coffeehouses, as is *koffein mentes* (decaffeinated coffee). *Tejeskávé,* a Hungarian version of café au lait, is another option.

Tea drinkers will have a less difficult time than in the past; most food establishments have come to recognize the tea drinker and offer a selection of teabags to choose from. Tea is now readily available in bars and cafes, plus there have been a number of tea cafes that have opened and are prospering (a few tea cafes are listed in chapter 6, "Where to Dine in Budapest"). For more variety and a peek at Hungary's burgeoning world of herbal medicine, look for teas in any of the numerous tea or herbal shops: *gyógynövény, herbárium,* or *gyógytea.*

WATER   While *csapvíz* (tap water) is safe to drink in Budapest, it isn't generally offered in restaurants because they would rather you order water, which is bottled and they charge for it. If you want to avoid the cost of water, ask for tap water specifically, stating "not bottled." Hungarians increasingly drink *Ásványvíz,* a carbonated mineral water; *szóda víz,* carbonated tap water; or *szénsav mentes* (purified bottled water). More of this specific water drinking is part fashion or enjoying the carbonation, and not due to the quality of the water. All of these varieties of water are available at all restaurants as well as at delicatessens and grocery stores.

Appendix C:
Hungary's Jewish History in Brief

During the Holocaust, Hungary had a unique situation concerning their Jewish citizens. In order to understand and appreciate the horrific events of World War II, it is important to know the Jewish history of the country.

The Jewish history in Hungary extends to the 2nd or 3rd century A.D., when the first Jewish people came to the area, mainly from Rome. Artifacts dating to 225 have been uncovered, showing a strong Jewish community long before the Magyars conquered the area in 896. When King István I adopted Christianity, declaring it the official religion, he also guaranteed the right to religious freedom, including the practice of Judaism. Religious freedom continued through the Árpád dynasty until it ended in 1301. András II, under pressure from the pope, created a prohibition on mixed marriages in the Golden Bull of 1222, an edict establishing the rights of noblemen. During his reign, he also restricted Jewish people from national and public office, forcing them to wear signs proclaiming their religion. Due to the economic services they provided, some remained in their appointed posts; one example is Count Teka, who was the Jewish royal chamberlain.

Under threat of invasion by the Mongols, King Béla IV implored Pope Gregory IX in 1239 to allow him to relax the laws, so the national revenues could be controlled by Jews. Béla accomplished this, so during his reign and the reign of his son, István V, there were many Hungarian coins minted with Hebrew characters inscribed on them. This attests to the privileged position of the Jews during this time.

Jewish and Hungarian history has been intertwined for centuries, with the Jews being the welcomed people or the outcasts, flipping back and forth. It was not until the early 20th century that Hungarian Jews were able to hold political positions, but even then, they were not able to make strongholds in creating changes.

The Hungarian regent Miklós Horthy of the right-wing Christianized government was in power from 1920 to 1944 and was heavily influenced by the Germans. He and the economic situation at the time pushed the country toward fascism. The Jews realized that efforts to assimilate had been in vain. Horthy aligned Hungary with the Germans and Italians. He had their promise that the land lost due to the Trianon Treaty after World War I, would be returned to Hungary. As Hungary aligned with Germany's Adolf Hitler and Italy's Benito Mussolini, the Jews were no longer in a position to strive for equality. Horthy had come to an agreement with Hitler to save the Hungarian Jews; however, Jews from all over the country were rounded up and many sent to Budapest to live in abandoned factories or "star houses" which were eventually ghettos. They lost everything. SS Colonel Adolf Eichmann was the official head of deportations from the countryside that started in March 1944.

During the last two months of World War II, Hungarian police, who were feeling the pressure of Soviet troops getting closer, successfully rounded up and deported 440,000 Jews in over 145 trains heading primarily to Auschwitz. Thousands of others were sent to the Hungary-Austrian border as workers to dig fortification trenches.

Those who could not be deported in time were lined up along the Danube by German soldiers and shot in the back, their bodies falling into the river. Those who were killed at the Dohány Synagogue were buried on the grounds against Jewish law.

Horthy, recognizing that the Axis Powers were not going to win the war, started secret negotiations with the Allied Powers. When this came to light in mid-May 1944, the German Security Police, with the assistance of the Hungarian authorities, began to methodically deport Hungarian Jews.

Horthy, under threat of war crime trials by the leaders of the Allied Powers, decided to stop the deportations on July 7, 1944. The following month, he dissolved his government, trying to create a resolution agreement with the Soviets, who were at Hungary's borders. After finalizing his negotiations with the Soviet commanders in October, Horthy was arrested by the Germans. They created a new government headed by Ferenc Szalasi, the leader of the fascist and radically anti-Semitic Arrow Cross Party.

Under the Arrow Cross regime, members of the party terrorized the Jewish population. Men and women were murdered by the hundreds. Hundreds more died from the brutal conditions of forced labor inflicted upon them. By November 1944, the Arrow Cross rounded up the balance of the 70,000 Jews in Budapest and forced them into a ghetto within an area of .3sq. km (.1 sq. mile). During November and December of the same year, several thousand more were forced to march from Budapest to the Austrian border. Those who could not keep up were shot along the way.

In January 1945, Soviet forces were in Pest and had signed a cease-fire. They liberated the Buda side of the city on February 13, 1945, driving out of Hungary the last of the German troops and their Arrow Cross compatriots by early April 1945.

In 1941, Hungary was home to approximately 825,000 Jews, but 63,000 were killed before the Germans arrived in March 1944. An additional 500,000 died under the Germans from murder or maltreatment. Less than one-third of the total Jewish population of Hungary prior to the war survived the Holocaust; about 255,000 Jews survived.

Many of the survivors owe a debt of gratitude to the Hungarian intellectual class and to government employees of neutral countries who intervened on their behalf, risking their lives in the process. The best known among them was Raoul Wallenberg, a Swedish diplomat who processed thousands of Swedish protectorate passports for Jews, so they could escape to Sweden safely. He was arrested by the Soviets in January 1947 and never heard from again. Under pressure, the Soviets claimed he died of a heart attack while in prison, yet this was never confirmed. Carl Lutz of Switzerland, as Swiss vice-consul to Hungary, saved Hungarian Jews from deportation by allowing them to immigrate to Palestine under protection of a Swiss safe-conduct, where he housed them in buildings that he declared part of the Swiss delegation. Ángel Sanz Briz was sent to Budapest in 1942 where it is estimated that he saved 5,200 Jews from the Holocaust through his influence as a Spanish diplomat and by using the Spanish embassy. He was aided by Giorgio Perlasca, an Italian veteran of the Spanish Civil War who was ordered to leave Budapest in 1944 but continued working with fake documents asserting he was a Spanish diplomat. Angelo Rotta, a Catholic priest and a member of the Vatican diplomatic corps, issued 15,000 protection letters to Hungarian Jews and gave them baptismal certificates from the Catholic Church. Friedrich Born, a Swiss citizen working for the International Committee of the Red Cross (ICRC), recruited 3,000 Jews as workers in his offices and declared those offices as under protection of the ICRC.

Several Hungarians were recognized as saviors of the Jews. Margit Slachta, who founded the religious order the Sisters of Social Service, was instrumental in saving many Jewish lives. She was an avid protester, raising objections against racial persecution, the anti-Jewish laws, and the deportations. Mother Slachta traveled to Rome in 1943 to appeal to Pope Pius XII to intercede against the persecution of Jews. From the spring of 1944 the mission of the sisters was fully directed at helping the Jews. They hid as many as 1,000. One sister, Sára Salkaházi, was murdered by Arrow Cross men on December 27, 1944. She was awarded the title "Righteous among the Nations" in 1969; Sister Margit received the honor 12 years after her death, in 1986.

General Tibor Almásy was an officer in the Hungarian army during World War II. He provided food, medical assistance, and certificates for his Jewish soldiers and was recognized as Righteous among the Nations in 1987. Because of his actions, he was arrested and imprisoned in March 1944. Following his release, he was commissioned as the garrison commander of Sopron's prison camp, where 400 Jews were forced laborers. Almásy reassured them that he would protect them as long as he was in charge. When he was ordered to exterminate his servicemen by the Arrow Cross, he saved them by declaring a typhoid quarantine of the entire barracks and erecting huge signs that said DANGER, TYPHOID FEVER: ENTRANCE FORBIDDEN.

Dr. József Antall, the father of a former Hungarian prime minister, was awarded the title Righteous among the Nations in 1989, posthumously. As head of the Department of Refugees and the Ministry of Interior, he issued legal permits for thousands of Jewish refugees from other occupied countries to stay in Hungary while at the same time Christianizing them. He opened a boarding school in Vác for Jewish children who had lost their parents. He was arrested by the Gestapo only to be released in September 1944.

Yad Vashem is Israel's official memorial to the victims of the Holocaust, established in 1953. Those declared as righteous by Jewish law are believed to be purified and deserving of entrance into paradise based on the merits in life. All of the above have received this honor.

Daily life did not improve for the Hungarian Jews after the war was over. When the communists came to power in 1948, many of the middle class, including a great number of Jews, were either deported or sent to labor camps. The Jews of the lower classes struggled to survive financially. Their shops were closed or their business licenses were withdrawn, causing further hardships. Religious practices were strictly regulated and limited to ceremonies within the synagogue. It was impossible to raise children in the traditional ways.

Many Jews took part in the unsuccessful revolution of October 23, 1956, including Auschwitz survivor István Angyal. He, among other Jews, was executed. International relations between Israel and Hungary were abolished and reinstated a number of times. As of 1994, they both abolished Visa requirements between the two countries and have a free trade agreement. This has created a boom in Jewish tourism to Hungary.

Today, there are approximately 100,000 Jews living in Hungary, with 80% to 90% living in Budapest, making this the largest population of Jews in Central Europe.

For more information on the Jewish sights in Budapest, see p. 185, "Walking Tour 4: The Jewish District."

Index

RESTAURANTS, COFFEEHOUSES & TEAHOUSES

I don't speak sign language.

A hotel can close for all kinds of reasons.
Our Guarantee ensures that if your hotel's undergoing construction, we'll let you know in advance. In fact, we cover your entire travel experience. See www.travelocity.com/guarantee for details.

travelocity
You'll never roam alone.